Instant Astrology

INSTANT ASTROLOGY

by
Mary Orser,
Rick and Glory Brightfield

First Harper Colophon Edition Published 1976

International Standard Book Number 0-917086-63-5

Cover Design by Larry Ortiz

Printed in the United States of America

Published by ACS Publications, Inc.
P.O. Box 16430
San Diego, CA 92116-0430

First Printing, February 1985
Second Printing, January 1986
Third Printing, May 1987

ACKNOWLEDGMENTS

The authors wish to thank the people who helped make this book a reality.

Dodie and Allan Edmands, fellow astrologers, who made many valuable suggestions as well as editing and proofreading sections of the book.

Donna Lawson, whose constructive criticism livened up the writing.

Zoltan Mason, who, after casting Mary Orser's chart, encouraged her to become an astrologer and was her first astrology teacher.

Dane Rudhyar, whose pioneer work in interpreting the meaning of the Moon phases is reflected in this book, and whose depth and breadth of astrological understanding is a continuing inspiration.

Dennis Drogseth, Pat Beckerman and Debra Lavaggi, who helped in various ways.

Randall Coleman Roffe for providing information on herbs and foods which, in chemical analysis, are found to be high in the minerals associated with the signs of the zodiac.

And finally, Mary Orser's students, who taught her what people really want to know about astrology.

Also by ACS Publications, Inc.

All About Astrology Series
The American Atlas: US Latitudes and Longitudes, Time Changes
    and Time Zones (Shanks)
The American Book of Nutrition & Medical Astrology (Nauman)
The American Book of Tables
The American Ephemeris Series 1901-2000
The American Ephemeris for the 20th Century [Midnight]
    1900 to 2000
The American Ephemeris for the 20th Century [Noon] 1900 to 2000
The American Ephemeris for the 21st Century 2001 to 2100
The American Heliocentric Ephemeris 1901-2000
The American Midpoint Ephemeris 1986-1990 (Michelsen)
The American Sidereal Ephemeris 1976-2000
The Asteroid Ephemeris: Dudu, Dembowska, Pittsburgh, & Frigga
    (Stark & Pottenger)
Asteroid Goddesses (George & Bloch)
Astrological Insights into Personality (Lundsted)
Astrological Predictions: A Revolutionary New Technique (Whitney)
Astrology: Old Theme, New Thoughts (March & McEvers)
Basic Astrology: A Guide for Teachers & Students (Negus)
Basic Astrology: A Workbook for Students (Negus)
The Body Says Yes (Kapel)
Comet Halley Ephemeris 1901-1996 (Michelsen)
Complete Horoscope Interpretation: Putting Together
    Your Planetary Profile (Pottenger)
Cosmic Combinations: A Book of Astrological Exercises (Negus)
Expanding Astrology's Universe (Dobyns)
The Fortunes of Astrology: A New Complete Treatment of the
    Arabic Parts (Granite)
The Gold Mine in Your Files (King)
Hands That Heal (Burns)
Healing with the Horoscope: A Guide to Counseling (Pottenger)
The Horary Reference Book (Ungar & Huber)
Horoscopes of the Western Hemisphere (Penfield)
The International Atlas: World Latitudes, Longitudes and
    Time Changes (Shanks)
Interpreting Solar Returns (Eshelman)
Interpreting the Eclipses (Jansky)
The Koch Book of Tables
The Mystery of Personal Identity (Mayer)
The Only Way to...Learn Astrology, Vol. I
    Basic Principles (March & McEvers)
The Only Way to...Learn Astrology, Vol. II
    Math & Interpretation Techniques (March & McEvers)
The Only Way to...Learn Astrology, Vol. III
    Horoscope Analysis (March & McEvers)
The Psychic and the Detective (Druffel with Marcotte)
Psychology of the Planets (F. Gauquelin)
Secrets of the Palm (Hansen)
Seven Paths to Understanding (Dobyns & Wrobel)
Spirit Guides: We Are Not Alone (Belhayes)
Stalking the Wild Orgasm (Kilham)
Tomorrow Knocks (Brunton)
12 Times 12 (McEvers)

EDITOR'S NOTE

This book will use the pronoun "she" as well as the generic "he" so that women are more clearly included. Since his/her or himself/herself are awkward constructions for the reader, these pronouns will be alternated according to chapters. Thus, one chapter will contain all "him's"; another all "her's." These pronouns are used in a universal way and are not intended to represent a specific sex.

CONTENTS

CHAPTER ONE

INTRODUCTION

Why "Instant Astrology"?

This book answers the need for a simple, instantly understandable "how-to" book on astrology — a book that lets you figure things out for yourself without wading through a lot of mathematics or complicated language. Or, if you want to find "instantly" the sections which apply specifically to you, there are diagrams and charts to show you how. The book also tells you how and when a professional astrologer or computer service can be of help, and how to judge their competence. Among the many questions that we answer are:

- Why is it that, when you know your Sun sign and those of your friends and family, some things you read about them fit like a glove while others miss the mark?

- How does your Sun sign react with other Sun signs? Can you be friends with an Aries? Lovers with a Cancer? What happens, for instance, when the parent is a Leo and the child is a Scorpio?

- What colors, gems, flowers, herbs and spices; and what countries have a special connection with your Sun sign?

- What other astrological positions besides your Sun sign are important to you? What is your Moon sign and what does it mean? How do the planets mirror your life?

- What is your Moon phase and what additional themes does it suggest?

- How do you understand and utilize a computer chart or one drawn up by an astrologer? How can your chart tell you what to expect in the future?

What Is Astrology?

Astrology is the study of how conditions in the universe are connected with particular conditions on Earth, and how you and I are affected.

How this study came to be developed goes back to the earliest attempts of people to understand themselves and the universe around them. Long before science became specialized, the observers of the stars were also observers of human behavior and were able to make connections between the two.

Even though astrology laid the groundwork for both modern astronomy and modern psychology, it fell out of favor during the period when "rational" science could not imagine the possibility of an interaction between human beings and the stars, planets, and greater span of the universe. However, modern science itself is gradually realizing that a broader and more comprehensive understanding of the universe reveals that its parts interact, in space-time, in ways never dreamed of before. Astrology can be thought of as an exploration into certain characteristics of time. In other words, the positions of the Sun, Moon, planets and stars, like notes on a musical score, indicate the "cosmic chord" of that moment in time; and any simultaneous event, such as the birth of a human being, is marked with that harmonic pattern.

Here are some of the studies which indicate that what's happening "out there" has a definite connection with what's happening here on Earth.

John H. Nelson, a scientist working for RCA Communications, was trying to find ways of predicting when radio reception would be bad. He discovered that when the planets are in certain positions, there are more disturbances in the electromagnetic envelope surrounding the Earth. These disturbances interfere with the transmission of radio waves. Other researchers have shown that changes in electromagnetic conditions have measurable effects on the biological activity of plants, animals and humans. Therefore, it is no longer a farfetched assumption that the positions of the planets, which affect electromagnetic conditions, are connected with both our biological and closely tied-in psychological functions.

Research scientist Frank A. Brown had some live oysters flown from the Atlantic Coast to his laboratory in Illinois. He set them up in a dark room to see how they would adjust to being separated from their natural ocean environment. At first, the oysters tried to keep the same schedule they were used to, opening their shells at the time of high tide on the Atlantic coast. Within two weeks, however, they seemed to sense that something was wrong and shifted their time of opening to fit with what would have been high tide in Illinois (had it been on the ocean). Since the Moon is the principal cause of high tides, the oysters seem to have been responding directly to the passage of the Moon over Illinois.

Michel and Francoise Gauquelin, two European scientific investigators, have done extensive studies on the connections between the positions of the planets at a person's birth and the profession which he or she enters. Working with thousands of cases, they noted when, at a person's birth, any planets had been on the eastern horizon (**rising**) or nearly overhead (**culminating**). The Gauquelins found undeniable evidence that, for example, persons born with Mars rising or culminating were more likely to become scientists, doctors, athletes or soldiers than writers, painters or musicians. The rising or culmination of other planets was shown to be connected with other professions. Further research found strong correlations between personality traits and planetary placements. (Francoise Gauquelin discusses some of their findings in *The Psychology of the Planets*.)

In addition to serious probing into questions of how and why astrology works, researchers are digging back through the vast store of astrological writings gathered over literally thousands of years, studying them with great care and checking the accuracy of their information by standard scientific techniques. They are finding that the ancients knew a lot more than the more conservative and conventional scientists have heretofore given them credit for.

Carl Jung, the highly respected psychoanalyst and deep observer of human nature, used astrology as one technique to understand his patients. An increasing number of people interested in what makes human beings tick, many psychologists included, are turning to astrology and finding that, both from tradition and new research, it has some very significant things to say about human beings and the world we live in.

Like other systems for understanding human behavior, astrology is not perfect. But the exciting news today is that astrology is being returned to its proper place as a deeply meaningful science and art.

What **Is** The Zodiac?

The ancients observed that the Sun, Moon and planets all appear to move in a relatively narrow band across the sky's background pattern of "fixed" stars. They found that each time the Sun returned to the same section of this band, people born at this time seemed to show similar characteristics. They could also connect the positions of the Moon and planets with certain characteristics.

The ancients called this highway through the sky the **zodiac** (from the same root as **zoo**), meaning "a band of animals." They divided it into twelve sections, or **signs**, and identified each sign according to the background pattern of fixed stars (**constellations**).

Today, of course, we know that the Sun seems to go through the signs of the zodiac because the Earth (like the other planets) revolves around the Sun. The Moon is the only heavenly body (aside from the artificial satellites) that revolves around the Earth, and, due to the marvelous construction of the universe, the path of the Moon also stays inside the zodiac "highway." For an astrological chart of an individual human being we work from an Earth-centered position because we are concerned with the position of the Sun, Moon and planets **as seen from the place and time of birth**.

Because of a slow "wobble" (or **precession**) of the Earth's axis, the Sun is not passing through the same constellations at the same seasons as it was when the constellations were named. Each complete wobble takes twenty-six thousand years, at the end of which the constellations will be back to the point in the cycle where the Sun enters the fixed star constellation of Aries at the spring equinox. At present, however, the spring equinox comes when the Sun is in the early part of the constellation Pisces.

This has brought about some confusion as to the sign designations. However, the majority of Western astrologers identify the astrological beginning of the year with the spring equinox, considering this point **the beginning of Aries** no matter what fixed star constellation is in the background. The sign designations are merely memory aids to designate parts of the yearly cycle. The sign of Cancer, for example, would still indicate summer in the northern hemisphere even if (because of the "wobble") the Sun were passing through the opposite constellation of Capricorn. A Scorpio is still formed in the late fall of the year even if the same background stars do not coincide with the period of the fall which we call "Scorpio."

CHAPTER TWO

WHAT IS THE MEANING OF YOUR SUN SIGN?

Your **Sun sign** is the sign of the zodiac the Sun was in when you were born. Most people know their Sun sign even if they know nothing else about themselves astrologically. This makes understanding the Sun signs a good place to start. There are many elements besides the Sun sign in a complete astrological chart, and we will go into these later on.

Over the thousands of years that astrology has existed, astrologers have developed certain principles which explain many of the personality differences that are noticeable in the different signs. To start with, some of the signs (Aries, Gemini, Leo, Libra, Sagittarius and Aquarius) are **extroverted**, that is, these signs tend to indicate personalities which are outgoing, very social and more assertive. The other signs (Taurus, Cancer, Virgo, Scorpio, Capricorn and Pisces) are **introverted**, that is, introspective, sometimes shy and less assertive.

Another classification of the signs is how they are distributed among the four **elements: fire, air, water** and **earth**. These are not meant to be taken literally but more as embodying types of approach. Thus, at a party, for instance, a fire-sign person (Aries, Leo or Sagittarius) would be drawn to a group discussing a subject with spirit, perhaps loudly. This is because a fire sign operates mainly from enthusiasms and is always asking such questions as: "Will I enjoy doing this?" or "Is this fulfilling?" At the same party, an air-sign person (Gemini, Libra or Aquarius) would connect with a group where a lot of ideas are being tossed around. This is because the air signs are concerned with the need to understand. They are asking themselves the questions: "What is the reason for this?'' and "What does this mean to me?'' A water-sign person (Cancer, Scorpio, or Pisces) will prefer a group that radiates "good vibes." Water signs operate from their emotions: "Does it feel right?'' "What is the atmosphere?'' Lastly, still at the party, an earth-sign person (Taurus, Virgo, or Capricorn) will gravitate to a group discussing practical problems. An Earth sign is, above all, practical, "What is the use of it?'', they ask, or "How does it work?''

Another important classification is the three qualities: **cardinal, fixed** and **mutable**. These are sometimes termed **generative, concentrative** and **distributive**. These characteristics are easy to understand if you think of them in terms of **action**. Thus, the cardinal signs (Aries, Cancer, Libra and Capricorn) **initiate** action. That is, these signs are usually active in starting projects. The fixed signs (Taurus, Leo, Scorpio and Aquarius) can **sustain** the action. They have the ability to follow through on things. The mutable signs (Gemini, Virgo, Sagittarius and Pisces) keep the action **moving** and steer it through its various changes. (See page 195)

These are basic principles involved in understanding the different signs. Your Sun sign characterizes your sense of yourself as an individual. Your Moon sign denotes instinctive and internal reactions. Your rising sign represents how your personality develops — how you relate to others. The Moon sign and the rising sign can be the same as your Sun sign or they can be completely different. The phase of the Moon (and even an eclipse of the Sun or Moon) as well as the positions of the planets further modify and complete the overall astrological picture. We will learn about all of these later on in this book.

If you are not sure of your Sun sign, or if you were born near the twenty-first of the month, when the signs usually change, turn to page 16 to find your Sun sign.

Aries ♈

Aries people are creative and action oriented. When an idea strikes them, they usually jump to their feet and dash off to implement it. That is, on the rare occasion that they are actually sitting, an untypical position for an Aries. They are natural self-starters. The problem is to get them to slow down or stop. Their courage and enthusiasm often borders on the foolhardy.

An Aries is quick to anger, like a firecracker with a short fuse, but it is an explosion which reaches its height suddenly and then is quick-ly over. The Aries will, of course, expect that anyone who is the object of the temper flash will realize that everything is forgotten and forgiven a few minutes later.

It is not in the Aries nature to be devious or subtle. They are usually blunt. When an Aries is self-centered (which they can be), it stands out like a sore thumb. On the other hand, their spontaneous approach to life can be very endearing.

IF YOU ARE AN ARIES:
You function best in a situation where your ability to get the ball rolling is needed. Along with this, you need a great deal of freedom of action. Avoid work situations calling for a lot of routine and detailed instructions. Both at work or with personal projects, you operate best when you have someone else who can follow through after you have set the direction and have gotten things started. If your job does not require much physical activity, try to get a good amount of it in your spare time.

Put some conscious attention to acquiring diplomacy and tact. Realize that there are times when your naturally competitive approach is out of place. Patience and the ability to plan ahead are two other areas in which you may have to put some effort. Also, the ability to follow through is not a natural Aries trait and needs to be developed. Restrain your impulse to dash on to something else rather than finish what you have already started. Stop sometimes and look at the map before you charge ahead.

Your particular gift is to overcome inertia and spark the flame of enthusiasm in other people.

Taurus ♉

Tauruses have a slow and unhurried natural rhythm. Attempts to speed them up are more likely to fluster them completely.

The essence of Taurus is stability. Taurus people are steady and patient, capable of hard work and sustained effort. On the other hand, when they relax, they are usually content with simple, quiet pleasures.

Tauruses carefully deliberate before starting any action or coming to a conclusion. But, once they have made up their minds, it is hard to change either their minds or their course of action.

Tauruses like their possessions to be, above all, practical, although they appreciate beautiful things. Once they have settled on their favorites, they are quite content with them forever or at least until they are completely worn out.

Tauruses have a close affinity to the Earth and nature. They take easily to the nurturing of plants, animals and other humans.

They are affectionate, good-natured, and slow to anger. Once angered, however, they can exhibit a sustained fury the likes of which are not soon forgotten.

IF YOU ARE A TAURUS:
You function best under conditions where there is a certain amount of control and predictability. You are not at your best when called upon to make instant decisions about constantly changing circumstances. However, you have the ability to sustain action and to follow through on projects.

Try to free yourself from being overly attached to specific things or ideas. Open yourself to different opinions, even when these run counter to your own. Try to distinguish between being good to yourself and being self-indulgent. Guard against holding grudges or other negative thought patterns.

Your particular gift is to serve as a steadying influence for others. Your practicality and steadfastness serve as an example.

Gemini ♊

Gemini minds are quick and curious. Geminis are interested in all kinds of people and ideas, and are fascinated with all aspects of communication. They are constantly intrigued by something new. They like plenty of variety in their day-to-day activities, friends and food. Above all, they enjoy reading and talking.

The typical Gemini is constantly aware of everything going on around him or her and wants to understand it all. Gemini people move quickly. They are outgoing and have a sparkling wit. They can turn with agility from one pursuit to another, oblivious of any inconsistency this may entail.

Geminis quickly grasp new knowledge and once something has been explained to them, they can usually turn around and explain it with great ease to someone else.

A characteristic of most Geminis to have several activities going at once. They are interested in virtually everything and have a strong desire to communicate it all to others.

IF YOU ARE A GEMINI:
It is against your nature to be working alone, particularly in a routine

job. Find some area of work in which you can communicate with others and which offers you sufficient variety.

You have a tendency to tackle too much at one time and to spread yourself too thin. You may need to pay conscious attention to limiting your activities. Try to be aware that below the surface of everything are depths which can only be reached by extended thought and concentration.

Try to deal with your problems with more than the superficiality of the intellect alone. Increase your sense of "feeling" in each situation. Develop an awareness of the need, at times, to relax and center yourself.

Your dual gifts, as a Gemini, are quick comprehension combined with the ability to communicate this comprehension to others.

Cancer ♋

Cancers are emotional barometers. They are constantly aware of the atmosphere of feelings surrounding them. They are sensitive to how something is said rather than the meanings of the words. If they perceive the emotional tone as insincere, they will distrust what is being said.

The Cancer moods are varied and changeable. They are capable of communicating their deepest feelings to others. However, if they sense that the atmosphere is not receptive, they can be unreachable.

Cancers have a special need to nurture. Home and the family are especially important to them. This is as true for Cancer males as it is for Cancer females.

Cancers are tenacious in pursuit of their objectives. Even the ebb and flow of their moods will not deter them.

IF YOU ARE A CANCER:
At work, you do not thrive under conditions of tension and crisis. However, you can be as comfortable working alone as with the public, the latter aided by your basically sympathetic nature. In your spare time, you probably take naturally to gardening as well as all types of collecting.

You may need to work on the ability to detach yourself from the emotions of others. Try to learn how to defeat a "crabby" mood. Avoid refocusing on the negative aspects of the past.

Your basic gifts are the abilities to nurture and to work creatively with emotional atmospheres.

Leo ♌

Leo people like to be at the hub of things. They have a sense of the dramatic and a tendency towards display. Warmth, a strong awareness of self and a natural dignity are their key characteristics. Usually they have a great deal of energy and can project the kind of confidence that strengthens others. Also, they have a natural authority which makes them good leaders, although this quality can appear overbearing at times.

Relationships are very important to Leos. They are not loners. They are generous, affectionate and very loyal toward those they love. In fact, they have a tendency to become overattached.

Leos retain much of the child, a quality which is usually more submerged in the rest of us. It is therefore easy for them to relate to children or to the childlike qualities in others. They appreciate play as a re-creation of the spirit, and see overseriousness as a state of imbalance. Like children, their basic nature is open and trusting. Craftiness is alien to them.

IF YOU ARE A LEO:
You are capable of hard work and do not mind a certain amount of routine so long as you are in a situation where you are not hurried and can relate to other people. Also, you enjoy a sense of responsibility. You can easily function in a position of authority, although you may find it difficult to delegate work.

Try to distinguish between giving direction to others when they need it and being overbearing. Guard against being self-centered. You may need to develop a sense of detachment and an appreciation of solitude.

Your greatest contribution is a warmth and understanding that can raise the spirits of those around you.

Virgo ♍

Typically, Virgos are perfectionists. They are also capable of the extremely hard work and dedication that is necessary to get all the details correct. Since they usually have varied interests, they can collect a remarkable amount of data about different things. A few are walking encyclopedias. At the very least, they can usually pop up with interesting facts on a great variety of subjects. This passion for data complements their analytical nature. They are not likely to make generalizations on the basis of too few facts, since they realize instinctively that understanding all the parts is necessary to grasping the whole picture. They can make exacting discriminations. Occasionally the pressure of too many details can cause a temporary confusion in their minds, but this is quickly overcome by their talents for systematization and organization.

IF YOU ARE A VIRGO:
You work best when meticulous attention to detail is called for. You can work both alone or with others, so long as you are not forced to work in a slipshod manner. You excel at technical work, research and analysis. The importance of Mercury to this sign shows special qualifications for teaching, communication and service. Spare-time activities also usually involve projects which lean heavily toward details and attempted perfection.

Try to avoid getting so involved in details that you lose track of the overall picture. This is often difficult for a Virgo, but it is something which can be developed. Keep in mind that the "feel" of something is often as important as the facts. Remember also that the ultimate perfection you envision is often not humanly possible. A Virgo has to guard against extremes of criticism, either of self or of others, particularly the tendency to keep mentally rehashing past errors instead of accepting them and going on to new things.

Your special talent is the ability to gather together all the elements of a situation and work toward its perfection.

Libra ♎

Libras are endowed with the kind of gentleness and charm that draws people to them. A Libra is also inclined to show consideration and tolerance toward others. Their most natural attributes are harmony and balance. They make good laywers, diplomats and peacemakers, but with a strong sense of justice. They try to see all sides of a question and strive for compromise. However, sometimes the Libra awareness of the "other" can express itself in vigorous competition rather than sweet cooperation.

Like the other air signs (Gemini and Aquarius), intellectual understanding and communication usually play a prominent role in their lives. The significance of Venus to this sign points to the many Libras with careers in the arts or, at the very least, to a strong appreciation of beauty.

IF YOU ARE A LIBRA:
You are most content working in a pleasant, clean and orderly atmosphere with others who do not put undue pressure on you. Because of your tact and diplomatic manner, you will have no difficulty in directing other people. However, you are not at your best when called upon to make frequent snap decisions without enough time to weigh the matters involved.

Attributes you may need to develop: the ability to make quick decisions and to take a firm stand when necessary, even though others may object; the ability to act independently and with consistency; and the ability to be candid and direct with others.

The gift of Libra is to communicate a sense of beauty and harmony to others.

Scorpio ♏

The intensity of Scorpio people is legendary. They are also strong-willed and determined. When necessary, they can act with great incisiveness.

Scorpios, like the other water signs (Cancer and Pisces), are deeply sensitive. They are capable of great insights into the underlying feelings and motives of others. Beware of trying to pull the wool over a Scorpio's eyes. The "scorpion sting" may be the result.

Scorpios have strong passions which run deep and often silently. They have strong energies which, when channeled, can give great qualities of endurance. They are most often self-sufficient but, on the other hand, can be firmly attached emotionally. Often their lives follow a cyclical pattern of depletion followed by periods of complete renewal.

IF YOU ARE A SCORPIO:
You will typically take to exacting work, particularly when it also challenges your resourcefulness and enables you to probe under the surface of what you are working on. In any event, work should channel your strong energies if they are to function well.

Try to develop a sense of detachment, as well as the ability to be tolerant and forgiving. Learn to share your feelings with others. Guard against paranoia and try not to hold grudges. If your work does not provide exercise for your whole body, try to get it in your spare time.

Your gifts are courage, intensity and depth of understanding.

Sagittarius ♐

Enthusiasm is one of the primary characteristics of a Sagittarius. Along with this is a determination to achieve perspective and to see the overall point of view. Their search for an ever broader understanding can often lead them to a serious study of religion, philosophy and/or sociology. They particularly appreciate the broadening effects of travel.

A Sagittarius is usually spontaneous, with an inclination to be straightforward and often bluntly honest. This inherent frankness is not motivated by a desire to wound but by a determination to find and tell the truth whatever it may be. What makes this tendency acceptable to others is the warmth and natural benevolence of the Sagittarians. They are inclined to be jovial, optimistic and outgoing.

Sagittarius people love the outdoors and often have a strong enthusiasm for sports and outdoor adventures. With this comes a certain amount of restlessness. Above all, they value their freedom.

IF YOU ARE A SAGITTARIUS:
In a work situation, you should avoid jobs where you have to deal with too many minor points. You can only handle them to the degree that you can fit them into the overall picture. You can think easily in broad abstractions but find it hard to focus in on details. Sagittarius people have a flair for management, teaching and working with people. You might like a job involving animals or one where you can travel.

Try not to go in too many directions at once. You may need to develop an ability to cope with details as well as a certain amount of fixity of purpose. Other areas to work on are tact, restraint and the ability to temper your enthusiasm with realism.

As a Sagittarius, you bring to the rest of us warmth and enthusiasm. You can lead us to insights into the broader perspective.

Capricorn ♑

Capricorns are strongly goal-directed. Whatever these goals are, they pursue them with determination, persistence and patience. They methodically plan ahead and then diligently work at executing their plan. They are usually practical and responsible and have a sense of the "right" way to do things. They abhor waste and frivolity. Capricorns judge things first by their usefulness. They approach anything new with caution. They most often achieve success through a slow and steady rise.

Capricorns tend to be serious. If they allow themselves to play, it is because they realize that recreation is necessary for efficient work. Their humor is straight-faced and dry.

IF YOU ARE A CAPRICORN:
You can work at a variety of occupations. You function best when you can apply your sense of organization and structure. You combine a talent for management with an ability to carry out instructions with care. When the purpose of the job seems objectively worthwhile to you, you work best; and when you are in an inherently chaotic situation, you work worst.

You may need to develop the ability to lighten up and not take life too seriously. Learn to counter the tendency toward depression with optimism. Try to learn to loosen up, relax and to show your affectionate feelings toward others.

As a Capricorn your contribution is the ability to help others envision and pursue their goals in spite of adversity.

Aquarius ≈

Aquarius people usually think in terms of "we." They are the cooperators of the zodiac. At the same time, though this may seem paradoxical, they have a strong need for personal freedom. They do not like to be fenced in.

Like the other air signs (Gemini and Libra), they lead with their ideas. With an Aquarius, these are likely to be, in some way or other, far out. They are good at envisioning completely unconventional solutions to human and other problems.

Aquarius people are inclined to be impersonal. This is the result of their instinctive awareness that all human beings are connected and that an overemphasis on the individual can create an imbalance. At the same time, they have a respect for the ideas of others.

There is an inventive element in the Aquarius makeup. They will always try to find a better way of doing something. When they do, it is often a concept "out of the blue" that sidesteps strictly logical methods of deduction.

IF YOU ARE AN AQUARIUS:
You enjoy working in organizations where you can come into contact with people. You are not likely to be happy when forced to work totally alone or when required to follow a set routine. An Aquarius thrives

on the unexpected.

Restrain your natural tendency to try to change everybody. Develop more flexibility in your opinions. Also, you need to develop a higher degree of sensitivity to the emotional content of many situations.

Your Aquarius gifts are the sense of human connections and the creation of new ways of working together.

Pisces ♓

Pisces people are acutely sensitive to their environment. They are strongly tuned in, consciously or unconsciously, to the people around them. Often they do not know what is coming from themselves and what is coming from others. They have a natural awareness of currents flowing underneath the surface of events and are extremely sympathetic to, and often identify with, the problems of others.

Pisceans are dreamers. It is not easy for them to deal with the practical world. They need a certain amount of escape time and solitude to adjust themselves to reality. More than any other sign, Pisceans need, both at home and at work, pleasant environments.

IF YOU ARE A PISCES:
You do not take well to strict discipline, routine or high pressure. You are most comfortable in work which involves service to others or where you can exercise your strong imagination.

You may need to develop the ability to act decisively, even when this could be upsetting to others. Do not let others impose on you. Keep a space for your dreams but try to consciously focus on the necessary practicalities of life. If it is not part of your regular occupation, try to engage in some form of the arts as an outlet for your imagination.

To the other signs of the zodiac, you can bring a sense of true sympathy and an insight into the realms of the imagination.

SUN SIGNS

Sign	Dates	Natural Qualities	May Need To Develop
Aries ♈	March 21- April 20	**assertiveness**: active, innovative, impulsive, exploring, energetic, forceful, alert, quick, outspoken, pioneering, direct, intense.	**control**: moderation, tolerance, patience, concentration, cooperation, restraint, planning, humility.
Taurus ♉	April 20- May 21	**persistence**: conservative, patient, practical, dogmatic, meticulous, careful, possessive, stable, deliberate, contented, stubborn, steadfast.	**flexibility**: adaptability, versatility, initiative, imagination, forgiveness, enterprise.
Gemini ♊	May 21- June 21	**inquisitiveness**: adaptable, alert, talkative, changeable, witty, restless, spontaneous, lively, intellectual, impatient, versatile, original.	**patience**: concentration, persistence, practicality, quietness, sympathy, forethought.
Cancer ♋	June 21- July 22	**sensitivity**: passive, romantic, sympathetic, dependable, reserved, reflective, nurturing, protective, receptive, cautious, timid, moody.	**logic**: assertiveness, forthrightness, daring, outspokeness, ability to let the past go.
Leo ♌	July 22- August 23	**self-expression**: creative, dramatic, ardent, exuberant, flamboyant, proud, broad-minded, expansive, dignified, loyal, generous, optimistic.	**humility**: adaptability, versatility, flexibility, sensitivity, thrift, cooperation.
Virgo ♍	August 23- September 23	**analytical**: practical, skeptical, systematic, industrious, fastidious, scientific, perfectionistic, methodical, meticulous, resourceful, calculating, orderly.	**tolerance**: optimism, confidence, instinct, sympathy, acceptance of imperfection, breadth of vision.

Sign	Dates	Natural Qualities	May Need To Develop
Libra ♎	September 23-October 23	**diplomatic**: friendly, easygoing, rational, amiable, considerate, helpful, sympathetic, artistic, idealistic, sensitive, generous, tolerant.	**decisiveness**: firmness, consistency, independence, application, depth, directness.
Scorpio ♏	October 23-November 22	**intensity**: incisive, passionate, courageous, determined, sensitive, perceptive, dominant, ambitious, sensual, enigmatic, mysterious, energetic.	**detachment**: forgiveness, cooperation, diplomacy, openness, right direction of energy.
Sagittarius ♐	November 22-December 21	**enthusiasm**: optimistic, versatile, restless, independent, inquisitive, spontaneous, intuitive, friendly, athletic, farsighted, buoyant, pioneering.	**restraint**: responsibility, sincerity, realism, tact, continuity, fixity of purpose.
Capricorn ♑	December 21-January 20	**seriousness**: cautious, economical, diligent, determined, orderly, reserved, ambitious, disciplined, diplomatic, steadfast, methodical, dependable.	**buoyancy**: sociability, optimism, playfulness, generosity, lightness of touch.
Aquarius ♒	January 20-February 19	**independence**: altruistic, sincere, logical, friendly, detached, versatile, generous, outgoing, visionary, eccentric, cooperative, liberal.	**predictability**: efficiency, tact, accuracy, quietness, flexibility, respect for meaningful conventions.
Pisces ♓	February 19-March 21	**sympathy**: understanding, imaginative, poetic, emotional, gentle, adaptable, receptive, creative, loyal, perceptive, intuitive, tolerant.	**practicality**: decisiveness, determination, logic, detachment, stability, not letting others impose on them.

CHAPTER THREE

SUN SIGN COMPATIBILITY

One sometimes hears such statements as: "I'm an Aquarius. I can't seem to get along with a Taurus or a Scorpio," or "I'm a Taurus and my best friends seem to be other Tauruses or Capricorns."

There is a widely held belief that certain Sun sign combinations should avoid each other and that other Sun sign combinations always hit it off. Unfortunately, when people feel this way and meet one of their "incompatible" Sun signs, they consciously or unconsciously look for negative characteristics. They often miss out on what could be a beautiful relationship.

In actuality, any two Sun signs can be compatible provided that each individual learns to understand, and develops sympathy for, the different modes of expression of the other. Also, there are many other elements in a complete chart, such as the rising sign, Moon sign and planets, which can mesh well together even if the Sun sign combination has problems. **Never judge a relationship by Sun signs alone**.

However, the Sun sign combination can be a guide to similarities or differences of approach which, if you understand them, can improve a relationship.

Comparing Sun signs is much like predicting how two people of different nationalities will react to each other, for example, a Japanese and an Italian. Certain generalizations can be made: the Japanese will probably talk more quietly, using fewer hand gestures than the Italian; the Italian will probably come to the point of the conversation with fewer formalities than the Japanese. However, both the Japanese and the Italian will also relate as individuals, over and beyond national habit patterns.

Here (in the following pages) are some ground rules for each particular Sun sign combination in friendship, love and marriage, and parent-child relationships.

FRIENDSHIP (starts page 19):
In the full-page chart at the beginning, the intersection of the horizontal column with the vertical one gives the page number for that particular combination.

LOVE AND MARRIAGE (starts page 41):

PARENT-CHILD RELATIONSHIPS (starts page 62):
The signs for the parents are across the top and the signs for the children are down the side.

Friendship

	Aries	Taurus	Gemini	Cancer	Leo	Virgo	Libra	Scorpio	Sagittarius	Capricorn	Aquarius	Pisces
Aries	20	20	20	20	21	21	21	22	22	22	23	23
Taurus	20	23	23	24	24	24	25	25	25	25	26	26
Gemini	20	23	26	26	27	27	27	27	28	28	28	29
Cancer	20	24	26	29	29	29	29	30	30	30	31	31
Leo	21	24	27	29	31	31	32	32	32	32	33	33
Virgo	21	24	27	29	31	33	33	34	34	34	34	35
Libra	21	25	27	29	32	33	35	35	35	36	36	36
Scorpio	22	25	27	30	32	34	35	37	37	37	37	38
Sagittarius	22	25	28	30	32	34	35	37	38	38	38	39
Capricorn	22	25	28	30	32	34	36	37	38	39	39	39
Aquarius	23	26	28	31	33	34	36	37	38	39	40	40
Pisces	23	26	29	31	33	35	36	38	39	39	40	40

ARIES — ARIES

This is likely to be a stormy relationship, even though two Aries Sun signs can become dedicated friends. There can be monumental quarrels, but these will be resolved quickly. Neither will feel deeply or permanently hurt by these collisions of temperament. Their other friends will be amazed by the violence of their disagreements, and even more amazed that the next day, or even hour, after an argument, two Aries people can be laughing together and even slapping each other's back in genuine comaraderie. In fact, what Aries likes is the "fizz" of the relationship.

A friendship between two Aries Sun signs can be just a bit standoffish at times. To keep from demolishing each other they need that little bit of insulation.

ARIES — TAURUS

Like a good many of the sign combinations, an Aries and a Taurus can become good friends if each understands the differences in temperament of the other. Also, each can find in the other what she may lack, or feels to be lacking in herself. In a combination like Aries-Taurus, with vast psychological differences, the two friends may remain somewhat of a mystery to each other. This quality can also be a big attraction.

A Taurus does not like to make split-second decisions the way an Aries does, which may sometimes dismay the Aries. However, the Aries will feel in the Taurus a dependable fixity, a needed friend when she needs to calm down.

ARIES — GEMINI

The Aries-Gemini relationship is likely to be an off-and-on one. The Aries may sometimes be a bit rash and headstrong for the reasoning Gemini. On the other hand, the Aries may find the Gemini too much up in the air. Their common enthusiasm for the new may form the basis for a lasting bond. However, one may periodically get fed up with the other and they may not see each other for months. Then they will run into each other on the street or at a party and a "new" friendship will start on some new basis or new interest. Each has a lot to learn from the other. The Gemini can help the Aries become more adaptable and less involved with personal temperament. The Aries can help the Gemini actually get moving with her ideas.

ARIES — CANCER

An Aries-Cancer relationship can go two ways. If the Cancer manages to douse the Aries fiery enthusiasms, then it can be destructive. But if the Cancer can slow the Aries down and enable her to follow through with what are sometimes overextended and naively optimistic plans, then the relationship can be very creative.

If the Aries's overassertive nature drives the introverted Cancer into her "shell," then the relationship will not work. But if the Aries's outgoing qualities bring the Cancer out of this shell, the relationship will work positively.

ARIES — LEO

Both of these signs, being fire signs, have a deep understanding of the other's needs and feelings. They have the same fire-sign intensity of enthusiasms. The most important thing for them to learn (with each other) is how to share the limelight. They are both temperamental and must avoid the feeling that one has an "edge" over the other.

They are very good companions for traveling, shopping and sports. The creativity and self-expression of the slower-paced Leo may often use the initiative abilities of the Aries to good advantage.

ARIES — VIRGO

On the face of it, Aries and Virgo are not the most likely combination. On the other hand, as is true with many "unlikely" combinations, they can learn a lot from each other. A Virgo needs everything to be perfect and correct to the last detail before going ahead. An Aries will usually go ahead no matter what the imperfections of a situation. If an Aries will let a Virgo friend organize all the details of a mutual enterprise, whether it is going to the theater or taking a long trip together, they will make a workable combination. Likewise, an Aries can activate a Virgo and provide the background energy for an ongoing activity, such as a sport or a hobby.

ARIES — LIBRA

These two signs (opposites in the zodiac) are truly complementary. Since they are both cardinal (initiating) and extroverted (outgoing) signs, they can move harmoniously in the same direction. Aries is able to add the vital emotional enthusiasm to Libra's essentially intellectual and elegantly balanced ideas.

The Aries's sometimes temperamental and touchy nature can be handled with diplomatic ease by the Libra. The usually impulsive Aries spirit can counterbalance the often wavering and indecisive Libra nature.

ARIES — SCORPIO

Any Aries-Scorpio relationship, whether friendship, love or otherwise, will be a very intense one. They have all the potentialities for being very close friends, with a great deal of mutual respect, or for becoming enemies. The Scorpio nature has the strength and will to absorb the intense psychic force-field of the Aries, often an effort for most of the other signs. The occasional flare-ups of temperament between these two signs are usually patched up quickly enough by the Aries, avoiding any lasting damage to the relationship.

Love and hate are always close at hand with the Scorpio, but an Aries will usually not let a disagreement stand long enough to solidify a turnabout in affection, and the deep loyalty of the Scorpio to friends will usually give a "grace period" in the relationship.

ARIES — SAGITTARIUS

Aries and Sagittarius operate on the same psychological level and share fire-sign enthusiasms. Their mutual taste for adventures of all kinds makes them great companions. However, their antics together often seem designed to annoy everyone else.

When the Sagittarius tendency toward "brutal honesty" becomes manifest, Aries may react badly. The Sagittarius will just be bewildered by the Aries outburst of anger, but because of the Sagittarius tendency to keep emotion on the surface, she will not be hurt by it.

At worst, the Aries-Sagittarius pair may develop prejudices toward other people or groups. At best, Aries can help Sagittarius focus in on mutual interests and projects, and the Sagittarius can broaden the intellectual horizons of the Aries.

ARIES — CAPRICORN

This is sometimes a difficult relationship where one strong force is working for or against another. They are similar in many ways and have a potential affinity, but there are also some strong differences that need to be resolved in a friendship. The impulsiveness and assertiveness of the Aries will either dismay the more down-to-earth Capricorn or will inspire her to get started. On the other hand, the Capricorn is a good listener and infinitely patient, and this is just what an Aries needs. The Aries must try to understand the basic Capricorn need for privacy and should leave her alone when she needs to be alone. The Aries may interpret this as indifference or coldness, but this is not the case. When the Capricorn is in the right mood, she can be as warmhearted and enthusiastic about the friendship as the Aries instinctively is.

ARIES — AQUARIUS

This is a definitely good relationship, particularly if it is combined with a common social cause or humanitarian endeavor. They make good companions to explore groups and activities, although the Aries may soon move on to a new group before the Aquarius has had time to fully settle down in the previous group.

The open, warmhearted, and generous nature of the Aries will superficially seem like the humanistic social consciousness of the Aquarian friend, but they come from different psychological sources. As long as the Aries-Aquarian friendship can operate on the external level of social action and agree not to examine basic motivations, the relationship is a very creative and productive one.

ARIES — PISCES

It is fortunate that there is a lot of understanding and sympathy in the Pisces nature, for otherwise it might be hard for a Pisces to deal with an Aries. A Pisces will always see the warm and generous side of an Aries. The occasional bluster, verbiage and impatience of the Aries can flow past the Pisces without a bad effect.

Aries is a fire sign and Pisces a water sign. But water does not necessarily douse a fire. It can be used to generate steam which can, in turn, activate an engine or sooth the nerves (as in a steambath). Like a steambath, the Pisces can relax the Aries and show her the more fanciful side of things.

TAURUS — TAURUS

These signs, when combined, make loyal old friends. The relationship may lack the verve and excitement that combinations with other signs will bring, as the Taurus is by nature conservative and placid. The two together make for a somewhat unexciting but dependable relationship. This combination is particularly good for such mutual activities as gardening, singing groups or playing music together. They will discuss new possessions and also enjoy exchanging gifts. Their unhurried pace will be a comfort to both, as no Taurus likes to rush. Each will have the feeling that she can rely on the other.

TAURUS — GEMINI

If they can learn to understand their differences, these are good zodiac signs for friendship. The Taurus tends to get in a rut occasionally, and having a Gemini friend can be very valuable. The imaginative Gemini will always be finding new, and usually exciting, projects for both and carry the Taurus along with the Gemini enthusiasm, although the

Gemini should realize that a Taurus can't jump into projects quite as quickly as she can. On the other hand, the Taurus can help the Gemini follow through on what she has started rather than leap from one thing to another.

TAURUS — CANCER
The Taurus-Cancer combination makes a great friendship. They will both love growing things, whether it be house plants in the city or a sizable vegetable garden in the country. They will be quiet friends, the kind who will like to sit together for hours without saying anything or will take long walks together. They particularly enjoy visiting each other's homes, both of which will probably be furnished with antiques (if they can afford them) or carefully restored "found" pieces if on a budget. They both admire old things as well as beautiful things, the Taurus perhaps for their actual value and the Cancer for their sentimental value. However, these somewhat separate motivations will seldom come into conflict.

TAURUS — LEO
Here is another pair of dependable friends. Both Taurus and Leo are known for their dependability and loyalty to friends. Unlike the Taurus-Taurus and the Taurus-Cancer combinations, which tend to be a bit placid, the outgoing Leo can add just enough fire to the relationship to give it some verve.

The more practical Taurus will particularly appreciate the generosity and honesty of the Leo, and the Leo will be able to participate, to some degree, in the Taurus preoccupation with exquisite possessions and love of beauty.

Both can be stubborn and they should understand that if they disagree, neither will give in easily.

TAURUS — VIRGO
Here are two friends who will be at their best when working together. Mutual hobbies are just up their alley. In some activity like gardening or crafts, the Taurus may end up doing all the heavy work, but the Virgo will be just as busy making sure that all the details are perfect. Both of these signs are "down to earth" and they make solid, enduring friends. The inherent patience of the Taurus combines well with the systematic nature of the Virgo. The Taurus steadiness can help to calm the Virgo worries and jittery nervousness. At the same time, the Virgo discernment and critical insights can provide the stimulus for change in a habit-bound Taurus.

TAURUS — LIBRA

This combination makes a good pair for participation together in some form of the arts. They both love beautiful things, which gives them many mutual interests. The determined nature of the Taurus will help the occasionally vacillating Libra make up her mind about a given project and then help to carry it through. There may be endless conversation between these two on aesthetics, but not too heavily or overseriously as they both have a good underlying sense of humor. Also, both Taurus and Libra enjoy meeting other people, so they will enjoy going places together. The Libra will be able to smooth over differences between the Taurus and others.

TAURUS — SCORPIO

Here again we run into a pair of opposites in the zodiac. Opposites can repel or attract, sometimes both at the same time. The Taurus is practical and down to earth, while the Scorpio is emotionally fluid and intense. If the Taurus can become a stabilizing influence for the Scorpio, this relationship will work well, as the Taurus can add humor and the Scorpio intensity to the relationship. Since both are capable of holding grudges, they must be careful to bring into the open any problems that might arise between them, and thus keep a good emotional flow.

TAURUS — SAGITTARIUS

This has the makings of a solid, generous relationship, although the Sagittarius, with her impulsiveness, may exasperate the conservative and more placid Taurus. A Sagittarius with a Taurus friend will quickly learn that, after an argument, all is forgiven with some small, practical gift.

    The Taurus is a good stabilizing influence for the unrestrained and sometimes impractical enthusiasm of the Sagittarius. In turn, the Sagittarius can get the Taurus out of some of her ruts and into new activities or off to new places.

TAURUS — CAPRICORN

These are two friends who will enoy down-to-earth pastimes together. Activities like crafts, hiking, and rock hunting are their forté. Both enjoy doing "practical" things and easily cooperate in building and completing do-it-yourself projects. The Capricorn will lead the way to new activities. The Taurus will be a relaxing, stabilizing influence. A Capricorn has a basic need to be alone some of the time, and this is an easy need for the Taurus to respect. Also, the Capricorn is often hard driving and needs a friend such as a Taurus to help her relax and enjoy what's happening now rather than continually focus on future goals.

TAURUS — AQUARIUS
An Aquarius has many friends but few close ones. This contrasts with the Taurus who may have fewer friends but more close ones. Nevertheless, there are many Taurus-Aquarius relationships that grow into close and long-lasting friendships. The Aquarius can often jolt the Taurus out of her outworn habits of thought. The basic danger in this relationship is that the Aquarius may spend a lot of time trying to "reform" the Taurus, which (in Aquarian terms) is likely to mean getting the Taurus to grasp the larger humanitarian, sociological picture. The Taurus (despite her personal and close-to-home generosity and instinctive humanitarianism) thinks in more personal terms.

TAURUS — PISCES
Here are a pair of low-key, easygoing friends. The Pisces is instinctively more imaginative than the Taurus but may lack determination and concentration. The Taurus can help her Pisces friend to bring dreams and poetic visions to some kind of practical reality. On the other hand, the Pisces can help keep the Taurus from getting completely bogged down in the practical and mundane. Both are likely to love animals, growing things, and nature in general. Probably they will enjoy quiet, at-home activities together.

GEMINI — GEMINI
Here are two perfect friends. Both have their carefree Gemini wit and charm. They reinforce each other's inquisitive nature. They can spend hours on the phone with each other and never run out of conversation, or they can write long, long letters to each other. They are at their best going to, or giving, parties together. They both like going places and trying new things. Long separations will not affect their friendship, and they will enjoy reunions, during which they can catch up on all the things that each has done in the interim.

GEMINI — CANCER
Gemini and Cancer people can be good friends if each is patient and understanding with the other. The cautious Cancer will be wary of the unpredictable nature of the Gemini. On the other hand, the Cancer can have a relaxing influence on the Gemini as well as making her aware of, and accepting of, the many shades of feeling. The Gemini can

sharpen the intellectual understanding of the Cancer. The Cancer will be amused by the Gemini's having to understand all about something before she does it, since the Cancer goes by what has the right "feel." On the other hand, sometimes Cancerian feelings may lead her off the track, and the Gemini approach can help to explain what is happening.

GEMINI — LEO
This is a good combination. Both enjoy sharing their dreams and plans with each other. There are long discussions that will range over the whole gamut of ideas and intellectual pursuits. The Gemini will furnish the variety in the relationship, while the Leo will give a degree of steadiness. They will enjoy going to movies and plays together, and both like meeting new people, if for different reasons (the Gemini for the variety and the Leo for the new audience). Gemini must not expect Leo to change plans at the drop of a new idea.

GEMINI — VIRGO
Here is an unlikely combination on the face of it, but (surprisingly enough) Gemini and Virgo are likely to have similar tastes in books, movies and other intellectual areas. This, at the very least, will give them plenty to talk about. On the other hand, the Gemini carefree sense of humor will often be lost on the Virgo cool and ultralogical mind. The Gemini is the extrovert and at her best at parties or social events; whereas the Virgo tends to be introverted and needs abundant time to be alone either to work or to worry. If they understand and can tolerate each other's needs in this respect, they can be valuable counterbalancing influences for each other.

GEMINI — LIBRA
This can be a very stimulating relationship, both from the standpoint of discussion and the use of intellectual and aesthetic ideas. The Gemini seems to collect ideas, often for the sheer fun of collecting them. Their novelty and, sometimes, humor amuse the Gemini. The Libra, on the other hand, will collect ideas to examine them and weigh them carefully to see how they fit with larger concepts, particularly in the arts. In discussions and activities the Libra can help the Gemini develop and organize ideas. Both enjoy going places together and meeting other people.

GEMINI — SCORPIO
This relationship might seem somewhat superficial, although there **is** a basis for a long-lasting and sincere friendship if each can develop

understanding and acceptance of the other. They have in common a hungry curiosity, though on different levels. The Gemini understanding of the inherent interconnectedness of everything and everyone in the world will help free the Scorpio of some of her jealous guardedness. The Scorpio will observe all of the Gemini activities, listening to her ideas, and try to figure out what is going on underneath. The Gemini can help the Scorpio achieve a lighter touch, and the Scorpio can help steady the Gemini's ever-active mind and help her see the deeper implications of ideas.

GEMINI — SAGITTARIUS

Here is a friendship that can be based on social activities and the sharing of ideas. As opposite signs in the zodiac, their minds truly complement each other. Both Gemini and Sagittarius enjoy traveling, parties and meeting all sorts of different people. They are both very active and extroverted and will enjoy doing things together. The Sagittarius can help the Gemini fit her many facets into wider horizons, and the Gemini can fill in the details of the Sagittarius tendency toward unclear generalization. Sagittarius can get Gemini into sports, which gives Gemini a needed change from too much thinking.

GEMINI — CAPRICORN

Here is another combination that requires a lot of mutual understanding. The Capricorn must accept the fact that the ever-experimenting Gemini never likes to do things the same way twice, while the Gemini must understand the satisfaction and security that a Capricorn gets from routine. In a workable friendship between these two, the Gemini can help the Capricorn occasionally break her routine and try something new. The Capricorn can organize some of the myriad ideas generated out of the head of the Gemini and help her follow through on them.

GEMINI — AQUARIUS

Here is another relationship that should produce a lot of conversation. The Aquarius will steer the conversation to the larger social implications. The Gemini will furnish many ideas to think about, much "food for thought," so to speak. The more serious and conceptual approach of the Aquarius will be tempered somewhat by the flexibility and wit of the Gemini, and the Aquarian grasp of the whole issue will help steady the Gemini tendency to flit from point to point. They will enjoy exploring new things together — new ideas, activities, people and places.

GEMINI — PISCES

Both of these signs like all sorts of people and all sorts of variety. They can have many enjoyable discussions. The Gemini will be able to explain to the Pisces the psychological motivations behind her feelings. The Pisces will be able to communicate her talent for fantasy and pure imagination, thus deepening the Gemini sensitivity.

At parties or other social functions, the Pisces is liable to be the quiet one but will enjoy observing and even sometimes participating in the vivacity of the Gemini. However, the Gemini must understand that the Pisces sometimes needs solitude.

CANCER — CANCER

Two Cancers make very compatible friends. They will enjoy visiting each other's homes as well as going places together, trying new restaurants, etc. They can be quiet together and are sensitive to each other's moods, sympathizing with each other's problems. They will particularly enjoy such activities as antique hunting and collecting all sorts of things. If either isn't feeling well, the other can be depended upon for a sympathetic visit or to run errands.

CANCER — LEO

What every Cancer needs is a good Leo friend to cheer up her when feeling low. In return, the Cancer is a good listener for the Leo when she needs an audience. A Cancer is particularly good at soothing the hurt pride of a sensitive Leo. The Cancer can sometimes be embarrassed by the Leo generosity, and there is a danger that the Leo will couple a flamboyant giving of gifts with a constant demand to be in the forefront. The Leo shouldn't urge the Cancer into sociable activities when the Cancer isn't in the mood. On the other hand, the Leo brightness can help the Cancer come out of herself.

CANCER — VIRGO

Here is a combination that relates easily. Both are often interested in food as well as health. They find talking together easy and stimulating. As both are collectors, they will naturally be interested in each other's collections. They will usually have a good understanding of each other's individual needs. The Cancer can help the Virgo get out of her squirrel-cage thinking and pay attention to feelings, and the Virgo can help the Cancer develop a much-needed logic.

CANCER — LIBRA

This relationship, given some tolerance and understanding from both sides, can be a deep and lasting one. The Libra is instinctively more open and diplomatic, while the Cancer tends to be more hidden and sometimes oversensitive. The Libra will be more talkative and extroverted and will weigh the pros and cons in each situation, while the Cancer tends to proceed from instinctive feelings. These tendencies can balance each other out nicely. The Cancer's enduring caringness will offset the Libra's occasional fickleness, whereas the Libra's poised detachment can sometimes help the Cancer gain some needed distance from her broodings. Both enjoy a peaceful atmosphere and are not likely to start an argument just to stir things up.

CANCER — SCORPIO

Cancer and Scorpio have an excellent chance of being good friends. Whether they are or not will probably be determined at the first meeting. Either of these signs, if initially "turned off," will not get a chance to develop a real friendship. On the other hand, if they "hit it off," they have a vast potential for deep friendship. Scorpio sensitivity to meaningless sentimentality can give a lot of strength to the relationship. The more easygoing Cancer can soothe some of the Scorpio intensity. Both work on an instinctive level. They can enjoy being with each other without having to talk all of the time.

CANCER — SAGITTARIUS

The Cancer, despite her cautious nature, has a definitely gregarious streak that will come out from time to time. This is when a Cancer will turn to a jovial Sagittarius friend to go out on the town or for help to get into a better mood. On the other hand, even the most frenetic and extroverted Sagittarius will now and again enjoy being at home, and a Cancer friend is a likely candidate to help her relax on these occasions. The Cancer can be a sounding board to test the "feel" of some of the Sagittarian's ambitious ideas.

CANCER — CAPRICORN

These two signs are opposites across the zodiac. This means that they basically complement each other. They are very compatible signs despite the more emotional bias of the Cancer and the greater concentration and practicality of the Capricorn. The Cancer can open up broader emotional realms for the more cautious and conservative Capricorn. Capricorn tends to focus on goals, losing a sense of emotional atmosphere. Despite this, their tastes might turn out to be surprisingly similar, and the Cancer will usually not resent having a certain amount of needed organization imposed upon her by the Capricorn.

CANCER — AQUARIUS

These two signs can make compatible friends, but only with understanding and some forebearance on both their parts. The Aquarius may be put off by the emotional nature of the Cancer, while the more conservative Cancer may find the Aquarius too unconventional and could be somewhat embarrassed by her when they are together in public. However, the Aquarius can help the Cancer see new ways of looking at and doing things, while the Cancer can help the Aquarius see the value of tradition. A definite plus in their relationship is that Aquarius likes to talk and Cancer is a good listener — more than a good listener, in fact, usually getting a genuine kick out of Aquarian's expansive ideas.

CANCER — PISCES

Here are two signs that fit perfectly into each other's moods. They typify old friends who like to be quiet together, perhaps while walking through the woods or by the sea. They will particularly like listening to music or playing quiet games at home. They can flow with each other so perfectly that they can switch without a hitch from doing a jigsaw puzzle together to working separately on personal projects in the same room. When they go out, they will likely have similar tastes in movies or other entertainment, and they also have the same instincts for knowing when they have had enough of a party and are ready to leave.

LEO — LEO

A Leo makes a good combination with another Leo. They enjoy sharing things and spending time together, particularly in the summer when they can lie out in the Sun. Also, they enjoy going to parties together, although there is always the danger that they may try to upstage each other. They have a good level of communication and usually can understand each other without having to talk. Leos always retain a sense of play and enjoy games of all kinds. They also understand that a negative attitude never solved anything, so two Leos have an unspoken agreement that they won't bring each other down.

LEO — VIRGO

There are potential areas of misunderstanding inherent in this relationship. The Leo by nature is indifferent to detail and cares only for the broader picture. A Virgo by nature is continuously fussing over details that would drive a Leo up the wall. However, this relationship can be a valuable one for both if they develop an understanding of each other's needs. The Leo's self-confidence can help to calm the Virgo's worried backtracking when they are engaged in a project together. The Virgo's perceptive criticisms, if delivered without malice, can help the Leo overcome her natural tendency toward naively pushing herself forward.

LEO — LIBRA

This is another good combination. Both have a sense of, and an appreciation of, beauty and are at their best when sharing aesthetic experiences. They are able to show each other much sympathy and kindness and are not likely to burden each other with their individual problems. They also share an ability to enjoy life and will bring out each other's best side. The Leo, being somewhat more decisive, can usually help the Libra make up her mind about important things. The Libra can help the Leo see both sides of a question.

LEO — SCORPIO

This, at its best, is a counterbalancing relationship where the Leo openness and cheerfulness can quiet the fears or suspicions of the Scorpio. The Leo can also bring warmth to the somewhat cool Scorpio nature. On the other hand, the Scorpio can offer important depth of feeling and understanding to the Leo. The Leo should be advised that with the Scorpio's insistence on purification she will not tolerate an unexamined pompous self-importance on the Leo's part. There may be times when a gloomy Scorpio mood will defy any attempt of the Leo to cheer up her, but in the long run the Leo will bring the Scorpio around. The Scorpio tendency to look beneath the surface of what is happening can balance the Leo's sometimes too trusting nature.

LEO — SAGITTARIUS

Both of these signs are good company and enjoy good company. Both are jovial and pleasure-loving and have no trouble expressing their feelings. They share an enthusiastic approach to life and enjoy games. Their other friends will find that the Leo-Sagittarius pair will liven up any party. The Leo can help steady the Sagittarian restlessness, and the Sagittarius can bring adventurousness to the Leo. They can fire each other up to accomplish things that either might find difficult to tackle alone.

LEO — CAPRICORN

Leo is warmer and more expansive in this relationship. Also, a Leo will usually bring out the best side of a Capricorn, that is, dependability and trustworthiness. A Leo will also bring out the latent sense of humor of the more serious Capricorn. The Capricorn can lend organization and practicality to this combination, while the Leo can help the

Capricorn relax and play once in a while. The Leo can bring the Capricorn out of gloomy moods. The Capricorn can be a good audience for the Leo but can also help the Leo see that she doesn't always need an audience.

LEO — AQUARIUS

These are opposite signs across the zodiac. But opposites attract for the most part. Both of these signs are outgoing and like all sorts of people. Both love the theater and other forms of drama. Both are doers and both are humanitarian, if from different viewpoints. Leo loves people and Aquarius loves humanity. Leo can help bring the sentiments of Aquarius down to the personal level, and Aquarius can help Leo learn the value of cooperation and when to take a more impersonal viewpoint. The Leo warmth can balance the Aquarius coolness.

LEO — PISCES

This is a good friendship combination. Leos certainly appreciate the quiet attention they usually get from a Pisces. Leo can also bring out and bolster the creativity and self-expression of Pisces. Pisces finds no problems with the Leonian need to feel regal. In joint projects, the Leo can supply the concentration and determination needed to finish them. It is very easy for this combination to relate on a level of fantasy, although the Leo's will be more childlike while that of the Pisces will be more whimsical. The Pisces can help the Leo overcome the destructive aspects of egocentricity and appreciate quietness. The Leo can brighten Piscean moods and help the Pisces overcome supersensitivity.

VIRGO — VIRGO

Virgo with Virgo makes a highly efficient combination. They will frequently get together to share information or to analyze in great detail what is wrong with the world. They integrate; they syncopate. They appreciate each other's mutual virtues. Among these are painstaking attention to detail, fastidiousness of dress, and high standards in general. If they happen to be women, they may admire each other's spotless housekeeping or discerning minds. Together they will likely be critical of themselves and everybody else, but at the same time, they will spend much time figuring out how to help their mutual friends with their problems. This is a good, lasting friendship.

VIRGO — LIBRA

Here is another combination that will talk a lot. The more relaxed Libra is very good at helping the more frenetic Virgo unwind. Their tastes can interlock in a very harmonious way. There are definite differences in temperament between these two, but each usually recognizes in the other the quality that she lacks and can help the other with. For example, the Virgo can help the Libra get things done, and the Libra can help the Virgo achieve a sense of balance and proportion. Neither sign is strong on decision making, so they should guard against building up each others indecisiveness.

VIRGO — SCORPIO
Here is a combination that sometimes likes to get together and talk about everyone else. The Virgo will ferret out all the juicy details, and the Scorpio will concentrate on seeing through motives. Both, in their own way, look for perfection. They can be perhaps a bit too critical of others, but they are also very perceptive and their perceptions usually dovetail. If they can use this combination of abilities in improving things rather than in demolishing them, they can be of great help to others as well as to each other.

VIRGO — SAGITTARIUS
This friendship has a lot to offer both. There will be much lively discussion about books, movies and experiences. The Virgo will come to admire the Sagittarian breadth of vision, while the Sagittarius will appreciate the amount of specific knowledge of the Virgo, even though the Sagittarius will feel its importance lies in documenting generalizations. The Sagittarius always tries to see "why" and the Virgo always tries to see "what," and this combination will give them a balanced understanding.

They can be very successful with mutual projects if the Sagittarius provides the energy and the Virgo works out the details.

VIRGO — CAPRICORN
These two Earth signs get along well together. Both are practical and like an organized approach to things. They tend to bring out the most positive and constructive side of each other's personality. In mutual projects the Capricorn will probably provide the basic structure with the whole picture in mind, while the Virgo will work out the various parts. The Capricorn can help the Virgo come to decisions by focusing on the essentials rather than in getting lost in all of these parts. The Virgo can help the Capricorn develop humility.

VIRGO — AQUARIUS
These two signs can make great friends. Both are analytical types and

prefer to discuss things objectively. The Aquarius will need to understand and respect the Virgoan drive for form and perfection, while the Virgo should understand the Aquarian need to find new ways of doing things. The Aquarius can help the Virgo broaden her viewpoint, and the Virgo can help the Aquarius see the practical applications to her theories.

VIRGO — PISCES
These two signs are opposites across the zodiac, which means that they complement and, in a sense, complete each other. Both are perfectionists in their own ways. Virgo will, of course, want to get all the details exactly right, while Pisces will feel for a clear expression of the total picture. Virgo can help Pisces, the perennial dreamer, bring reality to some of these dreams. Pisces can help Virgo see the magic in life and keep from getting wound up in an overanalytical approach. Both share a liking for quiet pursuits and also a desire to help others.

LIBRA — LIBRA
Two Libras are the least likely of any combination to disagree with each other unless they fall into competitiveness. Most Librans prefer peaceful activities, good company and pleasant surroundings. When two Libras become friends, therefore, they will usually be an easygoing, free-flowing pair. They both enjoy the arts and beautiful things in general. However, both being Libras, they may find it hard at times to make up their minds about what they want to do together. But since they both want, above all, to please each other, they will usually put off decision making and just enjoy what is happening at the moment.

LIBRA — SCORPIO
This relationship needs a certain amount of give and take, but given this, these two signs can become good friends. Libra can help — or a better term might be **inspire** — Scorpio to relax. Scorpio energy is proverbial, while Libra much prefers to take things easy. Scorpio, though, is much more decisive and, if diplomatic about it, can help her Libra friend make important decisions. Libra's gentle personality can help Scorpio pull out of dark moods.

LIBRA — SAGITTARIUS
The Libra may sometimes find her Sagittarius friend a little too energetic to keep up with. On the other hand, there is a common meeting ground if the Libra can convince the Sagittarius to slow down a bit and the Sagittarius can energize the Libra. They quite often have strong shared

interests on the artistic or the intellectual side. They both have a compelling desire that justice be done. Both enjoy parties and meeting people, although the Libra may prefer small intimate affairs while the Sagittarius likes large numbers of people. Each handles social situations slightly differently also; the Libra may find the Sagittarian candor too blunt and tactless, while the Sagittarius may disdain the Libra diplomacy as two-faced. All in all, however, this combination usually makes harmonious and sympathetic friends.

LIBRA — CAPRICORN

People of these two signs get on well together despite contrasting views of life, which, in this case, can also be complementary. In this combination the Libra will be the more talkative and outgoing while the Capricorn will do the listening. The Libra can certainly help the Capricorn to have a more balanced perspective on life's struggles and to relax. On the other hand, the Capricorn can certainly help the Libra direct her many interests in a more practical way. The Libra will constantly appreciate the common sense and earthiness of the Capricorn. The Libra can help the Capricorn appreciate beauty for beauty's sake.

LIBRA — AQUARIUS

This is often an intellectual friendship. They have a lot to talk about. The Libra ideas may sometimes be a bit conservative, and an Aquarian friend is often just the right catalyst to expand her concepts. The Aquarius can help the Libra take a more impersonal viewpoint, whereas the Libra can help the Aquarius achieve a balance when her ideas get too far out. The Libra's desire for harmony often inhibits her initiative; here the Aquarius can help by acting out of concrete conviction in an issue. On the other hand, the Aquarius may offend people by taking her convictions far too seriously, and here the Libra can be of service by smoothing over the irritations with old-fashioned diplomacy.

LIBRA — PISCES

A Libra and a Pisces can have a lot in common and definitely have many mutual interests. Both tune in to the arts and have a sense of harmony and balance. The Libra will be able to fit the Piscean imaginative fantasia into a coherent, balanced form. Both value peace and pleasantness. The Libra will be the more talkative and outgoing of the two. A Libran friend can certainly steady the course of a usually somewhat unsteady Pisces. The Libra will respond to the deep sense of devotion and friendship that a Pisces will develop as a result of Libran kindness.

SCORPIO — SCORPIO

This has the makings of a strong, extraordinary relationship. Each can understand what makes the other tick and can admire the other's better qualities. Of course, two Scorpios will have to "hit it off" when they meet for the first time; otherwise, they may always be somewhat wary of each other. In any event, this is a relationship that is bound to be intense. There may be a tendency to form a gossip club of two. They will certainly enjoy exploring many facets of life together as well as digging into the unknown. This relationship may sometimes be stormy, but it will be worthwhile for both.

SCORPIO — SAGITTARIUS

A friendship between a Scorpio and a Sagittarius demands a reconciliation of different temperaments. When there **is** a friendship, it is because the Scorpio appreciates the openness, candor and honesty of the Sagittarius, and the Sagittarius comes to understand that there is a great depth of understanding in the Scorpio. This means also that there must be a good deal of mutual acceptance and adaptability to the other's nature. Or more precisely, the Sagittarius will have to learn to respect the confidences of the Scorpio and not go around repeating them. The Sagittarius must learn to accept the secretiveness of the Scorpio. On the other side, the Scorpio must not be too possessive of her wide-ranging friend.

SCORPIO — CAPRICORN

Here are two signs that mesh well together. Both can throw themselves into all sorts of activities with great intensity. They may also share a somewhat cynical view of life, which means that they can bring out in each other a somewhat offbeat sense of humor. On the other hand, they can fall into being aloof and disdainful of the rest of humanity with a kind of oppressive seriousness. In any event, the relationship will most likely be a lively one. They will be able to approach any common endeavor, such as a business venture, with drive and ambition. They can enjoy being quiet together and can respect each other's need for solitude.

SCORPIO — AQUARIUS

This is a somewhat unlikely combination. However, a basis for a strong friendship does exist here in the joining of forces in the name of a social cause. As a team of sorts, the Aquarius can work out front in a political campaign while the Scorpio can be very effective maneuvering in the background. Both are interested in the attack on broad social problems, a sphere that Aquarius excels in and Scorpio can also become profoundly involved in. While the Aquarius is a skilled organizer, aware of group dynamics, her Scorpio friend is deeply sensitive to the hidden motivations of the individual members of the group. While working effectively together, these two can become devoted friends.

SCORPIO — PISCES
These two water signs make sincere friends who can tune into the nuances of each other's thoughts. A Scorpio friend is always a valuable one for a Pisces, as the Scorpio can give support and protection to the more vulnerable Pisces. In turn, the less intense and more easygoing Pisces can help the Scorpio become more mellow and less generally suspicious. This is another pair of friends who can enjoy each other's company without always needing to talk.

SAGITTARIUS — SAGITTARIUS
This pair of friends will always be ready for an adventure together, whether it's exploring new places and activities or broadening their concepts of what this world is really about. They will enjoy active sports together as well a a variety of social activities and work with groups. Their other friends will notice that whenever the Sagittarius pair arrives, the atmosphere becomes warmer and more friendly. Although they might have friendly arguments about philosophy, two Sagittarius people are not likely to get into personal conflicts with each other.

SAGITTARIUS — CAPRICORN
These two signs share a "look-at-the-whole-view" approach and therefore can have an instinctive understanding of each other. The Sagittarius good spirits are just what the sometimes overly sober Capricorn needs, and in turn, the Capricorn stability can help balance the restlessness of the Sagittarius. Each should understand that whereas expansion is basic to Sagittarius, contraction is basic to Capricorn. They can help each other balance these two tendencies out. An activity both will enjoy is long hikes together.

SAGITTARIUS — AQUARIUS
Both of these signs are outgoing people who love many kinds of social gatherings and will enjoy going with each other to whatever is happening, although the Aquarius may be more interested in the discussions of new ideas, while the Sagittarius may simply enjoy any kind of conviviality. Since both signs have a strong need for independence, they can form an easy relationship in which neither clings to the other. They

should be able to cooperate very well in group work, although the Aquarian ideas might sometimes seem a bit too advanced for the somewhat more traditional Sagittarius, and the Aquarius might become impatient with a dogmatic tendency in her Sagittarius friend.

SAGITTARIUS — PISCES
Both of these signs look to the broad horizons, although the approach of Sagittarius is more adventurous and that of Pisces more mystical. Together they can dream big dreams, as neither sign feels unduly confined to reality. Both also share an appreciation of nature. Friendship with a Sagittarius can develop warmth and outgoing qualities in a Pisces. In turn, some of the Pisces sensitivity and tact can rub off on the Sagittarius.

CAPRICORN — CAPRICORN
Two Capricorns can rely on each other to be on time and to do what each has promised. They can also have serious discussions without the necessity of "lightening up," which most other signs need. They will enjoy such activities as hiking and mountain climbing and will also like constructing things together. Each will appreciate the other's dry sense of humor. They will enjoy discussing each other's plans and ambitions, and celebrating when one of them has achieved a goal.

CAPRICORN — AQUARIUS
The Aquarius can jolt the Capricorn out of some of her set notions about how things ought to be done. On the other hand, the Capricorn can help the Aquarius organize her ideas and do something practical about them, but she should not press systematization on the Aquarius, who needs freedom. The Aquarius must be careful about trying to change the Capricorn set ways unless there is an excellent reason for doing so. If each of these signs understands the quirks of the other, they can have a good friendship.

CAPRICORN — PISCES
These two signs have a good potential for friendship. The Capricorn can help the Pisces organize and be practical, and the Pisces can help the Capricorn see the whimsical side of things when Capricorn gets too intent on goals. Pisces can also help Capricorn learn to flow rather than always plod. The Capricorn no-nonsense nature can help the Pisces keep from getting lost in a totally unrealistic project and put at least one foot on the ground.

AQUARIUS — AQUARIUS

This pair can spend hours figuring out how the world could be made better. They will appreciate each other's quick minds and inventive approaches. Neither is in danger of getting bogged down in traditional ideas. They can have a friendship without encroaching on each other's freedom and will enjoy working together in organizations for improving something or other. In fact, they will enjoy going together to all sorts of social gatherings and meeting new friends.

AQUARIUS — PISCES

A Pisces friend can help an Aquarius understand what she is feeling. On the other hand, an Aquarius can help a Pisces understand what she is thinking. Both might have a tendency to be unrealistic: the Aquarius may pursue unreachable goals while the Pisces may be absorbed in magical fantasies and dreams. The Pisces can help the Aquarius soften some of the hard corners in her personality and will also sympathize when no one else understands some of the far-out Aquarian ideas. Aquarius must guard against trying to give Pisces too much direction and should respect the dream space that a Pisces needs.

PISCES — PISCES

These two will take each other on wonderful flights of fancy and sympathize with each other no matter what happens. They will enjoy sitting quietly together, each doing her own thing but occasionally tuning in with a smile. They can be almost psychically sensitive to each other's moods and will enjoy working on beautiful things together. They will also enjoy working together in organizations.

Love and Marriage

		Aries ♈	Taurus ♉	Gemini ♊	Cancer ♋	Leo ♌	Virgo ♍	Libra ♎	Scorpio ♏	Sagittarius ♐	Capricorn ♑	Aquarius ♒	Pisces ♓
Aries	♈	41	41	42	42	42	43	43	43	43	44	44	44
Taurus	♉	41	45	45	45	45	46	46	46	46	47	47	47
Gemini	♊	42	45	47	48	48	48	48	49	49	49	49	50
Cancer	♋	42	45	48	50	50	50	51	51	51	52	52	52
Leo	♌	42	45	48	50	52	53	53	53	53	54	54	54
Virgo	♍	43	46	48	50	53	55	55	55	55	56	56	56
Libra	♎	43	46	48	51	53	55	57	57	57	57	58	58
Scorpio	♏	43	46	49	51	53	55	57	58	58	59	59	59
Sagittarius	♐	43	46	49	51	53	55	57	58	59	60	60	60
Capricorn	♑	44	47	49	52	54	56	57	59	60	60	60	61
Aquarius	♒	44	47	49	52	54	56	58	59	60	60	61	61
Pisces	♓	44	47	50	52	54	56	58	59	60	61	61	62

ARIES — ARIES

Both the men and the women of this sign tend to fall in love at first sight and then go all out in the pursuit of their amatory goals. They both like the direct approach with no beating around the bush. Sometimes sex, pure and simple, is a major preoccupation for an Aries. This, coupled with the high energy level of the sign, means that the Aries-Aries combination is quite likely to result in a quick affair, quick to begin and quick to end. If this relationship does end in marriage, however, it is usually one full of fun and excitement. If each makes allowances for a certain degree of shortness of temper and perhaps a bit of selfishness on the part of the other, it can become a stable and lasting relationship.

ARIES — TAURUS

These two signs have quite different outlooks on love and marriage. The Aries is likely to be more liberated in terms of sex, while the Taurus is usually far more conservative. The Aries reacts more immediately to his physical drives and desires while the Taurus is more concerned with permanence and stability, so that marriage may seem like a more natural state to a Taurus than to an Aries. However, once married, the Aries can turn around and be a most devoted and enthusiastic marriage partner, although perhaps with an occasional roving eye.

ARIES — GEMINI

Here is one sign where Aries has met his match. Like Aries, Gemini might have a bent toward sexual freedom. However, Gemini is in many ways a most congenial amatory sign for Aries, with plenty of energy and verve emanating on both sides. The Gemini, however, will add and cultivate a deeper level of friendship within the love relationship. If they **do** get married, then it is sure to be an exciting and rewarding relationship with never a dull moment. They will always have plenty to talk about, never get into a rut, and enjoy venturing together into new activities.

ARIES — CANCER

This love relationship will call for a lot of mutual tolerance. The Cancer can be erratic, moody and unpredictable in a romantic relationship, all of which an Aries may find hard to put up with. However, both signs have the ability to give deeply of themselves when the proper situation arises. The Aries can give the Cancer the aggressive affection that the Cancer often needs to feel reassured. The Cancer can give the Aries the nurturing affection and the stable home life that the Aries needs and may not be able to create for himself. The Aries should try to remember that his sudden bursts of temper can be quite painful to the sensitive Cancer nature.

ARIES — LEO

This can be a good love relationship provided there is a little understanding on both sides. Both may always want to be in the forefront, expecting the other to accept a place in the background, which is not an easy thing for either to accept. Given the Leo flair for drama and the Aries volatile temper, there can be quite a few scenes both in private and in public. However, both have passionate as well as generous natures, so that quarrels are usually quickly resolved and often produce a deeper level of love and understanding. The Aries pace is naturally quicker than that of the Leo, so they must find a mutual ground between the Aries instantaneous reactions and the Leo slower decision making.

ARIES — VIRGO

Aries and Virgo have very different temperaments when it comes to love and romance. The Aries will rush into love at first sight, while the typical Virgo needs time to analyze and adjust to any new relationship before committing himself to it. They also operate on different emotional levels. It is not that the Virgo is **never** as passionate as the Aries, it is just that he needs intellectual stimulation as well as physical stimulation to make sex a complete experience. If the Aries in the relationship can understand this, then things can work out. However, they will need to achieve a balance between the Aries spontaneity and decisiveness and the Virgoan tendency to put off decisions until there is no way to avoid them.

ARIES — LIBRA

In this love relationship each can bring qualities that complement those of the other. The Aries can bring passion and enthusiasm, while the Libra can add kindness and sympathy. Each can inspire these qualities in the other. Libra can be the most harmonious and balancing sign for an Aries. On the other hand, although both signs are true romantics, the Libra romanticism is on the idealistic level while the Aries is of the swept-away, head-over-heels variety. This can sometimes lead to a misunderstanding about the other's intentions. The Libran basic and fundamental need for a permanent relationship is sometimes difficult for the Aries to understand and accept.

ARIES — SCORPIO

This combination has all the makings of an intense and passionate relationship. It can, in fact, sometimes be a bit too intense. The Aries will meet his match in passion with a Scorpio. The relationship can be stormy, but, on the other hand, two people with strong emotional natures may have a deeper understanding of each other than if their intensity of response were less well matched. There is also the possibility of an "off-on" relationship in which they typically can't live with each other and can't live without each other. However, when they resolve these problems, this relationship can be a spectacular one.

ARIES — SAGITTARIUS

When an Aries meets a Sagittarius and becomes involved in a love affair, they both will feel that they have made a great find. They can meet each other on an equal level of energy since they both share the same enthusiasm for life and love. This should be a relationship full of good-hearted fun and spontaneity and also not lacking in love and romance. Neither will want to make it a "heavy" melodramatic affair. Marriage between an Aries and a Sagittarius will always be exciting, but they will have to put conscious effort into dealing with the practicalities, something which may not be easy for either.

ARIES — CAPRICORN
At first, a Capricorn may seem a little cool and distant to an Aries. The romantic intensity and enthusiasm of the Aries may be bewildering to the more steady and down-to-earth Capricorn. However, the Aries has the capacity in abundance to fire up the passionate depths beneath the Capricorn surface. The Capricorn calm, stable nature can blend very well with the Aries zest for life, particularly if they settle down for a long relationship. An Aries needs a steadying point, which a Capricorn can provide. Likewise, a Capricorn needs, sometimes, to be jolted out of his many practical concerns, and this is something an Aries does easily. However, for a successful relationship, the Aries must respect the Capricorn need for a certain amount of routine, and the Capricorn must make allowances for the erratic qualities of Aries.

ARIES — AQUARIUS
Both of these signs approach love as a great adventure. They are both ready to explore romance and sex, the Aries in a hot-blooded fashion and the Aquarius in a cooler and more detached way. Yet both have an innate need to retain a certain amount of freedom. This is another pair who will never lack for conversation. Since the Aries naturally focuses on "I" and the Aquarius on "we," they can balance each other out and teach each other a thing or two about when to take individual initiative and when to cooperate.

ARIES — PISCES
Here is another pair that couldn't be more different in basic romantic temperament. The emotions of the Aries are direct, fiery and enthusiastic. Those of the Pisces are subtle, complex and changeable. Pisces people can try to go in opposite directions at the same time. This applies equally to their romantic involvements. If the Aries "moves in" too quickly on the Pisces (an Aries tendency), then the Pisces may become nervous and confused. But if the Pisces vacillates too long, the Aries will tend to become impatient and dissatisfied. Perhaps it will help if the Aries tries to remember to allow the Pisces to relax and flow into a romantic mood, at which point he can be a marvelous lover with a capacity for great affection.

TAURUS — TAURUS

Two Tauruses might find their "soul mates" in each other. Romantically, they are perhaps the most blending of any of the same-sign combinations. They will share a sensuous and gracious approach to lovemaking as well as create for each other a deep-seated sense of emotional security. The Taurean psyche, particularly when doubled, is drawn to marriage. They can develop a comfortable "old-shoe" relationship with satisfying routines, each aware of the dependability of the other. However, since Taurus is probably the most stubborn sign of the zodiac, these lovers must learn how to avoid becoming an immovable object to each other's irresistible force.

TAURUS — GEMINI

The Gemini, though as capable of love and passion as anyone else, finds sex and romance more the expression of deep and abiding friendship. The Taurus may mistake the changeable and impulsive Gemini spirit for his own emotional "rushes." If a sudden, brief encounter is the only result, it can leave the Taurus bewildered, particularly when the Gemini ends the affair with a "can't we be friends?" appeal. In a lasting relationship, however, the Taurus can give much needed stability to the Gemini nerves, and the Gemini can keep the Taurus from settling into ruts that are too fixed.

TAURUS — CANCER

The Cancer has the water sign's tendency to take on the emotional coloration of whomever he is involved with romantically and sexually. The Taurus, on the other hand, bears the steadiness of Earth itself. The changeable and erratic Cancer, passionate one moment and then turned off the next, will benefit greatly from the Taurean ability to make him feel more secure emotionally. In turn, the grateful Cancer will show the Taurus great love and affection. Both share the desire to nurture whatever needs their care and to have a secure home.

TAURUS — LEO

Leos approach all situations, love and romance included, with a sense of pride and regal condescension. They can also be somewhat conventional and "proper." This gives the amorous Taurus problems to overcome. However, a Taurus can romantically capture a reluctant Leo by subtly catering to the Leo ego. In return, the Taurus will find the Leo very attentive and loyal. They are both home-loving, and this makes for successful marriages. Also, they both have a leisurely rhythm, so one will not always try to be hurrying the other.

TAURUS — VIRGO

The Virgo approach to love is somewhat on the intellectual side. Virgo is not carried away by romantic dreams. Taurus also has his share of common sense, so they share a certain practicality. Sex is likely to be more important to the Taurus than it is to the Virgo, although the Taurus will be able usually to raise the emotional level of the Virgo by patience and understanding. In an ongoing relationship the easy-going Taurus nature can help calm the sometimes jittery Virgo. The Virgo can contribute fastidiousness to the Taurean inclination to care for possessions.

TAURUS — LIBRA

In general, the Taurus is fairly certain what he wants out of love while the Libra is more typically confused and uncertain about the whole thing. On the other hand, Libras have very romantic feelings and are often "in love with love." When a Libra falls in love with a Taurus and the Taurus reciprocates, the Libra may not know what to do next. Fortunately, the Taurus **does** know what to do next. When this relationship leads to marriage, it can fulfill the need for a settled tie that both of these Venus-related signs have.

TAURUS — SCORPIO

This relationship is a bit like walking an emotional tightrope. They can both be passionate and loving but they can also be extremely stubborn, sometimes to the point of complete emotional paralysis. The Taurus possessiveness and the Scorpio jealousy might create a tense situation to say the least. On the other hand, if they can both relax a bit, the Scorpio may inspire the Taurus to heights of passion that he could not reach with another sign. Like other pairs of signs that are opposite on the zodiac, this pair can either seem like totally different beings or can complement each other's qualities marvelously.

TAURUS — SAGITTARIUS

This is a combination of rather different kinds of people. For a long-term romantic relationship, particularly a marriage, to work, it will take a lot of patience and understanding on the part of each one. The Taurus likes the idea of a settled, more or less permanent, state and tends to be quite possessive of his mate. But the Sagittarius, more than any other sign, needs space and freedom. While the Sagittarius can benefit from an element of stability in his life, the relationship will work best if a sense of change and adventure prevails from time to time.

TAURUS — CAPRICORN

This combination has great possibilities for a long-lasting love relationship. Since both are Earth signs, they can be practical, realistic and enduring. The Taurus can help the Capricorn appreciate the beautiful as well as the practical, and also develop a sense of when to take things easy. The Capricorn may be able to keep the Taurus from getting stuck in laziness. This is not only a good marriage combination but can also be successful as a business partnership where husband and wife work together.

TAURUS — AQUARIUS

This relationship has many similarities to that of the Taurus-Sagittarius combination. The Taurean tendency to jealousy could frustrate the forming of a good romantic relationship with either a Sagittarius or an Aquarius, two signs which are both notorious for their need for freedom. The Aquarian concept of romance might also seem a bit cool to the much more amorously inclined Taurus. On top of this, both Taurus and Aquarius tend to be stubborn. However, the warmly affectionate Taurus can often melt the "iceberg" facade of the Aquarius, while the Aquarius can teach the Taurus some much-needed detachment.

TAURUS — PISCES

This can be a very satisfying relationship on both a sexual and an emotional level. On a **practical** level they may not have such an easy time of it, as the Pisces is constantly changing direction, much to the consternation of the firmly rooted Taurus. However, the sympathetic and affectionate nature of the Pisces is usually much appreciated by the Taurus and helps him overlook the Piscean impracticality. Also, the Pisces appreciates a down-to-earth partner to take the load of practicalities off his shoulders. If married, they can be happily so, as they both make devoted mates.

GEMINI — GEMINI

These two people can be definitely in tune sexually. In a sense, only another Gemini can understand Gemini, something which is not necessarily true where other signs are doubled, or at least not to the extent that it is here. Only another Gemini can fathom the deep and complex interrelationship of romance and intellectual stimulation that a Gemini needs. Also, no matter how passionate and complex the Gemini-Gemini love games become, there will always be an underlying element of genuine friendship between them.

GEMINI — CANCER

As lovers, these two signs have a fifty-fifty chance together. They will either be on the same wavelength or completely out of phase with each other. Sexually they are stimulated by completely different things. The Gemini is usually first stimulated intellectually, while the Cancer is more typically engulfed by a sudden passion, without extended preliminaries. As a consequence, each may appear to the other as somewhat unpredictable. Although they both like and enjoy sex, they may not both feel like it at the same time. But the Cancer is capable of nourishing and protecting the high-strung Gemini, while the Gemini can divert the Cancer from negative moods.

GEMINI — LEO

This romantic pair may often succeed for the simple reason that the relationship offers a challenge to both. The Gemini is ingenious enough to get beneath the surface "pomposity" of the Leo and discover the potential wells of passion beneath his proud exterior. In turn, the direct and warmhearted devotion of the Leo can usually break down the often formidable mental barriers that a Gemini sometimes puts up. If the romance leads to marriage, this can be an exciting one, as each will constantly discover new facets in the other. However, the faster-moving Gemini must avoid trying to hurry the slower-paced Leo.

GEMINI — VIRGO

This combination will always be able to communicate with each other and, in fact, might be in danger of too much communication. While such stimulation can be highly satisfying to both, the Gemini's frequent changes of direction and lack of constancy and the Virgo's tendency to criticism may be irritants. However, if they can overcome the tendency to project onto each other their own changeability, they will find they have much in common, as both of these signs relate to Mercury.

GEMINI — LIBRA

These two air signs are almost always off to a good start when it comes to romance. Both are looking for the perfect balance of mental and emotional traits in a lover. The Gemini belief that deep friendship is the best foundation for romance sits very well with a Libra. Gemini needs only to remember that Libra is something of a romantic and will be tremendously delighted by an occasional sentimental gift with an affectionate note. All in all, this collaboration should work out very well for both.

GEMINI — SCORPIO

Gemini and Scorpio operate on completely different emotional levels. The sexual intensity of the Scorpio can most often confuse and possibly irritate the less intense, more casually romantic Gemini. The Gemini changeability and widespread interests can arouse the darker, jealous side of the Scorpio, who may feel that the Gemini is cool and unemotional. However, when both are blessed with deep understanding of the differences in temperament of their respective signs, a genuine romantic relationship will be possible and bring to each from the other qualities of loving of which they had no inkling.

GEMINI — SAGITTARIUS

These two signs have a strong attraction for each other. Although they are opposites across the zodiac, they actually share many qualities in the area of love. They both approach romance with a light touch and treasure a strong element of friendship within a relationship. They both feel the need to retain individuality and freedom and are adventurous and enthusiastic about life. In an ongoing relationship the Sagittarius can lend wisdom to the Gemini, who is sometimes so diversified in his many interests that he lacks a viewpoint. In turn, the Gemini can provide the Sagittarius with the fund of information the Sagittarius needs to build his overview of life.

GEMINI — CAPRICORN

This can be a satisfactory romantic union, though it is not without its difficulties. The affection of the Gemini is somewhat carefree and sometimes on the surface. That of the Capricorn, while not scorchingly passionate, is a good, solid, lasting love. The love of a Capricorn can often steady the sometimes wavering Gemini and inspire him to the deeper, more permanent values possible in human love. The Gemini spirited and adventurous approach to life can lighten up the Capricorn and keep him from getting lost in routine.

GEMINI — AQUARIUS

These two signs will find that they come together on all levels, including those of friendship, interests and romance. Although sex may be important to both, their deep, underlying friendship is sometimes even more important. Since they both tend to approach romance with something of a light touch, they should always be careful not to let their intellectual activities stifle their emotional needs. If they balance their intellectual natures with their sensual natures (which can be more important than either of them realizes), they will have a truly fabulous time together.

GEMINI — PISCES

Both of these signs are in search of sexual identity and both long to be "truly in love." They are also, each in their own ways, "split personalities," making the complexity of the interaction between them sometimes confusing to both. What often saves the situation is that both are easygoing and patient and therefore can develop a solid and endearing love relationship. Sometimes there are underlying emotional problems that need to be looked at and worked out. It may help if the Gemini realizes that the Pisces approaches life from a standpoint of deep feeling and if the Pisces realizes that the Gemini tendency to talk about everything that happens is his way of expressing affection.

CANCER — CANCER

Cancer doubled can create a situation where two people of high sensitivity and emotional vulnerability are thrown together. This has the danger of creating an atmosphere of negativity. On the other hand, two Cancers together have the capacity to tune in instinctively to each other's emotional and sexual needs. They will have an instinctive appreciation of each other's good qualities, particularly the gentle understanding and constant affection that both thrive on. They can be so much on the same wavelength that they become almost telepathic. This can be a good marriage combination but these partners should strive to "lighten" the climate of their relationship.

CANCER — LEO

This combination is potentially one of the warmest in the zodiac. Leo puts a premium on loving and being loved while Cancer values emotional closeness and caring. Authoritative, the Leo male can sometimes serve as a kindly father figure for his wife or sweetheart. On the other hand, the Leo of either sex can sometimes seem too domineering for the sensitivities of the Cancer. The attitudes of these two toward sex can differ considerably. The Leo is usually direct and basic, while the Cancer needs a much more delicate approach. If they can stay aware of the balance between Sun-ruled vibrant Leo energy and Moon-ruled gentle Cancer energy, however, these two signs can complement each other in a very special way.

CANCER — VIRGO

These two signs mesh well romantically. Virgo gives emotional control and stability to the sometimes sexually confused Cancer. The Virgo will allow the affair to develop at just the right pace and will not panic the supersensitive Cancer. If the relationship leads to marriage, there can be a genuine division of labor and sharing of work and responsibility. Both love the concepts of home and family and, if they control a mutual tendency to worry too much, theirs can be a satisfying long-term relationship. The Cancer can help the Virgo keep in touch with his feelings and not go overboard on the thinking side.

CANCER — LIBRA
These two signs can be a very romantic combination. The Libra will quickly learn, in Libra's usually balanced and easygoing way, what Cancer needs to be fulfilled emotionally and sexually. The Cancer, always something of a chameleon, will develop many Libra characteristics as well as many mutual interests, which in turn will be very gratifying to the Libra. These signs share an enthusiasm for life and love and can form a solid, long-term relationship. The Libra should understand that a Cancer handles moods better alone, and the Cancer should understand that a Libra often prefers to talk problems out.

CANCER — SCORPIO
The romantic inclinations of Cancer and Scorpio often interlock very well, since they are both very sensitive. However, for this very reason, there are also inevitable rough spots. Each must understand that, if hurt, the other tends to withdraw emotionally, the Cancer in a sulky mood and the Scorpio somewhat cold and restrained. If these understandings can be worked out, this combination can form a strong and long-lasting love. The passionate energy of the Scorpio can broaden the approach of Cancer to sex, because the Cancer can open up and express himself to the limit without fazing the Scorpio. The Cancer can teach the Scorpio sympathy and generosity of feeling. This is also an excellent marriage combination.

CANCER — SAGITTARIUS
This relationship often takes a lot of compromising. It is one of those situations where a couple can be very compatible in bed, but find it hard to adjust to each other's idiosyncrasies in everyday life. The Sagittarius will want to lead an active social life, while the Cancer will usually prefer to stay at home and relax. The Cancer may have a tendency to be overpossessive of his lover, while the most important thing to a Sagittarius is freedom, in love as in other areas of existence. However, if they can understand each other's differences, the Sagittarius can bring the Cancer out of "down" moods, and the Cancer can help the Sagittarius be more aware of nuances of feeling.

CANCER — CAPRICORN

This can be a stimulating, satisfying, and long-lasting romantic relationship. There are hurdles to overcome, as in any relationship, but the inherent loyalty of both signs should keep the combination stable. Being opposite signs in the zodiac, they both share something in common and complement each other. They can also be very compatible sexually and, when they do argue, the disagreements may very often be resolved in bed. Both need to guard against taking life too seriously. The Cancer sensitivity can soften the Capricorn tendency to sometimes push ahead without awareness of the atmosphere. On the other hand, the Capricorn logical practicality can balance the Cancer tendency to overemphasize the "feel" of a situation.

CANCER — AQUARIUS

Although these two signs can be sexually compatible, the Aquarius may need some coaxing to come home to bed. Aquarius, one suspects, would much rather be out with friends or working on some cause or other. However, this is not to say that once in bed, Aquarians are not good lovers. The Cancer will have to guard against feeling hurt and distressed by the Aquarian gregariousness and love of freedom. The Aquarius should accept the Cancer need for privacy. If they both believe strongly in the same things, this can be a good and long-lasting relationship.

CANCER — PISCES

These two signs are often an ideal romantic relationship. They both **feel** deeply and sincerely and have strong imaginative and instinctive powers. They both strive for emotional security, and they can find it in this relationship. There is a strong sexual attraction between these two signs that reinforces their emotional compatibility. They may find it a bit hard to be practical. If their romance leads to marriage, they may have to make a conscious effort to develop a constructive approach to all the inevitable daily problems and learn how to talk things out to clear the air.

LEO — LEO

Leo is the generous and loving sign. When doubled in this combination, these traits become predominant. In addition, Leos have a strong sex drive, and a great deal of time will be taken up by good, old-fashioned lovemaking. Their life, in fact, can resolve itself into a continuous romance and one with style and flair to boot. As long as they agree to share the spotlight equally, which — though difficult — is aided by Leo generosity, there will be great tranquility. In fact, the two contented lions will be able to spread good cheer to everyone around them.

LEO — VIRGO
There could scarcely be two temperaments so completely different as these two signs. Leo is one of the warmest signs, in love and in bed, while Virgo is one of the most detached, sometimes finding it difficult to express his emotions. Probably the best thing that can happen to a Virgo **is** to get romantically involved with a Leo. With the warm and passionate administrations of a Leo it will be found that Virgo **does** have a romantic streak under that cool and calculating exterior. Also, the Virgo natural bent for service can mesh nicely with the Leo regal side. However, the pair should try to reverse these roles periodically, just for balance.

LEO — LIBRA
These two signs are different in many ways but both are warmhearted and generous. Sexually they are well suited. Leo is open and enthusiastic in bed and Libra — though not usually so uninhibited — is capable of, and will enjoy, the higher level of unabashed passion. The main difficulty in a long-term romantic relationship will be the notorious Leo temper, which — although soon forgotten by the Leo — will be deeply disturbing to the Libra, who dislikes unpleasantness more than anything else. Also, the more decisive Leo could be put out by the inability of the Libra to make up his mind. All in all, though, it is an excellent sign combination.

LEO — SCORPIO
This relationship promises plenty of sex but might have problems in other areas. The Leo generous nature may constantly be seen as needless extravagance by the overcritical Scorpio, while Scorpio's secretive and jealous nature is the exact opposite of what a Leo really wants in a lover. However, if both signs are emotionally mature, then the strength and the security that a Scorpio can offer will outweigh the other tendencies, and the Leo extreme warmth and ability to give of himself will inspire the best in the Scorpio. In this case it can be a highly creative and energetic combination.

LEO — SAGITTARIUS
These two signs are good-natured, loving, and enthusiastic about sex. All in all, it can be a good, solid, emotional relationship. The Leo will have to remember that the Sagittarius needs a good deal of freedom. This does not necessarily mean that the Sagittarius will be off having

other affairs, but Sagittarians should always be allowed to feel that they **could** if they really wanted to. In turn, the Sagittarius will allow the Leo as much freedom as he wants and, if the Leo is a woman, will encourage her to develop an outside and independent career. If the Leo is a man, he need never fear that the Sagittarius will be jealous of anything he does.

LEO — CAPRICORN
This is another combination of rather different people. Leo's lighthearted but enthusiastic attitude toward romance may not be appreciated by the Capricorn. Leos have a profound sense of humor when it comes to sex, and this leads to a great deal of amorous teasing on their part. This may not sit well with the often more serious Capricorn. On the other hand, Leos are completely devoted to the care and comfort of their mate. There is no sign, in fact, better suited to warm up and "lighten" the personality of a Capricorn than a Leo. In turn, the Capricorn can help the Leo be aware of when he is overemphasizing the playful side of life.

LEO — AQUARIUS
Just as Leos find Capricorns somewhat overserious, they may also find Aquarians very detached and aloof. The problem for the Leo is similar in both cases. The instinct of the Leo is to meet this challenge with warmth and wholehearted generosity. This seldom fails to work, since Aquarius (like Capricorn) has latent potentialities for higher and more passionate emotional levels. If the Leo-Aquarius relationship leads to marriage, it can be very successful, as both possess qualities of loyalty. However, they can also be equally stubborn, and they will have to work to avoid friction over the tendencies of Leo to want to run things and of Aquarius to want personal freedom of action and a less possessive atmosphere.

LEO — PISCES
This relationship can be a confusing one for the Leo. Sometimes the Pisces will respond wholeheartedly to the generous love of the Leo, while other times the Pisces will seem to cut off the Leo completely, both mentally and physically. The Leo might sooner or later lose patience, and this could be an end to the affair. What can save this relationship, if the Leo can accept this Piscean changeability in daily life, is that it is natural for Pisces to nurture and sympathize, and Leo always loves the attention. Also, most Pisces people need some protection, and this is something Leo provides with ease.

VIRGO — VIRGO

Virgo and Virgo will naturally have similar attitudes toward life. They will both be ruled by practicality and common sense. This hardly seems like a very romantic beginning, but Virgos march to a different drummer, one that may forever seem incomprehensible to outsiders. When Virgo meets Virgo, there will not be a "head over heels" infatuation. The affair will develop slowly and cautiously. By the time that they are "in love," they will both have fully analyzed each other's virtues and failings and weighed the pros and cons of the relationship. Despite this, they can be surprisingly enthusiastic in bed, something which others, seeing only their cool and perfectionistic exteriors, would find hard to believe.

VIRGO — LIBRA

The thinking function is important to both of these signs, and neither will run out of topics of conversation. The Libra is inclined to be more of a romantic than the more analytical Virgo. Both have a strong sense of perfection, and this will be a point of rapport between them, so long as they don't become disappointed in the imperfections of each other. The Libra may be able to get the Virgo to relax and enjoy having sex as well as to enjoy being in love. The Virgo can help the Libra counteract his occasional lazy streak.

VIRGO — SCORPIO

These two signs are, in many ways, at opposite ends of the emotional spectrum. Virgo is cool and detached, while Scorpio is very passionate and intense. This does not rule out a relationship, although it indicates that both must show a great deal of understanding and patience. Like many combinations that seem somewhat difficult at first examination, they can learn from each other and thus grow. Their differences will actually complement each other if they just relax and enjoy themselves in the situation. The thorniest problem might be the basic difference in sexual needs. However, both share a thoroughness and the need to get to the bottom of any problems, and this should enable them to work out their problems creatively.

VIRGO — SAGITTARIUS

The nature of this relationship will depend primarily on the flexibility of the Virgo. If Sagittarius can inspire in Virgo the Sagittarian love of life and infectious enthusiasm, then it can be the best thing that ever happened to the Virgo, and if the Virgo can persuade the Sagittarius to pay a little more attention to the necessary specifics of things, the

Sagittarius may become happily more stabilized. However, there are difficulties inherent in this combination. The Sagittarius will definitely seem messy and disorganized (relatively speaking) to the supermeticulous Virgo. Their emotional levels are somewhat different, but not all that different to prevent achieving a balance between them. The Sagittarius always takes the overview of any situation, while the Virgo starts with the facts. If they can meet in the middle, they will be a fantastic combination.

VIRGO — CAPRICORN

Sexually, this is a low-key but harmonious relationship. There is a strong physical attraction between these two signs, and romantically they can create a deep and abiding love. Each will have to deal with moodiness and, occasionally, depressions on the part of the other. However, both are sensible Earth signs and inclined to come around to common sense before long. They will enjoy projects together, as they share a common joy in work. This pair of signs can usually mesh well in a long-term relationship.

VIRGO — AQUARIUS

Here is a relationship where deep and genuine friendship can grow into love. After they do become lovers or perhaps marry, friendship will still be the predominating factor in their relationship. The emotional and sexual sides of this combination will be low-key but adequate to their mutual needs. Both of these signs are more mentally oriented and are also somewhat independent. Trouble might arise when the Aquarius is off pursuing social or humanitarian causes to the neglect of the Virgo. The Aquarius will also have to understand the Virgo need for them to spend at least a couple of evenings a week alone together.

VIRGO — PISCES

This is a good relationship. If there is any sign that can "flow" with Virgo moods, it is Pisces. There is a natural rapport between these signs, as there is between most signs that are opposite across the zodiac. The Virgo, above all, needs the warmth and understanding that a Pisces can give. Virgo finds it easy to relax and even dream with a Pisces lover. That is, so long as the Virgo is given the opportunity at some point to organize and work out the details of the Pisces' life. They should make a conscious effort to help each other in those areas where one is stronger than the other, the Pisces in creativity and imagination and the Virgo in practical ability.

LIBRA — LIBRA

This doubling of signs should make for a beautiful mutual communication. Most Libras feel more at home within a love relationship than alone. Each will make a special effort to please the other, and they will enhance each other's appreciation of the beauty in the world around them. They are also likely to develop a good sexual communication. In a permanent relationship two Libras will have to learn how to strengthen their capacity to make decisions and not blame each other for the decisions they do make. They may also need to make a special effort to bring any disagreements to the surface without succumbing to a competitive outlook.

LIBRA — SCORPIO

This is a case of quite different temperaments that can either repel each other or create a more balanced whole. Emotionally and sexually the Scorpio could bring out depths of feeling the Libra didn't know he had. The Libra, on the other hand, can introduce a touch of play that is good for the Scorpio. In a relationship of some duration, the naturally decisive Scorpio can help the Libra learn to do less jumping back and forth over the fence. The diplomatic Libra can help the sharp-tongued Scorpio add grace to his speech.

LIBRA — SAGITTARIUS

Both of these signs enjoy social activities and are likely to have a positive approach to other people. They will enjoy going places and participating in many different activities together. In a romantic and sexual relationship the Libra might try to cling a little more than the naturally freer Sagittarius likes, but they should be able to work this out. In an ongoing relationship their home can become a gathering place for friends, a place of charm where many feel welcome.

LIBRA — CAPRICORN

In this combination the Libra is more likely to be talkative and outgoing, while the Capricorn will most probably be the better listener. On the surface the Libra is more of a romantic, but under the surface of every Capricorn sleeps a hidden romantic. Sexually, the affectionate Libra can balance the sometimes cool but intense Capricorn. As they get to know each other better in a long relationship, the Capricorn can help the Libra organize and move ahead on activities, and the Libra can help the Capricorn balance out a tendency toward too much overdrive and also keep in touch with beauty as well as practicality.

LIBRA — AQUARIUS

These two signs of the air element will find much to talk about, although the ideas of the Libra may seem somewhat conservative compared to the far-out notions of the Aquarius. In a romantic relationship the Libra grace can open up the personal feelings of the sometimes rather detached Aquarius. They should be able to establish a good sexual connection. There is an excellent potential here for a long-term relationship, although they should make a conscious effort to develop silent as well as verbal communication with each other. In many ways, however, the two signs have much in common.

LIBRA — PISCES

Both of these signs have a sense of harmony and balance and can develop a beautiful rapport — emotionally, sexually and as friends. They can be sensitive to each other's needs and can enhance each other's natural awareness of beauty. They both tend to be very romantic, and in glorifying their relationship they may tend to forget that they are two individuals. In an enduring relationship they will have to help each other come to clear-cut decisions and also learn to discuss problems in the open. Also, both signs can "put it off until tomorrow," and so they will have to strengthen each other in doing first things first. All in all, though, it is a nice sign combination.

SCORPIO — SCORPIO

Emotionally and sexually, this pair can be the most intense combination in the zodiac. Scorpio feelings run deep under the surface, and when these two underground streams flow together, the power generated can surprise both of them. In any relationship, either long-term or short-term, two Scorpios must guard against the temptation to continually test each other's intentions. Once they trust each other, however, the relationship will be a deeply meaningful one.

SCORPIO — SAGITTARIUS

A romantic connection between these two signs can make their differences quite exciting. The Scorpio looks into the emotional depths of a situation, while the natural approach of the Sagittarius is to accept any expressed feelings at face value. Sexually, the Sagittarius may seem a bit casual to the more intense Scorpio. In a more permanent relationship between these two signs, it is important for the Scorpio to understand that being with a Sagittarius can help open up some closed doors to areas of his psyche that probably need airing out. The Sagittarius will find that being with a Scorpio will increase his sensitivity to emotional atmospheres.

SCORPIO — CAPRICORN

This combination can be good together in many ways. Emotionally and sexually, the Scorpio should be able to probe underneath the cool Capricorn exterior to the strong and earthy Capricorn desires. Both natures are intense, although the Scorpio has more emotional intensity and the Capricorn more driving intensity to achieve his aims. Both share a cynicism about too much "sweetness and light." In a long-term relationship this pair can balance each other out very nicely, although they may need to consciously lighten up with their own particular brand of straight-faced humor.

SCORPIO — AQUARIUS

Here is another pair who can have a very intense relationship. The Scorpio is the more emotionally intense, whereas the Aquarius is more intent on following whatever ideas he is involved with. Sexually, the Aquarius is more casual and open than the Scorpio. In a long-term relationship the Aquarius will resist any move on the part of the Scorpio to be emotionally possessive, a situation that can help the Scorpio deal with this temptation.

SCORPIO — PISCES

This can be a good combination, since both signs have the potential for a deep emotional understanding of each other. Sexually, the more gentle Pisces can calm some of the Scorpio tendency to overreact. In an ongoing relationship these two signs can develop a strong intuitive connection with each other. The understanding nature of the Pisces can keep the Scorpio from being overly suspicious. Also, the Scorpio can protect the more vulnerable Pisces from being imposed upon. The Pisces will have to learn to be open with the Scorpio about what he is feeling, and the Scorpio must learn not to play emotional games with the Pisces.

SAGITTARIUS — SAGITTARIUS

This is a superadventurous pair, ready to explore romance and sex with plenty of good humor. They will probably both enjoy sports, social gatherings and traveling together. Romance between them will be kept on a somewhat light tone, as each has a need to retain an element of independence, and Sagittarius is not a sign inclined to get into heavy drama. Nevertheless, they will enjoy philosophizing about what the world is all about.

SAGITTARIUS — CAPRICORN

A romantic relationship between these two signs can be wonderful for both if they understand their differences. Emotionally and sexually, the more ardent Sagittarius can bring out the fire that smolders under the cool Capricorn surface. The Sagittarius can also bring out adventurousness in the more conservative Capricorn. On the other hand, the Capricorn can serve as a much-needed anchor point in reality to the Sagittarius, who is often likely to let his enthusiasms take over. The Sagittarius must be careful not to push the Capricorn into venturing beyond where the Capricorn feels secure, and the Capricorn must guard against throwing too much cold water on the Sagittarius dreams.

SAGITTARIUS — AQUARIUS

This is a pair with much in common. Both are outgoing, love social gatherings and are always ready to try something new. Romantically and sexually they should relate well, although the Sagittarius is warmer in his approach. Both have a touch of detachment, and there is an unspoken agreement between them that a clinging relationship is not where it's at. In a long-term connection they will enjoy each other's interest in broader social and philosophical issues.

SAGITTARIUS — PISCES

Since both of these signs are dreamers, a romance between them will take on something of a dream quality. The Sagittarius will explore the emotional depths of the Pisces and bring out his understanding of even the most fantastic Sagittarian dreams. The Sagittarius will also be able to raise the spirits of the sometimes moody Pisces. However, the Sagittarius must understand that a Pisces naturally holds things inside. The Pisces, who tends to be hypersensitive, should understand that the Sagittarius natural bluntness does not stem from malice.

CAPRICORN — CAPRICORN

Both can understand that still waters run deep, emotionally and sexually, and that love is there even if neither is overly demonstrative. They will be able to combine the Capricorn need for solitude with togetherness, pursuing different interests in the same room, yet tuning in on each other with an occasional look or quiet word. In a long-term relationship neither is particularly temperamental. Also, neither will be sloppy or annoy the other by losing things.

CAPRICORN — AQUARIUS

In a romantic relationship the quiet, usually understated Capricorn affection can be a balance for the rather flashy and demonstrative Aquarian temperament. Actually, the Capricorn can use being shaken — emotionally and sexually — out of routine habits, and the Aquarius will benefit by the Capricorn emotional steadiness. Although both of these signs are associated with Saturn, they are rather different. In an ongoing relationship each will have to make allowances for the fact that the Capricorn likes a good deal of order and planning in his or her life, while the Aquarius never likes to be pinned down to anything resembling a schedule.

CAPRICORN — PISCES
In a romantic relationship this can be an excellent combination, since the earthiness of the Capricorn serves as a much-needed anchor for the ethereal and often impractical Pisces. Likewise, the Capricorn needs the Pisces awareness of the beauty of dreams without concern for whether or not they can actually come true. The Pisces needs to understand that, romantically and sexually, the affections of the Capricorn can burn with a steady flame rather than a fireworks display. The Capricorn must realize that expressing his or her deeper feelings will mean a lot to the Pisces. Both signs can enjoy being quiet together.

AQUARIUS — AQUARIUS
Aquarius is not overly sentimental and, in a romantic and sexual relationship, each will understand the other's ability to be personal in what might seem to others a somewhat impersonal manner. This combination will have many surprises for both. They will enjoy social activities with a variety of friends, both old and new, and each will understand the other's need for an element of freedom in the relationship. They will always have plenty to talk about, since both are interested in how things would be in an ideal world.

AQUARIUS — PISCES
A relationship between these two signs can help sensitize the Aquarius, sexually and romantically, and help the Pisces become less acutely sensitive. The Aquarius should remember to bring the Pisces a purely sentimental gift from time to time, and the Pisces should accept that unpredictability is an Aquarian characteristic. In an on-going relationship the Aquarian should give the Piscesan space to dream, and the Piscesan should understand that an Aquarian often expresses affection by talking about his newest ideas and should not imagine that emotional coolness and seeming aloofness is a rejection.

PISCES — PISCES

This pair can understand each other far deeper than the need to talk about it and can be acutely sensitive to each other's moods, even when not together. Therefore, their romantic and sexual relationship and their shared good moods can be ecstatically out of this world, but they must learn not to amplify each other's depressions. They should also avoid building up an "us against the world" feeling, since it may sometimes seem (with some justification) that they understand each other better than anyone else. This is a combination for beautiful, shared dreams.

Parent-Child Relationships

PARENT

	Aries	Taurus	Gemini	Cancer	Leo	Virgo	Libra	Scorpio	Sagittarius	Capricorn	Aquarius	Pisces
Aries	62	64	66	68	69	71	73	74	76	78	79	81
Taurus	63	64	66	68	69	71	73	74	76	78	80	81
Gemini	63	65	66	68	70	71	73	75	76	78	80	81
Cancer	63	65	66	68	70	71	73	75	76	78	80	81
Leo	63	65	66	68	70	72	73	75	77	78	80	82
Virgo	63	65	67	68	70	72	73	75	77	78	80	82
Libra	63	65	67	68	70	72	73	75	77	79	80	82
Scorpio	64	65	67	69	70	72	74	75	77	79	80	82
Sagittarius	64	65	67	69	70	72	74	75	77	79	81	82
Capricorn	64	65	67	69	71	72	74	76	77	79	81	82
Aquarius	64	66	67	69	71	72	74	76	77	79	81	82
Pisces	64	66	67	69	71	72	74	76	78	79	81	83

CHILD

ARIES PARENT — ARIES CHILD

Both can be strong-willed, and the Aries parent must work on his or her own temper so as to help the child develop a controllable temper. Fortunately, the Aries parent can keep up with the fast-moving young Aries and can participate with her in vigorous games and sports, but the parent should try to set a good example of sportsmanship.

ARIES PARENT — TAURUS CHILD
The Aries parent must realize that any Taurus naturally has a much slower pace and should learn not to pull the Taurus child too abruptly from whatever she is doing in order to introduce the child to new things. The parent must learn to approach the child subtly; a Taurus cannot be pushed but can be led. Both can benefit: the Aries parent can learn to slow down, and the Taurus child won't grow up as rigidly set in her patterns.

ARIES PARENT — GEMINI CHILD
Both are lively and communicative, and the Aries parent enjoys introducing the Gemini child to the many things in the world around them. The parent must make a conscious effort to teach the young Gemini to complete activities rather than to keep moving to something else.

ARIES PARENT — CANCER CHILD
The Aries parent must tune in on the Cancer child's sensitivity and realize that she sometimes needs privacy to dream in. An indirect approach is often necessary. The child will inevitably benefit from the parent's example of courageous forthrightness, so long as the lesson is not force-fed. Also, the parent should beware lest she throw away the child's treasured collection of things. Rearing a Cancer child can help an Aries parent to learn the art of subtlety in human relations.

ARIES PARENT — LEO CHILD
The Aries parent can impart her enthusiasms to the Leo child, and they both enjoy games. The Aries parent should let the Leo child develop her own rhythm. The parent can help curb tendencies in the child toward egotism but should refrain from embarrassing the child in front of others.

ARIES PARENT — VIRGO CHILD
The Aries parent can help the young Virgo develop less fussiness and be more outgoing. Also, the Aries parent can encourage the Virgo child to be more physically active in order to balance the child's possible tendency to putter. However, the parent should respect the child's need for privacy and should be sensitive to the subtleties of the child's keen perceptions.

ARIES PARENT — LIBRA CHILD
A Libra child reacts better to a gentle and rational approach, so the Aries parent must learn to modify her natural inclination to issue

commands without explaining why. The Aries parent can help the Libra child develop more decisiveness.

ARIES PARENT — SCORPIO CHILD

The Scorpio child's rhythm is slower than that of the Aries parent, and the child will not want to be pulled quickly from one thing to another. The Aries parent can help the Scorpio child express her feelings rather than hiding them.

ARIES PARENT — SAGITTARIUS CHILD

The Aries parent can help the Sagittarius child to develop her natural love of exploring and also to learn to be more decisive. The parent should be patient with the child's thirst for greater understanding and should have some pretty good reasons behind expressions of parental authority.

ARIES PARENT — CAPRICORN CHILD

The Aries parent needs to realize that any Capricorn needs to know ahead of time what to expect rather than to act on the spur of the moment. The Aries parent can help the Capricorn child be spontaneous.

ARIES PARENT — AQUARIUS CHILD

The Aries parent can help the Aquarius child learn to do rather than just talk about it, although the child will have her own ideas about how to go about things, which the parent should respect if possible.

ARIES PARENT — PISCES CHILD

The Aries parent should make a point of giving the Pisces child dream space and treating her with gentleness. However, the Aries parent can help the Pisces child learn to make up her mind and connect with reality.

TAURUS PARENT — ARIES CHILD

The Taurus parent will have to speed up in order to keep ahead of his or her Aries offspring. The parent can help the child learn to follow through and not to go off half-cocked, but she should remember to not dampen the child's natural enthusiasm with too many restrictions.

TAURUS PARENT — TAURUS CHILD

This combination might reinforce each other's stubbornness, but the Taurus child will respond well to the Taurus parent's affection and patience. They can enjoy the physical world together.

TAURUS PARENT — GEMINI CHILD
The Taurus parent can help the Gemini child steady down and connect with the Earth. However, the Taurus parent should accept that it is natural for a Gemini child to be doing more than one thing at a time.

TAURUS PARENT — CANCER CHILD
The Taurus parent and Cancer child can enjoy quiet times together, doing things around the house. The Taurus parent can help steady some of the Cancer child's moodiness.

TAURUS PARENT — LEO CHILD
The Taurus parent and Leo child share similar rhythms and both tend to be pretty even-tempered. The Taurus parent can be strong enough to curb the Leo child's tyrant tendencies but should avoid stubborn and useless contests of will.

TAURUS PARENT — VIRGO CHILD
Both tend to have a natural respect for each other's possessions. The Taurus parent can, by calm and loving reassurance, help the Virgo child overcome a tendency to be finicky. However, the parent should remember to respect the child's occasional need for distance.

TAURUS PARENT — LIBRA CHILD
The Taurus parent and Libra child will appreciate each other's calmness and good humor. The Taurus parent can help the Libra child develop her sense of beauty.

TAURUS PARENT — SCORPIO CHILD
Both can be quite strong-minded. The Taurus parent can help the Scorpio child to relax some of her intensity but should not try to break her will.

TAURUS PARENT — SAGITTARIUS CHILD
The Taurus parent must learn to appreciate the Sagittarius child's need for adventure and to dream of far-off places and ideas. The Taurus parent can help the Sagittarius child learn to bring some of her dreams to reality.

TAURUS PARENT — CAPRICORN CHILD
Both are down-to-earth and not given to frivolous emotional displays. The Taurus parent's reassuring affection can calm the fears of a Capricorn child.

TAURUS PARENT — AQUARIUS CHILD
The Taurus parent can help the Aquarius child curb excessive talkativeness and also develop good habits rather than always trying something new. The parent should try to be patient with the child's tendency to experiment, for in it is the seed of originality and invention.

TAURUS PARENT — PISCES CHILD
The Taurus parent must realize that a Pisces child may never get her feet planted totally on the ground. However, the Taurus parent, while respecting her Pisces child's imagination, can help the child develop the necessary practicalities.

GEMINI PARENT — ARIES CHILD
Both can be quick-moving. The Gemini parent will be able to teach the Aries child to think before she plunges into action. But if the parent tries to explain too much, the child cannot be expected to sit still and listen.

GEMINI PARENT — TAURUS CHILD
The Gemini parent should realize that the Taurus child will not want to be introduced to many different things at the same time or to sudden changes of activity. In the effort to provide the child with the stable and quiet growing environment, the Gemini parent will be benefited in having her own restless pace slowed down.

GEMINI PARENT — GEMINI CHILD
The Gemini child will probably delight the Gemini parent by talking early and wanting to find out about everything that's happening. The Gemini parent should consciously teach the Gemini child more concentration than is natural to either of them.

GEMINI PARENT — CANCER CHILD
The Gemini parent should make a point of not constantly disturbing the Cancer child's attention without first tuning in on her mood. The Gemini parent can help a Cancer child to balance her strong instincts with logic.

GEMINI PARENT — LEO CHILD
The Leo child is usually charming and loves attention, but the Gemini parent must guard against letting the Leo child run the show. The Gemini parent can help the Leo child to look at all points of view.

GEMINI PARENT — VIRGO CHILD
The Gemini parent and Virgo child will always have lots to talk about. The Gemini parent should respect the Virgo child's possessions and fastidiousness.

GEMINI PARENT — LIBRA CHILD
The Gemini parent and Libra child have a good basis for understanding each other. The Libra child may even be able to teach her Gemini parent a thing or two about how to be neat. Communication can flow comfortably.

GEMINI PARENT — SCORPIO CHILD
The Gemini parent must not expect the Scorpio child to communicate everything she does or is thinking about. However, the Gemini parent can, with tact, help the Scorpio child to be more open and less attached.

GEMINI PARENT — SAGITTARIUS CHILD
The Gemini parent and the Sagittarius child share an ever-present curiosity about the world around them. The Gemini parent needs to answer the Sagittarius child's whys on a deeper level than the concrete reasons. At the same time, the parent can give the child an appreciation of the interconnectedness and relativity of different points of view, thus checking the child's tendency toward dogmatism.

GEMINI PARENT — CAPRICORN CHILD
The Gemini parent must respect the Capricorn child's need to organize her possessions and activities. However, the Gemini parent can teach the Capricorn child more flexibility.

GEMINI PARENT — AQUARIUS CHILD
This is a good combination for communication. The Gemini parent can help the Aquarius child develop flexibility in her opinions but will find it easy to be receptive to the child's original thinking. The parent should be sensitive to the things the child takes very seriously and not make light of them.

GEMINI PARENT — PISCES CHILD
The Gemini parent and the Pisces child can share an imaginative world. The Gemini parent can help the Pisces child be aware of what's going on around her in the everyday world as well as in dreams. The parent should allow the child enough solitude to adjust her dreams to practical reality and should try to appreciate the creative potential in the child's fantasies.

CANCER PARENT — ARIES CHILD

The Cancer parent will have the patience to deal with the strong will of the Aries child and, in time, will manage to see some of this patience rub off on the impulsive Aries nature. The parent must not tie down the child as a result of fond and sentimental memories of the child's babyhood; such smothering possessiveness will only be rewarded with open rebellion.

CANCER PARENT — TAURUS CHILD

The Taurus child will respond with affection to the affectionate Cancer parent, who can learn to wear away the stubborn Taurus edges by avoiding direct confrontations.

CANCER PARENT — GEMINI CHILD

The Cancer parent can help calm some of the Gemini child's fidgety nature and teach her to be aware of what she is feeling as well as thinking.

CANCER PARENT — CANCER CHILD

The Cancer parent and the Cancer child will have close, often nonspoken understanding of each other, tuning in instinctively on each other's moods.

CANCER PARENT — LEO CHILD

The Leo child will be a ray of sunshine to the Cancer parent. The Cancer parent can teach the Leo child to enjoy solitude as well as being the center of attention.

CANCER PARENT — VIRGO CHILD

The Cancer parent and the Virgo child are both "collectors" and will be interested in each other's collections. However, the Cancer parent must work consciously to keep this tendency within reasonable limits for the Virgo child. The parent can help the child deepen her emotional sensitivity but should not be hurt by the child's criticism of her parent's sentimental attachments.

CANCER PARENT — LIBRA CHILD

A Libra child likes to please and will rarely jar the deeper sensitivities of the Cancer parent. The Cancer parent can help the Libra child to be in touch with her feelings. The parent should be patient if the child sometimes finds outside relationships more important than home.

CANCER PARENT — SCORPIO CHILD

The Cancer parent will be able to tune in on the moods of the Scorpio child and help her pull out of the darker moods through gentle affection and acceptance. The parent should try to absorb with equanimity the child's sometimes ruthless drive for change and not be too bound by outworn family traditions.

CANCER PARENT — SAGITTARIUS CHILD

The Cancer parent must understand that the Sagittarius child will be quite adventurous and curious about everything. The Cancer parent can help the Sagittarius child learn to sense which of her enthusiasms are just passing fancies.

CANCER PARENT — CAPRICORN CHILD

The Cancer parent has the sympathetic and understanding nature necessary to coax the Capricorn child into expressing her feelings more freely and can make the child feel steadily loved, provided the child's fears are not reinforced by the parent's moodiness.

CANCER PARENT — AQUARIUS CHILD

The Cancer parent can help the Aquarius child learn to respect some of the tried-and-true ways of doing things in order to counteract the Aquarius child's fascination with the unusual and zany. But the parent should, nonetheless, try to be open to the child's original approach and encourage her inventiveness.

CANCER PARENT — PISCES CHILD

The Cancer parent can tune in on the Pisces child's extreme sensitivity and help her to be sympathetic without taking everything too much to heart.

LEO PARENT — ARIES CHILD

The Leo parent can help the Aries child steady her rhythms and learn to express herself with affection as well as enthusiasm. However, the parent should not expect the child to always behave with the parent's sense of dignity and decorum.

LEO PARENT — TAURUS CHILD

The Leo parent can help the Taurus child develop generosity. Confrontations should be avoided, since it will be difficult, if not impossible, for either parent or child to give in.

LEO PARENT — GEMINI CHILD

The Leo parent's affection and warmth can rub off on the Gemini child. The Leo parent's centeredness can help the Gemini child learn not to fritter away her energy. The child may resist the parent's domination unless she is advised of the reasons behind the rules.

LEO PARENT — CANCER CHILD

The Leo parent can use her warmth to help the Cancer child out of sulking, despondent moods but must realize that the child may not be as naturally outgoing as a Leo and that her need for seclusion some of the time is not antisocial.

LEO PARENT — LEO CHILD

The Leo parent can bring out the sunny nature of the Leo child but must be careful that she does not influence her toward too much self-centeredness.

LEO PARENT — VIRGO CHILD

The Leo parent's warmth can be calming to the nervous energy of the Virgo child. The Leo parent's centered nature can help the Virgo child find her own center. The parent should respect the reserve and the need for order in her child.

LEO PARENT — LIBRA CHILD

Both like the happy side of things. The Leo parent's natural gentleness is an approach to which the Libra child responds best. The Leo parent can help the Libra child learn to make up her mind.

LEO PARENT — SCORPIO CHILD

The Leo parent's openness can help keep the Scorpio child from developing an unduly suspicious temperament. However, the Leo parent must learn to respect a natural need for some secretiveness in the Scorpio child.

LEO PARENT — SAGITTARIUS CHILD

The Leo parent (who never loses her connection with childhood) should enjoy helping the Sagittarius child invent adventures. The Leo parent can also help the Sagittarius child tone down some of her restlessness. The parent should be ready with understandable answers when rules are met with the child's whys.

LEO PARENT — CAPRICORN CHILD
The Leo parent should understand that the Capricorn child is naturally serious and not be concerned if the child doesn't smile as much as is natural to Leo. However, the Leo parent can easily give the Capricorn child a needed feeling of security and warmth.

LEO PARENT — AQUARIUS CHILD
Both are naturally outgoing. The Leo parent can help the Aquarius child develop a warm heart to match her active brain. The parent should be prepared for occasional rebellions on the part of the child and should not insist unreasonably that arbitrary parental edicts be obeyed.

LEO PARENT — PISCES CHILD
The Leo parent's steady loving nature can help the Pisces child become more steady and secure. However, the Leo parent must learn to respect the Pisces child's sensitivities and not push her into the center of attention if the child is not ready.

VIRGO PARENT — ARIES CHILD
The Virgo parent may be able to instill some courtesy in the blunt Aries child, but the parent must realize that an Aries child will never be as fastidious as a Virgo. The parent should try to tolerate a little noise and chaos as natural manifestations of a healthy Aries child.

VIRGO PARENT — TAURUS CHILD
The Taurus child's placid nature can make the Virgo parent less nervous about the problems of parenthood, but the parent must remember that Taurus children particularly like affectionate hugs.

VIRGO PARENT — GEMINI CHILD
The Virgo parent will enjoy the Gemini child's sharp perceptions and quick comprehension. Since both are fidgety signs, the parent should put conscious attention toward helping the child learn to enjoy quiet pursuits and to concentrate.

VIRGO PARENT — CANCER CHILD
The Virgo parent must realize that the Cancer child is more easily influenced through an approach to feelings than to intellect, but at the same time the parent's natural logic can help the child learn to think clearly.

VIRGO PARENT — LEO CHILD
The Virgo parent will appreciate the affectionate nature of the Leo child. Without damaging the child's dignity the parent should be firm with important decisions and not let her tendency toward self-contradiction leave a power vacuum for the child to fill. The parent must also realize that the Leo pace is slower than that of the Virgo.

VIRGO PARENT — VIRGO CHILD
The Virgo parent will enjoy the Virgo child's intelligence and curiosity but must learn not to unconsciously strengthen the child's fussy whims about such things as what to eat and what to wear.

VIRGO PARENT — LIBRA CHILD
Since both might have trouble being decisive, the Virgo parent should make a conscious effort to teach the Libra child how to make decisions clearly. The parent should take care not to upset the delicate balance of the child's sensibilities with too many trifles.

VIRGO PARENT — SCORPIO CHILD
The Virgo parent can help the Scorpio child develop her natural capacity to be thorough. The parent must realize that firmness is important with a Scorpio child.

VIRGO PARENT — SAGITTARIUS CHILD
The Virgo parent can help the Sagittarius child to not neglect the details in her natural involvement with "what it means." The Virgo parent should accept that a Sagittarius child is naturally adventurous.

VIRGO PARENT — CAPRICORN CHILD
The Virgo parent will appreciate the Capricorn child's careful, serious nature. Since both have a tendency toward being worriers, the parent should make a conscious effort to keep things on the bright side and not instill any unnecessary fears in the child.

VIRGO PARENT — AQUARIUS CHILD
The Virgo parent must realize that the Aquarius child is naturally a breaker of rules and therefore the parent should be firm about the rules that count and not overload the child with unnecessary regulation.

VIRGO PARENT — PISCES CHILD
The Virgo parent can help bring a little order into the Pisces child's life but needs to understand that the child has her own way of learning

and is influenced much more by sympathies than by rules or reason.

LIBRA PARENT — ARIES CHILD
Some of the Libra parent's sense of fairness can be rubbed off on the "me first" nature of the Aries child, but the parent should realize that the fighting spirit of the Aries child must be properly channeled rather than squelched.

LIBRA PARENT — TAURUS CHILD
The Libra parent will find the Taurus child very responsive to beauty. The parent can help the child understand sharing but may find that an appeal to the child's affections is more effective than to reason.

LIBRA PARENT — GEMINI CHILD
The Libra parent and the Gemini child will have good verbal communication. The Libra parent can help the Gemini child learn something about neatness but must realize that a Gemini always has too many things happening at once to keep everything totally together.

LIBRA PARENT — CANCER CHILD
The Libra parent will appreciate the sympathetic side of the Cancer child's nature but needs to realize that it is natural for a Cancer to go through mood cycles and must not always insist upon communicating with her.

LIBRA PARENT — LEO CHILD
The Leo child's big smile is a delight to the Libra parent, but the Libra parent must help the young Leo to understand that in fairness to others she must not hog the limelight.

LIBRA PARENT — VIRGO CHILD
There is good basis for understanding in this combination. The Libra parent can help the Virgo child develop her appreciation for beauty to balance her practical mental orientation.

LIBRA PARENT — LIBRA CHILD
This is a pleasant combination. However, the Libra parent must make sure that she instills a clear sense of truthfulness in the Libra child, as the Libra natural bent toward diplomacy can sometimes unconsciously bend the facts.

LIBRA PARENT — SCORPIO CHILD
The Libra parent must understand that the Scorpio child may need help to develop a sense of justice and diplomacy but that a Scorpio has a natural respect for strength and honesty.

LIBRA PARENT — SAGITTARIUS CHILD
Both are basically happy-natured, and enjoy company. The Libra parent may be able to instill some tact in the naturally blunt Sagittarius child but should not try to curtail the child's healthy enthusiasm with too much concern for decorum.

LIBRA PARENT — CAPRICORN CHILD
The Libra parent will find the Capricorn child responsive in learning neatness and organization but should not be concerned if she often prefers to play alone quietly rather than with other children. The parent can help the child understand life's sufferings in more perspective.

LIBRA PARENT — AQUARIUS CHILD
The Libra parent should help her Aquarius child to sometimes laugh at herself instead of being intent on rebellion. But the parent should not expect the child to adhere to stuffy old rituals of politeness just because they are "nice." Both are talkative signs, so the Libra parent needs to put conscious attention toward helping the young Aquarius appreciate quiet and also learn to listen.

LIBRA PARENT — PISCES CHILD
The Libra parent will appreciate the Pisces child's quiet charm and sense of beauty. The Libra parent's gentle nature will help prevent emotional scars on the sensitive Pisces child.

SCORPIO PARENT — ARIES CHILD
Both are intense and can be combative; therefore the Scorpio parent must make a conscious effort to teach the Aries child an appreciation of peace and fairness. The parent will appreciate the high spirits of the young Aries.

SCORPIO PARENT — TAURUS CHILD
Both can be possessive and stubborn, but also loyal. The Scorpio parent needs to deliberately help the Taurus child learn how to compromise, but the parent will appreciate the child's strong-mindedness.

SCORPIO PARENT — GEMINI CHILD
The Scorpio parent can help the Gemini child learn to concentrate and to go into things more than surface-deep. On the other hand, the parent should make an effort to satisfy the child's wide-ranging curiosity and not be too condemning of the child's restless experimentation.

SCORPIO PARENT — CANCER CHILD
Both can be quite sensitive to each other's feelings. The Scorpio parent can help the child develop some needed emotional toughness, provided she approaches the child with tenderness. The child's need for security should never be disregarded. Since neither of these signs is naturally open and frank, the parent needs to make a disciplined effort to help the child develop these qualities.

SCORPIO PARENT — LEO CHILD
Since both are fixed signs, the Scorpio parent needs to make an effort to help the Leo child develop flexibility. The parent will appreciate the child's ability to be centered and can help the child enjoy solitude as well as being the center of attention.

SCORPIO PARENT — VIRGO CHILD
A Scorpio parent can set high standards, and a Virgo child will take seriously the challenge of improving her performance. Since Scorpio can be a rather "heavy" sign, the parent should work consciously to help the Virgo child counteract her tendencies to worry.

SCORPIO PARENT — LIBRA CHILD
The Scorpio parent can help the Libra child develop drive and good work habits, traits that are not built into the Libra makeup. The Scorpio parent needs to reexamine her strong and fixed opinions, as a Libra child always wants to see both sides of any question.

SCORPIO PARENT — SCORPIO CHILD
The Scorpio parent will find the Scorpio child taking after him or her in intensity and strength of will, and the parent needs to help the child, without maneuvering, to develop these traits positively.

SCORPIO PARENT — SAGITTARIUS CHILD
The Scorpio parent must realize that the Sagittarius child has a natural attraction to freedom and will never take too easily to discipline. The parent can help the child realize that self-discipline will give her more freedom.

SCORPIO PARENT — CAPRICORN CHILD
The natural concentration of the Scorpio parent can help develop the Capricorn child's potential for thoroughness. The parent should be wary lest her emotional intensity threaten the child's security. Since both are serious signs, the Scorpio parent should put considerable exertion toward helping the Capricorn child avoid building up a worry habit.

SCORPIO PARENT — AQUARIUS CHILD
The Scorpio parent must curb her tendency to demand too much, as this could strengthen the natural rebellion of an Aquarius child. The Scorpio parent can help the Aquarius child learn to appreciate solitude.

SCORPIO PARENT — PISCES CHILD
The Scorpio parent needs to realize that a too-strict approach to a Pisces child isn't a good idea, since no Pisces is comfortable in a set routine. The Pisces child responds more readily to an appeal to her sympathies, so long as the parent doesn't deliberately play on the child's emotions.

SAGITTARIUS PARENT — ARIES CHILD
Both love adventure, so the Sagittarius parent will enjoy introducing the Aries child to all the exciting things in the world around them. Since neither of these signs is noted for self-discipline, the parent may need to make a conscious effort to help the child develop this attribute.

SAGITTARIUS PARENT — TAURUS CHILD
The Sagittarius parent should not expect the Taurus child to be as fast-moving and adventurous as she is, but the parent can help the child develop flexibility.

SAGITTARIUS PARENT — GEMINI CHILD
Both are inquisitive and into a lot of activities. The Sagittarius parent can help the Gemini child see broader perspectives than the Gemini nature would naturally see but should not be perturbed if the child cannot adhere to all the parent's beliefs. The parent should work on helping the child learn to concentrate.

SAGITTARIUS PARENT — CANCER CHILD
The Sagittarius parent can help the Cancer child be more open but must also allow her to have secret time and space that is not shared by the parent.

SAGITTARIUS PARENT — LEO CHILD
Both know how to play, so they will naturally enjoy each other. The Sagittarius parent, with her natural optimism and ability to encourage, should guard against expanding the Leo child's egotistical tendencies.

SAGITTARIUS PARENT — VIRGO CHILD
The Sagittarius parent, whose nature it is to keep trying something new, can help the Virgo child not to be too finicky. The parent can also help the child see a broader perspective, but should respect the child's desire to perfect whatever she is working on.

SAGITTARIUS PARENT — LIBRA CHILD
Both are inclined to be friendly and optimistic and will enjoy each other's company. The Sagittarius parent should encourage independence in the Libra child but should try not to needlessly embarrass her with ill-considered bluntness.

SAGITTARIUS PARENT — SCORPIO CHILD
The Sagittarius parent should accept that whereas the Sagittarian nature is open, there is always a touch of secrecy about a Scorpio. However, the parent can help the Scorpio child learn to express his or her feelings more freely.

SAGITTARIUS PARENT — SAGITTARIUS CHILD
Both will enjoy sports and exploring with each other. The parent needs to help the child learn how to curb restlessness and to develop perseverance.

SAGITTARIUS PARENT — CAPRICORN CHILD
The Sagittarius parent can help the Capricorn child learn not to neglect sports and exercise, as well as to lighten up on some of the Capricorn seriousness. However, the Sagittarius parent should accept that the Capricorn nature is basically serious. The parent should make a conscious effort not to let her restlessness threaten the child's security.

SAGITTARIUS PARENT — AQUARIUS CHILD
This is a sociable combination, with a lot of interest in ideas, although the Sagittarius parent may find her Aquarius offspring has a few offbeat notions and should not expect the child to cling too rigidly to family traditions. The parent should consciously help the child learn to appreciate solitude.

SAGITTARIUS PARENT — PISCES CHILD

The Sagittarius parent can help the Pisces child not to live too much in a dream world, but the parent should tune into the Pisces child's sensitivity and not push her to show off when not so inclined.

CAPRICORN PARENT — ARIES CHILD

The Capricorn parent can help the Aries child learn to think before she acts. However, the parent should be careful not to suppress the child's enthusiasm and spontaneity in the process.

CAPRICORN PARENT — TAURUS CHILD

Both can enjoy with each other a variety of down-to-earth activities. The Capricorn parent can help the Taurus child develop the capacity to work but should guard against expecting too much drive and seriousness from an easygoing Taurus.

CAPRICORN PARENT — GEMINI CHILD

The Capricorn parent can help the Gemini child organize her many interests and learn to think sometimes before she speaks. However, the parent should accept that it is natural for a Gemini to keep her fingers in several pies at the same time. Moreover, the child cannot help but balk at authority, no matter how severely invoked, unless it is backed up with reason.

CAPRICORN PARENT — CANCER CHILD

The Capricorn parent must realize that the Cancer child operates best not on a strict schedule but by learning to catch the right mood for what she has to do. If the parent goes about it gently, she can instill in the child forethought and good working habits. The Cancer child opens up to affection.

CAPRICORN PARENT — LEO CHILD

The Capricorn parent will warm up to the naturally affectionate nature of the Leo child. The parent can help the child learn that she doesn't always need an audience.

CAPRICORN PARENT — VIRGO CHILD

The Capricorn parent can help the Virgo child learn how to structure her activities and how to put first things first. The parent may need to focus on helping the young Virgo learn how to express her affections and avoid self-criticism.

CAPRICORN PARENT — LIBRA CHILD
The Capricorn parent can help the Libra child learn good work habits but should make allowances for the easygoing streak in the Libra nature. The parent should allow the child to develop her natural appreciation of beauty as well as practicality.

CAPRICORN PARENT — SCORPIO CHILD
The Capricorn parent can help the Scorpio child channel her driving energy into worthwhile activities. The parent should encourage positive expression of the child's deep emotional sensitivity. However, since both are rather serious signs, the parent may need to make a conscious effort toward helping the young Scorpio lighten up.

CAPRICORN PARENT — SAGITTARIUS CHILD
The Capricorn parent can help the Sagittarius child learn to channel her restlessness by encouraging the child's desire to take part in active sports. The parent should take care not to be a wet blanket to the child's enthusiasms.

CAPRICORN PARENT — CAPRICORN CHILD
The parent will find the child ambitious, serious and easy to teach neatness to. However, since Capricorn can be an overserious sign, the parent should deliberately encourage play, warmth and humor in the child.

CAPRICORN PARENT — AQUARIUS CHILD
The Capricorn parent can help the Aquarius child learn to be more regular in her work habits but should allow her to experiment rather than always do things in the same way.

CAPRICORN PARENT — PISCES CHILD
The Capricorn parent needs to realize that the Pisces child is naturally a dreamer and should not be treated with undue strictness. However, the parent can help the child develop a certain amount of practicality without expecting her to come completely down to earth.

AQUARIUS PARENT — ARIES CHILD
The Aquarius parent can handle the adventurous nature of the Aries child and can help her to learn how to disagree with others without becoming angry. The parent should work on helping the child learn quietness as well as self-expression.

AQUARIUS PARENT — TAURUS CHILD

The Aquarius parent can help the Taurus child not become set in habit patterns. However, a Taurus does not take well to being forced to try something before she is ready for it.

AQUARIUS PARENT — GEMINI CHILD

The Aquarius parent will encourage the Gemini child to develop her various interests and sociability. The parent should not expect the child to hold too rigidly to convictions and should respect the child's right to change her mind.

AQUARIUS PARENT — CANCER CHILD

The Aquarius parent should not expect the Cancer child to be naturally outgoing and independent, but the parent can help the child develop these qualities to some extent. The parent should respect the child's quiet moods.

AQUARIUS PARENT — LEO CHILD

The Aquarius parent can help the Leo child learn cooperation and not become too self-centered. The child can teach the parent how to express warmth. The parent should pay attention to helping the child learn to enjoy being alone as well as with others.

AQUARIUS PARENT — VIRGO CHILD

The Aquarius parent can help the Virgo child overcome fears of trying something new and learn how to develop intuition as well as her analytical nature. Conscious effort may be needed to help the child learn to express her feelings freely.

AQUARIUS PARENT — LIBRA CHILD

The Aquarius parent will enjoy introducing the Libra child to all sorts of ideas. Effort should be made to encourage the child to develop her own beliefs, since in the light of her desire to please, the Libra child may otherwise grow up to be a mere mouthpiece of the parent's convictions.

AQUARIUS PARENT — SCORPIO CHILD

The Aquarius parent can help the Scorpio child become more open and cooperative, but the parent should also respect the child's need for privacy.

AQUARIUS PARENT — SAGITTARIUS CHILD
The Aquarius parent and Sagittarius child can communicate easily. The parent should encourage the child's participation in active sports but should help the child learn to steady a restless nature.

AQUARIUS PARENT — CAPRICORN CHILD
The Aquarius parent can help the Capricorn child not to become too set in established routines, but the parent should respect the child's need for organization and some solitude.

AQUARIUS PARENT — AQUARIUS CHILD
The Aquarius parent will naturally encourage the outgoing nature and inventiveness of the Aquarius child. However, the parent should also try to teach the child to enjoy being by herself.

AQUARIUS PARENT — PISCES CHILD
The Aquarius parent can help the Pisces child learn independence and become somewhat outgoing. However, the parent should respect the child's need for a certain amount of solitude and dream space.

PISCES PARENT — ARIES CHILD
The Pisces parent will enjoy the bright interest that the Aries child shows in her surroundings but will have to work on learning how to handle the headstrong Aries qualities. The Pisces parent can help the Aries child learn empathy.

PISCES PARENT — TAURUS CHILD
The Taurus child might teach the Pisces parent a thing or two about practicalities, but the parent will enjoy introducing the child to all the beautiful things in the world around them.

PISCES PARENT — GEMINI CHILD
The Pisces parent will enjoy the whimsical nature of the Gemini child but will have to make a special effort to help the child learn concentration and self-discipline. The parent can help the child deepen her sensitivities but should not be too surprised if the child is the clearer thinker.

PISCES PARENT — CANCER CHILD
Both will enjoy spinning dreams together, and each is likely to be sensitive to the other's moods. The parent may need to make a special effort to help the child develop the ability to think clearly, since both of them have a more predominant feeling nature.

PISCES PARENT — LEO CHILD

The Pisces parent will enjoy the cheery, affectionate qualities of the Leo child, but will have to make a real effort to be firm enough so that the child doesn't become ruler of the household.

PISCES PARENT — VIRGO CHILD

The Pisces parent can help the Virgo child tune into the magic of the world rather than get caught up in thinking and fiddling too much. However, the parent should try not to let the child's environment become too disorderly. The parent may need to make an effort to teach the child how to center herself.

PISCES PARENT — LIBRA CHILD

The Pisces parent will tune into the Libra child's affable nature and her ever-present sense of the beautiful. However, the parent may need to make a concerted effort to teach the child how to make decisions and how to develop good work habits.

PISCES PARENT — SCORPIO CHILD

Both should naturally be able to tune into each other's feelings, but the Pisces parent may have to make a special effort to keep the young Scorpio from developing the ability to manipulate the parent's good nature and become somewhat tyrannical.

PISCES PARENT — SAGITTARIUS CHILD

The Pisces parent will enjoy the warm enthusiasm of the Sagittarius child but may need to make an effort to teach the child to corral some of her energy and focus in on the details.

PISCES PARENT — CAPRICORN CHILD

The Pisces parent can help the down-to-earth Capricorn child keep in touch with the magic side of things and develop her feeling nature. However, the parent should also encourage the child's natural interest in practical things and endeavor to provide a secure environment for the child.

PISCES PARENT — AQUARIUS CHILD

The Pisces parent can help the Aquarius child to be in touch with his or her feeling nature, and both will enjoy going off on imaginative flights of fancy.

PISCES PARENT — PISCES CHILD
The Pisces parent will find it easy to tune in on the Pisces child's sensitive, dreamy nature. However, the parent may have to work on ways to help the child handle her excess sensitivity as well as deal with the practicalities of living.

CHAPTER FOUR

YOUR MOON SIGN AND PHASE

The zodiac sign in which the Moon was at your birth is your **Moon sign**. It can be the same as your Sun sign or any of the other eleven zodiac signs. In this book you will discover how to find your Moon sign and what it means.

Your Moon sign shows your immediate reactions, your instincts, what goes on underneath the surface of your Sun sign consciousness. The Moon sign indicates your feelings, moods, the rhythms of your bodily processes. When you were a baby or young child, you probably seemed more like your Moon sign than your Sun sign. As you began to recognize yourself as a separate individual, your Sun sign came to be more prominent. However, your Moon sign is always there, underneath, blending with the Sun sign in your personality.

The Moon sign is your atmosphere — the background feeling in which your Sun sign is focused. It often appears more clearly when your conscious mind is not so sharp, for instance when you are relaxed, tuning in on your own flow. It is also, of course, more in evidence when you are tired or ill.

The Moon sign is a key to your moods and feelings. It also relates to your bodily functions and your habits, how adaptable and changeable you are. Also the Moon sign is one indication, particularly in a man's chart, of the type of woman who is important in his life. This does not mean, necessarily, that he will relate only to women whose Sun sign is the same as his Moon sign, but that he will be drawn to women who, in one way or another, embody some of the strongest qualities of the zodiac sign in which his Moon is placed.

Knowing your own Moon sign and that of persons close to you

can give you insights into what goes on underneath the surface of the consciously expressed will of the Sun sign.

Beginning on page 89 are calendars from 1911 through 2000 which will enable you to find easily the Moon sign of anyone born in those years. To interpret the Moon sign meaning:

1. In the **Sun sign section** beginning on page 5, read the description of the sign of the zodiac which your Moon is in. The characteristics of this sign, expressed more directly and consciously when a Sun sign, will be the instinctual and unconscious background when a Moon sign.

2. In the **Moon sign section** beginning on page 88, read the characteristics for your Moon sign.

3. In the section beginning on page 140, read a description of how your **Sun sign-Moon sign combination** blends in your personality.

How To Find Your Sun Sign, Moon Sign and Moon Phase

If you were born after 1910, the calendar (pp. 89-133) will enable you to easily find your Moon sign and Moon phase (see page 137). If you are not sure of your Sun sign or were born near the 21st of the month (near a Sun sign change), the calendar will enable you to verify the correctness of your Sun sign.

Notice that each page of the calendar contains two years. Each third of a page has eight months, with every month having its own column. Each column is divided into four sections. The top section is a heading, giving you the month and year. The second section indicates symbols for the Sun and the sign into which it is changing that month. The date and time of the change (in Sun sign) is on the next line.

The third section in each column indicates changes in Moon signs. The date is given on the left, followed by the sign the Moon is changing into, followed by the time of that change.

The fourth section lists Moon phases. Each line gives the date of the phase, a symbol for the phase and the time the change in phase occurs. There are eight possible Moon phases:

New ●	Full ○
Crescent ☽	Disseminating ◑
First Quarter ◐	Third Quarter ◑
Gibbous ◐	Balsamic ☾

The time given in this calendar is United States Eastern Standard

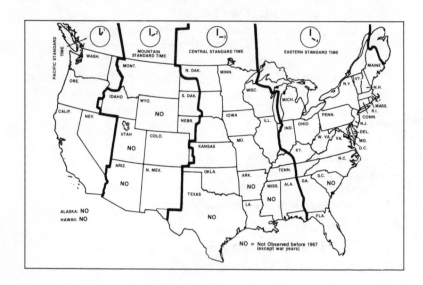

Outside Dates
for Daylight Savings Time

Year	Dates	Year	Dates	Year	Dates	Year	Dates
1920	3/28 - 10/31	1940	4/28 - 9/29	1961	4/30 - 10/29	1981	4/26 - 10/25
1921	4/24 - 9/25	1941	4/27 - 9/28	1962	4/29 - 10/28	1982	4/25 - 10/31
1922	4/30 - 9/24	1942	WAR TIME	1963	4/28 - 10/27	1983	4/24 - 10/30
1923	4/29 - 9/30	to		1964	4/25 - 10/25	1984	4/29 - 10/28
1924	4/27 - 9/28	1945		1965	4/25 - 10/31	1985	4/28 - 10/27
1925	4/26 - 9/27	1946	4/28 - 9/29	1966	4/24 - 10/30	1986	4/27 - 10/26
1926	4/25 - 9/26	1947	4/27 - 9/28	1967	4/30 - 10/29	1987	4/26 - 10/25
1927	4/24 - 9/25	1948	4/25 - 9/26	1968	4/28 - 10/27	1988	4/24 - 10/30
1928	4/29 - 9/30	1949	4/24 - 9/25	1969	4/27 - 10/26	1989	4/30 - 10/29
1929	4/28 - 9/29	1950	4/30 - 9/24	1970	4/26 - 10/25	1990	4/29 - 10/28
1930	4/27 - 9/28	1951	4/29 - 9/30	1971	4/25 - 10/21	1991	4/28 - 10/27
1931	4/26 - 9/27	1952	4/27 - 9/28	1972	4/30 - 10/29	1992	4/26 - 10/25
1932	4/24 - 9/25	1953	4/26 - 9/27	1973	4/29 - 10/28	1993	4/25 - 10/31
1933	4/30 - 9/24	1954	4/25 - 10/31	1974	1/6 - 10/27	1994	4/24 - 10/30
1934	4/29 - 9/30	1955	4/24 - 10/30	1975	2/23 - 10/26	1995	4/30 - 10/29
1935	4/28 - 9/29	1956	4/29 - 10/28	1976	4/25 - 10/31	1996	4/28 - 10/27
1936	4/26 - 9/27	1957	4/28 - 10/27	1977	4/24 - 10/30	1997	4/27 - 10/26
1937	4/25 - 9/26	1958	4/27 - 10/26	1978	4/30 - 10/29	1998	4/26 - 10/25
1938	4/24 - 10/2	1959	4/26 - 10/25	1979	4/29 - 10/28	1999	4/25 - 10/31
1939	4/30 - 9/24	1960	4/24 - 10/30	1980	4/27 - 10/26	2000	4/30 - 10/29

Time. This is always five hours less than Greenwich Mean Time, which is the "basic" standard time for the world. If you were born on or near the United States east coast (in the Eastern Time zone), you do not need to make any time corrections unless Daylight Saving Time or Wartime Daylight Saving Time was in effect at that particular time. If you were born in the Central Standard Time zone (unless Daylight Saving Time was in effect), add **one hour** to your birth time to convert to Eastern Standard Time. For Mountain Standard Time, add **two hours**, and for Pacific Standard Time, add **three hours**.

For Yukon Standard Time, add **four hours**. For Central Alaska Standard Time, add **five hours**. (Hawaii now uses Central Alaska Standard Time. However, before June 8, 1947, parts of Hawaii used Hawaiian Standard Time. For a birthplace in Hawaiian Standard Time, add **five and a half hours**.) For Nome Standard Time (western Alaska), add **six hours**.

If you were born in a place in the world with a different time zone, it may be more convenient to convert to Greenwich Mean Time (since this is the way most world time-conversion charts work) and then subtract five hours to get United States Eastern Standard Time.

After you correct your time for Eastern Standard Time and if you were born in the United States and if your birth time is **within an hour** of a Moon sign, Sun sign or Moon phase change, you should check to see if there is a possibility that Daylight Saving Time might have been in effect when you were born. This can be one of three kinds:

1. Summer Daylight Saving Time
2. Wartime Daylight Saving Time
3. Fuel crisis Daylight Saving Time

Although it is a very complex operation to determine whether any given locality did or did not have Daylight Saving Time (within a state different communities might elect, in a given year, to be on or off, or begin and end Daylight Saving Time on different dates), it is relatively simple to eliminate the possibility when and where it was not in effect. Find your state on the map on page 86. If there is "NO" indicated, it means that Daylight Saving Time was not observed anywhere in the state for the years before 1967 (except wartime). If your state does not have a "NO," you will have to check with relatives or local records to find out if you need to **subtract one hour** from the time of your birth (already corrected for time zone differences) to conform with Eastern Standard Time. If your state does not have a "NO" listed, you will still be all right if you were not born within the **outside dates** listed for each year below the map. These are the dates when summer Daylight Saving Time could have started and ended.

During both World War I and World War II, Wartime Daylight Saving Time was standard throughout the country during the following times:

1918, 3/31 to 10/27
1919, 3/30 to 10/26
1942 to 1945, 2/9/42 to 9/30/45

Since 1967, automatic nationwide Daylight Saving Time has been in effect from the last Sunday in April to the last Sunday in October. An exception was the fuel crisis Daylight Saving Time in 1974 and 1975 (see dates under map). An entire state can exempt itself. In 1967 Arizona and Hawaii were exempt, and in 1968 Michigan became exempt as well.

Sun and Moon Calendar (1911–2000)

(Beginning on page 89)

If Your Moon Sign is Aries ♈

Although an Aries Sun sign is more consciously action oriented, you, as an Aries Moon sign, have instantaneous reactions. If the cup falls off the table, you've caught it before it reaches the floor. Your emotional responses are just as quick. This may tend to confuse others because just as soon as your reaction has sparked a reaction in them, you've probably changed to another mood altogether. Try to counterbalance this by taking a conscious mental pause before launching into action. Recognize that there are times when careful consideration is necessary. However, don't let anyone stifle your high spirits, your independence, or your fresh way of looking at things.

If Your Moon Sign Is Taurus ♉

Your physical and emotional reactions are slow and steady. You are very practical and handle most problems with a great deal of common sense. You do not anger easily, although when aroused you can demonstrate a formidable wrath. You really enjoy comfort and, at the very least, need a certain degree of material security to be happy, although you may not realize this as consciously as a Taurus Sun sign. Your relaxed charm transmits to others a sense of peace and security. Your thumb is very likely green.

(Text continues on page 134)

JAN 1911 — ☉ → ♒ 20 10p51

☽ → SIGNS

Day	Sign	Time
2	♈	4a2
4	♉	12p50
6	♊	7p33
9	♋	12a1
11	♌	2a16
13	♍	3a3
15	♎	3a49
17	♏	6a30
19	♐	12p47
21	♑	11p5
24	♒	11a54
27	♓	12a30
29	♈	10a57
31	♉	6p55

☽ PHASES

Day	Phase	Time
4	☽	9a21
8	○	1a20
11	○	11a1
14	○	5p25
18	○	4a1
22	○	1a20
26	☾	5a11
30	●	4a44

FEB 1911 — ☉ → ♓ 19 1p20

☽ → SIGNS

Day	Sign	Time
3	♊	12a57
5	♋	5a36
7	♌	9a2
9	♍	11a27
11	♎	1p33
13	♏	1a4
15	♐	10p21
18	♑	7a39
20	♒	7p53
23	♓	8a37
25	♈	7p17
28	♉	2a50

☽ PHASES

Day	Phase	Time
2	☽	9p41
6	○	10a27
9	○	8p7
13	○	5a37
16	○	9p26
20	○	10p44
23	☾	1a5
28	●	7p30

MAR 1911 — ☉ → ♈ 21 12p54

☽ → SIGNS

Day	Sign	Time
2	♈	7a49
4	♉	11a21
6	♊	2p22
8	♋	5p23
10	♌	8p45
13	♍	1a4
15	♎	7a19
17	♏	4p20
20	♐	4a4
22	♑	4p53
25	♒	4a12
27	♓	12p13
29	♈	4p51
31	♉	7p13

☽ PHASES

Day	Phase	Time
4	☽	7a39
7	○	6p1
11	○	4a53
13	○	9a36
17	○	1p35
19	○	7p26
26	☾	6p17
30	●	7a37

APR 1911 — ☉ → ♉ 21 12a36

☽ → SIGNS

Day	Sign	Time
2	♊	8p49
4	♋	10p52
7	♌	2a14
9	♍	7a22
11	♎	2p35
13	♏	12a6
16	♐	11a46
18	♑	12a34
21	♒	12p33
23	♓	9p41
26	♈	3a2
28	♉	5a23
30	♊	5a39

☽ PHASES

Day	Phase	Time
2	☽	3p50
6	○	12a54
9	○	2p17
13	○	9a36
17	○	11a4
21	○	1p35
25	☾	8a16
28	●	5p24

MAY 1911 — ☉ → ♊ 22 12a18

☽ → SIGNS

Day	Sign	Time
2	♋	6a6
4	♌	8a8
6	♍	12p49
8	♎	8p26
11	♏	6a35
13	♐	6p32
16	♑	7a20
18	♒	7p40
21	♓	5a53
23	♈	12p40
25	♉	3p48
27	♊	4p12
29	♋	3p37
31	♌	4p2

☽ PHASES

Day	Phase	Time
1	☽	10p59
5	○	8a13
9	○	1a12
13	○	1a9
17	○	4a17
21	○	4a22
24	☾	7p12
28	●	1a24
31	○	5a58

JUN 1911 — ☉ → ♋ 22 8a35

☽ → SIGNS

Day	Sign	Time
2	♍	7p13
5	♎	2a6
7	♏	12p21
10	♐	12a37
12	♑	1p27
15	♒	1a44
17	♓	12p26
19	♈	8p31
22	♉	1a14
24	♊	2a45
26	♋	2a20
28	♌	1a54
30	♍	3a34

☽ PHASES

Day	Phase	Time
3	☽	5p4
7	○	2p7
11	○	4p50
15	○	7p2
19	○	3p50
23	☾	3a35
26	●	8a19
29	○	1p49

JUL 1911 — ☉ → ♌ 23 7p28

☽ → SIGNS

Day	Sign	Time
2	♎	8a59
4	♏	6p27
7	♐	6a39
9	♑	7p31
12	♒	7a33
14	♓	6p3
17	♈	2a34
19	♉	8a33
21	♊	11a41
23	♋	12p29
25	♌	12p24
27	♍	1p26
29	♎	5p31

☽ PHASES

Day	Phase	Time
3	○	4a20
7	○	4a57
11	○	7a53
15	○	7a12
19	○	12a30
22	☾	10a9
25	●	3p12
31	☽	1p28

AUG 1911 — ☉ → ♍ 24 2a13

☽ → SIGNS

Day	Sign	Time
1	♏	1a44
3	♐	1p20
6	♑	2a9
8	♒	2p12
11	♓	12a0
13	♈	7a3
15	♉	2p11
17	♊	4p29
19	♋	8p42
21	♌	9p54
23	♍	11p26
26	♎	3a5
28	♏	10a16
30	♐	9p0

☽ PHASES

Day	Phase	Time
1	○	6p29
5	○	9p6
9	○	9p54
13	○	5p13
17	○	7a10
20	☾	3p57
23	●	11p14
27	☽	12p17
31	○	11a20

SEP 1911 — ☉ → ♎ 23 11p17

☽ → SIGNS

Day	Sign	Time
2	♑	9a37
4	♒	9p35
7	♓	7a17
9	♈	2p31
11	♉	7p49
13	♊	11p47
16	♋	2a47
18	♌	5a17
20	♍	8a5
22	♎	12p21
24	♏	6p16
27	♐	5a20
29	♑	5p38

☽ PHASES

Day	Phase	Time
4	○	1p54
8	○	12p50
12	○	1a44
15	○	12p50
18	○	10p15
22	☾	9a37
26	●	4a7
30	☽	6a7

OCT 1911 — ☉ → ♏ 24 7a58

☽ → SIGNS

Day	Sign	Time
2	♒	5a56
4	♓	3p59
6	♈	10p56
9	♉	3a12
11	♊	5a55
13	♋	8a11
15	♌	10a54
17	♍	2p41
19	♎	8p7
22	♏	3a36
24	♐	1p34
27	♑	1a36
29	♒	2p14

☽ PHASES

Day	Phase	Time
4	○	6a46
7	○	11p11
11	○	9a32
14	○	6p26
18	○	6a27
22	☾	11p9
25	●	10p37
30	○	1a41

NOV 1911 — ☉ → ♐ 23 4a56

☽ → SIGNS

Day	Sign	Time
1	♓	1a11
3	♈	8a49
5	♉	12p54
7	♊	2p28
9	♋	3p10
11	♌	4p38
13	♍	8p5
16	♎	2a3
18	♏	10a27
20	♐	8p54
23	♑	8a55
25	♒	9p39
28	♓	9a32
30	♈	6p35

☽ PHASES

Day	Phase	Time
2	○	11p7
6	☾	10a48
9	○	5p28
13	○	2a19
16	○	5p45
20	●	3p49
24	☽	6p29
28	○	8p41

DEC 1911 — ☉ → ♑ 22 5p53

☽ → SIGNS

Day	Sign	Time
2	♉	11p43
5	♊	1a18
7	♋	12a55
9	♌	12a38
11	♍	2a1
13	♎	7a35
15	♏	3a8
18	♐	3a8
20	♑	3p24
23	♒	4a5
25	♓	4p36
28	♈	2a36
30	♉	9a30

☽ PHASES

Day	Phase	Time
2	○	2p17
6	○	9p51
9	○	2a26
12	○	12p45
16	○	8p39
20	●	10a40
24	☽	2p5
28	○	1p47

JAN 1912 — ☉ → ♒ 21 4a29

☽ → SIGNS

Day	Sign	Time
1	♊	12p28
3	♋	12p25
5	♌	11a17
7	♍	11a23
9	♎	2p42
11	♏	8a57
13	♐	6a18
16	♑	9p27
18	♒	10p5
21	♓	10p5
24	♈	8a41
26	♉	4p47
28	♊	9p45
30	♋	11p14

☽ PHASES

Day	Phase	Time
1	○	3a32
4	○	8a29
7	○	1p13
11	○	2a42
15	☾	2a38
19	●	9a7
23	☽	7a52
26	○	2p26
30	○	2p28

FEB 1912 — ☉ → ♓ 19 6p55

☽ → SIGNS

Day	Sign	Time
2	♌	10p47
4	♍	10p22
6	♎	12a12
8	♏	5a53
10	♐	3p35
13	♑	3a51
15	♒	4p33
18	♓	4a13
20	♈	2p9
22	♉	10p25
25	♊	4a14
27	♋	7a29
29	♌	8a42

☽ PHASES

Day	Phase	Time
2	○	6p57
6	○	2a11
9	○	7p50
13	○	10p7
18	●	10p17
21	☽	10p41
25	○	2p26
28	○	11p21

MAR 1912 — ☉ → ♈ 20 6p29

☽ → SIGNS

Day	Sign	Time
2	♍	9a13
4	♎	10a53
6	♏	3p25
8	♐	11p43
11	♑	11a12
13	♒	11p50
16	♓	11a28
18	♈	8p59
21	♉	3a37
23	♊	9a37
25	♋	12p17
27	♌	3p54
29	♍	5p35
31	♎	8p39

☽ PHASES

Day	Phase	Time
3	○	5a41
6	○	5p13
10	○	2p55
14	☾	5p8
18	●	5p8
22	○	10a4
26	○	10p1
30	○	7a0

APR 1912 — ☉ → ♉ 20 6a12

☽ → SIGNS

Day	Sign	Time
3	♏	1a15
5	♐	8a47
7	♑	7p23
10	♒	7a47
12	♓	7p42
15	♈	5a14
17	♉	11a50
19	♊	4p2
21	♋	6p53
23	♌	9p22
25	♍	12a17
28	♎	4a14
30	♏	2p31

☽ PHASES

Day	Phase	Time
1	○	5p4
5	○	9p38
9	○	10a23
13	○	12p6
17	☾	6p40
20	●	2p0
24	○	3a47
27	○	2p31

MAY 1912 — ☉ → ♊ 21 5a57

☽ → SIGNS

Day	Sign	Time
2	♐	5p30
5	♑	3a42
7	♒	3p50
10	♓	4a8
12	♈	2p20
14	♉	9p4
17	♊	12a32
19	♋	2a4
21	♌	3a18
23	♍	5a40
25	♎	9a59
27	♏	4p26
30	♐	12a56

☽ PHASES

Day	Phase	Time
1	○	5a19
5	○	2a34
9	○	4a55
13	○	3a49
16	☾	5p13
20	●	3p38
23	○	9a11
26	○	10p56
30	○	6p29

JUN 1912 — ☉ → ♋ 21 2p17

☽ → SIGNS

Day	Sign	Time
1	♑	11a17
3	♒	11p18
6	♓	11a54
8	♈	11p3
11	♉	6a46
13	♊	10a32
15	♋	11a24
17	♌	11a16
19	♍	12p2
21	♎	3p33
23	♏	9p57
26	♐	6a58
28	♑	5p49

☽ PHASES

Day	Phase	Time
3	○	7p16
7	○	9p35
11	○	4p37
15	☾	1a23
18	●	6a18
21	○	3p38
24	○	9a3
29	○	8a33

JUL 1912 — ☉ → ♌ 23 1a13

☽ → SIGNS

Day	Sign	Time
1	♒	5a57
3	♓	6p39
6	♈	6a30
8	♉	3p33
10	♊	8p34
12	♋	9p54
14	♌	9p15
16	♍	9p9
18	♎	10p36
21	♏	3a52
23	♐	12p34
25	♑	11p41
28	♒	12p1
31	♓	12a39

☽ PHASES

Day	Phase	Time
3	○	11a13
7	○	11a46
11	☾	2a39
14	●	8a13
17	○	12p38
21	○	12a18
24	○	9p22
27	○	2p58
31	○	3p1

AUG 1912 — ☉ → ♍ 23 8a1

☽ → SIGNS

Day	Sign	Time
2	♈	12p39
4	♉	10p37
7	♊	5a9
9	♋	7a56
11	♌	7a59
13	♍	7a14
15	♎	7a48
17	♏	11a28
19	♐	6p58
22	♑	5a42
24	♒	6p6
27	♓	6a49
29	♈	6p21

☽ PHASES

Day	Phase	Time
2	○	6a8
5	○	11p17
9	☾	10a37
12	●	2p57
15	○	8p54
19	○	11a56
23	○	12p8
26	○	2a15
31	○	3p1

SEP 1912 — ☉ → ♎ 23 5a8

☽ → SIGNS

Day	Sign	Time
1	♉	4a19
3	♊	11a45
5	♋	4p5
7	♌	5p42
9	♍	5p51
11	♎	6p18
13	♏	8p54
16	♐	2a49
18	♑	12p42
21	♒	12a51
23	♓	1p24
26	♈	1a10
28	♉	10a4
30	♊	5p12

☽ PHASES

Day	Phase	Time
4	○	8a23
7	☾	5p32
10	●	4p48
14	○	7a58
18	○	10p15
22	○	5a14
26	○	6a34
29	○	2a15

OCT 1912 — ☉ → ♏ 23 1p50

☽ → SIGNS

Day	Sign	Time
2	♋	10p9
5	♌	1a11
7	♍	2a54
9	♎	4a24
11	♏	7a4
13	♐	1p3
15	♑	10p13
17	♒	10p5
20	♓	9p7
23	♈	9p7
25	♉	5p14
28	♊	11p22
30	♋	3a35

☽ PHASES

Day	Phase	Time
3	○	9p48
7	☾	12a34
10	●	8p4
13	○	10p15
17	○	6a6
20	○	11p58
24	○	11a12
28	○	11a54

NOV 1912 — ☉ → ♐ 22 10a48

☽ → SIGNS

Day	Sign	Time
1	♌	6a46
3	♍	9a34
5	♎	12p31
7	♏	4p17
9	♐	9p43
12	♑	5a47
14	♒	4p44
17	♓	5a24
19	♈	5p16
22	♉	2a13
24	♊	7a40
26	♋	10a36
29	♌	12p33

☽ PHASES

Day	Phase	Time
2	○	6a46
5	☽	8a45
8	●	9p4
12	☽	3p39
16	○	5p43
20	○	7p0
24	○	11a12
27	○	8p43

DEC 1912 — ☉ → ♑ 21 11p45

☽ → SIGNS

Day	Sign	Time
1	♍	2a50
2	♎	6p26
4	♏	11p21
7	♐	5a48
9	♑	2p9
12	♒	12a50
14	♓	1p25
17	♈	1a59
19	♉	11a56
22	♊	5p50
24	♋	8p11
26	♌	8p35
29	♍	9p27

☽ PHASES

Day	Phase	Time
1	○	6a4
4	☾	6p53
8	●	8p6
12	☽	11a29
16	○	3p6
20	○	12p44
23	○	11p30
27	○	5a38
30	○	3p11

JAN 1913 — AUG 1913

	JAN 1913	FEB 1913	MAR 1913	APR 1913	MAY 1913	JUN 1913	JUL 1913	AUG 1913
☉ →	♒ 20 10a19	♓ 19 12a44	♈ 21 12a18	♉ 20 12p 2	♊ 21 11a49	♋ 21 8p 9	♌ 23 7a 3	♍ 23 1p48

☽ → SIGNS

JAN 1913	FEB 1913	MAR 1913	APR 1913	MAY 1913	JUN 1913	JUL 1913	AUG 1913
1 ♏ 4a49	2 ♑ 2a58	1 ♑ 8a52	1 ♓ 3p39	2 ♓ 11a38	1 ♉ 6a45	3 ♊ 4a29	1 ♌ 4p24
3 ♐ 12p 1	4 ♒ 2p25	4 ♒ 8p21	3 ♈ 4a21	4 ♈ 10p34	3 ♊ 2p42	5 ♋ 6a39	3 ♍ 4p43
5 ♑ 9p10	7 ♓ 3a 2	6 ♓ 9a10	5 ♉ 4p 4	7 ♉ 6a49	5 ♋ 7p40	7 ♌ 8a 0	5 ♎ 5p12
8 ♒ 8a 7	9 ♈ 3p59	8 ♈ 9p56	8 ♊ 12a30	9 ♊ 12p42	7 ♌ 10p51	9 ♍ 9a59	7 ♏ 7p22
10 ♓ 8p38	12 ♉ 3a47	11 ♉ 9a34	10 ♋ 7a 9	11 ♋ 4p57	10 ♍ 1a31	11 ♎ 1p26	10 ♐ 12a 3
13 ♈ 9a36	14 ♊ 12p37	13 ♊ 7p 0	12 ♌ 11a30	13 ♌ 8p 9	12 ♎ 4a27	13 ♏ 6p37	12 ♑ 7a24
15 ♉ 8p46	16 ♋ 5p29	16 ♋ 1a20	14 ♍ 11a30	15 ♍ 10p44	14 ♏ 8a 0	16 ♐ 1a39	14 ♒ 5p 9
18 ♊ 4a 6	18 ♌ 6p46	18 ♌ 4a27	16 ♎ 1p53	18 ♎ 1a14	16 ♐ 12p31	18 ♑ 10a48	17 ♓ 4a52
20 ♋ 7a14	20 ♍ 6p 8	20 ♍ 5a 8	18 ♏ 3p 2	20 ♏ 4a38	18 ♐ 6p41	20 ♒ 10p12	19 ♈ 5p47
22 ♌ 7a25	22 ♎ 5p37	22 ♎ 5a36	20 ♐ 4p14	22 ♐ 8a 0	21 ♑ 3a20	23 ♓ 11a29	22 ♉ 6a30
24 ♍ 6a47	24 ♏ 7p11	24 ♏ 5a59	22 ♑ 7p 2	24 ♑ 10a12	23 ♒ 2p45	25 ♈ 11p29	24 ♊ 5p 3
26 ♎ 7a25	27 ♐ 12a10	26 ♐ 9a 9	25 ♒ 12a56	27 ♒ 7p 0	26 ♓ 3a38	28 ♉ 8a57	26 ♋ 11p54
28 ♏ 10a49		28 ♑ 4p 8	27 ♓ 10a33	29 ♓ 7p36	28 ♈ 3p22	30 ♊ 2p29	29 ♌ 2a55
30 ♐ 5p30		31 ♒ 2a53	29 ♈ 10p54		30 ♉ 11p47		31 ♍ 3a16

☽ PHASES

JAN 1913	FEB 1913	MAR 1913	APR 1913	MAY 1913	JUN 1913	JUL 1913	AUG 1913
3 ☾ 7a27	1 ☾ 10p30	3 ☾ 3p42	2 ☾ 10a 6	2 ☾ 4a20	4 ● 2p56	4 ● 12a 6	2 ● 7a57
7 ● 5a28	6 ● 12a21	7 ● 12p47	6 ● 3a34	6 ● 3a24	7 ☽ 7p15	7 ☽ 7a36	8 ☽ 1p26
11 ☽ 8a21	10 ☽ 4a13	11 ☽ 9p 6	10 ☽ 7p17	9 ☽ 7p17	11 ○ 11a37	10 ○ 4p37	8 ○ 11p 2
15 ○ 11a 1	14 ○ 3a33	15 ○ 3p57	13 ○ 12a38	13 ○ 4a44	14 ○ 10p37	14 ○ 6a 9	12 ○ 3p56
19 ○ 3a57	17 ○ 4p15	19 ○ 1a54	17 ○ 9a35	16 ○ 4p 9	18 ○ 12p53	18 ○ 1a 6	16 ○ 3p26
22 ○ 10a39	20 ○ 9p 3	22 ○ 6a56	20 ○ 4p32	20 ○ 2a18	22 ○ 9a49	22 ○ 2a14	20 ○ 6p50
25 ○ 3p27	24 ○ 2a30	25 ○ 2p43	24 ○ 3a58	23 ○ 6a19	26 ☾ 12p40	26 ☾ 4a58	24 ○ 7p17
29 ☾ 2a34	27 ☾ 4p15	29 ☾ 7a57	28 ☾ 1a 8	27 ☾ 6p 3	30 ☾ 11a24	29 ☾ 11p27	28 ☾ 9a43
				31 ☾ 9p 2			31 ☾ 3p37

SEP 1913 — APR 1914

	SEP 1913	OCT 1913	NOV 1913	DEC 1913	JAN 1914	FEB 1914	MAR 1914	APR 1914
☉ →	♎ 23 10a53	♏ 23 7p35	♐ 22 4p35	♑ 22 5a35	♒ 20 4p12	♓ 19 6a38	♈ 21 6a10	♉ 20 5p53

☽ → SIGNS

SEP 1913	OCT 1913	NOV 1913	DEC 1913	JAN 1914	FEB 1914	MAR 1914	APR 1914
2 ♎ 2a46	1 ♏ 1p31	2 ♑ 5a 8	1 ♒ 9p42	3 ♈ 4a57	2 ♉ 1a54	1 ♉ 9a 7	2 ♋ 1p58
4 ♏ 3a21	3 ♐ 3p 7	4 ♒ 12p43	4 ♓ 8a 0	5 ♉ 5p43	4 ♊ 1p30	3 ♊ 9p14	4 ♌ 9p 5
6 ♐ 6a31	5 ♑ 8p10	7 ♓ 12a 1	6 ♈ 8p45	8 ♊ 4a13	7 ♋ 9p15	6 ♋ 6a34	7 ♍ 12a36
8 ♑ 1p 7	8 ♒ 5a 9	9 ♈ 1p 1	9 ♉ 9a11	10 ♋ 11a12	9 ♌ 2a46	8 ♌ 12p 3	9 ♎ 1a12
10 ♒ 10p56	10 ♓ 5p 6	12 ♉ 1a16	11 ♊ 7p 9	12 ♌ 3p 8	11 ♍ 5a 0	10 ♍ 2p 2	11 ♏ 12a22
13 ♓ 10a57	13 ♈ 6a 8	14 ♊ 11a24	14 ♋ 3a 2	14 ♍ 4p57	13 ♎ 5a37	12 ♎ 1p57	13 ♐ 12a22
15 ♈ 11p55	15 ♉ 6p30	16 ♋ 7p 9	16 ♌ 7a 9	16 ♎ 5p39	15 ♏ 4a55	14 ♏ 1p39	15 ♑ 2a58
18 ♉ 12p33	18 ♊ 5a13	19 ♌ 1a17	18 ♍ 11a 0	18 ♏ 10p44	17 ♐ 8a 3	16 ♐ 3p 0	17 ♒ 9a31
20 ♊ 11p34	20 ♋ 1p45	21 ♍ 5a40	20 ♎ 2p19	21 ♐ 2a39	19 ♑ 1p37	18 ♑ 7p23	19 ♓ 7p52
23 ♋ 7a44	22 ♌ 7p45	23 ♎ 8a30	22 ♏ 5p21	23 ♑ 7a58	21 ♒ 9p41	21 ♒ 3a15	22 ♈ 8a29
25 ♌ 12a26	24 ♍ 11p 9	25 ♏ 10a13	24 ♐ 8p28	25 ♒ 3p12	24 ♓ 8a30	23 ♓ 2p 1	24 ♉ 9p29
27 ♍ 2p 1	27 ♎ 12a17	27 ♐ 11a54	27 ♑ 12a35	28 ♓ 12a54	26 ♈ 8p 8	26 ♈ 2a29	27 ♊ 9a29
29 ♎ 1p47	29 ♏ 12a30	29 ♑ 3p11	29 ♒ 7a 0	30 ♈ 12p56		28 ♉ 3p26	29 ♋ 7p50
	31 ♐ 1a29		31 ♓ 4p38			31 ♊ 3a42	

☽ PHASES

SEP 1913	OCT 1913	NOV 1913	DEC 1913	JAN 1914	FEB 1914	MAR 1914	APR 1914
3 ● 8p36	3 ● 6a 1	1 ☽ 6p25	1 ☽ 10a12	4 ○ 8a 8	3 ○ 5a32	3 ○ 12a 2	2 ☾ 2p41
7 ○ 8a 5	6 ○ 8p45	5 ○ 1p34	5 ○ 9a58	8 ○ 8a52	6 ○ 2a 4	8 ○ 4p17	7 ● 3a23
11 ○ 4a57	10 ○ 9p31	9 ○ 4p54	9 ○ 10p21	12 ○ 12a38	10 ○ 12p34	12 ○ 9p 8	10 ● 8a28
15 ☽ 7a45	15 ○ 11a 6	13 ○ 6p11	13 ○ 10a 0	15 ○ 9a45	13 ○ 7p 2	14 ○ 4a 8	13 ☽ 1p30
19 ☾ 10a36	19 ☽ 12a46	17 ☽ 1p 7	16 ☽ 11p56	18 ☽ 7p29	17 ☽ 4a23	18 ☽ 2p39	16 ☽ 2p52
23 ○ 7a29	22 ● 5p52	20 ● 2a56	20 ● 11a15	22 ● 8a 7	20 ● 8p19	22 ● 2p39	21 ● 2a45
26 ● 6p57	26 ☾ 3a43	24 ☾ 12p30	23 ☾ 9p45	26 ☾ 1a33	24 ☾ 7p 1	26 ☾ 1p 8	24 ☾ 6a21
29 ☾ 11p56	29 ☾ 9a28	27 ● 8p41	27 ● 9a58	30 ☽ 1a56	28 ☽ 10p23	30 ☽ 4p26	29 ☾ 7a 1
			31 ☽ 5a 9				

MAY 1914 — DEC 1914

	MAY 1914	JUN 1914	JUL 1914	AUG 1914	SEP 1914	OCT 1914	NOV 1914	DEC 1914
☉ →	♊ 21 5p37	♋ 22 1a55	♌ 23 12p47	♍ 23 7p29	♎ 23 4p34	♏ 24 1a17	♐ 22 10p20	♑ 22 11a22

☽ → SIGNS

MAY 1914	JUN 1914	JUL 1914	AUG 1914	SEP 1914	OCT 1914	NOV 1914	DEC 1914
2 ♌ 3a53	1 ♎ 6p50	2 ♏ 3a19	2 ♑ 3p13	1 ♒ 3a 3	1 ♈ 4a37	1 ♉ 11p 8	1 ♊ 5p53
4 ♍ 9a 2	3 ♏ 8p30	4 ♐ 5a25	4 ♒ 8p26	3 ♓ 11a26	3 ♉ 4p58	4 ♊ 11a43	4 ♋ 5a19
6 ♎ 11a13	6 ♐ 9p12	6 ♑ 7a53	7 ♓ 4a 3	6 ♈ 10p 0	6 ♊ 5a45	6 ♋ 11p33	6 ♌ 3p13
8 ♏ 11a20	8 ♑ 10p40	8 ♒ 12p10	9 ♈ 2p25	8 ♉ 10a15	8 ♋ 5p26	9 ♌ 9a36	8 ♍ 11p 3
10 ♐ 11a 1	10 ♒ 2a46	10 ♓ 7p32	12 ♉ 2a46	11 ♊ 10p53	11 ♌ 2a36	11 ♍ 4p46	11 ♎ 4a 9
12 ♑ 12p30	13 ♓ 10a44	13 ♈ 6a 2	14 ♊ 3p 6	13 ♋ 9a41	13 ♍ 8a11	13 ♎ 8p36	13 ♏ 6a22
14 ♒ 5p28	15 ♈ 10p11	15 ♉ 6p49	17 ♋ 1a11	15 ♌ 5p41	15 ♎ 9a49	15 ♏ 9p41	15 ♐ 6a39
17 ♓ 2a39	18 ♉ 11a14	18 ♊ 6a46	19 ♌ 7a52	17 ♍ 10p41	17 ♏ 9a21	17 ♐ 9p42	17 ♑ 6a46
19 ♈ 2p54	20 ♊ 10p44	20 ♋ 4p12	21 ♍ 11a30	19 ♎ 10p51	19 ♐ 8a40	19 ♑ 7p42	19 ♒ 8a47
22 ♉ 3a51	23 ♋ 8a 7	23 ♌ 1a18	23 ♎ 1p18	21 ♏ 11p30	21 ♑ 8a40	21 ♒ 9p42	21 ♓ 2p24
24 ♊ 3p37	25 ♌ 3p13	25 ♍ 3a 0	25 ♏ 2p43	23 ♐ 11p35	23 ♒ 9a55	24 ♓ 2a 2	24 ♈ 12a 2
27 ♋ 1a28	27 ♍ 8p35	27 ♎ 6a 5	27 ♐ 4p59	25 ♑ 2a34	25 ♒ 2p39	26 ♈ 12p18	26 ♉ 12p18
29 ♌ 9a21	30 ♎ 12a32	29 ♏ 8a45	29 ♑ 8p57	28 ♒ 8a36	27 ♓ 11p13	29 ♉ 5a22	29 ♊ 12a53
31 ♍ 3p12		31 ♐ 11a35		30 ♓ 5p33	30 ♈ 10a34		31 ♋ 12p 1

☽ PHASES

MAY 1914	JUN 1914	JUL 1914	AUG 1914	SEP 1914	OCT 1914	NOV 1914	DEC 1914
3 ○ 1a28	1 ○ 9a 2	3 ○ 11p19	2 ○ 5a15	4 ● 9a 1	4 ● 12a58	2 ○ 6p48	2 ○ 1p20
6 ○ 11a42	4 ○ 5p57	7 ○ 8a59	6 ○ 7p40	8 ○ 12a58	8 ○ 4a 8	6 ○ 9p14	6 ○ 12p54
9 ○ 4p30	8 ○ 12a18	11 ○ 1a28	10 ○ 5p17	12 ○ 12p48	12 ○ 4a32	10 ○ 6p36	10 ○ 6a31
12 ○ 11p46	11 ○ 11a36	15 ○ 9a17	14 ○ 7p55	16 ☽ 7a31	16 ☽ 9a36	14 ☽ 11a 1	14 ☽ 4p12
16 ☽ 5p11	15 ☽ 9a19	19 ☽ 2a22	17 ☽ 6p16	19 ☽ 4p33	19 ☽ 1a33	17 ☽ 7p43	17 ☽ 9p34
20 ☾ 7p38	19 ☽ 12p13	22 ● 9p38	21 ● 7a26	22 ● 9p47	22 ● 7p37	21 ● 4p23	21 ● 7a 8
24 ● 9p34	22 ● 9a16	26 ☾ 9a16	24 ☾ 3p17	26 ☾ 7a 2	25 ☾ 5p43	24 ☾ 4p55	24 ☾ 3p24
28 ☽ 6p11	27 ☾ 2a36	29 ○ 6p50	27 ○ 11p52	30 ○ 12a37	29 ○ 3p45	28 ○ 10a13	28 ○ 6a37
	30 ○ 2p24		31 ○ 1p17				

JAN 1915 — ☉ → ♒ 20 9p59

D→SIGNS
```
 2 ♌  9p12
 5 ♍  4a28
 7 ♎  9a52
 9 ♏  1p24
11 ♐  3p24
13 ♑  4p51
15 ♒  7p16
18 ♓ 12a14
20 ♈  8a42
22 ♉  8p12
25 ♊  8a48
27 ♋  8p 7
30 ♌  4a55
```

D PHASES
```
 1 O  7a20
 5 C  2a27
 8 ●  4p12
12 C  1a15
15 O  9a41
19 C 12a23
23 C 12a32
27 O  3a12
30 C 11p41
```

FEB 1915 — ☉ → ♓ 19 12p23

D→SIGNS
```
 1 ♍ 11a10
 3 ♎  3p32
 5 ♏  6p47
 7 ♐  9p33
10 ♑ 12a25
12 ♒  4a 9
14 ♓  9a39
16 ♈  5p46
19 ♉  4a37
21 ♊  5p 5
24 ♋  4a57
26 ♌  2p10
28 ♍  8p 3
```

D PHASES
```
 3 O  1p35
 7 C 12a10
10 C 10a22
13 ● 11p31
17 D  7p31
21 O  9p58
25 O 10p12
```

MAR 1915 — ☉ → ♈ 21 11a51

D→SIGNS
```
 2 ♎ 11p14
 4 ♏  1a 5
 7 ♐  2a58
 9 ♑  5a58
11 ♒ 10a40
13 ♓  5p16
16 ♈  1a54
18 ♉ 12p38
21 ♊ 12a57
23 ♋  1p21
25 ♌ 11p37
28 ♍  6a13
30 ♎  9a 9
```

D PHASES
```
 1 C  1p32
 4 O 10p35
 8 C  7a27
11 C  8p21
15 ●  2p42
19 D  2p55
23 O  5p47
27 O  2p20
31 O 12a37
```

APR 1915 — ☉ → ♉ 20 11p28

D→SIGNS
```
 1 ♏  9a48
 3 ♐ 10a 5
 5 ♑ 11a46
 7 ♒  4p 3
 9 ♓ 11p 8
12 ♈  8a31
14 ♉  7p37
17 ♊  7a57
19 ♋  8p36
22 ♌  7a53
24 ♍  3p53
26 ♎  7p46
28 ♏  8p23
30 ♐  7p36
```

D PHASES
```
 3 O  6a13
 6 C  3p12
10 C  4a35
14 ●  6a35
18 D  8p21
22 O 10a38
26 O  2a56
29 C  9a19
```

MAY 1915 — ☉ → ♊ 21 11p10

D→SIGNS
```
 2 ♑  7p39
 4 ♒  4a40
 7 ♓  4a40
 9 ♈  2p 9
12 ♉  1a40
14 ♊  2p 9
17 ♋  2a47
19 ♌  2p31
21 ♍ 11p46
24 ♎  5a16
26 ♏  6a49
28 ♐  6a26
30 ♑  5a39
```

D PHASES
```
 2 O 11a32
 6 C 12a22
 8 C 11a 4
13 ●  8p41
17 D 10p30
21 O  1a21
26 O  6p56
30 O 11p27
```

JUN 1915 — ☉ → ♋ 22 7a29

D→SIGNS
```
 1 ♒  6a49
 3 ♓ 11a31
 5 ♈  8p 6
 8 ♉  7a30
10 ♊  8p 6
13 ♋  8a37
15 ♌  8p12
18 ♍  5a53
20 ♎ 12p39
22 ♏  4p 3
24 ♐  4p45
26 ♑  4p21
28 ♒  4p54
30 ♓  8p14
```

D PHASES
```
 2 O  1p34
 6 C 12a22
 8 C 11a 4
13 ●  8p41
17 D  1p57
20 O  2p51
24 O  6p56
30 O 11p27
```

JUL 1915 — ☉ → ♌ 23 6p26

D→SIGNS
```
 3 ♈  3a23
 5 ♉  2p 1
 8 ♊  2a30
10 ♋  2p56
13 ♌  2a 6
15 ♍ 11a22
17 ♎  6p21
19 ♏ 10p50
22 ♐  1a 6
24 ♑  2a10
26 ♒  3a10
28 ♓  6a 4
30 ♈ 12p 6
```

D PHASES
```
 2 O 12a54
 6 C  2a37
 9 C  1a37
12 D  1a37
17 ●  9p17
20 O  6a15
26 C  7a11
28 O  9a17
```

AUG 1915 — ☉ → ♍ 24 1a15

D→SIGNS
```
 1 ♉  9p39
 4 ♊  9a43
 6 ♋ 10p11
 9 ♌  9a 8
11 ♍  5p41
13 ♎ 11p55
16 ♏  4a16
18 ♐  7a18
20 ♑  9a38
22 ♒ 12p 3
24 ♓  3p35
26 ♈  9p21
29 ♉  6a 7
31 ♊  5p38
```

D PHASES
```
 4 O  4p27
 7 C  7p 0
10 C  5p52
14 D 10a 3
17 ●  9p17
21 O  6a15
24 C  4p40
28 O  9a17
```

SEP 1915 — ☉ → ♎ 23 10p24

D→SIGNS
```
 3 ♉  6a11
 5 ♊  5p24
 8 ♋  1a42
10 ♌  7a 0
12 ♍ 10a14
14 ♎ 12p41
16 ♏  3p20
18 ♐  6p49
20 ♑ 11p32
23 ♒  5a55
25 ♓  2p34
28 ♈  1a42
30 ♉  2p20
```

D PHASES
```
 1 O  9a56
 5 C 11a38
 9 ●  5a52
12 D  5p 3
16 O  2a21
19 O  1p30
23 O  4a35
27 C  1a57
```

OCT 1915 — ☉ → ♏ 24 7a 9

D→SIGNS
```
 3 ♊  2a13
 5 ♋ 11a 4
 7 ♌  4p 8
 9 ♍  6p19
11 ♎  7p21
13 ♏  8p56
16 ♐ 12a14
18 ♑  5a37
20 ♒  1p48
22 ♓ 10p 8
25 ♈  9a15
27 ♉  9p53
30 ♊ 10a26
```

D PHASES
```
 1 O  4a44
 5 C  3a46
 8 ●  4p41
11 D 11p54
15 O  8a51
18 O 11p19
22 O  7p15
26 O  8p36
30 O 11p39
```

NOV 1915 — ☉ → ♐ 23 4a13

D→SIGNS
```
 1 ♋  8p30
 4 ♌  2a29
 6 ♍  4a37
 8 ♎  4a35
10 ♏  4a33
12 ♐  6a22
14 ♑ 11a 4
16 ♒  6p40
19 ♓  4a29
21 ♈  3p56
24 ♉  4a33
26 ♊  5p22
29 ♋  4a33
```

D PHASES
```
 3 C  6p36
 7 ●  2a52
10 D  7a53
13 O  6p 2
17 O 12p21
21 O 12p36
25 O  5p10
29 C  7a58
```

DEC 1915 — ☉ → ♑ 22 5p16

D→SIGNS
```
 1 ♎ 12p 9
 3 ♏  3p33
 5 ♐  3p47
 7 ♑  2p52
 9 ♒  3p 0
11 ♓  5p57
14 ♈ 12a14
16 ♉ 10a14
18 ♊ 10p 2
21 ♋ 10a44
23 ♌ 11p23
26 ♍ 10a51
28 ♎  7p40
31 ♏ 12a55
```

D PHASES
```
 3 C  7a42
 6 ●  1p 3
10 D  5p58
13 O  6p38
17 O  4a46
21 O 10a52
26 O  7a58
```

JAN 1916 — ☉ → ♒ 21 3a53

D→SIGNS
```
 2 ♐  2a43
 4 ♑  2a25
 6 ♒  1a58
 8 ♓  3a21
10 ♈  9a 8
12 ♉  6p43
15 ♊  6a43
17 ♋  7p 7
20 ♌  5a32
22 ♍  1p 2
25 ♎  1a25
27 ♏  7a43
29 ♐ 11a18
31 ♑ 12p42
```

D PHASES
```
 1 C  7p 3
 4 ● 11p45
 8 D  6a32
11 O 10p37
16 O  6a 2
20 C  3a28
24 O  2a59
27 O  7p35
31 C  4a55
```

FEB 1916 — ☉ → ♓ 19 6p18

D→SIGNS
```
 2 ♒  1p 9
 4 ♓  2p16
 6 ♈  5p45
 9 ♉ 12a50
11 ♊ 11a31
13 ♋ 12p38
16 ♌  1a 7
18 ♍ 11p 8
21 ♎  7a13
23 ♏  1p 8
25 ♐  5p20
27 ♑  8p13
29 ♒ 10p17
```

D PHASES
```
 3 C 11a 5
 6 ●  9p17
10 D  8p35
14 O  9p28
18 O  3p39
22 O  4p23
25 C  1p45
29 O ——
```

MAR 1916 — ☉ → ♈ 20 5p47

D→SIGNS
```
 3 ♈ 12a26
 5 ♉  3a56
 7 ♊  9a43
 9 ♋  7p45
12 ♌  8a 3
14 ♍  8p41
17 ♎  7a12
19 ♏  2p37
21 ♐  7p26
23 ♑ 10p48
26 ♒  1a43
28 ♓  4a47
30 ♈  8a18
```

D PHASES
```
 3 C 10p57
 7 ●  1p38
11 D  1p32
15 O 12p26
19 O  8p 7
23 O 11a22
26 O ——
29 C 10p 5
```

APR 1916 — ☉ → ♉ 20 5a24

D→SIGNS
```
 1 ♉ 12p48
 3 ♊  7p11
 6 ♋  4a19
 8 ♌  4p10
11 ♍  5a 1
13 ♎  4p 7
16 ♏  3a47
18 ♐  5a52
20 ♑ 10a 7
22 ♒  7p34
24 ♓ 10a 7
26 ♈  2p 5
28 ♉  7p35
```

D PHASES
```
 2 ● 11a20
 6 D  6a58
10 O  9a35
14 O  9a47
18 O 12a 7
21 O  8a30
24 O  5p38
28 C  6a40
```

MAY 1916 — ☉ → ♊ 21 5a 5

D→SIGNS
```
 1 ♉  2a48
 3 ♊ 12p11
 5 ♋ 11p53
 8 ♌ 12p51
11 ♍ 12a45
13 ♎  1p42
15 ♏ 12p 8
17 ♐  3p30
19 ♑  3p30
21 ♒  4p33
23 ♓  7p34
26 ♈  1a 8
28 ♉  8a54
30 ♊  6p53
```

D PHASES
```
 2 ● 12a28
 6 D 12a36
10 O  3a46
13 O 11p41
17 O  9a11
20 O  2p55
23 C 12a18
27 C  2a18
31 ●  2p37
```

JUN 1916 — ☉ → ♋ 21 1p24

D→SIGNS
```
 2 ♋  6a45
 4 ♌  7p47
 7 ♍  8a15
 9 ♎  5p58
11 ♏ 11p40
13 ♐  1a40
16 ♑  1a32
18 ♒  1a16
20 ♓  2a39
22 ♈  6a55
24 ♉  2p25
27 ♊ 12a ——
29 ♋ 12p54
```

D PHASES
```
 4 D  5p36
 8 O  6a54
12 O 10a25
15 O  4p41
18 C  5a 8
22 ●  8a16
25 D  3a50
30 O  5a43
```

JUL 1916 — ☉ → ♌ 23 12a21

D→SIGNS
```
 2 ♌  1a57
 4 ♍  2p32
 7 ♎  1a 6
 9 ♏  7p56
11 ♐ 11a43
13 ♑ 12p20
16 ♒ 11a46
18 ♓ 12a 4
20 ♈  2p32
22 ♉ 10p15
24 ♊  6a35
26 ♋  7a56
29 ♌  7a56
31 ♍  8p18
```

D PHASES
```
 4 D  8a59
 8 O  6a48
11 O  6p48
14 C 11p40
18 ●  5a 1
21 D  5p32
24 O 10a 3
28 O 12p24
```

AUG 1916 — ☉ → ♍ 23 7a 8

D→SIGNS
```
 3 ♎  6a54
 5 ♏  2p56
 7 ♐  7p56
 9 ♑ 10p39
11 ♒ 10p28
13 ♓ 10p29
16 ♈  1a21
18 ♉  4a45
20 ♊ 11a27
23 ♋  1a21
25 ♌  1p21
28 ♍  2a 3
30 ♎ 12p34
```

D PHASES
```
 2 O  8p59
 6 O  4p 5
10 C  1a52
13 ● 10p46
17 D  2p42
20 O  7a52
23 O  3a57
27 ● 12p24
```

SEP 1916 — ☉ → ♎ 23 4a15

D→SIGNS
```
 1 ♏  8p24
 4 ♐  2a 5
 6 ♑  5a43
 8 ♒  7a39
10 ♓  8a41
12 ♈ 10a17
14 ♉  2p 9
16 ♊  9p38
19 ♋  8a45
21 ♌  9p19
24 ♍  9a46
27 ♎  8a 2
29 ♏  2a21
```

D PHASES
```
 1 D  8a59
 5 O 11p26
 8 C  3p30
11 ●  2a58
15 D  8p 8
18 O  3p36
22 O ——
26 O  3p36
29 D  6p13
```

OCT 1916 — ☉ → ♏ 23 12p57

D→SIGNS
```
 1 ♐  7a28
 3 ♑ 11a23
 5 ♒  2p28
 7 ♓  4p59
 9 ♈  7p40
11 ♉ 11p45
14 ♊  6a37
16 ♋  4p58
18 ♌  5a39
21 ♍  6p 3
23 ♎  3a45
26 ♏ 10a 8
28 ♐  2p 7
31 ♑  5p 0
```

D PHASES
```
 4 O  6a 0
 8 C  3p43
11 ●  2a 0
14 D  6p34
18 O  8p 8
22 C 10p 8
25 O  3p36
29 O  6p34
```

NOV 1916 — ☉ → ♐ 22 9a58

D→SIGNS
```
 1 ♒  7p50
 3 ♓ 11p 4
 5 ♈  2a59
 8 ♉  6a37
10 ♊  3p19
12 ♋ 10p48
15 ♌  1p44
17 ♍  2a33
20 ♎  2a33
22 ♏  7p48
24 ♐ 11p12
27 ♑  2a 5
29 ♒  4a29
```

D PHASES
```
 2 O 12p50
 6 C 12a20
 9 ●  9p17
13 D  9p17
17 O  6p ——
21 O  3p29
25 D  3a50
28 D 11a27
```

DEC 1916 — ☉ → ♑ 21 10p58

D→SIGNS
```
 1 ♓  4a29
 3 ♈  8a34
 5 ♉  2p35
 7 ♊ 10p40
 9 ♋  8a59
12 ♌  9p17
14 ♍ 10a18
17 ♎  9p49
20 ♏  5a52
22 ♐  9a57
24 ♑ 11a 6
26 ♒ 11a41
28 ♓ 12p18
31 ♈  7a 7
```

D PHASES
```
 1 O  8p55
 5 C 11a21
 9 ●  7a43
13 D 10a 8
17 O  1p 6
21 C  7a12
24 O  3p31
28 O  8p59
31 O  7a 7
```

```
 JAN 1917   FEB 1917   MAR 1917   APR 1917   MAY 1917   JUN 1917   JUL 1917   AUG 1917
 O -> ♒     O -> ♓     O -> ♈     O -> ö     O -> ∏     O -> ʂ     O -> ♌     O -> ♍
 20  9a37   19 12a 5   20 11p37   20 11a17   21 10a58   21  7p14   23  6a 8   23 12p53

 ))->SIGNS  ))->SIGNS  ))->SIGNS  ))->SIGNS  ))->SIGNS  ))->SIGNS  ))->SIGNS  ))->SIGNS
 1  ö 8p 4  2  ʂ 9p30  2  ʂ 3a52  2  ♍12p32  3  ≏ 7a52  1  ♏ 1a34  1  ♐ 5p14  2  ♒ 7a49
 4  ∏ 4a39  5  ♌10a16  4  ♌ 4p35  5  ≏11p53  5  ♏ 4p39  4  ♐ 7a27  3  ♑ 8p25  4  ♓ 7a20
 6  ʂ 3p34  7  ♍11p 9  7  ♍ 5a29  7  ♏ 8a54  7  ♐10p44  6  ♑10a45  5  ♒ 9p55  6  ♈ 7a18
 9  ♌ 4a 3 10  ≏11a 4  9  ≏ 5p 1 10  ♐ 3p50 10  ♑ 2a59  8  ♒12p45  7  ♓ 9p53  8  ö 9a36
11  ♍ 5p 1 12  ♏ 9p 6 12  ♏ 2a40 12  ♑ 8p47 12  ♒ 6a17 10  ♓ 2p59  9  ♈11p25 10  ∏ 3p23
14  ≏ 5a 4 15  ♐ 4a22 14  ♐10a18 15  ♒12a56 14  ♓ 9a10 12  ♈ 5p31 12  ö 3a12 13  ʂ12a39
16  ♏ 2p31 17  ♑ 8a24 16  ♑ 3p38 17  ♓ 3a24 16  ♈12p 4 14  ö 9p48 14  ∏ 9a47 15  ♌12p19
18  ♐ 8p17 19  ♒ 9a32 18  ♒ 6p32 19  ♈ 5a10 18  ö 3p38 17  ∏ 4a 2 16  ʂ 6p59 18  ♍ 1a 2
20  ♑10p28 21  ♓ 9a 5 20  ♓ 7p30 21  ö 7a30 20  ∏ 8p53 19  ʂ12p33 19  ♌ 6a17 20  ≏ 1p41
22  ♒10p19 23  ♈ 9a 6 22  ♈ 7p50 23  ∏12p 4 23  ʂ 4a49 21  ♌11p26 21  ♍ 6p51 23  ♏ 1a15
24  ♓ 9a41 25  ö11a19 24  ö 9p35 25  ʂ 8p 7 25  ♌ 3p42 24  ♍11a59 24  ≏ 7a32 25  ♐10a28
26  ♈10p33 27  ∏ 5p34 27  ∏ 2a28 28  ♌ 7p31 28  ♍ 4a20 27  ≏12a26 26  ♏ 6p40 27  ♑ 4p14
29  ö 2a34            29  ʂ11a28 30  ♍ 8p19 30  ≏ 4p20 29  ♏10a37 29  ♐ 2a38 29  ♒ 6p27
31  ∏10a26            31  ♌11p38                                  31  ♑ 6a48 31  ♓ 6p11

 )) PHASES  )) PHASES  )) PHASES  )) PHASES  )) PHASES  )) PHASES  )) PHASES  )) PHASES
 4  O 1a29  2  O 6p41  4  O 1p49  3  O 9a 0  3  O 2a35  1  O 5p49  1  O 6a40  3  O12a10
 8  ☽ 2a41  6  O10p28  7  O 8a48  7  O 8a48  6  O 9p43  5  O 8a 6  4  O 4p40  6  O 4a35
12  O 6a37 11  O12a42 12  O 3p16 11  O 2a19 10  O10a31  9  O 4p53  7  O10p30  9  O 2p56
16  O 6a42 14  O 8p53 14  O 7a33 14  O 3p12 17  ☾ 8p47 12  O 1a38 11  O 7a12 13  ( 11a 3
19  ( 8p52 17  ☾ 8a10 19  ( 5p 8 18  ( 12a20 20  ● 6a49 15  ( 1p57 14  ( 11p 4 17  ● 1p20
23  ● 2a39 22  ● 1p 8 22  ● 11p 4 21  ● 9a 1 24  ☽ 7p46 18  ● 6p24 17  ● 9p59 21  ☽ 4p 6
26  ☽ 7a39 24  ☽ 7p37 26  ☽ 9a 1 24  ☽ 11p54 28  O 6p33 23  ☽ 8a36 23  ☽12a51 25  ☽ 2p 8
29  O 8p 1 28  O11a43 30  O 5a36 29  O12a21            27  O 11a 8 27  O 1a40 29  O 2a42
                                                                 30  O 5p29
```

```
 SEP 1917   OCT 1917   NOV 1917   DEC 1917   JAN 1918   FEB 1918   MAR 1918   APR 1918
 O -> ≏     O -> ♏     O -> ♐     O -> ♑     O -> ♒     O -> ♓     O -> ♈     O -> ö
 23 10a 0   23  6p44   22  3p45   22  4a46   20  3p24   19  5a53   21  5a25   20  5p 5

 ))->SIGNS  ))->SIGNS  ))->SIGNS  ))->SIGNS  ))->SIGNS  ))->SIGNS  ))->SIGNS  ))->SIGNS
 2  ♈ 5p20  2  ö 4a25  1  ʂ11p 8  2  ♌ 5p32  1  ♍ 1p23  2  ♏ 9p51  2  ♏ 4a32  3  ʂ 6a59
 4  ö 6p 6  4  ∏ 7a13  5  ♌ 8a42  5  ♍ 5a 6  4  ≏ 1a56  5  ♐ 8a15  4  ♐ 3p47  5  ♌12p56
 6  ∏10p19  6  ʂ 2p 6  7  ♍ 8p56  7  ≏ 5p41  6  ♏ 1p50  7  ♑ 2p57  7  ♑12a 4  7  ♍ 3p22
 9  ʂ 6a40  9  ♌12a50 10  ≏ 9a26 10  ♏ 4a52  8  ♐10p57  9  ♒ 5p46  9  ♒ 4a23  9  ≏ 3p18
11  ♌ 6p12 11  ♍ 1p32 12  ♏ 8p12 12  ♐ 1p10 11  ♑ 4a23 11  ♓ 5p57 11  ♓ 5a12 11  ♏ 2p40
14  ♍ 7a 2 14  ≏ 1a58 15  ♐ 4a52 14  ♑ 7p25 13  ♒ 6a55 13  ♈ 6p 0 13  ♈ 5a15 13  ♐ 3p37
16  ≏ 7p30 16  ♏12p53 17  ♑10a55 16  ♒11p59 15  ♓ 7a30 15  ö 6p31 15  ö 3a48 15  ♑ 7p57
19  ♏ 6a55 19  ♐10p 0 19  ♒ 3p38 19  ♓ 2a51 17  ♈ 9a 3 17  ∏10p29 17  ∏ 5a57 18  ♒ 4a18
21  ♐ 4p32 21  ♑ 5a13 21  ♓ 7p 4 21  ♈ 5a 6 19  ö11a48 20  ʂ 5a50 19  ʂ11a57 20  ♓ 3p46
23  ♑11p37 23  ♒10a16 23  ♈ 9p35 23  ö 8a 6 21  ∏ 4p 2 22  ♌ 3p52 21  ♌ 9p33 22  ♈ 4p37
26  ♒ 3a33 25  ♓ 1p 2 26  ö11p55 25  ∏11a 2 23  ʂ12a17 25  ♍ 3a32 24  ♍ 9a31 24  ö 4p30
28  ♓ 4a39 27  ♈ 2p 8 28  ∏ 3a13 27  ʂ 5p29 26  ♌ 9a45            26  ≏10p 7 28  ∏ 3a30
30  ♈ 4a15 29  ö 2p59 30  ʂ 8a48 30  ♌ 2a15 28  ♍ 8p58            29  ♏10a20 30  ʂ12a33
           31  ∏ 5p26                       31  ≏ 9a26            31  ♐ 9p47

 )) PHASES  )) PHASES  )) PHASES  )) PHASES  )) PHASES  )) PHASES  )) PHASES  )) PHASES
 1  O 7a28  3  O11p 7  2  O 1p30  2  O 7a25  1  O 3a40  4  ● 2a51  1  O 7p46  4  ● 8a33
 4  O12p24  7  O 5p14  6  O12p 3  6  O 9a13  5  O 6a49  7  ( 9p 5  5  O 7p43  7  ( 7p12
 8  ● 2a 5 11  ( 7p52 10  ( 3p 9 10  (10a42  8  ( 7p 5 11  ● 5a 4 11  ● 2a46 11  ●11p34
12  ( 2a10 15  ●10p40 14  ● 1p28 14  ● 4a17 12  ●12a40 14  ☽ 9a47 15  ( 7p31 14  ( 6a23
16  ● 5p27 18  ☾ 5p35 17  ☾ 7p29 17  ☾ 3p29 15  ☾ 9p37 17  O 7p56 19  O 8a30 17  O11p 7
20  ☾ 6a 1 23  O 9a37 21  O 1a 7 21  O 1a 7 19  O 3p15 21  O 3p15 23  O 7a31 22  O12a39
24  O12a41 27  O 6p36 25  O 2a53 24  O12p43 26  O10p14 25  O 4p34 27  O12p22 26  O 3a 5
27  O10a50 30  O 1p 7 28  O 1p41 28  O 4a51                       31  O12p22 30  O 1a30
30  O 3p31
```

```
 MAY 1918   JUN 1918   JUL 1918   AUG 1918   SEP 1918   OCT 1918   NOV 1918   DEC 1918
 O -> ∏     O -> ʂ     O -> ♌     O -> ♍     O -> ≏     O -> ♏     O -> ♐     O -> ♑
 21  4p45   22 12a59   23 11a51   23  6p37   24  3p46   24 12a33   22  9p38   22 10a41

 ))->SIGNS  ))->SIGNS  ))->SIGNS  ))->SIGNS  ))->SIGNS  ))->SIGNS  ))->SIGNS  ))->SIGNS
 2  ♒ 7p12  1  ♓ 4a53  1  ♈ 3p44  1  ∏12a48  1  ♌ 7p53  1  ♍11a45  1  ♏ 6p31  2  ♐ 1p20
 4  ♓11p 7  3  ♈ 7a37  4  ∏ 7p 4  3  ʂ 6a21  3  ♍ 5a56  3  ≏11p43  4  ♐ 6a51  4  ♑11p41
 7  ♈12a40  5  ö 9a29  6  ʂ11p49  5  ♌ 1p49  6  ≏ 5p35  6  ♏12p27  6  ♑ 5p49  7  ♒ 7a52
 9  ö 1a 5  7  ∏11a35  9  ♌ 6a20  8  ♍11p17  8  ♏ 6a19  8  ♐12a 4  9  ♒ 2a25  9  ♓ 1p47
11  ∏ 2a 6  9  ʂ 3p13 11  ♍ 3p33 10  ≏11a 5 11  ♐ 6p35 10  ♑10a45 11  ♓ 9a 6 11  ♈ 5p33
13  ʂ 5a30 11  ♌ 9p35 14  ≏ 3a 9 13  ♏11p26 14  ♑ 4a49 13  ♒ 5p26 13  ♈ 1p45 13  ö 7p35
15  ♌12p31 14  ♍ 7a10 16  ♏ 3p41 15  ♐11a22 16  ♒11a26 15  ♓ 9p26 15  ö 4p 8 15  ∏ 8p49
17  ♍11p10 16  ≏ 7p 9 19  ♐ 2a48 17  ♑ 8p17 18  ♓ 1p41 17  ♈10p48 17  ∏ 4p25 17  ʂ10p14
20  ≏11a25 19  ♏ 7a30 21  ♑10a46 20  ♒ 1a11 20  ♈ 1p 7 19  ö10a28 20  ʂ 5p19 20  ♌ 2a25
22  ♏11p38 21  ♐ 6p 4 23  ♒ 3p19 22  ♓ 2a48 22  ö 1p20 21  ∏11p10 22  ♌ 4p23 22  ♍ 9a33
25  ♐10a 8 24  ♑ 1a51 25  ♓ 5p32 24  ♈ 2a56 24  ∏ 1p31 24  ʂ 1a39 25  ♍12p50 24  ≏ 8p10
27  ♑ 6p37 26  ♒ 7a 1 27  ♈ 6p59 26  ö 3a35 26  ʂ 4p20 26  ♌ 7a54 27  ♍12p25 27  ♏ 8a48
30  ♒12a38 28  ♓10a26 29  ö 8p33 28  ∏ 6a19 29  ♌ 1a25 28  ♍ 5p42 30  ♏ 1a13 29  ♐ 9p 3
           30  ♈ 1p 4            30  ʂ11a50            31  ≏ 5a45

 )) PHASES  )) PHASES  )) PHASES  )) PHASES  )) PHASES  )) PHASES  )) PHASES  )) PHASES
 3  ● 5p26  1  O11p20  1  O 3a42  1  ( 9p10  1  ( 7a 2  2  ● 10p 5  3  ● 4p 1  3  ☽10a19
 7  ( 2a 9  5  ( 7a53  5  ( 1p48  5  ● 3p29  5  ● 5a43  5  ☽ 1a23  7  ☽ 5p15  7  O 7a 7
10  ● 8a 0  8  ●  5p 2  8  ● 3a22  9  ☽ 8a27  9  ☽ 8a27  9  O12p 7  11  O11a46  9  O 9p31
13  ☽ 6p40 12  ☽ 8a22 11  ☽11p23 14  O 6p16 13  O10a 2 13  O12p 7 15  O 9p27 13  O 6a35
17  O 3p14 16  O 8a11 14  O 6p16 18  O 2p23 17  O 1a57 16  O 7p34 18  O 2a32 17  ♐ 2p17
21  O 5p32 20  O10a 5 18  O 2p23 22  O12a 2 22  O 8a 0 22  O10p 9 20  O11a 4 21  O 3a 3
25  O 5p32 24  O 5a38 22  O12a 2 26  O11p45 26  O12p25 26  O12p35 25  O 5a25 25  O 1a30
29  O11a12 27  O 6p12 26  O11p45 28  O 2p27 30  ( 11p38 30  (12p35 29  ● 8a 0 29  ( 4a56
                     30  O 8a13                       30  ♐ 8p 6
```

JAN 1919 — ☉→♒ 20 9p21

☽→SIGNS
1 ♉ 7a 1 · 3 ♊ 2p15 · 5 ♋ 7p18 · 7 ♌ 11p 0 · 10 ♍ 2a 1 · 12 ♎ 4a48 · 14 ♏ 7a56 · 16 ♐ 12p16 · 18 ♑ 6p56 · 21 ♒ 4a42 · 23 ♓ 4p59 · 26 ♈ 5a35 · 28 ♉ 3p53 · 30 ♊ 10p43

☽ PHASES
2 ● 3a24 · 5) 6p37 · 9 ○ 5a55 · 12 ◑ 4p 3 · 16 ○ 3a44 · 19 ○ 9p29 · 23 ◐ 11p22 · 28 (1a12 · 31 ● 6p 6

FEB 1919 — ☉→♓ 19 11a47

☽→SIGNS
2 ♓ 2a38 · 4 ♈ 5a 2 · 6 ♉ 7a22 · 8 ♊ 10a30 · 10 ♋ 2p46 · 12 ♌ 8p17 · 14 ♍ 3a31 · 17 ♎ 1p 6 · 19 ♏ 1a 3 · 22 ♐ 1p57 · 24 ♑ 1a 8 · 27 ♒ 8a36

☽ PHASES
4) 4a13 · 7 ○ 1p52 · 10 ◑ 2a17 · 14 ○ 6p38 · 18 ○ 5p17 · 22 ◐ 8p47 · 26 (6p50

MAR 1919 — ☉→♈ 21 11a19

☽→SIGNS
1 ♓ 12p14 · 3 ♈ 1p28 · 5 ♉ 2p14 · 7 ♊ 4p10 · 9 ♋ 8p 0 · 12 ♌ 2a18 · 14 ♍ 10a25 · 16 ♎ 8p29 · 19 ♏ 8a24 · 21 ♐ 9p23 · 24 ♑ 9a25 · 26 ♒ 6p11 · 28 ♓ 10p45 · 30 ♈ 11p57

☽ PHASES
2 ● 6a11 · 5) 12p46 · 7 ○ 9p 5 · 10 ◑ 1p38 · 14 ○ 10a41 · 18 ○ 10a 9 · 22 ◐ 2p59 · 26 (7p23 · 28 (8a50 · 31 ● 4p 4

APR 1919 — ☉→♉ 20 10p58

☽→SIGNS
1 ♉ 11p40 · 3 ♊ 11p56 · 6 ♋ 2a22 · 8 ♌ 7a48 · 10 ♍ 4p 7 · 13 ♎ 2a42 · 15 ♏ 2p54 · 18 ♐ 3a52 · 20 ♑ 4p13 · 23 ♒ 2a 9 · 25 ♓ 8a17 · 27 ♈ 10a40 · 29 ♉ 10a35

☽ PHASES
1 ○ 9p 5 · 7 ○ 7a38 · 11 ○ 2a26 · 15 ○ 3a25 · 19 ○ 6a57 · 23 ○ 6a21 · 26 (7p23 · 30 ● 12a30

MAY 1919 — ☉→♊ 21 10p39

☽→SIGNS
1 ♊ 10a 0 · 3 ♋ 10a50 · 5 ♌ 2p37 · 7 ♍ 10p 0 · 10 ♎ 8a32 · 12 ♏ 8p57 · 15 ♐ 9a46 · 17 ♑ 10p 6 · 20 ♒ 8a23 · 22 ♓ 3p44 · 24 ♈ 7p46 · 26 ♉ 9p 2 · 28 ♊ 8p53 · 30 ♋ 9p 4

☽ PHASES
3) 5a45 · 5 ○ 6p33 · 9 ○ 4p51 · 14 ◐ 8p 1 · 18 ○ 9p52 · 22 ○ 9p 4 · 29 (8a11

JUN 1919 — ☉→♋ 22 6a53

☽→SIGNS
1 ♌ 11p26 · 4 ♍ 5a18 · 6 ♎ 2p58 · 9 ♏ 3a15 · 11 ♐ 4p11 · 14 ♑ 4a 4 · 16 ♒ 1p58 · 18 ♓ 9p31 · 21 ♈ 2a38 · 23 ♉ 5a28 · 25 ♊ 6a42 · 27 ♋ 7a28 · 29 ♌ 9a23

☽ PHASES
1 ○ 3p17 · 5 ○ 7a21 · 9 ○ 8a39 · 13 ○ 11a28 · 17 ○ 9a22 · 21 ◐ 12a32 · 24 (9a31 · 27) 3p52

JUL 1919 — ☉→♌ 23 5p44

☽→SIGNS
1 ♍ 2p 6 · 3 ♎ 10p34 · 6 ♏ 10a18 · 8 ♐ 11p13 · 11 ♑ 10a56 · 13 ♒ 8p14 · 16 ♓ 3a 6 · 18 ♈ 8a 6 · 20 ♉ 11a43 · 22 ♊ 2p19 · 24 ♋ 4p25 · 26 ♌ 7p 0 · 28 ♍ 11p28 · 31 ♎ 7a 6

☽ PHASES
1) 2a12 · 4 ○ 10p17 · 9 ○ 1a13 · 13 ○ 1a 2 · 16 ○ 5p58 · 20 ○ 6a 3 · 23 ◐ 3p13 · 30) 3p 8

AUG 1919 — ☉→♍ 24 12a28

☽→SIGNS
2 ♏ 6p 8 · 4 ♐ 6a57 · 7 ♑ 6p52 · 9 ♒ 3a56 · 12 ♓ 9a59 · 14 ♈ 1p59 · 16 ♉ 5p 5 · 18 ♊ 8p 3 · 20 ♋ 11p13 · 23 ♌ 2a59 · 25 ♍ 8a 8 · 28 ♎ 3p41 · 30 ♏ 2a15

☽ PHASES
3 ○ 3p11 · 7 ○ 5p35 · 11 ○ 12p39 · 15 ○ 12a50 · 18 ○ 10a56 · 21 ◑ 9p28 · 25 ○ 10a37 · 29) 6a33

SEP 1919 — ☉→♎ 23 9p35

☽→SIGNS
1 ♐ 2p57 · 4 ♑ 3a21 · 6 ♒ 12p53 · 8 ♓ 6p45 · 10 ♈ 9p47 · 12 ♉ 11p35 · 15 ♊ 1a35 · 17 ♋ 4a38 · 19 ♌ 9a 7 · 21 ♍ 3p14 · 23 ♎ 11p24 · 26 ♏ 9a59 · 28 ♐ 10p36

☽ PHASES
2 ○ 9a21 · 6 ○ 4a 1 · 9 ○ 10p54 · 13 ◐ 7a18 · 17 ○ 4p31 · 20 (5p24 · 23 ● 11p33 · 28) 12a17

OCT 1919 — ☉→♏ 24 6a21

☽→SIGNS
1 ♑ 11a28 · 3 ♒ 10p 3 · 6 ♓ 4a44 · 8 ♈ 7a44 · 10 ♉ 8a32 · 12 ♊ 9a13 · 14 ♋ 10a39 · 16 ♌ 2p 6 · 18 ♍ 8p58 · 21 ♎ 5a45 · 23 ♏ 4p52 · 26 ♐ 5a30 · 28 ♑ 6a 8 · 31 ♒ ...

☽ PHASES
2 ○ 3a37 · 5 ○ 11p12 · 9 ○ 8a38 · 13 ◐ 2p33 · 16 (2a14 · 19 (4p30 · 23 ● 3p39 · 27) 7p17 · 31 ○ 8p43

NOV 1919 — ☉→♐ 23 3a25

☽→SIGNS
2 ♒ 2p19 · 4 ♓ 6p30 · 6 ♈ 7p31 · 8 ♉ 7p 3 · 10 ♊ 7p 3 · 12 ♋ 9p13 · 15 ♌ 2a41 · 17 ♍ 11a32 · 19 ♎ 10p58 · 22 ♏ 11a47 · 24 ♐ 12a45 · 27 ♑ 12p37 · 29 ♒ 10p 3

☽ PHASES
4 ○ 12p 9 · 7 ○ 6p35 · 11 ◐ 11p31 · 14 (10a40 · 18 (1a52 · 21 ● 1p50 · 26) 1p50 · 30 ○ 11a46

DEC 1919 — ☉→♑ 22 4p27

☽→SIGNS
2 ♈ 4a 2 · 4 ♉ 6a33 · 6 ♊ 6a36 · 8 ♋ 5a54 · 10 ♌ 6a40 · 12 ♍ 10a 6 · 15 ♎ 5a47 · 17 ♏ 5a 0 · 19 ♐ 5p59 · 22 ♑ 6a20 · 24 ♒ 6p20 · 27 ♓ 3a55 · 29 ♈ 11a 6 · 31 ♉ 3p28

☽ PHASES
3 ○ 11p59 · 7 ○ 5a 9 · 10 ◐ 10a42 · 14 (7a20 · 18 (1a52 · 22 ● 5a55 · 26) 1p50 · 30 ○ 12a24

JAN 1920 — ☉→♒ 21 3a 4

☽→SIGNS
2 ♊ 5p13 · 4 ♋ 5p19 · 6 ♌ 5p30 · 8 ♍ 7p46 · 11 ♎ 1a47 · 13 ♏ 11a57 · 16 ♐ 12a43 · 18 ♑ 1p33 · 21 ♒ 12a39 · 23 ♓ 9a34 · 25 ♈ 4p32 · 28 ♉ 9p43 · 30 ♊ 1a 9

☽ PHASES
2 ○ 10a39 · 5 ○ 4p 7 · 9 ◐ 12a23 · 12 (7p 8 · 16 (10p37 · 20 ● 12a26 · 24) 8p11 · 31 ○ 8p 8

FEB 1920 — ☉→♓ 19 5p29

☽→SIGNS
1 ♋ 2a53 · 3 ♌ 4a 5 · 5 ♍ 6a18 · 7 ♎ 11a19 · 9 ♏ 8p13 · 12 ♐ 8a21 · 14 ♑ 9p14 · 17 ♒ 8a20 · 19 ♓ 4p38 · 21 ♈ 10p36 · 24 ♉ 3a 5 · 26 ♊ 6a49

☽ PHASES
4 ○ 3a42 · 8 ○ 4p31 · 11 ◐ 3p49 · 15 (7p17 · 19 (4p34 · 23 ● 7a16 · 26) 6p49

MAR 1920 — ☉→♈ 20 4p59

☽→SIGNS
3 ♌ 12p22 · 5 ♍ 3p40 · 7 ♎ 8p53 · 10 ♏ 5a10 · 12 ♐ 5p25 · 15 ♑ 6a 6 · 17 ♒ 6a58 · 20 ♓ 6a43 · 22 ♈ 12p25 · 24 ♉ 3p 1 · 26 ♊ 5p58 · 28 ♋ 8p29 · 30 ♌ 10p47

☽ PHASES
4 ○ 4a49 · 8 ○ 10a33 · 11 ◐ 12p57 · 16 (1p51 · 19 ● 9p34 · 23) 4p10 · 27 ○ 1a44 · 30 ○ 1p31

APR 1920 — ☉→♉ 20 4a39

☽→SIGNS
2 ♎ 4a59 · 4 ♏ 1p33 · 7 ♐ 12a41 · 9 ♑ 1a31 · 12 ♒ 10a56 · 14 ♓ 4p29 · 16 ♈ 7p 8 · 18 ♉ 8p14 · 20 ♊ 9p22 · 22 ♋ 11p48 · 25 ♌ 3a18 · 27 ♍ 9a 4 · 29 ♎ 11a18

☽ PHASES
3 ○ 5a54 · 7 ○ 5p18 · 11 ◐ 8a24 · 15 (5a22 · 18 (8a43 · 21 ● 11p34 · 25) 8a27 · 28 ○ 11p16

MAY 1920 — ☉→♊ 21 4a21

☽→SIGNS
1 ♏ 8p37 · 4 ♐ 7a59 · 6 ♑ 8p39 · 9 ♒ 9a19 · 11 ♓ 7p32 · 14 ♈ 2a23 · 16 ♉ 5a35 · 18 ♊ 6a13 · 20 ♋ 6a49 · 22 ♌ 9a40 · 24 ♍ 10a10 · 26 ♎ 4p50 · 29 ♏ 2a23 · 31 ♐ 2p20

☽ PHASES
2 ● 8p47 · 6 ○ 11p16 · 11 ◐ 1p58 · 14 (5p45 · 18 (1a25 · 21 ● 6a18 · 24) 4p 7 · 28 ○ 10a52

JUN 1920 — ☉→♋ 21 12p40

☽→SIGNS
3 ♑ 3a 4 · 5 ♒ 3p38 · 8 ♓ 2a42 · 10 ♈ 10a57 · 12 ♉ 3p35 · 14 ♊ 4p57 · 16 ♋ 4p26 · 18 ♌ 3a12 · 20 ♍ 5p44 · 22 ♎ 11p 5 · 25 ♏ 8a19 · 27 ♐ 8p15 · 30 ♑ 9a 6

☽ PHASES
2 ○ 12p18 · 5 ○ 3p16 · 9 ◐ 1p58 · 13 (3a20 · 16 (8a41 · 19 ● 1p24 · 23) 1a49 · 27 ○ 12a34

JUL 1920 — ☉→♌ 22 11p35

☽→SIGNS
2 ♒ 9p30 · 5 ♓ 8a37 · 7 ♈ 5p38 · 9 ♉ 11p45 · 12 ♊ 3a 3 · 14 ♋ 3a 3 · 16 ♌ 2a31 · 18 ♍ 3a12 · 20 ♎ 7a 2 · 22 ♏ 3p 3 · 25 ♐ 2a31 · 27 ♑ 3p22 · 30 ♒ 3a37

☽ PHASES
1 ○ 3a40 · 5 ○ 4a47 · 9 ◐ 12a47 · 12 (10a47 · 17 ● 9a 3 · 19 ● 9p57 · 23) 2p20 · 26 ○ 4p 4 · 30 ○ 6p19

AUG 1920 — ☉→♍ 23 6a21

☽→SIGNS
1 ♓ 2p18 · 3 ♈ 11p 9 · 6 ♉ 5a56 · 8 ♊ 10a15 · 10 ♋ 12p41 · 12 ♌ 2a10 · 14 ♍ 1p27 · 16 ♎ 4p27 · 18 ♏ 11p12 · 21 ♐ 9p45 · 23 ♑ 10p22 · 26 ♒ 10a36 · 28 ♓ 8p55 · 31 ♈ 5a 3

☽ PHASES
3 ○ 4p 0 · 7 ○ 7a50 · 10 ◐ 4p56 · 14 (10p43 · 17 ● 9a 3 · 21) 5a51 · 25 ○ 8a 2 · 30 ○ 6p19

SEP 1920 — ☉→♎ 23 3a28

☽→SIGNS
2 ♉ 11a19 · 4 ♊ 3p57 · 6 ♋ 7p 3 · 8 ♌ 10p54 · 11 ♍ 2a10 · 13 ♎ 6a23 · 15 ♏ 1p27 · 18 ♐ 5p57 · 20 ♑ 6p32 · 22 ♒ 6p32 · 25 ♓ 4a57 · 27 ♈ 12p34 · 29 ♉ 5p49

☽ PHASES
2 ● 1a26 · 6 ○ 2p 4 · 10 ◐ 10p57 · 13 (6a10 · 15 ● 11p19 · 19) 11p55 · 23 ○ 9a 8 · 27 ○ 8p56

OCT 1920 — ☉→♏ 23 12p13

☽→SIGNS
1 ♊ 9p32 · 4 ♋ 12a28 · 6 ♌ 3a13 · 8 ♍ 6a23 · 10 ♎ 10a44 · 13 ♏ 5p13 · 15 ♐ 2a30 · 18 ♑ 2p16 · 20 ♒ 2a52 · 23 ♓ 1p 2 · 25 ♈ 7a45 · 27 ♉ 4a59 · 29 ♊ 4a59 · 31 ♋ 6a34

☽ PHASES
1 ○ 9a44 · 4 ○ 7p53 · 8 ◐ 6a10 · 11 (11a 5 · 15 ● 2p16 · 19) 3p12 · 22 ○ 11a 0 · 29 ○ 5p43

NOV 1920 — ☉→♐ 22 9a15

☽→SIGNS
2 ♌ 8a37 · 4 ♍ 12p 3 · 6 ♎ 5p23 · 9 ♏ 12a49 · 11 ♐ 10a26 · 13 ♑ 10p 3 · 16 ♒ 10a44 · 18 ♓ 10p39 · 21 ♈ 7a45 · 23 ♉ 1p 2 · 25 ♊ 3p 0 · 27 ♋ 3p12 · 29 ♌ 3p32

☽ PHASES
3 ○ 2a35 · 7 ○ 5p51 · 10 ◐ 11a 5 · 14 ● 1a16 · 18) 3p12 · 22 ○ 8p42 · 29 ○ 2a11

DEC 1920 — ☉→♑ 21 10p17

☽→SIGNS
1 ♍ 5p45 · 3 ♎ 10p21 · 6 ♏ 6a51 · 8 ♐ 5p 9 · 11 ♑ 4a59 · 13 ♒ 5p39 · 16 ♓ 6a 3 · 18 ♈ 4p30 · 21 ♉ 11p22 · 23 ♊ 2a15 · 25 ♋ 2a13 · 27 ♌ 1a16 · 29 ♍ 1a39 · 31 ♎ 5a 6

☽ PHASES
2 ○ 11a29 · 6 (4a57 · 10 ● 5a 3 · 14) 8a23 · 17 ○ 9a40 · 22 ○ 1a30 · 25 ○ 7a58 · 31 ○ 11p34

JAN 1921 – AUG 1921

JAN 1921
☉ → ♒ 20 8a55

D → SIGNS:
2 ♏ 12p27 · 4 ♐ 10p57 · 7 ♑ 11a 9 · 9 ♒ 11p49 · 12 ♓ 12p10 · 14 ♈ 11p14 · 17 ♉ 7a40 · 19 ♊ 12p23 · 21 ♋ 1p35 · 23 ♌ 12p45 · 25 ♍ 12p 4 · 27 ♎ 1p46 · 29 ♏ 7p24

D PHASES:
4 (9p26 · 9 ● 12a26 · 13) 3a23 · 17 O 1a30 · 20 O 1p41 · 23 O 6p 7 · 26 O 11p43 · 30) 3p 2

FEB 1921
☉ → ♓ 18 11p20

D → SIGNS:
1 ♐ 5a 3 · 3 ♑ 5p14 · 6 ♒ 5a59 · 8 ♓ 6p 3 · 11 ♈ 4a51 · 13 ♉ 1p44 · 15 ♊ 7p54 · 17 ♋ 10p57 · 19 ♌ 11p34 · 21 ♍ 11p20 · 23 ♎ 12a21 · 26 ♏ 4a28 · 28 ♐ 12p36

D PHASES:
3 (4p17 · 7 ● 7p36 · 11) 7p50 · 15 O 1p53 · 18 O 11p30 · 22 O 4a32 · 25 O 1p32

MAR 1921
☉ → ♈ 20 10p51

D → SIGNS:
3 ♑ 12a 3 · 5 ♒ 12p45 · 8 ♓ 12a44 · 10 ♈ 10a58 · 12 ♉ 7a15 · 15 ♊ 1a28 · 17 ♋ 7a51 · 19 ♌ 7a 1 · 21 ♍ 9a 7 · 23 ♎ 10a49 · 25 ♏ 2p33 · 27 ♐ 9p34 · 30 ♑ 7a58

D PHASES:
1 O 9a 3 · 5 (11a56 · 9 ● 1p 1 · 13) 8a55 · 17 O 10p48 · 20 O 7a30 · 23 O 3p18 · 27 O 5a 3 · 31 O 4a13

APR 1921
☉ → ♉ 20 10a32

D → SIGNS:
1 ♒ 8p21 · 4 ♓ 8a28 · 6 ♈ 6p31 · 9 ♉ 1a59 · 11 ♊ 7a15 · 13 ♋ 10a58 · 15 ♌ 1p47 · 17 ♍ 4p21 · 19 ♎ 7p24 · 21 ♏ 11p53 · 24 ♐ 6a45 · 26 ♑ 4p27 · 29 ♒ 4a25

D PHASES:
4 (6a49 · 8 ● 4a 5 · 11) 6p37 · 14 O 10a24 · 17 O 10p20 · 22 O 2p49 · 25 O 9p31 · 29 O 11p 8

MAY 1921
☉ → ♊ 21 10a16

D → SIGNS:
1 ♓ 4p46 · 4 ♈ 3a13 · 6 ♉ 10a31 · 8 ♊ 2p51 · 10 ♋ 5p19 · 12 ♌ 7p16 · 14 ♍ 9p51 · 17 ♎ 1a46 · 19 ♏ 7a21 · 21 ♐ 2p52 · 24 ♑ 12a34 · 26 ♒ 12p17 · 29 ♓ 12a50 · 31 ♈ 12p 5

D PHASES:
3 (11p45 · 7 ● 4p 1 · 10) 1a40 · 14 O 10a24 · 17 O 10p20 · 21 O 3p15 · 25 O 2p12 · 29 O 4p44

JUN 1921
☉ → ♋ 21 6p35

D → SIGNS:
2 ♉ 8p 3 · 5 ♊ 12a17 · 7 ♋ 1a46 · 9 ♌ 2a18 · 11 ♍ 3a41 · 13 ♎ 7a 9 · 15 ♏ 1p10 · 17 ♐ 9p28 · 20 ♑ 7a38 · 22 ♒ 7p24 · 25 ♓ 8a 2 · 27 ♈ 8p 2 · 30 ♉ 5a14

D PHASES:
2 (2p 1 · 6 ● 1a14 · 9) 7a20 · 12 O 3p59 · 16 O 7a18 · 20 O 4a41 · 24 O 6a31 · 28 O 8a16

JUL 1921
☉ → ♌ 23 5a30

D → SIGNS:
2 ♊ 10a23 · 4 ♋ 11a55 · 6 ♌ 11a33 · 8 ♍ 11a26 · 10 ♎ 1p28 · 12 ♏ 6p42 · 15 ♐ 1p43 · 17 ♑ 11p15 · 19 ♒ 7p 7 · 22 ♓ 2p23 · 24 ♈ 2a41 · 27 ♉ 12p58 · 29 ♊ 7p37 · 31 ♋ 10p18

D PHASES:
2 (1a28 · 6 ● 8a36 · 8) 1p 2 · 11 O 11p15 · 15 O 6p18 · 19 O 7p 7 · 23 O 10p 6 · 27 O 9p19 · 31 O 10a32

AUG 1921
☉ → ♍ 23 12p15

D → SIGNS:
2 ♌ 10p11 · 4 ♍ 9p18 · 6 ♎ 9p51 · 9 ♏ 1a33 · 11 ♐ 8a59 · 13 ♑ 7p30 · 16 ♒ 7a41 · 18 ♓ 8p20 · 21 ♈ 8a29 · 23 ♉ 7p 7 · 26 ♊ 2a58 · 28 ♋ 7a17 · 30 ♌ 8a30

D PHASES:
3 ● 3p17 · 7) 8p 9 · 10 O 9a13 · 14 O 7a46 · 18 O 10a28 · 22 O 12p11 · 25 O 7a51 · 29 (6p 2

SEP 1921 – APR 1922

SEP 1921
☉ → ♎ 23 9a20

D → SIGNS:
1 ♍ 8a 6 · 3 ♎ 8a 5 · 5 ♏ 10a24 · 7 ♐ 4p20 · 10 ♑ 1a58 · 12 ♒ 2p 0 · 15 ♓ 2a39 · 17 ♈ 2p29 · 20 ♉ 12a41 · 22 ♊ 8a41 · 24 ♋ 2p 6 · 26 ♌ 4p57 · 28 ♍ 6p 1 · 30 ♎ 6p41

D PHASES:
1 ● 10p32 · 5) 2a45 · 8 O 10p29 · 12 O 11p49 · 16 O 2a19 · 21 (12a40 · 24 O 4p17 · 28 (1a 5

OCT 1921
☉ → ♏ 23 6p 2

D → SIGNS:
2 ♏ 8p37 · 5 ♐ 1a22 · 7 ♑ 9a45 · 9 ♒ 9p12 · 12 ♓ 9a50 · 15 ♈ 9p34 · 17 ♉ 7a 8 · 19 ♊ 2p31 · 21 ♋ 7p21 · 23 ♌ 10p26 · 26 ♍ 1a40 · 28 ♎ 3a48 · 30 ♏ 6a33

D PHASES:
1 (7a26 · 4) 6p28 · 7 O 10a53 · 11 O 1p23 · 15 O 8a39 · 18 O 8p44 · 23 (11a22 · 27 (8a45 · 30 ● 6p38

NOV 1921
☉ → ♐ 22 3p 4

D → SIGNS:
1 ♐ 11a 8 · 3 ♑ 6p37 · 6 ♒ 5a17 · 8 ♓ 5p51 · 11 ♈ 5a52 · 13 ♉ 3p19 · 16 ♊ 9p40 · 18 ♋ 1a41 · 20 ♌ 4a32 · 22 ♍ 7a17 · 24 ♎ 10a31 · 26 ♏ 2p37 · 28 ♐ 8p 2

D PHASES:
3) 10a26 · 7 O 10a53 · 10 O 1p23 · 14 O 9p50 · 18 O 5a36 · 21 (6a41 · 25 ● 5p55 · 29) 8a25

DEC 1921
☉ → ♑ 22 4a 7

D → SIGNS:
1 ♑ 3a32 · 3 ♒ 1p41 · 6 ♓ 2a 3 · 8 ♈ 2p37 · 11 ♉ 12a45 · 13 ♊ 7a 7 · 15 ♋ 10a11 · 17 ♌ 11a34 · 19 ♍ 1p 2 · 21 ♎ 3p52 · 23 ♏ 8p33 · 26 ♐ 3a 1 · 28 ♑ 11a16 · 30 ♒ 9p31

D PHASES:
3) 5a15 · 7 O 8a19 · 10 O 8a12 · 14 O 9p50 · 18 O 8p12 · 22 ● 5a23 · 25 (5a13 · 29) 12a39

JAN 1922
☉ → ♒ 20 2p48

D → SIGNS:
2 ♓ 9a44 · 4 ♈ 10p42 · 7 ♉ 9a20 · 9 ♊ 5p27 · 11 ♋ 8p47 · 13 ♌ 9p16 · 15 ♍ 9p12 · 17 ♎ 10p16 · 20 ♏ 2a 2 · 22 ♐ 8a33 · 24 ♑ 6p19 · 27 ♒ 6a16 · 29 ♓ 6p47

D PHASES:
2) 1a51 · 6 O 5a23 · 10 O 12a55 · 16 O 9a36 · 20 (12a45 · 23 ● 6p53 · 27) 6p48 · 31) 10p29

FEB 1922
☉ → ♓ 19 5a16

D → SIGNS:
1 ♈ 5a35 · 3 ♉ 5p40 · 6 ♊ 2a41 · 8 ♋ 7a29 · 10 ♌ 8a39 · 12 ♍ 7a58 · 14 ♎ 7a34 · 16 ♏ 9a22 · 18 ♐ 2p31 · 20 ♑ 11p 5 · 23 ♒ 10a12 · 25 ♓ 10p45 · 28 ♈ 11a41

D PHASES:
4 O 11p52 · 9 O 2p43 · 15 O 1a 9 · 18 O 1p18 · 22 (10a49 · 26 ● 1p47

MAR 1922
☉ → ♈ 21 4a48

D → SIGNS:
2 ♉ 11p51 · 5 ♊ 9a49 · 7 ♋ 4p18 · 9 ♌ 7p 9 · 11 ♍ 7p22 · 13 ♎ 7p13 · 15 ♏ 10p33 · 17 ♐ 10p33 · 20 ♑ 5a41 · 22 ♒ 4p58 · 25 ♓ 4a56 · 27 ♈ 5p38 · 30 ♉ 5a38

D PHASES:
2) 5p 2 · 6 O 2p21 · 10 O 1a34 · 16 O 6a14 · 22 (11p17 · 24 ● 4a28 · 28) 8a 3

APR 1922
☉ → ♉ 20 4p28

D → SIGNS:
1 ♊ 3p29 · 3 ♋ 10p46 · 6 ♌ 3a12 · 8 ♍ 5a 9 · 10 ♎ 5a36 · 12 ♏ 6a 6 · 14 ♐ 8a25 · 16 ♑ 2p 1 · 18 ♒ 11p27 · 21 ♓ 11a43 · 23 ♈ 12a37 · 26 ♉ 12p 7 · 29 ♊ 9p19

D PHASES:
1) 7a56 · 5 O 12a45 · 11 O 3p43 · 15 O 7p53 · 18 (7p53 · 22 ● 10p43 · 27) 12a 3 · 30) 6p54

MAY 1922 – DEC 1922

MAY 1922
☉ → ♊ 21 4p10

D → SIGNS:
1 ♋ 4a12 · 3 ♌ 9a 5 · 5 ♍ 12p19 · 7 ♎ 2p21 · 9 ♏ 4p 0 · 11 ♐ 6p32 · 13 ♑ 11p25 · 16 ♒ 7a45 · 18 ♓ 7p20 · 21 ♈ 8a12 · 23 ♉ 8p12 · 26 ♊ 4a29 · 28 ♋ 11p26 · 30 ♌ 2p34

D PHASES:
4 O 7a55 · 7 O 4p53 · 11 (1a 6 · 14 O 2p26 · 18 ● 1p17 · 22) 4p12 · 26 O 1p 3 · 30 O 2a41

JUN 1922
☉ → ♋ 22 12a26

D → SIGNS:
1 ♍ 5p48 · 3 ♎ 8p43 · 5 ♏ 11p42 · 8 ♐ 3a18 · 10 ♑ 8a30 · 12 ♒ 4p25 · 15 ♓ 3a25 · 17 ♈ 4p12 · 20 ♉ 4a 9 · 22 ♊ 1p 2 · 24 ♋ 6p27 · 26 ♌ 9p28 · 28 ♍ 11p36

D PHASES:
2 O 9p 9 · 5 O 11p 8 · 9 (10a57 · 13 O 5a 8 · 17 ● 7a 3 · 21) 1a58 · 24 O 11p19 · 28 O 8a39

JUL 1922
☉ → ♌ 23 11a19

D → SIGNS:
1 ♎ 2a 4 · 3 ♏ 5a29 · 5 ♐ 10a 5 · 7 ♑ 4p18 · 10 ♒ 12a27 · 12 ♓ 11a16 · 14 ♈ 11p59 · 17 ♉ 12p28 · 20 ♊ 10p10 · 22 ♋ 3a56 · 24 ♌ 6a26 · 26 ♍ 7a21 · 28 ♎ 8a26 · 30 ♏ 10a58

D PHASES:
2 O 5p51 · 5 O 5a51 · 9 (10p 7 · 13 O 9p 4 · 17 ● 12a10 · 20) 9p 5 · 24 O 7a46 · 27 O 2p13 · 30 O 11p21

AUG 1922
☉ → ♍ 23 6p 4

D → SIGNS:
1 ♐ 3p35 · 3 ♑ 10p22 · 6 ♒ 7a18 · 8 ♓ 6p22 · 11 ♈ 7a 5 · 13 ♉ 7p57 · 16 ♊ 6a42 · 18 ♋ 1p40 · 20 ♌ 4p45 · 22 ♍ 5p15 · 24 ♎ 5p24 · 26 ♏ 6p 1 · 28 ♐ 9p26 · 30 ♑ 3a53

D PHASES:
3 O 2p56 · 7 O 11a18 · 11 (8a35 · 15 ● 3p45 · 18) 8a22 · 22 O 9p33 · 25) 8p38 · 29 O 6a54

SEP 1922
☉ → ♎ 23 3p10

D → SIGNS:
2 ♒ 1p12 · 4 ♓ 12a41 · 7 ♈ 1p29 · 9 ♉ 2a24 · 11 ♊ 1p50 · 14 ♋ 10p13 · 16 ♌ 2a48 · 18 ♍ 4a 8 · 20 ♎ 4a 2 · 22 ♏ 3a43 · 24 ♐ 5a27 · 27 ♑ 5p40

D PHASES:
1 O 1a32 · 4 O 2a47 · 8 (6a20 · 13 O 9a42 · 16 ● 7p38 · 20) 11p38 · 24 O 4a53 · 27 O 5p40

OCT 1922
☉ → ♏ 23 11p53

D → SIGNS:
2 ♒ 6a40 · 4 ♈ 7p36 · 7 ♉ 8a20 · 9 ♊ 7p44 · 12 ♋ 4a52 · 14 ♌ 11a 1 · 16 ♍ 2p43 · 18 ♎ 3p47 · 20 ♏ 3p48 · 22 ♐ 3p 5 · 24 ♑ 6p33 · 27 ♒ 2a 0 · 29 ♓ 1p 7

D PHASES:
1 O 4p23 · 5 O 7p58 · 8 (11a17 · 13 O 2a52 · 16 ● 11a28 · 20) 6p18 · 23 O 3a31 · 27 O 8a40 · 30 O 3a15

NOV 1922
☉ → ♐ 22 8p55

D → SIGNS:
1 ♈ 2p39 · 3 ♉ 3a 9 · 6 ♊ 2a33 · 8 ♋ 10a23 · 10 ♌ 5p 5 · 12 ♍ 9p36 · 15 ♎ 12a52 · 17 ♏ 2a59 · 19 ♐ 4a31 · 21 ♑ 8a39 · 23 ♒ 1a52 · 25 ♓ 8p39 · 28 ♈ 10p 0 · 30 ♉ 10p 0

D PHASES:
4 O 1p36 · 8 (11a17 · 11 O 12p28 · 15 ● 5p28 · 18) 7p 6 · 22 O 5a55 · 26 O 3a15 · 30 O 6a59

DEC 1922
☉ → ♑ 22 9a57

D → SIGNS:
3 ♊ 8a33 · 5 ♋ 4p33 · 7 ♌ 10p32 · 10 ♍ 3a 9 · 12 ♎ 6a39 · 14 ♏ 9a14 · 16 ♐ 11a27 · 18 ♑ 2p34 · 21 ♒ 8p 8 · 23 ♓ 5a14 · 25 ♈ 5p22 · 28 ♉ 6a 9 · 30 ♊ 5p 2

D PHASES:
4 O 6a23 · 7 O 11p 3 · 11 (9p31 · 14 ● 7a20 · 18) 11p22 · 21 O 12a53 · 26 O 12a53 · 30 O 3a20

JAN 1923 – AUG 1923

	JAN 1923	FEB 1923	MAR 1923	APR 1923	MAY 1923	JUN 1923	JUL 1923	AUG 1923
☉ →	♒ 20 8p35	♓ 19 11a 0	♈ 21 10a29	♉ 20 10p 5	♊ 21 9p45	♋ 22 6a 3	♌ 23 5p 0	♍ 23 11p52

☽ → SIGNS

JAN 1923	FEB 1923	MAR 1923	APR 1923	MAY 1923	JUN 1923	JUL 1923	AUG 1923
2 ♋ 12a39	2 ♍ 5p12	2 ♍ 3a41	2 ♏ 2p25	2 ♐ 12a59	2 ♒ 4p 3	2 ♓ 8a28	1 ♈ 3a11
4 ♌ 5a34	4 ♎ 6p38	4 ♎ 4a 0	4 ♐ 2p33	4 ♑ 2a14	4 ♓ 11p43	4 ♈ 6p51	3 ♉ 3p22
6 ♍ 8a59	6 ♏ 8p37	6 ♏ 4a16	6 ♑ 5p19	6 ♒ 7a 5	7 ♈ 11a 2	7 ♉ 7a25	6 ♊ 3a47
8 ♎ 11a58	8 ♐ 11p58	8 ♐ 6a 5	8 ♒ 11p48	8 ♓ 4p 6	9 ♉ 11p56	9 ♊ 7p37	8 ♋ 2p 7
10 ♏ 3p 4	11 ♑ 5a 8	10 ♑ 10a34	11 ♓ 9a50	11 ♈ 4a12	12 ♊ 12p 3	12 ♋ 5a33	10 ♌ 9p19
12 ♐ 6p34	13 ♒ 12p18	12 ♒ 6p 2	13 ♈ 10p 8	13 ♉ 5p 4	14 ♋ 10p22	14 ♌ 12p53	13 ♍ 1a44
14 ♑ 10p56	15 ♓ 9p43	15 ♓ 4a 7	16 ♉ 11a 7	16 ♊ 5a27	17 ♌ 6a11	16 ♍ 6p10	15 ♎ 4a27
17 ♒ 5a 5	18 ♈ 9a20	17 ♈ 4p 6	18 ♊ 11p33	18 ♋ 4p 3	19 ♍ 12p22	18 ♎ 10p 5	17 ♏ 6a38
19 ♓ 1p57	20 ♉ 10p15	20 ♉ 5a 0	21 ♋ 10a28	21 ♌ 12a40	21 ♎ 4p44	21 ♏ 1a 8	19 ♐ 9a12
22 ♈ 1a37	23 ♊ 10a31	22 ♊ 5p33	23 ♌ 6p50	23 ♍ 6a54	23 ♏ 7p20	23 ♐ 3a43	21 ♑ 12p49
24 ♉ 2p33	25 ♋ 7p57	25 ♋ 4a 5	25 ♍ 11p56	25 ♎ 10a25	25 ♐ 8p46	25 ♑ 6a32	23 ♒ 6p 3
27 ♊ 2a 7	28 ♌ 1a30	27 ♌ 11a13	28 ♎ 1a48	27 ♏ 11a35	27 ♑ 10p19	27 ♒ 10a42	26 ♓ 1a25
29 ♋ 10a19		29 ♍ 2p36	30 ♏ 1a32	29 ♐ 11a37	30 ♒ 1a44	29 ♓ 5p23	28 ♈ 11a15
31 ♌ 2p57		31 ♎ 3p 6		31 ♑ 12p27			30 ♉ 11p12

☽ PHASES

JAN 1923	FEB 1923	MAR 1923	APR 1923	MAY 1923	JUN 1923	JUL 1923	AUG 1923
2 O 9p33	1 O 10a53	2 ☽ 10p23	1 O 8a 9	3 O 10p15	2 O 8a58	1 O 9p34	4 O 2p22
6 O 9a26	4 O 6p54	6 O 3a53	4 O 12p49	7 O 1p18	6 O 4a19	5 O 8p56	8 ☾ 2p31
9 ☽ 7p54	8 ◐ 4a16	9 ◐ 1p31	8 ◐ 12a22	11 ☾ 2p31	10 ☾ 7a12	9 ☾ 11p21	12 ● 6a16
13 ☾ 7a12	11 ☾ 6p13	13 ☾ 7a11	11 ☾ 10p10	13 ● 5p38	14 ● 4a42	12 ● 3p44	15 ☽ 4p 9
16 ● 9p41	15 ● 2p 7	17 ● 7a51	16 ● 1a28	19 ☽ 4p36	18 ☽ 2a20	17 ☽ 9a50	19 O 1a 7
20 ☽ 7p23	18 ☽ 4p10	21 ☽ 11a30	20 ☽ 3a48	23 O 9a25	22 O 3p46	20 O 5p32	22 O 12p42
24 ◐ 10p59	23 O 7p 6	25 O 11a41	24 O 12a20	26 O 6p53	25 O 12a29	24 O 5p52	26 O 5a29
28 O 9p53	27 O 1p38	29 O 2a13	27 O 11a47	30 O 12a 7	28 O 8a 4	31 O 12p22	30 O 5a 3
			30 O 4p30				

SEP 1923 – APR 1924

	SEP 1923	OCT 1923	NOV 1923	DEC 1923	JAN 1924	FEB 1924	MAR 1924	APR 1924
☉ →	♎ 23 9p 4	♏ 24 5a51	♐ 23 2a54	♑ 22 3p53	♒ 21 2a28	♓ 19 4p51	♈ 20 4p20	♉ 20 3a58

☽ → SIGNS

SEP 1923	OCT 1923	NOV 1923	DEC 1923	JAN 1924	FEB 1924	MAR 1924	APR 1924
2 ♊ 11a50	2 ♋ 7a 0	1 ♑ 12a 0	2 ♏ 7p24	1 ♐ 5a23	1 ♒ 4p 3	2 ♓ 2a11	2 ♉ 10p45
5 ♋ 10p59	4 ♌ 4p14	3 ♒ 3p 0	4 ♐ 9p14	3 ♑ 6a48	3 ♓ 6p43	4 ♈ 7a44	5 ♊ 9a11
7 ♌ 6a54	7 ♍ 9p40	5 ♓ 10a24	6 ♑ 8p57	5 ♒ 7a21	5 ♈ 11p12	6 ♉ 3p26	7 ♋ 9p13
9 ♍ 11a16	9 ♎ 11p35	8 ♈ 10a37	8 ♒ 8p31	7 ♓ 8a54	8 ♉ 6a36	9 ♊ 1a35	10 ♌ 9a52
11 ♎ 1p 3	11 ♏ 11p25	10 ♉ 10p 9	10 ♓ 10p 9	9 ♈ 1p13	10 ♊ 5p 0	11 ♋ 1p43	12 ♍ 9p15
13 ♏ 1p47	13 ♐ 11p 8	13 ♊ 9a37	13 ♈ 3a35	11 ♉ 9p22	13 ♋ 5a34	14 ♌ 2a 8	15 ♎ 5a21
15 ♐ 3p 5	15 ♑ 12a42	15 ♋ 12p39	15 ♉ 1p 8	14 ♊ 8a48	15 ♌ 5p53	16 ♍ 12p31	17 ♏ 9a27
17 ♑ 6p14	18 ♒ 5a29	18 ♌ 7p46	18 ♊ 1a21	16 ♋ 9p27	18 ♍ 3a 9	18 ♎ 7p27	19 ♐ 10a32
19 ♒ 11p52	20 ♓ 1p 5	20 ♍ 6a25	20 ♋ 2p 3	19 ♌ 9a 5	20 ♎ 11a 0	20 ♏ 11p 0	21 ♑ 10a34
22 ♓ 8a 3	22 ♈ 12a33	23 ♎ 7a33	23 ♌ 1a40	21 ♍ 6p33	22 ♏ 1p57	22 ♐ 12a27	23 ♒ 11a39
24 ♈ 7p22	24 ♉ 12p48	25 ♏ 7p27	25 ♍ 11a40	24 ♎ 1a49	24 ♐ 4p16	24 ♑ 1a29	25 ♓ 1p30
27 ♉ 6a22	27 ♊ 1a28	27 ♐ 7p21	27 ♎ 7p51	26 ♏ 7a14	26 ♑ 7p 4	26 ♒ 3a37	27 ♈ 7p39
29 ♊ 7p 6	29 ♋ 1p39	29 ♑ 2p18	30 ♏ 1a51	28 ♐ 11a 8	28 ♒ 10p12	28 ♓ 7a47	30 ♉ 4a39
		30 ♍ —		30 ♑ 1p52		31 ♈ 2p13	

☽ PHASES

SEP 1923	OCT 1923	NOV 1923	DEC 1923	JAN 1924	FEB 1924	MAR 1924	APR 1924
3 O 7p47	2 O 12a29	1 O 3p49	1 O 5a 9	3 ☾ 1a17	1 ☾ 10a12	1 ☾ 7p28	2 ● 2a17
7 ☾ 4a36	6 ☾ 5p36	5 ☾ 5a23	4 ☾ 3p52	6 ● 7a47	4 ● 8p38	4 ● 10a57	8 O 3a47
10 ● 3p52	10 ● 1a 5	8 ● 10a27	7 ● 8p30	9 O 7p34	8 O 1p47	9 O 9a 0	10 O 6a12
13 O 10p23	13 O 5a43	11 O 3p15	11 O 3a49	13 O 5p44	12 O 3p 9	12 O 11a50	16 O 12a50
17 O 7a14	17 O 3p53	16 O 4a41	14 O 9p38	17 O 8p57	15 O 11a50	15 O 3a14	19 O 9a10
20 O 10p16	20 O 11a33	19 O 4a32	19 O 12a14	21 O 7p56	20 O 11a11	20 O 11p30	22 O 1p53
24 O 8p48	24 O 1p26	23 O 2a33	23 O 2a33	25 O 12p43	23 O 10p41	24 O 6a45	25 O 11p28
	28 O 4p35	27 O 9a23	27 O 12a17	29 O 12a53	28 O 8a15	27 O 3p24	29 ☾ 5p40
			30 O 4p 7			31 ☾ 5a49	

MAY 1924 – DEC 1924

	MAY 1924	JUN 1924	JUL 1924	AUG 1924	SEP 1924	OCT 1924	NOV 1924	DEC 1924
☉ →	♊ 21 3a40	♋ 21 11a59	♌ 22 10p57	♍ 23 5a48	♎ 23 2a58	♏ 23 11a44	♐ 22 8a46	♑ 21 9p45

☽ → SIGNS

MAY 1924	JUN 1924	JUL 1924	AUG 1924	SEP 1924	OCT 1924	NOV 1924	DEC 1924
2 ♊ 3p37	1 ♋ 9a47	1 ♌ 4a28	2 ♎ 8a 5	3 ♐ 1a54	2 ♒ 10a54	1 ♓ 9p53	2 ♉ 8a38
5 ♋ 3a48	3 ♌ 10p27	3 ♍ 4p11	4 ♏ 3p19	5 ♑ 5a 0	4 ♓ 1p 2	5 ♈ 2a34	4 ♊ 3p10
7 ♌ 4p30	6 ♍ 10a29	6 ♎ 2a15	6 ♐ 8p24	7 ♒ 7a40	6 ♈ 4p19	7 ♉ 9a39	7 ♋ 12a33
10 ♍ 4a30	8 ♎ 8p40	8 ♏ 9a55	8 ♑ 11p32	9 ♓ 10a33	8 ♉ 9p 6	9 ♊ 6p44	9 ♌ 11a52
12 ♎ 1p57	11 ♏ 3a41	10 ♐ 2p36	11 ♒ 1a20	11 ♈ 1p30	11 ♊ 3a30	12 ♋ 5p44	12 ♍ 12a21
14 ♏ 7p28	13 ♐ 7a16	12 ♑ 4p31	13 ♓ 2a52	13 ♉ 7p42	13 ♋ 11a50	14 ♌ 5p56	14 ♎ 1p12
16 ♐ 9p10	15 ♑ 7a57	14 ♒ 4p48	15 ♈ 5a28	16 ♊ 3a50	15 ♌ 10p23	17 ♍ 6p 1	17 ♏ 1a 7
18 ♑ 8p33	17 ♒ 6a42	16 ♓ 5p11	17 ♉ 10a32	18 ♋ 2p24	18 ♍ 10a48	19 ♎ 6p 1	19 ♐ 10a15
20 ♒ 7p48	19 ♓ 6a28	18 ♈ 7p30	19 ♊ 6p54	21 ♌ 2p52	20 ♎ 11p21	22 ♏ 1a51	21 ♑ 3p25
22 ♓ 9p 4	21 ♈ 9a32	21 ♉ 1a12	22 ♋ 6a14	23 ♍ 3p49	23 ♏ 9a33	24 ♐ 5a38	23 ♒ 4p55
25 ♈ 1a49	23 ♉ 4p56	23 ♊ 10a 6	24 ♌ 6p48	26 ♎ 12a 6	25 ♐ 5a28	26 ♑ 6a26	25 ♓ 4p18
27 ♉ 10a16	26 ♊ 3a51	25 ♋ 11p18	27 ♍ 6a18	28 ♏ 5a53	27 ♑ 7p 3	28 ♒ 5a25	27 ♈ 3p41
29 ♊ 9p23	28 ♋ 3p51	28 ♌ 11a11	29 ♎ 3p18	30 ♐ 9a37	29 ♒ 7p39	30 ♓ 5a25	29 ♉ 5p 6
		30 ♍ 9p37	31 ♏ 9p37		31 ♑ 7a56		31 ♊ 9p57

☽ PHASES

MAY 1924	JUN 1924	JUL 1924	AUG 1924	SEP 1924	OCT 1924	NOV 1924	DEC 1924
3 ● 6p 0	2 ● 9a34	2 ● 12a35	4 ● 9a44	2 O 5p32	2 O 12a30	3 O 5p18	3 O 4a10
7 O 8p57	6 O 11a48	6 O 12a 2	7 O 10p41	6 O 3a45	6 O 5p 9	7 O 4a30	7 O 12a15
11 O 9p13	10 O 8a36	9 O 4p46	11 O 7a 7	9 O 1p34	9 O 10p 4	11 O 7a30	11 O 2a 3
15 O 11a39	13 O 7p31	13 O 6a49	13 O 3p19	12 O 3p21	12 O 3p21	15 O 10a11	15 O 5a47
18 O 4p52	16 O 11p41	16 O 8a49	18 O 5a15	16 O 8p46	16 O 2p40	19 O 12p38	18 O 5a11
21 O 9p13	20 O 4p46	20 O 4p18	22 O 6a37	20 O 5p54	20 O 5p54	22 O 12p15	22 O 5p58
25 O 9a16	23 O 9p16	23 O 11a36	26 O 6a37	24 ☾ 11p22	24 ☾ 11p22	26 ☾ 12p15	25 O 10p45
29 ☾ 7a 3	27 ☾ 9p52	27 ☾ 1p52	28 ● 3p15	28 ● 3p15	28 ● 1a57	29 O 4p59	29 O 4a19
		31 ● 2p42			31 O 7a56		

1925 (January – August)

	JAN 1925	FEB 1925	MAR 1925	APR 1925	MAY 1925	JUN 1925	JUL 1925	AUG 1925
O →	♒ 20 8a20	♓ 18 10p43	♈ 20 10p12	♉ 20 9a51	♊ 21 9a33	♋ 21 5p50	♌ 23 4a45	♍ 23 11a33

D→SIGNS

JAN 1925	FEB 1925	MAR 1925	APR 1925	MAY 1925	JUN 1925	JUL 1925	AUG 1925
3 ♉ 6a31	2 ♊ 12a32	1 ♊ 8a26	2 ♌ 5p32	2 ♍ 1p38	1 ♎ 7a30	3 ♏ 1a54	1 ♑ 12p46
5 ♊ 5p52	5 ♋ 1p10	3 ♋ 8p38	5 ♍ 4a55	5 ♎ 10p26	3 ♏ 1p21	5 ♐ 2a24	3 ♒ 12p40
8 ♋ 6a32	7 ♌ 1a49	6 ♌ 9a22	7 ♎ 1p 4	7 ♏ 3a21	5 ♐ 3p33	7 ♑ 1a49	5 ♓ 12p23
10 ♌ 7p14	9 ♍ 1p 1	8 ♍ 8p24	9 ♏ 6p 4	9 ♐ 5a27	7 ♑ 3p45	9 ♒ 2a 6	7 ♈ 1p46
13 ♍ 6a54	11 ♎ 10p 6	11 ♎ 4a44	11 ♐ 9p 5	11 ♑ 6a30	9 ♒ 3p53	11 ♓ 4a53	9 ♉ 6p24
15 ♎ 4p32	14 ♏ 4a54	13 ♏ 10a37	13 ♑ 11p32	13 ♒ 8a 8	11 ♓ 5p40	13 ♈ 11a 5	12 ♊ 2a57
17 ♏ 11p11	16 ♐ 9a27	15 ♐ 2p51	16 ♒ 2a23	15 ♓ 11a23	13 ♈ 10p 3	15 ♊ 8p37	14 ♋ 2p39
20 ♐ 2a34	18 ♑ 12p 2	17 ♑ 6p 7	18 ♓ 6a 2	17 ♈ 4p34	16 ♉ 5a15	18 ♋ 8a32	17 ♌ 3a41
22 ♑ 3a22	20 ♒ 1p21	19 ♒ 8p51	20 ♈ 10a45	19 ♉ 11p41	18 ♊ 2p57	20 ♌ 9p32	19 ♍ 4p13
24 ♒ 3a 9	22 ♓ 2p36	21 ♓ 11p33	22 ♉ 4p59	22 ♊ 8a50	21 ♋ 2a36	23 ♍ 10a17	22 ♎ 3a 5
26 ♓ 3a45	24 ♈ 5p21	24 ♈ 3a 4	25 ♊ 1a33	24 ♋ 8p 7	23 ♌ 3p30	25 ♎ 9p30	24 ♏ 11a44
28 ♈ 6a59	26 ♉ 11p 3	26 ♉ 8a34	27 ♋ 1p 0	27 ♌ 8a59	26 ♍ 4a21	28 ♏ 5a56	26 ♐ 5p49
30 ♉ 1p58		28 ♊ 5p 7	30 ♌ 1a36	29 ♍ 9p35	28 ♎ 3p15	30 ♐ 10a56	28 ♑ 9p19
		31 ♋ 4a42			30 ♏ 10p32		30 ♒ 10p41

D PHASES

JAN 1925	FEB 1925	MAR 1925	APR 1925	MAY 1925	JUN 1925	JUL 1925	AUG 1925
1 ◐ 6p25	4 ○ 2p10	2 ○ 7a 6	1 ○ 3a12	4 ○ 8p41	3 ○ 8a56	2 ○ 6p27	2 ○ 2a11
5 ○ 6p33	8 ☾ 4p49	6 ○ 10a30	5 ○ 5a 8	8 ○ 8a42	6 ○ 4a47	5 ○ 11p53	4 ☾ 6a59
9 ○ 9p47	12 ○ 9p10	10 ○ 9a21	8 ○ 10p32	11 ○ 3p42	9 ○ 9p55	9 ○ 4a48	7 ○ 1p14
13 ○ 11p31	16 ○ 4a41	14 ○ 12a57	12 ○ 9a 7	15 ○ 12a45	13 ○ 7a44	12 ○ 4p34	11 ○ 4a10
17 ○ 6p33	20 ◖ 9a45	17 ○ 12p21	15 ○ 6p40	18 ☽ 2p59	16 ☾ 1a10	16 ☽ 1p46	15 ☽ 4a54
21 ◖ 4a36	22 ☾ 9p12	20 ◖ 10p 9	19 ◖ 6a16	22 ○ 10a48	20 ○ 1a17	20 ☽ 4p40	19 ○ 8a14
24 ☾ 9a45	26 ☾ 9a17	24 ☽ 9a 3	24 ☾ 9a 3	26 ☾ 12p27	25 ◖ 4a44	24 ◖ 7p11	22 ☾ 3p30
27 ◖ 5p54		28 ◖ 1a53	26 ◖ 7p11	30 ○ 3p 4	29 ○ 4a43	28 ○ 3p22	26 ○ 11p46
31 ◐ 11a43			30 ○ 10p19				30 ○ 9a 7

1925 (September – December) / 1926 (January – April)

	SEP 1925	OCT 1925	NOV 1925	DEC 1925	JAN 1926	FEB 1926	MAR 1926	APR 1926
O →	♎ 23 8a43	♏ 23 5p31	♐ 22 2p36	♑ 22 3a37	♒ 20 2p12	♓ 19 4a35	♈ 21 4a 1	♉ 20 3p36

D→SIGNS

SEP 1925	OCT 1925	NOV 1925	DEC 1925	JAN 1926	FEB 1926	MAR 1926	APR 1926
1 ♓ 11p 2	1 ♈ 10a 6	2 ♊ 4a44	1 ♋ 10p19	3 ♍ 6a26	2 ♎ 1a10	1 ♏ 7a 3	2 ♑ 7a 8
4 ♈ 12a12	3 ♉ 1p19	4 ♋ 2p 6	4 ♌ 10a13	5 ♎ 6p44	4 ♏ 11a39	3 ♐ 5p28	4 ♒ 11p 4
6 ♉ 3a27	5 ♊ 7p34	7 ♌ 2a16	6 ♍ 11p13	8 ♏ 4a19	6 ♐ 7p 2	6 ♑ 1a40	6 ♓ 5p 0
8 ♊ 10a39	8 ♋ 5a33	9 ♍ 3p 7	9 ♎ 10a52	10 ♐ 10a 1	9 ♑ 11p37	8 ♒ 7a 6	8 ♈ 7p 3
10 ♋ 9p35	10 ♌ 6p 9	12 ♎ 1a52	11 ♏ 7p 3	12 ♑ 12p 9	11 ♒ 1a10	10 ♓ 9a40	10 ♉ 8p 2
13 ♌ 10a30	13 ♍ 6a43	14 ♏ 9a 5	13 ♐ 11p23	14 ♒ 12p 6	13 ♓ 1a20	12 ♈ 10a 3	12 ♊ 9p31
15 ♍ 10p56	15 ♎ 4p57	16 ♐ 1p12	16 ♑ 12a59	16 ♓ 11a48	14 ♈ 10p47	14 ♉ 9a51	15 ♋ 1a20
18 ♎ 9a18	18 ♏ 12a12	18 ♑ 3p38	18 ♒ 1a35	18 ♈ 1p 3	17 ♉ 8a22	16 ♊ 11a 6	17 ♌ 8a54
20 ♏ 5p18	20 ♐ 5a11	20 ♒ 5p48	20 ♓ 1a47	20 ♉ 5p15	19 ♊ 7a22	18 ♋ 3p41	19 ♍ 8p 7
22 ♐ 11p17	22 ♑ 8a57	22 ♓ 8p37	22 ♈ 5a57	23 ♊ 12a55	21 ♋ 5p28	21 ♌ 12a30	22 ♎ 8p59
25 ♑ 3a37	24 ♒ 12p12	25 ♈ 12a31	24 ♉ 11a25	25 ♋ 11a30	24 ♌ 6a 0	23 ♍ 12p35	24 ♏ 8p52
27 ♒ 6a29	26 ♓ 3p14	27 ♉ 5a46	26 ♊ 7p18	27 ♌ 11p52	26 ♍ 6p59	26 ♎ 1a36	27 ♐ 6a18
29 ♓ 8a19	28 ♈ 6p23	29 ♊ 12p50	29 ♋ 5a26	30 ♍ 12p49		28 ♏ 1p 7	29 ♑ 1p 9
	30 ♉ 10p29		31 ♌ 5p26			30 ♏ 11p17	

D PHASES

SEP 1925	OCT 1925	NOV 1925	DEC 1925	JAN 1926	FEB 1926	MAR 1926	APR 1926
2 ○ 2p53	2 ○ 12a23	4 ○ 7a22	4 ○ 3a30	3 ○ 12a31	1 ○ 8p 5	3 ○ 12p28	2 ○ 1a10
6 ○ 12a 3	5 ○ 2p 0	8 ○ 10a13	8 ○ 7a10	7 ○ 2a22	5 ○ 6p25	7 ○ 6a49	5 ○ 3p50
9 ○ 7p11	9 ○ 1p34	12 ○ 10a51	11 ○ 4a 7	10 ○ 6p36	9 ○ 7a 8	10 ○ 5p11	9 ☽ 1a 1
13 ○ 10p15	13 ☽ 4p41	16 ☾ 1a57	15 ◖ 2p 5	14 ◖ 1a34	12 ○ 12p20	13 ○ 10p20	12 ○ 7a56
17 ☽ 11p12	17 ○ 1p 5	19 ☽ 1a23	18 ○ 8p33	17 ○ 6a36	15 ○ 5p43	17 ☽ 6a 7	15 ○ 7p57
21 ☾ 5p38	21 ☾ 2a40	22 ○ 9p 5	22 ○ 6a 8	20 ○ 5p31	17 ○ 7a36	21 ○ 12a11	19 ○ 6p23
25 ◖ 6a51	24 ○ 1p37	26 ○ 9a47	25 ○ 10p15	24 ○ 1p51	20 ○ 8a 0	25 ○ 3a 8	23 ○ 9p29
28 ○ 4p 7	28 ○ 12a 1	30 ○ 3a11	29 ○ 9p 1	28 ☾ 4p35	23 ◖ 11a50	29 ○ 5a 0	27 ○ 7p16
	31 ○ 12p16						

1926 (May – December)

	MAY 1926	JUN 1926	JUL 1926	AUG 1926	SEP 1926	OCT 1926	NOV 1926	DEC 1926
O →	♊ 21 3p14	♋ 21 11p30	♌ 23 10a25	♍ 23 5p14	♎ 23 2p27	♏ 23 11p18	♐ 22 8p28	♑ 22 9a33

D→SIGNS

MAY 1926	JUN 1926	JUL 1926	AUG 1926	SEP 1926	OCT 1926	NOV 1926	DEC 1926
1 ♉ 6p32	2 ♓ 6a53	1 ♈ 3p14	2 ♊ 6a24	3 ♌ 8a 1	3 ♍ 2a49	1 ♎ 10p22	1 ♏ 5p39
3 ♊ 10p31	4 ♈ 9a45	3 ♉ 6p59	4 ♋ 3p 8	5 ♍ 8p40	5 ♎ 3p28	4 ♏ 9a37	4 ♐ 2a32
6 ♋ 1a31	6 ♉ 1p28	6 ♊ 12a57	7 ♌ 2a12	8 ♎ 9a23	8 ♏ 2a58	6 ♐ 6p51	6 ♑ 8a52
8 ♌ 3a55	8 ♊ 6p43	8 ♋ 9a16	9 ♍ 2p39	10 ♏ 9p15	10 ♐ 12p54	9 ♑ 2a11	8 ♒ 1p21
10 ♍ 6a33	11 ♋ 2a14	10 ♌ 7p50	12 ♎ 2p39	12 ♐ 7a21	12 ♑ 8p47	11 ♒ 7a41	10 ♓ 4p43
12 ♎ 10a46	13 ♌ 12p29	13 ♍ 8a 7	14 ♏ 2p39	15 ♑ 2p37	15 ♒ 2a 8	13 ♓ 11a 2	12 ♈ 7p33
14 ♏ 5p53	16 ♍ 12a48	15 ♎ 8p52	17 ♐ 2a39	17 ♒ 6p23	17 ♓ 4a29	15 ♈ 1p28	14 ♉ 10p23
17 ♐ 4a20	18 ♎ 1p40	18 ♏ 8a 7	20 ♑ 4p10	19 ♓ 7p 6	19 ♈ 5a 1	17 ♉ 2p53	16 ♊ 1a59
19 ♑ 4p54	20 ♏ 11p40	20 ♐ 4p10	22 ♒ 8p28	21 ♈ 8a31	21 ♉ 5a 1	19 ♊ 5p10	18 ♋ 7a19
22 ♒ 5a 4	23 ♑ 6a35	22 ♑ 9p48	23 ♓ 9p49	23 ♉ 6p12	23 ♊ 6p12	21 ♋ 9p54	20 ♌ 3p16
24 ♓ 2p41	25 ♒ 10a18	24 ♒ 9p48	25 ♈ 9p28	25 ♊ 8a31	25 ♋ 12p 8	24 ♌ 6a10	23 ♍ 2a 2
26 ♈ 9p14	27 ♓ 12p 1	26 ♓ 9p46	27 ♉ 9p28	28 ♋ 12p39	27 ♌ 9p10	26 ♍ 5p36	25 ♎ 2p35
29 ♉ 1a24	29 ♓ 1p13	28 ♈ 10p13	29 ♊ 12a39	30 ♌ 10p10	30 ♍ 9a43	29 ♎ 6a13	27 ♏ 2a15
31 ♊ 4a18		31 ♉ 12a46	31 ♋ 8p48				31 ♐ 11a50

D PHASES

MAY 1926	JUN 1926	JUL 1926	AUG 1926	SEP 1926	OCT 1926	NOV 1926	DEC 1926
1 ○ 10a38	3 ○ 3a 9	2 ○ 8a 2	4 ◖ 8a 9	2 ○ 2p45	2 ○ 2p17	1 ◖ 9a 6	1 ◖ 4a53
4 ○ 10p13	6 ◖ 1p59	5 ◖ 9p47	8 ● 8a48	7 ● 12a45	6 ● 5p13	5 ● 9a34	5 ● 1a11
8 ◖ 7a32	10 ● 5a 8	9 ● 9p 0	12 ○ 3a...	11 ○ 2a48	10 ○ 4p19	9 ○ 2a24	8 ○ 3p 4
11 ● 5p55	14 ○ 3a20	13 ○ 7p58	16 ○ 11a38	15 ○ 11p26	14 ○ 9a27	12 ○ 6p 1	12 ○ 1a47
15 ○ 11a12	18 ○ 6a13	17 ○ 9p55	20 ○ 5p39	19 ○ 3p19	18 ○ 10a51	16 ○ 3a10	15 ○ 12p 0
19 ○ 12p48	21 ○ 9p48	21 ○ 3p48	23 ○ 7a37	23 ○ 9p11	21 ○ 9a44	20 ○ 2a15	19 ○ 1p 9
23 ○ 1p51	25 ☾ 4p12	25 ☾ 12a13	26 ○ 12p 0	26 ○ 9p...	24 ○ 9p23	23 ○ 2a 1	22 ○ 11p59
27 ○ 6a48	28 ○ 11p32	28 ○ 5a12	29 ○ 11p40	30 ○ 4a59	27 ○ 2a15		26 ○ 9p16
30 ○ 5p44		29 ◖ 2p25					31 ◖ 12a12

1927 (Jan – Aug)

JAN 1927
☉ → ♒ 20 8p12

☽ → SIGNS
2 ♑ 5p51 · 4 ♒ 9p10 · 6 ♓ 11p 5 · 9 ♈ 12a59 · 11 ♉ 3a56 · 13 ♊ 8a30 · 15 ♋ 2p59 · 17 ♌ 11p31 · 20 ♍ 10a10 · 22 ♎ 10p27 · 25 ♏ 3a54 · 27 ♐ 9p21 · 30 ♑ 4a12

☽ PHASES
3 ♐ 3p28 · 7 ♑ 12a38 · 10 ○ 9a43 · 13 ○ 10p49 · 17 ○ 5p27 · 21 ○ 6p 1 · 25 ● 2p59 · 29 ☽ 5p37

FEB 1927
☉ → ♓ 19 10a34

☽ → SIGNS
1 ♒ 7a22 · 3 ♓ 8a 6 · 5 ♈ 8a19 · 7 ♉ 9a50 · 9 ♊ 1p54 · 11 ♋ 8p51 · 13 ♌ 6a11 · 16 ♍ 5p15 · 18 ♎ 5a31 · 21 ♏ 6p 8 · 23 ♐ 5a34 · 26 ♑ 1p56 · 28 ♒ 6p14

☽ PHASES
2 ● 3a54 · 5 ♑ 9a38 · 8 ○ 6p53 · 12 ○ 11a55 · 15 ○ 11a18 · 20 ○ 2p12 · 22 ○ 3p42 · 25 ● 8a14 · 28 ☽ 7a59

MAR 1927
☉ → ♈ 21 9a59

☽ → SIGNS
2 ♓ 7p 5 · 4 ♈ 6p19 · 6 ♉ 6p 7 · 8 ♊ 8p29 · 11 ♋ 2a29 · 13 ♌ 11a51 · 15 ♍ 11p22 · 18 ♎ 11a48 · 20 ♏ 11p49 · 23 ♐ 12p 6 · 26 ♑ 8p 2 · 28 ♒ 3a39 · 30 ♓ 5a52

☽ PHASES
2 ● 2p24 · 6 ♑ 6p47 · 9 ○ 6a 2 · 13 ○ 5a24 · 16 ○ 10p35 · 20 ○ 11p 6 · 24 ○ 5p21 · 29 ☽ 6p56

APR 1927
☉ → ♉ 20 9p31

☽ → SIGNS
1 ♈ 5a30 · 3 ♉ 4a36 · 5 ♊ 5a25 · 7 ♋ 9a42 · 9 ♌ 6p 0 · 12 ♍ 5a19 · 14 ♎ 5p53 · 17 ♏ 6a20 · 19 ♐ 5p49 · 22 ♑ 3a35 · 24 ♒ 10a43 · 26 ♓ 2p37 · 28 ♈ 3p43 · 30 ♉ 3p28

☽ PHASES
1 ● 11p24 · 4 ♑ 4a46 · 8 ○ 7p20 · 12 ○ 7p36 · 16 ○ 10p35 · 20 ○ 11p 6 · 24 ○ 5p21 · 27 ● 2a53

MAY 1927
☉ → ♊ 21 9p 8

☽ → SIGNS
2 ♊ 3p52 · 4 ♋ 6p51 · 7 ♌ 1a39 · 9 ♍ 12p 3 · 12 ♎ 12a27 · 14 ♏ 12p52 · 16 ♐ 11p57 · 19 ♑ 9a11 · 21 ♒ 4p16 · 23 ♓ 9p 1 · 25 ♈ 11p37 · 28 ♉ 12a50 · 30 ♊ 2a 2

☽ PHASES
1 ● 7a40 · 4 ♐ 4p 2 · 10 ○ 10a27 · 12 ○ 12p34 · 16 ○ 2p 2 · 20 ○ 10a27 · 24 ○ 12a33 · 27 ☽ 8a58 · 30 ● 4p 6

JUN 1927
☉ → ♋ 22 5a22

☽ → SIGNS
1 ♋ 4a50 · 3 ♌ 10a37 · 5 ♍ 7p55 · 8 ♎ 7a49 · 10 ♏ 8p16 · 13 ♐ 7a16 · 15 ♑ 3p51 · 17 ♒ 10p 9 · 20 ♓ 2a25 · 22 ♈ 5a29 · 24 ♉ 7a54 · 26 ♊ 10a26 · 28 ♋ 2p 3 · 30 ♌ 7p48

☽ PHASES
2 ♐ 4a45 · 7 ♑ 2a48 · 9 ○ 5a14 · 18 ○ 6p42 · 21 ○ 5a29 · 25 ○ 2p32 · 27 ♐ 1a32

JUL 1927
☉ → ♌ 23 4p17

☽ → SIGNS
3 ♍ 4a27 · 5 ♎ 3p47 · 8 ♏ 4a17 · 10 ♐ 3p37 · 13 ♑ 12a 6 · 15 ♒ 5a31 · 17 ♓ 8a43 · 19 ♈ 10a58 · 21 ♉ 1p24 · 23 ♊ 4p46 · 25 ♋ 9p30 · 28 ♌ 4a 0 · 30 ♍ 12p41

☽ PHASES
2 ♑ 6p57 · 6 ♒ 7p52 · 9 ○ 8p59 · 18 ○ 2p22 · 21 ○ 9a43 · 24 ● 8p57 · 28 ● 12p36

AUG 1927
☉ → ♍ 23 11p 5

☽ → SIGNS
1 ♎ 11p44 · 4 ♏ 12p16 · 7 ♐ 12a14 · 9 ♑ 9a23 · 11 ♒ 2p46 · 13 ♓ 5p 4 · 15 ♈ 5p57 · 17 ♉ 7p12 · 19 ♊ 10p 8 · 22 ♋ 3a19 · 24 ♌ 10a39 · 26 ♍ 7p55 · 29 ♎ 7a 2 · 31 ♏ 7p36

☽ PHASES
1 ♓ 10a31 · 5 ○ 1p 5 · 9 ○ 11a21 · 12 ○ 11p37 · 16 ○ 6a19 · 19 ○ 2p54 · 23 ● 5a25 · 27 ● 1a45 · 31 ☽ 3a13

1927 (Sep – Dec) · 1928 (Jan – Apr)

SEP 1927
☉ → ♎ 23 8p17

☽ → SIGNS
3 ♐ 8a10 · 5 ♑ 6p28 · 8 ♒ 12a50 · 10 ♓ 3a18 · 12 ♈ 3a18 · 14 ♉ 3a 2 · 16 ♊ 4a28 · 18 ♋ 8a49 · 20 ♌ 4p13 · 23 ♍ 2a 1 · 25 ♎ 1p30 · 28 ♏ 2a 1 · 30 ♐ 2p54

☽ PHASES
4 ○ 5a44 · 8 ○ 12a 3 · 11 ○ 7a 4 · 14 ○ 12p34 · 17 ○ 10p29 · 21 ○ 4p50 · 25 ● 5p11 · 28 ☽ 8p30

OCT 1927
☉ → ♏ 24 5a 7

☽ → SIGNS
3 ♑ 2a13 · 5 ♒ 10a 7 · 7 ♓ 1p50 · 9 ♈ 2p14 · 11 ♉ 1p17 · 13 ♊ 1p 2 · 15 ♋ 3p50 · 17 ♌ 10p 7 · 20 ♍ 7a43 · 22 ♎ 7p27 · 25 ♏ 8a 8 · 27 ♐ 8p48 · 30 ♑ 8a22

☽ PHASES
3 ○ 9p 1 · 7 ○ 11a 9 · 10 ○ 4p14 · 14 ○ 2a39 · 17 ○ 9a31 · 21 ● 7a40 · 25 ● 10a37 · 29 ☽ 1p23

NOV 1927
☉ → ♐ 24 2a14

☽ → SIGNS
1 ♒ 5p26 · 3 ♓ 10p55 · 6 ♈ 12a53 · 8 ♉ 12a34 · 10 ♊ 12a 3 · 12 ♋ 1a15 · 14 ♌ 5a48 · 16 ♍ 1p22 · 19 ♎ 1a40 · 21 ♏ 2p26 · 24 ♐ 2a53 · 26 ♑ 2p 1 · 28 ♒ 11p 6

☽ PHASES
2 ○ 10a15 · 5 ○ 9p 6 · 9 ○ 4p14 · 12 ○ 8a19 · 16 ○ 12a28 · 20 ○ 1a49 · 24 ● 5a 9 · 29 ☽ 4a39

DEC 1927
☉ → ♑ 22 3p18

☽ → SIGNS
1 ♓ 5a37 · 3 ♈ 9a39 · 5 ♉ 10a46 · 7 ♊ 11a 6 · 9 ♋ 12p11 · 11 ♌ 3p31 · 13 ♍ 9p31 · 16 ♎ 8a55 · 18 ♏ 9p57 · 21 ♐ 9a59 · 23 ♑ 8p37 · 26 ♒ 6a 2 · 28 ♓ 11a 0 · 30 ♈ 3p19

☽ PHASES
1 ○ 9p15 · 5 ○ 9p 6 · 8 ♈ 12p32 · 11 ○ 10p50 · 15 ○ 7p56 · 20 ○ 1a49 · 23 ♐ 11p13 · 27 ● 5p32 · 31 ○ 6a22

JAN 1928
☉ → ♒ 21 1a57

☽ → SIGNS
1 ♉ 6p14 · 3 ♊ 8p20 · 5 ♋ 10p28 · 8 ♌ 1a52 · 10 ♍ 7a53 · 12 ♎ 5p18 · 15 ♏ 5a26 · 17 ♐ 6p 6 · 20 ♑ 4a49 · 22 ♒ 12p27 · 24 ♓ 5p48 · 26 ♈ 9p42 · 28 ♉ 11p42 · 31 ♊ 2a47

☽ PHASES
3 ○ 3p45 · 7 ♑ 1a 7 · 10 ○ 4p 5 · 14 ○ 4p13 · 18 ○ 7p16 · 22 ♐ 3p18 · 26 ☽ 4a 4 · 29 ● 2p25

FEB 1928
☉ → ♓ 19 4p19

☽ → SIGNS
2 ♋ 6a21 · 4 ♌ 10a53 · 6 ♍ 5p 9 · 9 ♎ 2a 3 · 11 ♏ 1p41 · 14 ♐ 2a32 · 16 ♑ 1p54 · 19 ♒ 9p47 · 21 ♓ 3p51 · 23 ♈ 4a 9 · 25 ♉ 5a42 · 27 ♊ 8a 7 · 29 ♋ 12p 4

☽ PHASES
2 ○ 1a28 · 5 ○ 3p11 · 10 ○ 11a12 · 14 ○ 2p 5 · 17 ♑ 2p48 · 21 ♐ 4a40 · 24 ☽ 3p29 · 26 ● 4a 4

MAR 1928
☉ → ♈ 20 3p44

☽ → SIGNS
2 ♌ 5p38 · 5 ♍ 12a51 · 7 ♎ 10a 4 · 9 ♏ 9p31 · 12 ♐ 10a24 · 14 ♑ 10p33 · 17 ♒ 7a31 · 19 ♓ 12p20 · 21 ♈ 1p54 · 23 ♉ 2p 6 · 25 ♊ 2p53 · 27 ♋ 4p46 · 29 ♌ 11p 4

☽ PHASES
2 ○ 12p 0 · 6 ○ 6a27 · 10 ○ 6a57 · 14 ○ 10a20 · 17 ○ 6a13 · 21 ○ 3p29 · 24 ♐ 9p 8 · 27 ● 10p20 · 31 ○ 11p44

APR 1928
☉ → ♉ 20 3a17

☽ → SIGNS
1 ♍ 6a53 · 3 ♎ 4p47 · 6 ♏ 4a27 · 8 ♐ 5p20 · 11 ♑ 5a56 · 13 ♒ 4p 7 · 15 ♓ 10p19 · 18 ♈ 12a36 · 20 ♉ 12a36 · 22 ♊ 12a 9 · 24 ♋ 1a14 · 26 ♌ 5a11 · 28 ♍ 12p28 · 30 ♎ 10p36

☽ PHASES
4 ○ 10p38 · 9 ○ 1a49 · 13 ○ 3a 8 · 16 ○ 6p22 · 20 ○ 12a25 · 24 ○ 5a19 · 26 ● 4p41 · 30 ○ 1p 0

1928 (May – Dec)

MAY 1928
☉ → ♊ 21 2a52

☽ → SIGNS
3 ♏ 10a38 · 5 ♐ 11p32 · 8 ♑ 12p 9 · 10 ♒ 10p57 · 13 ♓ 6a35 · 15 ♈ 11a25 · 17 ♉ 11a25 · 19 ♊ 11a40 · 21 ♋ 1p16 · 23 ♌ 7p 7 · 26 ♍ 4a36 · 28 ♎ 4p40

☽ PHASES
4 ○ 3p12 · 8 ○ 6p18 · 12 ○ 3p50 · 16 ○ 3a25 · 19 ♈ 8a14 · 22 ○ 2p 6 · 26 ○ 4a11 · 30 ○ 3a53

JUN 1928
☉ → ♋ 21 11a 6

☽ → SIGNS
2 ♏ 5a38 · 4 ♐ 6p 0 · 7 ♑ 4a41 · 9 ♒ 12p54 · 11 ♓ 6p13 · 13 ♈ 8p46 · 15 ♉ 9p24 · 17 ♊ 9p34 · 19 ♋ 11p 2 · 22 ♌ 3a27 · 24 ♍ 11a42 · 26 ♎ 11p27 · 29 ♏ 12p13

☽ PHASES
3 ♐ 7a13 · 7 ○ 7a31 · 10 ○ 5p34 · 14 ○ 10a20 · 17 ○ 11p13 · 20 ○ 1p12 · 24 ● 5p47 · 28 ○ 8p 2

JUL 1928
☉ → ♌ 22 10p 2

☽ → SIGNS
2 ♐ 12a23 · 4 ♑ 10a32 · 6 ♒ 6p22 · 9 ♓ 12a 4 · 11 ♈ 3a59 · 13 ♉ 5a59 · 15 ♊ 7a 6 · 17 ♋ 9a 6 · 19 ♌ 12p52 · 21 ♍ 8p 2 · 24 ♎ 6a47 · 26 ♏ 7p34 · 29 ♐ 8a 7 · 31 ♑ 5p33

☽ PHASES
2 ○ 9p48 · 7 ○ 3a 2 · 10 ○ 7a16 · 13 ○ 4p11 · 17 ○ 1p35 · 20 ● 11a44 · 24 ○ 9a38 · 28 ● 12p38

AUG 1928
☉ → ♍ 23 4a53

☽ → SIGNS
1 ♒ 12a34 · 3 ♓ 5a33 · 5 ♈ 9a18 · 7 ♉ 12p22 · 9 ♊ 3p 3 · 11 ♋ 5p57 · 13 ♌ 10p 7 · 16 ♍ 4a53 · 18 ♎ 2p57 · 21 ♏ 3a29 · 23 ♐ 3p59 · 26 ♑ 1a57 · 28 ♒ 8a30

☽ PHASES
1 ○ 10a30 · 5 ○ 1a18 · 8 ○ 9p24 · 12 ○ 10p 3 · 15 ● 8a48 · 19 ○ 1a50 · 23 ○ 3a21 · 27 ○ 4a48 · 30 ○ 9p34

SEP 1928
☉ → ♎ 23 2a 6

☽ → SIGNS
1 ♓ 12p26 · 3 ♈ 3p 7 · 5 ♉ 5p43 · 7 ♊ 8p51 · 9 ♋ 12a49 · 12 ♌ 6a 1 · 14 ♍ 1p12 · 16 ♎ 11p 4 · 19 ♏ 11a23 · 21 ♐ 12a16 · 24 ♑ 11a 1 · 26 ♒ 6p 1 · 28 ♓ 9p57 · 30 ♈ 10p59

☽ PHASES
2 ○ 7a58 · 6 ○ 6p35 · 10 ○ 5a 5 · 13 ♍ 8p20 · 17 ♏ 1p20 · 21 ○ 4p 6 · 25 ○ 9a48 · 29 ○ 7a42

OCT 1928
☉ → ♏ 23 10a55

☽ → SIGNS
1 ♉ 11p 0 · 3 ♊ 12a 9 · 5 ♋ 2a21 · 7 ♌ 6a18 · 9 ♍ 12p13 · 11 ♎ 8p14 · 14 ♏ 6a28 · 16 ♐ 7p33 · 19 ♑ 7a50 · 21 ♒ 5p13 · 24 ♓ 3a50 · 26 ♈ 8a 4 · 28 ♉ 9a16 · 30 ♊ 9a11

☽ PHASES
2 ○ 2p52 · 6 ○ 12a 6 · 10 ☽ 5p 2 · 13 ♏ 4p35 · 17 ○ 1p20 · 21 ● 4p 6 · 25 ○ 5p43 · 28 ○ 5p43

NOV 1928
☉ → ♐ 22 8a 0

☽ → SIGNS
1 ♋ 9a40 · 3 ♌ 12p14 · 5 ♍ 5p 2 · 8 ♎ 1a 5 · 10 ♏ 12p53 · 13 ♐ 1a20 · 15 ♑ 2p25 · 18 ♒ 2a40 · 20 ♓ 12p19 · 22 ♈ 6p14 · 24 ♉ 8p30 · 26 ♊ 8p23 · 28 ♋ 7p43 · 30 ♌ 8p28

☽ PHASES
4 ○ 9a 8 · 8 ☽ 3a25 · 12 ♐ 4a35 · 16 ○ 10a51 · 20 ○ 10p28 · 23 ♐ 9a 7 · 27 ● 9p43 · 30 ● 9p30

DEC 1928
☉ → ♑ 21 9p 4

☽ → SIGNS
1 ♍ 12a16 · 3 ♎ 7a52 · 5 ♏ 6p46 · 8 ♐ 7a29 · 10 ♑ 8p29 · 13 ♒ 8a35 · 15 ♓ 6p49 · 18 ♈ 2a15 · 20 ♉ 6a25 · 22 ♊ 7a40 · 24 ♋ 7a16 · 26 ♌ 7a 6 · 28 ♍ 9a12 · 30 ♎ 3p...

☽ PHASES
3 ○ 9p31 · 7 ○ 9p12 · 12 ○ 12a 6 · 16 ○ 2p32 · 19 ○ 10p43 · 23 ○ 2p54 · 27 ● 2p54 · 30 ● 9p30

JAN 1929 – AUG 1929

	JAN 1929	FEB 1929	MAR 1929	APR 1929	MAY 1929	JUN 1929	JUL 1929	AUG 1929
☉ →	≈	♓	♈	♉	♊	♋	♌	♍
	20 7a42	18 10p 7	20 9p35	20 9a10	21 8a47	21 5p 0	23 3a53	23 10a41

☽ → SIGNS

- **JAN:** 1 ♎ 3p 8 · 3 ♏ 1a10 · 6 ♐ 1p50 · 8 ♑ 2a50 · 11 ≈ 2p33 · 14 ♓ 12a21 · 16 ♈ 8a 7 · 18 ♉ 1p37 · 20 ♊ 4p43 · 22 ♋ 5p56 · 24 ♌ 6p16 · 26 ♍ 7p47 · 29 ♎ 12a19 · 31 ♏ 8a57
- **FEB:** 2 ♐ 8p59 · 5 ♑ 10a 0 · 7 ≈ 9p34 · 10 ♓ 6a42 · 12 ♈ 1p41 · 14 ♉ 7p 2 · 16 ♊ 11p 1 · 19 ♋ 1a45 · 21 ♌ 3a41 · 23 ♍ 5a58 · 25 ♎ 10a15 · 27 ♏ 5p54
- **MAR:** 2 ♐ 5a 3 · 4 ♑ 5p55 · 7 ≈ 5a44 · 9 ♓ 2p44 · 11 ♈ 8p51 · 14 ♉ 1a 4 · 16 ♊ 4a23 · 18 ♋ 7a23 · 20 ♌ 10a27 · 22 ♍ 2p 5 · 24 ♎ 7p11 · 27 ♏ 2a49 · 29 ♐ 1p26
- **APR:** 1 ♑ 2a 2 · 3 ≈ 2p17 · 6 ♓ 12a26 · 8 ♈ 5a57 · 10 ♉ 9a17 · 12 ♊ 11a12 · 14 ♋ 1p 4 · 16 ♌ 3p50 · 18 ♍ 8p 5 · 21 ♎ 1a10 · 23 ♏ 10a34 · 25 ♐ 9p16 · 28 ♑ 9a43 · 30 ≈ 10p19
- **MAY:** 3 ♓ 8a51 · 5 ♈ 3p51 · 7 ♉ 7p18 · 9 ♊ 8p22 · 11 ♋ 8p44 · 13 ♌ 10p 3 · 15 ♍ 1a33 · 18 ♎ 7a52 · 20 ♏ 4p53 · 23 ♐ 4a 3 · 25 ♑ 4p34 · 28 ≈ 5a17 · 30 ♓ 4p37
- **JUN:** 2 ♈ 12a58 · 4 ♉ 5a34 · 6 ♊ 6a57 · 8 ♋ 6a35 · 10 ♌ 6a25 · 12 ♍ 8a20 · 14 ♎ 1p38 · 16 ♏ 10p32 · 19 ♐ 10a 3 · 21 ♑ 10p45 · 24 ≈ 11a24 · 26 ♓ 10p59 · 29 ♈ 8a21
- **JUL:** 1 ♉ 2p31 · 3 ♊ 5p14 · 5 ♋ 5p20 · 7 ♌ 4p37 · 9 ♍ 5p 9 · 11 ♎ 8p54 · 14 ♏ 4a 0 · 16 ♐ 4p47 · 19 ♑ 5a20 · 21 ≈ 5p22 · 24 ♓ 4a39 · 26 ♈ 2p13 · 28 ♉ 9p25 · 31 ♊ 1a43
- **AUG:** 2 ♋ 3a15 · 4 ♌ 3a11 · 6 ♍ 3a22 · 8 ♎ 5a55 · 10 ♏ 12p22 · 12 ♐ 10p44 · 15 ♑ 11a20 · 17 ≈ 11p50 · 20 ♓ 10a46 · 22 ♈ 7p47 · 25 ♉ 2a55 · 27 ♊ 8a 3 · 29 ♋ 11a 4 · 31 ♌ 12p26

☽ PHASES

- **JAN:** 2 ◐ 1p44 · 6 ◑ 4p 3 · 10 ● 7p28 · 14 ☽ 5p55 · 18 ○ 10a15 · 21 ○ 8p 0 · 25 ○ 2a 9 · 28 ◐ 12p17
- **FEB:** 1 ◐ 9a10 · 5 ◑ 12p58 · 8 ● 12p55 · 13 ☽ 6a21 · 16 ○ 7p22 · 20 ○ 4a54 · 23 ○ 1p58 · 27 ○ 5a14
- **MAR:** 3 ◐ 6a 9 · 7 ◑ 8a40 · 11 ● 3a36 · 13 ☽ 4p12 · 18 ○ 2a41 · 21 ○ 1p16 · 25 ○ 2a46 · 28 ○ 11p31
- **APR:** 2 ◐ 2a29 · 6 ◑ 1a41 · 9 ● 3p32 · 13 ☽ 12a 7 · 16 ○ 9a 9 · 19 ○ 10p 5 · 23 ○ 4p47 · 27 ◐ 5p50
- **MAY:** 1 ◐ 8p25 · 5 ◑ 3p33 · 9 ● 1a 7 · 12 ☽ 6a53 · 15 ○ 3p56 · 19 ○ 8a23 · 23 ○ 7a50 · 27 ○ 10a49 · 31 ○ 11a13
- **JUN:** 4 ◑ 2a29 · 7 ● 8a56 · 10 ☽ 1p30 · 13 ○ 10a14 · 17 ○ 8p47 · 20 ○ 11p15 · 26 ○ 1a38 · 29 ◐ 10p53
- **JUL:** 3 ☽ 10a59 · 6 ● 3p47 · 9 ◑ 9p 2 · 13 ○ 11a 5 · 17 ○ 11a19 · 21 ○ 2p20 · 25 ○ 9p 8 · 29 ☽ 7a55
- **AUG:** 1 ◐ 5p47 · 4 ◑ 10p40 · 8 ● 6a40 · 12 ☽ 1a 1 · 16 ○ 3a31 · 20 ○ 4a42 · 24 ○ 2a37 · 30 ◑ 11p51

SEP 1929 – APR 1930

	SEP 1929	OCT 1929	NOV 1929	DEC 1929	JAN 1930	FEB 1930	MAR 1930	APR 1930
☉ →	♎	♏	♐	♑	≈	♓	♈	♉
	23 7a52	23 4p41	22 1p48	22 2a53	20 1p33	19 4a 0	21 3a30	20 3p 6

☽ → SIGNS

- **SEP:** 2 ♍ 1p26 · 4 ♎ 3p51 · 6 ♏ 9p20 · 9 ♐ 6a38 · 11 ♑ 6p44 · 14 ≈ 7a16 · 16 ♓ 6p 7 · 19 ♈ 2a30 · 21 ♉ 8a45 · 23 ♊ 1p25 · 25 ♋ 4p52 · 27 ♌ 7p28 · 29 ♍ 9p52
- **OCT:** 2 ♎ 1a 9 · 4 ♏ 6a40 · 6 ♐ 3p18 · 9 ♑ 2a49 · 11 ≈ 3p25 · 14 ♓ 2a40 · 16 ♈ 11a 2 · 18 ♉ 4p29 · 20 ♊ 7p54 · 22 ♋ 10p24 · 25 ♌ 12a55 · 27 ♍ 4a 8 · 29 ♎ 8a39 · 31 ♏ 3p 1
- **NOV:** 2 ♐ 11p47 · 5 ♑ 10a57 · 7 ≈ 11p33 · 10 ♓ 11a30 · 12 ♈ 8p43 · 15 ♉ 2a19 · 17 ♊ 4a53 · 19 ♋ 5a53 · 21 ♌ 6a58 · 23 ♍ 9a31 · 25 ♎ 2p23 · 27 ♏ 9p40 · 30 ♐ 7a 8
- **DEC:** 2 ♑ 6p25 · 5 ≈ 6a57 · 7 ♓ 7p27 · 10 ♈ 5a57 · 12 ♉ 12p49 · 14 ♊ 3p49 · 16 ♋ 4p 4 · 18 ♌ 3p34 · 20 ♍ 4p22 · 22 ♎ 8p 3 · 25 ♏ 3a11 · 27 ♐ 1p11 · 30 ♑ 12a56
- **JAN:** 1 ≈ 1p29 · 4 ♓ 2a 4 · 6 ♈ 1p27 · 9 ♉ 9p55 · 11 ♊ 2a34 · 13 ♋ 3a55 · 15 ♌ 3a37 · 17 ♍ 1a56 · 19 ♎ 3a44 · 21 ♏ 9a25 · 23 ♐ 6p56 · 26 ♑ 6a25 · 28 ≈ 7p35 · 31 ♓ 7a59
- **FEB:** 2 ♈ 7p23 · 5 ♉ 4a48 · 7 ♊ 11a 8 · 9 ♋ 1p55 · 11 ♌ 2p 0 · 13 ♍ 1p14 · 15 ♎ 1p50 · 17 ♏ 5p44 · 20 ♐ 1a48 · 22 ♑ 1p13 · 25 ≈ 1a57 · 27 ♓ 2p13
- **MAR:** 2 ♈ 1a 8 · 4 ♉ 10a18 · 6 ♊ 5p16 · 8 ♋ 9p34 · 10 ♌ 11p25 · 12 ♍ 11p54 · 15 ♎ 12a43 · 17 ♏ 3a46 · 19 ♐ 10a23 · 21 ♑ 8p40 · 24 ≈ 9a 5 · 26 ♓ 9p24 · 29 ♈ 8a 0 · 31 ♉ 4p23
- **APR:** 2 ♊ 10p42 · 5 ♋ 3a11 · 7 ♌ 6a 9 · 9 ♍ 8a 4 · 11 ♎ 10a17 · 13 ♏ 1p45 · 15 ♐ 7p49 · 18 ♑ 5a 7 · 20 ≈ 4p58 · 23 ♓ 5a23 · 25 ♈ 4p10 · 28 ♉ 12a 8 · 30 ♊ 5a26

☽ PHASES

- **SEP:** 3 ● 6a47 · 7 ○ 7p18 · 10 ○ 5p57 · 14 ○ 8p40 · 18 ○ 6p16 · 22 ○ 9a40 · 25 ○ 9p 7 · 29 ◑ 6a25
- **OCT:** 2 ● 5p19 · 6 ○ 11a16 · 10 ○ 1p 5 · 14 ○ 6p 1 · 18 ○ 7a16 · 21 ○ 5p56 · 25 ○ 3a21 · 28 ● 2p49
- **NOV:** 1 ◑ 7a 1 · 5 ● 6a 3 · 9 ☽ 4a41 · 12 ○ 7p14 · 16 ○ 6a38 · 20 ○ 2a13 · 23 ○ 9p27 · 27 ◑ 2a11 · 30 ○ 11p48
- **DEC:** 2 ● 2a16 · 6 ◑ 4a41 · 9 ☽ 9p 9 · 12 ○ 10p44 · 16 ○ 6a38 · 22 ○ 9p27 · 26 ● 4p58 · 30 ● 6p41
- **JAN:** 3 ◐ 10p 9 · 7 ◑ 10p11 · 11 ● 12p16 · 14 ○ 9p57 · 17 ○ 9p57 · 20 ○ 1a 7 · 25 ◑ 10a40 · 29 ● 2p 7
- **FEB:** 2 ◐ 4p 5 · 6 ◑ 12p26 · 9 ● 11p14 · 13 ○ 3a38 · 17 ○ 1a 0 · 20 ○ 3a44 · 24 ◑ 5a55 · 28 ● 8a32
- **MAR:** 4 ◐ 6a55 · 7 ◑ 11p 0 · 11 ● 10a13 · 14 ○ 1p58 · 18 ○ 1a 0 · 21 ○ 10p12 · 25 ◑ 1a 9 · 28 ● 12a46
- **APR:** 2 ◐ 6p13 · 6 ◑ 8a24 · 9 ● 3p14 · 13 ○ 12a48 · 16 ○ 4p46 · 20 ○ 5p 8 · 24 ◑ 7p 1 · 28 ● 9p 9

MAY 1930 – DEC 1930

	MAY 1930	JUN 1930	JUL 1930	AUG 1930	SEP 1930	OCT 1930	NOV 1930	DEC 1930
☉ →	♊	♋	♌	♍	♎	♏	♐	♑
	21 2p42	21 10p53	23 9a42	23 4p26	23 1p36	23 10p26	22 7p35	22 8a40

☽ → SIGNS

- **MAY:** 2 ♋ 8a54 · 4 ♌ 11a32 · 6 ♍ 2p10 · 8 ♎ 5p30 · 10 ♏ 10p 6 · 13 ♐ 4a39 · 15 ♑ 1p39 · 18 ≈ 1a 3 · 20 ♓ 1p34 · 23 ♈ 12a55 · 25 ♉ 9a15 · 27 ♊ 2p 7 · 29 ♋ 4p25 · 31 ♌ 5p45
- **JUN:** 2 ♍ 7p37 · 4 ♎ 11p 4 · 7 ♏ 4a30 · 9 ♐ 11a56 · 11 ♑ 9p20 · 14 ≈ 8a39 · 16 ♓ 9p12 · 19 ♈ 9a15 · 21 ♉ 7p39 · 24 ♊ 2a 0 · 26 ♋ 5a57 · 28 ♌ 6a25 · 30 ♍ 6a28
- **JUL:** 2 ♎ 4a47 · 4 ♏ 9a56 · 6 ♐ 5p49 · 9 ♑ 3a49 · 11 ≈ 3p23 · 14 ♓ 3a57 · 16 ♈ 4p26 · 19 ♉ 2a54 · 21 ♊ 9a39 · 23 ♋ 12p22 · 25 ♌ 12p19 · 27 ♍ 11a34 · 29 ♎ 11a38 · 31 ♏ 4p 5
- **AUG:** 2 ♐ 11p24 · 4 ♑ 9a34 · 6 ≈ 9p28 · 9 ♓ 10a 3 · 12 ♈ 10p32 · 14 ♉ 9a38 · 17 ♊ 5p46 · 19 ♋ 11p58 · 21 ♌ 10p13 · 23 ♍ 9p58 · 25 ♎ 10p 7 · 28 ♏ 2a34 · 30 ♐ 4p 5
- **SEP:** 2 ♑ 3p35 · 4 ≈ 3a27 · 6 ♓ 4p 6 · 9 ♈ 4a21 · 11 ♉ 3p18 · 14 ♊ 12a 1 · 16 ♋ 5a42 · 18 ♌ 8a18 · 20 ♍ 8a45 · 22 ♎ 8a43 · 24 ♏ 10a 7 · 26 ♐ 2p34 · 28 ♑ 10p48
- **OCT:** 1 ≈ 10a 9 · 4 ♓ 10p48 · 6 ♈ 10a52 · 9 ♉ 9p14 · 11 ♊ 5p 5 · 14 ♋ 11a58 · 16 ♌ 2a27 · 18 ♍ 5a36 · 21 ♎ 4p 3? · 23 ♏ 7a27 · 25 ♐ 9p24 · 28 ♑ 8a 2 · 31 ♓ 6a23
- **NOV:** 2 ♈ 6p34 · 5 ♉ 4a37 · 7 ♊ 11a58 · 9 ♋ 5p 5 · 11 ♌ 8p 5 · 14 ♍ 11p42 · 16 ♎ 2a27 · 18 ♏ 5a36 · 20 ♐ 10a 0 · 22 ♑ 4p42 · 25 ≈ 2a23 · 27 ♓ 2p32 · 30 ♈ 3a 6
- **DEC:** 2 ♉ 2p31 · 4 ♊ 8p32 · 7 ♋ 12a31 · 9 ♌ 2a52 · 11 ♍ 5a 4 · 13 ♎ 8a 5 · 16 ♏ 12p19 · 18 ♐ 5p54 · 20 ♑ 1a11 · 22 ♈ 10a43 · 25 ≈ 10p35 · 27 ♓ 11a29 · 30 ♉ 10p51

☽ PHASES

- **MAY:** 2 ☽ 2a23 · 5 ● 11a53 · 8 ○ 10p18 · 12 ○ 12p29 · 16 ○ 9a 9 · 20 ○ 11a21 · 24 ◑ 10a38 · 28 ● 12a36 · 31 ☽ 8a28
- **JUN:** 3 ○ 4p56 · 7 ○ 6a15 · 11 ○ 1a11 · 15 ○ 1a35 · 19 ○ 4a 0 · 22 ◑ 11p32 · 26 ● 8a46 · 30 ☽ 1p53
- **JUL:** 2 ○ 11p 3 · 6 ○ 3p59 · 10 ○ 3p 1 · 14 ○ 5p34 · 18 ○ 6p29 · 22 ◑ 9a52 · 25 ● 3p42 · 27 ◐ 4a19 · 30 ☽ 8p 5
- **AUG:** 1 ○ 7a26 · 5 ○ 4a 5 · 9 ○ 5a57 · 13 ○ 6a30 · 17 ○ 1a35 · 20 ◑ 10p37 · 23 ● 3p27 · 27 ☽ 4a19 · 30 ○ 6p56
- **SEP:** 3 ○ 6p51 · 7 ○ 9p48 · 11 ○ 10p19 · 15 ◑ 4p12 · 18 ◑ 9a 1 · 22 ● 6a41 · 25 ☽ 5p52 · 29 ○ 4a22
- **OCT:** 3 ○ 12p12 · 7 ○ 1p55 · 11 ○ 10a13 · 14 ◑ 7a27 · 18 ◑ 9a 1 · 22 ● 4p47 · 25 ☽ 5p28 · 28 ○ 1a17
- **NOV:** 2 ○ 7a23 · 5 ○ 5a28 · 9 ○ 8p26 · 13 ◑ 7a27 · 16 ◑ 5p28 · 20 ● 5a21 · 24 ☽ 2a23 · 28 ○ 7p21
- **DEC:** 2 ○ 2a55 · 5 ○ 7p40 · 9 ○ 5a37 · 13 ○ 3p 6 · 16 ◑ 3a40 · 20 ● 8p24 · 23 ☽ 7p21 · 27 ○ 10p58 · 30 ○ 9p 2

JAN 1931 – AUG 1931

	JAN 1931	FEB 1931	MAR 1931	APR 1931	MAY 1931	JUN 1931	JUL 1931	AUG 1931
☉ →	♒ 20 7p18	♓ 19 9a40	♈ 21 9a 6	♉ 20 8p40	♊ 21 8p15	♋ 22 4a28	♌ 23 3p21	♍ 23 10p10

JAN 1931 D→SIGNS
1 ♊ 6a34 · 3 ♋ 10a21 · 5 ♌ 11a32 · 7 ♍ 12p 6 · 9 ♎ 1p48 · 11 ♏ 5p40 · 13 ♐ 11p50 · 16 ♑ 8a 1 · 18 ♒ 6p 4 · 21 ♓ 5a55 · 23 ♈ 6p55 · 26 ♉ 7a10 · 28 ♊ 4p18 · 30 ♋ 9p 9

FEB 1931 D→SIGNS
1 ♌ 10p24 · 3 ♍ 9p56 · 5 ♎ 9p54 · 8 ♏ 12a 4 · 10 ♐ 5a21 · 12 ♑ 1p39 · 15 ♒ 12a14 · 17 ♓ 12p23 · 20 ♈ 1a21 · 22 ♉ 1p54 · 25 ♊ 12a13 · 27 ♋ 6a47

MAR 1931 D→SIGNS
1 ♌ 9a25 · 3 ♍ 9a21 · 5 ♎ 8a32 · 7 ♏ 9a 2 · 9 ♐ 12p30 · 11 ♑ 7p39 · 14 ♒ 6a 3 · 16 ♓ 6p26 · 19 ♈ 7a24 · 21 ♉ 7p44 · 24 ♊ 6a19 · 26 ♋ 2p 4 · 28 ♌ 6p29 · 30 ♍ 7p58

APR 1931 D→SIGNS
1 ♎ 7p49 · 3 ♏ 7p50 · 5 ♐ 9p52 · 8 ♑ 3a20 · 10 ♒ 12p49 · 13 ♓ 12a49 · 15 ♈ 1p48 · 18 ♉ 1a50 · 20 ♊ 11a56 · 22 ♋ 7p42 · 25 ♌ 1a 4 · 27 ♍ 4a10 · 29 ♎ 5a35

MAY 1931 D→SIGNS
1 ♏ 6a26 · 3 ♐ 8a14 · 5 ♑ 12p35 · 7 ♒ 8p36 · 10 ♓ 8a 2 · 12 ♈ 8p56 · 15 ♉ 8a54 · 17 ♊ 6p26 · 20 ♋ 1a26 · 22 ♌ 6a27 · 24 ♍ 10a 7 · 26 ♎ 12p51 · 28 ♏ 3p 7 · 30 ♐ 5p48

JUN 1931 D→SIGNS
2 ♑ 10p 7 · 4 ♒ 5a23 · 6 ♓ 4p 1 · 9 ♈ 4a44 · 11 ♉ 4p54 · 14 ♊ 2a21 · 16 ♋ 8a38 · 18 ♌ 12p36 · 20 ♍ 3p32 · 22 ♎ 6p23 · 24 ♏ 9p34 · 27 ♐ 1a26 · 29 ♑ 6a35

JUL 1931 D→SIGNS
1 ♒ 1p56 · 4 ♓ 12a 9 · 6 ♈ 12p40 · 9 ♉ 1a14 · 11 ♊ 11a14 · 13 ♋ 5p30 · 15 ♌ 8p41 · 17 ♍ 10p22 · 19 ♎ 12a 6 · 22 ♏ 2a56 · 24 ♐ 7a18 · 26 ♑ 1p22 · 28 ♒ 9p24 · 31 ♓ 7a45

AUG 1931 D→SIGNS
2 ♈ 8p10 · 5 ♉ 9a 5 · 7 ♊ 8p 1 · 10 ♋ 3a10 · 12 ♌ 6a31 · 14 ♍ 7a25 · 16 ♎ 7a45 · 18 ♏ 9a10 · 20 ♐ 12p47 · 22 ♑ 6p58 · 25 ♒ 3a38 · 27 ♓ 2p27 · 30 ♈ 2a56

D PHASES

JAN	FEB	MAR	APR	MAY	JUN	JUL	AUG
4 ○ 8a15	2 ○ 7p26	1 ○ 12a41	2) 3p 5	2 ○ 12a14	4 ○ 12a57	3 ○ 4p 8	2 ○ 8a33
7 ○ 2p38	6 ○ 12a17	4 ○ 5a36	5 ○ 10p31	5 ○ 11a 8	8 ○ 1a18	7 ○ 6p51	6 ○ 11a28
11 ○ 12a 9	9 ○ 11a 9	7 ○ 10a54	9 ○ 3p15	9 (7a48	12 (3a30	11 (6p 2	10 (6a28
14 ● 4p 2	13 ● 6a40	11 (11p16	11 (5p 6	13 (10a56	15 ● 10p 1	15 ● 10p 9	13 (3p27
18 ● 1p35	17 ● 8a11	17 ● 7p59	17 ● 7p59	17 ● 10a28	19 ● 9a37	18 ● 3p14	16 ● 9p 7
22 ● 4p14	21 ● 12p 3	21 ● 5p42	21 ● 5p42	21 ● 2a55	23 ● 7p23	22 ● 12a16	20 ● 6a36
26 ○ 7p 5	25 ○ 11a42	25 ● 8a40	25 ● 8a40	25 ○ 2p39	26 ○ 6a 6	25 ○ 1p25	23 ○ 11p 4
30 ○ 12p25		29 ○ 10a10	28 ○ 5p36	29 ○ 11p54	29 ○ 7p47	29 ○ 7a47	27 ○ 10p 9

SEP 1931 – APR 1932

	SEP 1931	OCT 1931	NOV 1931	DEC 1931	JAN 1932	FEB 1932	MAR 1932	APR 1932
☉ →	♎ 23 7p23	♏ 24 4a16	♐ 23 1a25	♑ 22 2p30	♒ 21 1a 7	♓ 19 3p28	♈ 20 2p53	♉ 20 2a28

SEP 1931 D→SIGNS
1 ♉ 3p59 · 4 ♊ 3a43 · 6 ♋ 12p15 · 8 ♌ 4p47 · 10 ♍ 6p 4 · 12 ♎ 5p43 · 14 ♏ 5p40 · 16 ♐ 7p39 · 19 ♑ 12a47 · 21 ♒ 9a18 · 23 ♓ 8p28 · 26 ♈ 9a 9 · 28 ♉ 10p 7

OCT 1931 D→SIGNS
1 ♊ 10a 3 · 3 ♋ 7p37 · 6 ♌ 1a49 · 8 ♍ 4a34 · 10 ♎ 4a50 · 12 ♏ 4a17 · 14 ♐ 4a51 · 16 ♑ 8a18 · 18 ♒ 3p39 · 21 ♓ 2a32 · 23 ♈ 3p21 · 26 ♉ 4a12 · 28 ♊ 3p47 · 31 ♋ 1a26

NOV 1931 D→SIGNS
2 ♌ 8a39 · 4 ♍ 1p 8 · 6 ♎ 3p 3 · 8 ♏ 3p21 · 10 ♐ 3p39 · 12 ♑ 5p52 · 14 ♒ 11p40 · 17 ♓ 9a32 · 19 ♈ 10p 8 · 22 ♉ 11a 0 · 24 ♊ 10p11 · 27 ♋ 6a 6 · 29 ♌ 2p 6

DEC 1931 D→SIGNS
1 ♍ 7p16 · 3 ♎ 10p44 · 6 ♏ 12a43 · 8 ♐ 2a 4 · 10 ♑ 4a17 · 12 ♒ 9a 9 · 14 ♓ 5p50 · 17 ♈ 5a49 · 19 ♉ 6p45 · 22 ♊ 5a59 · 24 ♋ 2p 5 · 26 ♌ 8p23 · 29 ♍ 12a41 · 31 ♎ 4a17

JAN 1932 D→SIGNS
1 ♏ 7a24 · 4 ♐ 10a15 · 6 ♑ 1p37 · 8 ♒ 6p43 · 11 ♓ 2a49 · 13 ♈ 2p 7 · 16 ♉ 3a 7 · 18 ♊ 2p47 · 20 ♋ 11p22 · 23 ♌ 4a39 · 25 ♍ 7a46 · 27 ♎ 10a 7 · 29 ♏ 12p43 · 31 ♐ 4p 7

FEB 1932 D→SIGNS
2 ♑ 8p39 · 5 ♒ 2a48 · 7 ♓ 11a15 · 9 ♈ 10p17 · 12 ♉ 11a 5 · 15 ♊ 11p27 · 17 ♋ 9a 2 · 19 ♌ 5p25 · 22 ♍ 4a18 · 25 ♎ 7p20 · 27 ♏ 9p38

MAR 1932 D→SIGNS
1 ♑ 2a 6 · 3 ♒ 9a 0 · 5 ♓ 6p15 · 8 ♈ 5a35 · 10 ♉ 6p19 · 13 ♊ 7a 3 · 15 ♋ 5p46 · 18 ♌ 12a56 · 20 ♍ 4a18 · 22 ♎ 4a56 · 24 ♏ 4a35 · 26 ♐ 5a 6 · 28 ♑ 8a 8 · 30 ♒ 2p30

APR 1932 D→SIGNS
2 ♓ 12a 5 · 4 ♈ 11a53 · 7 ♉ 12a43 · 9 ♊ 1p27 · 11 ♋ 12a47 · 14 ♌ 9a22 · 16 ♍ 2p21 · 18 ♎ 4p 0 · 20 ♏ 3p33 · 22 ♐ 2p57 · 24 ♑ 4p15 · 26 ♒ 9p 4 · 29 ♓ 5a55

D PHASES

SEP	OCT	NOV	DEC	JAN	FEB	MAR	APR
1 ○ 1a29	4 ○ 3p15	3 ○ 2a17	2 ○ 11a50	4 (6a43	2 (4p51	3 (4a32	1 (6p13
5 ○ 2a21	8 (3a 3	6 (12p19	5 (9p25	7 (6p28	6 (6p45	7 (2a44	5 ● 8p21
8 (5p16	11 (8a 6	9 (5p55	9 (5a16	11 ● 1p 8	10 ● 10a11	11 ● 5a51	9 ○ 11p41
11 (11p26	14 ● 1p58	13 ● 2a29	12 ● 6p18	15 ○ 3p55	14 ○ 1p15	14 ○ 7a41	13 ○ 10p15
15 ● 4a24	18 ● 4a20	16 ● 9p13	16 ● 5p43	19 ○ 4p57	18 ○ 10a47	18 ○ 3p29	16 ○ 11a17
18 ● 3p37	22 ○ 4a50	20 ○ 10a30	20 ○ 9p14	23 ○ 8a44	21 ○ 9p 7	22 ○ 7a37	20 ○ 4p27
22 ○ 12p 6	26 ○ 8a34	24 ○ 2a10	24 ○ 6p23	26 ○ 6p44	25 ○ 12p29	25 ○ 10p43	23 ○ 9p19
26 ○ 2p45	30 ○ 8a42	28 ○ 6p38	28 ○ 8a50	30 ○ 4a32	28 ○ 1p 3	28 ○ 10p43	28 ○ 10a14
30 ○ 5p51			31 ○ 8p23				

MAY 1932 – DEC 1932

	MAY 1932	JUN 1932	JUL 1932	AUG 1932	SEP 1932	OCT 1932	NOV 1932	DEC 1932
☉ →	♊ 21 2a 6	♋ 21 10a22	♌ 22 9p18	♍ 23 4a 6	♎ 23 1a16	♏ 23 10a 4	♐ 22 7a10	♑ 21 8p14

MAY 1932 D→SIGNS
1 ♈ 5p46 · 4 ♉ 6a46 · 6 ♊ 7p20 · 9 ♋ 6a34 · 11 ♌ 3p46 · 13 ♍ 10p13 · 16 ♎ 1a32 · 18 ♏ 2a15 · 20 ♐ 1a47 · 22 ♑ 2a12 · 24 ♒ 5a30 · 26 ♓ 12p57 · 29 ♈ 12a 9 · 31 ♉ 1p 4

JUN 1932 D→SIGNS
1 ♊ 1a32 · 3 ♋ 12p21 · 5 ♌ 9p14 · 8 ♍ 4a 6 · 10 ♎ 8a11 · 12 ♏ 11a 0 · 14 ♐ 11a45 · 16 ♑ 12p31 · 18 ♒ 3p12 · 20 ♓ 9p25 · 23 ♈ 7a34 · 25 ♉ 8p 8 · 28 ♊ 8a35

JUL 1932 D→SIGNS
2 ♋ 7p 6 · 5 ♌ 3a18 · 7 ♍ 9a33 · 9 ♎ 2p12 · 11 ♏ 5p27 · 13 ♐ 7p38 · 15 ♑ 10p 4 · 18 ♒ 12a44 · 20 ♓ 6a34 · 22 ♈ 3p52 · 25 ♉ 3a54 · 27 ♊ 4p26 · 30 ♋ 3a 7

AUG 1932 D→SIGNS
1 ♌ 10a57 · 3 ♍ 4p15 · 5 ♎ 7p56 · 7 ♏ 10p49 · 9 ♐ 1a32 · 12 ♑ 4a38 · 14 ♒ 8a54 · 16 ♓ 3p13 · 18 ♈ 12a44 · 21 ♉ 11a56 · 23 ♊ 12a33 · 26 ♋ 11a50 · 28 ♌ 8p 3 · 31 ♍ 2a58

SEP 1932 D→SIGNS
2 ♎ 3a32 · 4 ♏ 5a 6 · 6 ♐ 6a59 · 8 ♑ 10a11 · 10 ♒ 2p35 · 12 ♓ 10p31 · 15 ♈ 8a 1 · 17 ♉ 7p33 · 20 ♊ 8a13 · 22 ♋ 8p13 · 25 ♌ 5a32 · 27 ♍ 11a 7 · 29 ♎ 1p22

OCT 1932 D→SIGNS
1 ♏ 1p44 · 3 ♐ 2p 2 · 5 ♑ 4p 0 · 7 ♒ 8p43 · 10 ♓ 4a26 · 12 ♈ 2p35 · 15 ♉ 2a24 · 17 ♊ 3p 2 · 20 ♋ 3a26 · 22 ♌ 1p57 · 24 ♍ 8p21 · 27 ♎ 12a30 · 29 ♏ 1a26

NOV 1932 D→SIGNS
1 ♐ 1p54 · 3 ♑ 3a 6 · 6 ♒ 8p 4 · 8 ♓ 8a24 · 11 ♈ 9p13 · 13 ♉ 9p35 · 16 ♊ 9p13 · 18 ♋ 8p35 · 20 ♌ 5a 8 · 23 ♎ 11a38 · 25 ♏ 10a58 · 27 ♐ 10a58 · 29 ♑ 11a54

DEC 1932 D→SIGNS
1 ♑ 11a54 · 3 ♒ 5p 8 · 6 ♓ 2a35 · 8 ♈ 2p41 · 11 ♉ 3a26 · 13 ♊ 3p28 · 16 ♋ 2a13 · 18 ♌ 11a 9 · 20 ♍ 5p31 · 22 ♎ 9p42 · 24 ♏ 11p31 · 26 ♐ 10p23 · 28 ♑ 10p23 · 31 ♒ 2a16

D PHASES

MAY	JUN	JUL	AUG	SEP	OCT	NOV	DEC
1 ○ 9a40	4 ● 4a16	3 ● 5p19	2 ● 4a42	3) 11p10	3) 5a56	1) 2p21	1) 1a23
5 ○ 1p11	8) 1a23	7) 9a59	5) 4p53	7 ○ 7a49	6 ○ 3p 5	5 ○ 1a50	4 ○ 4p45
9) 2p11	11 ○ 4p39	10 ○ 10p 7	9 ○ 2a40	10 ○ 8a17	10 ○ 8a17	9 ○ 9p 3	8 ○ 6p 6
13 ○ 9a 2	15 ○ 1a36	13 ○ 1a36	12 ○ 12p51	14 ○ 4p 6	13 ○ 5a 9	13 ○ 9p20	12 ○ 9p20
16 ○ 7p27	18 ○ 7a38	17 ○ 4p 6	16 ○ 2a41	18 ○ 11a26	18 ○ 11a26	17 ○ 9p 9	16 ○ 9p20
20 ○ 12a24	21 ○ 6p23	21 ○ 7a57	20 ○ 11p46	22 ○ 7p47	22 ○ 12p13	20 ○ 5a 8	20 ○ 3p22
23 ○ 7a 1	25 ○ 9p36	25 ○ 8a41	24 ○ 2a21	26 (3p 1	26 (3a45	24 (3p 8	24 (1a11
26 ○ 11p54	29 (6p30	29 (10a17	28 (1a 9	30 ● 12a29	29 ● 9a56	27 ● 7p43	27 ● 6a22
31 (2a 5			31 ● 2p54				31) 3p32

JAN 1933 – AUG 1933

	JAN 1933	FEB 1933	MAR 1933	APR 1933	MAY 1933	JUN 1933	JUL 1933	AUG 1933
☉ →	♒	♓	♈	♉	♊	♋	♌	♍
	20 6a53	18 9p16	20 8p43	20 8a18	21 7a57	21 4p12	23 3a 5	23 9a52

☽→SIGNS

JAN: 2 ♈ 10a13 · 4 ♉ 9p36 · 7 ♊ 10a19 · 9 ♋ 10p16 · 12 ♌ 8a26 · 14 ♍ 4p42 · 16 ♎ 11p 3 · 19 ♏ 3a24 · 21 ♐ 5a54 · 23 ♑ 7a17 · 25 ♒ 8a56 · 27 ♓ 12p31 · 29 ♈ 7p21

FEB: 1 ♉ 5a40 · 3 ♊ 6p 5 · 6 ♋ 6a13 · 8 ♌ 4p16 · 10 ♍ 11p43 · 13 ♎ 4a59 · 15 ♏ 8a46 · 17 ♐ 11a42 · 19 ♑ 2p22 · 21 ♒ 5p29 · 23 ♓ 9p56 · 26 ♈ 4a42 · 28 ♉ 2p20

MAR: 3 ♊ 2a17 · 5 ♋ 2p43 · 8 ♌ 1a18 · 10 ♍ 8a42 · 12 ♎ 1p 3 · 14 ♏ 3p27 · 16 ♐ 5p18 · 18 ♑ 7p47 · 20 ♒ 11p39 · 23 ♓ 5a15 · 25 ♈ 12p49 · 27 ♉ 10p31 · 30 ♊ 10a13

APR: 1 ♋ 10p50 · 4 ♌ 10a16 · 6 ♍ 6p33 · 8 ♎ 11p 0 · 11 ♏ 1a 3 · 13 ♐ 12a52 · 15 ♑ 5a 2 · 17 ♒ 7p14 · 19 ♓ 10a54 · 21 ♈ 7p14 · 24 ♉ 5a31 · 26 ♊ 5p18 · 29 ♋ 5a58

MAY: 1 ♌ 6p 6 · 3 ♍ 3a41 · 5 ♎ 9a17 · 8 ♏ 11a 7 · 10 ♐ 10a43 · 12 ♑ 10a15 · 14 ♒ 11a45 · 16 ♓ 4p33 · 18 ♈ 1a53 · 21 ♉ 11a26 · 23 ♊ 11p31 · 26 ♋ 12p12 · 29 ♌ 12p33 · 31 ♍ 11a 6

JUN: 2 ♎ 6p15 · 4 ♏ 9p25 · 6 ♐ 9p32 · 8 ♑ 8p33 · 10 ♒ 8p41 · 12 ♓ 11p49 · 15 ♈ 6a50 · 17 ♉ 5p12 · 20 ♊ 5a35 · 22 ♋ 6p 6 · 25 ♌ 6p17 · 27 ♍ 5p 1 · 30 ♎ 1a11

JUL: 2 ♏ 5a57 · 4 ♐ 7a31 · 6 ♑ 7a15 · 8 ♒ 7a 5 · 10 ♓ 9a 1 · 12 ♈ 2p31 · 15 ♉ 11a44 · 17 ♊ 11a44 · 20 ♋ 12p19 · 22 ♌ 10p35 · 24 ♍ 6a44 · 26 ♎ 12p21 · 29 ♏ 3p26 · 31 ♐ 9p26

AUG: 2 ♑ 4p40 · 4 ♒ 5p22 · 6 ♓ 7p10 · 9 ♈ 11p40 · 11 ♉ 7a44 · 13 ♊ 6p57 · 16 ♋ 7a32 · 18 ♌ 7p22 · 21 ♍ 5a 7 · 23 ♎ 12p29 · 25 ♏ 5p37 · 27 ♐ 9p21 · 29 ♑ 11p52

☽ PHASES

JAN: 3 ● 11a23 · 7 ○ 2p32 · 11 ○ 3p35 · 15 ○ 11a12 · 19 ○ 1a15 · 22 ☾ 10a15 · 25 ● 6p19 · 29 ☽ 8a30

FEB: 2 ● 8a16 · 6 ○ 1a 2 · 10 ● 8a 0 · 15 ○ 9a55 · 17 ○ 9a 8 · 22 ☾ 7p 6 · 24 ● 7a44 · 28 ☽ 3a10

MAR: 4 ● 5a23 · 8 ○ 5a55 · 11 ● 9p45 · 16 ○ 3a37 · 18 ○ 4p 4 · 22 ☾ 4a35 · 25 ● 10p20 · 29 ☽ 10p 6

APR: 3 ● 12a56 · 6 ○ 9p53 · 8 ○ 8a37 · 13 ○ 2p20 · 16 ○ 11p17 · 20 ☾ 3p20 · 24 ● 1p38 · 28 ☽ 4p 0

MAY: 2 ● 5p39 · 6 ○ 10a22 · 9 ○ 5p 4 · 16 ○ 9p21 · 16 ○ 7a50 · 20 ☾ 3a38 · 24 ● 5a 7 · 28 ☽ 8a 1

JUN: 1 ● 6a53 · 4 ○ 7p36 · 8 ○ 1a44 · 11 ○ 4a58 · 15 ○ 4p 5 · 18 ☾ 5p32 · 22 ● 8p22 · 26 ☽ 8a44 · 30 ● 4p40

JUL: 4 ○ 2a26 · 7 ○ 6a50 · 10 ○ 2p16 · 14 ○ 7a23 · 18 ☾ 8a53 · 22 ● 11a 3 · 26 ☽ 8a44 · 29 ○ 11p43

AUG: 2 ○ 8a 9 · 5 ○ 2p31 · 9 ○ 1a52 · 12 ○ 10p49 · 17 ☾ 1a25 · 21 ● 12a48 · 24 ☽ 5p37 · 28 ● 5p13 · 31 ○ 2p 7

SEP 1933 – APR 1934

	SEP 1933	OCT 1933	NOV 1933	DEC 1933	JAN 1934	FEB 1934	MAR 1934	APR 1934
☉ →	♎	♏	♐	♑	♒	♓	♈	♉
	23 7a 1	23 3p48	22 12p54	22 1a58	20 12p37	19 3a 2	21 2a28	20 2p 0

☽→SIGNS

SEP: 1 ♒ 1a59 · 3 ♓ 4a44 · 5 ♈ 9a14 · 7 ♉ 4p35 · 10 ♊ 3a 1 · 12 ♋ 3p25 · 15 ♌ 3a30 · 17 ♍ 1p13 · 19 ♎ 7p51 · 22 ♏ 12a 0 · 24 ♐ 2a48 · 26 ♑ 5a23 · 28 ♒ 8a26 · 30 ♓ 12p27

OCT: 2 ♈ 5p51 · 5 ♉ 1a18 · 7 ♊ 11a18 · 9 ♋ 11p29 · 12 ♌ 12p 2 · 14 ♍ 10p24 · 17 ♎ 5a 7 · 19 ♏ 8a54 · 21 ♐ 9a54 · 23 ♑ 11a13 · 25 ♒ 1p48 · 27 ♓ 6p17 · 30 ♈ 12a40

NOV: 1 ♉ 8a53 · 3 ♊ 7p 2 · 6 ♋ 7a 5 · 8 ♌ 7p58 · 11 ♍ 7a24 · 13 ♎ 3p12 · 15 ♏ 6p52 · 17 ♐ 7p34 · 19 ♑ 7p23 · 21 ♒ 8p21 · 23 ♓ 11p49 · 26 ♈ 6a12 · 28 ♉ 3p 3

DEC: 1 ♊ 1a44 · 3 ♋ 1p53 · 6 ♌ 2a49 · 8 ♍ 2p49 · 11 ♎ 12a18 · 13 ♏ 5a27 · 15 ♐ 6a48 · 17 ♑ 6a38 · 19 ♒ 5a37 · 21 ♓ 7a15 · 23 ♈ 12p15 · 26 ♉ 8p42 · 28 ♊ 7p43 · 31 ♋ 8p 6

JAN: 2 ♌ 8a56 · 4 ♍ 9p 9 · 7 ♎ 7a20 · 9 ♏ 2p11 · 11 ♐ 5p18 · 13 ♑ 5p37 · 15 ♒ 4p57 · 17 ♓ 4p39 · 19 ♈ 8p28 · 22 ♉ 3a26 · 24 ♊ 1p54 · 27 ♋ 2a24 · 29 ♌ 3p11

FEB: 1 ♍ 3a 0 · 3 ♎ 12p59 · 5 ♏ 8p31 · 8 ♐ 1a14 · 10 ♑ 3a23 · 12 ♒ 3a57 · 14 ♓ 4a27 · 16 ♈ 6a39 · 18 ♉ 12p 3 · 20 ♊ 9p16 · 23 ♋ 9a22 · 25 ♌ 10p13 · 28 ♍ 9p46

MAR: 2 ♎ 7p 2 · 5 ♏ 1a59 · 7 ♐ 6a58 · 9 ♑ 10a22 · 11 ♒ 12p36 · 13 ♓ 2p37 · 15 ♈ 5p 0 · 17 ♉ 9p33 · 20 ♊ 5a51 · 22 ♋ 5p13 · 25 ♌ 6a 2 · 27 ♍ 6p21 · 30 ♎ 2a37

APR: 1 ♏ 8a35 · 3 ♐ 12p37 · 5 ♑ 3p45 · 7 ♒ 6p43 · 9 ♓ 9p52 · 12 ♈ 1a40 · 14 ♉ 6a55 · 16 ♊ 2p41 · 19 ♋ 1a26 · 21 ♌ 2p10 · 24 ♍ 2a20 · 26 ♎ 11a52 · 28 ♏ 5p 7 · 30 ♐ 8p 2

☽ PHASES

SEP: 4 ☾ 12a 4 · 7 ● 4p 8 · 11 ○ 4p30 · 15 ☾ 6p30 · 19 ● 1p21 · 23 ☽ 1a 5 · 26 ○ 10a36 · 29 ○ 9p34

OCT: 3 ☾ 12p 2 · 7 ● 9a 1 · 11 ○ 11a45 · 15 ☾ 11a15 · 19 ● 12a44 · 22 ☽ 8a20 · 25 ○ 5p20 · 29 ○ 7a31

NOV: 2 ○ 2a59 · 6 ● 4a 4 · 10 ○ 7a18 · 14 ☾ 2a43 · 17 ● 11a24 · 20 ☽ 4p35 · 24 ○ 2a38 · 27 ○ 8p36

DEC: 1 ○ 8p31 · 6 ● 12a 3 · 10 ○ 1a23 · 13 ☾ 4p19 · 16 ● 9p53 · 20 ☽ 3p 9 · 23 ○ 3p54 · 27 ○ 3p54

JAN: 4 ○ 7p 7 · 8 ● 4p36 · 11 ☾ 4a21 · 15 ● 6a50 · 19 ☽ 7p43 · 22 ○ 5a29 · 25 ○ 1a 4 · 30 ● 11a31

FEB: 3 ○ 11a25 · 7 ● 4a10 · 10 ☾ 1p46 · 13 ● 8a 0 · 17 ☽ 5a29 · 21 ○ 1a 4 · 25 ● 4a12

MAR: 1 ○ 5a25 · 5 ● 2p15 · 11 ☾ 10p20 · 14 ● 7a 8 · 18 ☽ 9p15 · 22 ○ 8p44 · 26 ○ 11p45 · 30 ○ 8p14

APR: 3 ○ 9a26 · 7 ● 7p48 · 10 ☾ 6a15 · 13 ● 6p57 · 17 ☽ 1p59 · 21 ○ 4p20 · 25 ○ 4p51 · 29 ○ 7p45

MAY 1934 – DEC 1934

	MAY 1934	JUN 1934	JUL 1934	AUG 1934	SEP 1934	OCT 1934	NOV 1934	DEC 1934
☉ →	♊	♋	♌	♍	♎	♏	♐	♑
	21 1p35	21 9p48	23 8a42	23 3p32	23 12p45	23 9p36	22 6p44	22 7a49

☽→SIGNS

MAY: 2 ♑ 9p53 · 5 ♒ 12a 6 · 7 ♓ 3a26 · 9 ♈ 8a 8 · 11 ♉ 2p24 · 13 ♊ 10p38 · 16 ♋ 9a17 · 18 ♌ 9p55 · 21 ♍ 10a35 · 23 ♎ 8p43 · 26 ♏ 2a52 · 28 ♐ 5a28 · 30 ♑ 6a12

JUN: 1 ♒ 6a55 · 3 ♓ 9a 6 · 5 ♈ 1p31 · 7 ♉ 8p17 · 9 ♊ 5a13 · 12 ♋ 4p14 · 15 ♌ 4a52 · 17 ♍ 5p51 · 20 ♎ 4a59 · 22 ♏ 12p25 · 24 ♐ 3p49 · 26 ♑ 4p24 · 28 ♒ 4p 2 · 30 ♓ 4p38

JUL: 2 ♈ 7p39 · 5 ♉ 1a47 · 7 ♊ 10a55 · 9 ♋ 10p20 · 12 ♌ 11a 7 · 15 ♍ 12a 7 · 17 ♎ 11a47 · 19 ♏ 8p31 · 22 ♐ 1a28 · 24 ♑ 3a 3 · 26 ♒ 2a43 · 28 ♓ 2a20 · 30 ♈ 3a45

AUG: 1 ♉ 8a26 · 3 ♊ 4p48 · 6 ♋ 4a13 · 8 ♌ 5p 8 · 11 ♍ 5a59 · 13 ♎ 5p33 · 16 ♏ 2a51 · 18 ♐ 9a11 · 20 ♑ 12p27 · 22 ♒ 1p18 · 24 ♓ 1p 8 · 26 ♈ 1p44 · 28 ♉ 4p54 · 30 ♊ 11p55

SEP: 2 ♋ 10a40 · 5 ♌ 11p32 · 7 ♍ 12p16 · 9 ♎ 11p23 · 12 ♏ 8a19 · 14 ♐ 3p 3 · 16 ♑ 7p35 · 18 ♒ 10p 6 · 20 ♓ 11p44 · 23 ♈ 1a46 · 25 ♉ 5a 7 · 27 ♊ 11a 1 · 30 ♋ 7a29

OCT: 2 ♌ 6a44 · 5 ♍ 7p31 · 7 ♎ 6a20 · 10 ♏ 2p33 · 12 ♐ 8p32 · 14 ♑ 1a 4 · 17 ♒ 4a32 · 19 ♓ 7a 9 · 22 ♈ 10a 1 · 24 ♉ 2p34 · 27 ♊ 9p42

NOV: 2 ♌ 3a36 · 4 ♍ 2p41 · 7 ♎ 1a20 · 9 ♏ 10p32 · 11 ♐ 3a33 · 13 ♑ 6a56 · 16 ♒ 9a52 · 18 ♓ 12p46 · 20 ♈ 4p26 · 22 ♉ 9p 3 · 25 ♊ 10p54 · 28 ♍ 11a52 · 30 ♎ 11p39

DEC: 3 ♍ 8a 6 · 5 ♎ 12p52 · 7 ♏ 9p 9 · 9 ♐ 4p34 · 11 ♓ 6p31 · 13 ♈ 9p51 · 16 ♉ 2a56 · 18 ♊ 9a58 · 23 ♋ 6a37 · 25 ♌ 7p32 · 28 ♍ 8p 4 · 30 ♏ 5p41

☽ PHASES

MAY: 2 ● 4p32 · 6 ○ 1a41 · 9 ☾ 2p19 · 13 ● 7a30 · 17 ☽ 7a 8 · 21 ○ 10a20 · 25 ○ 6a42 · 28 ● 4p41 · 30 ○ 10p40

JUN: 4 ○ 7a53 · 7 ☾ 11p26 · 11 ● 9p11 · 15 ☽ 11p57 · 20 ○ 11p57 · 23 ○ 5p32 · 27 ● 1a29 · 30 ○ 4a58

JUL: 3 ○ 3p28 · 7 ☾ 10a33 · 11 ● 12p 6 · 15 ☽ 3p30 · 19 ○ 1p53 · 23 ○ 2a10 · 26 ● 7a 8 · 29 ○ 12p27

AUG: 2 ○ 1a27 · 6 ☾ 12a18 · 10 ● 3a45 · 13 ☽ 7p33 · 18 ○ 9a34 · 21 ○ 2p37 · 26 ● 9p56 · 31 ○ 2p40

SEP: 4 ☾ 4p42 · 8 ● 7p20 · 12 ☽ 4p31 · 17 ○ 7a26 · 20 ○ 4p38 · 26 ○ 11p19 · 30 ● 10a17

OCT: 4 ☾ 10a56 · 8 ● 10a 5 · 12 ☽ 2a20 · 15 ○ 9p39 · 19 ○ 10a 1 · 22 ○ 11p26 · 27 ● 3a22

NOV: 3 ☾ 5a41 · 6 ● 6p 9 · 10 ☽ 11a21 · 13 ○ 9p39 · 17 ○ 8a57 · 20 ○ 11p26 · 24 ● 9p 3 · 30 ☾ 11p39

DEC: 2 ● 11p34 · 6 ☽ 12p25 · 10 ○ 8p22 · 13 ○ 5a51 · 16 ○ 7p58 · 20 ● 6p 1 · 28 ○ 9p 8

JAN 1935 – AUG 1935

Sun ingress (☉ →)
JAN 1935	FEB 1935	MAR 1935	APR 1935	MAY 1935	JUN 1935	JUL 1935	AUG 1935
☉→♒ 20 6p28	☉→♓ 19 8a52	☉→♈ 21 8a18	☉→♉ 20 7p50	☉→♊ 21 7p25	☉→♋ 22 3a38	☉→♌ 23 2p33	☉→♍ 23 9p24

☽ → SIGNS

JAN 1935: 1 ♐ 11p27 · 4 ♑ 1a44 · 6 ♒ 2a 4 · 8 ♓ 2a17 · 10 ♈ 4a 3 · 12 ♉ 8a24 · 14 ♊ 3p43 · 17 ♋ 1a37 · 19 ♌ 1p27 · 22 ♍ 2a19 · 24 ♎ 2p59 · 27 ♏ 1a46 · 29 ♐ 9a11 · 31 ♑ 12p47

FEB 1935: 2 ♒ 1p26 · 4 ♓ 12p47 · 6 ♈ 12p49 · 8 ♉ 3p22 · 10 ♊ 9p35 · 13 ♋ 7a24 · 15 ♌ 7p35 · 18 ♍ 8a33 · 20 ♎ 9p 2 · 23 ♏ 8a 4 · 25 ♐ 4p40 · 27 ♑ 10p 4

MAR 1935: 2 ♒ 12a16 · 4 ♓ 12a13 · 5 ♈ 11p40 · 8 ♉ 12a43 · 10 ♊ 5a11 · 12 ♋ 1p51 · 15 ♌ 1a48 · 17 ♍ 2p51 · 20 ♎ 3a 8 · 22 ♏ 1p44 · 24 ♐ 10p23 · 27 ♑ 4a48 · 29 ♒ 8a41 · 31 ♓ 10a14

APR 1935: 2 ♈ 10a31 · 4 ♉ 11a18 · 6 ♊ 2p35 · 8 ♋ 9p49 · 11 ♌ 8a52 · 13 ♍ 9p46 · 16 ♎ 10a 1 · 18 ♏ 8p 9 · 21 ♐ 4a 6 · 23 ♑ 10a13 · 25 ♒ 2p43 · 27 ♓ 5p39 · 29 ♈ 7p26

MAY 1935: 1 ♉ 9p 9 · 4 ♊ 12a26 · 6 ♋ 6a50 · 8 ♌ 4p55 · 11 ♍ 5a26 · 14 ♎ 6p 3 · 16 ♏ 3a54 · 18 ♐ 11a13 · 20 ♑ 4p20 · 22 ♒ 8p 8 · 24 ♓ 11p13 · 27 ♈ 1a58 · 29 ♉ 4a59 · 31 ♊ 9a11

JUN 1935: 2 ♋ 3p43 · 4 ♌ 1a19 · 7 ♍ 1p25 · 10 ♎ 1a59 · 12 ♏ 12p35 · 14 ♐ 7p57 · 17 ♑ 12a21 · 19 ♒ 2a56 · 21 ♓ 4a55 · 23 ♈ 7a21 · 25 ♉ 10a54 · 27 ♊ 4p 9 · 29 ♋ 11p26

JUL 1935: 2 ♌ 9a13 · 4 ♍ 9p 8 · 7 ♎ 9a52 · 9 ♏ 9p15 · 12 ♐ 5a27 · 14 ♑ 10a 3 · 16 ♒ 11a53 · 18 ♓ 12p30 · 20 ♈ 1p32 · 22 ♉ 4p21 · 24 ♊ 9p42 · 27 ♋ 5a43 · 29 ♌ 4p 4

AUG 1935: 1 ♍ 4a 6 · 3 ♎ 4p55 · 6 ♏ 4a57 · 8 ♐ 2p25 · 10 ♑ 8p10 · 12 ♒ 10p21 · 14 ♓ 10p19 · 16 ♈ 9p55 · 18 ♉ 11p 7 · 21 ♊ 3a25 · 23 ♋ 11a17 · 25 ♌ 10p 0 · 28 ♍ 10a20 · 30 ♎ 11p 8

☽ PHASES

JAN 1935: 1 (3p40 · 5 ✓ 12a20 · 8) 5a57 · 11 O 3p55 · 15 O 9a53 · 19 O 10a44 · 23 O 2p37 · 27 O 2p58 · 31 (5a29

FEB 1935: 3 ✓ 11a27 · 6) 4p23 · 10 O 4a24 · 14 O 6a17 · 18 O 8a43 · 26 O 5a14

MAR 1935: 1 (4p44 · 4) 9p40 · 8) 3a52 · 11 O 7p30 · 15 O 9p16 · 20 O 12a31 · 23 O 1p14 · 27 O 3p50 · 31 (1a29

APR 1935: 3 ● 7a10 · 6 O 4p38 · 10 O 12p42 · 14 O 3p58 · 18 O 4p 9 · 22 O 10a10 · 25 O 11p20 · 29 (8a22

MAY 1935: 2 ● 4p36 · 6 O 6a53 · 10 O 6a54 · 14 O 9a17 · 18 O 4a57 · 22 O 6p17 · 25 O 4a44 · 28 ℂ 2p30

JUN 1935: 4) 10p29 · 9 O 12a49 · 13 O 12a28 · 16 O 3p20 · 20 O 12a33 · 23 O 9a21 · 26 ℂ 9p17 · 30 ✓ 2p44

JUL 1935: 4) 2p52 · 9 O 1p30 · 13 O 11p 0 · 16 ✓ 12a 0 · 19 O 6a 6 · 22 O 2p42 · 26 (6a 7 · 30 ● 4a32

AUG 1935: 3) 7a15 · 7 O 8a23 · 11 O 12a42 · 14 O 7a43 · 17 O 12p11 · 20 O 10p17 · 24 (5p59 · 28 ● 8p 0

SEP 1935 – APR 1936

Sun ingress (☉ →)
SEP 1935	OCT 1935	NOV 1935	DEC 1935	JAN 1936	FEB 1936	MAR 1936	APR 1936
☉→♎ 23 6p38	☉→♏ 24 3a29	☉→♐ 23 12a35	☉→♑ 22 1p37	☉→♒ 21 12a12	☉→♓ 19 2p33	☉→♈ 20 1p58	☉→♉ 20 1a31

☽ → SIGNS

SEP 1935: 2 ♏ 11a22 · 4 ♐ 9p48 · 7 ♑ 5a 8 · 9 ♒ 8a44 · 11 ♓ 9a15 · 13 ♈ 8a20 · 15 ♉ 8a30 · 17 ♊ 10a48 · 19 ♋ 5p27 · 22 ♌ 3a50 · 24 ♍ 4p18 · 27 ♎ 5p 6

OCT 1935: 2 ♐ 3a41 · 4 ♑ 12p 2 · 6 ♒ 5p20 · 8 ♓ 7p27 · 10 ♈ 7p20 · 12 ♉ 6p53 · 15 ♊ 8p17 · 17 ♋ 1a21 · 19 ♌ 10p44 · 21 ♍ 10p 0 · 24 ♎ 11a31 · 26 ♏ 11p14 · 29 ♐ 9a17 · 31 ♑ 5p31

NOV 1935: 3 ♒ 11p38 · 5 ♓ 3a20 · 7 ♈ 4a54 · 9 ♉ 5a28 · 11 ♊ 6a36 · 13 ♋ 10a56 · 15 ♌ 6p50 · 18 ♍ 6a10 · 20 ♎ 6p52 · 23 ♏ 6a36 · 25 ♐ 4p 8 · 27 ♑ 11p28 · 30 ♒ 5a 0

DEC 1935: 2 ♓ 9a 3 · 4 ♈ 11a53 · 6 ♉ 2p 3 · 8 ♊ 4p36 · 10 ♋ 8p54 · 13 ♌ 4a 6 · 15 ♍ 2p32 · 18 ♎ 2a58 · 20 ♏ 3p 2 · 23 ♐ 12a44 · 25 ♑ 7a27 · 27 ♒ 11a46 · 29 ♓ 2p42 · 31 ♈ 5p15

JAN 1936: 2 ♉ 8p11 · 5 ♊ 12a 4 · 7 ♋ 5a29 · 9 ♌ 1p 2 · 11 ♍ 11p 5 · 14 ♎ 11a10 · 16 ♏ 11p38 · 19 ♐ 10a11 · 21 ♑ 5p18 · 23 ♒ 9p 2 · 25 ♓ 10p35 · 27 ♈ 11p36 · 30 ♉ 1a37

FEB 1936: 1 ♊ 5a38 · 3 ♋ 11a58 · 5 ♌ 8p26 · 8 ♍ 6a48 · 10 ♎ 7p45 · 13 ♏ 6p56 · 15 ♐ 8p41 · 18 ♑ 3a21 · 20 ♒ 7p59 · 22 ♓ 8a55 · 24 ♈ 8a35 · 26 ♉ 8a51 · 28 ♊ 11a30

MAR 1936: 1 ♋ 5p25 · 3 ♌ 2a20 · 5 ♍ 1p18 · 8 ♎ 1a26 · 11 ♏ 2p 3 · 14 ♐ 2a 6 · 16 ♑ 11a51 · 18 ♒ 5p52 · 20 ♓ 7p59 · 22 ♈ 7p31 · 24 ♉ 6p37 · 26 ♊ 7p31 · 28 ♋ 11p52 · 31 ♌ 8a 3

APR 1936: 2 ♍ 7p 7 · 5 ♎ 7a31 · 7 ♏ 8p 5 · 10 ♐ 8a 2 · 12 ♑ 6p23 · 15 ♒ 1a49 · 17 ♓ 5a37 · 19 ♈ 6a20 · 21 ♉ 5a37 · 23 ♊ 5a37 · 25 ♋ 3p 3 · 28 ♌ 6a16

☽ PHASES

SEP 1935: 1 O 10p56 · 5 O 9p26 · 9 O 10a28 · 12 O 3p18 · 15 ● 8p 4 · 19 O 9a23 · 23 ℂ 9a 9 · 27 ● 12p29

OCT 1935: 1 O 1p29 · 5 O 8a39 · 9 O 7p 4 · 12 O 11p39 · 15 O 6a54 · 19 O 12a36 · 23 ℂ 3a 8 · 27 ● 5a15 · 31 O 2a38

NOV 1935: 3 O 6p12 · 6 O 11a48 · 9 O 9a42 · 13 O 9p24 · 17 O 7p36 · 21 ℂ 10p48 · 25 ● 9p36 · 29) 2p15

DEC 1935: 3 O 2a28 · 6 O 11a48 · 9 O 10p10 · 13 O 3p23 · 17 O 4p57 · 21 ℂ 6p43 · 25 ● 9p15 · 29) 12a28

JAN 1936: 1 O 10a14 · 4 O 9p36 · 8 ✓ 1p14 · 12 O 11a36 · 16 O 2p41 · 20 ℂ 1p22 · 24 ● 2a18 · 27) 9a40 · 30 O 6p35

FEB 1936: 3 O 9a23 · 7 O 6a19 · 11 O 8a12 · 15 O 10a45 · 19 ℂ 5a23 · 25 ● 6p31 · 29) 4a28

MAR 1936: 3 O 11p18 · 7 O 12a13 · 11 O 3a35 · 16 ℂ 5p58 · 20 ● 3p46 · 26) 11p13 · 30 O 4p22

APR 1936: 2 O 2p55 · 6 O 7p48 · 11 O 4p21 · 15 ℂ 3a13 · 18 ● 7a32 · 24) 2p 2 · 28 O 6a16

MAY 1936 – DEC 1936

Sun ingress (☉ →)
MAY 1936	JUN 1936	JUL 1936	AUG 1936	SEP 1936	OCT 1936	NOV 1936	DEC 1936
☉→♊ 21 1a 7	☉→♋ 21 9a21	☉→♌ 22 8p18	☉→♍ 23 3a10	☉→♎ 23 12a26	☉→♏ 23 9a18	☉→♐ 22 6a25	☉→♑ 21 7p27

☽ → SIGNS

MAY 1936: 2 ♎ 1p43 · 5 ♏ 2a16 · 7 ♐ 1p54 · 9 ♑ 11p57 · 12 ♒ 7a47 · 14 ♓ 12p52 · 16 ♈ 3p14 · 18 ♉ 3p47 · 20 ♊ 4p12 · 22 ♋ 6p 6 · 24 ♌ 11p41 · 27 ♍ 8a47 · 29 ♎ 8p38

JUN 1936: 1 ♏ 9a11 · 3 ♐ 8p37 · 6 ♑ 6a 2 · 8 ♒ 1p17 · 10 ♓ 6p27 · 12 ♈ 9p46 · 14 ♉ 11p48 · 17 ♊ 1a29 · 19 ♋ 4a 8 · 21 ♌ 9a 6 · 23 ♍ 5p15 · 26 ♎ 4a23 · 28 ♏ 4p52

JUL 1936: 1 ♐ 4a27 · 3 ♑ 1p34 · 5 ♒ 7p56 · 8 ♓ 12a10 · 10 ♈ 3a10 · 12 ♉ 5a45 · 14 ♊ 8a38 · 16 ♋ 12p27 · 18 ♌ 5p58 · 21 ♍ 2a 6 · 23 ♎ 12p30 · 26 ♏ 1a 6 · 28 ♐ 12p55 · 30 ♑ 10p24

AUG 1936: 2 ♒ 4a25 · 4 ♓ 7a36 · 6 ♈ 9a21 · 8 ♉ 11a11 · 10 ♊ 2p12 · 12 ♋ 6p52 · 15 ♌ 1a20 · 17 ♍ 9a44 · 19 ♎ 8p17 · 22 ♏ 8a36 · 24 ♐ 9p 9 · 27 ♑ 7a35 · 29 ♒ 2p12 · 31 ♓ 5p 5

SEP 1936: 2 ♈ 5p43 · 4 ♉ 6p 4 · 6 ♊ 7p54 · 8 ♋ 11p56 · 11 ♌ 7a13 · 13 ♍ 4p19 · 16 ♎ 4a 4 · 18 ♏ 4p53 · 21 ♐ 4a24 · 23 ♑ 3p53 · 25 ♒ 11p53 · 28 ♓ 4a34 · 30 ♈ 4a10

OCT 1936: 2 ♉ 3a25 · 4 ♊ 3a37 · 6 ♋ 6a28 · 8 ♌ 12p 0 · 10 ♍ 9p10 · 13 ♎ 9a19 · 15 ♏ 9p46 · 18 ♐ 10a37 · 20 ♑ 10p37 · 23 ♒ 8a 0 · 25 ♓ 1p28 · 27 ♈ 3p 9 · 29 ♉ 2p34 · 31 ♊ 1p49

NOV 1936: 1 ♋ 3p 0 · 3 ♌ 8p37 · 6 ♍ 4a 0 · 8 ♎ 3p15 · 11 ♏ 3a52 · 13 ♐ 4p33 · 16 ♑ 4a20 · 18 ♒ 2p 6 · 21 ♓ 9p 4 · 23 ♈ 12a27 · 25 ♉ 1a29 · 27 ♊ 1a29 · 29 ♋ 1a40

DEC 1936: 2 ♌ 4a43 · 4 ♍ 11a30 · 6 ♎ 9p55 · 9 ♏ 10a25 · 11 ♐ 11p 7 · 14 ♑ 10a25 · 16 ♒ 7p42 · 19 ♓ 2a43 · 21 ♈ 7p26 · 23 ♉ 10a 5 · 25 ♊ 11a24 · 27 ♋ 12p26 · 29 ♌ 3p14 · 31 ♍ 8p45

☽ PHASES

MAY 1936: 2 O 7a28 · 6 O 10a 1 · 10 O 8a52 · 14 O 1a12 · 17 O 9a59 · 20 ● 3p34 · 27) 9p46

JUN 1936: 4 O 12a11 · 8 O 10a43 · 12 O 7a 5 · 16 ℂ 9p19 · 19 ● 10a18 · 24) 2p58 · 26 O 2p22 · 30 O 4p26

JUL 1936: 4 ℂ 12p34 · 8 O 1a43 · 14 ℂ 9p19 · 18 ● 10a18 · 22) 5a45 · 26 O 7a36 · 28 O 7a40

AUG 1936: 2 O 10p47 · 6 O 7a25 · 9 O 3p59 · 13 ℂ 4a35 · 16 ● 10p21 · 20) 9p59 · 25 O 12a49 · 27 O 9p27

SEP 1936: 1 O 7a37 · 4 O 9p11 · 8 ℂ 12p41 · 12 ● 12p41 · 17) 3p17 · 19 O 9p38 · 25 O 4p 1

OCT 1936: 3 O 8p28 · 8 ℂ 3a34 · 12 ● 5a20 · 15 ● 8a48 · 19 O 7a53 · 25 O 6a12 · 30 O 9p 0

NOV 1936: 2 O 6a23 · 6 O 8p28 · 9 ℂ 11p42 · 15 ● 8p19 · 21 O 8p19 · 27 O 6a30 · 28 O 11p 0

DEC 1936: 1 O 7p22 · 5 O 1p20 · 9 ℂ 3p48 · 13 ✓ 6p25 · 17 ● 3p43 · 24 O 6p30 · 27 O 9p36 · 31 O 11a18

JAN 1937
☉ → ♒ 20 6a 1

☽ → SIGNS
3 ♎ 5a55 / 5 ♏ 5p58 / 8 ♐ 6a43 / 10 ♑ 5p53 / 13 ♒ 2a25 / 15 ♓ 8a28 / 17 ♈ 12p48 / 19 ♉ 4p 7 / 21 ♊ 6p53 / 23 ♋ 9p38 / 26 ♌ 1a 8 / 28 ♍ 6a30 / 30 ♎ 2p49

☽ PHASES
4 ◐ 9a22 / 8 (12p51 / 12 ● 11a47 / 16) 3a30 / 19 ○ 3p 2 / 23 ○ 1a 2 / 26 ○ 12p15 / 30 ○ 5a28

FEB 1937
☉ → ♓ 18 8p21

☽ → SIGNS
2 ♏ 2a10 / 4 ♐ 2p59 / 7 ♑ 2a34 / 9 ♒ 11a 0 / 11 ♓ 4p10 / 13 ♈ 7p12 / 15 ♉ 9p34 / 18 ♊ 12a22 / 20 ♋ 4a 4 / 22 ♌ 8a51 / 24 ♍ 3p 4 / 26 ♎ 11p26

☽ PHASES
3 ○ 7a 4 / 7 (9a 9 / 11 ● 2a34 / 14) 1p 6 / 17 ○ 10p49 / 21 ○ 10a56 / 25 ○ 2a43

MAR 1937
☉ → ♈ 20 7p45

☽ → SIGNS
1 ♏ 10a23 / 3 ♐ 11p 8 / 6 ♑ 11a23 / 8 ♒ 8p35 / 11 ♓ 1a50 / 13 ♈ 4a 0 / 15 ♉ 4a54 / 17 ♊ 6a19 / 19 ♋ 9a25 / 21 ♌ 2p35 / 23 ♍ 9p44 / 26 ♎ 6a47 / 28 ♏ 5p51 / 31 ♐ 6a32

☽ PHASES
1 ○ 12a53 / 5 (4a17 / 9 ● 2a42 / 12) 2p31 / 15 ○ 9p24 / 19 ○ 6a46 / 22 ○ 9p43 / 26 ○ 6p12 / 30 ○ 8p11

APR 1937
☉ → ♉ 20 7a19

☽ → SIGNS
2 ♑ 7p16 / 5 ♒ 5a38 / 7 ♓ 11a59 / 9 ♈ 2p28 / 11 ♉ 2p39 / 13 ♊ 2p34 / 15 ♋ 4p 2 / 17 ♌ 8p11 / 20 ♍ 3a16 / 22 ♎ 12p51 / 25 ♏ 12a20 / 27 ♐ 1p 5 / 30 ♑ 1a56

☽ PHASES
3 ○ 10p53 / 7 (4p35 / 11 ● 12a10 / 14) 5a16 / 17 ○ 3p34 / 21 ○ 9a51 / 25 ○ 10a23 / 29 ○ 1p53

MAY 1937
☉ → ♊ 21 6a57

☽ → SIGNS
2 ♒ 1p 8 / 5 ♓ 8p57 / 7 ♈ 12a47 / 9 ♉ 1a32 / 11 ♊ 12a56 / 13 ♋ 1a 0 / 15 ♌ 3a27 / 17 ♍ 9a19 / 19 ♎ 6p34 / 22 ♏ 6a18 / 24 ♐ 7p10 / 27 ♑ 7a53 / 29 ♒ 7p13

☽ PHASES
3 ○ 1p36 / 7 (3a 1 / 10 ● 8a17 / 13) 1p26 / 17 ○ 1a49 / 20 ○ 11p37 / 25 ○ 2a37 / 29 ○ 4a46

JUN 1937
☉ → ♋ 21 3p12

☽ → SIGNS
1 ♓ 3a57 / 3 ♈ 9a22 / 5 ♉ 11a36 / 7 ♊ 11a45 / 9 ♋ 11a31 / 11 ♌ 12p44 / 13 ♍ 5p 1 / 16 ♎ 1a 8 / 18 ♏ 12p31 / 21 ♐ 1a25 / 23 ♑ 1p58 / 26 ♒ 12a54 / 28 ♓ 9a37 / 30 ♈ 3p50

☽ PHASES
2 ○ 12a23 / 5 (10a51 / 8 ♪ 3p43 / 11) 10p28 / 15 ○ 2p 3 / 19 ○ 5p19 / 23 ○ 5p11 / 27 ○ 4p25

JUL 1937
☉ → ♌ 23 2a 7

☽ → SIGNS
2 ♉ 7p34 / 4 ♊ 9p15 / 6 ♋ 9p53 / 8 ♌ 10p59 / 11 ♍ 2a15 / 13 ♎ 9a 4 / 15 ♏ 7p36 / 18 ♐ 8a20 / 20 ♑ 8p50 / 23 ♒ 7a20 / 25 ♓ 3p21 / 28 ♈ 9p15 / 30 ♉ 1a31

☽ PHASES
1 ○ 8a 2 / 4 (5p 7 / 7 ● 11p12 / 11) 9a 2 / 15 ○ 4a36 / 19 ○ 7a28 / 23 ○ 7a45 / 27 ○ 1a19 / 30 ○ 1p46

AUG 1937
☉ → ♍ 23 8a58

☽ → SIGNS
1 ♊ 4a29 / 3 ♋ 6a34 / 5 ♌ 8a35 / 7 ♍ 11a46 / 9 ♎ 5p58 / 12 ♏ 3a36 / 14 ♐ 3p59 / 17 ♑ 4a37 / 19 ♒ 3p 5 / 21 ♓ 10p28 / 24 ♈ 3a23 / 26 ♉ 6a57 / 28 ♊ 10a 1 / 30 ♋ 1p 3

☽ PHASES
2 (10p54 / 6 ● 7a37 / 9) 9p48 / 13 ○ 9p28 / 18 ○ 12a 6 / 21 ○ 7p47 / 25 ○ 8a33 / 28 ○ 6p54

SEP 1937
☉ → ♎ 23 6a13

☽ → SIGNS
1 ♌ 4p21 / 3 ♍ 8p34 / 6 ♎ 2a48 / 8 ♏ 11a59 / 10 ♐ 11p59 / 13 ♑ 12p51 / 15 ♒ 11p51 / 18 ♓ 7a19 / 20 ♈ 11a31 / 22 ♉ 1p49 / 24 ♊ 3p46 / 26 ♋ 6p24 / 28 ♌ 10p14

☽ PHASES
1 (5a16 / 4 ● 5p53 / 8) 1p17 / 12 ○ 3p57 / 16 ○ 4p 3 / 20 ○ 6a32 / 23 ○ 3p23 / 27 ○ 12a43 / 30 (1p25

OCT 1937
☉ → ♏ 23 3p 6

☽ → SIGNS
1 ♍ 3a28 / 3 ♎ 10a31 / 5 ♏ 7p55 / 8 ♐ 7a44 / 10 ♑ 8p46 / 13 ♒ 8a37 / 15 ♓ 5p 3 / 17 ♈ 9p32 / 20 ♉ 11p 9 / 22 ♊ 11p40 / 24 ♋ 12a46 / 26 ♌ 3a42 / 28 ♍ 9a 1 / 30 ♎ 4p47

☽ PHASES
4 ● 6a58 / 8) 7a19 / 12 ○ 10a47 / 16 ○ 4p47 / 20 ○ 10p57 / 26 ○ 12a56 / 30 (12a31

NOV 1937
☉ → ♐ 22 12p17

☽ → SIGNS
2 ♏ 2a48 / 4 ♐ 2p46 / 7 ♑ 3a50 / 9 ♒ 4p19 / 12 ♓ 2a 7 / 14 ♈ 7a59 / 16 ♉ 10a12 / 18 ♊ 10a 9 / 20 ♋ 9a47 / 22 ♌ 10a55 / 24 ♍ 2p55 / 26 ♎ 10p21 / 29 ♏ 8a46

☽ PHASES
2 ● 11p16 / 7) 2a48 / 11 ○ 4a33 / 14 ○ 8p27 / 18 ○ 3a 9 / 24 ○ 7p 4 / 28 (9a52

DEC 1937
☉ → ♑ 22 1a22

☽ → SIGNS
1 ♐ 9p 5 / 4 ♑ 10a 7 / 6 ♒ 10p40 / 9 ♓ 9a21 / 11 ♈ 4p55 / 13 ♉ 8p50 / 15 ♊ 9p42 / 17 ♋ 9p 3 / 19 ♌ 8p48 / 21 ♍ 10p57 / 24 ♎ 2a53 / 26 ♏ 2p44 / 29 ♐ 3a11 / 31 ♑ 4p17

☽ PHASES
2 ● 6p10 / 6) 9p51 / 10 ○ 8p12 / 14 ○ 8a44 / 17 ○ 1p52 / 20 ○ 7p21 / 24 ○ 4p24 / 28 (9a52

JAN 1938
☉ → ♒ 20 11a59

☽ → SIGNS
2 ♒ 4a31 / 4 ♓ 3p 6 / 7 ♈ 11p29 / 10 ♉ 5a 6 / 12 ♊ 7a50 / 14 ♋ 8a41 / 16 ♌ 9a12 / 18 ♍ 9a12 / 20 ♎ 1p27 / 22 ♏ 9p55 / 25 ♐ 9a51 / 27 ♑ 10p58 / 30 ♒ 11a 0

☽ PHASES
1 ● 1p58 / 5) 2p48 / 9 ○ 9a13 / 12 ○ 7p36 / 16 ○ 12a53 / 19 ○ 8a50 / 23 ○ 3a 9 / 27 (6a28 / 31 ● 8a35

FEB 1938
☉ → ♓ 19 2a20

☽ → SIGNS
1 ♓ 8p58 / 4 ♈ 4a54 / 6 ♉ 10a58 / 8 ♊ 3p 7 / 10 ♋ 5p25 / 12 ♌ 6p33 / 14 ♍ 7p57 / 16 ♎ 11p28 / 19 ♏ 6a37 / 21 ♐ 5p33 / 24 ♑ 6a 1 / 26 ♒ 6p36

☽ PHASES
4) 4a47 / 7 ○ 7p32 / 11 ○ 5a 1 / 14 ○ 12p14 / 18 ○ 12a32 / 21 ○ 11p24 / 26 (2a54

MAR 1938
☉ → ♈ 21 1a43

☽ → SIGNS
1 ♓ 4a13 / 4 ♈ 11a16 / 6 ♉ 4p29 / 8 ♊ 8p33 / 11 ♋ 11p46 / 13 ♌ 2a23 / 15 ♍ 4a35 / 17 ♎ 9a 8 / 19 ♏ 3p53 / 21 ♐ 2a 1 / 23 ♑ 2p32 / 26 ♒ 2a56 / 28 ♓ 12p52 / 30 ♈ 7p33

☽ PHASES
2 ● 12a40 / 5) 3p51 / 9 ○ 3a35 / 12 ○ 1p22 / 16 ○ 12a15 / 19 ○ 6p 0 / 23 ○ 9p16 / 27 (9p16 / 31 ● 1p52

APR 1938
☉ → ♉ 20 1p14

☽ → SIGNS
2 ♉ 11p43 / 4 ♊ 2a33 / 6 ♋ 5a 7 / 8 ♌ 8a 4 / 10 ♍ 11a51 / 12 ♎ 5p 2 / 15 ♏ 12a21 / 17 ♐ 10a19 / 19 ♑ 10p31 / 22 ♒ 11a10 / 24 ♓ 9p53 / 27 ♈ 5a 8 / 29 ♉ 9a 1

☽ PHASES
3 ○ 12a32 / 7 ○ 10a10 / 10 ○ 9p34 / 14 ○ 1p21 / 18 ○ 12p13 / 22 ○ 3p14 / 26 (12p37 / 29 ○ 9p53

MAY 1938
☉ → ♊ 21 12p50

☽ → SIGNS
1 ♊ 10a45 / 3 ♋ 11a50 / 5 ♌ 1p42 / 7 ♍ 5p17 / 9 ♎ 11p 5 / 12 ♏ 7a16 / 14 ♐ 5p40 / 17 ♑ 5a51 / 19 ♒ 6p37 / 22 ♓ 6a 8 / 24 ♈ 2p35 / 26 ♉ 7p17 / 28 ♊ 8p52 / 30 ♋ 8p52

☽ PHASES
3) 7a36 / 6 ○ 4p24 / 10 ○ 6a44 / 14 ○ 3a39 / 18 ○ 5a50 / 22 ○ 1a 6 / 26 (12a57 / 29 ● 8a59

JUN 1938
☉ → ♋ 21 9p 3

☽ → SIGNS
1 ♌ 9p 8 / 3 ♍ 11p21 / 6 ♎ 4a35 / 8 ♏ 1p 1 / 10 ♐ 11p57 / 13 ♑ 12p21 / 15 ♒ 1a 7 / 18 ♓ 1p31 / 20 ♈ 10p39 / 23 ♉ 4a50 / 25 ♊ 7a25 / 27 ♋ 8a20 / 29 ♌ 6a45

☽ PHASES
1) 1p59 / 4 ○ 11p32 / 8 ○ 5p46 / 12 ○ 7p18 / 16 ○ 9p46 / 20 ○ 7a18 / 24 (10a38 / 28 ● 4p10 / 30) 8p46

JUL 1938
☉ → ♌ 23 7a57

☽ → SIGNS
1 ♍ 7a23 / 3 ♎ 11a 9 / 5 ♏ 6p48 / 8 ♐ 5a45 / 10 ♑ 6p22 / 13 ♒ 7a 5 / 15 ♓ 6p55 / 18 ♈ 4a31 / 20 ♉ 12p31 / 23 ♊ 4p43 / 25 ♋ 5p54 / 27 ♌ 5p26 / 29 ♍ 5p17 / 31 ♎ 7p28

☽ PHASES
4 ○ 8a47 / 8 ○ 6a 4 / 12 ○ 10a 4 / 16 ○ 11a32 / 20 (6p18 / 23 ● 10p53 / 26) 5a 6

AUG 1938
☉ → ♍ 23 2p46

☽ → SIGNS
2 ♏ 1a49 / 4 ♐ 12p 2 / 6 ♑ 12a33 / 9 ♒ 1p15 / 12 ♓ 1a15 / 14 ♈ 10a11 / 16 ♉ 6p25 / 19 ♊ 12a? / 21 ♋ 2a39 / 23 ♌ 3a42 / 25 ♍ 10a26 / 27 ♎ 10a26 / 29 ♏ 10a26 / 31 ♐ 7p28

☽ PHASES
2 ○ 9p 0 / 6 ○ 10p28 / 11 ○ 12a57 / 15 ○ 3p30 / 18 ○ 3p30 / 22 (12a45 / 24 ● 6a17 / 28) 4p 7

SEP 1938
☉ → ♎ 23 11a59

☽ → SIGNS
3 ♑ 7a30 / 5 ♒ 8p10 / 8 ♓ 7a28 / 10 ♈ 4p40 / 12 ♉ 11p54 / 15 ♊ 5a23 / 17 ♋ 9a 9 / 19 ♌ 11a26 / 21 ♍ 1p 1 / 23 ♎ 3p19 / 25 ♏ 7p56 / 28 ♐ 4a 2 / 30 ♑ 3p20

☽ PHASES
1 ○ 12p28 / 5 ○ 3p20 / 9 ○ 3p 8 / 13 ○ 9a? / 16 ○ 10p12 / 20 (7a 3 / 23 ● 3p34 / 27) 6a28

OCT 1938
☉ → ♏ 23 8p54

☽ → SIGNS
3 ♒ 3a57 / 5 ♓ 3p27 / 8 ♈ 12a22 / 10 ♉ 6a42 / 12 ♊ 11a10 / 15 ♋ 2p31 / 17 ♌ 5p19 / 19 ♍ 8p 9 / 21 ♎ 11p43 / 24 ♏ 5a 0 / 26 ♐ 1p 8 / 28 ♑ 11p? / 31 ♒ 12p 8

☽ PHASES
1 ○ 6a45 / 5 ○ 8a57 / 9 ○ 4a37 / 13 ○ 11a20 / 16 (4a24 / 19 ● 12a20 / 23) 3a42 / 27 ○ 12a 5 / 31 ○ 2a45

NOV 1938
☉ → ♐ 22 6p 6

☽ → SIGNS
2 ♓ 12a 9 / 4 ♈ 9a35 / 6 ♉ 3p41 / 8 ♊ 7p 3 / 10 ♋ 8p59 / 12 ♌ 10p50 / 15 ♍ 1a38 / 17 ♎ 6a 3 / 19 ♏ 12p25 / 21 ♐ 8p56 / 24 ♑ 7a37 / 26 ♒ 7p58 / 29 ♓ 8a30

☽ PHASES
4 ○ 2a32 / 7 (5p23 / 11 ● 11a20 / 14 (12a20 / 18) 6p? / 21 ○ 7p 5 / 25 ○ 7p56 / 29 ○ 10p59

DEC 1938
☉ → ♑ 22 7a13

☽ → SIGNS
1 ♈ 7p 2 / 4 ♉ 2a 0 / 6 ♊ 5a18 / 8 ♋ 6a 7 / 10 ♌ 6a17 / 12 ♍ 7a37 / 14 ♎ 11a27 / 16 ♏ 6p13 / 19 ♐ 3a31 / 21 ♑ 2p39 / 24 ♒ 2a59 / 26 ♓ 3p14 / 29 ♈ 3a14 / 31 ♉ 11a47

☽ PHASES
3 ○ 7p15 / 7 ○ 5a22 / 11 ○ 11a 3 / 14 (8p16 / 17 ● 1p23 / 21) 1p 7 / 25 ○ 4p20 / 29 ○ 9p53

JAN 1939 – AUG 1939

JAN 1939
O -> ≈ 20 5p51

D->SIGNS
2 II 4p19
4 S 5p20
6 Ω 4p32
8 m 4p 8
10 ≏ 6p10
12 m 11p54
15 ✗ 9a 9
17 ✗ 8p43
20 ≈ 9a15
22 ≈ 9p51
25 ↑ 9a42
27 ŏ 7p29
30 II 1a50

D PHASES
2 O 10a 7
5 O 8p 0
9 O 8p10
12 O 8a10
16 C 5a38
20 ● 8a26
24 D 11a31
28 O 9a59
31 O 10p26

FEB 1939
O -> H 19 8a 9

D->SIGNS
1 S 4a22
3 Ω 4a 6
5 m 3a 2
7 ≏ 3a29
9 m 7a22
11 ✗ 3p24
14 ✗ 2a41
16 ≈ 3p22
19 H 3a52
21 ↑ 3p23
24 ŏ 1a19
26 II 8a47
28 S 1p 6

D PHASES
4 O 2a55
7 O 8a17
10 O 11p12
15 C 12a 7
19 ● 3a28
23 D 4a 2
26 O 10p26

MAR 1939
O -> ↑ 21 7a28

D->SIGNS
2 Ω 2p30
4 m 2p25
6 ≏ 2p55
8 m 4p59
10 ✗ 11p23
13 ✗ 9a35
15 ≈ 10p 1
18 H 10a31
20 ↑ 9p41
23 ŏ 7p23
25 II 2p14
27 S 7p19
29 Ω 10p15
31 m 11p39

D PHASES
2 O 8a 9
5 O 1p 0
9 O 9p36
12 O 4p37
15 C 7p19
19 ● 11a35
23 D 2a39
26 O 10p26

APR 1939
O -> ŏ 20 6p55

D->SIGNS
1 ≏ 12a48
3 m 3a21
5 ✗ 8a47
7 ✗ 5p46
10 ≈ 5a33
12 H 6p 4
15 ↑ 5a13
17 ŏ 1p56
19 II 8p16
21 S 12a43
23 Ω 3a55
25 m 6a26
28 m 9a 2

D PHASES
3 O 11p18
7 O 12p29
11 O 11a11
15 (1p50
19 (11a35
23 D 2a39
26 O 1p25
29 O 10p43

MAY 1939
O -> II 21 6p26

D->SIGNS
2 m 12p36
4 ✗ 6p11
7 ✗ 2a33
9 ≈ 1p41
12 H 2a 9
14 ↑ 1p41
16 ŏ 10p28
19 II 4a 6
21 S 7a23
23 Ω 9a33
25 m 11a50
27 ≏ 3p 6
29 m 7p47

D PHASES
3 ✗ 10a15
7 O 4a21
11 O 5a40
15 O 6a33
18 (8a37
22 ● 9a32
26 D 6p20
29 O 5a34

JUN 1939
O -> S 22 2a39

D->SIGNS
1 ✗ 2a15
4 ✗ 10a50
6 ≈ 9p40
9 ↑ 10p10
11 ŏ 7a43
13 II 1p32
15 S 4p 6
17 Ω 4p58
19 m 5p56
21 ≏ 8p30
23 m 1a25
26 ✗ 8a39
28 ✗ 5p53

D PHASES
1 O 10p11
5 O 8p37
9 O 9p 7
13 (8p51
17 ● 8a37
20 D 3p 1
23 O 11p35
27 O 2p26

JUL 1939
O -> Ω 23 1p36

D->SIGNS
3 ≈ 4a54
5 ↑ 5p17
8 ŏ 5a50
10 II 4p27
13 S 2a16
15 Ω 9a 2
17 m 2a30
19 ≏ 7a 4
23 m 7a 4
27 ✗ 11p50
30 ≈ 11a15

D PHASES
1 O 11a16
5 O 12p49
9 O 8a31
13 (4p 3
17 ● 8p35
20 D 6a34
23 O 1a 8
27 O 1a36
31 O 1a36

AUG 1939
O -> m 23 8p31

D->SIGNS
1 H 11p41
4 ↑ 12p22
6 ŏ 11p47
9 II 8a 6
11 S 12p21
13 Ω 1p 9
15 m 12p19
17 ≏ 12p 3
19 m 2p20
21 ✗ 8p13
24 ✗ 5a33
26 ≈ 5p 9
29 H 5a42
31 ↑ 6p15

D PHASES
4 O 4a32
8 O 4a18
11 (5p57
14 ● 10p53
18 D 3a38
21 O 4p20
25 O 2p51
29 O 5p 8

SEP 1939 – APR 1940

SEP 1939
O -> ≏ 23 5p49

D->SIGNS
3 ŏ 5a47
5 II 3p 2
7 S 8p52
9 Ω 11p11
11 m 11p 9
13 ≏ 10p38
15 m 11p43
18 ✗ 4a 2
20 ✗ 12p11
22 ≈ 11p24
25 H 12a12
28 ↑ 12a22
30 ŏ 11a28

D PHASES
2 O 7p13
6 O 3p24
10 (1a54
13 ● 6a22
16 D 1p16
20 O 5a34
24 O 6a42
28 O 9a27

OCT 1939
O -> m 24 2a46

D->SIGNS
1 II 8p38
3 S 3a16
5 Ω 7a10
7 m 8a46
9 ≏ 9a15
11 m 9a35
13 ✗ 10a18
16 ✗ 1p36
18 ≈ 8p22
21 H 6a40
23 ↑ 7p 5
26 ŏ 7p28
28 II 6p 9
31 S 2a31

D PHASES
2 O 8a20
6 O 12a27
9 (9a23
12 ● 3p30
16 D 2a 4
19 O 10p24
24 O 1a17
28 O 1a41
31 O 7p40

NOV 1939
O -> ✗ 22 11p59

D->SIGNS
1 Ω 8p38
3 Ω 1p 1
5 m 3p57
7 ≏ 6p 3
9 m 8p14
11 ✗ 11p41
13 ✗ 5a42
16 ≈ 3p 0
18 H 3p 0
21 ↑ 3p35
23 ŏ 2a23
26 II 10a 9
28 S 3p11
30 Ω 6p34

D PHASES
2 O 8a20
4 O 8a12
7 (7p24
11 ● 2a54
14 D 6p10
18 O 6p21
22 O 9p 5
26 O 6a28
30 O 5a30

DEC 1939
O -> ✗ 22 1p 6

D->SIGNS
2 m 9p23
5 ≏ 12a22
7 m 3a57
9 ✗ 8a32
11 ✗ 2p51
13 ≈ 11p48
16 H 11p48
19 ↑ 12a 3
21 ŏ 11a32
23 II 7p37
26 S 12a 3
28 Ω 3a 5
30 m 3a28

D PHASES
3 O 3p40
7 O 2a44
10 ● 4p45
14 D 1p 6
18 O 4p 3
22 O 4p19
26 O 6a28
29 O 2p35

JAN 1940
O -> ≈ 20 11p44

D->SIGNS
1 ≏ 5a43
3 m 9a36
5 ✗ 3p12
7 ✗ 10p29
10 ≈ 9a36
12 H 7a42
15 ↑ 7p33
17 ŏ 7a55
20 II 5a32
22 S 10a35
24 Ω 12p10
26 m 12p43
28 ≏ 12p43
30 m 3p17

D PHASES
1 O 11p56
5 (1p56
9 ● 8a52
13 D 9a44
17 O 1p21
21 O 9a17
24 O 6p22
27 O 11p49
31 O 9a47

FEB 1940
O -> H 19 2p 4

D->SIGNS
1 ✗ 8p36
4 ✗ 4a27
6 ≈ 2p49
9 H 1a58
11 ↑ 2p49
14 ŏ 3a36
16 II 2p10
19 S 8p46
21 Ω 11p19
24 m 11p11
26 ≏ 11p13
28 m 2a54

D PHASES
4 (3a15
8 ● 2a45
12 D 6a19
16 O 7a55
19 O 11p 8
23 O 4a55
26 O 9p35

MAR 1940
O -> ↑ 20 1p24

D->SIGNS
2 ✗ 10a 2
4 ✗ 8a 7
7 ≈ 9p 1
9 H 9a44
11 ↑ 9a 2
14 ŏ 8p53
16 S 4a57
19 Ω 10a20
21 m 9a47
23 ≏ 9a33
25 m 9a33
27 ✗ 11a31
29 ✗ 4p59

D PHASES
4 (6p39
8 ● 9p22
13 D 12a45
16 O 10p25
20 O 9a52
23 O 2p33
26 O 8p36
29 O 9p35

APR 1940
O -> ŏ 20 12a51

D->SIGNS
2 ≈ 2a13
4 H 2p11
7 ↑ 3a10
9 ŏ 3p38
12 II 2a32
14 S 10a44
16 Ω 4p44
19 m 7p34
21 ≏ 8p33
23 m 9p48
25 ✗ 1a49
28 ✗ 9a39
30 H 8p56

D PHASES
3 (11a42
7 ● 3p18
11 D 9a34
15 O 8p45
18 O 6p 7
21 O 11p37
25 O 8a24
29 O 2a49

MAY 1940 – DEC 1940

MAY 1940
O -> II 21 12a23

D->SIGNS
3 ↑ 9a52
5 ŏ 10p12
8 II 8a33
10 S 4p33
12 Ω 10p22
15 m 2a17
17 ≏ 4a40
19 m 6a12
21 ✗ 8a 0
23 ✗ 11a34
25 ≈ 6p19
28 H 4a39
30 ↑ 5p18

D PHASES
3 (5a26
7 ● 7a 6
11 D 3p50
18 O 12a45
21 O 8a33
24 O 9p18
28 O 7p40

JUN 1940
O -> S 21 8a36

D->SIGNS
2 ŏ 5a44
4 II 3p56
6 Ω 11p 2
8 m 4a 0
11 ≏ 7a41
13 m 10a43
15 ✗ 1p31
17 ≏ 4p34
19 ✗ 8p44
21 ≈ 3a15
24 H 12p55
26 ↑ 12a 4
29 ŏ 1p52

D PHASES
2 (10p40
5 ● 8p 5
10 D 3a15
12 O 8p59
16 O 6a 1
19 O 6p 1
23 O 11a35
27 O 1p13

JUL 1940
O -> Ω 22 7p34

D->SIGNS
2 II 12a15
4 S 7a10
6 Ω 11a12
8 m 1p44
10 ≏ 4p 7
12 m 7p13
15 ✗ 2a38
17 ✗ 4a17
19 ≈ 11a22
21 H 8p58
24 ↑ 9a 1
26 ŏ 9p56
29 II 9a 4
31 S 4p32

D PHASES
2 (2p18
5 ● 6a27
9 D 4p17
12 O 1a35
15 O 1p15
19 O 4a55
21 O 8p16
25 O 10p32
29 (3p41

AUG 1940
O -> m 23 2a28

D->SIGNS
2 Ω 8p20
4 m 9p50
6 ≏ 10p49
9 ✗ 1a29
11 m 4a29
13 ✗ 10a15
15 ≈ 6p 7
18 H 4a10
20 ↑ 4p14
23 ŏ 5a 6
25 II 5p 3
28 S 1a53
30 Ω 6a31

D PHASES
3 ● 3p 9
6 D 7p 9
7 D 9p55
10 O 7a 0
13 O 9p31
16 O 9a41
20 O 1p19
24 O 12p47
29 (3p41

SEP 1940
O -> ≏ 22 11p46

D->SIGNS
1 m 7a57
3 ≏ 8a16
5 m 10a36
7 ✗ 3p45
9 ≈ 11p33
12 H 9a45
14 ↑ 10a25
17 ŏ 10a43
19 II 11p25
22 S 12a35
24 Ω 9a57
26 m 3p13
28 ≏ 6p41
30 ≏ 6p46

D PHASES
1 ● 11p15
4 D 4a26
8 O 2p32
12 O 8a45
16 O 9a41
20 O 5a21
24 O 12p47
27 (11a57
30 ● 5p 3

OCT 1940
O -> m 23 8a39

D->SIGNS
2 m 6p12
4 ✗ 6p54
6 ≈ 10p28
9 H 5a44
11 ↑ 4a50
14 ŏ 4a50
16 II 5p49
19 S 5a59
21 Ω 3p18
24 m 9p51
28 ≏ 5a37
30 m 5a25

D PHASES
2 ● 7a41
4 D 12p50
8 O 1a18
12 O 11p42
14 O 9p23
18 O 7p34
20 O 5a21
22 O 11a36
25 (9p18
29 ● 3a42

NOV 1940
O -> ✗ 22 5a49

D->SIGNS
1 ✗ 5a21
3 ≈ 7a22
5 H 1p 3
7 ↑ 10p45
10 ŏ 11a13
13 II 12p13
15 S 12p 0
18 Ω 9p52
20 m 5a38
22 ≏ 11a10
24 m 2p25
26 ✗ 3p44
29 ≈ 4p18

D PHASES
2 D 11p53
6 O 4p 8
10 O 9p23
14 O 10p30
18 O 7p34
22 O 11a36
25 (9p18
29 ● 3a42

DEC 1940
O -> ✗ 21 6p55

D->SIGNS
1 ≈ 10p12
3 H 6a35
5 ↑ 6p26
8 ŏ 7a27
10 II 7p 7
13 S 4a20
15 Ω 11a16
17 m 4p35
19 ≏ 8p37
21 m 11p30
24 ✗ 1a36
26 ≈ 3a58
30 H 8a 8

D PHASES
2 O 2p 4
6 O 11a 1
10 O 2p47
14 O 2p37
18 O 7a49
21 O 8p45
25 (6a31
29 ● 3p56

JAN 1941 – AUG 1941

	JAN 1941	FEB 1941	MAR 1941	APR 1941	MAY 1941	JUN 1941	JUL 1941	AUG 1941
O →	≈ 20 5a34	✶ 18 7p56	♈ 20 7p20	♉ 20 6a50	♊ 21 6a23	♋ 21 2p33	♌ 23 1a26	♍ 23 8a17

JAN 1941 D→SIGNS: 1 ✶ 3p35 · 4 ♈ 2a34 · 6 ♉ 3p28 · 9 ♊ 3a27 · 11 ♋ 12p33 · 13 ♌ 6p39 · 15 ♍ 10p45 · 18 ♎ 2a 0 · 20 ♏ 5a 4 · 22 ♐ 8a16 · 24 ♑ 12p 1 · 26 ≈ 5p 6 · 29 ✶ 12a34 · 31 ♈ 11a32
JAN 1941 D PHASES: 1 D 7a27 · 5 O 8a40 · 9 O 11a20 · 13 O 6a 4 · 16 O 6p24 · 20 O 5a 1 · 23 C 4p 4 · 27 ● 6a 3 · 31 D 3a15

FEB 1941 D→SIGNS: 2 ♉ 11p41 · 5 ♊ 12p 9 · 7 ♋ 9p57 · 10 ♌ 4a 7 · 12 ♍ 7a21 · 14 ♎ 9a 7 · 16 ♏ 10a51 · 18 ♐ 1p37 · 20 ♑ 5p53 · 23 ≈ 12a 1 · 25 ✶ 8a18 · 27 ♈ 6p54
FEB 1941 D PHASES: 4 O 6a43 · 8 O 5a57 · 11 O 7p26 · 15 O 3a47 · 18 ● 1p 7 · 22 C 2a41 · 25 ● 10p 2

MAR 1941 D→SIGNS: 2 ♉ 7a23 · 4 ♊ 8p12 · 7 ♋ 7a 4 · 9 ♌ 2p19 · 11 ♍ 5p51 · 13 ♎ 6p51 · 15 ♏ 7p 3 · 17 ♐ 8p 7 · 19 ♑ 11p25 · 22 ≈ 5a34 · 24 ✶ 2p30 · 27 ♈ 1a39 · 29 ♉ 2p13
MAR 1941 D PHASES: 1 D 11p43 · 6 O 2a42 · 9 O 9p38 · 13 ● 6a47 · 16 O 12p26 · 19 O 9p51 · 23 C 3p 2 · 27 ● 3p14 · 31 D 6p45

APR 1941 D→SIGNS: 1 ♊ 3a 6 · 3 ♋ 2p43 · 5 ♌ 11p26 · 8 ♍ 4a21 · 10 ♎ 5a54 · 12 ♏ 5a51 · 14 ♐ 5a 7 · 16 ♑ 6a38 · 18 ≈ 11a31 · 20 ✶ 8p 7 · 23 ♈ 7a34 · 25 ♉ 8p22 · 28 ♊ 9a11 · 30 ♋ 8p56
APR 1941 D PHASES: 4 O 7p12 · 8 O 10a 6 · 11 O 4p15 · 14 O 8p51 · 18 ● 11p 9 · 22 C 5a20 · 26 ● 12a18 · 30 D 11p42

MAY 1941 D→SIGNS: 3 ♌ 6a34 · 5 ♍ 1p 5 · 7 ♎ 4p11 · 9 ♏ 4p33 · 11 ♐ 3p49 · 13 ♑ 4p 3 · 15 ≈ 7p15 · 18 ✶ 2a33 · 20 ♈ 1p 8 · 23 ♉ 2a26 · 25 ♊ 3p10 · 28 ♋ 2a36 · 30 ♌ 12p15
MAY 1941 D PHASES: 4 O 7a48 · 7 O 7p32 · 11 O 12a15 · 14 O 5a44 · 18 ● 8p17 · 21 C 9p 6 · 26 ● 12a18 · 29 D 11p42

JUN 1941 D→SIGNS: 1 ♍ 7p38 · 4 ♎ 12a17 · 6 ♏ 2a13 · 8 ♐ 2a23 · 10 ♑ 2a31 · 12 ≈ 4a41 · 14 ✶ 10a33 · 16 ♈ 8p30 · 19 ♉ 9a 3 · 21 ♊ 9p44 · 24 ♋ 8a51 · 26 ♌ 5p55 · 29 ♍ 1a 3
JUN 1941 D PHASES: 2 O 4p56 · 6 O 2a32 · 9 O 7a34 · 12 O 3p56 · 17 ● 10a45 · 20 C 1p29 · 24 ● 2p22 · 28 D 9a35

JUL 1941 D→SIGNS: 1 ♎ 6a17 · 3 ♏ 9a33 · 5 ♐ 11a13 · 7 ♑ 12p20 · 9 ≈ 2p36 · 11 ✶ 7p42 · 14 ♈ 4a34 · 16 ♉ 4p30 · 19 ♊ 5a 9 · 21 ♋ 4p15 · 24 ♌ 12p48 · 26 ♍ 7a 3 · 28 ♎ 11a40 · 30 ♏ 3p 9
JUL 1941 D PHASES: 2 O 11p24 · 5 O 8a 6 · 9 O 3p17 · 12 O 4a11 · 16 ● 3a 7 · 20 C 5a40 · 24 ● 2a39 · 27 D 5p20 · 31 O 4a19

AUG 1941 D→SIGNS: 1 ♐ 5p49 · 3 ♑ 8p 7 · 5 ≈ 11p32 · 8 ✶ 4a51 · 10 ♈ 1p13 · 12 ♉ 12a32 · 15 ♊ 1p 9 · 17 ♋ 12a37 · 20 ♌ 9a15 · 22 ♍ 2p53 · 24 ♎ 6p21 · 26 ♏ 8p48 · 28 ♐ 11p13 · 31 ♑ 2a17
AUG 1941 D PHASES: 3 O 1p32 · 7 O 12a38 · 10 O 6p52 · 14 O 8p40 · 18 ● 7p11 · 22 ● 1p34 · 25 D 11p56 · 29 O 9a 3

SEP 1941 – APR 1942

	SEP 1941	OCT 1941	NOV 1941	DEC 1941	JAN 1942	FEB 1942	MAR 1942	APR 1942
O →	♎ 23 5a33	♏ 23 2p27	♐ 22 11a38	♑ 22 12a44	≈ 20 11a24	✶ 19 1a47	♈ 21 1a11	♉ 20 12p39

SEP 1941 D→SIGNS: 2 ≈ 6a38 · 4 ✶ 12p52 · 6 ♈ 9p28 · 9 ♉ 8a32 · 11 ♊ 9p 5 · 14 ♋ 9a 9 · 16 ♌ 6p56 · 19 ♍ 12a29 · 21 ♎ 3a17 · 23 ♏ 4a23 · 25 ♐ 5a24 · 27 ♑ 7a34 · 29 ≈ 12p17
SEP 1941 D PHASES: 1 O 8p22 · 5 ● 12p36 · 9 O 11a43 · 13 O 8a31 · 17 C 11a51 · 20 ● 11p38 · 24 O 6a28 · 27 O 3p 9

OCT 1941 D→SIGNS: 1 ✶ 7p18 · 4 ♈ 4a37 · 6 ♉ 3p52 · 9 ♊ 4a22 · 11 ♋ 4p52 · 14 ♌ 3a29 · 16 ♍ 10a36 · 18 ♎ 1p54 · 20 ♏ 2p25 · 22 ♐ 2p 0 · 24 ♑ 2p40 · 26 ≈ 6p 2 · 29 ✶ 12a51 · 31 ♈ 10a38
OCT 1941 D PHASES: 1 O 6a 0 · 5 O 3a32 · 9 O 5a54 · 13 O 7a52 · 17 C 1a29 · 20 ● 9a20 · 23 D 2p 3 · 27 O 12a 4 · 30 O 7p22

NOV 1941 D→SIGNS: 2 ♉ 10p19 · 5 ♊ 10a52 · 7 ♋ 11p 5 · 10 ♌ 10a49 · 12 ♍ 7p29 · 15 ♎ 12a21 · 17 ♏ 1a40 · 19 ♐ 12a53 · 21 ♑ 12a11 · 23 ≈ 1a46 · 25 ✶ 7a 3 · 27 ♈ 4p26 · 30 ♉ 4a18
NOV 1941 D PHASES: 3 O 9p 0 · 8 O 12a15 · 11 O 11p53 · 15 C 12a45 · 18 ● 7p 3 · 21 D 11p45 · 25 O 12p52 · 29 O 12p26

DEC 1941 D→SIGNS: 2 ♊ 5p 0 · 5 ♋ 5a21 · 7 ♌ 4p43 · 10 ♍ 2a12 · 12 ♎ 8a46 · 14 ♏ 11a51 · 16 ♐ 12p10 · 18 ♑ 11a26 · 20 ≈ 11a53 · 22 ✶ 3p33 · 24 ♈ 11p24 · 27 ♉ 10a43 · 29 ♊ 11p27
DEC 1941 D PHASES: 3 O 3p51 · 7 O 5p35 · 11 O 1p48 · 15 C 12a45 · 18 ● 5a18 · 21 D 12p19 · 25 O 5a43 · 29 O 8a 9

JAN 1942 D→SIGNS: 1 ♋ 11a41 · 3 ♌ 10p32 · 6 ♍ 7a42 · 8 ♎ 2p48 · 10 ♏ 7p24 · 12 ♐ 9p31 · 14 ♑ 10p 7 · 16 ≈ 10p52 · 19 ✶ 1a43 · 21 ♈ 8a 8 · 23 ♉ 6p18 · 26 ♊ 6a44 · 28 ♋ 7p 3 · 31 ♌ 5a37
JAN 1942 D PHASES: 2 O 10a42 · 6 O 8a53 · 10 O 1a 4 · 13 C 10a17 · 16 ● 4p31 · 20 D 3a51 · 24 O 1a35 · 28 O 4a48

FEB 1942 D→SIGNS: 2 ♍ 1p57 · 4 ♎ 8p18 · 7 ♏ 12a56 · 9 ♐ 4a 6 · 11 ♑ 6a19 · 13 ≈ 8a27 · 15 ✶ 11a50 · 17 ♈ 5p46 · 20 ♉ 2a47 · 22 ♊ 2p47 · 25 ♋ 3a11 · 27 ♌ 2p 6
FEB 1942 D PHASES: 1 O 4a12 · 4 O 9p28 · 8 O 9a52 · 11 C 7p31 · 15 ● 5a 2 · 18 D 9p37 · 22 O 10p40 · 27 O 12a36

MAR 1942 D→SIGNS: 2 ♍ 10p 6 · 4 ♎ 3a23 · 6 ♏ 6a50 · 8 ♐ 9a28 · 10 ♑ 12p 8 · 12 ≈ 3p30 · 14 ✶ 8p 9 · 17 ♈ 2a41 · 19 ♉ 11a39 · 21 ♊ 11p 0 · 24 ♋ 11a33 · 26 ♌ 11p 4 · 29 ♍ 9p36 · 31 ♎ 12p36
MAR 1942 D PHASES: 2 ● 7p20 · 6 O 7a20 · 9 O 5p 0 · 13 C 3a55 · 16 ● 6p50 · 20 D 4p21 · 24 O 7p 1 · 28 O 6p 3

APR 1942 D→SIGNS: 2 ♏ 2p54 · 4 ♐ 4p 4 · 6 ♑ 5p41 · 8 ≈ 8p56 · 11 ✶ 2a19 · 13 ♈ 9a49 · 15 ♉ 7p18 · 18 ♊ 6a36 · 20 ♋ 7p 1 · 23 ♌ 7a21 · 25 ♍ 6p55 · 27 ♎ 10p50 · 30 ♏ 12a59
APR 1942 D PHASES: 1 O 7a32 · 4 O 3p 7 · 7 O 11p43 · 11 C 1p43 · 15 ● 9a33 · 18 D 10a40 · 23 O 1p10 · 27 O 8a15 · 30 O 4p59

MAY 1942 – DEC 1942

	MAY 1942	JUN 1942	JUL 1942	AUG 1942	SEP 1942	OCT 1942	NOV 1942	DEC 1942
O →	♊ 21 12p 8	♋ 21 8p16	♌ 23 7a 7	♍ 23 1p58	♎ 23 11a17	♏ 23 8p15	♐ 22 5p30	♑ 22 6a40

MAY 1942 D→SIGNS: 2 ♐ 1a 3 · 4 ♑ 1a 4 · 6 ≈ 2a55 · 8 ✶ 7a43 · 10 ♈ 3p31 · 13 ♉ 1a37 · 15 ♊ 1p15 · 18 ♋ 1a49 · 20 ♌ 2p21 · 23 ♍ 1a 7 · 25 ♎ 8a22 · 27 ♏ 11a32 · 29 ♐ 1a39 · 31 ♑ 10a43
MAY 1942 D PHASES: 3 O 9p51 · 7 O 7a13 · 11 C 12a53 · 15 ● 12a45 · 18 D 3a36 · 23 O 4a10 · 26 O 7p 1 · 30 O 12a29

JUN 1942 D→SIGNS: 2 ≈ 10a59 · 4 ✶ 4a10 · 6 ♈ 9p11 · 9 ♉ 9a10 · 11 ♊ 9p11 · 14 ♋ 7a50 · 16 ♌ 6p19 · 18 ♍ 3a58 · 21 ♎ 9a 2 · 23 ♏ 1p35 · 25 ♐ 4p41 · 27 ♐ 9p30 · 29 ♑ 9p 0
JUN 1942 D PHASES: 2 O 4a46 · 5 O 4p26 · 9 C 1p44 · 13 ● 4p 2 · 17 D 6p29 · 21 O 3p44 · 25 O 2a58 · 28 O 2p14

JUL 1942 D→SIGNS: 2 ✶ 10p46 · 4 ♈ 4a10 · 6 ♉ 1p22 · 9 ♊ 1a10 · 11 ♋ 1p51 · 14 ♌ 2a 8 · 16 ♍ 9a38 · 18 ♎ 1p35 · 20 ♏ 3p46 · 22 ♐ 5p 7 · 24 ♑ 6p55 · 26 ≈ 7p37 · 28 ✶ 10p39 · 30 ♈ 5a29 · 31 D 12p55
JUL 1942 D PHASES: 1 O 12p58 · 5 O 3a58 · 9 C 4a15 · 13 ● 7a 3 · 16 D 5p 7 · 20 O 6a30 · 24 O 2p14 · 27 O 11p15

AUG 1942 D→SIGNS: 2 ♊ 8p47 · 4 ♋ 7a54 · 7 ♌ 8p30 · 9 ♍ 8a39 · 12 ♎ 7p 9 · 14 ♏ 3a31 · 17 ♐ 9a38 · 18 ♑ 1p35 · 20 ≈ 4p15 · 22 ✶ 5p 7 · 24 ♈ 6p55 · 27 ♉ 10p39 · 30 ♊ 5a29
AUG 1942 D PHASES: 2 O 6p 4 · 6 C 1p18 · 11 ● 9p28 · 15 D 5p 7 · 19 O 6a30 · 22 O 2p57 · 26 O 9a30 · 29 O 10p46

SEP 1942 D→SIGNS: 1 ♋ 3p40 · 4 ♌ 4a 0 · 6 ♍ 4p15 · 9 ♎ 2a31 · 11 ♏ 10a 5 · 13 ♐ 3p18 · 15 ♑ 6p58 · 17 ≈ 9p48 · 20 ✶ 12a47 · 22 ♈ 3a43 · 24 ♉ 7a57 · 26 ♊ 1p35 · 29 ♋ 12a 5
SEP 1942 D PHASES: 1 O 6p28 · 5 C 1p18 · 10 ● 5p 7 · 14 D 1a25 · 17 O 9p38 · 20 O 9a34 · 24 O 3a48 · 29 O 10p46

OCT 1942 D→SIGNS: 1 ♌ 12p 3 · 4 ♍ 12a35 · 6 ♎ 11a13 · 8 ♏ 6p33 · 10 ♐ 10p46 · 13 ♑ 1a10 · 15 ≈ 3a13 · 17 ✶ 6a 1 · 19 ♈ 10a 5 · 21 ♉ 3p36 · 23 ♊ 10p52 · 26 ♋ 8a18 · 28 ♌ 8p 0 · 31 ♍ 8a48
OCT 1942 D PHASES: 1 O 5a27 · 5 C 6a37 · 8 ● 11p 6 · 13 O 8a50 · 16 O 5p58 · 20 O 6a18 · 23 O 11p 5 · 27 O 10p 1

NOV 1942 D→SIGNS: 2 ♎ 8p19 · 5 ♏ 4a21 · 7 ♐ 8a27 · 9 ♑ 9a47 · 11 ≈ 10a18 · 13 ✶ 11a48 · 15 ♈ 3p28 · 17 ♉ 9p30 · 20 ♊ 5a37 · 22 ♋ 3p34 · 25 ♌ 3a16 · 27 ♍ 3p36 · 30 ♎ 4a29
NOV 1942 D PHASES: 1 O 1a18 · 4 C 11p 8 · 8 ● 10a19 · 11 O 4p36 · 15 O 5p49 · 18 O 5p49 · 22 O 3p54 · 30 O 8p37

DEC 1942 D→SIGNS: 2 ♏ 1p55 · 4 ♐ 7p 6 · 6 ♑ 8p34 · 8 ≈ 8p 7 · 10 ✶ 7p57 · 12 ♈ 9p56 · 15 ♉ 3a 4 · 17 ♊ 11a46 · 19 ♋ 9p46 · 22 ♌ 10a35 · 24 ♍ 10p35 · 26 ♎ 11a10 · 29 ♏ 9p44
DEC 1942 D PHASES: 1 O 1a18 · 7 O 6p59 · 14 O 12p47 · 18 O 8a31 · 22 O 10a 3 · 26 O 1p51 · 30 O 1p37

JAN 1943 – AUG 1943

JAN 1943 — ⊙ -> ≈ 20 5p19

D->SIGNS			D PHASES		
1	♏	4a40	3	(	2a43
3	♐	7a34	6	●	7a37
5	♑	7a35	9	)	1p 3
7	≈	6a42	13	○	2a48
9	♓	7a 3	17	○	2a12
11	♈	10a20	21	◑	5a48
13	♉	5p21	25	○	7a50
16	♊	3a39	29	◑	3a13
18	♋	3p53			
21	♌	4a43			
23	♍	5p 3			
26	♎	3a47			
28	♏	11a50			
30	♐	4p34			

FEB 1943 — ⊙ -> ♓ 19 7a40

D->SIGNS			D PHASES		
1	♑	6p15	1	(	1p26
3	≈	6p10	5	●	5a34
5	♓	6p 7	8	)	2a18
7	♈	8p 0	11	○	7p40
10	♉	1a17	15	○	9p53
12	♊	10a25	20	◑	12a45
14	♋	5a50	23	○	10p23
17	♌	11a18	27	◑	1p22
19	♍	11p20			
22	♎	9a30			
24	♏	5p25			
26	♐	10p59			

MAR 1943 — ⊙ -> ♈ 21 7a 2

D->SIGNS			D PHASES		
1	♑	2a19	2	(	10p30
3	≈	3a56	6	●	5p 8
5	♓	4a54	9	)	5p 8
7	♈	6a41	13	○	2p30
9	♉	10a53	17	○	5p51
11	♊	6p39	21	◑	5p 8
14	♋	5a50	25	○	9a14
16	♌	6p41	28	◑	8p52
19	♍	6a43			
21	♎	4p21			
23	♏	11p23			
26	♐	4a23			
28	♑	8a 5			
30	≈	10a57			

APR 1943 — ⊙ -> ♉ 20 6p31

D->SIGNS			D PHASES		
1	♓	1p27	1	(	6a29
3	♈	4p17	4	●	4p53
5	♉	8p37	8	)	9a 8
8	♊	2a53	12	○	10a 4
10	♋	2a39	16	○	12p12
12	♌	2p59	20	◑	6a10
15	♍	4p19	23	○	5p12
17	♎	12a41	27	◑	2a51
20	♏	7a 4	30	(	2p 8
22	♐	10a56			
24	♑	1p39			
26	≈	4p21			
28	♓	7p36			
30	♈	11p39			

MAY 1943 — ⊙ -> ♊ 21 6p 3

D->SIGNS			D PHASES		
3	♉	4a57	4	●	4a43
5	♊	12p16	8	)	1a52
8	♋	10p17	12	○	4a52
10	♌	10a38	16	○	3a39
13	♍	11p21	20	◑	4p13
15	♎	9a44	22	○	8a34
17	♏	4p19	29	(	10p21
19	♐	7p33			
21	♑	9p 0			
23	≈	10p23			
25	♓	12a57			
28	♈	4a 3			
30	♉	11a25			

JUN 1943 — ⊙ -> ♋ 22 2a12

D->SIGNS			D PHASES		
1	♊	7p29	2	●	5p33
4	♋	5a45	6	)	6p49
6	♌	6p 3	10	○	9p35
9	♍	7a 3	14	○	3p57
11	♎	6p22	18	◑	12a14
14	♏	1a59	20	○	5a31
16	♐	5a36	24	◑	3p 8
18	♑	6a29	28	(	8a 9
20	≈	6a33			
22	♓	7a36			
24	♈	10a52			
26	♉	4p52			
29	♊	1a27			

JUL 1943 — ⊙ -> ♌ 23 1p 4

D->SIGNS			D PHASES		
1	♋	12p13	2	●	7a44
4	♌	12a39	5	)	11a 7
6	♍	1p45	10	○	11a29
9	♎	1a 1	14	○	1a41
11	♏	10a40	17	◑	7a21
13	♐	5p 6	20	○	12p13
15	♑	5p 6	23	◑	11p38
17	≈	4p45	27	(	7p 6
19	♓	4p30	31	●	11p 6
21	♈	6p 8			
23	♉	10p52			
26	♊	6a53			
28	♋	6p 4			
31	♌	6a43			

AUG 1943 — ⊙ -> ♍ 23 7p55

D->SIGNS			D PHASES		
2	♍	7p45	5	●	1a54
5	♎	7a51	8	)	10p36
7	♏	5p40	12	○	9a45
9	♐	12a 8	15	○	2p34
12	♑	3a 9	18	◑	8p33
14	≈	3a 6	21	○	11a 4
16	♓	3a32	26	(	11a30
18	♈	3a32	30	●	2p59
20	♉	6a39			
22	♊	1p34			
25	♋	12a 7			
27	♌	12p49			
30	♍	1a47			

SEP 1943 – APR 1944

SEP 1943 — ⊙ -> ♎ 23 5p12

D->SIGNS			D PHASES		
1	♎	1p33	3	☽	2p40
3	♏	11p20	7	●	7a32
6	♐	6a38	10	○	5p 5
8	♑	11a13	13	○	10p40
10	≈	1p18	17	◑	7a24
12	♓	1p46	21	○	2a 6
14	♈	2p 8	25	(	2a56
16	♉	4p 0	29	●	6a29
18	♊	9p42			
21	♋	7a34			
23	♌	7p34			
26	♍	8p 4			
28	♎	7p56			

OCT 1943 — ⊙ -> ♏ 24 2a 8

D->SIGNS			D PHASES		
1	♏	5a 4	3	☽	1a32
3	♐	12p 3	6	●	3p10
5	♑	5p11	10	○	12a27
8	≈	8p39	13	○	8a23
9	♓	10p44	17	◑	9p28
12	♈	12a12	20	○	8p42
14	♉	2a26	24	(	12a13
16	♊	7a 7	28	●	8p59
18	♋	3p28			
21	♌	3a12			
23	♍	4p 0			
26	♎	3a38			
28	♏	12p14			
30	♐	6p14			

NOV 1943 — ⊙ -> ♐ 22 11p22

D->SIGNS			D PHASES		
1	♑	10p36	1	☽	11a 7
4	≈	2a 9	4	●	10p22
6	♓	5a16	8	○	8a39
8	♈	8a10	11	○	11a20
10	♉	11a32	15	◑	11a20
12	♊	4p31	19	○	5p43
14	♋	12a 5	26	(	10p50
17	♌	11a21			
19	♍	12p19			
22	♎	12a19			
24	♏	9p 9			
27	♐	2a35			
29	♑	5a43			

DEC 1943 — ⊙ -> ♑ 22 12p29

D->SIGNS			D PHASES		
1	≈	8a 1	1	☽	6a 3
3	♓	10a35	7	●	6p30
5	♈	2p 0	11	○	11a24
7	♉	6p30	15	◑	11a20
10	♊	12a32	19	○	3p 3
12	♋	8a46	23	(	12p 1
14	♌	7p37	26	●	10p50
17	♍	8a22	30	☽	5a33
19	♎	8p55			
22	♏	6a46			
24	♐	12p44			
26	♑	3p24			
28	≈	4p21			
30	♓	5p17			

JAN 1944 — ⊙ -> ≈ 20 11p 7

D->SIGNS			D PHASES		
1	♈	7p34	2	●	3p 4
3	♉	11p58	6	○	6a50
6	♊	6a44	10	○	5a 9
8	♋	3p48	14	◑	8a28
11	♌	2a57	18	○	10a32
13	♍	3p38	22	(	3a 9
16	♎	4a29	25	☽	10a24
18	♏	3p27	29	●	3p28
20	♐	10p53			
23	♑	2a26			
25	≈	3a 9			
27	♓	2a47			
29	♈	3a14			
31	♉	6a 7			

FEB 1944 — ⊙ -> ♓ 19 1p27

D->SIGNS			D PHASES		
2	♊	12p17	1	☽	2a 8
4	♋	9p40	4	○	10p 3
7	♌	9a20	9	◑	4a 3
9	♍	10p 8	13	○	4a31
12	♎	10a54	17	○	2a41
14	♏	10p24	20	(	3p42
17	♐	7a13	24	●	8p59
19	♑	1p 4	27	☽	2a12
21	≈	2p27			
23	♓	1p31			
25	♈	1p17			
27	♉	2a12			

MAR 1944 — ⊙ -> ♈ 20 12p48

D->SIGNS			D PHASES		
3	♊	3a38	1	☽	3p40
5	♋	3p19	5	○	7p28
8	♌	4a18	9	◑	8p23
10	♍	4p55	13	○	3p 5
13	♎	4a12	17	○	1a34
15	♏	1p31	20	(	6a36
17	♐	8p13	24	●	2p 0
19	♑	11p55	27	☽	7p34
22	≈	12a59			
24	♓	12a42			
26	♈	1a 1			
28	♉	3a58			
30	♊	10a59			

APR 1944 — ⊙ -> ♉ 20 12a18

D->SIGNS			D PHASES		
1	♋	9p54	4	○	10a15
4	♌	10a49	8	◑	12p22
6	♍	11p22	12	○	11p59
9	♎	10a12	15	○	9p 3
11	♏	7p 2	18	(	9p43
14	♐	1a56	22	●	3a10
16	♑	6a46	26	☽	3a10
18	≈	9a28			
20	♓	10a35			
22	♈	11a28			
24	♉	1p58			
26	♊	7p49			
29	♋	5a36			

MAY 1944 – DEC 1944

MAY 1944 — ⊙ -> ♊ 20 11p51

D->SIGNS			D PHASES		
1	♋	6p 4	4	○	4a12
4	♌	6a39	8	◑	2a28
6	♍	5p18	11	○	6p22
9	♎	1a27	15	○	6a12
11	♏	7a33	18	(	3p20
13	♐	12p10	21	●	1a12
15	♑	3p35	25	☽	5p51
17	≈	6p 9	29	○	7p 6
19	♓	8p15			
21	♈	11p26			
24	♉	5a 4			
26	♊	2p 4			
29	♋	1a58			
31	♌	2p37			

JUN 1944 — ⊙ -> ♋ 21 8a 2

D->SIGNS			D PHASES		
3	♍	1a32	2	○	8p25
5	♎	9a27	6	○	1p57
7	♏	2p41	10	○	1a23
9	♐	6p12	13	◑	10a56
11	♑	8p58	16	(	9p27
13	≈	11p54	19	●	12p 0
16	♓	2a52	24	☽	9a46
18	♈	7a11	28	○	12p27
20	♉	1p28			
22	♊	10p25			
25	♋	9a58			
27	♌	10p39			
30	♍	10a10			

JUL 1944 — ⊙ -> ♌ 22 6p56

D->SIGNS			D PHASES		
2	♍	6p38	2	○	10a33
4	♎	11p42	6	○	11p27
7	♏	2a14	9	◑	9p52
9	♐	3a39	13	(	3p38
11	♑	5a18	16	●	4a59
13	≈	8a16	20	☽	12a42
15	♓	1p11	23	○	2a14
17	♈	8p21	27	○	4a23
20	♉	5a51	31	○	10p48
22	♊	5p24			
25	♋	6a16			
27	♌	6p16			
30	♍	3a50			

AUG 1944 — ⊙ -> ♍ 23 1a46

D->SIGNS			D PHASES		
1	♎	9a42	4	☾	7a39
3	♏	12p16	7	●	12p49
5	♐	12p35	10	○	9p52
7	♑	12p43	14	◑	3p 9
9	≈	2p19	18	(	3p25
11	♓	6p38	21	☽	9a58
14	♈	2a 0	26	○	6p31
16	♉	12p 0	30	○	9p28
19	♊	12a45			
21	♋	1p45			
24	♌	1a13			
26	♍	11a51			
28	♎	7p12			
30	♏	10p44			

SEP 1944 — ⊙ -> ♎ 22 11p 2

D->SIGNS			D PHASES		
1	♐	11p14	2	○	3p21
3	♑	10p27	5	○	7p41
5	≈	10p28	9	◑	7a 3
8	♓	1a13	13	(	4a41
10	♈	7a47	17	☽	2a37
12	♉	5p50	21	●	9a58
15	♊	6a 0	25	○	7a 7
17	♋	6p48	28	○	6p52
20	♌	7a11			
22	♍	4p16			
24	♎	2a55			
27	♏	8a10			
29	♐	9a58			

OCT 1944 — ⊙ -> ♏ 23 7a56

D->SIGNS			D PHASES		
1	♑	9a30	1	○	11p22
3	≈	8a46	5	○	4a58
5	♓	9a59	9	◑	8p12
7	♈	2p36	12	(	9p27
9	♉	12a55	15	☽	5p59
12	♊	12p 4	19	●	12p52
14	♋	12a55	24	○	12p11
17	♌	1p 3	28	○	3a27
19	♍	11p50	31	○	8a35
22	♎	8a48			
24	♏	3p19			
26	♐	6p53			
28	♑	7p54			
30	≈	8a35			

NOV 1944 — ⊙ -> ♐ 22 5a 8

D->SIGNS			D PHASES		
1	♓	8p28	3	○	5p40
3	♈	12a12	7	○	1p28
6	♉	7a44	11	◑	4p36
8	♊	6p59	15	(	12p52
11	♋	7a44	18	☽	8p47
13	♌	7p47	23	●	2p12
16	♍	6a 2	26	○	11a51
18	♎	2p20	30	○	7p52
20	♏	8p47			
23	♐	1a18			
25	♑	3a57			
27	≈	5a22			
29	♓	6a55			

DEC 1944 — ⊙ -> ♑ 21 6p15

D->SIGNS			D PHASES		
1	♈	10a16	3	○	10a 2
3	♉	4p53	7	○	9a56
5	♊	3a 4	11	◑	12p45
8	♋	3p28	15	(	9a34
11	♌	3a42	18	☽	11p58
13	♍	1p50	23	○	10a54
15	♎	9p22	25	○	8p57
18	♏	2a44	29	●	9a38
20	♐	6a39			
22	♑	9a42			
24	≈	12p24			
26	♓	3p26			
28	♈	7p44			
31	♉	2a19			

JAN 1945 – AUG 1945

JAN 1945	FEB 1945	MAR 1945	APR 1945	MAY 1945	JUN 1945	JUL 1945	AUG 1945
☉→♒ 20 4a54	☉→♓ 18 7p15	☉→♈ 20 6p37	☉→♉ 20 6a 7	☉→♊ 21 5a40	☉→♋ 21 1p52	☉→♌ 23 12a45	☉→♍ 23 7a35

☽→SIGNS

JAN 1945	FEB 1945	MAR 1945	APR 1945	MAY 1945	JUN 1945	JUL 1945	AUG 1945
2 ♍ 11a49	1 ♎ 7a46	3 ♏ 3a32	1 ♐ 10p 7	1 ♑ 2p40	2 ♓ 10a25	1 ♈ 7p29	2 ♊ 6a23
4 ♎ 11p44	3 ♏ 8p22	5 ♐ 3p45	4 ♑ 8a51	3 ♒ 11p 6	4 ♈ 1p51	3 ♉ 10p 4	4 ♋ 10a22
7 ♏ 12p13	6 ♐ 7a57	8 ♑ 1a37	6 ♒ 4p28	6 ♓ 4a21	6 ♉ 3p23	6 ♊ 12a19	6 ♌ 3p52
9 ♐ 10p55	8 ♑ 4p29	10 ♒ 7a40	8 ♓ 8p10	8 ♈ 6a25	8 ♊ 4p15	8 ♋ 3a10	9 ♍ 9a21
12 ♑ 6a28	10 ♒ 9p12	12 ♓ 9a50	10 ♈ 8p38	10 ♉ 6a24	10 ♋ 6p20	10 ♌ 7a43	11 ♎ 9p21
14 ♒ 10a57	12 ♓ 10p55	14 ♈ 9a32	12 ♉ 8p18	12 ♊ 6a12	12 ♌ 10p20	12 ♍ 2p58	13 ♏ 9a56
16 ♓ 1p27	14 ♈ 11p12	16 ♉ 8a54	14 ♊ 7p40	14 ♋ 7a51	15 ♍ 6a 7	15 ♎ 1a13	16 ♐ 8p31
18 ♈ 3p20	17 ♉ 11a 6	18 ♊ 10a 4	16 ♋ 7p31	16 ♌ 12p57	17 ♎ 5p 6	17 ♏ 1p29	18 ♑ 8p30
20 ♉ 5p48	19 ♊ 3a 1	20 ♋ 2p31	18 ♌ 10p13	18 ♍ 9p56	20 ♏ 5a36	20 ♐ 1a36	20 ♒ 7a 5
22 ♊ 9p34	21 ♋ 8a42	22 ♌ 10p31	21 ♍ 4a52	21 ♎ 9a43	22 ♐ 5p27	22 ♑ 11a29	23 ♓ 7a 5
25 ♋ 3a 5	23 ♌ 4p58	25 ♍ 9a11	23 ♎ 3a15	23 ♏ 10p20	25 ♑ 3a14	24 ♒ 6p16	25 ♈ 8a30
27 ♌ 10a33	26 ♍ 3a13	27 ♎ 9p15	26 ♏ 3p52	26 ♐ 10a11	27 ♒ 10a36	26 ♓ 10p26	27 ♉ 9a33
29 ♍ 8p 9	28 ♎ 2p57	30 ♏ 9a50	29 ♐ 3a56	28 ♑ 8p24	29 ♓ 3p51	29 ♈ 1a 7	29 ♊ 11a47
				31 ♒ 4a35		31 ♉ 3a29	31 ♋ 4p 0

☽ PHASES

JAN 1945	FEB 1945	MAR 1945	APR 1945	MAY 1945	JUN 1945	JUL 1945	AUG 1945
2 ○ 5a18	1 ○ 1a51	2 ○ 9p49	1 ○ 3p38	1 ○ 6a23	3 ☾ 8a15	2 ☾ 1p13	4 ☾ 4a27
6 ○ 7a47	5 ○ 4a55	6 ☾ 11p30	5 ☾ 2p18	4 ☾ 4p39	6 ● 11p26	5 ● 10p 6	7 ● 7p32
10 ☾ 8a20	9 ☾ 1a50	10 ● 4p10	9 ● 2a57	8 ● 10a44	9 ☽ 11a31	9 ☽ 1a23	11 ☽ 4p55
14 ● 12a 6	12 ● 12p33	13 ☽ 10p51	12 ☽ 7a29	11 ☽ 3p21	13 ○ 9a 5	13 ○ 3a25	15 ○ 7p26
17 ☽ 9a39	15 ☽ 6p30	17 ○ 3a15	15 ○ 12p40	14 ○ 11p18	17 ○ 11a32	17 ○ 2a 1	19 ○ 6p11
20 ○ 6p48	19 ○ 12a36	20 ○ 2p11	18 ○ 2a46	18 ○ 5p12	21 ○ 10a 8	21 ○ 9p25	23 ○ 7a 3
24 ○ 7a34	22 ○ 8p13	24 ○ 10a45	23 ○ 2a36	22 ○ 7p 4	25 ♐ 10a 8	24 ○ 3a25	26 ○ 2p 7
28 ○ 1a41	26 ○ 7p 7	28 ○ 12p44	27 ○ 5a33	26 ○ 8p49	29 ○ 2a 7	28 ○ 8a27	29 ○ 10p44
				30 ○ 5p45		31 ○ 5p30	

SEP 1945 – APR 1946

SEP 1945	OCT 1945	NOV 1945	DEC 1945	JAN 1946	FEB 1946	MAR 1946	APR 1946
☉→♎ 23 4a50	☉→♏ 23 1p44	☉→♐ 22 10a55	☉→♑ 22 12a 4	☉→♒ 20 10a45	☉→♓ 19 1a 9	☉→♈ 21 12a33	☉→♉ 20 12p 2

☽→SIGNS

SEP 1945	OCT 1945	NOV 1945	DEC 1945	JAN 1946	FEB 1946	MAR 1946	APR 1946
2 ♌ 10p19	2 ♍ 12p34	1 ♎ 5a 8	3 ♐ 12p30	2 ♑ 7a11	1 ♒ 12a23	2 ♓ 3p25	1 ♈ 4a16
5 ♍ 6a36	4 ♎ 11p16	3 ♏ 5p29	6 ♑ 12a23	4 ♒ 4p38	3 ♓ 6a32	4 ♈ 6p23	3 ♉ 4a56
7 ♎ 4p48	7 ♏ 11a24	6 ♐ 6a18	8 ♒ 10a34	6 ♓ 11p47	5 ♈ 10a38	6 ♉ 8p 8	5 ♊ 5a25
10 ♏ 4a48	10 ♐ 12a17	8 ♑ 6p35	10 ♓ 6p20	9 ♈ 4a56	7 ♉ 1p46	8 ♊ 10p12	7 ♋ 7a21
12 ♐ 5p37	12 ♑ 12p33	11 ♒ 4a59	12 ♈ 11p15	11 ♉ 8a25	9 ♊ 4p45	11 ♋ 1a28	9 ♌ 11a37
15 ♑ 5a11	15 ♒ 10p 7	13 ♓ 12p35	15 ♉ 1a30	13 ♊ 10a42	11 ♋ 7p59	13 ♌ 6a14	11 ♍ 6p20
17 ♒ 1p19	17 ♓ 3a34	15 ♈ 5p17	17 ♊ 2a 2	15 ♋ 12p32	13 ♌ 11p50	15 ♍ 12p32	14 ♎ 3a13
19 ♓ 5p19	19 ♈ 6a34	17 ♉ 8p48	19 ♋ 3a 2	17 ♌ 3p 3	16 ♍ 5a 3	17 ♎ 8p40	16 ♏ 2p 3
21 ♈ 6p10	21 ♉ 8a30	19 ♊ 3p 2	21 ♌ 4a30	19 ♍ 7p40	18 ♎ 12p36	20 ♏ 7a 4	19 ♐ 2a30
23 ♉ 5p53	23 ♊ 11a30	21 ♋ 3p14	23 ♍ 9a30	22 ♎ 3a31	20 ♏ 10p 5	22 ♐ 7p30	21 ♑ 3p28
25 ♊ 6p31	25 ♋ 5a11	23 ♌ 6p12	25 ♎ 6p45	24 ♏ 2p40	23 ♐ 11a41	25 ♑ 8a17	24 ♒ 2a56
27 ♋ 9p38	27 ♌ 9a55	25 ♍ 12a59	28 ♏ 11a18	27 ♐ 3a27	26 ♑ 12a 1	27 ♒ 6p51	26 ♓ 10a54
30 ♌ 3a47	29 ♍ 6p12	28 ♎ 11a18	30 ♐ 7p32	29 ♑ 3p18	28 ♒ 9a34	30 ♓ 1a26	28 ♈ 2p45
		30 ♏ 11p43					30 ♉ 3p31

☽ PHASES

SEP 1945	OCT 1945	NOV 1945	DEC 1945	JAN 1946	FEB 1946	MAR 1946	APR 1946
2 ☾ 12p54	2 ☾ 12a22	4 ● 6p11	4 ● 1p 6	3 ☽ 7a30	1 ● 1p43	3 ● 1p 1	1 ● 11p37
6 ● 8a43	6 ● 8a22	8 ☽ 9p13	8 ☽ 1p 3	7 ○ 2a18	5 ☽ 12p56	9 ○ 9p40	5 ☽ 5a28
10 ☽ 9a54	10 ☽ 3a42	12 ○ 6a14	15 ○ 6a 4	10 ○ 3p27	8 ○ 11p27	10 ○ 7a 3	8 ○ 3p 4
14 ○ 12p38	14 ○ 4a38	16 ○ 5a43	15 ○ 3p24	14 ○ 12a47	12 ○ 10a58	13 ○ 8p19	12 ○ 7a 2
18 ○ 7a29	17 ○ 7p14	19 ○ 10a13	18 ♐ 9p17	17 ○ 9a47	15 ○ 11p28	17 ○ 2p11	16 ○ 5a47
21 ○ 3p45	21 ○ 12a32	22 ○ 4p41	22 ○ 7a11	21 ○ 12a13	19 ○ 6p56	21 ○ 2p15	20 ○ 8a45
24 ○ 8p36	24 ○ 5a12	26 ○ 8a28	26 ○ 3a 0	25 ○ 12a 3	23 ○ 9p36	25 ○ 5p37	24 ○ 10a18
28 ○ 6a24	27 ○ 5p30	29 ☾ 9a37	30 ☾ 6a13	29 ☾ 3a10	27 ☾ 10p14	29 ☾ 1p55	28 ☾ 1a57
	31 ☾ 3p19						

MAY 1946 – DEC 1946

MAY 1946	JUN 1946	JUL 1946	AUG 1946	SEP 1946	OCT 1946	NOV 1946	DEC 1946
☉→♊ 21 11a34	☉→♋ 21 7p44	☉→♌ 23 6a37	☉→♍ 23 1p26	☉→♎ 23 10a41	☉→♏ 23 7p35	☉→♐ 22 4p46	☉→♑ 22 5a53

☽→SIGNS

MAY 1946	JUN 1946	JUL 1946	AUG 1946	SEP 1946	OCT 1946	NOV 1946	DEC 1946
2 ♊ 3p 3	1 ♋ 1a28	2 ♍ 3p45	1 ♎ 7a 5	2 ♐ 12p31	2 ♑ 9a29	1 ♒ 5a36	3 ♈ 7a 5
4 ♋ 3p22	3 ♌ 2a39	4 ♎ 10p21	4 ♏ 4p23	5 ♑ 1a24	4 ♒ 9p27	3 ♓ 3p32	5 ♉ 10a48
6 ♌ 6p 4	5 ♍ 6a57	7 ♏ 8a41	6 ♐ 4a36	7 ♒ 12p41	7 ♓ 6a 9	5 ♈ 9p28	7 ♊ 11a30
8 ♍ 11p57	7 ♎ 2p57	9 ♐ 9p20	8 ♑ 5p23	9 ♓ 8p46	9 ♈ 11a 5	7 ♉ 11p49	9 ♋ 11a50
11 ♎ 8a15	10 ♏ 2a 4	12 ♑ 10a 5	11 ♒ 5a13	12 ♈ 1a49	11 ♉ 1p20	10 ♊ 12a17	11 ♌ 10a46
13 ♏ 8p 8	12 ♐ 2p50	14 ♒ 9p17	13 ♓ 12p41	14 ♉ 5a 3	13 ♊ 2p36	12 ♋ 12a15	13 ♍ 1p 9
16 ♐ 8a46	15 ♑ 3a39	17 ♈ 6a15	15 ♈ 6p37	16 ♊ 5a37	15 ♋ 4p23	14 ♌ 1a53	15 ♎ 7p 7
18 ♑ 9p42	17 ♒ 3p16	19 ♉ 12p59	17 ♉ 10p59	18 ♋ 5a10	17 ♌ 7p35	16 ♍ 6a 5	18 ♏ 4a43
21 ♒ 9a31	20 ♓ 12a43	21 ♊ 5p35	20 ♊ 2p13	20 ♌ 12a35	20 ♍ 12a18	18 ♎ 1p12	20 ♐ 4p48
23 ♓ 6p39	22 ♈ 7p 9	23 ♋ 8p18	22 ♋ 5a 6	22 ♍ 6p38	22 ♎ 7a33	20 ♏ 10p58	23 ♑ 5a50
26 ♈ 12a 5	24 ♉ 10a56	25 ♌ 9a43	24 ♌ 7a38	24 ♎ 9a12	24 ♏ 4a 3	23 ♐ 10a44	25 ♒ 6p29
28 ♉ 2a 3	26 ♊ 12p10	27 ♍ 10p57	26 ♍ 10a54	27 ♏ 5a 6	26 ♐ 5a 3	25 ♑ 11p39	28 ♓ 5a43
30 ♊ 1a54	28 ♋ 12p10	30 ♎ 1a32	28 ♎ 4p15	29 ♐ 8p32	29 ♑ 4p59	28 ♒ 12p30	30 ♈ 2p31
	30 ♌ 12p47		31 ♏ 1a49			30 ♓ 11p30	

☽ PHASES

MAY 1946	JUN 1946	JUL 1946	AUG 1946	SEP 1946	OCT 1946	NOV 1946	DEC 1946
1 ● 8a16	2 ☽ 9p28	2 ☽ 7a 0	4 ○ 3p55	3 ○ 9a49	3 ○ 4a53	1 ○ 11p40	1 ○ 4p47
4 ☽ 1p11	6 ○ 11a 6	6 ○ 12a15	7 ○ 7p 0	7 ○ 11a36	7 ○ 3a20	5 ○ 5p52	5 ○ 7a 4
8 ○ 12a13	10 ○ 10a22	10 ○ 2a17	11 ○ 4a59	11 ○ 11p11	10 ○ 9p40	8 ☾ 2a10	8 ☾ 12p52
11 ○ 8p 0	14 ♐ 4a22	14 ○ 12a44	15 ○ 1a44	13 ☾ 8a28	12 ☾ 7a37	10 ● 1a32	15 ● 5a57
15 ○ 9p52	18 ○ 2p24	18 ○ 12a44	19 ☾ 8a17	17 ☾ 1p 6	15 ● 5p35	15 ● 1p 9	15 ● 5p49
20 ○ 11p 1	21 ☾ 2p52	21 ☾ 2p52	23 ● 6a47	21 ● 1p 1	19 ☽ 11a32	19 ☽ 4a17	19 ☽ 4a17
23 ☾ 10a56	25 ☽ 5p52	25 ☽ 11p49	26 ● 4p 7	24 ☽ 3a45	26 ☽ 6p32	23 ☽ 12p24	23 ☽ 8a 6
30 ☽ 3p49	28 ♐ 1p 6	28 ● 6a54	30 ☽ 8a34	29 ☽ 1a30	28 ☽ 8p40	27 ☽ 4p25	27 ☽ 10a48
		31 ☽ 6p29					31 ○ 7a22

BAND 1 — 1947

JAN 1947
☉ -> ≈ 20 4p32

D -> SIGNS
1 ♉ 8p 6 · 3 ♊ 10p26 · 5 ♋ 10p28 · 7 ♌ 9p53 · 9 ♍ 10p44 · 12 ♎ 2a54 · 14 ♏ 11a15 · 16 ♐ 11p 3 · 19 ♑ 12p10 · 22 ♒ 12a37 · 24 ♓ 11a23 · 26 ♈ 8p10 · 29 ♉ 2a45 · 31 ♊ 6a52

D PHASES
3 ○ 6p48 · 6 ◐ 11p47 · 10 ○ 6a 6 · 13 ● 9p56 · 18 ☾ 12a 0 · 22 ● 3a34 · 26 ☽ 2a26 · 29 ◐ 7p 7

FEB 1947
☉ -> ♓ 19 6a52

D -> SIGNS
2 ♋ 8a38 · 4 ♌ 9a 1 · 6 ♍ 9a42 · 8 ♎ 12p39 · 11 ♏ 7p28 · 13 ♐ 6a15 · 15 ♑ 7p12 · 18 ♒ 7p38 · 20 ♓ 5p57 · 23 ♈ 1a57 · 25 ♉ 8a 8 · 27 ♊ 12p47

D PHASES
2 ○ 4a55 · 5 ◐ 10a50 · 8 ○ 8p32 · 12 ● 4p58 · 16 ☾ 8p41 · 20 ● 9p 0 · 24 ☽ 2p55 · 28 ◐ 4a12

MAR 1947
☉ -> ♈ 21 6a13

D -> SIGNS
1 ♋ 3p59 · 3 ♌ 6p 0 · 5 ♍ 7p46 · 7 ♎ 10p51 · 10 ♏ 4a51 · 12 ♐ 2p34 · 15 ♑ 3a 0 · 17 ♒ 3p35 · 20 ♓ 1a57 · 22 ♈ 9a23 · 24 ♉ 2p29 · 26 ♊ 6p16 · 28 ♋ 9p26 · 31 ♌ 12a22

D PHASES
3 ○ 1p36 · 6 ◐ 10p15 · 10 ○ 12p56 · 13 ● 11p28 · 18 ☾ 4p 7 · 22 ● 11a34 · 26 ☽ 12a38 · 29 ◐ 11a15

APR 1947
☉ -> ♉ 20 5p39

D -> SIGNS
2 ♍ 3a30 · 4 ♎ 7a39 · 6 ♏ 1p56 · 8 ♐ 11p12 · 11 ♑ 11a51 · 13 ♒ 11p51 · 16 ♓ 10a47 · 18 ♈ 6p25 · 20 ♉ 10p56 · 23 ♊ 1a27 · 25 ♋ 3a22 · 27 ♌ 5a44 · 29 ♍ 9a15

D PHASES
1 ○ 9p32 · 4 ◐ 11p53 · 9 ○ 6a38 · 12 ● 9a23 · 17 ☾ 8a55 · 20 ● 11p19 · 24 ☽ 8a16 · 27 ◐ 5p18

MAY 1947
☉ -> ♊ 21 5p 9

D -> SIGNS
1 ♎ 2a24 · 3 ♏ 9p35 · 6 ♐ 6p55 · 8 ♑ 7a41 · 11 ♒ 7p20 · 13 ♓ 3a56 · 16 ♈ 8a51 · 18 ♉ 10a51 · 20 ♊ 11a27 · 22 ♋ 12p18 · 24 ♌ 3p20 · 26 ♍ 7p54 · 28 ♎ 3a42 · 31 ♏ 3a42

D PHASES
1 ○ 5a49 · 4 ◐ 11p53 · 9 ○ 12a29 · 11 ● 9a41 · 16 ☾ 10p42 · 18 ● 4p26 · 23 ☽ 9p 0 · 25 ◐ 7a25 · 30 ○ 3p32

JUN 1947
☉ -> ♋ 22 1a19

D -> SIGNS
2 ♐ 1p54 · 5 ♑ 1a51 · 7 ♒ 2a38 · 9 ♓ 2a47 · 12 ♈ 12p34 · 14 ♉ 6p45 · 16 ♊ 9p21 · 18 ♋ 9p32 · 20 ♌ 9p 6 · 22 ♍ 10p 1 · 25 ♎ 1a51 · 27 ♏ 9a17 · 29 ♐ 7p46

D PHASES
3 ◐ 2p27 · 7 ○ 5p16 · 11 ○ 5p58 · 15 ☾ 9a41 · 18 ● 4p26 · 21 ☽ 9p 0 · 25 ◐ 7a25 · 29 ○ 3a28

JUL 1947
☉ -> ♌ 23 12p14

D -> SIGNS
2 ♑ 8a 3 · 4 ♒ 8p50 · 7 ♓ 9a 3 · 9 ♈ 7p34 · 12 ♉ 3a12 · 14 ♊ 8a14 · 16 ♋ 11a34 · 18 ♌ 1p41 · 20 ♍ 7a19 · 22 ♎ 10p 1 · 24 ♏ 3p41 · 27 ♐ 1a40 · 29 ♑ 2p 1

D PHASES
3 ○ 5a38 · 7 ◐ 8a12 · 11 ○ 5a54 · 14 ● 11p15 · 18 ☾ 4a18 · 21 ● 9p 0 · 24 ☽ 4a18 · 28 ◐ 5p46

AUG 1947
☉ -> ♍ 23 7p 9

D -> SIGNS
1 ♒ 2a50 · 3 ♓ 2p49 · 6 ♈ 1a20 · 8 ♉ 9a43 · 10 ♊ 3p17 · 12 ♋ 6p 6 · 14 ♌ 6p49 · 16 ♍ 5p49 · 18 ♎ 7p 4 · 20 ♏ 11p44 · 23 ♐ 8a34 · 25 ♑ 8p31 · 28 ♒ 9a18 · 30 ♓ 9p 3

D PHASES
1 ○ 8p50 · 5 ◐ 9p 4 · 9 ○ 3p22 · 13 ● 1a27 · 16 ☾ 6a12 · 19 ☽ 1p47 · 23 ● 7a40 · 27 ◐ 10a 1 · 31 ○ 11a34

BAND 2 — 1947–1948

SEP 1947
☉ -> ♎ 23 4p29

D -> SIGNS
2 ♈ 7a 2 · 4 ♉ 3p10 · 6 ♊ 9p18 · 9 ♋ 1a12 · 11 ♌ 3a 3 · 13 ♍ 3a51 · 15 ♎ 5a16 · 17 ♏ 9a10 · 19 ♐ 4p49 · 22 ♑ 3a57 · 24 ♒ 4p37 · 27 ♓ 4a24 · 29 ♈ 1p58

D PHASES
4 ○ 8a 4 · 7 ◐ 10p57 · 11 ○ 7a51 · 14 ● 2p28 · 17 ☾ 2a26 · 21 ☽ 12a42 · 26 ○ 3a33 · 30 ◐ 1a41

OCT 1947
☉ -> ♏ 24 1a26

D -> SIGNS
1 ♉ 9p15 · 4 ♊ 2a44 · 6 ♋ 6a47 · 8 ♌ 9a41 · 10 ♍ 11a57 · 12 ♎ 2p31 · 14 ♏ 6p45 · 17 ♐ 1a53 · 19 ♑ 12p14 · 22 ♒ 12a39 · 24 ♓ 12p45 · 27 ♈ 10p31 · 29 ♉ 5a16 · 31 ♊ 9a36

D PHASES
5 ○ 5p41 · 7 ◐ 5a29 · 10 ○ 2p43 · 14 ● 1a10 · 17 ☾ 6p35 · 21 ☽ 8p11 · 26 ○ 9p32 · 29 ◐ 3p 7

NOV 1947
☉ -> ♐ 24 10p38

D -> SIGNS
2 ♋ 12p32 · 4 ♌ 3p 3 · 6 ♍ 5p55 · 8 ♎ 9p42 · 11 ♏ 3a 2 · 13 ♐ 10a25 · 15 ♑ 8p37 · 18 ♒ 8a48 · 20 ♓ 9p15 · 23 ♈ 7a53 · 25 ♉ 3p 6 · 27 ♊ 6p55 · 29 ♋ 8p31

D PHASES
2 ○ 2a27 · 5 ◐ 12p 3 · 8 ○ 11p18 · 12 ● 3p 1 · 16 ☾ 1p37 · 20 ☽ 4p44 · 25 ○ 3p27 · 28 ◐ 3a45

DEC 1947
☉ -> ♑ 22 11a43

D -> SIGNS
1 ♌ 9p30 · 3 ♍ 11p 8 · 6 ♎ 3a14 · 8 ♏ 9a24 · 10 ♐ 5p49 · 13 ♑ 4a14 · 15 ♒ 4p16 · 18 ♓ 4a59 · 20 ♈ 4p37 · 23 ♉ 1a11 · 25 ♊ 5a47 · 27 ♋ 7a 3 · 29 ♌ 6a41 · 31 ♍ 6a47

D PHASES
2 ○ 2a26 · 4 ◐ 7p55 · 8 ○ 10a43 · 12 ● 7a53 · 16 ☾ 10a 6 · 20 ☽ 12p44 · 24 ○ 7a12 · 27 ◐ 3p27 · 30 ● 8p14

JAN 1948
☉ -> ≈ 20 10p19

D -> SIGNS
2 ♎ 9a10 · 4 ♏ 2p51 · 6 ♐ 11p40 · 9 ♑ 10a41 · 11 ♒ 10p54 · 14 ♓ 11a35 · 16 ♈ 11p44 · 19 ♉ 9a42 · 21 ♊ 4p 1 · 23 ♋ 6p23 · 25 ♌ 6p 0 · 27 ♍ 4p56 · 29 ♎ 5p29 · 31 ♏ 9p27

D PHASES
3 ○ 6a13 · 7 ◐ 1a21 · 11 ○ 2a45 · 15 ● 6a12 · 19 ☾ 6a32 · 22 ☽ 8p58 · 26 ○ 2a11 · 30 ◐ 6a42

FEB 1948
☉ -> ♓ 19 12p37

D -> SIGNS
3 ♐ 4p30 · 6 ♑ 4a59 · 8 ♒ 5p37 · 11 ♓ 5a37 · 13 ♈ 5p12 · 16 ♉ 3a11 · 18 ♊ 11a19 · 20 ♋ 4p 9 · 22 ♌ 4a22 · 24 ♍ 3p 1 · 26 ♎ 6a24 · 28 ♏ 6a24

D PHASES
1 ○ 7p31 · 5 ◐ 6p41 · 10 ○ 2p 2 · 14 ● 12a14 · 17 ☾ 7a55 · 21 ☽ 12p16 · 24 ○ 6p52

MAR 1948
☉ -> ♈ 20 11a57

D -> SIGNS
1 ♐ 1a22 · 3 ♑ 10p50 · 6 ♒ 11a14 · 8 ♓ 11p53 · 11 ♈ 11a33 · 13 ♉ 9p40 · 16 ♊ 5a45 · 18 ♋ 11a14 · 20 ♌ 1p58 · 22 ♍ 2p42 · 24 ♎ 3p 1 · 26 ♏ 4p49 · 28 ♐ 9p46 · 31 ♑ 6a34

D PHASES
2 ○ 11a35 · 6 ◐ 1p29 · 10 ○ 4p15 · 14 ● 3p 2 · 17 ☾ 7a27 · 21 ○ 4p24 · 24 ☽ 10p10 · 28 ◐ 8a42

APR 1948
☉ -> ♉ 19 11p25

D -> SIGNS
2 ♒ 6p18 · 5 ♓ 6a56 · 7 ♈ 6p28 · 10 ♉ 3a58 · 12 ♊ 11a20 · 14 ♋ 4p16 · 16 ♌ 8p16 · 18 ♍ 10p49 · 21 ♎ 12a16 · 23 ♏ 2a49 · 25 ♐ 7a31 · 27 ♑ 3p21 · 30 ♒ 2a16

D PHASES
1 ○ 8a25 · 5 ◐ 8a16 · 9 ○ 2a14 · 13 ● 2p42 · 16 ☾ 2a28 · 20 ☽ 11p49 · 26 ○ 1p49 · 30 ◐ 4p45

BAND 3 — 1948

MAY 1948
☉ -> ♊ 20 10p57

D -> SIGNS
2 ♓ 2p44 · 5 ♈ 2a28 · 7 ♉ 11a48 · 9 ♊ 6p20 · 11 ♋ 10p38 · 14 ♌ 1a39 · 16 ♍ 4a14 · 18 ♎ 6a55 · 20 ♏ 10a55 · 22 ♐ 4p22 · 25 ♑ 12a 8 · 27 ♒ 10a31 · 29 ♓ 10p46

D PHASES
1 ◐ 1a50 · 8 ◐ 9p30 · 12 ○ 10a15 · 15 ● 7p55 · 19 ☾ 6a 2 · 22 ☽ 7p37 · 26 ○ 3p42 · 30 ◐ 5p43

JUN 1948
☉ -> ♋ 21 7a10

D -> SIGNS
1 ♈ 10a55 · 3 ♉ 8p43 · 6 ♊ 3a 6 · 8 ♋ 6a28 · 10 ♌ 8a11 · 12 ♍ 9a48 · 14 ♎ 12p33 · 16 ♏ 5p 3 · 18 ♐ 11p28 · 21 ♑ 7a51 · 23 ♒ 6p15 · 26 ♓ 6a23 · 28 ♈ 6p56

D PHASES
3 ◐ 5p22 · 7 ◐ 7a55 · 10 ○ 9p29 · 14 ● 12a40 · 17 ☾ 1p35 · 21 ☽ 7a54 · 25 ○ 7a52 · 29 ◐ 10a23

JUL 1948
☉ -> ♌ 22 6p 8

D -> SIGNS
1 ♉ 5a40 · 3 ♊ 12p48 · 5 ♋ 4p 7 · 7 ♌ 4p53 · 9 ♍ 5p 3 · 11 ♎ 6p31 · 13 ♏ 10p28 · 16 ♐ 5a11 · 18 ♑ 1p48 · 21 ♒ 1a 2 · 23 ♓ 1p13 · 26 ♈ 1a57 · 28 ♉ 1p34 · 30 ♊ 10p 1

D PHASES
3 ◐ 6a25 · 6 ◐ 4p 9 · 10 ○ 1p35 · 13 ● 6a 3 · 16 ☾ 10p58 · 20 ☽ 11p56 · 25 ○ 1a 7 · 29 ◐ 10a23

AUG 1948
☉ -> ♍ 23 1a 3

D -> SIGNS
2 ♋ 2a20 · 4 ♌ 3a13 · 6 ♍ 2a32 · 8 ♎ 2a29 · 10 ♏ 4a56 · 12 ♐ 10a23 · 14 ♑ 7p51 · 17 ♒ 7a35 · 19 ♓ 7p23 · 22 ♈ 8a 5 · 24 ♉ 8p 3 · 27 ♊ 5a40 · 29 ♋ 11a34 · 31 ♌ 1p41

D PHASES
1 ● 5p 4 · 5 ◐ 11p13 · 8 ○ 3a37 · 11 ● 2p40 · 14 ☾ 4a43 · 19 ☽ 3a25 · 23 ○ 3p25 · 27 ◐ 9a43 · 31 ● 1a53

SEP 1948
☉ -> ♎ 22 10p22

D -> SIGNS
2 ♍ 1p20 · 4 ♎ 12p35 · 6 ♏ 1p34 · 8 ♐ 5p52 · 11 ♑ 1a56 · 13 ♒ 12p58 · 16 ♓ 1a27 · 18 ♈ 2p 2 · 21 ♉ 1a45 · 23 ♊ 12p21 · 25 ♋ 5p14 · 27 ♌ 8p35 · 29 ♍ 11p40

D PHASES
2 ● 6a21 · 6 ◐ 2a 5 · 10 ○ 1a42 · 14 ● 4a43 · 17 ☾ 9p23 · 22 ☽ 6a16 · 26 ○ 8a41 · 30 ◐ 4p22

OCT 1948
☉ -> ♏ 23 7a18

D -> SIGNS
1 ♎ 11p30 · 3 ♏ 11p58 · 6 ♐ 2a55 · 8 ♑ 9a31 · 10 ♒ 7p42 · 13 ♓ 8a 1 · 15 ♈ 8p36 · 18 ♉ 7a54 · 20 ♊ 5p14 · 23 ♋ 12a21 · 25 ♌ 5a10 · 27 ♍ 7a53 · 29 ♎ 9a16 · 31 ♏ 10a31

D PHASES
2 ● 2p42 · 5 ◐ 11p 5 · 9 ○ 7p19 · 13 ● 9p35 · 17 ☾ 7p23 · 22 ☽ 12a 7 · 25 ○ 8a11 · 28 ◐ 5p34

NOV 1948
☉ -> ♐ 22 4a29

D -> SIGNS
2 ♐ 1p10 · 4 ♑ 6p39 · 7 ♒ 3a41 · 9 ♓ 3p33 · 12 ♈ 4a12 · 14 ♉ 3p40 · 17 ♊ 12a 2 · 19 ♋ 7a11 · 21 ♌ 10a32 · 23 ♍ 1p48 · 25 ♎ 4p33 · 27 ♏ 7p52 · 29 ♐ 10p52

D PHASES
1 ● 1a 3 · 4 ◐ 1p38 · 8 ○ 11a46 · 12 ● 2p55 · 16 ☾ 1p31 · 20 ☽ 6p30 · 24 ○ 2a17 · 27 ● 1p44

DEC 1948
☉ -> ♑ 21 5p33

D -> SIGNS
2 ♑ 4a16 · 4 ♒ 12p32 · 6 ♓ 11p46 · 9 ♈ 12p30 · 11 ♉ 12a 9 · 14 ♊ 8a44 · 16 ♋ 2p 1 · 18 ♌ 5p 3 · 20 ♍ 7p19 · 22 ♎ 9p59 · 25 ♏ 1a39 · 27 ♐ 6a29 · 29 ♑ 12p46 · 31 ♒ 9p 3

D PHASES
4 ● 7a18 · 8 ◐ 8a57 · 12 ○ 10a53 · 16 ● 4a11 · 19 ☾ 2p34 · 22 ☽ 12p31 · 26 ○ 12p31 · 30 ● 4a45

1949

JAN 1949
☉ → ♒ 20 4a 9

☽→SIGNS
| 3 ♓ 7a58 | 5 ♈ 8p40 | 8 ♉ 9a 3 | 10 ♊ 6p31 | 12 ♋ 11p57 | 15 ♌ 2a 8 | 17 ♍ 2a52 | 19 ♎ 4a 3 | 21 ♏ 6a59 | 23 ♐ 12p 9 | 25 ♑ 7p21 | 28 ♒ 4a26 | 30 ♓ 3p26 |

☽ PHASES
| 3 ☽ 3a16 | 7 ○ 6a51 | 14 ○ 5a18 | 17 ○ 11p40 | 21 ○ 9a 3 | 25 ☽ 12a38 | 28 ● 9p42 |

FEB 1949
☉ → ♓ 18 6p27

☽→SIGNS
| 2 ♈ 4a 4 | 4 ♉ 4p57 | 7 ♊ 3a40 | 9 ♋ 10a22 | 11 ♌ 1p 1 | 13 ♍ 1p 5 | 15 ♎ 12p44 | 17 ♏ 1p53 | 19 ♐ 5p49 | 22 ♑ 12a50 | 24 ♒ 10a15 | 26 ♓ 9p54 |

☽ PHASES
| 2 ☽ 12a 5 | 6 ○ 3a 5 | 9 ○ 8p49 | 16 ○ 4a 8 | 20 ○ 7p43 | 23 ☽ 3p55 |

MAR 1949
☉ → ♈ 20 5p48

☽→SIGNS
| 1 ♈ 10a36 | 3 ♉ 11p33 | 6 ♊ 11a 5 | 8 ♋ 7p21 | 10 ♌ 11p33 | 13 ♍ 12a24 | 16 ♎ 11p25 | 19 ♏ 1a30 | 21 ♐ 7a 4 | 24 ♑ 4p10 | 26 ♒ 3a50 | 28 ♓ 4p41 | 31 ♈ 5a29 |

☽ PHASES
| 3 ☽ 7p46 | 7 ○ 7p42 | 11 ○ 9a 1 | 14 ○ 2p 3 | 17 ○ 7p13 | 21 ○ 8a10 | 25 ☽ 6a45 | 29 ● 10a11 |

APR 1949
☉ → ♉ 20 5a17

☽→SIGNS
| 2 ♊ 5p 3 | 5 ♋ 2a10 | 7 ♌ 7a59 | 9 ♍ 10a32 | 11 ♎ 11a23 | 13 ♏ 10a27 | 15 ♐ 11a23 | 17 ♑ 3p16 | 19 ♒ 10p59 | 22 ♓ 10a 8 | 24 ♈ 11p 1 | 27 ♉ 11a41 | 29 ♊ 10p48 |

☽ PHASES
| 2 ☽ 12p26 | 6 ○ 8a 1 | 9 ○ 6p19 | 11 ♊ 2p 3 | 13 ○ 6a13 | 16 ○ 10p27 | 23 ☽ 11p58 | 28 ● 3a 2 |

MAY 1949
☉ → ♊ 21 4a51

☽→SIGNS
| 2 ♋ 7a43 | 4 ♌ 2p11 | 6 ♍ 6p11 | 8 ♎ 8p 7 | 10 ♏ 8p54 | 12 ♐ 9p57 | 15 ♑ 12a57 | 17 ♒ 7a19 | 19 ♓ 5p26 | 22 ♈ 6a 2 | 24 ♉ 6p42 | 27 ♊ 5a27 | 29 ♋ 1p38 | 31 ♌ 7p36 |

☽ PHASES
| 2 ☽ 1a13 | 5 ○ 4p33 | 12 ○ 7a51 | 15 ○ 6p13 | 19 ○ 2p22 | 23 ☽ 5p25 | 27 ● 5p24 | 31 ☽ 10a26 |

JUN 1949
☉ → ♋ 21 1p 3

☽→SIGNS
| 2 ♍ 11p53 | 5 ♎ 2a57 | 7 ♏ 5a13 | 9 ♐ 7a23 | 11 ♑ 10a40 | 13 ♒ 4p26 | 15 ♓ 1a38 | 18 ♈ 1p45 | 20 ♉ 2a30 | 23 ♊ 1p20 | 25 ♋ 9p16 | 27 ♌ 12p36 | 28 ♍ 2a 0 |

☽ PHASES
| 3 ○ 10p27 | 10 ○ 7a35 | 14 ○ 1a31 | 18 ○ 2a32 | 22 ☽ 9a54 | 26 ● 5a 2 | 29 ☽ 5p10 |

JUL 1949
☉ → ♌ 22 11p57

☽→SIGNS
| 2 ♎ 8a22 | 4 ♏ 11a22 | 6 ♐ 2p45 | 8 ♑ 7p 2 | 11 ♒ 1a 9 | 13 ♓ 10a 1 | 15 ♈ 9p43 | 18 ♉ 10a36 | 20 ♊ 9p57 | 23 ♋ 5a52 | 25 ♌ 10a19 | 27 ♍ 12p36 | 29 ♎ 2p20 | 31 ♏ 4p44 |

☽ PHASES
| 3 ○ 3a 8 | 6 ○ 1p35 | 10 ○ 2a41 | 13 ○ 10a27 | 18 ○ 1a 1 | 22 ☽ 12a39 | 25 ● 2p33 | 28 ☽ 10p52 |

AUG 1949
☉ → ♍ 23 6a48

☽→SIGNS
| 2 ♐ 8p25 | 4 ♑ 1a36 | 7 ♒ 8a34 | 9 ♓ 5p45 | 12 ♈ 5a20 | 14 ♉ 6p18 | 17 ♊ 6a23 | 19 ♋ 3p15 | 21 ♌ 9p55 | 23 ♍ 10p24 | 25 ♎ 10p24 | 27 ♏ 11p19 | 29 ♐ 2a 0 |

☽ PHASES
| 1 ○ 7a57 | 4 ○ 8p45 | 8 ○ 2p33 | 12 ○ 5p55 | 16 ○ 5p59 | 20 ☽ 1p32 | 24 ● 10p59 | 27 ☽ 4a53 | 30 ○ 2p16 |

SEP 1949
☉ → ♎ 23 4a 6

☽→SIGNS
| 1 ♑ 7a 5 | 3 ♒ 2p27 | 6 ♓ 12a26 | 8 ♈ 12p13 | 11 ♉ 1a12 | 13 ♊ 1p47 | 15 ♋ 11p52 | 18 ♌ 6a 5 | 20 ♍ 8a34 | 22 ♎ 8a41 | 24 ♏ 8a20 | 26 ♐ 9a21 | 28 ♑ 1p 7 | 30 ♒ 8p13 |

☽ PHASES
| 3 ○ 6a21 | 7 ○ 4a59 | 11 ○ 8a14 | 15 ○ 12a53 | 19 ☽ 12a53 | 22 ☽ 7a21 | 25 ● 12p20 | 28 ○ 11p18 |

OCT 1949
☉ → ♏ 23 1p 3

☽→SIGNS
| 3 ♓ 6a19 | 5 ♈ 6p27 | 8 ♉ 7a26 | 10 ♊ 8p 2 | 13 ♋ 6a51 | 15 ♌ 2p35 | 17 ♍ 6p42 | 19 ♎ 7p48 | 21 ♏ 7p18 | 23 ♐ 7p 8 | 26 ♑ 9p10 | 28 ♒ 2a20 | 30 ♓ 12p21 |

☽ PHASES
| 2 ○ 7p25 | 6 ○ 9p52 | 11 ○ 1a13 | 14 ○ 11p 6 | 18 ○ 11a16 | 21 ☽ 4p23 | 24 ☽ 10p 3 | 28 ● 12p 2 |

NOV 1949
☉ → ♐ 22 10a16

☽→SIGNS
| 2 ♈ 12a34 | 4 ♉ 1p37 | 7 ♊ 1a55 | 9 ♋ 12p35 | 11 ♌ 9p 0 | 14 ♍ 2a42 | 16 ♎ 5a 6 | 18 ♏ 6a15 | 20 ♐ 6a18 | 22 ♑ 7a19 | 24 ♒ 11a24 | 26 ♓ 7p35 | 29 ♈ 7a18 |

☽ PHASES
| 1 ○ 12p19 | 5 ○ 4p 9 | 9 ○ 4p44 | 13 ○ 10a47 | 16 ○ 6a24 | 20 ☽ 2a29 | 23 ☽ 10a40 | 27 ○ 5a 1 |

DEC 1949
☉ → ♑ 21 11p23

☽→SIGNS
| 1 ♉ 8p22 | 4 ♊ 8a28 | 6 ♋ 6p31 | 9 ♌ 2a27 | 11 ♍ 8a31 | 13 ♎ 12p45 | 15 ♏ 3p13 | 17 ♐ 4p32 | 19 ♑ 6p 0 | 21 ♒ 9p24 | 24 ♓ 4a20 | 26 ♈ 3p 5 | 29 ♉ 3a58 | 31 ♊ 4p13 |

☽ PHASES
| 1 ○ 8a13 | 5 ○ 10a13 | 9 ○ 9a44 | 13 ○ 8p48 | 16 ○ 6a24 | 19 ☽ 1p56 | 23 ☽ 2a28 | 27 ○ 1a31 | 31 ○ 5a 9 |

1950

JAN 1950
☉ → ♒ 20 10a 0

☽→SIGNS
| 3 ♋ 1a56 | 5 ♌ 8a58 | 7 ♍ 2p 6 | 9 ♎ 6p 8 | 11 ♏ 9p28 | 14 ♐ 12a16 | 16 ♑ 3a 6 | 18 ♒ 7a 7 | 20 ♓ 1p41 | 22 ♈ 11p37 | 25 ♉ 12p 8 | 28 ♊ 12a43 | 30 ♋ 10a50 |

☽ PHASES
| 4 ○ 2a48 | 7 ○ 5p44 | 14 ○ 1a32 | 18 ○ 2a59 | 21 ☽ 9p 7 | 25 ● 11p39 | 30 ○ 12a58 |

FEB 1950
☉ → ♓ 19 12a18

☽→SIGNS
| 1 ♌ 5p34 | 3 ♍ 9p37 | 6 ♎ 12a19 | 8 ♏ 2a50 | 10 ♐ 5a51 | 12 ♑ 9a45 | 14 ♒ 2p57 | 16 ♓ 10p11 | 19 ♈ 8a11 | 21 ♉ 8p12 | 24 ♊ 9a 3 | 26 ♋ 8p 3 |

☽ PHASES
| 2 ○ 5p16 | 5 ○ 5p44 | 13 ○ 1p32 | 16 ○ 5p53 | 20 ☽ 5p21 | 24 ☽ 8p52 | 28 ○ 6p11 |

MAR 1950
☉ → ♈ 20 11p35

☽→SIGNS
| 1 ♌ 3a30 | 3 ♍ 7a24 | 5 ♎ 9a 0 | 7 ♏ 9a55 | 9 ♐ 11a37 | 11 ♑ 3p 7 | 13 ♒ 8p52 | 16 ♓ 4a59 | 18 ♈ 3p21 | 21 ♉ 3a32 | 23 ♊ 4p28 | 26 ♋ 4a17 | 28 ♌ 1p 4 | 30 ♍ 6p 1 |

☽ PHASES
| 4 ○ 5a34 | 7 ○ 12p30 | 10 ○ 9p38 | 14 ○ 12p40 | 17 ☽ 10a20 | 21 ☽ 1p10 | 26 ● 3p10 | 30 ○ 8a11 |

APR 1950
☉ → ♉ 20 10a59

☽→SIGNS
| 2 ♎ 7p40 | 5 ♏ 7p35 | 7 ♐ 7p37 | 9 ♑ 9p29 | 11 ♒ 2a24 | 14 ♓ 10a38 | 17 ♈ 9p32 | 19 ♉ 9a59 | 21 ♊ 10p54 | 24 ♋ 11a 2 | 27 ♌ 9p49 | 29 ♎ 6a25 |

☽ PHASES
| 2 ☽ 3p49 | 5 ○ 8p45 | 9 ○ 6a42 | 13 ☽ 1a41 | 17 ☽ 5p20 | 21 ☽ 6a46 | 25 ○ 5a40 | 28 ○ 7p 1 |

MAY 1950
☉ → ♊ 21 10a27

☽→SIGNS
| 1 ♏ 6a37 | 3 ♐ 5a50 | 5 ♑ 6a 8 | 7 ♒ 9a22 | 9 ♓ 4p34 | 12 ♈ 3a18 | 14 ♉ 3p59 | 17 ♊ 4a52 | 19 ♋ 4p50 | 22 ♌ 3a 6 | 24 ♍ 10a50 | 26 ♎ 3p26 | 28 ♏ 5p 1 | 30 ♐ 6p43 |

☽ PHASES
| 2 ○ 12a19 | 5 ○ 5a 3 | 9 ○ 5p32 | 12 ☽ 4p29 | 16 ☽ 7p54 | 19 ☽ 9p12 | 24 ● 4p28 | 28 ○ 3a 6 | 31 ○ 7a43 |

JUN 1950
☉ → ♋ 21 6p36

☽→SIGNS
| 1 ♑ 4p27 | 3 ♒ 6p18 | 5 ♓ 11p57 | 8 ♈ 9a44 | 10 ♉ 10p12 | 13 ♊ 11a 5 | 15 ♋ 10p52 | 18 ♌ 8a37 | 20 ♍ 4p31 | 22 ♎ 10p 9 | 24 ♏ 1a19 | 27 ♐ 2a26 | 29 ♑ 2a48 |

☽ PHASES
| 3 ○ 2p14 | 7 ○ 6a 9 | 11 ☽ 8a28 | 15 ☽ 10a53 | 19 ☽ 8a31 | 22 ☽ 12a12 | 25 ● 9a14 | 29 ○ 2p58 |

JUL 1950
☉ → ♌ 23 5a30

☽→SIGNS
| 1 ♒ 4a19 | 3 ♓ 8a51 | 5 ♈ 5p24 | 8 ♉ 5a13 | 10 ♊ 6p 2 | 13 ♋ 5a33 | 15 ♌ 2p52 | 17 ♍ 10p 5 | 20 ♎ 3a34 | 22 ♏ 7a27 | 24 ♐ 9a55 | 26 ♑ 11a39 | 28 ♒ 3a14 | 30 ♓ 6p19 |

☽ PHASES
| 3 ○ 1a10 | 6 ○ 9p53 | 11 ☽ 12a47 | 15 ☽ 12a 5 | 18 ☽ 5p21 | 22 ● 5a50 | 25 ○ 2p34 | 28 ○ 11p18 |

AUG 1950
☉ → ♍ 23 12p23

☽→SIGNS
| 2 ♈ 2a54 | 4 ♉ 1p 6 | 7 ♊ 1a44 | 9 ♋ 1p27 | 12 ♌ 10p36 | 14 ♍ 5a 3 | 16 ♎ 9a31 | 18 ♏ 12p49 | 20 ♐ 3p36 | 22 ♑ 6p23 | 24 ♒ 9p53 | 27 ♓ 3a 2 | 29 ♈ 10a44 | 31 ♉ 9p19 |

☽ PHASES
| 1 ○ 12a 2 | 5 ○ 8a53 | 8 ○ 8a 8 | 11 ☽ 10p29 | 15 ☽ 12a34 | 17 ☽ 3p54 | 20 ● 10p35 | 23 ○ 8p33 | 27 ○ 9a51 | 30 ○ 6a24 |

SEP 1950
☉ → ♎ 23 9a44

☽→SIGNS
| 3 ♊ 9a45 | 5 ♋ 9p54 | 7 ♌ 7a34 | 10 ♍ 1p55 | 12 ♎ 5p28 | 14 ♏ 7p27 | 16 ♐ 9p12 | 18 ♑ 11p59 | 21 ♒ 3a59 | 23 ♓ 10a 9 | 25 ♈ 6p32 | 28 ♉ 5a 8 | 30 ♊ 5p26 |

☽ PHASES
| 3 ○ 6p45 | 7 ○ 8a 8 | 11 ☽ 10p29 | 14 ☽ 7a10 | 18 ☽ 3p54 | 22 ● 4a40 | 26 ○ 8p33 | 30 ○ 12p12 |

OCT 1950
☉ → ♏ 23 6p45

☽→SIGNS
| 3 ♋ 5a59 | 5 ♌ 4p40 | 7 ♍ 11p54 | 10 ♎ 3a29 | 12 ♏ 4a31 | 14 ♐ 4a44 | 16 ♑ 5a55 | 18 ♒ 9a26 | 20 ♓ 3p53 | 23 ♈ 12a59 | 25 ♉ 12p 3 | 28 ♊ 1a 6 | 30 ♋ 1p 3 |

☽ PHASES
| 2 ○ 2a53 | 7 ○ 10p38 | 11 ☽ 8a33 | 14 ☽ 2p14 | 17 ☽ 11p18 | 21 ● 4p 9 | 25 ○ 3p46 | 29 ○ 6p52 |

NOV 1950
☉ → ♐ 22 4p 3

☽→SIGNS
| 2 ♌ 12a38 | 4 ♍ 9a21 | 6 ♎ 2p10 | 8 ♏ 3p29 | 11 ♐ 3p11 | 13 ♑ 2p51 | 15 ♒ 2p25 | 17 ♓ 9p38 | 19 ♈ 6p 8 | 21 ♉ 6a38 | 24 ♊ 7p13 | 26 ♋ 7a 2 | 29 ♌ 7a 2 |

☽ PHASES
| 2 ○ 8p 0 | 6 ☽ 11a59 | 9 ☽ 6p25 | 12 ☽ 10p51 | 16 ● 10a 6 | 20 ○ 7a28 | 24 ○ 10a14 | 28 ○ 1p 7 |

DEC 1950
☉ → ♑ 22 5a14

☽→SIGNS
| 1 ♍ 4p53 | 3 ♎ 11p29 | 6 ♏ 2a19 | 8 ♐ 2a17 | 10 ♑ 1a16 | 12 ♒ 1a34 | 14 ♓ 5a10 | 16 ♈ 12p58 | 19 ♉ 12a10 | 21 ♊ 12p49 | 23 ♋ 1a18 | 26 ♌ 12p45 | 28 ♍ 10p41 | 31 ♎ 6a20 |

☽ PHASES
| 2 ○ 11a22 | 5 ☽ 11p51 | 9 ● 4a28 | 12 ○ 9a56 | 16 ○ 12a56 | 20 ○ 2a 2 | 24 ○ 5a23 | 28 ○ 5a46 |

JAN 1951 — ☉ → ≈ 20 3p52

☽ → SIGNS: 2 ♏ 10a58; 4 ♐ 12p38; 6 ♑ 12p32; 8 ♒ 12p35; 10 ♓ 2p56; 12 ♈ 9p 5; 15 ♉ 7a10; 17 ♊ 7p36; 20 ♋ 8a 6; 22 ♌ 7p12; 25 ♍ 4a26; 27 ♎ 11a46; 29 ♏ 5p 4; 31 ♐ 8p16

☽ PHASES: 1 ◑ 12a11; 4 ◐ 10a 8; 7 ● 3p10; 10 ◑ 11p57; 14 ○ 7p23; 18 ◑ 10p25; 22 ○ 11p47; 26 ○ 7p52; 30 ◑ 10a13

FEB 1951 — ☉ → ♓ 19 6a10

☽ → SIGNS: 2 ♑ 9p52; 4 ♒ 11p 4; 7 ♓ 1a29; 9 ♈ 6a43; 11 ♉ 3p33; 13 ♊ 3a18; 16 ♋ 3p51; 18 ♌ 3a 1; 21 ♍ 11a43; 23 ♎ 6p 1; 25 ♏ 10p31; 28 ♐ 1a49

☽ PHASES: 2 ◐ 7p10; 6 ● 2a54; 9 ◑ 4p33; 13 ○ 3p55; 17 ○ 6p46; 21 ◐ 4p12; 25 ○ 7a 3; 28 ◐ 5p59

MAR 1951 — ☉ → ♈ 21 5a26

☽ → SIGNS: 2 ♑ 4a29; 4 ♒ 7a11; 6 ♓ 10a45; 9 ♈ 4p16; 11 ♉ 12a33; 13 ♊ 11a36; 16 ♋ 12a 6; 18 ♌ 11a44; 20 ♍ 8p39; 23 ♎ 2a21; 25 ♏ 5a36; 27 ♐ 7a40; 29 ♑ 9a51; 31 ♒ 1p 2

☽ PHASES: 4 ◐ 3a43; 7 ● 1p56; 11 ○ 10a43; 15 ◐ 12p40; 19 ◐ 1p27; 23 ● 5a50; 26 ○ 9p39; 30 ◐ 12a35

APR 1951 — ☉ → ♉ 20 4p48

☽ → SIGNS: 2 ♓ 5p44; 4 ♈ 12a16; 7 ♉ 8a52; 9 ♊ 7p41; 12 ♋ 8a 4; 14 ♌ 8p18; 17 ♍ 6a 7; 19 ♎ 12p13; 21 ♏ 2p55; 23 ♐ 3p40; 25 ♑ 4p19; 27 ♒ 6p32; 29 ♓ 11p13

☽ PHASES: 2 ◐ 12p42; 5 ● 6a52; 10 ○ 5a 8; 14 ◐ 7a55; 18 ◐ 5a16; 21 ● 4p30; 24 ○ 10p36; 28 ◐ 7a18

MAY 1951 — ☉ → ♊ 21 4p15

☽ → SIGNS: 2 ♈ 6a26; 5 ♉ 3p46; 7 ♊ 2a51; 9 ♋ 3p13; 12 ♌ 3a49; 14 ♍ 2p44; 16 ♎ 10p 5; 19 ♏ 1a23; 21 ♐ 1a44; 23 ♑ 1a 7; 25 ♒ 1a41; 27 ♓ 5a 5; 29 ♈ 11a53; 31 ♉ 9p33

☽ PHASES: 1 ◐ 10p50; 5 ● 8p36; 10 ○ 9p10; 14 ◐ 12a32; 17 ● 9a50; 21 ○ 12a45; 24 ◐ 5a 5; 27 ● 9p17; 31 ● 10a34

JUN 1951 — ☉ → ♋ 22 12a25

☽ → SIGNS: 3 ♊ 9a 3; 5 ♋ 9p31; 8 ♌ 10a12; 10 ♍ 9p46; 13 ♎ 6a31; 15 ♏ 11a17; 17 ♐ 12p26; 19 ♑ 12p13; 21 ♒ 11a 4; 23 ♓ 12p49; 25 ♈ 6p13; 27 ♉ 3a17; 30 ♊ 2p51

☽ PHASES: 4 ● 11a40; 8 ○ 2p37; 12 ◐ 1p52; 16 ● 2a58; 19 ○ 7a36; 22 ◐ 12p20; 26 ● 1a21; 29 ◐ 3p15

JUL 1951 — ☉ → ♌ 23 11a21

☽ → SIGNS: 3 ♋ 3a27; 5 ♌ 4p 0; 8 ♍ 3a36; 10 ♎ 1p19; 12 ♏ 7p19; 14 ♐ 10p 3; 16 ♑ 10p14; 18 ♒ 10p17; 20 ♓ 10a 7; 22 ♈ 2p17; 25 ♉ 10a 7; 27 ♊ 9a42; 30 ♋ 9a42

☽ PHASES: 4 ○ 2a48; 8 ◐ 4a25; 11 ● 11p56; 15 ○ 6a16; 18 ◐ 2p17; 21 ● 9p20; 25 ◐ 1p59; 29 ○ 3p15

AUG 1951 — ☉ → ♍ 23 6p16

☽ → SIGNS: 1 ♌ 10p 7; 3 ♍ 9a18; 6 ♎ 6p34; 8 ♏ 1a24; 11 ♐ 5a31; 13 ♑ 7a18; 15 ♒ 7a53; 17 ♓ 8a52; 19 ♈ 11a58; 21 ♉ 6p26; 24 ♊ 4a27; 26 ♋ 4p44; 28 ♌ 5a10; 31 ♍ 4p 0

☽ PHASES: 2 ● 5p39; 6 ○ 3p54; 9 ◐ 7a22; 13 ● 3p55; 16 ◐ 9p59; 20 ● 8a50; 24 ○ 5a20; 28 ◐ 7a57

SEP 1951 — ☉ → ♎ 23 3p37

☽ → SIGNS: 3 ♎ 12a32; 5 ♏ 6a49; 7 ♐ 11a11; 9 ♑ 2p 6; 11 ♒ 4p11; 13 ♓ 6p21; 15 ♈ 9p47; 18 ♉ 3a41; 20 ♊ 12p27; 23 ♋ 12a34; 25 ♌ 1p 8; 28 ♍ 12a 5; 30 ♎ 8a 8

☽ PHASES: 1 ● 7a50; 5 ◐ 1a16; 8 ○ 1p 6; 11 ◐ 10p 7; 15 ● 7a38; 18 ○ 11p 9; 22 ◐ 11a29; 26 ● 1a29; 30 ◐ 8p57

OCT 1951 — ☉ → ♏ 24 12a36

☽ → SIGNS: 2 ♏ 1p23; 4 ♐ 4p48; 6 ♑ 7p30; 8 ♒ 10p19; 11 ♓ 1a46; 13 ♈ 6a19; 15 ♉ 12p37; 17 ♊ 9p22; 20 ♋ 8a42; 22 ♌ 9p25; 25 ♍ 9a 1; 27 ♎ 5p25; 29 ♏ 10p 9

☽ PHASES: 4 ◐ 9a14; 7 ○ 7p 0; 11 ◐ 5a47; 14 ● 7p51; 18 ○ 4p15; 22 ◐ 6p55; 26 ● 6p51; 30 ◐ 8a54

NOV 1951 — ☉ → ♐ 22 9p51

☽ → SIGNS: 1 ♐ 12a20; 3 ♑ 1a40; 5 ♒ 3a43; 7 ♓ 7a23; 9 ♈ 12p52; 11 ♉ 8p 7; 14 ♊ 8p19; 16 ♋ 4p27; 19 ♌ 4a27; 21 ♍ 5p35; 23 ♎ 6p38; 25 ♏ 9p24; 28 ♐ 8a32; 30 ♑ 10a22

☽ PHASES: 2 ◐ 4p53; 6 ○ 1a59; 9 ◐ 3p52; 13 ○ 10a52; 17 ● 11a38; 21 ◐ 3p 1; 25 ○ 10a55; 28 ● 8p 0

DEC 1951 — ☉ → ♑ 22 11a 0

☽ → SIGNS: 1 ♒ 10a45; 4 ♓ 1p 8; 6 ♈ 6p18; 8 ♉ 2a 4; 11 ♊ 11a54; 13 ♋ 11p22; 16 ♌ 12p 5; 18 ♍ 12a52; 21 ♎ 11a41; 23 ♏ 6p38; 26 ♐ 9p27; 28 ♑ 9p24; 30 ♒ 9p10

☽ PHASES: 2 ◐ 1a23; 5 ○ 11a20; 9 ● 4a57; 13 ○ 4a30; 17 ● 7a58; 21 ◐ 9a37; 25 ● 6a43; 28 ● 6a43; 31 ◑ 11a35

JAN 1952 — ☉ → ♒ 20 9p39

☽ → SIGNS: 3 ♓ 12a42; 5 ♈ 7a43; 7 ♉ 5p42; 10 ♊ 5a34; 12 ♋ 6p19; 15 ♌ 7a 0; 17 ♍ 6p19; 20 ♎ 2a44; 22 ♏ 7a22; 24 ♐ 8a39; 26 ♑ 8a 6; 28 ♒ 7a45; 30 ♓ 9a32

☽ PHASES: 3 ◐ 11p42; 7 ○ 9p 8; 11 ● 11p55; 16 ○ 1a 9; 20 ◐ 1a18; 24 ● 12p44; 26 ◑ 5p26; 31 ◐ 11p45

FEB 1952 — ☉ → ♓ 19 11a57

☽ → SIGNS: 1 ♈ 2p51; 3 ♉ 11p55; 6 ♊ 11a44; 8 ♋ 12a36; 11 ♌ 1p17; 13 ♍ 12a20; 16 ♎ 11a17; 18 ♏ 5p42; 20 ♐ 8p45; 22 ♑ 9p 2; 24 ♒ 8p42; 26 ♓ 8p11; 29 ♈ 12a 2

☽ PHASES: 2 ○ 3p 1; 6 ● 3p50; 10 ○ 7p28; 14 ◐ 7p44; 18 ◐ 1p 1; 21 ◐ 10p31; 25 ● 4a16; 28 ◑ 1p36

MAR 1952 — ☉ → ♈ 20 11a14

☽ → SIGNS: 2 ♉ 7a36; 4 ♊ 6p40; 7 ♋ 7a30; 9 ♌ 7p51; 12 ♍ 6a16; 14 ♎ 2p20; 16 ♏ 8p15; 18 ♐ 12a42; 21 ♑ 2a55; 23 ♒ 4a39; 25 ♓ 6a34; 27 ♈ 10a 5; 29 ♉ 4p36

☽ PHASES: 3 ○ 8a43; 7 ● 11a42; 11 ○ 1p14; 14 ◐ 8a22; 18 ● 9p40; 21 ● 4p33; 25 ◐ 3p13; 28 ● 4a46

APR 1952 — ☉ → ♉ 19 10p37

☽ → SIGNS: 1 ♊ 2a39; 3 ♋ 3p10; 6 ♌ 3a40; 8 ♍ 1p56; 10 ♎ 9p13; 13 ♏ 2a 8; 15 ♐ 5a41; 17 ♑ 8a43; 19 ♒ 11a40; 21 ♓ 2p15; 23 ♈ 7p15; 26 ♉ 1a40; 28 ♊ 11a12; 30 ♋ 11p12

☽ PHASES: 2 ○ 3a48; 6 ● 6a54; 10 ○ 3a53; 13 ◐ 5p34; 17 ● 4a 7; 20 ◐ 2p19; 24 ● 2a27; 27 ◑ 8p51

MAY 1952 — ☉ → ♊ 20 10p 4

☽ → SIGNS: 3 ♌ 11a57; 5 ♍ 10p39; 8 ♎ 5a49; 10 ♏ 9a50; 12 ♐ 12p 9; 14 ♑ 2p14; 16 ♒ 5p 8; 18 ♓ 9p 7; 21 ♈ 2a29; 23 ♉ 9a37; 25 ♊ 9p22; 28 ♋ 6a59; 30 ♌ 7p57

☽ PHASES: 1 ○ 10p58; 5 ● 11p47; 9 ○ 3p16; 13 ◐ 12a27; 16 ● 9a39; 19 ◐ 9p54; 23 ● 2p28; 27 ◑ 1p36; 31 ◑ 4p46

JUN 1952 — ☉ → ♋ 21 6a12

☽ → SIGNS: 2 ♍ 7a26; 4 ♎ 2p 7; 6 ♏ 7p21; 8 ♐ 9p 2; 10 ♑ 9p26; 12 ♒ 10p43; 15 ♓ 1a 6; 17 ♈ 6a15; 19 ♉ 1p49; 22 ♊ 12a 4; 24 ♋ 12p26; 27 ♌ 1a29; 29 ♍ 3p18

☽ PHASES: 4 ○ 1p37; 8 ○ 12a 7; 11 ● 6a21; 15 ◐ 6a33; 18 ◐ 6a33; 21 ● 6a16; 26 ◑ 9a16; 30 ○ 8a11

JUL 1952 — ☉ → ♌ 22 5p 7

☽ → SIGNS: 1 ♎ 12a25; 4 ♏ 5a27; 6 ♐ 7a 2; 8 ♑ 6a54; 10 ♒ 6a59; 12 ♓ 8a56; 14 ♈ 1p45; 16 ♉ 9p37; 19 ♊ 8a20; 21 ♋ 9p24; 24 ♌ 9a24; 26 ♍ 8p10; 29 ♎ 2a24; 31 ♏ 2p37

☽ PHASES: 4 ○ 12a37; 7 ● 7a33; 10 ○ 12p28; 13 ◐ 10p42; 17 ● 5p19; 21 ● 6p31; 25 ◑ 10p 0; 29 ○ 8p51

AUG 1952 — ☉ → ♍ 23 12a 3

☽ → SIGNS: 2 ♐ 5p27; 4 ♑ 5p27; 6 ♒ 5p 5; 8 ♓ 5p33; 11 ♈ 8p46; 13 ♉ 3a36; 16 ♊ 1p52; 18 ♋ 2a19; 20 ♌ 3p22; 23 ♍ 3a42; 25 ♎ 2p10; 27 ♏ 9p53; 30 ♐ 2a24

☽ PHASES: 2 ● 9a34; 5 ○ 2p40; 8 ○ 7p49; 12 ◐ 11p26; 16 ◐ 6a55; 19 ● 10a20; 24 ● 12p 3; 27 ◑ 7a 3; 31 ○ 5p21

SEP 1952 — ☉ → ♎ 23 9p24

☽ → SIGNS: 1 ♑ 4a 3; 3 ♒ 4a 0; 5 ♓ 3a57; 7 ♈ 5a48; 9 ♉ 11a 6; 11 ♊ 8p24; 14 ♋ 8a38; 16 ♌ 9p41; 19 ♍ 9a41; 21 ♎ 7p43; 24 ♏ 3a33; 26 ♐ 9a 7; 28 ♑ 12p24; 30 ♒ 1p52

☽ PHASES: 3 ○ 10p19; 7 ● 5a19; 10 ○ 2p33; 14 ◐ 4p13; 18 ● 5p42; 22 ● 10a33; 26 ◑ 3p31; 30 ○ 12a50

OCT 1952 — ☉ → ♏ 23 6a22

☽ → SIGNS: 2 ♓ 2p34; 4 ♈ 4p 0; 6 ♉ 8p15; 9 ♊ 3a50; 11 ♋ 4p45; 14 ♍ 4a51; 16 ♎ 4p44; 19 ♏ 2a10; 21 ♐ 9a12; 23 ♑ 2p28; 25 ♒ 6p28; 27 ♓ 9p23; 29 ♈ 11p34

☽ PHASES: 3 ○ 7a15; 6 ● 5p45; 10 ○ 2p33; 14 ◐ 1p19; 18 ● 5p42; 22 ◐ 10a33; 25 ● 11p 4; 29 ○ 8a41

NOV 1952 — ☉ → ♐ 22 3a36

☽ → SIGNS: 1 ♈ 1a58; 3 ♉ 5p 8; 5 ♊ 1p12; 7 ♋ 12p47; 9 ♌ 1p56; 12 ♍ 1p56; 14 ♎ 10a18; 16 ♏ 4p33; 19 ♐ 8p40; 21 ♑ 11p52; 24 ♒ 2a55; 26 ♓ 6a 9; 28 ♈ 9a54; 30 ♉ 2p53

☽ PHASES: 1 ○ 6p10; 5 ○ 9a40; 8 ● 10a43; 11 ◐ 1p19; 17 ◐ 7a56; 20 ● 8p 3; 24 ○ 6a34; 27 ○ 5p20

DEC 1952 — ☉ → ♑ 21 4p43

☽ → SIGNS: 2 ♊ 10p 9; 5 ♋ 8a23; 7 ♌ 8p57; 10 ♍ 9a35; 12 ♎ 7p35; 15 ♏ 2a 0; 17 ♐ 5a17; 19 ♑ 7a 2; 21 ♒ 7a46; 23 ♓ 9p 2; 25 ♈ 9p 2; 28 ♉ 3a46; 30 ♊ 12a 6

☽ PHASES: 1 ○ 7a41; 5 ● 4a51; 9 ○ 8a22; 13 ◐ 7a41; 16 ● 9p 2; 20 ● 5a20; 23 ○ 2p52; 27 ○ 4a40; 31 ○ 12a 6

JAN 1953 – AUG 1953

JAN 1953
☉ → ♒ 20 3a22

☽ → SIGNS
1	Ω	4p17
4	♏	4a41
6	♏	5p36
9	♏	4a44
11	♐	12p14
13	♑	3p55
15	♒	4p57
17	♓	5p 7
19	♈	6p 8
21	♉	9p20
24	♊	3a21
26	♋	12p 7
28	Ω	11p 6
31	♍	11a35

☽ PHASES
4 ○ 1a54 / 8 ○ 5a 9 / 12 (12a 6 / 15 ● 9a 8 / 18) 2p54 / 22 ○ 12a43 / 25 ○ 6p17 / 29 ♐ 6p44

FEB 1953
☉ → ♓ 18 5p41

☽ → SIGNS
3	♏	12a31
5	♏	12p21
7	♐	9p20
10	♑	2a32
12	♒	4a17
14	♓	3a58
16	♈	3a30
18	♉	4a50
20	♊	9a27
22	♋	5p45
25	Ω	5a 5
27	♍	5p51

☽ PHASES
2 ○ 10p32 / 6 ○ 11p 9 / 10 (2p 1 / 13 ♐ 8p10 / 17) 1a 2 / 20 ○ 12p45 / 24 ○ 10a34 / 28 ○ 1p59

MAR 1953
☉ → ♈ 20 5p 1

☽ → SIGNS
2	♏	6a41
4	♏	6p31
7	♐	4a20
9	♑	11a10
11	♒	2p37
13	♓	3p17
15	♈	2p39
17	♉	2p44
19	♊	5p35
22	♋	12a29
24	Ω	11a14
27	♍	12a 4
29	♎	12p51

☽ PHASES
4 ○ 4p35 / 8 ○ 1p26 / 12 (1a 9 / 13 ♐ 3p 9 / 18) 12p 0 / 22 ○ 3a11 / 26 ○ 4a35 / 30 ○ 7a55

APR 1953
☉ → ♉ 20 4a25

☽ → SIGNS
1	♏	12a19
3	♐	9a58
5	♑	5p29
7	♒	10p27
10	♓	12a49
12	♈	1a19
14	♉	1a31
16	♊	3a27
18	♋	8a53
20	Ω	6p27
23	♍	6a25
25	♎	7p 0
28	♏	6a52
30	♐	3p52

☽ PHASES
3 ○ 7a 1 / 6 ○ 11p58 / 10 (9a41 / 13 ♐ 3p 9 / 17) 12a 8 / 20 ○ 7p40 / 24 ○ 10p48 / 28 ○ 11p20

MAY 1953
☉ → ♊ 21 3a53

☽ → SIGNS
2	♑	10p55
5	♒	4a12
7	♓	7a46
9	♈	9a49
11	♉	11a12
13	♊	1p27
15	♋	6p16
18	Ω	2a47
20	♍	2p31
23	♎	3a16
25	♏	2p32
27	♐	11p 8
30	♑	5a17

☽ PHASES
2 ○ 5p52 / 6 ○ 7a21 / 9 (4p17 / 13 ● 12a 6 / 16) 1p46 / 20 ○ 1p20 / 24 ○ 3p50 / 27 ○ 12p 3

JUN 1953
☉ → ♋ 21 12p 0

☽ → SIGNS
1	♒	9a45
3	♓	1p12
5	♈	4p 1
7	♉	6p41
9	♊	10p 3
12	♋	3a39
14	Ω	11a27
16	♍	10p37
19	♎	11a16
21	♏	10p57
24	♐	7a48
26	♑	1p29
28	♒	4p51
30	♓	7p 8

☽ PHASES
1 ○ 1a55 / 4 ○ 3p29 / 8 (10p 7 / 11 ● 9a55 / 15) 4a54 / 19 ○ 7a 1 / 22 ○ 8p19 / 26 ○ 10p29 / 30 ♐ 8a10

JUL 1953
☉ → Ω 22 10p52

☽ → SIGNS
2	♈	9p23
5	♉	12a23
7	♊	4a42
9	♋	10a54
11	Ω	7p28
14	♍	6a28
16	♎	7p 4
19	♏	7a17
21	♐	4p59
24	♑	11p 7
26	♒	2a 3
28	♓	3a 7
30	♈	3a56

☽ PHASES
3 ○ 5p 3 / 7 (4a38 / 10 ● 9p28 / 14) 9p 7 / 18 ○ 11p47 / 22 ○ 8p19 / 26 ♐ 7a21 / 29 ○ 1p45

AUG 1953
☉ → ♍ 23 5a45

☽ → SIGNS
1	♉	5a57
3	♊	10a10
5	♋	4p59
8	Ω	2a16
10	♍	1p33
13	♎	2a 8
15	♏	2p43
18	♐	1a30
20	♑	8a53
22	♒	1p12
24	♓	12p46
26	♈	1p10
28	♉	1p10
30	♊	4p 7

☽ PHASES
1 ○ 10p16 / 5 (1p16 / 9 ♐ 11a10 / 13) 1p41 / 17 ○ 3p 8 / 21 ○ 7a57 / 24 ○ 3p21 / 27 ○ 5a46 / 31 ○ 5a46

SEP 1953 – APR 1954

SEP 1953
☉ → ♎ 23 3a 6

☽ → SIGNS
1	♋	10p30
4	Ω	8a 5
6	♍	7p47
9	♎	8a27
11	♏	9p 5
14	♐	8a32
16	♑	5p21
18	♒	10p30
21	♓	12a 6
24	♈	10p45
27	♊	12a 1
29	♋	4a56

☽ PHASES
4 (1a 3 / 8 ● 2a48 / 12) 5a52 / 16 ○ 4a49 / 19 ○ 6p13 / 22 ○ 3a53 / 26 ○ 2p50 / 29 ○ 4p51

OCT 1953
☉ → ♏ 23 12p 6

☽ → SIGNS
1	Ω	1p53
3	♍	1a40
6	♎	2p28
8	♏	2a56
11	♐	2p19
13	♑	11p51
16	♒	6a34
18	♓	9a55
20	♈	10a27
22	♉	9a47
24	♊	10a 4
26	♋	1p24
28	Ω	8p 0
31	♍	8a 4

☽ PHASES
3 (4p19 / 7 ● 7p40 / 11) 9p 4 / 15 ○ 4p44 / 19 ○ 3a25 / 22 ○ 7a56 / 26 ○ 2p52 / 29 ○ 8a 9

NOV 1953
☉ → ♐ 22 9a22

☽ → SIGNS
2	♎	8p51
5	♏	3a 9
7	♐	8p 6
10	♑	5a18
12	♒	12p31
14	♓	5p17
16	♈	7p35
18	♉	8p15
20	♊	8p54
22	♋	11p31
25	Ω	5a40
27	♍	3p41
30	♎	4a 6

☽ PHASES
2 (10a33 / 6 ● 12p58 / 10) 10a52 / 14 ○ 2a52 / 17 ○ 12p 2 / 20 ○ 6p12 / 24 ○ 5a27 / 28 ○ 12a43

DEC 1953
☉ → ♑ 21 10p32

☽ → SIGNS
2	♏	4p30
5	♐	3a 9
7	♑	11a33
9	♒	5p59
11	♓	10p46
14	♈	2a 6
16	♉	4a22
18	♊	6a27
20	♋	9a 0
22	Ω	3p23
25	♍	12a24
27	♎	12p11
30	♏	12a43

☽ PHASES
2 (6a32 / 6 ● 5a48 / 10) 11p 0 / 13 ○ 11a30 / 17 ○ 8p45 / 20 ○ 6a44 / 24 ○ 11p25 / 28 ○ 12a43

JAN 1954
☉ → ♒ 20 9a11

☽ → SIGNS
1	♐	11a39
3	♑	7p45
6	♒	1a 9
8	♓	4a43
10	♈	7a27
12	♉	10a10
14	♊	1p29
16	♋	6p 0
19	Ω	12a24
21	♍	9a14
23	♎	8p30
26	♏	9a 3
28	♐	8p42
31	♑	5a27

☽ PHASES
1 (2a44 / 4 ● 9p21 / 8) 9a27 / 11 ○ 7p22 / 15 ○ 6a28 / 18 ○ 9p37 / 22 ○ 7p30 / 26 ○ 10p28 / 30 ○ 9p30

FEB 1954
☉ → ♓ 18 11p32

☽ → SIGNS
2	♒	10a38
4	♓	1p 3
6	♈	2p14
8	♉	3p47
10	♊	6p54
13	♋	12a10
15	Ω	3a17
17	♍	7a35
19	♎	12a24
22	♎	4a14
25	♐	5a 0
28	♑	2p58

☽ PHASES
3 ● 10a55 / 7) 6p36 / 10 ○ 3a29 / 13 ○ 5p53 / 17 ○ 2p17 / 21 ○ 3p50 / 25 ○ 6p29

MAR 1954
☉ → ♈ 20 10p53

☽ → SIGNS
1	♒	9p 7
3	♓	11p32
5	♈	11p40
7	♉	11p48
10	♊	1a 6
12	♋	5a31
14	Ω	1p17
16	♍	11p21
19	♎	10a57
21	♏	11p56
24	♐	10p55
26	♑	10p55
29	♒	6a37
31	♓	10a16

☽ PHASES
1 (1p30 / 3 ● 3a 8 / 11 ○ 12p52 / 15 ○ 7a13 / 19 ○ 7a42 / 23 ○ 10a45 / 27 (11a14 / 31 (1a58

APR 1954
☉ → ♉ 20 10a19

☽ → SIGNS
2	♈	10a40
4	♉	9a43
6	♊	9a40
8	♋	12p29
10	Ω	7p 5
13	♍	5a 3
15	♎	4p58
18	♏	5a32
20	♐	5p55
23	♑	2p 2
25	♒	2p 2
27	♓	9p 8
29	♈	9p 8

☽ PHASES
3 ● 7a25 / 10 ○ 11a53 / 10 ○ 1p10 / 18 ○ 12a48 / 22 ○ 3a 2 / 25 (11a 5

MAY 1954 – DEC 1954

MAY 1954
☉ → ♊ 21 9a47

☽ → SIGNS
1	♉	8p42
3	♊	8p 6
5	♋	9p30
8	Ω	2a29
10	♍	11a23
12	♎	11p 3
15	♏	11a42
17	♐	11p53
20	♑	10a49
22	♒	7p48
25	♓	2a 8
27	♈	5a32
29	♉	6a33
31	♊	6a40

☽ PHASES
1 ● 3p22 / 5) 9p34 / 9 ○ 1p17 / 13 ○ 2p 8 / 17 ○ 4p47 / 21 ○ 4p 5 / 25 (8a49 / 28 (5p42 / 31 ● 11p 3

JUN 1954
☉ → ♋ 21 5p54

☽ → SIGNS
2	♋	7a46
4	Ω	11a34
6	♍	7p 6
9	♎	5a59
11	♏	6p30
14	♐	7a 9
16	♑	6p 0
19	♒	2a19
21	♓	7a37
23	♈	11a28
25	♉	2p 9
27	♊	3p41
29	♋	5p35

☽ PHASES
4) 8a42 / 8 ○ 4a14 / 12 ○ 6a31 / 15 ○ 7p29 / 20 ○ 1a55 / 23 (2p46 / 26 (11p10 / 30 ♐ 7a26

JUL 1954
☉ → Ω 23 4a45

☽ → SIGNS
1	Ω	9p16
4	♍	3a56
6	♎	1p53
9	♏	2a 1
11	♐	2p19
14	♑	12a40
16	♒	8a19
18	♓	1p33
20	♈	5p 7
22	♉	7p52
24	♊	10p30
27	♋	1a41
29	Ω	6a10
31	♍	12p49

☽ PHASES
3) 9p33 / 7 ○ 7p14 / 11 ○ 10p46 / 15 ○ 9a13 / 19 ○ 9p14 / 22 (3p10 / 24 (11p51 / 26 (4a53 / 28 ● 12p 9

AUG 1954
☉ → ♍ 23 11a36

☽ → SIGNS
1	♎	10p14
4	♏	10a12
6	♐	10p32
9	♑	9a20
11	♒	4p54
13	♓	9p17
16	♈	11p ?
18	♉	1a33
20	♊	3a56
22	♋	7a 1
24	Ω	11p ?
26	♍	8p44
30	♎	6a12

☽ PHASES
2) 12p12 / 6 ○ 1p51 / 10 ○ 2p18 / 14 ○ 6a 3 / 17 ○ 3p10 / 21 ○ 11p51 / 24 (12p 9 / 28 ● 5a21

SEP 1954
☉ → ♎ 23 8a55

☽ → SIGNS
1	♏	5p48
4	♐	6a32
6	♑	6p10
9	♒	2a31
11	♓	6a55
13	♈	8a22
15	♉	8a28
17	♊	9a55
19	♋	1p13
21	Ω	7p50
23	♍	3a11
26	♎	1p13
28	♏	1a52

☽ PHASES
1) 4a34 / 5 ○ 7p28 / 9 ○ 4a38 / 12 ○ 3p19 / 19 ○ 6a11 / 22 (10p 2 / 26 ● 7p50 / 30) 10p16

OCT 1954
☉ → ♏ 23 5p57

☽ → SIGNS
1	♐	1p41
4	♑	2a 4
6	♒	11a45
8	♓	5p17
10	♈	7p58
12	♉	6p32
14	♊	7p50
16	♋	10p 7
19	Ω	1a59
21	♍	8a44
23	♎	7p12
26	♏	7a11
28	♐	7p59
31	♑	8a36

☽ PHASES
5 ○ 12a31 / 7 ○ 4a48 / 12 ○ 2a10 / 13 ○ 2p46 / 21 (11a15 / 24 (12p47 / 30) 4p23

NOV 1954
☉ → ♐ 22 3p14

☽ → SIGNS
2	♒	7p22
5	♓	2a34
7	♈	5a42
9	♉	5a48
11	♊	4a50
13	♋	4a59
15	Ω	8a 3
17	♍	2p52
19	♎	1a 2
22	♏	1p13
25	♐	2a24
27	♑	2p27
30	♒	1a19

☽ PHASES
3 ○ 3p55 / 7 ○ 4a48 / 10 ○ 9a29 / 19 ○ 2p21 / 21 (3a59 / 25 (7a30 / 28 (2a11

DEC 1954
☉ → ♑ 22 4a25

☽ → SIGNS
2	♓	9a38
4	♈	2p35
6	♉	4p23
8	♊	4p16
10	♋	4p 6
12	Ω	5p48
15	♍	10p54
17	♎	7a51
19	♏	7p43
22	♐	8a35
24	♑	8p40
27	♒	7a 0
29	♓	3p56
31	♈	8p56

☽ PHASES
3 ○ 4a56 / 6 ○ 3p 3 / 9 ○ 7p57 / 13 ○ 3a48 / 16 ○ 9p21 / 22 (11p40 / 25 ● 2a33 / 29) 12a20

JAN 1955
☉ → ♒ 20 3p 2

☽→SIGNS
3 ♉ 12a24 · 5 ♊ 2a 4 · 7 ♋ 3a 0 · 9 ♌ 4a41 · 11 ♍ 8a43 · 13 ♎ 4p15 · 16 ♏ 3a15 · 18 ♐ 4p 1 · 21 ♑ 4a 9 · 23 ♒ 1p58 · 25 ♓ 9p11 · 28 ♈ 2a19 · 30 ♉ 6a 4

☽ PHASES
1 ○ 3p29 · 5 ☽ 12a37 · 8 ✶ 7a44 · 11 ○ 7p34 · 15 ○ 5p14 · 19 ☾ 8p45 · 23 ● 8p 7 · 27 ☽ 12p19 · 31 ☾ 12a 5

FEB 1955
☉ → ♓ 19 5a19

☽→SIGNS
1 ♊ 9a 2 · 3 ♋ 11a36 · 5 ♌ 2p28 · 7 ♍ 6p43 · 10 ♎ 1a33 · 12 ♏ 11a38 · 15 ♐ 12a 7 · 17 ♑ 12p34 · 19 ♒ 10p33 · 22 ♓ 5a 9 · 24 ♈ 9a 6 · 26 ♉ 11a46 · 28 ♊ 2p24

☽ PHASES
3 ○ 9a56 · 6 ● 8p43 · 10 ○ 1p23 · 14 ○ 2p40 · 18 ☽ 4p58 · 22 ● 10a54 · 25 ☽ 9p52

MAR 1955
☉ → ♈ 21 4a35

☽→SIGNS
2 ♋ 5p40 · 4 ♌ 9p48 · 7 ♍ 3a 9 · 9 ♎ 10a20 · 12 ♏ 8p 4 · 14 ♐ 8a13 · 17 ♑ 9p 1 · 19 ♒ 7a47 · 22 ♓ 2p45 · 24 ♈ 6p 9 · 27 ♉ 8p42 · 29 ♊ 11p 5

☽ PHASES
1 ○ 7a40 · 4 ○ 7p28 · 10 ○ 10a41 · 12 ○ 8a20 · 16 ○ 11a36 · 20 ☽ 10a23 · 23 ● 10p42 · 27 ☽ 5a52 · 30 ○ 3p10

APR 1955
☉ → ♉ 20 3p58

☽→SIGNS
1 ♋ 3a20 · 3 ♌ 9a31 · 5 ♍ 5p34 · 8 ♎ 3a38 · 10 ♏ 3p41 · 13 ♐ 4a40 · 15 ♑ 4p20 · 18 ♒ 12a28 · 20 ♓ 4a29 · 22 ♈ 5a29 · 24 ♉ 5a24 · 26 ♊ 6a 9 · 28 ♋ 9a 8 · 30 ♌ 2p58

☽ PHASES
3 ○ 5a41 · 7 ○ 1a35 · 11 ○ 3a12 · 15 ○ 6a 1 · 19 ☾ 12a 3 · 22 ● 8a 6 · 25 ☽ 1p19 · 28 ○ 11p23

MAY 1955
☉ → ♊ 21 3p24

☽→SIGNS
2 ♎ 11p26 · 5 ♏ 10a 4 · 7 ♐ 10p19 · 10 ♑ 11a19 · 12 ♒ 11p29 · 15 ♓ 8a53 · 17 ♈ 2p21 · 19 ♉ 4p12 · 21 ♊ 3p56 · 23 ♋ 3p22 · 25 ♌ 4p52 · 27 ♍ 9p 5 · 30 ♎ 5a 8

☽ PHASES
2 ○ 5p 9 · 6 ○ 5p14 · 9 ○ 11a32 · 13 ○ 8a42 · 18 ☾ 10a31 · 22 ☽ 3p59 · 24 ○ 9a 1 · 30 ○ 9p21

JUN 1955
☉ → ♋ 21 11p31

☽→SIGNS
1 ♏ 3p54 · 4 ♐ 4a24 · 6 ♑ 5p21 · 9 ♒ 5a30 · 11 ♓ 3p32 · 13 ♈ 10p24 · 16 ♉ 1a50 · 18 ♊ 2a37 · 20 ♋ 2a15 · 22 ♌ 2a36 · 24 ♍ 5a26 · 26 ♎ 11a55 · 28 ♏ 10p 4

☽ PHASES
1 ○ 6a20 · 4 ○ 9a 8 · 8 ○ 1a11 · 11 ○ 11p32 · 16 ○ 6p21 · 19 ✶ 11p12 · 23 ☽ 5a39 · 26 ○ 8p44 · 29 ○ 9p21

JUL 1955
☉ → ♌ 23 10a25

☽→SIGNS
1 ♐ 10a34 · 4 ♑ 11p29 · 6 ♒ 11a18 · 9 ♓ 9p 9 · 11 ♈ 4a33 · 13 ♉ 9a20 · 15 ♊ 11a43 · 17 ♋ 12p30 · 19 ♌ 1p 3 · 21 ♍ 3p 6 · 23 ♎ 8p16 · 26 ♏ 5a19 · 28 ♐ 5p24 · 31 ♑ 6a18

☽ PHASES
3 ○ 12a29 · 8 ○ 11p25 · 12 ○ 3p31 · 16 ○ 12a43 · 19 ☽ 6a35 · 22 ☽ 11a 0 · 26 ☽ 11a 0 · 30 ○ 1p46

AUG 1955
☉ → ♍ 23 5p19

☽→SIGNS
2 ♒ 5p52 · 5 ♓ 3a 4 · 7 ♈ 10a 0 · 9 ♉ 3p 3 · 11 ♊ 6p33 · 13 ♋ 8p50 · 15 ♌ 10p34 · 18 ♍ 12a57 · 20 ♎ 5a34 · 22 ♏ 1p37 · 25 ♐ 1a 3 · 27 ♑ 1p57 · 30 ♒ 1a35

☽ PHASES
3 ○ 2p30 · 8 ○ 8a41 · 10 ○ 9p33 · 14 ○ 6a39 · 17 ● 2p58 · 21 ☽ 4a35 · 25 ○ 3a52 · 29 ○ 6a42

SEP 1955
☉ → ♎ 23 2p41

☽→SIGNS
1 ♓ 10a23 · 3 ♈ 4p24 · 5 ♉ 8p36 · 7 ♊ 11p58 · 10 ♋ 3a 1 · 12 ♌ 6a 2 · 14 ♍ 9a33 · 16 ♎ 2p35 · 18 ♏ 10p18 · 21 ♐ 9a11 · 23 ♑ 10p 1 · 26 ♒ 10a 7 · 28 ♓ 7p12

☽ PHASES
2 ○ 2a59 · 5 ○ 4p21 · 9 ○ 2a59 · 12 ☾ 1p12 · 16 ● 1a19 · 19 ✶ 8p 9 · 23 ○ 10p41 · 26 ○ 11p12

OCT 1955
☉ → ♏ 23 11p43

☽→SIGNS
1 ♈ 12a46 · 3 ♉ 3a52 · 5 ♊ 5a59 · 7 ♋ 8a23 · 9 ♌ 11a41 · 11 ♍ 4p01 · 13 ♎ 10p13 · 16 ♏ 6a44 · 18 ♐ 5p 7 · 21 ♑ 5a52 · 23 ♒ 6p33 · 26 ♓ 5a29 · 28 ♈ 10a46 · 30 ♉ 1p30

☽ PHASES
1 ○ 2p17 · 4 ○ 11p35 · 8 ○ 9a 4 · 11 ☾ 9p30 · 15 ● 2p32 · 19 ☽ 9p20 · 23 ○ 6p 5 · 27 ○ 1a 4

NOV 1955
☉ → ♐ 22 9p 1

☽→SIGNS
1 ♊ 2p23 · 3 ♋ 3p11 · 5 ♌ 5p20 · 7 ♍ 9p36 · 10 ♎ 4a15 · 12 ♏ 1p12 · 15 ♐ 12a17 · 17 ♑ 12p59 · 20 ♒ 1a58 · 22 ♓ 1p10 · 24 ♈ 8p47 · 27 ♉ 12a27 · 29 ♊ 1a11

☽ PHASES
3 ○ 7a30 · 6 ○ 4p56 · 10 ○ 8a42 · 14 ☾ 7a14 · 18 ● 10a25 · 22 ☽ 12p29 · 26 ○ 4a50 · 29 ✶ 11a50

DEC 1955
☉ → ♑ 22 10a11

☽→SIGNS
1 ♋ 12a46 · 3 ♌ 1a 7 · 5 ♍ 3a50 · 7 ♎ 9a48 · 9 ♏ 6p59 · 12 ♐ 6a34 · 14 ♑ 7p23 · 17 ♒ 8p 2 · 19 ♓ 8p 2 · 22 ♈ 5a 5 · 24 ♉ 10a33 · 26 ♊ 12p33 · 28 ♋ 12p17 · 30 ♌ 11a36

☽ PHASES
2 ○ 4p51 · 6 ○ 3a35 · 9 ☾ 11p33 · 13 ● 5a 5 · 18 ☽ 5a55 · 25 ○ 5p31 · 28 ○ 10p44

JAN 1956
☉ → ♒ 20 8p49

☽→SIGNS
1 ♍ 12p31 · 3 ♎ 4p44 · 6 ♏ 1a 0 · 8 ♐ 12p32 · 11 ♑ 1a33 · 13 ♒ 2p19 · 16 ♓ 1a47 · 18 ♈ 11a17 · 20 ♉ 6p11 · 22 ♊ 11p20 · 25 ♋ 11p 6 · 27 ♌ 11p17 · 29 ♍ 2p29 · 31 ♎ 1a56

☽ PHASES
1 ○ 4a 3 · 4 ○ 5p41 · 7 ☾ 2p15 · 12 ● 10p11 · 20 ○ 5p58 · 24 ○ 4a31 · 30 ○ 5p16

FEB 1956
☉ → ♓ 19 11a 5

☽→SIGNS
2 ♏ 8a33 · 4 ♐ 7p13 · 7 ♑ 8a 8 · 9 ♒ 8p52 · 12 ♓ 7a52 · 14 ♈ 4p48 · 16 ♉ 11p48 · 19 ♊ 4a50 · 21 ♋ 7a50 · 23 ♌ 9a10 · 25 ♍ 10a 5 · 27 ♎ 12p20 · 29 ♏ 5p45

☽ PHASES
3 ○ 11a 8 · 7 ☾ 2p15 · 11 ● 4p38 · 19 ○ 4a21 · 22 ○ 1p48 · 25 ○ 8p42 · 29 ○ 8a29

MAR 1956
☉ → ♈ 20 10a20

☽→SIGNS
3 ♐ 3a 9 · 5 ♑ 4a19 · 8 ♒ 4a33 · 10 ♓ 3p11 · 13 ♈ 11p26 · 15 ♉ 5a32 · 17 ♊ 10a11 · 19 ♋ 1p47 · 21 ♌ 4p31 · 23 ♍ 6p53 · 25 ♎ 10p 0 · 28 ♏ 3a18 · 30 ♐ 11a56

☽ PHASES
3 ○ 6a53 · 8 ☾ 10a24 · 12 ● 8a37 · 16 ○ 12a17 · 22 ○ 12p14 · 26 ○ 8a11 · 29 ○ 1a20

APR 1956
☉ → ♉ 19 9p43

☽→SIGNS
1 ♑ 11p37 · 4 ♒ 12p24 · 6 ♓ 11p37 · 9 ♈ 7a47 · 11 ♉ 1p 3 · 13 ♊ 4p30 · 15 ♋ 7p15 · 17 ♌ 10p 0 · 20 ♍ 1a17 · 22 ♎ 5a34 · 24 ♏ 11a44 · 26 ♐ 8p21 · 29 ♑ 7a44

☽ PHASES
3 ○ 3a 6 · 7 ☾ 4a30 · 10 ● 9p39 · 18 ○ 8a45 · 20 ○ 6p28 · 24 ○ 5a31 · 28 ○ 7p 0

MAY 1956
☉ → ♊ 20 9p12

☽→SIGNS
1 ♒ 8p27 · 4 ♓ 8a15 · 6 ♈ 5p 5 · 8 ♉ 10p24 · 11 ♊ 1a 0 · 13 ♋ 2a21 · 15 ♌ 3a52 · 17 ♍ 6a40 · 19 ♎ 11p26 · 22 ♏ 6p25 · 24 ♐ 3a46 · 26 ♑ 3p11 · 29 ♒ 3a52 · 31 ♓ 4p 9

☽ PHASES
2 ○ 9p55 · 6 ☾ 7p43 · 10 ● 8a 4 · 13 ☽ 3p32 · 17 ○ 12a15 · 20 ○ 2p 7 · 24 ✶ 10a26 · 28 ○ 12p18

JUN 1956
☉ → ♋ 21 5a24

☽→SIGNS
3 ♈ 2a57 · 5 ♉ 8a22 · 7 ♊ 11a42 · 9 ♋ 11a45 · 11 ♌ 11a45 · 13 ♍ 1p 3 · 15 ♎ 4p58 · 18 ♏ 12a38 · 20 ♐ 9a55 · 22 ♑ 9p43 · 25 ♒ 10a26 · 27 ♓ 10p54 · 30 ♈ 9a43

☽ PHASES
1 ○ 2p13 · 5 ☾ 8a 3 · 8 ● 4p29 · 11 ☽ 9p37 · 15 ○ 12a38 · 19 ○ 12a38 · 23 ○ 1a14 · 27 ○ 4a13

JUL 1956
☉ → ♌ 22 4a20

☽→SIGNS
2 ♉ 5p26 · 4 ♊ 9p26 · 6 ♋ 8a27 · 9 ♌ 9p42 · 11 ♍ 1p54 · 13 ♎ 5a56 · 15 ♏ 3p38 · 18 ♐ 3a41 · 20 ♑ 4p13 · 23 ♒ 5a10 · 25 ♓ 6p15 · 28 ♈ 5a 5 · 30 ♉ 2a40

☽ PHASES
4 ☾ 5p53 · 8 ● 4p29 · 11 ☽ 9p37 · 14 ○ 4a 8 · 18 ○ 3p47 · 21 ○ 7p38 · 25 ○ 6p15 · 26 ○ 6p15

AUG 1956
☉ → ♍ 22 11p15

☽→SIGNS
1 ♊ 6a16 · 3 ♋ 8a32 · 5 ♌ 8a27 · 7 ♍ 7a50 · 9 ♎ 8a50 · 11 ♏ 1p20 · 13 ♐ 9p56 · 16 ♑ 9p47 · 18 ♒ 10p38 · 21 ♓ 10a47 · 23 ♈ 9p30 · 26 ♉ 6a23 · 28 ♊ 12p59 · 30 ♋ 4p51

☽ PHASES
3 ☾ 1a50 · 6 ● 6a25 · 9 ☽ 12p20 · 13 ○ 3a45 · 20 ○ 7p38 · 25 ○ 6a23 · 28 ● 11p23

SEP 1956
☉ → ♎ 22 8p35

☽→SIGNS
1 ♌ 6p14 · 3 ♍ 6p20 · 5 ♎ 7p 4 · 7 ♏ 10p26 · 10 ♐ 4a50 · 12 ♑ 4p46 · 15 ♒ 5a28 · 17 ♓ 5p34 · 20 ♈ 4a29 · 22 ♉ 12p 1 · 24 ♊ 6p25 · 26 ♋ 9p12 · 29 ♌ 1a49

☽ PHASES
1 ● 8a37 · 4 ☽ 1p57 · 7 ○ 11p18 · 11 ○ 7p13 · 15 ○ 10p 9 · 19 ○ 10p19 · 23 ○ 2a20 · 26 ☾ 11p 2 · 30 ☾ 3p17

OCT 1956
☉ → ♏ 23 5a35

☽→SIGNS
1 ♍ 3a24 · 3 ♎ 5a 1 · 5 ♏ 7p 4 · 7 ♐ 2p46 · 10 ♑ 12a48 · 12 ♒ 1p 9 · 15 ♓ 11a35 · 17 ♈ 11a35 · 19 ♉ 7p 7 · 22 ♊ 12a29 · 24 ♋ 4a23 · 26 ♌ 7a27 · 28 ♍ 10a 9 · 30 ♎ 1p10

☽ PHASES
3 ● 11p25 · 6 ☽ 7p46 · 11 ○ 1p44 · 15 ○ 4p10 · 19 ○ 12p25 · 23 ○ 2a20 · 26 ☾ 11p 2

NOV 1956
☉ → ♐ 22 2a50

☽→SIGNS
1 ♏ 5p24 · 3 ♐ 11p56 · 6 ♑ 9p19 · 8 ♒ 9p19 · 11 ♓ 8p36 · 13 ♈ 8p36 · 16 ♉ 4a12 · 18 ♊ 8a45 · 20 ♋ 1p10 · 22 ♌ 1p10 · 24 ♍ 2a34 · 26 ♎ 7p11 · 29 ♏ 2a34

☽ PHASES
2 ● 11a44 · 4 ☽ 7a36 · 10 ○ 10a19 · 14 ○ 10a20 · 18 ○ 11a 8 · 22 ○ 1p 2 · 28 ☾ 8a57

DEC 1956
☉ → ♑ 21 4p 0

☽→SIGNS
1 ♐ 7a59 · 3 ♑ 5p36 · 6 ♒ 5a16 · 8 ♓ 5p57 · 11 ♈ 5a37 · 13 ♉ 2p15 · 15 ♊ 7p 6 · 17 ♋ 8p52 · 19 ♌ 9p11 · 21 ♍ 9p56 · 24 ♎ 12a39 · 26 ♏ 6a 9 · 28 ♐ 2p20 · 31 ♑ 12a37

☽ PHASES
2 ☽ 3a13 · 4 ● 3a42 · 9 ○ 6a51 · 14 ○ 10a33 · 17 ○ 8p 1 · 20 ○ 8p 1 · 24 ○ 5a10 · 27 ☾ 9p55 · 31 ● 9p14

JAN 1957 — ☉ → ♒ 20 2a39

D→SIGNS
2 ♏ 12p25
5 ♐ 1a 4
7 ♑ 1p23
9 ♒ 11p27
12 ♓ 5a44
14 ♈ 8a 6
16 ♉ 7a50
18 ♊ 7a 3
20 ♋ 7a55
22 ♌ 12p 2
24 ♍ 7p52
27 ♎ 6a32
29 ♏ 6p42

D PHASES
5 ☽ 12a19
9 ○ 2a 6
12 ○ 6p43
16 ○ 1a21
19 ○ 5a43
22 ○ 4p48
26 ☾ 1p51
30 ● 4p25

FEB 1957 — ☉ → ♓ 18 4p58

D→SIGNS
1 ♐ 7a20
3 ♑ 7p42
6 ♒ 6a37
8 ♓ 2p34
10 ♈ 6p39
12 ♉ 7p19
14 ♊ 6p17
16 ♋ 5p50
18 ♌ 8p 6
21 ♍ 2a23
23 ♎ 12p27
26 ♏ 12a42
28 ♐ 1p25

D PHASES
3 ☽ 7p35
7 ○ 6p23
11 ○ 7a 6
14 ○ 11a38
17 ○ 4p49
21 ○ 7a19
25 ☾ 7a51

MAR 1957 — ☉ → ♈ 20 4p16

D→SIGNS
3 ♑ 1a31
5 ♒ 12p20
7 ♓ 9p 3
10 ♈ 2a45
12 ♉ 5a12
14 ♊ 5a20
16 ♋ 4a59
18 ♌ 6a15
20 ♍ 10a53
22 ♎ 7p34
25 ♏ 7a17
27 ♐ 8p 0
30 ♑ 7a55

D PHASES
1 ● 11a12
5 ☽ 12p 5
9 ○ 6a50
12 ○ 4p40
15 ○ 9p22
19 ○ 5a33
23 ☾ 12a 4
27 ☽ 2a33
31 ● 4a19

APR 1957 — ☉ → ♉ 20 3a41

D→SIGNS
1 ♒ 6p11
4 ♓ 2a30
6 ♈ 8a37
8 ♉ 12p24
10 ♊ 2p13
12 ♋ 3p 8
14 ♌ 4p45
16 ♍ 8p43
19 ♎ 2p53
21 ♏ 3a23
24 ♐ 3p22
26 ♑ ...
29 ♒ 1a18

D PHASES
4 ☽ 1a 3
7 ○ 3p33
10 ○ 6a 6
13 ○ 7a 9
17 ○ 7p46
21 ○ 6p 1
25 ☾ 8p40
29 ☽ 6p54

MAY 1957 — ☉ → ♊ 21 3a10

D→SIGNS
1 ♊ 8a47
3 ♋ 2p 8
5 ♌ 5p54
7 ♍ 8p37
9 ♎ 10p57
12 ♏ 1a48
14 ♐ 6a13
16 ♑ 1p13
18 ♒ 11p12
21 ♓ 11a20
23 ♈ 11p34
26 ♉ 9a43
28 ♊ 4p47
30 ♋ 9p 6

D PHASES
3 ☽ 10a30
6 ○ 9p29
10 ○ 6a35
13 ○ 5p34
17 ○ 11a 3
21 ○ 12p 3
24 ☾ 1p12
29 ● 6a39

JUN 1957 — ☉ → ♋ 21 11a20

D→SIGNS
1 ♌ 11p45
4 ♍ 1a59
6 ♎ 4a45
8 ♏ 8a41
10 ♐ 2p 9
12 ♑ 9p36
15 ♒ 7a23
17 ♓ 7p15
20 ♈ 7a46
22 ♉ 6p38
25 ♊ 2a 7
27 ♋ 6a 1
29 ♌ 7a31

D PHASES
1 ☽ 5p15
5 ○ 2a10
8 ○ 1p22
12 ○ 5a 2
16 ○ 2a56
20 ○ 5a22
24 ☾ 3a33
27 ● 3p53
30 ☽ 10p38

JUL 1957 — ☉ → ♌ 22 10p15

D→SIGNS
1 ♍ 8a23
3 ♎ 10a16
5 ♏ 2p10
7 ♐ 8p20
10 ♑ 4a35
12 ♒ 2p43
15 ♓ 2a32
17 ♈ 3p14
20 ♉ 2a58
22 ♊ 11a34
24 ♋ 5p16
26 ♌ 9p17
28 ♍ 8p59
30 ♎ 5p20

D PHASES
4 ○ 7a 9
7 ○ 9p34
11 ○ 5p50
15 ○ 7p 5
18 ○ 11a 4
23 ☾ 3p32
26 ● 11p28
30 ☽ 4a 9

AUG 1957 — ☉ → ♍ 23 5a 8

D→SIGNS
1 ♏ 8p 1
3 ♐ 1a47
6 ♑ 10a23
8 ♒ 9p 1
11 ♓ 9a 2
13 ♈ 9p46
16 ♉ 7p51
18 ♊ 7p51
21 ♋ 3a51
23 ♌ 3a26
25 ♍ 2a41
27 ♎ 3a45
29 ♏ ...
31 ♐ 8a 7

D PHASES
2 ○ 1p55
6 ○ 8a 3
10 ○ 8a 4
14 ○ 11a 4
18 ○ 11a16
22 ☾ 1a24
25 ● 6a33
28 ☽ 11a13
31 ○ 11p35

SEP 1957 — ☉ → ♎ 23 2a26

D→SIGNS
2 ♍ 4p 5
5 ♎ 2a50
7 ♏ 3p 4
10 ♐ 3a45
12 ♑ 3p57
15 ♒ 2a26
17 ♓ 9a50
19 ♈ 1p31
21 ♉ 2p11
23 ♊ 1p33
25 ♋ 1p40
27 ♌ 7a41
29 ♍ 10p59

D PHASES
4 ○ 9p23
8 ○ 11p55
13 ○ 2a19
16 ○ 11p 2
20 ☾ 9p52
23 ● 2p18
26 ☽ 8p55
30 ○ 12p49

OCT 1957 — ☉ → ♏ 23 11a24

D→SIGNS
2 ♎ 9a 4
4 ♏ 9p17
7 ♐ 9a57
9 ♑ 9p 8
12 ♒ 8a 1
14 ♓ 3p54
16 ♈ 9p19
18 ♉ 11p23
21 ♊ 12a 3
23 ♋ 12a31
25 ♌ 2a33
27 ♍ 7a41
29 ♎ 4p32

D PHASES
4 ○ 1p45
8 ○ 4p42
12 ○ 4p 7
16 ○ 8a44
19 ☾ 5p49
22 ● 11p43
26 ☽ 9a52
30 ○ 5a48

NOV 1957 — ☉ → ♐ 22 8a39

D→SIGNS
1 ♏ 4a18
3 ♐ 5p 0
6 ♑ 4a38
8 ♒ 2p 9
10 ♓ 9p24
13 ♈ 2a36
15 ♉ 6a 7
17 ♊ 8a55
19 ♋ 10a17
21 ♌ 12p52
23 ♍ 5p29
26 ♎ 1a 5
28 ♏ 12p16

D PHASES
3 ○ 8a41
7 ☾ 9a32
11 ○ 4a 5
14 ○ 4p59
18 ☾ 2a11
21 ● 11a19
25 ☽ 2a 5
30 ○ 1a58

DEC 1957 — ☉ → ♑ 21 9p49

D→SIGNS
1 ♐ 12a56
3 ♑ 12p48
6 ♒ 10p 0
8 ♓ 4a16
10 ♈ 8a23
12 ♉ 11a28
14 ♊ 2p23
16 ♋ 5p35
18 ♌ 9p30
21 ♍ 2a47
23 ♎ 10a19
25 ♏ 8p41
28 ♐ 9a13
30 ♑ 9p37

D PHASES
3 ○ 4a54
7 ○ 7a10
10 ○ 2p22
17 ☾ 11a39
21 ● 1a12
24 ☽ 9p 3
28 ○ 11p52

JAN 1958 — ☉ → ♒ 20 8a29

D→SIGNS
2 ♒ 7a21
4 ♓ 1p22
6 ♈ 4p21
8 ♉ 5p59
10 ♊ 7p52
12 ♋ 11p 2
15 ♌ 3a49
17 ♍ 10a13
19 ♎ 6p22
22 ♏ 5p 3
24 ♐ 5p 3
27 ♑ 5p33
29 ♒ 4p47
31 ♓ 11p41

D PHASES
2 ○ 12a29
5 ○ 3p 9
8 ○ 11p38
12 ● 6p34
15 ☾ 10p42
19 ● 5p 8
23 ☽ 5p37
31 ○ 5p37

FEB 1958 — ☉ → ♓ 18 10p49

D→SIGNS
3 ♈ 2a38
5 ♉ 3a11
7 ♊ 3a23
9 ♋ 5a 3
11 ♌ 9a11
13 ♍ 3p55
16 ♎ 12a51
18 ♏ 11a39
21 ♐ 12a 2
23 ♑ 1p 5
26 ♒ 1a52
28 ♓ 9a17

D PHASES
4 ○ 3a 5
8 ○ 8a44
10 ● 6p34
16 ☾ 10a38
18 ● 4a50
22 ☽ 2p 2
26 ○ 3p52

MAR 1958 — ☉ → ♈ 20 10p 6

D→SIGNS
2 ♈ 1p27
4 ♉ 2p15
6 ♊ 1p34
8 ♋ 1p34
10 ♌ 3p56
12 ♍ 9p51
14 ♎ 6a28
17 ♏ 5p41
20 ♐ 6a17
22 ♑ 7p16
25 ♒ 7a20
27 ♓ 4p53
29 ♈ 10p46

D PHASES
2 ○ 7a26
5 ○ 1p28
10 ● 6p17
16 ☾ 5a48
18 ● 4a50
24 ☽ 8a10
28 ○ 6a18
31 ○ 6p 2

APR 1958 — ☉ → ♉ 20 9a27

D→SIGNS
1 ♉ 1a 1
3 ♊ 12a54
5 ♋ 1a16
7 ♌ 1a 7
9 ♍ 3p56
11 ♎ 1p38
13 ♏ 12p23
16 ♐ 1a16
18 ♑ 1p46
20 ♒ 10p46
22 ♓ 5a44
26 ♈ 9a41
28 ♉ ...
30 ♊ 11a 6

D PHASES
1 ☽ 10p45
4 ○ 4a34
10 ● 6p50
14 ☾ 6p47
18 ● 11p 2
22 ☽ 11p 2
26 ○ 4p36
30 ○ 2a 5

MAY 1958 — ☉ → ♊ 21 8a51

D→SIGNS
2 ♋ 11a14
4 ♌ 11a43
6 ♍ 2p21
8 ♎ 8p29
11 ♏ 6a27
13 ♐ 6p58
16 ♑ 7a50
18 ♒ 7p14
21 ♓ 4a23
23 ♈ 11a15
25 ♉ 4p 0
27 ♊ 6p55
29 ♋ 8p33
31 ♌ 9p54

D PHASES
3 ☾ 7a23
6 ○ 3p45
10 ● 9a38
14 ☾ 12p 2
18 ● 2p 0
22 ☽ 9a55
25 ○ 11p38
29 ○ 8a30

JUN 1958 — ☉ → ♋ 21 4p57

D→SIGNS
3 ♍ 12a23
5 ♎ 5a34
7 ♏ 2p24
10 ♐ 2a20
12 ♑ 3p12
15 ♒ 3a31
17 ♓ 1p15
19 ♈ 8p22
21 ♉ 12a42
24 ♊ 3a30
26 ♋ 6a12
28 ♌ 9a32
30 ♍ 10p52

D PHASES
1 ○ 9p55
5 ○ 4a 6
8 ● 11a59
13 ☾ 5a 2
16 ● 6p 1
20 ☽ 7p46
24 ○ 4a45
28 ○ 2p19

JUL 1958 — ☉ → ♌ 23 3a51

D→SIGNS
2 ♎ 2p44
4 ♏ 10p57
7 ♐ 10a18
9 ♑ 11p 9
12 ♒ 10a47
14 ♓ 7p15
17 ♈ 12a31
19 ♉ 2a31
21 ♊ 3a42
23 ♋ 6a11
25 ♌ 8a57
27 ♍ 12p25
29 ♎ 4p53
31 ♏ 1a35

D PHASES
2 ○ 1a 5
6 ○ 6p 1
10 ☾ 7p21
12 ● 8p46
18 ☽ 1p33
22 ○ 11p52
25 ○ 9p20
29 ○ 8p42

AUG 1958 — ☉ → ♍ 23 10a46

D→SIGNS
1 ♐ 7a11
3 ♑ 6p14
6 ♒ 7a 4
8 ♓ 7p16
11 ♈ 4a25
13 ♉ 9a43
15 ♊ 12p 7
17 ♋ 1p17
19 ♌ 2p50
21 ♍ 5p48
23 ♎ 10p38
26 ♏ 5a28
28 ♐ 2p25
31 ♑ 1a35

D PHASES
3 ○ 9a44
7 ☾ 12p50
9 ● 10p33
14 ☽ 10p33
16 ○ 5a39
18 ○ 5a39
21 ○ 2p45
25 ○ 4a53
31 ○ ...

SEP 1958 — ☉ → ♎ 23 8a 9

D→SIGNS
2 ♒ 2p24
5 ♓ 3a 7
7 ♈ 2p42
9 ♉ 11p42
11 ♊ 10p19
13 ♋ 9a43
15 ♌ 12p 7
18 ♍ 12a16
20 ♎ 2p50
22 ♏ 5p48
25 ♐ 10p38
27 ♑ 2p25
29 ♒ ...

D PHASES
2 ○ 2a52
6 ○ 5a24
9 ☾ 11p 5
13 ● 7a 2
17 ☽ 12p21
22 ○ 10p18
25 ○ 4p 8
27 ○ 4p44

OCT 1958 — ☉ → ♏ 23 5p12

D→SIGNS
2 ♓ 9a50
4 ♈ 9p 0
7 ♉ 4a51
9 ♊ 8a49
11 ♋ 9a44
13 ♌ 9a11
15 ♍ 11a23
17 ♎ 11a23
19 ♏ 5p 4
22 ♐ 2a19
24 ♑ 2p10
27 ♒ 3a 7
29 ♓ 3p49

D PHASES
1 ○ 8p26
5 ○ 8p30
9 ☾ 10a12
12 ● 3p52
19 ☽ 8p57
22 ○ 1a52
27 ☽ 10a41
31 ○ 1p 7

NOV 1958 — ☉ → ♐ 22 2p29

D→SIGNS
3 ♉ 3a 9
5 ♊ 12p 2
7 ♋ 5p45
9 ♌ 8p16
11 ♍ 8p30
14 ♎ 8p 3
16 ♏ 8p54
18 ♐ 8a56
20 ♑ 8p28
23 ♒ 9a11
25 ♓ 10p 0
28 ♈ 8a56
30 ♉ 5p41

D PHASES
4 ○ 9a19
7 ☾ 8p30
11 ● 1a34
18 ☽ 8a 7
20 ○ 11p59
25 ○ 1a52
30 ○ 3a57

DEC 1958 — ☉ → ♑ 22 3a40

D→SIGNS
2 ♊ 12a18
4 ♋ 4a31
6 ♌ 6a28
8 ♍ 7a 2
10 ♎ 8a30
13 ♏ 10a38
15 ♐ 5p12
18 ♑ 3a45
20 ♒ 4p38
23 ♓ 5a 9
25 ♈ 5p12
27 ♉ 11p33
30 ♊ 5a41

D PHASES
3 ○ 8p24
7 ☾ 6a13
10 ● 12p23
18 ☽ 10p20
20 ○ 10p39
25 ○ 10p54
29 ○ 4p37

JAN 1959 — AUG 1959

	JAN 1959	FEB 1959	MAR 1959	APR 1959	MAY 1959	JUN 1959	JUL 1959	AUG 1959
☉ ->	♒ 20 2p19	♓ 19 4a38	♈ 21 3a55	♉ 20 3p17	♊ 21 2p42	♋ 21 10p50	♌ 23 9a46	♍ 23 4p44

☽ -> SIGNS

JAN 1959: 1 ♎ 10a21 / 3 ♏ 1p42 / 5 ♐ 3p56 / 7 ♑ 5p50 / 9 ♒ 8p52 / 12 ♓ 2a39 / 14 ♈ 12p 9 / 17 ♉ 12a33 / 19 ♊ 1p16 / 21 ♋ 11p47 / 24 ♌ 7a13 / 26 ♍ 12p13 / 28 ♎ 3p54 / 30 ♏ 7p 5

FEB 1959: 1 ♐ 10p11 / 3 ♑ 1a29 / 5 ♒ 5a40 / 8 ♓ 11a50 / 10 ♈ 8p55 / 13 ♉ 8a47 / 15 ♊ 9p39 / 18 ♋ 8a51 / 20 ♌ 4p38 / 22 ♍ 9p 6 / 24 ♎ 11p29 / 27 ♏ 1a15

MAR 1959: 1 ♐ 3a33 / 3 ♑ 7a 6 / 5 ♒ 12p16 / 7 ♓ 7p25 / 10 ♈ 4a54 / 12 ♉ 4p37 / 15 ♊ 5a31 / 17 ♋ 5p28 / 20 ♌ 2a22 / 22 ♍ 8a 4 / 24 ♎ 9a27 / 26 ♏ 9a54 / 28 ♐ 10a31 / 30 ♑ 12p49

APR 1959: 1 ♒ 5p41 / 4 ♓ 1a23 / 6 ♈ 11a33 / 8 ♉ 11p32 / 11 ♊ 12p25 / 14 ♋ 12a48 / 16 ♌ 10a55 / 18 ♍ 5p28 / 20 ♎ 8p19 / 22 ♏ 8p34 / 24 ♐ 7p59 / 26 ♑ 8p32 / 29 ♒ 11p55

MAY 1959: 1 ♓ 6a58 / 3 ♈ 5p19 / 6 ♉ 5a39 / 8 ♊ 6a34 / 11 ♋ 6a57 / 13 ♌ 5p40 / 16 ♍ 1a38 / 18 ♎ 6a 6 / 20 ♏ 7a24 / 22 ♐ 6a51 / 24 ♑ 6a24 / 26 ♒ 8a 9 / 28 ♓ 1p42 / 30 ♈ 11p18

JUN 1959: 2 ♉ 11a37 / 5 ♊ 12a35 / 7 ♋ 12p44 / 9 ♌ 11p19 / 12 ♍ 7a50 / 14 ♎ 1p42 / 16 ♏ 4p38 / 18 ♐ 5p14 / 20 ♑ 5p 1 / 22 ♒ 6p 0 / 24 ♓ 10p 9 / 27 ♈ 6a28 / 29 ♉ 6p11

JUL 1959: 2 ♊ 7a 5 / 4 ♋ 7p 3 / 7 ♌ 5a 8 / 9 ♍ 1p15 / 11 ♎ 7p26 / 14 ♏ 11p33 / 16 ♐ 1a42 / 18 ♑ 2a42 / 20 ♒ 4a 5 / 22 ♓ 7a41 / 24 ♈ 2p53 / 27 ♉ 1a43 / 29 ♊ 2p23

AUG 1959: 1 ♋ 2a24 / 3 ♌ 12p 9 / 5 ♍ 7p59 / 8 ♎ 12a56 / 10 ♏ 5a 0 / 12 ♐ 7a58 / 14 ♑ 10a19 / 16 ♒ 12p53 / 18 ♓ 4p59 / 20 ♈ 11p51 / 23 ♉ 9a58 / 25 ♊ 10p18 / 28 ♋ 10a33 / 30 ♌ 8p33

☽ PHASES

JAN 1959: 2 ☉ 5a50 / 5 ☽ 3p33 / 9 ● 12a34 / 12 ☽ 3p34 / 16 ○ 4p27 / 20 ○ 7p18 / 24 ○ 2p33 / 28 ○ 3a20 / 31 ○ 2p 6

FEB 1959: 4 ☽ 12a55 / 7 ● 2p22 / 11 ☽ 11a 3 / 15 ○ 2p20 / 19 ○ 1p55 / 26 ● 12p35

MAR 1959: 1 ○ 9p54 / 5 ☽ 11a 4 / 9 ● 5a51 / 13 ☽ 7a 8 / 17 ○ 10a10 / 21 ○ 5a30 / 24 ○ 3p 2 / 27 ○ 8p52 / 31 ○ 6a 7

APR 1959: 3 ☽ 10p47 / 7 ● 10p29 / 12 ☽ 1a51 / 15 ○ 7p49 / 19 ○ 2a33 / 22 ○ 12a13 / 26 ○ 4a48 / 29 ○ 3p38

MAY 1959: 3 ☽ 12p24 / 7 ● 3p11 / 11 ☽ 5p51 / 15 ○ 3p 9 / 19 ○ 3a10 / 22 ○ 7a56 / 25 ○ 1p10 / 29 ○ 3a14

JUN 1959: 2 ☽ 3a39 / 6 ● 6a53 / 10 ☽ 6a42 / 14 ○ 12a22 / 17 ○ 10a 9 / 20 ○ 3p 0 / 23 ○ 10p55 / 27 ○ 5p12

JUL 1959: 1 ☽ 7p46 / 5 ● 9p 0 / 9 ☽ 4p47 / 13 ○ 7a 1 / 16 ○ 3p44 / 20 ○ 10p33 / 23 ○ 10a52 / 27 ○ 9p12 / 31 ☽ 12p 2

AUG 1959: 4 ● 9a34 / 8 ☽ 12a51 / 11 ○ 12p10 / 14 ○ 9p15 / 18 ○ 7a51 / 22 ○ 1a29 / 26 ○ 3a 3 / 30 ☽ 3a56

SEP 1959 — APR 1960

	SEP 1959	OCT 1959	NOV 1959	DEC 1959	JAN 1960	FEB 1960	MAR 1960	APR 1960
☉ ->	♎ 23 2p 9	♏ 23 11p11	♐ 22 8p27	♑ 22 9a35	♒ 20 8p10	♓ 19 10a26	♈ 20 9a43	♉ 19 9p 6

☽ -> SIGNS

SEP 1959: 2 ♍ 3a31 / 4 ♎ 7a56 / 6 ♏ 10a53 / 8 ♐ 1p20 / 10 ♑ 4p 5 / 12 ♒ 7p43 / 15 ♓ 12a54 / 17 ♈ 8a16 / 19 ♉ 6p12 / 22 ♊ 6a16 / 24 ♋ 6p49 / 27 ♌ 5a36 / 29 ♍ 1p 4

OCT 1959: 1 ♎ 6p54 / 3 ♏ 9p54 / 5 ♐ 7p54 / 7 ♑ 9p38 / 10 ♒ 1a12 / 12 ♓ 6a33 / 14 ♈ 2p20 / 17 ♉ 1a40 / 19 ♊ 2p 6 / 22 ♋ 2a22 / 24 ♌ 1p41 / 26 ♍ 10p48 / 29 ♎ 5a 4 / 31 ♏ 5a14

NOV 1959: 2 ♐ 5a 2 / 4 ♑ 5a 5 / 6 ♒ 7a16 / 8 ♓ 12p35 / 11 ♈ 9p10 / 13 ♉ 8a16 / 16 ♊ 8p56 / 18 ♋ 9p 4 / 20 ♌ 9p 4 / 23 ♍ 7a 8 / 25 ♎ 1p41 / 27 ♏ 4p22 / 29 ♐ 4p12

DEC 1959: 1 ♑ 3p11 / 3 ♒ 3p35 / 5 ♓ 7p16 / 8 ♈ 2a59 / 10 ♉ 1p56 / 13 ♊ 2a24 / 15 ♋ 3p 6 / 18 ♌ 2a58 / 20 ♍ 9p29 / 22 ♎ 2a 1 / 25 ♏ 3a16 / 27 ♐ 2a38 / 29 ♑ 2a15

JAN 1960: 2 ♒ 4a19 / 4 ♓ 10a21 / 6 ♈ 8p22 / 9 ♉ 8a45 / 11 ♊ 9p23 / 14 ♋ 8a59 / 16 ♌ 7p 3 / 19 ♍ 3a14 / 21 ♎ 8a55 / 23 ♏ 12p 3 / 25 ♐ 1p19 / 27 ♑ 1p19 / 29 ♒ 2p56 / 31 ♈ 7p39

FEB 1960: 3 ♈ 4a16 / 5 ♉ 3p58 / 8 ♊ 4a37 / 10 ♋ 4p 8 / 13 ♌ 1a35 / 15 ♍ 8a55 / 17 ♎ 2p24 / 19 ♏ 6p12 / 21 ♐ 8p39 / 23 ♑ 10p32 / 26 ♒ 1a 4 / 28 ♓ 5a38

MAR 1960: 1 ♈ 1p18 / 3 ♉ 12a 8 / 6 ♊ 12p37 / 8 ♋ 12a25 / 11 ♌ 9a47 / 13 ♍ 4p37 / 15 ♎ 8p37 / 17 ♏ 11p27 / 20 ♐ 2a14 / 22 ♑ 5a10 / 24 ♒ 8a38 / 26 ♓ 2p30 / 28 ♈ 10p13 / 31 ♉ 8a32

APR 1960: 2 ♊ 8p46 / 5 ♋ 9p 1 / 7 ♌ 7p 2 / 10 ♍ 1a36 / 12 ♎ 5a 1 / 14 ♏ 6a37 / 16 ♐ 8a32 / 18 ♑ 10a32 / 20 ♒ 2p55 / 22 ♓ 9p23 / 25 ♈ 5a51 / 27 ♉ 4p16 / 30 ♊ 4a22

☽ PHASES

SEP 1959: 2 ● 8p56 / 6 ☽ 7a31 / 9 ○ 5p 7 / 13 ○ 4a10 / 16 ○ 7p52 / 20 ○ 6p32 / 24 ○ 9p22 / 28 ☽ 7p11

OCT 1959: 1 ● 6p54 / 5 ☽ 2p41 / 8 ● 11p22 / 12 ○ 1p54 / 15 ○ 10a59 / 19 ○ 8a 1 / 23 ○ 8a 3 / 26 ● 10p24 / 31 ☽ 5p41

NOV 1959: 3 ○ 10p32 / 7 ☽ 8a24 / 11 ● 3a21 / 15 ○ 4a42 / 19 ○ 8a 1 / 23 ○ 8a 3 / 26 ○ 10p24 / 30 ☽ 3a46

DEC 1959: 3 ○ 8a22 / 6 ● 9p12 / 10 ○ 8p27 / 14 ○ 11p49 / 19 ○ 1a51 / 22 ○ 10p28 / 26 ● 9a39 / 29 ☽ 2p 9

JAN 1960: 1 ☽ 8p52 / 5 ● 1p53 / 10 ○ 9a26 / 13 ○ 6p51 / 18 ○ 5p28 / 21 ○ 10a 1 / 24 ● 7p16 / 28 ☽ 1a15 / 31 ☽ 12p 7

FEB 1960: 4 ● 9a26 / 9 ○ 12p24 / 12 ○ 9a26 / 16 ○ 9a46 / 19 ○ 6p47 / 23 ☽ 3a50 / 26 ● 1p24

MAR 1960: 1 ☽ 5p25 / 5 ● 6a 5 / 10 ○ 8a12 / 13 ○ 3p54 / 18 ○ 1a40 / 20 ○ 1a40 / 23 ☽ 12p17 / 27 ● 2a37 / 30 ☽ 11p35

APR 1960: 4 ● 2a 5 / 8 ○ 1a27 / 11 ○ 3p27 / 16 ○ 11p23 / 18 ○ 7a57 / 21 ☽ 9p28 / 25 ● 4p44 / 29 ☽ 5p27

MAY 1960 — DEC 1960

	MAY 1960	JUN 1960	JUL 1960	AUG 1960	SEP 1960	OCT 1960	NOV 1960	DEC 1960
☉ ->	♊ 20 8p33	♋ 21 4a42	♌ 22 3p38	♍ 22 10p35	♎ 22 7p59	♏ 23 5a 2	♐ 22 2a19	♑ 21 3p26

☽ -> SIGNS

MAY 1960: 2 ♋ 4p59 / 5 ♌ 3a59 / 7 ♍ 11a30 / 9 ♎ 3p 7 / 11 ♏ 3p55 / 13 ♐ 3p50 / 15 ♑ 4p51 / 17 ♒ 8p23 / 20 ♓ 2a55 / 22 ♈ 12p 0 / 24 ♉ 10p55 / 27 ♊ 11a 6 / 29 ♋ 11p50

JUN 1960: 1 ♍ 11a38 / 3 ♎ 8p20 / 5 ♏ 1a20 / 7 ♐ 2a31 / 9 ♑ 1a48 / 11 ♒ 1a23 / 13 ♓ 3a17 / 15 ♈ 8p? / 18 ♉ 5p33 / 20 ♊ 5p10 / 23 ♋ 5p10 / 25 ♌ 5p? / 28 ♍ 5p53

JUL 1960: 1 ♎ 3a46 / 3 ♏ 10a 8 / 5 ♐ 12p42 / 7 ♑ 12p34 / 9 ♒ 11a43 / 11 ♓ 12p19 / 13 ♈ 4p 7 / 15 ♉ 11p? / 18 ♊ 11a? / 20 ♋ 11a? / 22 ♌ 11p? / 25 ♍ 12a? / 27 ♎ 1p54 / 29 ♏ 9a? / 31 ♐ 7a38

AUG 1960: 1 ♐ 9p 4 / 3 ♑ 10p26 / 5 ♒ 10p21 / 7 ♓ 10p42 / 10 ♈ 1a21 / 12 ♉ 7a36 / 14 ♊ 5p29 / 17 ♋ 5a43 / 19 ♌ 6p18 / 22 ♍ 5a41 / 24 ♎ 3p 9 / 26 ♏ 10p24 / 29 ♐ 3a19 / 31 ♑ 6a 9

SEP 1960: 2 ♒ 7a35 / 4 ♓ 8p46 / 6 ♈ 11a26 / 8 ♉ 4p44 / 11 ♊ 1a31 / 13 ♋ 1p10 / 16 ♌ 1a46 / 18 ♍ 1p 7 / 20 ♎ 9p58 / 23 ♏ 4a18 / 25 ♐ 8a42 / 27 ♑ 11a24 / 29 ♒ 1p?

OCT 1960: 1 ♓ 5p14 / 3 ♈ 8p46 / 6 ♉ 2a 9 / 8 ♊ 10a16 / 10 ♋ 9p18 / 13 ♌ 9a55 / 15 ♍ 9p40 / 18 ♎ 6a32 / 20 ♏ 12p 6 / 22 ♐ 5p28 / 24 ♑ 5p28 / 26 ♒ 7p57 / 28 ♓ 11p26 / 31 ♈ 4a11

NOV 1960: 2 ♉ 10a27 / 4 ♊ 6p44 / 7 ♋ 5a26 / 9 ♌ 5p59 / 12 ♍ 6a24 / 14 ♎ 6p? / 16 ♏ 9p53 / 19 ♐ 12a17 / 21 ♑ 1a 2 / 23 ♒ 2a 4 / 25 ♓ 4a49 / 27 ♈ 9a51 / 29 ♉ 5p 0

DEC 1960: 2 ♊ 2a 1 / 4 ♋ 12p52 / 7 ♌ 1a21 / 9 ♍ 2p13 / 12 ♎ 2a10 / 14 ♏ 8a13 / 16 ♐ 11a 7 / 18 ♑ 10a49 / 20 ♒ 10a30 / 22 ♓ 11a? / 24 ♈ 3p34 / 27 ♉ 10p30 / 29 ♊ 8a 1 / 31 ♋ 7p22

☽ PHASES

MAY 1960: 3 ○ 8p 0 / 7 ○ 3p32 / 10 ○ 12a42 / 14 ○ 5a45 / 17 ○ 2p54 / 21 ☽ 8a 4 / 25 ● 7a26 / 29 ☽ 10a 9

JUN 1960: 2 ○ 11a 1 / 6 ● 2a18 / 9 ○ 8a 2 / 12 ○ 12p17 / 15 ○ 11p35 / 19 ☽ 6p? / 23 ● 10p27 / 28 ☽ 1a 5

JUL 1960: 1 ○ 10p48 / 5 ○ 10a23 / 8 ○ 2p37 / 11 ○ 8p 9 / 15 ○ 10a43 / 19 ☽ 10a38 / 23 ● 1p31 / 27 ☽ 1p54 / 31 ○ 7a38

AUG 1960: 3 ○ 4p48 / 6 ○ 9p41 / 8 ○ 6a16 / 12 ○ 12a37 / 18 ○ 2a40 / 20 ☽ 6a? / 22 ● 4a15 / 26 ☽ 12a31 / 29 ○ 2p22

SEP 1960: 1 ○ 10p51 / 5 ● 6a19 / 8 ○ 7p 9 / 12 ○ 12p25 / 16 ○ 1p57 / 20 ☽ 6p13 / 24 ● 9a21 / 27 ○ 8p13

OCT 1960: 3 ○ 5a47 / 5 ○ 5p16 / 8 ○ 10a58 / 12 ○ 12p25 / 15 ☽ 7a 6 / 20 ● 2a 7 / 22 ○ 5p15 / 25 ○ 2a34 / 30 ○ 2p40

NOV 1960: 3 ○ 6a58 / 5 ○ 5p28 / 11 ○ 8a47 / 15 ☽ 6p46 / 18 ● 2p19 / 22 ○ 10a42 / 25 ○ 2a15 / 29 ○ 5p 0

DEC 1960: 2 ○ 11p24 / 5 ○ 1a42 / 10 ○ 4a38 / 14 ○ 10p27 / 18 ● 5a47 / 21 ○ 9p30 / 28 ○ 4p51

JAN 1961 — ☉ -> ♒ 20 2a 1

☽->SIGNS
3	♌	7a54
5	♍	9p56
8	♎	8a31
10	♏	5p 9
12	♐	9p40
14	♑	10p41
16	♒	9p55
18	♓	9p32
20	♈	11p26
23	♉	4a51
25	♊	1p50
28	♋	1a22
30	♌	2p 5

☽ PHASES
1	O	6p 6
5	O	9p56
9	◐	10p 2
13	◑	11a29
16	●	4p30
19	◐	9p48
23	O	11a14
27	O	10a15
31	O	1p47

FEB 1961 — ☉ -> ♓ 18 4p17

☽->SIGNS
2	♍	2a48
4	♎	2p27
6	♏	11p51
9	♐	6a 1
11	♑	8a48
13	♒	9a15
15	♓	8a53
17	♈	9a41
19	♉	1p21
21	♊	8p51
24	♋	7a49
26	♌	8p34

☽ PHASES
4	O	4p 5
8	◐	11a49
11	◑	10p13
15	☽	3a10
18	●	10a40
22	O	3a35
26	O	5a32

MAR 1961 — ☉ -> ♈ 20 3p32

☽->SIGNS
1	♍	9a12
3	♎	8p21
6	♏	5a24
8	♐	12p 4
10	♑	4p19
12	♒	6p29
14	♓	7p26
16	♈	8p32
18	♉	11p25
21	♊	5a32
23	♋	3p22
26	♌	3a49
28	♍	4p30
31	♎	3a21

☽ PHASES
2	♐	8a35
6	◐	6a38
9	◑	9p57
13	☽	7a 5
16	●	6p51
20	O	12a55
22	O	9p48
28	O	1a 5

APR 1961 — ☉ -> ♉ 20 2a55

☽->SIGNS
2	♏	11a37
4	♐	5p34
6	♑	9p52
9	♒	1a 3
11	♓	3a31
13	♈	5a55
15	♉	9a16
17	♊	2p55
19	♋	11p50
22	♌	11a43
24	♍	12a31
27	♎	11a34
29	♏	7p27

☽ PHASES
1	O	12a47
4	O	5p24
8	◐	5a16
11	◑	2p43
18	●	4p16
22	O	4p49
26	O	10a29
30	O	1p40

MAY 1961 — ☉ -> ♊ 21 2a22

☽->SIGNS
2	♐	12a25
4	♑	3a40
6	♒	6a24
8	♓	9a23
10	♈	12p56
12	♉	5a55
14	♊	11p34
16	♋	3a16
18	♌	4p12
21	♍	7p45
24	♎	4a32
25	♏	7p 5
29	♐	9a11
31	♑	11a20

☽ PHASES
2	O	7a19
5	◐	5a40
10	●	11a54
17	O	1a 8
24	O	1a11
29	O	11p37

JUN 1961 — ☉ -> ♋ 21 10a30

☽->SIGNS
2	♒	12p45
4	♓	2p50
6	♈	6p23
9	♉	11p38
11	♊	6a40
13	♋	3p50
16	♌	3a16
18	♍	4p 4
21	♎	4a32
23	♏	1p51
25	♐	7p 5
27	♑	9p 0
29	♒	9p18

☽ PHASES
2	O	7a19
5	◐	5a40
9	●	11a54
17	O	1a 8
24	O	10p53
28	O	7a38

JUL 1961 — ☉ -> ♌ 22 9p24

☽->SIGNS
1	♓	9p52
4	♈	12a12
6	♉	5a 2
8	♊	12p27
10	♋	10p13
13	♌	10a55
15	♍	10p55
18	♎	11a39
20	♏	10p 5
23	♐	4a42
25	♑	7a29
27	♒	7a41
29	♓	7a13
31	♈	7a56

☽ PHASES
1	O	1p 6
4	◐	10p32
8	●	3p 5
16	O	2p11
24	O	8a54
27	O	2p50
30	O	7p40

AUG 1961 — ☉ -> ♍ 23 4a19

☽->SIGNS
2	♉	11a19
4	♊	6p 4
6	♋	3a56
9	♌	5a 0
11	♍	5p44
14	♎	4a44
17	♏	4p44
19	♐	12p44
21	♑	5p 7
23	♒	6p25
25	♓	6p 2
27	♈	5p49
29	♉	7p37

☽ PHASES
3	O	6a47
7	◐	3a 6
11	●	5a36
15	D	8a39
19	O	5a51
22	O	5p22
25	♐	10p13
29	O	3a59

SEP 1961 — ☉ -> ♎ 23 1a43

☽->SIGNS
1	♊	12a53
3	♋	10a 0
5	♌	10p 1
8	♍	11a 5
10	♎	11p23
13	♏	11p33
15	♐	6p54
17	♑	12a42
20	♒	3a43
22	♓	4a36
24	♈	4a40
26	♉	5a42
28	♊	9a31
30	♋	5p19

☽ PHASES
1	●	6p 5
5	◐	6p13
9	O	9p50
13	D	10p 0
17	O	3p23
24	O	1a 8
24	O	6a33
27	O	2p54

OCT 1961 — ☉ -> ♏ 23 10a48

☽->SIGNS
3	♌	4a44
5	♍	5p46
8	♎	6a 4
10	♏	4p19
12	♐	12a21
15	♑	6a24
17	♒	10a37
19	♓	1p10
21	♈	2p36
23	♉	4p 7
25	♊	7p24
28	♋	2a 3
30	♌	12p30

☽ PHASES
1	O	9a10
5	◐	12p 5
9	●	1p52
13	D	9a31
16	O	11p34
20	O	8a55
23	O	4p31
27	O	3a58

NOV 1961 — ☉ -> ♐ 22 8a 8

☽->SIGNS
1	♍	1a18
4	♎	1p42
6	♏	11p40
9	♐	6a51
11	♑	11a59
13	♒	3p59
15	♓	7p18
17	♈	10p10
20	♉	1a 3
22	♊	4a59
24	♋	11a20
26	♌	9p 1
29	♍	9a25

☽ PHASES
4	O	7a27
8	●	4a58
11	D	7p40
15	O	7a12
18	O	5p22
22	O	4a44
25	O	10p48
29	O	9a25

DEC 1961 — ☉ -> ♑ 21 9p20

☽->SIGNS
1	♎	10p 8
4	♏	8a30
6	♐	3p25
8	♑	7p31
10	♒	10p11
13	♓	12a41
15	♈	3a44
17	♉	7a39
19	♊	12p50
21	♋	7p50
24	♌	5a26
26	♍	5p29
29	♎	6a11
31	♏	5p42

☽ PHASES
4	(	2a40
7	●	6p52
11	D	5a 9
14	O	3p 6
17	O	7p42
21	O	10p47
25	O	10p57

JAN 1962 — ☉ -> ♒ 20 7a58

☽->SIGNS
3	♐	1a23
5	♑	5a24
7	♒	7a 0
9	♓	7a53
11	♈	9a34
13	♉	1p 1
15	♊	6p42
18	♋	2a40
20	♌	12p50
23	♍	12a53
25	♎	1p52
28	♏	1a59
30	♐	10a59

☽ PHASES
2	●	8p20
6	D	7a35
13	O	12a 1
16	O	3p24
20	O	1p16
23	O	11a53
27	O	10a50

FEB 1962 — ☉ -> ♓ 18 10p15

☽->SIGNS
1	♑	4p10
3	♒	5p57
5	♓	5p53
7	♈	5p50
9	♉	7p35
12	♊	12a18
14	♋	8a20
16	♌	7p 4
19	♍	7a27
21	♎	8p22
24	♏	8a36
26	♐	6p46

☽ PHASES
1	(	11a37
4	●	7p10
11	O	10a43
15	O	6a11
19	O	8a18
23	O	11a53
27	O	10a50

MAR 1962 — ☉ -> ♈ 20 9p30

☽->SIGNS
1	♑	1a38
3	♒	4a52
5	♓	5a16
7	♈	4a32
9	♉	4a40
11	♊	7a35
13	♋	2p26
16	♌	1a 2
18	♍	1p33
21	♎	2a28
23	♏	2p29
26	♐	12a49
28	♑	8a46
30	♒	1p43

☽ PHASES
3	(	12a 8
6	●	5a31
12	O	10a35
16	O	11p39
20	O	11p12
23	O	2a55
28	O	11p11

APR 1962 — ☉ -> ♉ 20 8a51

☽->SIGNS
1	♓	3p42
3	♈	3p41
5	♉	3p25
7	♊	5p 0
9	♋	10p12
12	♌	7a36
14	♍	7p57
17	♎	8a54
19	♏	8p37
22	♐	6a27
24	♑	2p20
26	♒	8p 8
28	♓	11p40

☽ PHASES
1	O	9a50
4	●	2p45
11	O	9p47
15	O	2p50
19	O	7p33
23	O	4p40
27	O	7a59
30	(	5p10

MAY 1962 — ☉ -> ♊ 21 8a17

☽->SIGNS
1	♈	1a12
3	♉	1a46
5	♊	3a16
7	♋	7a28
9	♌	3p35
12	♍	3a11
14	♎	4p 3
17	♏	4a43
19	♐	1p 2
21	♑	8p 8
24	♒	1a31
26	♓	5a29
28	♈	8a15
30	♉	10a17

☽ PHASES
3	●	11p25
7	D	10a19
11	O	7a44
15	O	10a48
19	O	9a32
23	O	2p 5
29	(	1p 5

JUN 1962 — ☉ -> ♋ 21 4p24

☽->SIGNS
1	♊	12p40
3	♋	4p56
6	♌	12a23
8	♍	11a12
11	♎	11p51
13	♏	11a45
16	♐	9p 4
18	♑	3a30
20	♒	7a49
22	♓	10a59
24	♈	1p43
26	♉	4p34
28	♊	8p 9

☽ PHASES
2	●	8a27
6	D	12a27
10	O	1a21
14	O	9p 2
21	O	8a59
24	O	6p43
28	(	4a56

JUL 1962 — ☉ -> ♌ 23 3a18

☽->SIGNS
1	♋	1a19
3	♌	8a55
5	♍	7p22
8	♎	7a48
10	♏	8p 5
13	♐	6a 0
15	♑	12p32
17	♒	4p41
19	♓	6p 0
21	♈	7p34
23	♉	9p57
26	♊	1a57
28	♋	8a 0
30	♌	4p21

☽ PHASES
1	●	6p52
5	D	4p 4
9	O	6p39
13	O	5p13
17	O	6a41
20	O	2p46
23	O	1p18
31	(	7a24

AUG 1962 — ☉ -> ♍ 23 10a13

☽->SIGNS
2	♍	2a57
4	♎	3p18
7	♏	3a56
9	♐	2p48
11	♑	10p18
14	♒	2a 7
16	♓	3a17
18	♈	3a25
20	♉	4a20
22	♊	7a28
24	♋	1p34
26	♌	10p30
29	♍	9a36
31	♎	10p 1

☽ PHASES
4	D	8a35
8	O	10a55
12	O	5a50
15	O	3p 9
19	O	8p31
22	O	2a 7
29	●	10p 9

SEP 1962 — ☉ -> ♎ 23 7a35

☽->SIGNS
3	♏	10a46
5	♐	10p26
8	♑	7a20
10	♒	12p26
12	♓	2p 2
14	♈	1p33
16	♉	1p 1
18	♊	2p29
20	♋	7p26
23	♌	4a 7
25	♍	3p31
28	♎	4a 8
30	♏	4p49

☽ PHASES
3	D	1a13
7	O	1a44
10	O	5p 2
13	O	11p11
17	O	3a30
20	O	2p36
24	O	11a51
28	●	2p39

OCT 1962 — ☉ -> ♏ 23 4p40

☽->SIGNS
3	♐	4a40
5	♑	2p35
7	♒	9p22
10	♓	12a29
12	♈	12a41
14	♉	12a41
15	♊	11p50
17	♋	3a 5
20	♌	10a30
22	♍	9p31
25	♎	10a14
27	♏	10p19
30	♐	10a19

☽ PHASES
2	D	5p16
6	O	2p54
10	O	3a 0
13	O	7a33
16	O	12p56
20	O	1a45
24	(	4a49
28	●	8a 5

NOV 1962 — ☉ -> ♐ 22 2p 2

☽->SIGNS
1	♑	8p17
4	♒	4a 2
6	♓	8a52
8	♈	10a45
10	♉	10a45
12	♊	10a43
14	♋	12p49
16	♌	6p40
19	♍	4a33
21	♎	4p58
24	♏	5a33
26	♐	4p43
29	♑	2a 0

☽ PHASES
1	D	8a 9
5	O	2a15
8	O	12p 5
11	O	5p 3
15	O	1a45
18	O	5p 0
23	(	12a14
27	●	1a29
30	D	9p25

DEC 1962 — ☉ -> ♑ 22 3a16

☽->SIGNS
1	♒	9a26
3	♓	2p53
5	♈	6p17
7	♉	7p59
9	♊	9p 7
11	♋	11p21
14	♌	4a20
16	♍	12p59
19	♎	12a41
21	♏	1p18
24	♐	12a33
26	♑	9a19
28	♒	3p42
30	♓	8p20

☽ PHASES
4	O	11a48
7	O	8p47
11	O	4a27
15	O	6p 8
18	O	5p42
22	(	8p39
26	●	5p59
30	D	8a52

JAN 1963 – AUG 1963

	JAN 1963	FEB 1963	MAR 1963	APR 1963	MAY 1963	JUN 1963	JUL 1963	AUG 1963
☉ ingress	☉ -> ♒ 20 1p54	☉ -> ♓ 19 4a 9	☉ -> ♈ 21 3a20	☉ -> ♉ 20 2p36	☉ -> ♊ 21 1p58	☉ -> ♋ 21 10p 4	☉ -> ♌ 23 8a59	☉ -> ♍ 23 3p58

☽ -> SIGNS

JAN 1963	FEB 1963	MAR 1963	APR 1963	MAY 1963	JUN 1963	JUL 1963	AUG 1963
1 ♈ 11p48	2 ♊ 11a 3	1 ♊ 4p39	2 ♌ 9a46	1 ♍ 1a13	3 ♏ 7a39	3 ♐ 3a11	1 ♑ 10p12
4 ♉ 2a34	4 ♋ 3p40	3 ♋ 9p 8	4 ♍ 7p20	4 ♎ 12p42	5 ♐ 8p 1	5 ♑ 2p 3	4 ♒ 6a25
6 ♊ 5a14	6 ♌ 10p 6	6 ♌ 4a15	7 ♎ 6a50	6 ♏ 1a16	8 ♑ 7a 7	8 ♒ 10p36	6 ♓ 11a46
8 ♋ 8a41	8 ♍ 6a36	8 ♍ 1p34	9 ♏ 7p14	9 ♐ 1p42	10 ♒ 4p22	10 ♓ 4a53	8 ♈ 3p 7
10 ♌ 2p 1	11 ♎ 5p18	11 ♎ 12a35	12 ♐ 7a48	12 ♑ 1a13	12 ♓ 11p21	12 ♈ 9a16	10 ♉ 5p37
12 ♍ 10p 7	13 ♏ 5a38	13 ♏ 12p51	14 ♑ 7p27	14 ♒ 10a51	15 ♈ 3a46	14 ♉ 12p15	12 ♊ 8p16
15 ♎ 9a 5	16 ♐ 5p57	16 ♐ 1a27	17 ♒ 4a34	16 ♓ 5p32	17 ♉ 5a54	16 ♊ 2p27	14 ♋ 11p39
17 ♏ 9p36	19 ♑ 4a 0	18 ♑ 12p35	19 ♓ 9a53	18 ♈ 8p48	19 ♊ 6a44	18 ♋ 5p 5	17 ♌ 4a40
20 ♐ 9a21	21 ♒ 10a23	20 ♒ 8p21	21 ♈ 11a30	20 ♉ 9p21	21 ♋ 7a46	20 ♌ 8p15	19 ♍ 10a40
22 ♑ 6p24	23 ♓ 1p17	23 ♓ 12a 4	23 ♉ 10a51	22 ♊ 8p53	23 ♌ 10a44	23 ♍ 2a 7	21 ♎ 7p25
25 ♒ 12a14	25 ♈ 2p 5	25 ♈ 12a38	25 ♊ 10a 6	24 ♋ 9p29	25 ♍ 4p56	25 ♎ 11a 2	24 ♏ 6a39
27 ♓ 3a35	27 ♉ 2p38	27 ♉ 12a36	27 ♋ 11a27	27 ♌ 12a59	28 ♎ 2a41	27 ♏ 10p38	26 ♐ 7p15
29 ♈ 5a44		29 ♊ 12a13	29 ♌ 4p25	29 ♍ 8a22	30 ♏ 2p48	30 ♐ 11a 8	29 ♑ 6a57
31 ♉ 7a55		31 ♋ 3a14		31 ♎ 7p 9			31 ♒ 3p37

☽ PHASES

JAN 1963	FEB 1963	MAR 1963	APR 1963	MAY 1963	JUN 1963	JUL 1963	AUG 1963
2 ● 8p 2	1 ○ 3a50	2 ○ 12p17	4 ○ 6p18	3 ○ 9a31	3 ○ 1a32	2 ○ 5p50	1 ○ 9a53
6 ○ 5a55	4 ○ 4p17	6 ○ 4a25	8 ○ 7p57	7 ○ 12p23	7 ○ 3a31	6 ○ 4p55	5 ○ 4a31
9 ☽ 6p 8	8 ○ 9a52	10 ○ 2a49	12 ○ 10p53	11 ○ 1p32	10 ○ 12a58	10 ○ 9a31	8 ○ 4p 6
13 ○ 1p17	12 ○ 9a36	12 ○ 10p53	16 ○ 9p52	14 ○ 12a58	14 ○ 3p53	13 ○ 8p57	12 ◑ 12p 3
17 ◑ 3p34	16 ◑ 12p39	16 ◑ 9p52	20 ◐ 10a50	19 ◑ 6p30	18 ◑ 12a20	17 ◑ 5p43	15 ◑ 3p43
21 ◐ 4a25	20 ◐ 9a57	18 ◐ 7a 8	23 ● 3p29	21 ◐ 11p 0	21 ◐ 6a46	20 ◐ 7a55	19 ◐ 2a55
25 ● 8a42	23 ● 9p 6	22 ● 12a11	26 ● 8p28	26 ● 6a33	24 ● 6p18	24 ● 7a55	22 ● 11p27
28 ☽ 6p38	27 ☽ 3a16	25 ◑ 7a10	30 ○ 10a 8	29 ☽ 11p55	28 ○ 3p24	28 ○ 8a13	27 ○ 1a54
		28 ☽ 11a36					31 ○ 1a 6
		31 ○ 10p15					

SEP 1963 – APR 1964

	SEP 1963	OCT 1963	NOV 1963	DEC 1963	JAN 1964	FEB 1964	MAR 1964	APR 1964
☉ ingress	☉ -> ♎ 23 1p24	☉ -> ♏ 23 10p29	☉ -> ♐ 22 7p50	☉ -> ♑ 22 9a 2	☉ -> ♒ 20 7p41	☉ -> ♓ 19 9a58	☉ -> ♈ 20 9a10	☉ -> ♉ 19 8p27

☽ -> SIGNS

SEP 1963	OCT 1963	NOV 1963	DEC 1963	JAN 1964	FEB 1964	MAR 1964	APR 1964
2 ♓ 8p37	2 ♈ 8a54	2 ♊ 6p48	2 ♋ 5a45	2 ♍ 9p48	1 ♎ 2p25	2 ♏ 8a54	1 ♐ 4a41
4 ♈ 10p52	4 ♉ 8a50	4 ♋ 7p 8	4 ♌ 7a20	5 ♎ 5a10	3 ♏ 12a13	4 ♐ 8p47	3 ♑ 5p36
7 ♉ 12a 2	6 ♊ 10p24	6 ♌ 10p24	6 ♍ 12p26	7 ♏ 4p 4	6 ♐ 12p35	7 ♑ 9a35	6 ♒ 5a24
9 ♊ 1a46	8 ♋ 11a 1	9 ♍ 5a14	8 ♎ 9p21	10 ♐ 4a49	8 ♑ 1a11	9 ♒ 8p36	8 ♓ 1p47
11 ♋ 5a38	10 ♌ 3p54	11 ♎ 3p 8	11 ♏ 9a 4	12 ♑ 5p14	11 ♒ 11a39	12 ♓ 4a 5	10 ♈ 6p 8
13 ♌ 10a30	12 ♍ 11p34	14 ♏ 2a57	13 ♐ 9p53	15 ♒ 3a48	13 ♓ 7p 9	14 ♈ 8a15	12 ♉ 7p37
15 ♍ 5p47	15 ♎ 9a24	16 ♐ 3p40	16 ♑ 10a21	17 ♓ 12p 4	16 ♈ 12a10	16 ♉ 10a36	14 ♊ 8p 6
18 ♎ 3a 0	17 ♏ 8p53	19 ♑ 4a23	18 ♒ 9p29	19 ♈ 6p10	18 ♉ 3a45	18 ♊ 12p26	16 ♋ 9p23
20 ♏ 2p10	20 ♐ 9a32	21 ♒ 3p51	21 ♓ 6a 7	21 ♉ 10p23	20 ♊ 6a48	20 ♋ 3p12	18 ♌ 12a40
23 ♐ 2a50	22 ♑ 10p21	24 ♓ 12a32	23 ♈ 12p41	24 ♊ 1a 5	22 ♋ 9a49	22 ♌ 7p15	21 ♍ 6a17
25 ♑ 3p15	25 ♒ 9a20	26 ♈ 5a25	25 ♉ 3p57	26 ♋ 2a51	24 ♌ 1p11	24 ♍ 12a42	23 ♎ 2p 8
28 ♒ 1a 3	27 ♓ 4p36	28 ♉ 6a49	27 ♊ 4p58	28 ♌ 4a45	26 ♍ 5p30	27 ♎ 7a48	26 ♏ 12a 1
30 ♓ 6a47	29 ♈ 7p40	30 ♊ 6a15	29 ♋ 4p26	30 ♍ 8a 9	28 ♎ 11p46	29 ♏ 5p 3	28 ♐ 11a46
	31 ♉ 7p42		31 ♌ 6p 9				

☽ PHASES

SEP 1963	OCT 1963	NOV 1963	DEC 1963	JAN 1964	FEB 1964	MAR 1964	APR 1964
3 ○ 2p34	2 ○ 11p44	1 ○ 8a55	4 ◑ 1a 9	2 ○ 3p34	1 ○ 8a18	2 ○ 2a34	3 ◑ 12a45
6 ○ 10p 2	6 ○ 4a46	4 ○ 1p34	7 ○ 9p34	5 ○ 10a58	5 ○ 7a42	5 ○ 5a 0	5 ○ 9p28
10 ○ 6a42	9 ○ 2p27	8 ○ 1a37	10 ○ 8a35	9 ◑ 10a59	9 ◑ 3a17	9 ◑ 6p39	8 ◑ 7a37
13 ◑ 8p32	13 ◑ 8a 4	11 ◑ 11p 6	15 ◑ 9p 6	12 ○ 8a 1	11 ○ 9p43	12 ◑ 6a16	10 ○ 1p42
17 ◐ 3p51	17 ● 7a43	16 ● 1a50	19 ● 9p29	18 ◑ 1a11	16 ● 8a24	16 ● 4a32	14 ○ 11p 9
21 ● 4p42	21 ● 11a 1	20 ● 5a 7	23 ○ 2p54	22 ● 12a29	20 ● 6p59	20 ● 9p48	19 ● 3p 0
25 ○ 7p38	25 ○ 12p20	23 ○ 2p54	30 ○ 6a42	26 ○ 9a45	24 ○ 7a39	24 ○ 4p20	22 ○ 12p50
29 ○ 3p 1	29 ○ 3a23	27 ○ 2p23		30 ○ 6p23	27 ○ 4p59	31 ○ 9p24	30 ○ 3p33
		30 ○ 6p54					

MAY 1964 – DEC 1964

	MAY 1964	JUN 1964	JUL 1964	AUG 1964	SEP 1964	OCT 1964	NOV 1964	DEC 1964
☉ ingress	☉ -> ♊ 20 7p50	☉ -> ♋ 21 3a57	☉ -> ♌ 22 2p53	☉ -> ♍ 22 9p51	☉ -> ♎ 23 7p17	☉ -> ♏ 23 4a21	☉ -> ♐ 22 1a39	☉ -> ♑ 21 2p50

☽ -> SIGNS

MAY 1964	JUN 1964	JUL 1964	AUG 1964	SEP 1964	OCT 1964	NOV 1964	DEC 1964
1 ♑ 12a42	2 ♓ 6a 1	1 ♈ 7p52	2 ♊ 10a28	2 ♋ 9p36	2 ♌ 7a42	1 ♍ 3a25	2 ♐ 8p24
3 ♒ 1p 6	4 ♈ 1p 3	4 ♉ 12a42	4 ♋ 12p12	5 ♌ 12a12	4 ♍ 12p45	3 ♎ 1p43	5 ♑ 8a53
5 ♓ 10p43	6 ♉ 4p20	6 ♊ 2a43	6 ♌ 1p11	7 ♍ 4a19	6 ♎ 7p57	5 ♏ 2a 6	7 ♒ 9p57
8 ♈ 4a16	8 ♊ 4p50	8 ♋ 2a57	8 ♍ 2p50	9 ♎ 11a20	9 ♏ 6a 2	8 ♐ 2p43	10 ♓ 10a 0
10 ♉ 6a 9	10 ♋ 4p16	10 ♌ 3a 1	10 ♎ 6p51	11 ♏ 9p47	11 ♐ 6p32	10 ♑ 3a28	12 ♈ 7p12
12 ♊ 6a 1	12 ♌ 4p35	12 ♍ 5a 3	13 ♏ 2a31	14 ♐ 10a30	14 ♑ 7a16	13 ♒ 3p59	15 ♉ 12a33
14 ♋ 5a53	14 ♍ 7p27	14 ♎ 9a41	15 ♐ 1p44	16 ♑ 10p47	16 ♒ 5p33	15 ♓ 2a28	17 ♊ 2a21
16 ♌ 7a31	17 ♎ 1a54	16 ♏ 6p28	18 ♑ 2a38	19 ♒ 8a22	19 ♓ 10a43	17 ♈ 1p57	19 ♋ 2a 2
18 ♍ 12p 2	19 ♏ 11a49	19 ♐ 6a28	20 ♒ 2p39	21 ♓ 2p39	21 ♈ 11p45	19 ♉ 2p59	21 ♌ 1a31
20 ♎ 7p41	21 ♐ 12a 3	21 ♑ 7p27	23 ♓ 12a25	23 ♈ 5p46	23 ♉ 5a22	21 ♊ 2a42	23 ♍ 2a42
23 ♏ 5a58	24 ♑ 1p 2	24 ♒ 7a31	25 ♈ 7a15	25 ♉ 6p37	25 ♊ 9a14	23 ♋ 3p59	25 ♎ 7a11
25 ♐ 6p 3	26 ♒ 1a45	26 ♓ 5p36	28 ♉ 12p24	27 ♊ 9p14	27 ♋ 1p25	25 ♌ 12a24	27 ♏ 3p11
28 ♑ 7a 0	29 ♓ 11a56	29 ♈ 1a25	30 ♊ 4p16	30 ♋ 3a53	30 ♌ 3a53	28 ♍ 12a24	29 ♐ 2a21
30 ♒ 7p33		31 ♉ 7a 0				30 ♎ 9a31	

☽ PHASES

MAY 1964	JUN 1964	JUL 1964	AUG 1964	SEP 1964	OCT 1964	NOV 1964	DEC 1964
4 ○ 5p20	3 ○ 6a 7	2 ○ 3p31	4 ♐ 7a31	2 ♐ 1p44	4 ● 2a16	4 ● 2a16	3 ♐ 8p18
8 ○ 9a24	6 ○ 1a25	6 ♐ 1a25	8 ● 11a34	5 ● 11p34	8 ◐ 11a56	8 ◐ 12a19	8 ● 12a19
11 ● 4p 2	9 ♐ 6a31	9 ♐ 11p22	11 ◐ 1a20	9 ◐ 3p26	12 ○ 7a20	12 ○ 7a20	12 ◐ 1a 1
14 ◑ 8p58	13 ◐ 4a50	13 ◐ 4a50	15 ○ 10p19	13 ○ 8a35	16 ○ 10a43	16 ○ 10a43	15 ○ 3p42
18 ○ 7p42	16 ● 6p 2	16 ● 6p47	19 ○ 1a27	17 ○ 6p30	20 ○ 11p45	20 ○ 4p20	19 ○ 9p41
22 ○ 4a58	20 ○ 4p52	19 ● 1a27	23 ○ 12p25	20 ○ 12p31	24 ○ 4p20	22 ○ 2a36	22 ○ 2a36
26 ○ 4a29	24 ○ 8p 8	23 ○ 12p25	26 ○ 4a27	24 ○ 11p59	27 ○ 4p59	25 ○ 2p27	25 ○ 2p27
30 ○ 7a47	28 ○ 9p14	26 ○ 4a27	30 ○ 4a15	28 ○ 10a 8	31 ◐ 6a48	29 ○ 7p47	29 ◐ 12p26
		30 ○ 10p29					

JAN 1965 ☉ -> ♒ 20 1a29

☽ -> SIGNS

Day	Sign	Time
1	♉	3p 6
4	♊	4a 4
6	♋	4p 6
9	♌	2a 8
11	♍	9a10
13	♎	12p48
15	♏	1p35
17	♐	1a45
19	♑	12p55
21	♒	3p28
23	♓	10p 1
26	♈	8a32
28	♉	9p21
31	♊	10a18

PHASES: 2 ● 4p 7 / 6 ◐ 7p 2 / 10 ◑ 4p 0 / 14 ○ 3a40 / 17 ○ 8a37 / 20 ◐ 2p42 / 24 ◑ 6a 7 / 28 ◖ 7a54

FEB 1965 ☉ -> ♓ 18 3p48

☽ -> SIGNS

Day	Sign	Time
2	♋	9p56
5	♌	7a43
7	♍	3p24
9	♎	8p36
11	♏	11p14
13	♐	11p54
16	♑	12a 5
18	♒	1a45
20	♓	6a45
22	♈	3p57
25	♉	4a17
27	♊	5p14

PHASES: 1 ● 11a36 / 5 ◑ 10a51 / 9 ○ 3a53 / 13 ○ 1p45 / 15 ◐ 7p27 / 19 ◑ 4a42 / 23 ● 12a39 / 27 ◖ 4a16

MAR 1965 ☉ -> ♈ 20 3p 5

☽ -> SIGNS

Day	Sign	Time
2	♋	4a38
4	♌	1p45
7	♍	8p49
9	♎	2a14
11	♏	6a 3
13	♐	8a23
15	♑	9a55
17	♒	12p 4
19	♓	4p32
22	♈	12p37
24	♉	12p 7
27	♊	12a59
29	♋	12p32
31	♌	9p19

PHASES: 3 ● 4a56 / 6 ◑ 11p20 / 10 ○ 12p52 / 13 ○ 10p10 / 17 ◐ 6a24 / 19 ◑ 8p30 / 24 ● 8p37 / 27 ◖ 11p23

APR 1965 ☉ -> ♉ 20 2a26

☽ -> SIGNS

Day	Sign	Time
3	♌	3a29
5	♍	11a15
7	♎	11a54
9	♏	2p24
11	♐	5p14
13	♑	8p38
16	♒	1a42
18	♓	9a31
20	♈	8p24
23	♉	9a 4
25	♊	9p 2
28	♋	12a59
30	♌	12p 4

PHASES: 1 ● 7p21 / 5 ◑ 4p16 / 8 ○ 7p40 / 12 ○ 6p 2 / 15 ◐ 1p51 / 19 ◑ 9a40 / 23 ● 4p 7 / 27 ◖ 3p59

MAY 1965 ☉ -> ♊ 21 1a50

☽ -> SIGNS

Day	Sign	Time
2	♍	3p27
4	♎	5p39
6	♏	7p50
8	♐	10p47
11	♑	3a 4
13	♒	9a10
15	♓	5p32
18	♈	4a20
20	♉	4p51
23	♊	5a14
25	♋	3p19
27	♌	9p48
30	♍	12a58

PHASES: 1 ● 6a56 / 4 ◐ 4p16 / 8 ○ 1a20 / 11 ○ 1p26 / 15 ◐ 6a52 / 19 ◑ 7a 0 / 23 ● 9a40 / 27 ◖ 5a42 / 30 ◐ 4p13

JUN 1965 ☉ -> ♋ 21 9a56

☽ -> SIGNS

Day	Sign	Time
1	♎	2a 5
3	♏	2a47
5	♐	4a33
7	♑	8a30
9	♒	3p 4
12	♓	12a10
14	♈	11a20
16	♉	11p51
19	♊	12p29
21	♋	11p29
24	♌	7a16
26	♍	11a18
28	♎	12p20
30	♏	11a59

PHASES: 2 ◑ 10p26 / 6 ○ 7a11 / 9 ○ 10p38 / 13 ◐ 10a 9 / 17 ◑ 11p38 / 21 ◐ 12a36 / 25 ◐ 4p47 / 28 ● 11p52

JUL 1965 ☉ -> ♌ 22 8p48

☽ -> SIGNS

Day	Sign	Time
2	♍	12p11
4	♎	2p43
6	♏	8p38
9	♐	5a53
11	♑	5p29
14	♒	6a 8
16	♓	6p45
19	♈	6a13
21	♉	3p14
23	♊	8p48
26	♋	10p53
29	♌	10p37
29	♍	9p55
31	♎	10p54

PHASES: 2 ◑ 10p26 / 5 ○ 4a29 / 9 ○ 2p36 / 13 ◐ 10a 3 / 17 ◐ 12p 1 / 21 ◐ 12p44 / 25 ◐ 12p53 / 29 ◖ 1a44 / 31 ◐ 11a37

AUG 1965 ☉ -> ♍ 23 3a43

☽ -> SIGNS

Day	Sign	Time
3	♏	3a20
5	♐	11a49
7	♑	11p22
10	♒	12a38
12	♓	11a57
15	♈	9p27
17	♉	...
20	♊	8a 4
22	♋	9a 1
24	♌	8a36
26	♍	9a 1
28	♎	9a54
30	♏	11a54

PHASES: 4 ○ 12a47 / 8 ◐ 12a16 / 12 ○ 3a22 / 16 ○ 4a 1 / 19 ◐ 10p50 / 23 ◐ 9a11 / 26 ● 1p51 / 29 ◖ 9p 3

SEP 1965 ☉ -> ♎ 23 1a 6

☽ -> SIGNS

Day	Sign	Time
1	♍	7p 0
4	♎	5a51
6	♏	6p34
9	♐	6a57
11	♑	5p50
14	♒	2a56
16	♓	9a 6
18	♈	3p 1
20	♉	5p35
22	♊	6p30
24	♋	7p15
26	♌	9p47
29	♍	3a42

PHASES: 2 ● 2p27 / 6 ◐ 4p40 / 10 ○ 6p32 / 14 ○ 9p37 / 18 ◐ 6a58 / 21 ◑ 3p58 / 24 ● 10p18 / 28 ◖ 9p45

OCT 1965 ☉ -> ♏ 23 10a10

☽ -> SIGNS

Day	Sign	Time
1	♎	1p29
4	♏	1a48
6	♐	2p14
9	♑	12a54
11	♒	9a17
13	♓	3p40
15	♈	8p27
17	♉	11p51
20	♊	2a13
22	♋	4a21
24	♌	7a31
26	♍	1p 9
28	♎	10p 5
31	♏	9a50

PHASES: 2 ○ 7a37 / 6 ◐ 10a35 / 10 ○ 9a14 / 14 ○ 1a50 / 18 ◐ 2p 0 / 20 ◑ 11p 9 / 24 ● 9a11 / 28 ◖ 2a 4

NOV 1965 ☉ -> ♐ 22 7a30

☽ -> SIGNS

Day	Sign	Time
2	♐	10p23
5	♑	9a22
7	♒	6p30
9	♓	10p54
12	♈	2a29
14	♉	5a14
16	♊	7a55
18	♋	11a10
20	♌	3p37
22	♍	9p57
24	♎	6a45
27	♏	6p 3
30	♐	6a40

PHASES: 1 ● 3a26 / 5 ◐ 3a 6 / 8 ○ 10p15 / 12 ○ 11a 8 / 16 ◐ 4a52 / 19 ◑ 7a57 / 22 ● 6p 0 / 26 ◖ 9p19

DEC 1965 ☉ -> ♑ 21 8p41

☽ -> SIGNS

Day	Sign	Time
2	♑	12p22
5	♒	3a11
7	♓	1p36
9	♈	4p33
11	♉	9p40
13	♊	10p15
15	♋	5a 1
17	♌	9p40
20	♍	5a 1
22	♎	2p27
25	♏	1a44
27	♐	2p17
30	♑	2a40

PHASES: 2 ● 12a34 / 4 ◐ 1p10 / 11 ○ 7p59 / 18 ◐ 7p20 / 23 ◑ 4p 3 / 26 ● 6p 0 / 30 ◐ 8p46

JAN 1966 ☉ -> ♒ 20 7a20

☽ -> SIGNS

Day	Sign	Time
2	♑	12p46
3	♒	7p 6
5	♓	9p40
7	♈	9p50
9	♉	9p34
11	♊	10p53
14	♋	3a 9
16	♌	10a40
18	♍	8p45
21	♎	8a26
23	♏	8p59
26	♐	9a33
28	♑	8p43
31	♒	4a44

PHASES: 3 ○ 3p40 / 7 ◐ 12a16 / 10 ○ 5a11 / 13 ○ 3p 0 / 17 ◐ 9a44 / 21 ◑ 10a46 / 25 ● 2p11 / 29 ● 2p48

FEB 1966 ☉ -> ♓ 18 9p38

☽ -> SIGNS

Day	Sign	Time
2	♓	8a41
4	♈	9a14
6	♉	8a11
8	♊	7a50
10	♋	10a15
12	♌	4p33
14	♍	2a26
16	♎	2p26
19	♏	3a 5
21	♐	3p30
24	♑	2a53
26	♒	12p 3

PHASES: 2 ○ 5a34 / 5 ◐ 10a58 / 8 ○ 3p24 / 12 ○ 3a53 / 16 ◐ 2a38 / 20 ◑ 5a49 / 24 ● 8a13 / 26 ● 5a15

MAR 1966 ☉ -> ♈ 20 8p53

☽ -> SIGNS

Day	Sign	Time
1	♓	5p48
3	♈	7p57
5	♉	7p59
7	♊	6p49
9	♋	7p47
12	♌	12a18
14	♍	8a55
16	♎	8p35
19	♏	9a19
21	♐	9p33
24	♑	8a32
26	♒	5p41
29	♓	12a23
31	♈	4a12

PHASES: 3 ○ 4p28 / 6 ◐ 8p45 / 10 ○ 3a 4 / 13 ○ 7p19 / 17 ◐ 8p53 / 21 ◑ 11p46 / 25 ● 10p58 / 29 ● 3p43

APR 1966 ☉ -> ♉ 20 8a12

☽ -> SIGNS

Day	Sign	Time
2	♉	5a31
4	♊	5a40
6	♋	6a30
8	♌	9a54
10	♍	5p 2
13	♎	4a13
15	♏	4a27
18	♐	4a27
20	♑	3p27
23	♒	11p27
25	♓	5a48
27	♈	10a 9
29	♉	12p50

PHASES: 2 ○ 12a43 / 5 ◐ 6a13 / 8 ○ 4p16 / 12 ○ 12p28 / 16 ◐ 3p12 / 20 ◑ 3p35 / 24 ● 10p49

MAY 1966 ☉ -> ♊ 21 7a32

☽ -> SIGNS

Day	Sign	Time
1	♎	2p31
3	♏	4p23
5	♐	7p52
8	♑	2a12
10	♒	11a52
12	♓	11p55
15	♈	12p15
17	♉	10p49
20	♊	6a40
22	♋	12p 0
24	♌	3p37
26	♍	6p22
28	♎	9p 0
31	♏	12a11

PHASES: 1 ○ 7a22 / 4 ◐ 4p 1 / 8 ○ 6a45 / 12 ○ 6a19 / 16 ◐ 8a29 / 20 ◑ 4a42 / 23 ● 6p 0 / 27 ● 3a50 / 30 ○ 1p41

JUN 1966 ☉ -> ♋ 21 3p34

☽ -> SIGNS

Day	Sign	Time
2	♐	4a39
4	♑	11a10
6	♒	8p21
9	♓	7a57
11	♈	8p26
14	♉	7a20
16	♊	3p26
18	♋	8p 5
20	♌	10p29
22	♍	12a 8
24	♎	2a23
26	♏	5a 5
29	♐	11a31

PHASES: 3 ○ 2a40 / 6 ◐ 10p10 / 10 ○ 11p58 / 14 ○ 11p59 / 18 ◐ 3p 9 / 21 ◑ 5a 6 / 25 ● 8a23 / 28 ● 8p53

JUL 1966 ☉ -> ♌ 23 2a23

☽ -> SIGNS

Day	Sign	Time
1	♑	6p51
4	♒	4a 4
6	♓	3p39
9	♈	4a16
11	♉	4p 4
14	♊	12a51
16	♋	5a44
18	♌	7a28
20	♍	7a47
22	♎	8a38
24	♏	11a32
26	♐	5p 5
29	♑	1a 4
31	♒	11a 2

PHASES: 2 ○ 2p36 / 6 ◐ 2p 9 / 10 ○ 4p43 / 14 ○ 1p15 / 18 ◐ 11p30 / 21 ◑ 5a 6 / 24 ● 2p 0

AUG 1966 ☉ -> ♍ 23 9a18

☽ -> SIGNS

Day	Sign	Time
1	♓	10p36
4	♈	11a15
7	♉	11p38
9	♊	9a38
12	♋	3p42
14	♌	6p35
16	♍	7p37
18	♎	7p40
20	♏	8p 5
22	♐	10p51
25	♑	4a38
27	♒	1p26
30	♓	4a48

PHASES: 1 ○ 4a 5 / 5 ◐ 6a21 / 9 ○ 7a56 / 13 ○ 12a19 / 17 ◐ 7p32 / 20 ◑ 9p25 / 24 ● 8a44 / 26 ● 5p50 / 30 ○ 7p14

SEP 1966 ☉ -> ♎ 23 6a44

☽ -> SIGNS

Day	Sign	Time
1	♈	5p28
4	♉	6a11
6	♊	4p52
9	♋	1a 4
11	♌	4a26
13	♍	3a33
16	♎	3a34
18	♏	3a59
21	♐	6a21
23	♑	10a48
26	♒	8p49
29	♓	11a47

PHASES: 3 ○ 10p16 / 7 ◐ 9p 7 / 11 ○ 9a39 / 14 ○ 2p13 / 18 ◐ 7p32 / 22 ◑ 10p 2 / 25 ● 8a44 / 29 ● 11a47

OCT 1966 ☉ -> ♏ 23 3p51

☽ -> SIGNS

Day	Sign	Time
1	♈	11a47
3	♉	10p43
6	♊	7a12
8	♋	12p25
11	♌	2p27
14	♍	2p21
16	♎	2p 0
18	♏	3p55
21	♐	5a41
23	♑	5p20
25	♒	1a37
28	♓	6p 6
31	♈	4a28

PHASES: 3 ○ 1p12 / 7 ◐ 8a 8 / 10 ○ 6p 0 / 14 ○ 10p52 / 18 ◐ 6a53 / 21 ◑ 12a34 / 25 ● 2a37 / 29 ● 5a10

NOV 1966 ☉ -> ♐ 22 1p15

☽ -> SIGNS

Day	Sign	Time
2	♉	12p43
4	♊	6p36
6	♋	10p10
8	♌	11p54
10	♍	12a53
13	♎	2a36
15	♏	6a37
17	♐	2p 3
19	♑	9a...
22	♒	12a53
24	♓	1a37
27	♈	6p50
29	♉	...

PHASES: 2 ○ 2a26 / 5 ◐ 5p18 / 9 ○ 2a15 / 12 ○ 9p33 / 17 ◐ 3p16 / 19 ◑ 7p20 / 23 ● 10p35 / 27 ● 9p40

DEC 1966 ☉ -> ♑ 22 2a29

☽ -> SIGNS

Day	Sign	Time
2	♊	12a 2
3	♋	3a48
6	♌	6a43
8	♍	9a18
10	♎	12p13
12	♏	4p30
14	♐	11p19
17	♑	9a17
19	♒	9p39
21	♓	9a17
24	♈	8p14
27	♉	...
29	♊	6a57
31	♋	9a33

PHASES: 1 ○ 1p45 / 5 ◐ 1a22 / 8 ○ 11a12 / 11 ○ 10p13 / 15 ◐ 3p16 / 19 ◑ 4p41 / 23 ● 6p54 / 27 ● 12p43 / 30 ○ 11p33

JAN 1967 – AUG 1967

	JAN 1967	FEB 1967	MAR 1967	APR 1967	MAY 1967	JUN 1967	JUL 1967	AUG 1967
☉ ->	♒ 20 1p 8	♓ 19 3a24	♈ 21 2a37	♉ 20 1p55	♊ 21 1p18	♋ 21 9p23	♌ 23 8a16	♍ 23 3p13

☽ -> SIGNS

JAN 1967	FEB 1967	MAR 1967	APR 1967	MAY 1967	JUN 1967	JUL 1967	AUG 1967
2 ♏ 12p 4	3 ♐ 12a56	1 ♐ 6a53	2 ♒ 2a49	2 ♓ 8p51	1 ♈ 3p 7	1 ♉ 11a43	2 ♋ 5p32
4 ♐ 3p16	5 ♑ 7a10	3 ♑ 12p35	5 ♓ 1p29	5 ♈ 8a10	4 ♉ 4a 4	3 ♊ 11p39	4 ♌ 11p26
6 ♐ 7p28	7 ♒ 3p17	6 ♒ 9p 4	8 ♈ 1a57	7 ♉ 9p 9	6 ♊ 3p52	6 ♋ 8a52	7 ♍ 2a36
9 ♑ 12a53	10 ♓ 1a19	8 ♓ 7a41	10 ♉ 2p56	10 ♊ 9a 8	9 ♋ 1a18	8 ♌ 2p59	9 ♎ 4a35
11 ♒ 8a 5	12 ♈ 1p17	11 ♈ 7p53	13 ♊ 3a15	12 ♋ 7p11	11 ♌ 8a19	10 ♍ 7p 8	11 ♏ 6a44
13 ♓ 5p45	15 ♉ 2a19	13 ♉ 8a54	15 ♋ 1p37	15 ♌ 2a49	13 ♍ 1p24	12 ♎ 10p20	13 ♐ 9a52
16 ♈ 5a48	17 ♊ 2p16	16 ♊ 9p19	17 ♌ 8p54	17 ♍ 7a52	15 ♎ 4p58	15 ♏ 1a18	15 ♑ 2p18
18 ♉ 6p39	19 ♋ 10p48	19 ♋ 7a10	20 ♍ 12a43	19 ♎ 10a31	17 ♏ 7p25	17 ♐ 4a22	17 ♒ 8p17
21 ♊ 6a38	22 ♌ 3a 4	21 ♌ 1p30	22 ♎ 1a41	21 ♏ 11a30	19 ♐ 9p20	19 ♑ 7a59	20 ♓ 4a18
23 ♋ 12p51	24 ♍ 4a 4	23 ♍ 3p 8	24 ♏ 1a19	23 ♐ 12p 6	21 ♑ 11p46	21 ♒ 12p59	22 ♈ 2p48
25 ♌ 4p20	26 ♎ 3a44	25 ♎ 2p50	26 ♐ 1a27	25 ♑ 1p58	24 ♒ 4a11	23 ♓ 8p24	25 ♉ 3a21
27 ♍ 5p36	28 ♏ 4a 9	27 ♏ 2p10	28 ♑ 3a54	27 ♒ 6p44	26 ♓ 11a49	26 ♈ 7a 0	27 ♊ 4p 8
29 ♎ 6p33		29 ♐ 3p 8	30 ♒ 9a57	30 ♓ 3a18	28 ♈ 10p53	28 ♉ 7p49	30 ♋ 2a35
31 ♏ 8p44		31 ♑ 7p11				31 ♊ 8a 1	

☽ PHASES

JAN 1967	FEB 1967	MAR 1967	APR 1967	MAY 1967	JUN 1967	JUL 1967	AUG 1967
3 ○ 9a19	1 ○ 6p 3	1 ○ 4a10	1 ○ 3p58	1 ○ 5a33	3 ☾ 11p48	3 ☾ 4p16	2 ☾ 7a18
6 ☾ 9p23	5 ☾ 9a10	6 ☾ 10p45	5 ☾ 2p 5	6 ☾ 6a43	8 ● 12a14	7 ● 12p 0	5 ● 9p48
10 ● 1p 6	9 ● 5a44	9 ● 11p30	8 ● 5p20	8 ● 9a55	11 ☽ 5p50	11 ☽ 12a42	9 ☽ 6a34
14 ☽ 11a10	13 ☽ 7a49	15 ☽ 3a18	13 ☽ 7p50	13 ☽ 8a35	15 ○ 6a12	14 ○ 10a53	13 ○ 3p44
18 ○ 2p41	17 ○ 10a56	17 ○ 3a31	17 ○ 3p48	17 ○ 12a18	18 ○ 3p13	17 ○ 9p 7	16 ○ 4a13
22 ○ 1p31	21 ○ 5a 4	21 ○ 5p10	21 ○ 2a18	20 ○ 9a19	22 ○ 11p57	21 ○ 9a39	19 ○ 9p27
26 ○ 1a40	25 ○ 12p43	25 ○ 3a24	24 ☾ 7a 4	23 ○ 3p22	25 ○ 2p 7	25 ○ 4a50	22 ○ 9p24
29 ○ 8a38	27 ○ 5p46		27 ○ 1p49	25 ○ 2p 7	28 ○ 1p40	29 ○ 7a14	28 ○ 12a35
				30 ○ 8p52			31 ☾ 8p40

SEP 1967 – APR 1968

	SEP 1967	OCT 1967	NOV 1967	DEC 1967	JAN 1968	FEB 1968	MAR 1968	APR 1968
☉ ->	♎ 23 12p38	♏ 23 9p44	♐ 22 7p 5	♑ 22 8a17	♒ 20 6p54	♓ 19 9a 9	♈ 20 8a22	♉ 19 7p41

☽ -> SIGNS

SEP 1967	OCT 1967	NOV 1967	DEC 1967	JAN 1968	FEB 1968	MAR 1968	APR 1968
1 ♌ 9a 8	2 ♎ 11p34	1 ♏ 10a26	2 ♑ 9p25	1 ♒ 10a24	2 ♈ 9a39	1 ♉ 5a28	2 ♊ 1a40
3 ♍ 12p 7	4 ♏ 11p14	3 ♐ 9a51	4 ♒ 11p57	3 ♓ 3p35	4 ♉ 9p15	3 ♊ 6p17	4 ♋ 2p13
5 ♎ 1p 3	6 ♐ 11p32	5 ♑ 10a44	7 ♓ 6a19	6 ♈ 12a45	7 ♊ 10a 9	6 ♋ 6a 7	7 ♌ 12a28
7 ♏ 1p44	9 ♑ 2a 4	7 ♒ 2p45	9 ♈ 4p43	8 ♉ 1p 3	9 ♋ 9p34	8 ♌ 3p27	9 ♍ 7a 4
9 ♐ 3p40	11 ♒ 7a45	9 ♓ 10p43	12 ♉ 5a32	11 ♊ 1a54	12 ♌ 5a50	10 ♍ 8p51	11 ♎ 10a 1
11 ♑ 7p43	13 ♓ 4p38	12 ♈ 9a58	14 ♊ 6p18	13 ♋ 12p54	14 ♍ 11a 3	12 ♎ 11p 9	13 ♏ 10a32
13 ♒ 4p38	16 ♈ 3a58	14 ♉ 10p52	17 ♋ 5a23	15 ♌ 9p 9	16 ♎ 2p21	14 ♏ 11p23	15 ♐ 10a23
16 ♓ 10a53	18 ♉ 4p30	17 ♊ 11a40	19 ♌ 2p21	18 ♍ 3a11	18 ♏ 5p 0	16 ♐ 11p38	17 ♑ 11a23
18 ♈ 9p46	21 ♊ 5a38	19 ♋ 11p13	21 ♍ 9p21	20 ♎ 7a47	20 ♐ 7p48	19 ♑ 1a35	19 ♒ 2p57
21 ♉ 10a21	23 ♋ 5p20	22 ♌ 8a47	24 ♎ 2a27	22 ♏ 11a28	22 ♑ 11p12	21 ♒ 4a55	21 ♓ 9p46
23 ♊ 11p21	26 ♌ 2a40	24 ♍ 3p46	26 ♏ 5a36	24 ♐ 2p24	25 ♒ 3a37	23 ♓ 9a17	24 ♈ 7a32
26 ♋ 10a45	28 ♍ 8p13	26 ♎ 7p48	28 ♐ 7a 9	26 ♑ 4p57	27 ♓ 9a42	25 ♈ 4p35	26 ♉ 7p22
28 ♌ 6p41	30 ♎ 10a31	28 ♏ 9p13	30 ♑ 8a11	28 ♒ 8p 6		28 ♉ 12p55	29 ♊ 8a11
30 ♍ 10p38		30 ♐ 9p10		31 ♓ 1a16			

☽ PHASES

SEP 1967	OCT 1967	NOV 1967	DEC 1967	JAN 1968	FEB 1968	MAR 1968	APR 1968
4 ● 6a37	3 ● 3p24	2 ☾ 12a48	1 ● 11a10	3 ☽ 10a43	2 ☽ 5a 5	3 ☽ 12a54	1 ☽ 8p20
7 ☽ 12p 6	7 ☽ 8p25	5 ● 6a19	4 ☽ 7p57	7 ○ 9a23	6 ○ 7a20	7 ○ 4a10	5 ○ 10p28
10 ○ 10p 6	10 ○ 7a11	8 ○ 8p 0	8 ○ 12p57	11 ○ 1p 5	10 ○ 8a54	11 ○ 2a 1	9 ○ 3p54
14 ○ 1p48	14 ○ 2a56	12 ○ 7p58	12 ○ 4p 2	15 ○ 5p40	14 ○ 12p32	17 ○ 9p 5	12 ☽ 11p52
18 ○ 12p 0	18 ☽ 5a11	16 ○ 11p53	16 ○ 6p21	19 ○ 2a38	17 ○ 10p28	21 ○ 6a 4	16 ○ 4a53
22 ○ 3p 7	22 ○ 8a43	19 ○ 9p21	20 ○ 2p22	22 ○ 12p32	20 ○ 10p28	24 ☾ 8p42	19 ○ 2p35
26 ○ 4p44	26 ○ 7a 4	24 ○ 7p23	24 ○ 5a48	26 ☾ 12a39	24 ☾ 10a 8	28 ● 5p48	23 ☾ 9a 2
30 ☾ 8a38	29 ☾ 7p36	29 ☾ 5a49	27 ☾ 3p25	29 ● 11a29	28 ● 1a56		27 ● 10a21
			30 ● 10p39				

MAY 1968 – DEC 1968

	MAY 1968	JUN 1968	JUL 1968	AUG 1968	SEP 1968	OCT 1968	NOV 1968	DEC 1968
☉ ->	♊ 20 7p 6	♋ 21 3a13	♌ 22 2p 8	♍ 22 9p 3	♎ 22 6p27	♏ 23 3a30	♐ 22 12a49	♑ 21 2p 0

☽ -> SIGNS

MAY 1968	JUN 1968	JUL 1968	AUG 1968	SEP 1968	OCT 1968	NOV 1968	DEC 1968
1 ♋ 8p50	2 ♍ 10p52	2 ♎ 11a10	3 ♐ 12a11	1 ♑ 8a22	2 ♓ 10p21	1 ♈ 11a51	1 ♉ 3a58
4 ♌ 7a54	5 ♎ 4a49	4 ♏ 3p20	5 ♑ 1a57	3 ♒ 11a19	5 ♈ 5a35	3 ♉ 10p 1	3 ♊ 4p 6
6 ♍ 3p58	7 ♏ 7a30	6 ♐ 5p 5	7 ♒ 3a37	5 ♓ 3p27	7 ♉ 3p 7	6 ♊ 9a48	6 ♋ 4a43
8 ♎ 8p21	9 ♐ 7a42	8 ♑ 5p24	9 ♓ 6a46	7 ♈ 9p49	10 ♊ 2a44	8 ♋ 10p27	8 ♌ 5p 3
10 ♏ 9p30	11 ♑ 7a 5	10 ♒ 6p 3	11 ♈ 12p53	10 ♉ 7a 6	12 ♋ 3p23	11 ♌ 10a45	11 ♍ 4a 0
12 ♐ 8p53	13 ♒ 7a46	12 ♓ 9p 3	13 ♉ 10p36	12 ♊ 7p23	15 ♌ 3a 8	13 ♍ 8p55	13 ♎ 12p 9
14 ♑ 8p31	15 ♓ 11a42	15 ♈ 3a52	16 ♊ 11a05	15 ♋ 7a28	17 ♍ 11a59	16 ♎ 3a26	15 ♏ 5p28
16 ♒ 10p22	17 ♈ 7p50	17 ♉ 2p31	18 ♋ 11p15	17 ♌ 6p25	19 ♎ 5p 5	18 ♏ 6a 6	17 ♐ 7p41
19 ♓ 3a53	20 ♉ 7a25	20 ♊ 3a13	21 ♌ 9a40	20 ♍ 2a16	21 ♏ 7p40	20 ♐ 6a 7	19 ♑ 7p32
21 ♈ 1p14	22 ♊ 8p22	22 ♋ 3p31	23 ♍ 5p21	22 ♎ 7a 0	23 ♐ 7p32	22 ♑ 5a20	21 ♒ 7p 6
24 ♉ 1a16	25 ♋ 8a43	25 ♌ 1a55	25 ♎ 10p45	24 ♏ 9a39	25 ♑ 7p 6	24 ♒ 9a53	23 ♓ 9p59
26 ♊ 2p12	27 ♌ 7p31	27 ♍ 10a10	28 ♏ 2a38	26 ♐ 11a30	27 ♒ 10p43	26 ♓ 5p26	26 ♈ 6a 1
29 ♋ 2a43	30 ♍ 4a26	29 ♎ 4p32	30 ♐ 5a41	28 ♑ 1p44	30 ♓ 3a54	29 ♈ 3a 2	28 ♉ 5p26
31 ♌ 1p53		31 ♏ 9p11		30 ♒ 5p11			30 ♊ 10p11 (*)

(*) 30 ○ 10a 3

☽ PHASES

MAY 1968	JUN 1968	JUL 1968	AUG 1968	SEP 1968	OCT 1968	NOV 1968	DEC 1968
1 ☽ 1p41	3 ● 7a42	2 ○ 7a42	1 ○ 1p34	2 ○ 4a21	2 ○ 12p36	1 ○ 12a10	4 ○ 6p 7
5 ○ 12p54	7 ○ 6p50	6 ○ 4p50	4 ○ 10p15	6 ○ 5p 7	6 ☽ 6a46	4 ☽ 11p25	8 ○ 9p11
9 ○ 2a 7	10 ○ 3p13	10 ○ 10p18	8 ○ 6a32	10 ○ 1p 8	9 ○ 7a16	9 ○ 9a48	12 ○ 7p49
12 ○ 8a 5	13 ○ 7a59	13 ○ 7a59	11 ○ 9p10	14 ○ 3p31	14 ○ 10a 5	13 ○ 3a53	16 ☽ 8a38
15 ○ 12p41	15 ○ 1p14	17 ☽ 4a11	15 ○ 11p19	18 ○ 3p12	18 ○ 8p19	18 ○ 8p19	19 ● 1p19
19 ○ 12a44	19 ○ 11a01	21 ☽ 7a 3	19 ☽ 11p19	22 ☽ 6a 8	21 ☾ 4p44	21 ☾ 7a28	22 ☽ 6p35
22 ☽ 11p13	21 ☾ 2p48	25 ● 5p25	23 ● 6p57	26 ● 3p16	24 ○ 10p39	24 ○ 6p30	26 ○ 9a15
27 ○ 2a30	25 ● 5p25	29 ☽ 6p35	27 ☾ 8a17	29 ○ 12a 7	28 ○ 7a40	26 ○ 6p30	30 ○ 10a 3
31 ☽ 4a 5	29 ☽ 3p34		30 ● 6p35				

1969 (January – August)

	JAN 1969	FEB 1969	MAR 1969	APR 1969	MAY 1969	JUN 1969	JUL 1969	AUG 1969
☉ ->	≈	♓	♈	♉	♊	♋	♌	♍
	20 12a39	18 2p55	20 2p 8	20 1a27	21 12a50	21 8a55	22 7p48	23 2a44

D->SIGNS

JAN 1969	FEB 1969	MAR 1969	APR 1969	MAY 1969	JUN 1969	JUL 1969	AUG 1969
2 ♌ 10a53	1 ♍ 5a29	2 ♎ 11p 7	1 ♏ 3p 3	1 ♏ 4a50	1 ♑ 4p 7	1 ♒ 1a49	1 ♈ 2p55
4 ♍ 10p55	3 ♎ 3p41	5 ♏ 6a34	3 ♐ 7p22	3 ♐ 6a19	3 ♒ 4p 4	3 ♓ 2a26	3 ♉ 9p 2
7 ♎ 9a42	6 ♏ 12a 0	7 ♐ 11a56	5 ♑ 9p57	5 ♑ 6a57	5 ♓ 6p13	5 ♈ 6a16	6 ♊ 6a49
9 ♏ 6p33	8 ♐ 6a18	9 ♑ 3p48	7 ♒ 12a 5	7 ♒ 8a28	7 ♈ 11p37	7 ♉ 1p53	8 ♋ 6p57
12 ♐ 12a32	10 ♑ 10a23	11 ♒ 6p40	10 ♓ 2a46	9 ♓ 12p 4	10 ♉ 8a 6	10 ♊ 12a31	11 ♌ 7a38
14 ♑ 3a19	12 ♒ 12p28	13 ♓ 9p 9	12 ♈ 6a41	11 ♈ 6p 9	12 ♊ 6p49	12 ♋ 12p47	13 ♍ 7p33
16 ♒ 3a39	14 ♓ 1p31	16 ♈ 12a 4	14 ♉ 12p13	14 ♉ 2a28	15 ♋ 6a52	15 ♌ 1a29	16 ♎ 5a51
18 ♓ 3a17	16 ♈ 3p 3	18 ♉ 4a27	16 ♊ 7p43	16 ♊ 12p41	17 ♌ 7p35	17 ♍ 1p42	18 ♏ 1p54
20 ♈ 4a21	18 ♉ 6p49	20 ♊ 11a20	18 ♋ 5a28	19 ♋ 12a31	20 ♍ 7a54	20 ♎ 12a20	20 ♐ 7p12
22 ♉ 8a43	21 ♊ 2a 2	22 ♋ 9p13	21 ♌ 5p17	21 ♌ 1p12	22 ♎ 6p 4	22 ♏ 8a 4	22 ♑ 9p49
24 ♊ 5p13	23 ♋ 12p41	25 ♌ 9a19	24 ♍ 5a51	24 ♍ 1a 7	25 ♏ 12a31	24 ♐ 12p11	24 ♒ 10p36
27 ♋ 4a53	26 ♌ 1a11	27 ♍ 9p37	26 ♎ 4p57	26 ♎ 10a 8	27 ♐ 3a 0	26 ♑ 1p 9	26 ♓ 11p 3
29 ♋ 5p36	28 ♍ 1p12	30 ♎ 7a54	29 ♎ 12a44	28 ♏ 3p 5	29 ♑ 2a44	28 ♒ 12p35	28 ♈ 12a57
				30 ♐ 4p30		30 ♓ 12p31	31 ♉ 5a50

D PHASES

JAN 1969	FEB 1969	MAR 1969	APR 1969	MAY 1969	JUN 1969	JUL 1969	AUG 1969
3 ○ 1p28	2 ○ 7a56	4 ○ 12a17	2 ● 1p45	2 ○ 12a13	3 ○ 12p44	2 ○ 7p39	1 ○ 4a28
7 ◐ 2p12	6 ◐ 4a29	7 ◐ 3p37	6 ◐ 12a 0	5 ◐ 6a36	6 ○ 10p39	6 ○ 8a17	4 ○ 8p39
11 ● 9a 0	9 ● 7p 8	11 ● 2a44	9 ○ 8a58	9 ● 3p12	10 ◑ 6p 9	10 ◐ 6a32	8 ◑ 9p39
14 ◑ 7p 6	13 ◑ 4a 2	14 ◑ 12p15	12 ◑ 8p43	12 ◑ 6a15	14 ● 6p 9	14 ● 9a11	13 ● 12a17
17 ● 11p59	17 ● 11a25	17 ● 11p51	16 ● 1p16	16 ● 3a26	18 ◐ 11a 8	18 ◑ 11a 8	17 ◐ 11p 4
21 ◐ 8a23	20 ◐ 12a33	21 ◐ 6p 9	20 ◐ 12p 2	20 ◐ 5a14	22 ○ 8p44	22 ○ 7a10	20 ○ 3p 3
25 ○ 3a23	23 ○ 11p30	25 ○ 7p48	24 ○ 2p45	24 ○ 7a15	26 ○ 10a16	25 ○ 5p29	23 ○ 11p43
29 ◑ 6a16	26 ◑ 2a24	29 ◑ 8p51	28 ◑ 12p30	28 ◑ 12a53	29 ○ 3p 4	28 ○ 9p45	27 ◑ 5a33
				31 ○ 8a18			30 ○ 3p54

1969 (September – December) / 1970 (January – April)

	SEP 1969	OCT 1969	NOV 1969	DEC 1969	JAN 1970	FEB 1970	MAR 1970	APR 1970
☉ ->	♎	♏	♐	♑	≈	♓	♈	♉
	23 12a 7	23 9a12	22 6a32	21 7p44	20 6a24	18 8p42	20 7p57	20 7a15

D->SIGNS

SEP 1969	OCT 1969	NOV 1969	DEC 1969	JAN 1970	FEB 1970	MAR 1970	APR 1970
2 ♊ 2p24	2 ♋ 9a52	1 ♌ 6a35	1 ♍ 3a14	2 ♏ 7a 3	2 ♑ 11p22	1 ♑ 7a54	2 ♓ 7p 1
5 ♋ 1a57	4 ♌ 10p25	3 ♍ 7p 0	3 ♎ 2p 0	4 ♐ 11a33	4 ♒ 11p20	4 ♒ 9a35	4 ♈ 8p32
7 ♌ 2p36	7 ♍ 10a21	6 ♎ 4a59	5 ♏ 9p30	6 ♑ 12p30	6 ♓ 10p37	6 ♓ 9a49	6 ♉ 11p 2
10 ♍ 2a20	9 ♎ 7p48	8 ♏ 11a18	8 ♐ 12a43	8 ♒ 11a48	8 ♈ 11p17	8 ♈ 10a16	9 ♊ 4a 2
12 ♎ 2p19	12 ♏ 2a19	10 ♐ 2p30	10 ♑ 1a20	10 ♓ 11a37	11 ♉ 2a59	10 ♉ 12p43	11 ♋ 12p33
14 ♏ 7p25	14 ♐ 6a33	12 ♑ 4p 9	12 ♒ 1a27	12 ♈ 1p17	13 ♊ 10a29	13 ♊ 6p 7	14 ♌ 12a16
17 ♐ 12a42	16 ♑ 9a35	14 ♒ 5p53	14 ♓ 2a56	14 ♉ 7p20	15 ♋ 9p17	15 ♋ 4a19	16 ♍ 1p 7
19 ♑ 4a14	18 ♒ 12p21	16 ♓ 8p52	16 ♈ 6a56	17 ♊ 4a 7	18 ♌ 9a53	18 ♌ 4p 9	19 ♎ 12a35
21 ♒ 6a31	20 ♓ 3p26	19 ♈ 1a32	18 ♉ 1p35	19 ♋ 3p14	20 ♍ 10a30	20 ♍ 5a30	21 ♏ 9a15
23 ♓ 8a42	22 ♈ 7p17	21 ♉ 7a52	21 ♊ 10p28	22 ♌ 3a40	23 ♎ 10a33	23 ♎ 2a10	23 ♐ 3p15
25 ♈ 10a56	25 ♉ 12a33	23 ♊ 3p59	23 ♋ 9a 9	24 ♍ 4p33	25 ♏ 8a23	25 ♏ 2a10	25 ♑ 7p26
27 ♉ 3p29	27 ♊ 8a 0	26 ♋ 2a10	26 ♌ 9p21	27 ♎ 2p34	28 ♐ 3a38	27 ♐ 2p 0	27 ♒ 10p43
29 ♊ 11p 6	29 ♋ 6p13	28 ♌ 2p22	28 ♍ 10a20	29 ♏ 8p50		29 ♑ 2p 0	30 ♓ 1a38
			30 ♎ 10p18			31 ♒ 5p 8	

D PHASES

SEP 1969	OCT 1969	NOV 1969	DEC 1969	JAN 1970	FEB 1970	MAR 1970	APR 1970
3 ◐ 11a58	3 ◐ 6a 5	2 ◐ 2a14	1 ◐ 10p50	4 ◑ 9a35	2 ◑ 9p29	4 ◑ 7a 9	2 ◑ 3p 9
7 ● 2p34	7 ● 4a36	5 ● 2a35	5 ● 9p 0	7 ● 3p36	6 ● 3p36	7 ● 12p43	5 ● 11p10
11 ◑ 2p56	11 ◑ 4a39	9 ● 5p12	9 ◐ 4a42	10 ◐ 8p27	9 ◐ 8a13	10 ◐ 9p38	9 ◐ 11p10
15 ○ 9a 0	15 ○ 5p30	13 ◑ 10a45	12 ○ 10a17	13 ○ 8a18	12 ○ 11p10	14 ○ 4p16	13 ○ 10a44
18 ◐ 9p25	18 ◐ 3a32	16 ◐ 8p10	16 ◐ 10a45	17 ◑ 5a21	16 ◑ 11p38	18 ◑ 7p 1	17 ◑ 1p52
22 ● 6a13	21 ● 2p 9	20 ● 12a22	19 ● 1p25	22 ● 5a55	19 ● 3a19	22 ● 4p30	21 ● 11a21
25 ◑ 3p21	25 ◑ 3a44	23 ◑ 6p54	23 ◐ 12p23	26 ◐ 11a27	22 ◐ 3a56	26 ◐ 6a 5	25 ◐ 1a34
29 ○ 6a19	28 ○ 11p40	27 ○ 7p20	27 ○ 7p20	30 ○ 9a39	25 ○ 9p33	30 ○ 6a 5	29 ○ 12p18
			31 ◐ 5p52				

1970 (May – December)

	MAY 1970	JUN 1970	JUL 1970	AUG 1970	SEP 1970	OCT 1970	NOV 1970	DEC 1970
☉ ->	♊	♋	♌	♍	♎	♏	♐	♑
	21 6a37	21 2p43	23 1a37	23 8a34	23 5a59	23 3p 5	22 12p25	22 1a36

D->SIGNS

MAY 1970	JUN 1970	JUL 1970	AUG 1970	SEP 1970	OCT 1970	NOV 1970	DEC 1970
2 ♈ 4a32	2 ♊ 9p10	2 ♋ 12p21	1 ♌ 5a44	2 ♎ 1p26	2 ♏ 6a35	3 ♑ 3a33	2 ♒ 1p45
4 ♉ 5a25	5 ♋ 5a25	4 ♌ 11p26	3 ♍ 6p34	4 ♏ 12a54	4 ♐ 3p31	5 ♒ 8a11	4 ♓ 4p55
6 ♊ 9p17	7 ♌ 4p17	7 ♍ 12p11	6 ♎ 7a33	7 ♐ 9a58	7 ♑ 10p10	7 ♓ 11a33	6 ♈ 8p 3
8 ♋ 9p17	10 ♍ 5a 2	10 ♎ 1a 3	8 ♏ 6p57	9 ♑ 3p52	9 ♒ 2a26	9 ♈ 1p52	8 ♉ 11p24
11 ♌ 8a22	12 ♎ 5p28	12 ♏ 11a41	11 ♐ 3a 7	11 ♒ 6p34	11 ♓ 4a30	11 ♉ 3p50	11 ♊ 3a33
13 ♍ 9p11	15 ♏ 3a 2	14 ♐ 6p26	13 ♑ 7a25	13 ♓ 6p57	13 ♈ 5a12	13 ♊ 6p48	13 ♋ 9a32
16 ♎ 9a 3	17 ♐ 8a39	17 ♑ 9p30	15 ♒ 8a31	15 ♈ 6p17	15 ♉ 6a 0	16 ♋ 12a23	15 ♌ 6p22
18 ♏ 5p49	19 ♑ 11a 5	19 ♒ 9p45	17 ♓ 8a 1	17 ♉ 7p21	17 ♊ 9a36	18 ♌ 9a36	18 ♍ 6a 5
20 ♐ 11p21	21 ♒ 12p 1	21 ♓ 9p59	19 ♈ 7a50	19 ♊ 11p 2	19 ♋ 2p59	20 ♍ 9p13	20 ♎ 7p 1
23 ♑ 2a13	23 ♓ 1p12	23 ♈ 6a10	21 ♉ 9a46	22 ♋ 6a41	22 ♌ 1a12	23 ♎ 10a39	23 ♏ 6a27
25 ♒ 4a26	25 ♈ 3p52	25 ♉ 6a 0	23 ♊ 3p 8	24 ♌ 5p 6	24 ♍ 1p57	25 ♏ 9p25	25 ♐ 2p51
27 ♓ 6a59	27 ♉ 8p35	27 ♊ 8a53	26 ♋ 11p58	27 ♍ 5a33	27 ♎ 2a37	28 ♐ 5a 2	27 ♑ 7p 1
29 ♈ 10a27	30 ♊ 3a24	29 ♋ 6p14	28 ♌ 11a38	29 ♎ 7p33	29 ♏ 1p15	30 ♑ 10a 6	29 ♒ 9p49
31 ♉ 3p 3			31 ♍ 12a36		31 ♐ 9p24		31 ♓ 11p 8

D PHASES

MAY 1970	JUN 1970	JUL 1970	AUG 1970	SEP 1970	OCT 1970	NOV 1970	DEC 1970
1 ◑ 10p16	3 ● 9p21	2 ● 10a18	2 ● 12a58	4 ◐ 7p 6	4 ◐ 2a28	2 ◐ 6p54	2 ◑ 4a52
5 ● 9a51	7 ◐ 7p58	7 ◐ 12p32	6 ◐ 4a32	8 ○ 2p38	7 ○ 11p43	6 ○ 7a47	5 ○ 3p36
9 ◐ 3a40	11 ○ 11p 7	11 ○ 2p43	10 ○ 3a50	11 ◑ 11p43	11 ◑ 9a10	9 ◑ 5p22	9 ◐ 2a32
13 ○ 5a26	15 ◑ 8p26	15 ◑ 7a40	13 ◑ 4p59	15 ● 6a10	14 ● 9p21	13 ● 2a28	12 ● 4p 4
17 ◑ 6a34	19 ● 7a28	18 ● 10p59	16 ● 10p16	18 ◐ 12p51	18 ◐ 1a24	16 ◐ 5p27	16 ◐ 12p44
20 ● 10p38	22 ◐ 2p 0	21 ◐ 7p59	20 ○ 3a18	22 ○ 4a42	22 ○ 9p47	20 ○ 6p13	20 ○ 4p 9
24 ◐ 8a16	25 ◑ 6a 0	25 ◑ 6a 0	23 ◑ 3p35	26 ● 6a20	26 ● 1a21	24 ◑ 9p 4	24 ◑ 3p51
27 ◑ 5p32	29 ○ 1p40	29 ○ 1p39	27 ◐ 1p39	30 ◐ 9a32	30 ◐ 1a28	28 ● 4p14	28 ● 5a43
31 ◑ 5a24			30 ● 9a32				31 ◑ 2p21

JAN 1971 — ☉→♒ 20, 12p13
☽→Signs: 3 ♈ 1a26 · 5 ♉ 5a 0 · 7 ♊ 10a 8 · 9 ♋ 5p 9 · 12 ♌ 2a24 · 14 ♍ 1p58 · 17 ♎ 2a53 · 19 ♏ 3p 4 · 22 ♐ 12a16 · 24 ♑ 5a33 · 26 ♒ 7a36 · 28 ♓ 8a 2 · 30 ♈ 8a36
☽ Phases: 3 ● 11p55 · 7 ○ 1p24 · 15 ○ 8a20 · 19 ○ 9a49 · 19 ○ 1p 8 · 23 ○ 8a30 · 26 ○ 9p55 · 29 ☽ 11p51

FEB 1971 — ☉→♓ 19, 2a27
☽→Signs: 1 ♉ 10a49 · 3 ♊ 3p35 · 5 ♋ 11p 7 · 8 ♌ 9a 6 · 10 ♍ 8p58 · 13 ♎ 9a50 · 15 ♏ 10p22 · 18 ♐ 8a46 · 20 ♑ 3p37 · 22 ♒ 6p43 · 24 ♓ 7p 5 · 26 ♈ 6p30 · 28 ♉ 6p54
☽ Phases: 2 ○ 9a31 · 6 ○ 2a40 · 10 ☽ 2a42 · 14 ○ 6a22 · 18 ○ 7a14 · 25 ○ 4a49 · 28 ☽ 9a39

MAR 1971 — ☉→♈ 21, 1a38
☽→Signs: 2 ♊ 10p 2 · 5 ♋ 4a47 · 7 ♌ 2p55 · 10 ♍ 3a10 · 12 ♎ 4p 6 · 15 ♏ 4a31 · 17 ♐ 3p24 · 20 ♑ 11p38 · 22 ♒ 4a29 · 24 ♓ 6a 8 · 26 ♈ 5a46 · 28 ♉ 5a 6 · 30 ♊ 6a44
☽ Phases: 3 ○ 9p 1 · 6 ○ 6p23 · 11 ○ 9p34 · 13 ○ 2p39 · 18 ○ 12a19 · 26 ○ 2p24 · 28 ☽ 8p 4

APR 1971 — ☉→♉ 20, 12p54
☽→Signs: 1 ♋ 11a51 · 3 ♌ 9p 6 · 6 ♍ 9a16 · 8 ♎ 10p17 · 11 ♏ 10a28 · 13 ♐ 9p 3 · 16 ♑ 5a38 · 18 ♒ 11a46 · 20 ♓ 3p 8 · 22 ♈ 4p 7 · 24 ♉ 4p 7 · 26 ♊ 5p14 · 28 ♋ 8p43
☽ Phases: 2 ○ 10a46 · 5 ○ 11a47 · 10 ○ 3p10 · 14 ○ 2p39 · 21 ● 11p 2 · 28 ☽ 7a34

MAY 1971 — ☉→♊ 21, 12p15
☽→Signs: 1 ♌ 4a35 · 3 ♍ 4p 3 · 6 ♎ 4a59 · 8 ♏ 5p 4 · 11 ♐ 3a 8 · 13 ♑ 11a 9 · 15 ♒ 5p20 · 17 ♓ 9p39 · 20 ♈ 12a11 · 22 ♉ 1a31 · 24 ♊ 3a 1 · 26 ♋ 6a26 · 28 ♌ 1p16 · 30 ♍ 11p48
☽ Phases: 2 ○ 2a34 · 5 ○ 5a30 · 10 ○ 6a24 · 14 ○ 1a27 · 21 ○ 3p15 · 24 ● 12a 8 · 27 ○ 8p36 · 31 ○ 7p42

JUN 1971 — ☉→♋ 21, 8p20
☽→Signs: 2 ♎ 12p27 · 5 ♏ 12a36 · 7 ♐ 10a28 · 9 ♑ 5p45 · 11 ♒ 11p 3 · 14 ♓ 3a 1 · 16 ♈ 6a 6 · 18 ♉ 8a39 · 20 ♊ 11a24 · 22 ♋ 3p30 · 24 ♌ 10p12 · 27 ♍ 8a 6 · 29 ♎ 8p22
☽ Phases: 4 ○ 10p18 · 8 ○ 7p 4 · 12 ○ 4p49 · 19 ○ 5a44 · 22 ● 12p 2 · 26 ☽ 11a19 · 30 ○ 1p11

JUL 1971 — ☉→♌ 23, 7a15
☽→Signs: 2 ♏ 8a46 · 4 ♐ 6p59 · 7 ♑ 2a 3 · 9 ♒ 6a27 · 11 ♓ 9a14 · 13 ♈ 11a32 · 15 ♉ 2p10 · 17 ♊ 5p47 · 19 ♋ 10p52 · 22 ♌ 6a17 · 24 ♍ 4p 9 · 27 ♎ 4a12 · 29 ♏ 4p50
☽ Phases: 4 ○ 1p32 · 8 ○ 5a37 · 11 ○ 3p46 · 18 ○ 12a47 · 22 ● 4a15 · 26 ☽ 3a25 · 30 ○ 6a 7

AUG 1971 — ☉→♍ 23, 2p16
☽→Signs: 1 ♐ 3a50 · 3 ♑ 11a32 · 5 ♒ 3p47 · 7 ♓ 6p27 · 9 ♈ 7p55 · 11 ♉ 7p55 · 13 ♊ 11p11 · 16 ♋ 4a50 · 18 ♌ 12p58 · 21 ♍ 11a23 · 23 ♎ 11a23 · 26 ♏ 11a57 · 28 ♐ 11a57 · 30 ♑ 6p54
☽ Phases: 3 ○ 3a 8 · 6 ○ 2p42 · 9 ○ 9p26 · 16 ○ 5a55 · 22 ● 8p30 · 24 ☽ 9p54 · 28 ○ 9p 5

SEP 1971 — ☉→♎ 23, 11a45
☽→Signs: 2 ♒ 2a 4 · 4 ♓ 3a51 · 6 ♈ 3a43 · 8 ♉ 3a38 · 10 ♊ 10a21 · 12 ♋ 6p38 · 14 ♌ 5a29 · 17 ♍ 5p47 · 19 ♎ 6p33 · 22 ♏ 6a33 · 24 ♐ 6p43 · 27 ♑ 4a53 · 29 ♒ 11a39
☽ Phases: 1 ○ 3p17 · 4 ○ 11p 3 · 8 ○ 3a42 · 11 ○ 1p23 · 15 ○ 8a15 · 19 ○ 9a42 · 23 ○ 12p53 · 27 ○ 12p17

OCT 1971 — ☉→♏ 23, 8p54
☽→Signs: 1 ♓ 2p37 · 3 ♈ 2p41 · 5 ♉ 1p42 · 7 ♊ 1p53 · 10 ♋ 5p44 · 12 ♌ 12a30 · 15 ♍ 11a16 · 17 ♎ 11p47 · 20 ♏ 12p31 · 22 ♐ 12a32 · 25 ♑ 11a 5 · 27 ♒ 7p11 · 30 ♓ 1a26
☽ Phases: 1 ○ 2a 7 · 4 ○ 7a20 · 7 ○ 11a51 · 11 ○ 12a29 · 14 ○ 11p38 · 19 ○ 2a59 · 23 ○ 4a44 · 27 ○ 12a54 · 30 ○ 11a52

NOV 1971 — ☉→♐ 22, 6p14
☽→Signs: 2 ♈ 12a55 · 4 ♉ 12a27 · 6 ♊ 12a15 · 8 ♋ 1a41 · 10 ♌ 6p50 · 13 ♍ 6a50 · 15 ♎ 7p37 · 18 ♏ 8a 2 · 20 ♐ 4p36 · 23 ♑ 12a52 · 26 ♒ 6a48 · 28 ♓ 10a 4 · 30 ♈ 11a 8
☽ Phases: 2 ○ 4p20 · 5 ○ 10p57 · 9 ○ 3p52 · 13 ○ 6p 6 · 15 ○ 8p46 · 21 ○ 7p10 · 25 ○ 11a37 · 29 ○ 8p52

DEC 1971 — ☉→♑ 22, 7a24
☽→Signs: 1 ♉ 11a25 · 3 ♊ 12p51 · 5 ♋ 5p17 · 8 ♌ 1a 1 · 10 ♍ 12p19 · 13 ♎ 1a 2 · 15 ♏ 1p37 · 18 ♐ 11p 7 · 20 ♑ 6a33 · 22 ♒ 12p10 · 24 ♓ 4p 9 · 26 ♈ 6p45 · 28 ♉ 9p20 · 30 ♊ 11p 1
☽ Phases: 2 ○ 2a48 · 5 ○ 1p37 · 9 ○ 11a 3 · 13 ○ 2p21 · 17 ○ 2p 3 · 21 ○ 7p46 · 25 ○ 8p35 · 28 ○ 5a45 · 31 ○ 3p20

JAN 1972 — ☉→♒ 20, 5p59
☽→Signs: 2 ♋ 3a22 · 4 ♌ 10a50 · 6 ♍ 9p33 · 9 ♎ 10a 3 · 11 ♏ 9p57 · 14 ♐ 8a11 · 16 ♑ 3p28 · 18 ♒ 8p28 · 21 ♓ 12a17 · 23 ♈ 3a11 · 25 ♉ 6a11 · 27 ♊ 9a33 · 29 ♋ 12p21 · 31 ♌ 7p56
☽ Phases: 3 ○ 3a21 · 7 ○ 6a12 · 12 ○ 10a44 · 16 ○ 5a33 · 19 ○ 6p26 · 23 ○ 4a29 · 26 ○ 3p37 · 30 ○ 5a58

FEB 1972 — ☉→♓ 19, 8a12
☽→Signs: 3 ♍ 6a 7 · 5 ♎ 6p18 · 8 ♏ 6a38 · 10 ♐ 4p50 · 13 ♑ 11p36 · 15 ♒ 3a11 · 17 ♓ 4a51 · 19 ♈ 6a28 · 21 ♉ 8a36 · 23 ♊ 12p52 · 25 ♋ 6p24 · 28 ♌ 3a39
☽ Phases: 2 ○ 5p27 · 6 ○ 1p37 · 11 ○ 5a34 · 14 ○ 7p29 · 18 ○ 3a29 · 21 ○ 12p20 · 25 ○ 2a21 · 28 ○ 10p12

MAR 1972 — ☉→♈ 20, 7a22
☽→Signs: 1 ♎ 2a 0 · 3 ♏ 12p36 · 6 ♐ 2p37 · 8 ♑ 11p33 · 11 ♒ 11p36 · 14 ♓ 1p39 · 16 ♈ 2p37 · 19 ♉ 3a11 · 21 ♊ 5p26 · 23 ♋ 9p26 · 26 ♌ 12a46 · 28 ♍ 9a48 · 31 ♎ 8a49
☽ Phases: 3 ○ 11p23 · 7 ○ 2a 6 · 11 ○ 9p30 · 14 ○ 11a40 · 18 ○ 9p12 · 21 ○ 3p 4 · 25 ○ 3p 6

APR 1972 — ☉→♉ 19, 6p38
☽→Signs: 2 ♏ 9p27 · 5 ♐ 9p21 · 7 ♑ 6p38 · 9 ♒ 11p58 · 12 ♓ 1a32 · 14 ♈ 12a55 · 16 ♉ 12a17 · 18 ♊ 1a46 · 20 ♋ 6a47 · 22 ♌ 3p24 · 25 ♍ 2a34 · 27 ♎ 2p56 · 30 ♏ 3a31
☽ Phases: 2 ○ 6p 1 · 6 ○ 6p45 · 10 ○ 9a52 · 13 ○ 9p31 · 17 ○ 7p55 · 20 ○ 7p45 · 24 ○ 5a20

MAY 1972 — ☉→♊ 20, 6p 0
☽→Signs: 2 ♐ 3p29 · 5 ♑ 1a35 · 7 ♒ 8a28 · 9 ♓ 11a35 · 11 ♈ 11a48 · 13 ♉ 10a57 · 15 ♊ 11a16 · 17 ♋ 2p38 · 19 ♌ 9p56 · 22 ♍ 8a36 · 24 ♎ 9p 1 · 27 ♏ 9a33 · 29 ♐ 9p13
☽ Phases: 2 ○ 10a 8 · 6 ○ 7a26 · 9 ○ 6p51 · 12 ○ 11p 8 · 16 ○ 5a 3 · 19 ☽ 8p16 · 23 ○ 8p45 · 27 ○ 11p28 · 31 ○ 11p11

JUN 1972 — ☉→♋ 21, 2a 6
☽→Signs: 1 ♑ 7a15 · 3 ♒ 2p52 · 5 ♓ 7p28 · 7 ♈ 9p15 · 9 ♉ 9p24 · 11 ♊ 10a 5 · 14 ♋ 12a10 · 16 ♌ 3p16 · 18 ♍ 3p39 · 20 ♎ 3p43 · 23 ♏ 4p14 · 25 ♐ 4p 2 · 28 ♑ 1p 3 · 30 ♒ 8p19
☽ Phases: 4 ○ 4p22 · 8 ○ 6a30 · 11 ☽ 2p39 · 14 ○ 3p41 · 18 ○ 10a41 · 22 ○ 12p50 · 26 ○ 1p46 · 30 ○ 9a11

JUL 1972 — ☉→♌ 22, 1p 3
☽→Signs: 3 ♓ 1a22 · 5 ♈ 4a25 · 7 ♉ 6a 5 · 9 ♊ 7a29 · 11 ♋ 10a 5 · 13 ♌ 3p16 · 16 ♍ 11p49 · 18 ♎ 11a55 · 20 ♏ 11p46 · 23 ♐ 4p19 · 25 ♑ 8p 7 · 28 ♒ 2a29 · 30 ♓ 6a50
☽ Phases: 3 ○ 10p26 · 7 ○ 6a48 · 10 ☽ 2p39 · 14 ○ 4a11 · 18 ○ 2a46 · 22 ○ 5a 6 · 26 ○ 2a24 · 29 ○ 4p44

AUG 1972 — ☉→♍ 22, 8p 3
☽→Signs: 1 ♈ 9a58 · 3 ♉ 12p33 · 5 ♊ 3p18 · 7 ♋ 6p56 · 9 ♌ 12a23 · 12 ♍ 8a15 · 14 ♎ 7p20 · 17 ♏ 7p38 · 19 ♐ 7p38 · 22 ♑ 10a29 · 24 ♒ 10a29 · 26 ♓ 3p43 · 28 ♈ 5p56 · 31 ♊ 7a48
☽ Phases: 2 ○ 3a 2 · 5 ○ 12p31 · 9 ○ 12a26 · 12 ○ 4p13 · 16 ○ 8p 9 · 20 ○ 1p22 · 24 ○ 1p22 · 29 ○ 2p16

SEP 1972 — ☉→♎ 22, 5p33
☽→Signs: 1 ♋ 9p12 · 4 ♌ 1a54 · 6 ♍ 8a15 · 8 ♎ 4p37 · 11 ♏ 3a15 · 13 ♐ 3p42 · 16 ♑ 4a 8 · 18 ♒ 2p 5 · 20 ♓ 8p 9 · 22 ♈ 10p45 · 24 ♉ 11p20 · 27 ♊ 12a41 · 29 ♋ 2a39
☽ Phases: 3 ☽ 5a47 · 7 ○ 8a36 · 11 ○ 1a16 · 15 ○ 2p13 · 19 ○ 11a54 · 22 ○ 11p 7 · 26 ○ 5a17 · 29 ○ 2p16

OCT 1972 — ☉→♏ 23, 2a42
☽→Signs: 1 ♌ 7a25 · 3 ♍ 2p31 · 5 ♎ 11p35 · 8 ♏ 10a27 · 10 ♐ 10p53 · 13 ♑ 11a40 · 15 ♒ 10p51 · 18 ♓ 6a13 · 20 ♈ 9a43 · 22 ♉ 9a37 · 24 ♊ 9a 2 · 26 ♋ 9a15 · 28 ♌ 1p14 · 30 ♍ 7p59
☽ Phases: 1 ○ 7p 5 · 4 ○ 8p21 · 7 ○ 5a23 · 10 ☽ 12a 1 · 14 ○ 12a 1 · 17 ○ 1p18 · 20 ○ 7p40 · 23 ○ 11p16 · 28 ○ 11p41

NOV 1972 — ☉→♐ 22, 12a 3
☽→Signs: 2 ♎ 5a27 · 4 ♏ 4p46 · 7 ♐ 5a17 · 9 ♑ 6p11 · 12 ♒ 6a 3 · 14 ♓ 2p56 · 16 ♈ 7p44 · 18 ♉ 8p53 · 20 ♊ 8p 5 · 22 ♋ 7p31 · 24 ♌ 9p12 · 27 ♍ 2a24 · 29 ♎ 11a15
☽ Phases: 1 ☽ 7p 5 · 5 ○ 8p21 · 9 ○ 12a 1 · 13 ○ 12a 1 · 16 ○ 5p44 · 20 ○ 6p 7 · 23 ○ 11p16 · 29 ○ 12p45

DEC 1972 — ☉→♑ 21, 1p13
☽→Signs: 1 ♏ 10p42 · 4 ♐ 11a23 · 7 ♑ 12a 7 · 9 ♒ 11a54 · 11 ♓ 9p33 · 14 ♈ 4a 0 · 16 ♉ 7a24 · 18 ♊ 7a24 · 20 ♋ 6a57 · 22 ♌ 7a34 · 24 ♍ 11a 3 · 26 ♎ 6p22 · 29 ♏ 5a10 · 31 ♐ 5p52
☽ Phases: 1 ☽ 11a54 · 5 ○ 3p24 · 9 ○ 5p44 · 13 ○ 1p36 · 17 ○ 10p 6 · 20 ○ 12p18 · 23 ○ 5a28 · 31 ☽ 7a36

JAN 1973 – AUG 1973

JAN 1973
☉ -> ♒   19   11p49

☽ -> SIGNS
| 3 ♉ 6a30 | 5 ♊ 5p47 | 8 ♋ 3a 3 | 10 ♌ 9a58 | 12 ♍ 2p25 | 14 ♎ 4p41 | 16 ♏ 5p39 | 18 ♐ 6p40 | 20 ♑ 9p24 | 23 ♒ 1a10 | 25 ♓ 12p52 | 28 ♈ 1a10 | 30 ♉ 1p54 |

☽ PHASES
4 ♐ 10a43 · 8 ♑ 8a57 · 12 ● 12a27 · 15 ♒ 9a38 · 18 ♐ 4p29 · 22 ○ 3a51 · 26 ◑ 1a 5 · 30 ◐ 4a36

FEB 1973
☉ -> ♓   18   2p 2

☽ -> SIGNS
| 2 ♊ 12a55 | 4 ♋ 9a22 | 7 ♌ 3p29 | 9 ♍ 7p54 | 12 ♎ 1p10 | 13 ♏ 1a44 | 15 ♐ 4a12 | 17 ♑ 7a31 | 19 ♒ 12p58 | 21 ♓ 9p35 | 24 ♈ 9a14 | 26 ♉ 10p 4 |

☽ PHASES
3 ● 4a23 · 6 ♑ 9p 5 · 10 ♒ 9a 6 · 13 ♐ 6p48 · 17 ○ 5a 7 · 20 ◑ 9p14 · 24 ◐ 10p10

MAR 1973
☉ -> ♈   20   1p13

☽ -> SIGNS
| 1 ♊ 9a22 | 3 ♋ 5p31 | 5 ♌ 10p37 | 8 ♍ 1a51 | 10 ♎ 4a31 | 12 ♏ 7a29 | 14 ♐ 11a 8 | 16 ♑ 3p42 | 18 ♒ 9p48 | 21 ♓ 6a16 | 23 ♈ 5p26 | 26 ♉ 6a13 | 28 ♊ 6p13 | 31 ♋ 2a55 |

☽ PHASES
1 ♐ 12a40 · 4 ● 7p 8 · 8 ♑ 6a31 · 11 ♒ 4p26 · 15 ♐ 3a54 · 18 ○ 6p34 · 22 ◑ 3p39 · 26 ◐ 6p46 · 30 ♐ 5p55

APR 1973
☉ -> ♉   20   12a31

☽ -> SIGNS
| 2 ♊ 7a48 | 4 ♋ 9a58 | 6 ♌ 11a12 | 8 ♍ 1p 5 | 10 ♎ 4p31 | 12 ♏ 9p47 | 15 ♐ 4a50 | 17 ♑ 1p51 | 20 ♒ 1a 2 | 22 ♓ 1p49 | 25 ♈ 2a21 | 27 ♉ 12p10 | 29 ♊ 5p53 |

☽ PHASES
3 ● 6a45 · 6 ♑ 2p14 · 9 ♒ 11p28 · 13 ♐ 1p32 · 17 ○ 8a51 · 21 ◑ 10a 5 · 25 ◐ 12p59 · 29 ♐ 7a33

MAY 1973
☉ -> ♊   20   11p54

☽ -> SIGNS
| 1 ♉ 8p 2 | 3 ♊ 8p16 | 5 ♋ 8p35 | 7 ♌ 10p36 | 10 ♍ 3a13 | 12 ♎ 10a31 | 14 ♏ 8p 9 | 17 ♐ 7a42 | 19 ♑ 8p30 | 22 ♒ 9p17 | 24 ♓ 8p 5 | 27 ♈ 3a15 | 29 ♉ 6a28 | 31 ♊ 6a53 |

☽ PHASES
2 ● 3p55 · 5 ♑ 9p17 · 9 ♒ 7a 7 · 13 ♐ 12a22 · 16 ○ 11p58 · 21 ◑ 3a17 · 24 ◐ 3a40 · 27 ♐ 1a48 · 30 ♐ 6a39

JUN 1973
☉ -> ♋   21   8a 1

☽ -> SIGNS
| 2 ♋ 6a21 | 4 ♌ 6a49 | 6 ♍ 9a51 | 8 ♎ 4p16 | 11 ♏ 1a52 | 13 ♐ 1p43 | 16 ♑ 2a37 | 18 ♒ 3p19 | 21 ♓ 2a29 | 23 ♈ 10a48 | 25 ♉ 3p37 | 27 ♊ 5p18 | 29 ♋ 5p 8 |

☽ PHASES
4 ♑ 4a33 · 7 ♒ 4p11 · 11 ♐ 1p 0 · 15 ♐ 3p35 · 19 ○ 6p13 · 23 ◑ 2p45 · 27 ◐ 1a48 · 30 ♐ 6a39

JUL 1973
☉ -> ♌   22   6p56

☽ -> SIGNS
| 1 ♌ 4p56 | 3 ♍ 6p31 | 5 ♎ 11p24 | 8 ♏ 7p48 | 10 ♐ 7p48 | 13 ♑ 8a46 | 15 ♒ 9p15 | 18 ♓ 8a 7 | 20 ♈ 4p44 | 22 ♉ 10p58 | 25 ♊ 1a58 | 27 ♋ 3a29 | 29 ♌ 4a35 |

☽ PHASES
3 ◐ 12p49 · 7 ♒ 10p 7 · 11 ♐ 3a26 · 15 ♐ 3a42 · 19 ○ 6a56 · 23 ◑ 6a23 · 26 ◑ 8a20 · 29 ● 1p59

AUG 1973
☉ -> ♍   23   1a54

☽ -> SIGNS
| 2 ♎ 8a12 | 4 ♏ 3p36 | 7 ♐ 2a37 | 9 ♑ 3p30 | 12 ♒ 3a52 | 14 ♓ 2p14 | 16 ♈ 10p16 | 19 ♉ 4a14 | 21 ♊ 8a26 | 23 ♋ 12p49 | 27 ♍ 2p33 | 29 ♎ 5p52 |

☽ PHASES
1 ◐ 10p52 · 5 ♒ 5p27 · 9 ♐ 8p 7 · 13 ♐ 9p10 · 17 ○ 4p 5 · 21 ◑ 5a22 · 24 ◑ 2p29 · 27 ● 10p26 · 31 ♐ 11a28

SEP 1973 – APR 1974

SEP 1973
☉ -> ♎   22   11p22

☽ -> SIGNS
| 1 ♏ 12a18 | 3 ♐ 10a24 | 5 ♑ 11p 1 | 8 ♒ 11a31 | 10 ♓ 9p40 | 13 ♈ 4a56 | 15 ♉ 9a59 | 17 ♊ 1p48 | 19 ♋ 5p 1 | 21 ♌ 7p56 | 23 ♍ 10p59 | 26 ♎ 3a 1 | 28 ♏ 9a18 | 30 ♐ 6p47 |

☽ PHASES
4 ◐ 10a22 · 8 ♒ 1p23 · 12 ♐ 10a16 · 16 ♐ 11a11 · 19 ○ 9p15 · 22 ◑ 8a54 · 26 ● 10p17 · 30 ◐ 3a11

OCT 1973
☉ -> ♏   23   8a31

☽ -> SIGNS
| 3 ♑ 7a 2 | 5 ♒ 7p49 | 8 ♓ 6a14 | 10 ♈ 1p29 | 12 ♉ 5p36 | 14 ♊ 8p 9 | 16 ♋ 10p29 | 19 ♌ 1a25 | 21 ♍ 5a19 | 23 ♎ 10a57 | 25 ♏ 6p59 | 28 ♐ 2a58 | 30 ♑ 2p57 |

☽ PHASES
4 ♑ 5a32 · 8 ♒ 6a28 · 11 ♐ 10p 9 · 15 ♐ 7a55 · 18 ○ 5p33 · 22 ◑ 5a44 · 26 ● 10p17 · 29 ◐ 9p51

NOV 1973
☉ -> ♐   22   5a55

☽ -> SIGNS
| 2 ♒ 3a58 | 4 ♓ 3p26 | 7 ♈ 11p19 | 9 ♉ 3a26 | 11 ♊ 5a 0 | 13 ♋ 5a47 | 15 ♌ 7a20 | 17 ♍ 10a41 | 19 ♎ 4p16 | 22 ♏ 12a 7 | 24 ♐ 10a11 | 26 ♑ 10p13 | 29 ♒ 11a17 |

☽ PHASES
3 ♑ 1a29 · 6 ♒ 10p35 · 10 ♐ 9a27 · 13 ♐ 4p10 · 17 ○ 1a35 · 20 ◑ 5p 1 · 24 ● 2p55 · 28 ◐ 6p 9

DEC 1973
☉ -> ♑   21   7p 8

☽ -> SIGNS
| 1 ♓ 11p32 | 4 ♈ 8a50 | 6 ♉ 2p 9 | 8 ♊ 3p58 | 10 ♋ 3p44 | 12 ♌ 3p44 | 14 ♍ 5p21 | 16 ♎ 9p53 | 19 ♏ 6a 4 | 21 ♐ 4p20 | 24 ♑ 4a41 | 26 ♒ 5p43 | 29 ♓ 4a34 | 31 ♈ 4p34 |

☽ PHASES
2 ♑ 8p29 · 6 ♒ 8p17 · 9 ♐ 9a27 · 13 ♐ 1a40 · 16 ♐ 12p13 · 20 ◑ 7a49 · 24 ● 4p 1a · 28 ◐ 2p 1

JAN 1974
☉ -> ♒   20   5a46

☽ -> SIGNS
| 2 ♉ 11p38 | 5 ♊ 3a 0 | 7 ♋ 3a28 | 9 ♌ 2a42 | 11 ♍ 2a42 | 13 ♎ 5a21 | 15 ♏ 11a53 | 17 ♐ 10p12 | 20 ♑ 10a47 | 22 ♒ 11p50 | 25 ♓ 12p 1 | 27 ♈ 10p 9 | 30 ♉ 6a42 |

☽ PHASES
1 ♐ 1p 7 · 5 ♒ 2a17 · 8 ♐ 7a30 · 11 ♐ 12p47 · 15 ♐ 2a 4 · 19 ◑ 12a53 · 23 ● 6a 2 · 27 ◐ 7a30 · 31 ♐ 2a39

FEB 1974
☉ -> ♓   18   7p59

☽ -> SIGNS
| 1 ♊ 11a53 | 3 ♋ 2p 6 | 5 ♌ 2p12 | 7 ♍ 1p52 | 9 ♎ 3p10 | 11 ♏ 7p58 | 14 ♐ 5a 1 | 16 ♑ 5p16 | 19 ♒ 6a21 | 21 ♓ 6p15 | 24 ♈ 4a13 | 26 ♉ 12p11 | 28 ♊ 6p10 |

☽ PHASES
3 ♑ 1p22 · 6 ♒ 6p24 · 10 ♐ 1a39 · 13 ♐ 7p 4 · 17 ◑ 9p58 · 22 ● 12a34 · 25 ◐ 9p41

MAR 1974
☉ -> ♈   20   7p 7

☽ -> SIGNS
| 2 ♋ 10p 0 | 4 ♌ 11p49 | 7 ♍ 12a33 | 9 ♎ 1a52 | 11 ♏ 5a40 | 13 ♐ 1p20 | 16 ♑ 12a41 | 18 ♒ 1p38 | 21 ♈ 1a34 | 23 ♈ 11a 3 | 25 ♉ 11p33 | 28 ♊ 6a23 | 30 ♋ 3a40 |

☽ PHASES
1 ♑ 10p 3 · 4 ♒ 10p28 · 8 ♐ 5a 3 · 11 ♐ 4p19 · 15 ◑ 2p15 · 19 ◑ 5p45 · 23 ● 4p24 · 27 ◐ 8a35 · 30 ◐ 8p44

APR 1974
☉ -> ♉   20   6a19

☽ -> SIGNS
| 2 ♌ 6a41 | 4 ♍ 8a57 | 6 ♎ 11a23 | 8 ♏ 3p25 | 10 ♐ 10p27 | 12 ♑ 8a56 | 15 ♒ 9p34 | 17 ♓ 9p20 | 20 ♈ 7p20 | 22 ♉ 1a54 | 24 ♊ 6a11 | 26 ♋ 9a18 | 28 ♌ 12p 4 | 30 ♍ 3p 1 |

☽ PHASES
3 ♑ 6a 8 · 6 ♒ 4p 1 · 10 ♐ 8a33 · 14 ♐ 9a58 · 18 ◑ 11a35 · 22 ◑ 5a17 · 25 ● 4p51 · 29 ◐ 2a40

MAY 1974 – DEC 1974

MAY 1974
☉ -> ♊   21   5a36

☽ -> SIGNS
| 2 ♎ 6p39 | 4 ♏ 11p43 | 7 ♐ 7a 5 | 9 ♑ 5p15 | 12 ♒ 5a34 | 14 ♓ 6p 3 | 17 ♈ 4a20 | 19 ♉ 11a10 | 21 ♊ 2p55 | 23 ♋ 4p46 | 25 ♌ 6p12 | 27 ♍ 8p49 | 30 ♎ 12a16 |

☽ PHASES
2 ♑ 1p22 · 6 ♒ 3a55 · 10 ♐ 1a40 · 14 ♐ 2a49 · 18 ◑ 2a41 · 21 ● 3p34 · 24 ◑ 11p23 · 28 ● 8a 3 · 31 ♐ 9p28

JUN 1974
☉ -> ♋   21   1p38

☽ -> SIGNS
| 1 ♏ 6a10 | 3 ♐ 2p22 | 6 ♑ 12a48 | 8 ♒ 1p 2 | 11 ♓ 1a44 | 13 ♈ 12p53 | 15 ♉ 8p47 | 18 ♊ 12a59 | 20 ♋ 2a21 | 22 ♌ 2a30 | 24 ♍ 3a11 | 26 ♎ 5a57 | 28 ♏ 11a40 | 30 ♐ 8p21 |

☽ PHASES
4 ♑ 5p10 · 8 ♒ 6p40 · 12 ♐ 8p45 · 16 ♐ 3p 4 · 19 ♐ 11p56 · 23 ◑ 5a13 · 26 ● 2p20 · 30 ♐ 7a32

JUL 1974
☉ -> ♌   23   12a31

☽ -> SIGNS
| 3 ♑ 7a19 | 5 ♒ 7p41 | 8 ♓ 8a26 | 10 ♈ 8p10 | 13 ♉ 5a21 | 15 ♊ 10a54 | 17 ♋ 12p56 | 19 ♌ 12p10 | 21 ♍ 12p10 | 23 ♎ 1p19 | 25 ♏ 5p46 | 28 ♐ 1a10 | 30 ♑ 1p11 |

☽ PHASES
4 ♑ 7a41 · 8 ♒ 10a37 · 12 ♐ 10a28 · 16 ♐ 1a 9 · 19 ♐ 9a25 · 22 ◑ 11a34 · 26 ● 10a39 · 29 ♐ 8p14

AUG 1974
☉ -> ♍   23   7a29

☽ -> SIGNS
| 2 ♒ 1a46 | 4 ♓ 2p27 | 7 ♈ 2a15 | 9 ♉ 12p13 | 11 ♊ 7p15 | 13 ♋ 10p49 | 16 ♌ 11p27 | 18 ♍ 11p14 | 19 ♎ 10p43 | 22 ♏ 1a37 | 24 ♐ 8a34 | 26 ♑ 7p15 | 29 ♒ 7a53 | 31 ♓ 8p29 |

☽ PHASES
2 ♑ 10p57 · 6 ♒ 1a 0 · 10 ♐ 9p46 · 14 ♐ 9a25 · 17 ♐ 2p 2 · 20 ◑ 6a40 · 24 ♐ 10a39 · 28 ● 11a34

SEP 1974
☉ -> ♎   23   4a59

☽ -> SIGNS
| 3 ♈ 7a58 | 5 ♉ 5p50 | 8 ♊ 1a36 | 10 ♋ 6a40 | 12 ♌ 8a54 | 14 ♍ 9a12 | 16 ♎ 9a17 | 18 ♏ 11a14 | 20 ♐ 4p46 | 22 ♑ 2p39 | 24 ♒ 12p54 | 27 ♓ 3a26 | 29 ♈ 4a58 |

☽ PHASES
1 ♑ 2p25 · 5 ♒ 1p41 · 9 ♐ 7a 1 · 12 ♐ 4p37 · 15 ● 9p45 · 18 ◑ 9p15 · 22 ● 8p53 · 26 ♐ 11p32 · 30 ♐ 8p19

OCT 1974
☉ -> ♏   23   2p11

☽ -> SIGNS
| 2 ♉ 11p39 | 5 ♊ 7a 1 | 7 ♋ 12p30 | 9 ♌ 3p56 | 11 ♍ 5p11 | 13 ♎ 5p38 | 15 ♏ 6a23 | 18 ♐ 10a44 | 20 ♑ 10p20 | 23 ♒ 10a57 | 25 ♓ 10p13 | 28 ♈ 9p58 |

☽ PHASES
1 ♑ 5a38 · 5 ♒ 12a51 · 8 ♐ 2p46 · 11 ♐ 11p39 · 15 ♐ 7a25 · 18 ● 9p15 · 22 ♐ 8p53 · 26 ♐ 11p32 · 30 ♐ 8p19

NOV 1974
☉ -> ♐   22   11p39

☽ -> SIGNS
| 1 ♊ 11p23 | 3 ♋ 6p 1 | 5 ♌ 9p30 | 8 ♍ 12a18 | 10 ♎ 2a59 | 12 ♏ 6a23 | 14 ♐ 11a39 | 16 ♑ 7p42 | 19 ♒ 6a39 | 21 ♓ 7p11 | 22 ♈ 4p 5 | 28 ♉ 9p58 |

☽ PHASES
3 ♑ 10a48 · 6 ♒ 9p47 · 10 ♐ 7a37 · 13 ♐ 7p53 · 17 ♐ 3p16 · 21 ● 5p40 · 25 ♐ 6p13 · 29 ♐ 10a10

DEC 1974
☉ -> ♑   22   12a57

☽ -> SIGNS
| 1 ♋ 1a22 | 3 ♌ 3a31 | 5 ♍ 5a40 | 7 ♎ 8a43 | 9 ♏ 1p14 | 11 ♐ 7p35 | 14 ♑ 4a 4 | 16 ♒ 2p48 | 19 ♓ 3a12 | 21 ♈ 3p35 | 24 ♉ 1a45 | 26 ♊ 8a16 | 28 ♋ 11a16 | 30 ♌ 12p 5 |

☽ PHASES
2 ♑ 7p59 · 6 ♒ 5a10 · 9 ♐ 5p39 · 13 ♐ 11a25 · 17 ♐ 11a32 · 21 ● 2p44 · 25 ♐ 4a13 · 28 ♐ 10p51

JAN 1975	FEB 1975	MAR 1975	APR 1975	MAY 1975	JUN 1975	JUL 1975	AUG 1975
☉ -> ♒	☉ -> ♓	☉ -> ♈	☉ -> ♉	☉ -> ♊	☉ -> ♋	☉ -> ♌	☉ -> ♍
20 11a37	19 1a50	21 12a57	20 12p 8	21 11a24	21 7p27	23 6a22	23 1p24

☽->SIGNS (JAN 1975)
```
 1 ♏ 12p33      3 ♎  2p22      5 ♏  6p39      8 ♐  1a39
10 ♑ 10a58     12 ♒ 10p 3     15 ♓ 10a23     17 ♈ 11p 4
20 ♉ 10a21     22 ♊  6p23     24 ♋ 10p20     26 ♌ 11p 0
28 ♍ 10p14     30 ♎ 10p13
```

☽->SIGNS (FEB 1975)
```
 2 ♏ 12a53      4 ♐  7a10      6 ♑  4p42      9 ♒  4a17
11 ♓  4p45     14 ♈  5a22     16 ♉  5p 9     19 ♊  2a35
21 ♋  8a19     23 ♌ 10a13     25 ♍  9p37     27 ♎  8a38
```

☽->SIGNS (MAR 1975)
```
 1 ♏  9a34      3 ♐  2p 6      5 ♑ 10p40      8 ♒ 10a10
10 ♓ 10p49     13 ♈ 11a18     15 ♉ 10p53     18 ♊  8a43
20 ♋  3p49     22 ♌  7p31     24 ♍  8p21     26 ♎  7p51
28 ♏  8p 8     30 ♐ 11p10
```

☽->SIGNS (APR 1975)
```
 2 ♑  6a 8      4 ♒  4p45      7 ♓  5a17      9 ♈  5p44
12 ♉  4a53     14 ♊  2p14     16 ♋  9p27     19 ♌  2a14
21 ♍  4a43     23 ♎  5a42     25 ♏  6a40     27 ♐  9a20
29 ♑  3p 9
```

☽->SIGNS (MAY 1975)
```
 2 ♒ 12a34      4 ♓ 12p34      7 ♈  1a 3      9 ♉ 12p 4
11 ♊  8p44     14 ♋  3a 8     16 ♌  7a39     18 ♍ 10a46
20 ♎  1p 5     21 ♏  2a35     24 ♐  6p41     27 ♑ 12a31
29 ♒  9a 9     31 ♓  8p32
```

☽->SIGNS (JUN 1975)
```
 3 ♈  9a 1      5 ♉  8p19      8 ♊  4a49     10 ♋ 10a22
12 ♌  1p45     14 ♍  4p11     16 ♎  6p41     18 ♏  9p59
21 ♐  2a35     23 ♑  8a56     25 ♒  5p33     28 ♓  4a33
30 ♈  5p 2
```

☽->SIGNS (JUL 1975)
```
 3 ♉  4a54      5 ♊  1p59      7 ♋  7p23     10 ♌  9p50
12 ♍ 10p56     14 ♎ 12a21     16 ♏  3a23     18 ♐  8a32
20 ♑  3p46     23 ♒ 12a56     25 ♓ 11a59     28 ♈ 12a27
30 ♉ 12p54
```

☽->SIGNS (AUG 1975)
```
 1 ♊ 11p 2      4 ♋  5a17      6 ♌  7a44      8 ♍  7a54
10 ♎  7a51     12 ♏  9a30     14 ♐  2p 0     16 ♑  9p25
19 ♒  7a 9     21 ♓  6p32     24 ♈  7a 3     26 ♉  8p 4
29 ♊  6a54     31 ♋  2p35
```

☽ PHASES

JAN 1975	FEB 1975	MAR 1975	APR 1975	MAY 1975	JUN 1975	JUL 1975	AUG 1975
1 ○ 5a 0	3 ○ 1a23	1 ○ 1a15	3 ○ 7a25	3 ◑ 12a44	1 ○ 6p23	1 ○ 11a37	3 ◑ 10p34
4 ◑ 2p 4	6 ◐ 10p 1	4 ◐ 7a49	7 ● 9a39	5 ◐ 7p47	5 ◐ 7p49	5 ◐ 10a15	7 ● 6a58
8 ◐ 6a27	11 ● 12a17	8 ● 3p29	11 ● 11a39	7 ● 1a 5	9 ● 1p49	8 ● 11p10	11 ○ 11a48
12 ● 8a14	15 ☽ 3a32	12 ● 6p48	15 ☽ 8a52	14 ☽ 6p14	13 ☽ 12a56	12 ☽ 6a17	13 ○ 3p 6
16 ☽ 8a14	19 ○ 2a39	16 ☽ 7p59	18 ○ 11p41	18 ○ 5a29	16 ○ 9a59	15 ○ 2p47	17 ○ 3p 6
20 ○ 10a15	22 ○ 3p39	20 ○ 8p 5	22 ○ 8a14	21 ○ 2a24	19 ○ 8p51	19 ○ 4a46	21 ○ 2p48
24 ○ 3a15	25 ○ 8p15	24 ○ 1a 3	25 ○ 2p55	24 ◑ 12a51	23 ○ 11a 4	23 ○ 12a29	25 ○ 5p43
27 ○ 10a10		27 ○ 5a36	29 ○ 2a59	28 ○ 5p42	27 ○ 1a25	27 ○ 1a 25	29 ○ 6p20
30 ○ 2p33		30 ☽ 1p24				31 ◐ 3a49	

SEP 1975	OCT 1975	NOV 1975	DEC 1975	JAN 1976	FEB 1976	MAR 1976	APR 1976
☉ -> ♎	☉ -> ♏	☉ -> ♐	☉ -> ♑	☉ -> ♒	☉ -> ♓	☉ -> ♈	☉ -> ♉
23 10a56	23 8p 7	22 5p31	22 6a46	20 5p26	19 7a40	20 6a50	19 6p 3

☽->SIGNS (SEP 1975)
```
 2 ♌  6p 8      4 ♍  5a 3      6 ♎  6p30      8 ♏  5p38
 8 ♐  5p46     10 ♑  8p41     13 ♒  3a11     15 ♓ 12p51
18 ♈ 12a32     20 ♉  1p 7     23 ♊  1a43     25 ♋ 1p13
27 ♌ 10p 7     30 ♎  3a21
```

☽->SIGNS (OCT 1975)
```
 2 ♍  5a 3      4 ♎  4a39      6 ♏  4a 9      8 ♐  5a36
10 ♑  9p10     12 ♒  7p10     15 ♓  6a40     17 ♈  7p20
20 ♉  7a43     22 ♊  6p51     25 ♋  3a57     27 ♌  9p18
29 ♍  5p 7     31 ♎  2p55
```

☽->SIGNS (NOV 1975)
```
 2 ♏  3p 8      4 ♐  4p10      6 ♑  7p45      9 ♒  2a59
11 ♓  1p42     14 ♈  2a17     16 ♉  2p38     19 ♊  1a14
21 ♋  9a36     23 ♌  3p48     25 ♍  7p19     27 ♎ 10p48
30 ♏ 12a37
```

☽->SIGNS (DEC 1975)
```
 2 ♐  2a33      4 ♑  5a58      6 ♒ 12p12      8 ♓  9p52
11 ♈ 10a 6     13 ♉ 10p38     16 ♊  9a12     18 ♋  4p49
20 ♌  9p30     23 ♍  1a28     25 ♎  4a27     27 ♏  6a48
29 ♐ 10p 3     31 ♑  3p17
```

☽->SIGNS (JAN 1976)
```
 2 ♒  9p33      5 ♓  6a35      7 ♈  6p21      9 ♉  7a10
11 ♊  7p45     14 ♋  5a 8     16 ♌  1p45     18 ♍  8a25
21 ♎ 10a11     23 ♏ 12p48     25 ♐  4p51     27 ♑ 10p18
30 ♒  5a34
```

☽->SIGNS (FEB 1976)
```
 1 ♓  2p47      4 ♈  2a17      6 ♉  3p13      9 ♊  3a16
11 ♋ 11a59     13 ♌  4p33     15 ♍  5p59     17 ♎  6p14
19 ♏  7p14     21 ♐ 10p18     24 ♑  3a54     26 ♒ 11a49
28 ♓  9p42
```

☽->SIGNS (MAR 1976)
```
 2 ♈  9a22      4 ♉ 10p18      7 ♊ 10a56      9 ♋  8p59
12 ♌  2a56     14 ♍  4a44     16 ♎  4a44     18 ♏  5a34
20 ♐  9a48     22 ♑  5p20     24 ♒  5a31     27 ♓  3p37
29 ♈  3p37
```

☽->SIGNS (APR 1976)
```
 1 ♉  4a34      3 ♊  5p16      6 ♋  4a 7      8 ♌ 11a37
10 ♍  3p16     12 ♎  3p55     14 ♏  3p15     16 ♐  3p15
18 ♑  5p44     20 ♒ 11p48     23 ♓  9a28     25 ♈  9p37
28 ♉ 10a 4     30 ♊ 11p 5
```

☽ PHASES

SEP 1975	OCT 1975	NOV 1975	DEC 1975	JAN 1976	FEB 1976	MAR 1976	APR 1976
2 ● 8a56	1 ☽ 5p56	3 ☽ 8a 5	2 ● 7p50	1 ☽ 9a40	4 ○ 1a25	4 ☽ 9p36	3 ☽ 3p41
5 ● 2p19	4 ● 10p24	6 ○ 5p48	6 ○ 10a 6	5 ○ 5a 1	8 ○ 5a 5	8 ○ 11p38	7 ○ 2p 2
8 ● 6p55	8 ○ 4a44	10 ○ 1p21	10 ○ 9a11	9 ○ 7a40	12 ○ 1a50	12 ○ 9p36	11 ○ 2a 3
12 ● 6a59	11 ○ 8p15	14 ○ 4p13	14 ○ 12p47	13 ○ 8a36	15 ○ 11a43	15 ○ 9p53	14 ○ 6a49
16 ○ 4a25	15 ○ 8p58	18 ◑ 5p28	18 ○ 9p40	16 ○ 11p47	18 ○ 5p34	19 ○ 2a43	17 ◑ 12p26
20 ○ 6a51	20 ○ 12a 6	22 ◐ 12p35	21 ○ 11p15	20 ○ 8a38	22 ◐ 3a16	22 ◐ 1p55	21 ◐ 2a14
24 ○ 9a32	24 ◑ 12a 1	26 ◐ 1a52	25 ◑ 9a52	23 ◑ 6p 5	25 ◑ 7p52	26 ◑ 10a 1	25 ◑ 1a46
28 ◐ 6a46	27 ◐ 5p 7	29 ◐ 11a 3	28 ◐ 8p35	31 ☽ 1a20	29 ● 6p25	30 ● 12p 8	29 ● 5a20
	31 ◐ 2a22						

MAY 1976	JUN 1976	JUL 1976	AUG 1976	SEP 1976	OCT 1976	NOV 1976	DEC 1976
☉ -> ♊	☉ -> ♋	☉ -> ♌	☉ -> ♍	☉ -> ♎	☉ -> ♏	☉ -> ♐	☉ -> ♑
20 5p21	21 1a24	22 12p19	22 7p19	22 4p49	23 1a59	21 11p22	21 12p36

☽->SIGNS (MAY 1976)
```
 3 ♋  9a54      5 ♌  6p 9      7 ♍ 11p25     10 ♎  1a40
12 ♏  2a 3     14 ♐  2a 4     16 ♑  3a32     18 ♒  7a40
20 ♓  3a32     23 ♈  3a 3     25 ♉  5p 7     28 ♊  5a22
30 ♋  3p39
```

☽->SIGNS (JUN 1976)
```
 1 ♌ 11p38      3 ♍  5a21      6 ♎  9a 0      8 ♏ 11a28
10 ♐  1p46     12 ♑  4p 7     14 ♒  8p10     17 ♓  2a53
19 ♈ 11a32     22 ♉ 12a22     24 ♊ 12p37     27 ♋ 10p29
29 ♌  5a40
```

☽->SIGNS (JUL 1976)
```
 1 ♍ 10a46      3 ♎  2a35      5 ♏  5a55      7 ♐  8p 6
 9 ♑ 10p50     11 ♒  9a15     14 ♓  9a36     16 ♈  7p40
19 ♉  8a11     21 ♊  8p11     24 ♋  6a40     26 ♌  2p 4
28 ♍  5p23     30 ♎  8p14
```

☽->SIGNS (AUG 1976)
```
 1 ♏ 10p56      4 ♐  2a 3      6 ♑  5a55      8 ♒ 10a57
11 ♓  6p 1     13 ♈  3a49     16 ♉  4p 5     18 ♊  4a54
21 ♋  3p34     23 ♌ 10p51     25 ♍  2a 4     27 ♎  3a42
29 ♏  5a 5     31 ♐  7a28
```

☽->SIGNS (SEP 1976)
```
 2 ♑ 11a29      4 ♒  5p20      7 ♓  1a12      9 ♈ 11a18
11 ♉ 11p30     14 ♊ 12p32     17 ♋ 12a 7     19 ♌  8a11
21 ♍ 12p16     23 ♎  1p28     25 ♏  1p34     27 ♐  2p22
29 ♑  5p13
```

☽->SIGNS (OCT 1976)
```
 1 ♒ 10p49      4 ♓  7a10      6 ♈  5p50      9 ♉  6a11
11 ♊  7p15     14 ♋  7a24     16 ♌  4p50     18 ♍ 10p25
21 ♎ 12a27     23 ♏  1p28     25 ♐  1p34     27 ♑ 12a56
29 ♒  5a 5     31 ♓ 12p53
```

☽->SIGNS (NOV 1976)
```
 2 ♈ 11p46      5 ♉ 12p23      8 ♊  1a21     10 ♋  1p36
12 ♌ 11p36     15 ♍ 11a32     17 ♎ 10a34     19 ♏ 11a 4
21 ♐ 11a 4     23 ♑  1p30     25 ♒  5p30     28 ♈  4a36
30 ♈  6a32
```

☽->SIGNS (DEC 1976)
```
 2 ♉  6p41      5 ♊  7a38      7 ♋  7p21     10 ♌  5a12
12 ♍ 12p55     14 ♎  6p13     16 ♏  9p 2     18 ♐ 10p37
20 ♑ 10p54     22 ♒ 11p48     24 ♓  4a36     27 ♈  1p32
30 ♉  1a43
```

☽ PHASES

MAY 1976	JUN 1976	JUL 1976	AUG 1976	SEP 1976	OCT 1976	NOV 1976	DEC 1976
3 ☽ 6a19	1 ☽ 5p15	1 ☽ 1a13	2 ○ 5p 7	4 ○ 12p23	3 ○ 11p40	2 ○ 2p50	2 ○ 9a39
7 ○ 12a17	5 ○ 7a20	4 ○ 12p29	6 ○ 4a13	8 ○ 7a52	7 ○ 11p56	6 ○ 2p52	6 ○ 1p15
10 ○ 9a56	8 ○ 4p12	7 ○ 9p54	9 ○ 6p44	12 ○ 9a33	12 ○ 3a39	10 ◑ 8p59	10 ◑ 12p23
13 ◑ 4p 4	11 ◑ 11p15	11 ◑ 5a52	13 ◐ 4p 8	16 ○ 12p20	16 ◑ 3a59	14 ◑ 5p39	14 ◑ 5a14
16 ◐ 11p 1	15 ◐ 10a52	15 ◐ 12a28	17 ◐ 7p13	20 ◐ 6a33	19 ◐ 6p17	18 ◐ 5a 7	17 ◐ 3p10
20 ◐ 4p22	19 ◐ 8a16	18 ◐ 10a52	21 ● 5p38	23 ● 2p55	23 ● 12a10	21 ● 7a35	20 ● 9p 8
24 ● 6p31	23 ● 11a20	23 ● 3a13	25 ● 6a 1	26 ● 8p24	26 ● 5a11	24 ● 4p29	24 ● 6a40
28 ● 8p47	27 ● 9a50	26 ● 8p39	28 ● 1p29	30 ● 6a13	29 ● 5p 9	28 ● 7a59	28 ● 2a48
		30 ☽ 7a29	31 ○ 10p36				

1977

JAN 1977 — ☉→♒ 19, 11p15
☽→SIGNS
1 ♊ 2p43 · 4 ♋ 2a13 · 6 ♌ 11a21 · 8 ♍ 6p23 · 10 ♎ 11p48 · 13 ♏ 3a44 · 15 ♐ 6a18 · 17 ♑ 8a 2 · 19 ♒ 10a12 · 21 ♓ 2p30 · 23 ♈ 10p20 · 26 ♉ 9a41 · 28 ♊ 10p37 · 31 ♋ 10a20

☽ PHASES
1 ○ 6a32 · 5 ○ 7a11 · 9 ● 1a24 · 12 C 2p55 · 16 ○ 12a33 · 19 ● 9a11 · 22 D 11p40 · 27 ○ 12a12 · 31 ○ 3a12

FEB 1977 — ☉→♓ 18, 1p31
☽→SIGNS
2 ♌ 7p12 · 4 ♍ 1a17 · 7 ♎ 5a36 · 9 ♏ 9a 4 · 11 ♐ 12p11 · 13 ♑ 3p14 · 15 ♒ 6p45 · 17 ♓ 11p45 · 20 ♈ 7a23 · 22 ♉ 6p 6 · 25 ♊ 6a50 · 27 ♋ 7p 2

☽ PHASES
3 ○ 10p56 · 7 ○ 12p12 · 10 ○ 11p 7 · 14 C 9a41 · 17 ○ 10p37 · 21 ● 6p45 · 25 ○ 9p50

MAR 1977 — ☉→♈ 20, 12p43
☽→SIGNS
2 ♌ 4a25 · 4 ♍ 10a19 · 6 ♎ 1p35 · 8 ♏ 3p37 · 10 ♐ 5p42 · 12 ♑ 8p40 · 15 ♒ 1a 0 · 17 ♓ 7a 6 · 19 ♈ 3p23 · 22 ♉ 2a39 · 24 ♊ 2p39 · 27 ♋ 3a17 · 29 ♌ 1p41 · 31 ♍ 8p25

☽ PHASES
1 ○ 9p44 · 5 ○ 12p13 · 10 ○ 9p16 · 12 C 6a35 · 15 ○ 7p21 · 18 ● 1p33 · 23 D 2p23 · 27 ○ 5p27 · 31 ○ 1p11

APR 1977 — ☉→♉ 19, 11p58
☽→SIGNS
2 ♎ 11p39 · 5 ♏ 12a40 · 7 ♐ 1a 9 · 9 ♑ 2a41 · 11 ♒ 6a24 · 13 ♓ 12p50 · 15 ♈ 9p52 · 18 ♉ 9a 3 · 20 ♊ 9p37 · 23 ♋ 10a25 · 25 ♌ 9p43 · 28 ♍ 5a52 · 30 ♎ 10a13

☽ PHASES
3 ○ 11p 9 · 7 ○ 5a11 · 10 ○ 2p15 · 14 C 6a26 · 18 ● 5a36 · 22 D 8a47 · 26 ○ 9a42 · 30 ○ 1a23

MAY 1977 — ☉→♊ 20, 11p15
☽→SIGNS
2 ♏ 11a24 · 4 ♐ 10a59 · 6 ♑ 10a54 · 8 ♒ 1p 0 · 10 ♓ 6p29 · 13 ♈ 3a30 · 15 ♉ 3p 4 · 18 ♊ 3a51 · 20 ♋ 4p36 · 23 ♌ 4a13 · 25 ♍ 1p31 · 27 ♎ 7p29 · 29 ♏ 9p57 · 31 ♐ 9p54

☽ PHASES
3 ○ 8a 4 · 6 ○ 12p38 · 9 ○ 11p 9 · 13 C 7p23 · 17 ● 9p52 · 22 D 12a39 · 25 ○ 10p20 · 29 ○ 10a41

JUN 1977 — ☉→♋ 21, 7a14
☽→SIGNS
2 ♑ 9p 7 · 4 ♒ 9p44 · 7 ♓ 1a36 · 9 ♈ 9a34 · 11 ♉ 8p57 · 14 ♊ 9a50 · 16 ♋ 10p35 · 19 ♌ 9a54 · 21 ♍ 7p29 · 24 ♎ 2a36 · 26 ♏ 6a42 · 28 ♐ 8a 2 · 30 ♑ 7a48

☽ PHASES
1 ○ 3p31 · 4 ○ 8p32 · 8 ○ 10a 7 · 12 C 11a 6 · 16 ● 1p23 · 20 D 1p36 · 24 ○ 7a44 · 27 ○ 10p24

JUL 1977 — ☉→♌ 22, 6p 4
☽→SIGNS
2 ♒ 7a56 · 4 ♓ 10a31 · 6 ♈ 5p 3 · 9 ♉ 3a33 · 11 ♊ 4p15 · 14 ♋ 4a50 · 16 ♌ 3p51 · 19 ♍ 12a59 · 21 ♎ 8a10 · 23 ♏ 1p14 · 25 ♐ 4p 5 · 27 ♑ 5p15 · 29 ♒ 6p 5 · 31 ♓ 8p24

☽ PHASES
4 ○ 5a54 · 8 ○ 11p40 · 12 C 2a 2 · 16 ● 3a37 · 19 D 11p58 · 23 ○ 11p24 · 26 ○ 11p24 · 30 ○ 5a53

AUG 1977 — ☉→♍ 23, 1a 1
☽→SIGNS
1 ♈ 1a54 · 3 ♉ 11a18 · 5 ♊ 11p30 · 8 ♋ 12p 4 · 10 ♌ 10p57 · 13 ♍ 7a26 · 15 ♎ 1p49 · 17 ♏ 1p49 · 19 ♐ 10p 3 · 21 ♑ 12a31 · 24 ♒ 2a41 · 26 ♓ 5a47 · 28 ♈ 11a12 · 30 ♉ —

☽ PHASES
2 ○ 5p37 · 6 ○ 3p40 · 10 C 6p27 · 14 ● 4p31 · 18 D 8a25 · 21 ○ 8p 5 · 25 ○ 5a 4 · 28 ○ 3p10

1977 – 1978

SEP 1977 — ☉→♎ 22, 10p30
☽→SIGNS
1 ♉ 7p52 · 4 ♊ 7a27 · 6 ♋ 8p 3 · 9 ♌ 7a14 · 11 ♍ 3p35 · 13 ♎ 9p 8 · 16 ♏ 12a46 · 18 ♐ 3a28 · 20 ♑ 6a 4 · 22 ♒ 9a12 · 24 ♓ 1p30 · 27 ♈ 7p41 · 29 ♉ 4a22

☽ PHASES
1 ○ 8a14 · 5 ○ 9a33 · 9 C 10a47 · 13 D 3p48 · 20 ○ 1a18 · 23 ○ 12p 8 · 27 ● 3a18

OCT 1977 — ☉→♏ 23, 7a41
☽→SIGNS
1 ♊ 3p34 · 4 ♋ 4a 9 · 6 ♌ 3p58 · 9 ♍ 12a59 · 11 ♎ 6a30 · 13 ♏ 9a11 · 15 ♐ 10a27 · 17 ♑ 11a51 · 19 ♒ 1p28 · 21 ♓ 4p29 · 24 ♈ 2a34 · 26 ♉ 11a53 · 29 ♊ 11p 8 · 31 ♋ 11a40

☽ PHASES
1 ○ 1a30 · 5 ○ 4a21 · 9 C 2a38 · 12 D 3p31 · 19 ○ 7p46 · 22 ○ 9p59 · 26 ○ 6p36 · 30 ● 8p31

NOV 1977 — ☉→♐ 22, 5a 8
☽→SIGNS
3 ♌ 12a 3 · 5 ♍ 10a17 · 7 ♎ 4p51 · 9 ♏ 7p42 · 11 ♐ 8p 4 · 13 ♑ 7p51 · 15 ♒ 9p 0 · 18 ♓ 12a59 · 20 ♈ 8a13 · 22 ♉ 6p10 · 25 ♊ 5a49 · 27 ♋ 6p20 · 30 ♌ 6a53

☽ PHASES
3 ○ 10p59 · 7 C 5p34 · 11 ● 2a10 · 14 D 7a 9 · 17 ○ 4p53 · 21 ○ 11a29 · 25 ○ 12p32 · 29 ● 9p53

DEC 1977 — ☉→♑ 21, 6p24
☽→SIGNS
2 ♍ 6p 6 · 5 ♎ 2a18 · 7 ♏ 6a33 · 9 ♐ 7a22 · 11 ♑ 6a26 · 13 ♒ 6a 0 · 15 ♓ 8a 7 · 17 ♈ 2p11 · 20 ♉ 11p54 · 22 ♊ 11a52 · 25 ♋ 12a30 · 27 ♌ 12p52 · 30 ♍ 12a14

☽ PHASES
3 ○ 4p16 · 7 C 7a 1 · 11 ● 8p33 · 13 D 5p 4 · 17 ○ 6a37 · 21 ○ 4a32 · 25 ○ 7a49 · 29 ● 10a 7

JAN 1978 — ☉→♒ 20, 5a 5
☽→SIGNS
1 ♎ 9a32 · 3 ♏ 3p35 · 5 ♐ 6p40 · 7 ♑ 6p55 · 9 ♒ 6p47 · 11 ♓ 5p51 · 13 ♈ 10p 5 · 16 ♉ 6a31 · 18 ♊ 6p51 · 21 ♋ 6a51 · 23 ♌ 7p 4 · 26 ♍ 5a56 · 28 ♎ 2p27 · 30 ♏ 10p 4

☽ PHASES
2 ○ 7a 7 · 5 ○ 6p32 · 12 ● 11p10 · 18 D 5p11 · 20 ○ 12a 2 · 24 ○ 2a56 · 28 ○ 1a58 · 31 ○ 6p51

FEB 1978 — ☉→♓ 18, 7p21
☽→SIGNS
2 ♐ 2a14 · 4 ♑ 3a50 · 6 ♒ 4a 4 · 8 ♓ 4a48 · 10 ♈ 7a57 · 12 ♉ 2p51 · 15 ♊ 1a24 · 17 ♋ 1p56 · 20 ♌ 2a10 · 22 ♍ 12p40 · 24 ♎ 9p 4 · 27 ♏ 3a28

☽ PHASES
4 ○ 4a 9 · 10 ● 8p19 · 18 D 8p17 · 22 ○ 8p27 · 26 ○ 2p41

MAR 1978 — ☉→♈ 20, 6p34
☽→SIGNS
1 ♐ 8a 2 · 3 ♑ 10a58 · 5 ♒ 12p51 · 7 ♓ 2p46 · 9 ♈ 6p 8 · 12 ♉ 2a18 · 14 ♊ 9a49 · 16 ♋ 9p49 · 19 ♌ 10a12 · 21 ♍ 8p50 · 24 ♎ 10a 1 · 26 ♏ 10a 1 · 28 ♐ 1p38 · 30 ♑ 4p24

☽ PHASES
2 ○ 3a34 · 5 C 12p29 · 12 ● 1p 4 · 20 D 8p50 · 22 ○ 9p37 · 26 ○ 1p21 · 28 ○ 12a16 · 31 ○ 10a11

APR 1978 — ☉→♉ 20, 5a50
☽→SIGNS
2 ♒ 7p 5 · 4 ♓ 10p21 · 6 ♈ 2a21 · 8 ♉ 9a22 · 10 ♊ 6p28 · 13 ♋ 5a59 · 15 ♌ 6p31 · 18 ♍ 5a44 · 20 ♎ 1p53 · 22 ♏ 6p39 · 24 ♐ 9p 0 · 26 ♑ 10p28 · 29 ♒ 12a28

☽ PHASES
3 D 8p29 · 7 ○ 10a15 · 11 C 6a39 · 15 ● 8a56 · 19 D 6a38 · 22 ○ 11p11 · 26 ○ 7p29 · 29 ○ 4p 2

1978

MAY 1978 — ☉→♊ 21, 5a 9
☽→SIGNS
1 ♓ 4a 0 · 3 ♈ 9a27 · 5 ♉ 4p52 · 8 ♊ 2a19 · 10 ♋ 1p42 · 13 ♌ 2a17 · 15 ♍ 2p15 · 17 ♎ 11p25 · 20 ♏ 4a39 · 22 ♐ 6a31 · 24 ♑ 6a42 · 26 ♒ 7a10 · 28 ♓ 9a37 · 30 ♈ 2p53

☽ PHASES
3 C 5a 8 · 6 ● 11p47 · 11 D 12a 4 · 15 ○ 10p38 · 18 ○ 10p38 · 22 ○ 8a17 · 25 ○ 1p32 · 28 ○ 10p31

JUN 1978 — ☉→♋ 21, 1p10
☽→SIGNS
1 ♉ 10p50 · 4 ♊ 8a54 · 6 ♋ 8p30 · 9 ♌ 9a 6 · 11 ♍ 9p35 · 14 ♎ 7a56 · 16 ♏ 2p50 · 18 ♐ 5p 1 · 20 ♑ 4p52 · 22 ♒ 4p 8 · 24 ♓ 4p57 · 26 ♈ 8p53 · 29 ♉ 4a21

☽ PHASES
1 C 3p10 · 5 ● 2p 2 · 9 D 4p35 · 14 ○ 5p44 · 17 ○ 9p30 · 20 ○ 7p45 · 23 ○ 6a44

JUL 1978 — ☉→♌ 23, 12a 1
☽→SIGNS
1 ♊ 2p38 · 4 ♋ 2a34 · 6 ♌ 3p13 · 9 ♍ 3a45 · 11 ♎ 2p48 · 13 ♏ 10p47 · 16 ♐ 2a50 · 18 ♑ 3a33 · 20 ♒ 2a42 · 22 ♓ 2a26 · 24 ♈ 4a46 · 26 ♉ 10a51 · 28 ♊ 8p31 · 31 ♋ 8a28

☽ PHASES
1 C 3a 4 · 4 ● 4a51 · 9 D 7a39 · 14 ○ 5a49 · 16 ○ 5p47 · 19 ○ 10p 5 · 23 ○ 3a24 · 26 ○ 5p31 · 30 C 5p 6

AUG 1978 — ☉→♍ 23, 6a57
☽→SIGNS
2 ♌ 9p10 · 5 ♍ 9a29 · 7 ♎ 8p30 · 10 ♏ 5a12 · 12 ♐ 10a43 · 14 ♑ 1p 3 · 16 ♒ 1p10 · 18 ♓ 1p10 · 20 ♈ 2p30 · 22 ♉ 7p30 · 25 ♊ 3a31 · 27 ♋ 2p 9 · 30 ♌ 3a40

☽ PHASES
3 ● 8p 1 · 6 D 10p20 · 12 ○ 12a30 · 14 ○ 5a14 · 18 ○ 5a14 · 21 ○ 7a18 · 24 ○ 12a 8 · 29 C 9a13

SEP 1978 — ☉→♎ 23, 4a26
☽→SIGNS
1 ♍ 3p47 · 4 ♎ 2a16 · 6 ♏ 10a38 · 8 ♐ 4p40 · 10 ♑ 8p20 · 12 ♒ 10p 9 · 14 ♓ 11p10 · 17 ♈ 12a50 · 19 ♉ 4a43 · 21 ♊ 11a31 · 23 ♋ 10p31 · 26 ♌ 11a 2 · 28 ♍ 11p11

☽ PHASES
2 ● 11a 9 · 5 D 5p26 · 10 ○ 10p20 · 13 ○ 6a54 · 18 ○ 2p 1 · 20 ○ 2a20 · 24 ○ 12a 8 · 27 C 9p26 · 31 ○ 3p 7

OCT 1978 — ☉→♏ 23, 1p38
☽→SIGNS
1 ♎ 9a17 · 3 ♏ 4p48 · 6 ♐ 1a53 · 8 ♑ 4a43 · 10 ♒ 6a16 · 12 ♓ 7a13 · 14 ♈ 10a 6 · 16 ♉ 2p22 · 18 ♊ 9p 5 · 21 ♋ 6a53 · 23 ♌ 7p 4 · 26 ♍ 7a32 · 28 ♎ 5p51 · 31 ♏ 12a53

☽ PHASES
2 ● 1a41 · 5 D 4a38 · 10 ○ 3p 0 · 14 ○ 1a10 · 16 ○ 6p20 · 20 ○ 6p20 · 23 ○ 7p34 · 27 C 9p26 · 30 ● 3a20

NOV 1978 — ☉→♐ 22, 11a 5
☽→SIGNS
2 ♐ 5a 4 · 4 ♑ 7a41 · 6 ♒ 10a 4 · 8 ♓ 1p 6 · 10 ♈ 5p12 · 12 ♉ 10p35 · 15 ♊ 5a45 · 17 ♋ 3p16 · 20 ♌ 3a 9 · 22 ♍ 3p57 · 25 ♎ 3a 7 · 27 ♏ 10a39 · 29 ♐ 2p24

☽ PHASES
2 D 1a48 · 10 ○ 11p12 · 14 ○ 3p 0 · 18 ○ 1p 5 · 22 ○ 4p24 · 26 C 3p10 · 30 ● 3a20

DEC 1978 — ☉→♑ 22, 12a22
☽→SIGNS
1 ♑ 4p44 · 3 ♒ 4p36 · 5 ♓ 7p34 · 7 ♈ 10p40 · 10 ♉ 3a 8 · 12 ♊ 12p55 · 14 ♋ 12p55 · 17 ♌ 11p34 · 19 ♍ 11p34 · 22 ♎ 11a40 · 24 ♏ 8p32 · 26 ♐ 2a16 · 29 ♑ 6a56 · 31 ♒ 1a53

☽ PHASES
3 D 10a13 · 6 ○ 7p34 · 10 ○ 10a48 · 14 ○ 7a31 · 18 ○ 9a34 · 22 ○ 12p42 · 25 C 6a56 · 29 ● 2p36

JAN 1979

☉ → ♒ 20 11a 1

☽ → SIGNS
- 2 ♓ 2a 8
- 4 ♈ 4a41
- 6 ♉ 10a18
- 8 ♊ 6p43
- 11 ♋ 5a15
- 13 ♌ 5p16
- 16 ♍ 6a10
- 18 ♎ 6p41
- 21 ♏ 4a51
- 23 ♐ 11a 8
- 25 ♑ 1p28
- 27 ♒ 1p12
- 29 ♓ 12p25
- 31 ♈ 1p12

☽ PHASES
- 1 ☽ 7p37
- 4 ● 6a15
- 9 ○ 1a13
- 13 ◐ 2a 9
- 17 ○ 5a59
- 21 ◑ 8a24
- 24 ◐ 8p10
- 28 ● 1a20
- 31 ☽ 6a32

FEB 1979

☉ → ♓ 19 1a14

☽ → SIGNS
- 2 ♉ 5p 3
- 5 ♊ 12a33
- 7 ♋ 11a 6
- 9 ♌ 11p26
- 12 ♍ 12p18
- 15 ♎ 12a37
- 17 ♏ 11a12
- 19 ♐ 6p51
- 21 ♑ 11p 1
- 24 ♒ 12a12
- 26 ♓ 11p53
- 27 ♈ 11p54

☽ PHASES
- 3 ● 7p37
- 7 ○ 6p15
- 11 ○ 9p40
- 16 ○ 12a12
- 19 ◑ 8p17
- 23 ◐ 6a52
- 26 ☽ 11a46

MAR 1979

☉ → ♈ 21 12a22

☽ → SIGNS
- 2 ♉ 2a 9
- 4 ♊ 7a58
- 6 ♋ 5p34
- 9 ♌ 5a48
- 11 ♍ 6p43
- 14 ♎ 6a42
- 16 ♏ 4p49
- 19 ♐ 12a38
- 21 ♑ 5a57
- 23 ♒ 8a52
- 25 ♓ 10a 5
- 27 ♈ 10a48
- 29 ♉ 12p36
- 31 ♊ 5p 9

☽ PHASES
- 1 ○ 6p56
- 5 ◐ 11a23
- 9 ○ 1p 3
- 13 ○ 4p15
- 17 ○ 2p41
- 21 ◑ 6a22
- 24 ◐ 3p31
- 27 ● 10p 0
- 31 ☽ 8a35

APR 1979

☉ → ♉ 20 11a36

☽ → SIGNS
- 3 ♋ 1a24
- 5 ♌ 12p58
- 8 ♍ 1a52
- 10 ♎ 1p45
- 12 ♏ 11p16
- 15 ♐ 6a18
- 17 ♑ 11a23
- 19 ♒ 3p 2
- 21 ♓ 5p41
- 23 ♈ 7p51
- 25 ♉ 10p27
- 28 ♊ 2a49
- 30 ♋ 10a12

☽ PHASES
- 4 ○ 4a58
- 8 ◐ 8a 9
- 12 ○ 8a15
- 15 ○ 11p31
- 19 ◑ 1p31
- 22 ◐ 10p48
- 26 ● 1p17
- 29 ☽ 11p17

MAY 1979

☉ → ♊ 21 10a54

☽ → SIGNS
- 2 ♌ 8p57
- 5 ♍ 9a42
- 7 ♎ 9p48
- 10 ♏ 7a10
- 12 ♐ 1p25
- 14 ♑ 5p26
- 16 ♒ 8p26
- 18 ♓ 11p19
- 21 ♈ 2a30
- 23 ♉ 6a21
- 25 ♊ 11a28
- 28 ♋ 6p51
- 30 ♌ 5a 8

☽ PHASES
- 3 ○ 11p26
- 6 ○ 1a55
- 11 ○ 9p 1
- 14 ○ 9a 2
- 18 ○ 6p57
- 21 ◑ 5a37
- 25 ● 7p 1
- 29 ☽ 2p59

JUN 1979

☉ → ♋ 21 6p56

☽ → SIGNS
- 1 ♍ 5p41
- 4 ♎ 6a12
- 6 ♏ 4p 5
- 9 ♐ 10p15
- 11 ♑ 1a24
- 13 ♒ 3a 6
- 15 ♓ 4a56
- 17 ♈ 7a53
- 19 ♉ 12p18
- 21 ♊ 6p23
- 24 ♋ 2a25
- 26 ♌ 12p47
- 29 ♍ 1a14

☽ PHASES
- 2 ○ 5p38
- 6 ○ 5p13
- 10 ○ 6a56
- 13 ○ 3p 1
- 17 ◑ 12a 1
- 20 ◐ 12p59
- 24 ● 6a58
- 28 ☽ 7a24

JUL 1979

☉ → ♌ 23 5a49

☽ → SIGNS
- 1 ♎ 2p 8
- 3 ♏ 12a57
- 6 ♐ 7a56
- 8 ♑ 11a 8
- 10 ♒ 11a59
- 12 ♓ 12p23
- 14 ♈ 1p57
- 16 ♉ 5p43
- 19 ♊ 12a 0
- 21 ♋ 8a41
- 23 ♌ 7p30
- 26 ♍ 8a 1
- 28 ♎ 9p 6
- 31 ♏ 8a46

☽ PHASES
- 2 ○ 10a24
- 6 ○ 5a47
- 9 ○ 3p 0
- 13 ○ 8p41
- 16 ◑ 5a59
- 19 ◐ 10p 4
- 23 ● 8p41
- 27 ☽ 11p51

AUG 1979

☉ → ♍ 23 12p47

☽ → SIGNS
- 1 ♐ 5p 6
- 4 ♑ 9p23
- 6 ♒ 10p28
- 8 ♓ 10p10
- 10 ♈ 10p10
- 13 ♉ 12a22
- 15 ♊ 5a41
- 17 ♋ 2p17
- 20 ♌ 1a29
- 22 ♍ 2p11
- 25 ♎ 3a14
- 27 ♏ 3p13
- 30 ♐ 12a40

☽ PHASES
- 1 ○ 12a58
- 4 ○ 4p 8
- 7 ○ 10p21
- 11 ○ 3a12
- 14 ○ 2p 2
- 18 ◑ 9a55
- 22 ● 12p11
- 25 ● 3p27
- 30 ○ 1p 9

SEP 1979

☉ → ♎ 23 10a17

☽ → SIGNS
- 1 ♑ 6a34
- 3 ♒ 8a59
- 5 ♓ 9a 3
- 7 ♈ 8a29
- 9 ♉ 9a43
- 11 ♊ 12p54
- 13 ♋ 8p27
- 16 ♌ 7a25
- 18 ♍ 8p16
- 21 ♎ 9a11
- 23 ♏ 8p54
- 26 ♐ 6a36
- 28 ♑ 1p40
- 30 ♒ 5p49

☽ PHASES
- 3 ○ 1a 3
- 6 ○ 5a59
- 9 ○ 11a32
- 17 ○ 1a 5
- 21 ○ 4a47
- 25 ◑ 5a26
- 28 ● 11p20

OCT 1979

☉ → ♏ 23 7p28

☽ → SIGNS
- 2 ♓ 7p23
- 4 ♈ 7p28
- 6 ♉ 7p 7
- 8 ♊ 10p 7
- 11 ♋ 4a 9
- 13 ♌ 2p12
- 16 ♍ 2a52
- 18 ♎ 3p45
- 21 ♏ 3a 4
- 23 ♐ 12p 9
- 25 ♑ 7p11
- 28 ♒ 12a17
- 30 ♓ 3a29

☽ PHASES
- 2 ○ 9a18
- 5 ○ 2p36
- 8 ○ 10p33
- 11 ◑ 3p 2
- 16 ○ 4p24
- 20 ◑ 9p56
- 24 ● 6p26
- 28 ● 8a 6
- 31 ○ 5p30

NOV 1979

☉ → ♐ 22 4p55

☽ → SIGNS
- 1 ♈ 5a 9
- 3 ♉ 6a16
- 5 ♊ 8a26
- 7 ♋ 1p24
- 9 ♌ 10p15
- 12 ♍ 10a21
- 14 ♎ 11p17
- 17 ♏ 10a30
- 19 ♐ 6p57
- 22 ♑ 1a 2
- 24 ♒ 5a37
- 26 ♓ 9a17
- 28 ♈ 12p17
- 30 ♉ 2p55

☽ PHASES
- 4 ○ 12a47
- 7 ○ 12p53
- 11 ○ 11a24
- 19 ○ 10a39
- 22 ◑ 1p 8
- 26 ● 6a42
- 29 ○ 12p 7

DEC 1979

☉ → ♑ 22 6a10

☽ → SIGNS
- 2 ♊ 6p 2
- 4 ♋ 11p 2
- 7 ♌ 6p33
- 9 ♍ 7a29
- 12 ♎ 8p13
- 14 ♏ 8a55
- 17 ♐ 3a37
- 19 ♑ 8a55
- 23 ♒ 2p50
- 25 ♓ 5p40
- 27 ♈ 9p 8
- 30 ♉ 1a32

☽ PHASES
- 3 ○ 1p 8
- 6 ○ 6a42
- 10 ○ 11a24
- 19 ◐ 10a39
- 22 ◑ 2p 7
- 26 ● 12a11
- 29 ○ 12p 7

JAN 1980

☉ → ♒ 20 4p49

☽ → SIGNS
- 1 ♊ 7a29
- 3 ♋ 9p47
- 6 ♌ 2a49
- 8 ♍ 3p38
- 11 ♎ 3a56
- 13 ♏ 1p17
- 16 ♐ 6p52
- 18 ♑ 8a43
- 19 ♒ 10p33
- 21 ♓ 11p52
- 24 ♈ 2a32
- 26 ♉ 7a35
- 28 ♊ 5a10
- 30 ♋ 11p 9

☽ PHASES
- 2 ○ 4a 2
- 6 ○ 3a 7
- 10 ○ 6a50
- 14 ◐ 4p20
- 20 ○ 9a 3
- 22 ◑ 7p14
- 26 ● 2p15

FEB 1980

☉ → ♓ 19 7a 2

☽ → SIGNS
- 2 ♌ 10a21
- 4 ♍ 11p 4
- 7 ♎ 11a46
- 9 ♏ 9p42
- 12 ♐ 5a12
- 14 ♑ 8a20
- 16 ♒ 8a54
- 18 ♓ 8a43
- 20 ♈ 9a35
- 22 ♉ 12p58
- 25 ♊ 7p35
- 27 ♋ 5a10
- 29 ♌ 4p53

☽ PHASES
- 5 ○ 12a12
- 9 ○ 2a35
- 12 ◐ 7p59
- 16 ○ 3a51
- 18 ◐ 4p20
- 20 ◑ 9a 3
- 26 ● 2p15

MAR 1980

☉ → ♈ 20 6a10

☽ → SIGNS
- 3 ♍ 5a40
- 5 ♎ 6p23
- 8 ♏ 5a39
- 10 ♐ 2p 2
- 12 ♑ 6p45
- 14 ♒ 8p11
- 16 ♓ 7p41
- 18 ♈ 7p18
- 20 ♉ 8p48
- 23 ♊ 1a56
- 25 ♋ 10a59
- 27 ♌ 10p52
- 30 ♎ 11a49

☽ PHASES
- 1 ◐ 4p 0
- 5 ○ 7p35
- 9 ◐ 8a25
- 13 ○ 1p56
- 19 ◑ 5p20
- 22 ◑ 7p32
- 27 ● 6a38
- 31 ○ 10a 4

APR 1980

☉ → ♉ 19 5p23

☽ → SIGNS
- 2 ♏ 12a22
- 4 ♐ 11a35
- 6 ♑ 8p43
- 9 ♒ 3a 0
- 11 ♓ 6a 7
- 13 ♈ 6a40
- 15 ♉ 6a11
- 17 ♊ 6a41
- 19 ♋ 10a12
- 21 ♌ 5p52
- 24 ♎ 5a12
- 26 ♏ 6p10
- 29 ♐ 6a35

☽ PHASES
- 4 ○ 11a42
- 8 ◐ 7a 7
- 11 ◑ 5p57
- 14 ○ 10p47
- 18 ◑ 10p 0
- 26 ○ 12a 5
- 30 ◐ 2a36

MAY 1980

☉ → ♊ 20 4p42

☽ → SIGNS
- 1 ♐ 5p22
- 4 ♑ 2a14
- 6 ♒ 9a 4
- 8 ♓ 1p34
- 10 ♈ 3p45
- 12 ♉ 4p24
- 14 ♊ 5p 8
- 16 ♋ 7p52
- 19 ♌ 2a15
- 21 ♍ 12p33
- 24 ♎ 1a11
- 26 ♏ 1p37
- 29 ♐ 12a 5
- 31 ♑ 8a15

☽ PHASES
- 4 ○ 12a10
- 7 ○ 3p51
- 11 ○ 1a 4
- 14 ○ 7a 1
- 17 ◑ 5p23
- 21 ● 2p16
- 25 ○ 5p17
- 29 ○ 4p28

JUN 1980

☉ → ♋ 21 12a47

☽ → SIGNS
- 2 ♒ 2p30
- 4 ♓ 7p10
- 6 ♈ 10p24
- 8 ♉ 12a30
- 11 ♊ 2a23
- 13 ♋ 5a30
- 15 ♌ 11a22
- 17 ♍ 8p47
- 20 ♎ 8a55
- 22 ♏ 9p27
- 25 ♐ 8a 2
- 27 ♑ 4p36
- 29 ♒ 9p 4

☽ PHASES
- 2 ○ 9a28
- 5 ○ 9a46
- 9 ◐ 6a46
- 12 ● 3p30
- 16 ☽ 7a 1
- 19 ○ 7a32
- 24 ○ 9a19
- 28 ○ 4a 2

JUL 1980

☉ → ♌ 22 11a42

☽ → SIGNS
- 2 ♓ 2a49
- 4 ♈ 3a47
- 6 ♉ 6a30
- 8 ♊ 9a34
- 10 ♋ 1p45
- 12 ♌ 8p 3
- 15 ♍ 5a30
- 17 ♎ 4p55
- 20 ♏ 5a33
- 22 ♐ 4p42
- 25 ♑ 12a45
- 27 ♒ 5a35
- 29 ♓ 8a11
- 31 ♈ 9a53

☽ PHASES
- 1 ○ 4p32
- 4 ○ 7p35
- 8 ◐ 12p26
- 14 ○ 1a46
- 15 ☽ 10p23
- 18 ○ 5p28
- 22 ○ 12p55
- 25 ○ 10p42
- 29 ○ 4a19

AUG 1980

☉ → ♍ 22 6p41

☽ → SIGNS
- 2 ♉ 11a55
- 4 ♊ 3p10
- 7 ♋ 8p12
- 9 ♌ 3a24
- 11 ♍ 12p55
- 14 ♎ 12a32
- 16 ♏ 1p15
- 19 ♐ 1a 8
- 21 ♑ 10a12
- 23 ♒ 3p53
- 25 ♓ 5p44
- 27 ♈ 6p11
- 29 ♉ 6p41
- 31 ♊ 8p50

☽ PHASES
- 3 ○ 7a 1
- 7 ○ 7p35
- 10 ◐ 2p10
- 14 ● 2p59
- 18 ○ 5p28
- 22 ○ 10p42
- 25 ○ 10p42
- 29 ○ 4a19

SEP 1980

☉ → ♎ 22 4p 9

☽ → SIGNS
- 3 ♋ 1a40
- 5 ♌ 9a22
- 7 ♍ 7p31
- 10 ♎ 7a22
- 12 ♏ 8p 6
- 15 ♐ 8a28
- 17 ♑ 6p45
- 20 ♒ 1a31
- 22 ♓ 4a27
- 24 ♈ 4a37
- 26 ♉ 3a53
- 28 ♊ 4a21
- 30 ♋ 7a47

☽ PHASES
- 1 ○ 1p 8
- 5 ○ 5a35
- 9 ◐ 5a 1
- 13 ● 8a 1
- 17 ○ 8a55
- 24 ○ 7a 8
- 30 ○ 10p18

OCT 1980

☉ → ♏ 23 1a18

☽ → SIGNS
- 2 ♌ 2p57
- 5 ♍ 1a31
- 7 ♎ 2a15
- 9 ♏ 2p38
- 12 ♐ 3a 1
- 14 ♑ 1p43
- 17 ♒ 9a54
- 19 ♓ 2p32
- 21 ♈ 3p43
- 23 ♉ 3p17
- 25 ♊ 2p19
- 27 ♋ 4p 0
- 29 ♌ 9p39

☽ PHASES
- 4 ◐ 7p12
- 7 ● 3p35
- 13 ☽ 12a40
- 16 ○ 10p47
- 20 ○ 11a16
- 23 ○ 3p52
- 26 ○ 9p 4
- 30 ◐ 11a33

NOV 1980

☉ → ♐ 22 10p42

☽ → SIGNS
- 1 ♍ 7a19
- 3 ♎ 7p32
- 6 ♏ 8a19
- 8 ♐ 8p26
- 11 ♑ 7a15
- 13 ♒ 4p10
- 15 ♓ 10p21
- 18 ♈ 1a22
- 20 ♉ 1a51
- 22 ♊ 1a27
- 24 ♋ 2a19
- 26 ♌ 6a23
- 28 ♍ 2p38

☽ PHASES
- 3 ◐ 12p20
- 7 ● 3p43
- 11 ☽ 4p13
- 15 ○ 8p49
- 18 ○ 8p49
- 21 ○ 1p 9
- 26 ○ 9a58
- 30 ◐ 4a59

DEC 1980

☉ → ♑ 21 11a57

☽ → SIGNS
- 1 ♎ 2a14
- 3 ♏ 3p 0
- 6 ♐ 2a58
- 8 ♑ 1p12
- 10 ♒ 9p36
- 13 ♓ 4a22
- 15 ♈ 8a22
- 17 ♉ 11a40
- 19 ♊ 1p 3
- 21 ♋ 4p34
- 23 ♌ 9p30
- 25 ♍ 11p33
- 28 ♎ 10a 5
- 30 ♏ 10p36

☽ PHASES
- 3 ◐ 7a59
- 7 ● 9a35
- 11 ☽ 6a 2
- 15 ○ 4p47
- 17 ○ 5p47
- 21 ○ 1p 8
- 25 ○ 2a19
- 29 ◐ 1a40

JAN 1981 – AUG 1981

	JAN 1981	FEB 1981	MAR 1981	APR 1981	MAY 1981	JUN 1981	JUL 1981	AUG 1981
☉ →	♒	♓	♈	♉	♊	♋	♌	♍
	19 10p37	18 12p52	20 12p 3	19 11p19	20 10p40	21 6a45	22 5p40	23 12a39

☽ → SIGNS

JAN 1981	FEB 1981	MAR 1981	APR 1981	MAY 1981	JUN 1981	JUL 1981	AUG 1981
2 ♐ 10a42	1 ♑ 5a37	2 ♒ 10p51	1 ♓ 1p41	1 ♈ 1a58	1 ♊ 11a49	2 ♌ 11p47	1 ♍ 1p55
4 ♑ 8p41	4 ♒ 12p55	5 ♓ 3a12	3 ♈ 3p25	3 ♉ 2a 0	3 ♋ 11a39	4 ♍ 4a26	3 ♎ 9p24
7 ♒ 4a13	6 ♓ 5p22	7 ♈ 4a49	5 ♉ 3p 4	5 ♊ 1a 1	5 ♌ 1p43	7 ♎ 12p42	6 ♏ 7a58
9 ♓ 9a47	8 ♈ 8p 2	9 ♉ 5a23	7 ♊ 2p47	7 ♋ 1a 0	7 ♍ 7p26	9 ♏ 12a 2	8 ♐ 8p23
11 ♈ 1p44	9 ♉ 10p11	11 ♊ 6a42	9 ♋ 4p34	9 ♌ 4a40	10 ♎ 4a55	12 ♐ 12p35	11 ♑ 8a20
13 ♉ 4p45	11 ♊ 12a51	13 ♋ 10a 6	11 ♌ 9p37	11 ♍ 11a55	12 ♏ 4p55	14 ♑ 12a20	13 ♒ 5p56
15 ♊ 7p18	14 ♋ 4a43	15 ♌ 4p 3	14 ♍ 5a57	13 ♎ 10p24	15 ♐ 5a32	17 ♒ 10a 2	16 ♓ 12a35
17 ♋ 10p 8	16 ♌ 10a10	17 ♍ 11p30	16 ♎ 4p38	16 ♏ 10a38	17 ♑ 5p21	19 ♓ 5p26	18 ♈ 4a49
20 ♌ 2a21	18 ♍ 5p34	20 ♎ 10a31	19 ♏ 4a39	18 ♐ 11p14	20 ♒ 3a36	21 ♈ 10p44	20 ♉ 7a44
22 ♍ 9a 3	21 ♎ 3a12	22 ♏ 10p14	21 ♐ 5p15	21 ♑ 11a20	22 ♓ 11a44	24 ♉ 1a42	22 ♊ 10a18
24 ♎ 6p45	23 ♏ 2p55	25 ♐ 10a51	24 ♑ 5a31	23 ♒ 10p 1	24 ♈ 5p18	26 ♊ 4a42	24 ♋ 1p17
27 ♏ 6a49	26 ♐ 3a29	27 ♑ 10p53	26 ♒ 3p 2	26 ♓ 6a 6	26 ♉ 8p17	28 ♋ 6a34	26 ♌ 5p10
29 ♐ 7p12	28 ♑ 2p47	30 ♒ 8a16	28 ♓ 10p56	28 ♈ 10a44	28 ♊ 9p21	30 ♌ 9a21	28 ♍ 10p32
				30 ♉ 12p11	30 ♋ 9p57		31 ♎ 6a 3

☽ PHASES

JAN 1981	FEB 1981	MAR 1981	APR 1981	MAY 1981	JUN 1981	JUL 1981	AUG 1981
2 (4a36	1 (12a26	2 (5p55	3 ● 11p20	2 ● 6a32	1 ● 2p 3	1 ○ 11p20	3) 2p29
6 ● 2a24	4 ● 5p14	4 ● 6a31	6) 2a24	5) 1p42	5) 1a 3	6 ○ 2a32	7 ○ 2p26
9) 5p47	8) 3a34	7) 7p49	10 ○ 5p22	9 ○ 6a34	9 ○ 9p40	10 ○ 4a 1	11 ○ 4p22
13 ○ 5a10	11 ○ 12p49	11 ○ 6a11	14 ○ 4p18	13 ○ 7a53	13 ○ 12a 5	13 ○ 10p47	15 ○ 11a13
16 ○ 2p54	15 ○ 12p43	15 ○ 1a43	18 ○ 7p 4	17 ○ 10a 5	16 ○ 11p39	16) 11p39	18 ○ 11p47
20 ○ 2p48	18 ○ 5p59	19 ○ 2a59	22 ● 8p31	21 ● 8a 4	20 ● 4p52	20 (4p52	22 ● 9a16
23 ○ 9p17	22 ○ 5p15	23 ○ 5a56	26 (4p 1	24 (11p25	24 (4a40	24 (4a40	25 (7p45
27 (11p19	25 ● 8p14	27 ● 5a15	30 (2a 8	28 (7a56	27 (1p21	27 ● 1p22	29 ● 9a44
		30 (6p34			30) 10p52	30 ● 2p54	

SEP 1981 – APR 1982

	SEP 1981	OCT 1981	NOV 1981	DEC 1981	JAN 1982	FEB 1982	MAR 1982	APR 1982
☉ →	♎	♏	♐	♑	♒	♓	♈	♉
	22 10p 6	23 7a14	22 4a37	21 5p51	20 4a32	18 6p47	20 5p56	20 5a 8

☽ → SIGNS

SEP 1981	OCT 1981	NOV 1981	DEC 1981	JAN 1982	FEB 1982	MAR 1982	APR 1982
2 ♏ 4p10	2 ♐ 12p 0	1 ♑ 7a46	1 ♒ 2a 9	2 ♈ 1a33	1 ♉ 3p20	1 ♊ 8p50	2 ♋ 8a37
5 ♐ 4a24	4 ♑ 12a49	3 ♒ 7p51	3 ♓ 12p16	4 ♉ 6a 3	3 ♊ 5p18	3 ♋ 10p50	5 ♌ 1p19
7 ♑ 4p49	7 ♒ 12p 1	6 ♓ 4a53	5 ♈ 6p49	6 ♊ 7a49	5 ♋ 6p50	5 ♌ 10p15	7 ♍ 7p27
10 ♒ 2a59	9 ♓ 7p33	8 ♈ 9a39	7 ♉ 9p32	8 ♋ 8a 1	7 ♌ 9p15	8 ♍ 6a27	9 ♎ 3a33
12 ♓ 9a34	12 ♈ 11p11	10 ♉ 10a45	9 ♊ 9p30	10 ♌ 8a21	9 ♍ 9p45	11 ♎ 11a34	11 ♏ 2p 7
14 ♈ 12p56	14 ♉ 11p41	12 ♊ 10a 1	11 ♋ 8p40	12 ♍ 10a37	11 ♎ 2a 2	14 ♏ 7p17	14 ♐ 2a42
16 ♉ 2p30	16 ♊ 12a53	14 ♋ 9a37	13 ♌ 9p 9	14 ♎ 4p17	13 ♏ 10a16	17 ♐ 6a47	16 ♑ 3p18
18 ♊ 3p59	18 ♋ 4a35	16 ♌ 11a33	16 ♍ 12a38	17 ♏ 1a47	16 ♐ 10a36	19 ♑ 6p40	19 ♒ 3a20
20 ♋ 6p40	20 ♌ 11a 5	18 ♍ 4p53	18 ♎ 7a58	19 ♐ 2p 0	18 ♑ 10p 5	22 ♒ 6a53	21 ♓ 1p23
22 ♌ 11p 9	22 ♍ 11a 5	21 ♎ 1a33	20 ♏ 6p59	22 ♑ 2a50	20 ♒ 10p15	24 ♓ 4p 2	23 ♈ 9a59
25 ♍ 5a29	24 ♎ 7p57	23 ♏ 12p37	23 ♐ 7a11	24 ♒ 2p25	23 ♓ 7a 9	27 ♈ 12a40	25 ♉ 11a44
27 ♎ 1p40	27 ♏ 6a38	26 ♐ 1a 1	25 ♑ 8p 0	26 ♓ 11p50	25 ♈ 1p17	29 ♉ 5a43	27 ♊ 2p10
29 ♏ 11p53	29 ♐ 6p49	28 ♑ 1p53	28 ♒ 7a54	29 ♈ 5a32	27 ♉ 5p32	31 ♊ 5a 9	29 ♋ 2p10
			30 ♓ 6p 1				

☽ PHASES

SEP 1981	OCT 1981	NOV 1981	DEC 1981	JAN 1982	FEB 1982	MAR 1982	APR 1982
2) 6a 5	1 ○ 11p39	4 ○ 8p 9	4 ○ 11a23	2 ○ 11p46	1 ○ 9a28	2 ○ 5p15	1 ○ 12a 9
8 ○ 8a26	6 ○ 2a46	8 ○ 11a40	7 ○ 11p 8	6 ○ 9a21	4 ○ 6p42	5 ○ 3a36	5 ○ 12p38
10 ○ 8a 6	9 ○ 10p39	11 ○ 5p27	11 ○ 3a42	9) 2p53	8 ○ 2a57	9 ○ 3a05	8 ○ 5a19
13 ○ 10p 9	13 ○ 7a50	14 ○ 10p 5	14 ○ 9a44	13 (12a10	11 (4p21	13 (10a 6	12 (4a24
17 ○ 6a 3	18 ○ 10p 1	18 ○ 1p 5	18 ○ 12a48	16 ● 6p58	15 ● 3p21	15 (12p15	16 (7a43
20 ○ 2p48	19 (10p41	22 ○ 7a 4	22 (1a27	24 (11p56	19 (6p43	21 (1p27	20 (4a50
24 (4a19	23 (3p57	26 ● 9a39	26 ● 8p58	24 (11p56	23 ● 4p13	21 (1p27	23 ● 3p29
27 ● 11p 8	27 ● 3p14	30 ● 6p29	30 ● 5a56	28) 7p44	27) 6a24	28) 2p43	26) 9p48
	31) 6p29						30) 7a 8

MAY 1982 – DEC 1982

	MAY 1982	JUN 1982	JUL 1982	AUG 1982	SEP 1982	OCT 1982	NOV 1982	DEC 1982
☉ →	♊	♋	♌	♍	♎	♏	♐	♑
	21 4a23	21 12p23	22 11p16	23 6a16	23 3a47	23 12p59	22 10a24	21 11p39

☽ → SIGNS

MAY 1982	JUN 1982	JUL 1982	AUG 1982	SEP 1982	OCT 1982	NOV 1982	DEC 1982
1 ♍ 6p45	2 ♏ 4p12	2 ♐ 9a26	1 ♑ 4a36	2 ♓ 11a11	2 ♈ 3a 6	1 ♊ 7p23	2 ♋ 5a58
4 ♎ 1a33	5 ♐ 3a32	4 ♑ 10p15	3 ♒ 5p17	4 ♈ 7p24	4 ♉ 8a 9	3 ♋ 8p59	4 ♌ 6a26
6 ♏ 10a24	7 ♑ 4p12	7 ♒ 11a 3	6 ♓ 4a24	7 ♉ 1a27	6 ♊ 11a39	5 ♌ 11p10	6 ♍ 8a33
8 ♐ 9p17	10 ♒ 4a44	9 ♓ 10p36	8 ♈ 1p 0	9 ♊ 5a58	8 ♋ 2p40	8 ♍ 2a40	8 ♎ 1p11
11 ♑ 9a50	12 ♓ 4p44	12 ♈ 7a49	10 ♉ 8p 0	11 ♋ 9a18	10 ♌ 5p44	10 ♎ 7a46	10 ♏ 8p35
13 ♒ 10p44	15 ♈ 1a20	14 ♉ 2p 0	13 ♊ 12a22	13 ♌ 11a46	12 ♍ 9p 9	12 ♏ 2p43	13 ♐ 6p27
16 ♓ 9a47	17 ♉ 6a 7	16 ♊ 5p 4	15 ♋ 2a41	15 ♍ 1p58	15 ♎ 1a23	15 ♐ 11p52	15 ♑ 6p15
18 ♈ 5p 4	19 ♊ 7a34	18 ♋ 5p46	17 ♌ 3a40	17 ♎ 5p 3	17 ♏ 7p11	18 ♑ 11a22	18 ♒ 7a13
20 ♉ 8p22	21 ♋ 7a13	20 ♌ 5p36	19 ♍ 4a40	19 ♏ 10p33	19 ♐ 3p42	21 ♒ 12a21	20 ♓ 7p56
22 ♊ 8p55	23 ♌ 6a57	22 ♍ 6p20	21 ♎ 7a 7	22 ♐ 7a31	22 ♑ 3a38	23 ♓ 12p49	23 ♈ 6a34
24 ♋ 8p39	25 ♍ 8a36	24 ♎ 9p45	23 ♏ 1p21	24 ♑ 7p32	24 ♒ 4a13	25 ♈ 10p 7	25 ♉ 1p37
26 ♌ 9p27	27 ♎ 1p31	27 ♏ 4a58	26 ♐ 11p11	27 ♒ 8a22	27 ♓ 4a13	28 ♉ 3a32	27 ♊ 4p49
29 ♍ 12a43	29 ♏ 10p 2	29 ♐ 3p48	28 ♑ 11a42	29 ♓ 7p19	29 ♈ 12p25	30 ♊ 5a36	29 ♋ 5p18
31 ♎ 7a 3			31 ♒ 12a24		31 ♉ 5p 4		31 ♌ 4p33

☽ PHASES

MAY 1982	JUN 1982	JUL 1982	AUG 1982	SEP 1982	OCT 1982	NOV 1982	DEC 1982
3 ○ 10p29	2 ○ 9a52	1 ○ 11p20	4 ○ 5p34	3 ○ 7a29	2 ○ 8p 9	1 ○ 7a57	4 ○ 1a 9
7 ○ 7p45	6 ○ 11a 0	6 ○ 2a32	8 ○ 9p 5	7 ○ 12p 9	6 ○ 6p 9	4 ○ 4p13	6 ○ 10a54
10 ○ 10p12	10 ○ 2p21	10 ○ 4a 1	12 ○ 6a 9	9 ○ 9p44	9 ○ 6p27	7 ○ 1a38	11 ○ 4a 9
16 (12a12	14 (1p 6	13 (10p47	15 (9p45	12 (9p44	11 (3p10	11 (4a 9	11 (4a18
19 (4p43	18 (1a45	17 (8a56	18 (7a 9	16 (7p 4	16 ● 7p 4	19 (11a43	19 ● 8a15
22) 11p41	21 ● 6a52	20 ● 1p57	22 ● 8a18	20 ● 10p27	20 ● 11p27	23 ● 3p 6	27 ● 12a20
29 ● 3p 7	24 ● 12p10	23 ● 9p 6	26 ● 4a50	24 ● 1a32	24) 6p31	27) 10a15	30) 6a33
	28 ● 12a57	27 ● 1p22	30 ○ 7a59		30) 7p21		
		30 ● 2p54					

JAN 1983 – AUG 1983

	JAN 1983	FEB 1983	MAR 1983	APR 1983	MAY 1983	JUN 1983	JUL 1983	AUG 1983
⊙ →	≈	♓	♈	♉	♊	♋	♌	♍
	20 10a18	19 12a31	20 11p39	20 10a51	21 10a 7	21 6p 9	23 5a 5	23 12p 8

☽ → SIGNS

JAN 1983: 2 ♏ 4p50 · 4 ♐ 7p45 · 7 ♑ 2a16 · 9 ♒ 12p14 · 12 ♓ 12a26 · 14 ♈ 1p27 · 17 ♉ 2a 3 · 19 ♊ 1p 8 · 21 ♋ 9p36 · 24 ♌ 2a40 · 26 ♍ 4a29 · 28 ♎ 4a10 · 30 ♏ 3a35

FEB 1983: 1 ♎ 4a47 · 3 ♐ 9a32 · 5 ♑ 6p29 · 8 ♒ 6a34 · 10 ♓ 7p41 · 13 ♈ 8a 2 · 15 ♉ 7p 1 · 17 ♊ 1a 1 · 18 ♋ 3a31 · 20 ♌ 9a52 · 22 ♍ 1p31 · 24 ♎ 2p47 · 26 ♏ 2p49 · 28 ♎ 3p30

MAR 1983: 2 ♐ 6p51 · 5 ♑ 2a15 · 7 ♒ 1p29 · 10 ♓ 2a30 · 12 ♈ 2p47 · 15 ♉ 1a 1 · 17 ♊ 9a 5 · 19 ♋ 1a14 · 21 ♌ 7p53 · 23 ♍ 10p43 · 26 ♎ 12a18 · 28 ♏ 1a49 · 30 ♐ 4a57

APR 1983: 1 ♑ 11a20 · 3 ♒ 9p30 · 6 ♓ 10a 7 · 8 ♈ 10p31 · 11 ♉ 8a37 · 13 ♊ 3p59 · 15 ♋ 9p15 · 18 ♌ 1a14 · 20 ♍ 4a27 · 22 ♎ 7a12 · 24 ♏ 10a 4 · 26 ♐ 2p 5 · 28 ♑ 8p29

MAY 1983: 1 ♒ 6a 2 · 3 ♓ 6p 9 · 6 ♈ 6a44 · 8 ♉ 5p17 · 11 ♊ 12a36 · 13 ♋ 5a 4 · 15 ♌ 7a48 · 17 ♍ 10a 1 · 19 ♎ 12p37 · 21 ♏ 4p12 · 23 ♐ 9p17 · 26 ♑ 4a28 · 28 ♒ 2p 7 · 31 ♓ 2a 0

JUN 1983: 2 ♈ 2p42 · 5 ♉ 1a59 · 7 ♊ 10a 5 · 9 ♋ 2p38 · 11 ♌ 4p33 · 13 ♍ 5p22 · 15 ♎ 6p38 · 17 ♏ 9p37 · 20 ♐ 3a 0 · 22 ♑ 10a55 · 24 ♒ 9p 9 · 27 ♓ 9a 7 · 29 ♈ 9p52

JUL 1983: 2 ♉ 9a48 · 4 ♊ 7p 6 · 7 ♋ 12a41 · 9 ♌ 2a51 · 11 ♍ 2a54 · 13 ♎ 2a43 · 15 ♏ 4a10 · 17 ♐ 8a38 · 19 ♑ 4p32 · 22 ♒ 3a11 · 24 ♓ 3p27 · 27 ♈ 4a21 · 29 ♉ 4p21

AUG 1983: 1 ♊ 2a37 · 3 ♋ 9a43 · 5 ♌ 1p 9 · 7 ♍ 2a51 · 9 ♎ 1p27 · 11 ♏ 12p52 · 13 ♐ 3p44 · 15 ♑ 10p34 · 18 ♒ 9a 0 · 20 ♓ 9p26 · 23 ♈ 10a10 · 25 ♉ 10p 8 · 28 ♊ 8a38 · 30 ♋ 4p49

☽ PHASES

JAN 1983: 2 O 11a26 · 5 ◑ 11p 0 · 9 ● 8p37 · 14 ◐ 12a 8 · 18 O 3a14 · 22 ◑ 12a26 · 25 ● 12p29 · 28 ◐ 5p27 · 31 O 11p16

FEB 1983: 4 O 2p17 · 8 ◑ 3p46 · 12 ● 7p10 · 16 ◐ 7p32 · 20 O 12p32 · 27 ◑ 10p30

MAR 1983: 2 O 12p48 · 6 ◑ 3a39 · 9 ● 6a31 · 13 ◐ 2a59 · 16 O 5p 1 · 20 ● 3a58 · 23 ◐ 1p43 · 27 O 1a31 · 30 ● 8p27

APR 1983: 1 O 3a59 · 4 ◑ 10p43 · 8 ● 2p25 · 12 ◐ 11p49 · 19 ● 9a17 · 21 ◐ 9p 0 · 26 O 1p26

MAY 1983: 4 ◑ 10p43 · 8 ◐ 10p55 · 12 ● 2p25 · 15 ◑ 11p38 · 17 O 2p46 · 21 ● 5a44 · 26 O 5a58

JUN 1983: 3 O 4p 8 · 7 ◑ 12p37 · 10 ● 11p38 · 14 ◐ 6a 8 · 17 O 12p 0 · 21 ● 5a44 · 24 ◑ 3a32 · 28 O 9p17

JUL 1983: 3 O 7a12 · 6 ◑ 11p53 · 10 ● 10 · 13 ◐ 12p 0 · 16 O 9p51 · 20 ● 4p54 · 24 ◑ 6p24 · 28 O 9p17

AUG 1983: 1 O 7p53 · 5 ◑ 9a 9 · 8 ● 2p18 · 11 ◐ 7p 1 · 15 O 7a47 · 19 ● 6a54 · 23 ◑ 10a 0 · 27 O 11a 3 · 31 ● 6a23

SEP 1983 – APR 1984

	SEP 1983	OCT 1983	NOV 1983	DEC 1983	JAN 1984	FEB 1984	MAR 1984	APR 1984
⊙ →	♎	♏	♐	♑	≈	♓	♈	♉
	23 9a42	23 6p55	22 4p19	22 5a31	20 4p 6	19 6a17	20 5a25	19 4p39

☽ → SIGNS

SEP 1983: 1 ♋ 9p53 · 3 ♌ 11p48 · 5 ♍ 11p36 · 7 ♎ 11p13 · 10 ♏ 12a49 · 12 ♐ 6a 8 · 14 ♑ 3p34 · 17 ♒ 3a46 · 19 ♓ 4p30 · 22 ♈ 5a 3 · 24 ♉ 2p13 · 26 ♊ 10p25 · 29 ♋ 4a25

OCT 1983: 1 ♌ 7a55 · 3 ♍ 9a15 · 5 ♎ 9a42 · 7 ♏ 11a 6 · 9 ♐ 3p21 · 11 ♑ 11p31 · 14 ♒ 11a 0 · 16 ♓ 11p42 · 19 ♈ 11a59 · 21 ♉ 8p48 · 24 ♊ 4a10 · 26 ♋ 9a47 · 28 ♌ 1p51 · 30 ♍ 4p33

NOV 1983: 1 ♎ 6p31 · 3 ♏ 8p53 · 6 ♐ 1a 9 · 8 ♑ 8a32 · 10 ♒ 7p11 · 13 ♓ 7p37 · 15 ♈ 7p37 · 18 ♉ 5a 7 · 20 ♊ 11a45 · 22 ♋ 4p11 · 24 ♌ 7p20 · 26 ♍ 10p 2 · 29 ♎ 12a57

DEC 1983: 1 ♏ 4a41 · 3 ♐ 9a56 · 5 ♑ 5p28 · 8 ♒ 3a40 · 10 ♓ 3p53 · 13 ♈ 4a17 · 15 ♉ 2p33 · 17 ♊ 9p54 · 20 ♋ 1a 3 · 22 ♌ 2a44 · 24 ♍ 4a 2 · 26 ♎ 6a19 · 28 ♏ 10a27 · 30 ♐ 4p44

JAN 1984: 2 ♑ 1a 8 · 4 ♒ 11a31 · 6 ♓ 11p35 · 9 ♈ 12p16 · 11 ♉ 12a36 · 14 ♊ 7a41 · 16 ♋ 11a48 · 18 ♌ 12p50 · 20 ♍ 12p36 · 22 ♎ 1p 7 · 24 ♏ 4p 4 · 26 ♐ 10p13 · 29 ♑ 7a13 · 31 ♒ 6p11

FEB 1984: 1 ♓ 6a22 · 3 ♈ 7p 4 · 6 ♉ 7a 6 · 8 ♊ 4p40 · 10 ♋ 11p30 · 13 ♌ 2a10 · 15 ♍ 2a20 · 17 ♎ 1a58 · 19 ♏ 2p50 · 21 ♐ 6a 3 · 23 ♑ 4a23 · 25 ♒ 12p50 · 27 ♓ 12a12

MAR 1984: 1 ♓ 12p30 · 4 ♈ 1a 7 · 6 ♉ 1p 6 · 9 ♊ 11p30 · 11 ♋ 6a48 · 13 ♌ 10a21 · 15 ♍ 10a47 · 17 ♎ 9a52 · 19 ♏ 9a49 · 21 ♐ 12p41 · 23 ♑ 7p36 · 26 ♒ 6a 9 · 28 ♓ 6p37 · 31 ♈ 7a14

APR 1984: 2 ♉ 6p56 · 5 ♊ 5a 5 · 7 ♋ 11p46 · 9 ♌ 6p 2 · 11 ♍ 8p11 · 13 ♎ 8p30 · 15 ♏ 8p41 · 17 ♐ 10p43 · 19 ♑ 4a11 · 22 ♒ 1p27 · 24 ♓ 2p 3 · 27 ♈ 2p 3 · 30 ♉ 1a31

☽ PHASES

SEP 1983: 3 ● 5p 0 · 6 ◐ 9p35 · 10 O 4a26 · 13 ◑ 9p24 · 17 ● 11p26 · 22 O 1a37 · 25 ◑ 11p15 · 29 ● 3p 6

OCT 1983: 3 ◐ 12a12 · 6 O 6a16 · 9 ◑ 5p14 · 13 ● 2p43 · 17 O 5p45 · 21 ◑ 4p54 · 25 ● 10a 5 · 28 ◐ 10p37

NOV 1983: 1 O 7a44 · 4 ◑ 5p22 · 8 ● 9a42 · 12 O 10a50 · 16 ◑ 12p46 · 19 ● 9p 1 · 23 ◐ 4a58 · 26 O 1p53 · 30 ● 4a 2

DEC 1983: 4 ◑ 7a26 · 8 ● 5a 8 · 12 O 8a 9 · 16 ◑ 7a20 · 19 ● 9p 1 · 23 ◐ 4a58 · 26 O 1p53 · 30 ● 4p42

JAN 1984: 3 ◑ 12a16 · 7 ● 1a55 · 11 O 9a48 · 15 ◑ 12a 8 · 18 ● 9a 5 · 21 ◐ 9p 9 · 24 O 11p48 · 31 ◑ 3p12

FEB 1984: 1 ● 6p47 · 5 O 10p 7 · 9 ◑ 11p 0 · 13 ◐ 2p 7 · 16 ● 7p41 · 20 O 1a 3 · 23 ◑ 12p12 · 27 ● 10a31

MAR 1984: 2 ◐ 1p31 · 6 O 9p38 · 10 ◑ 1p28 · 14 ● 12a54 · 17 O 5a10 · 20 ◑ 11a12 · 24 ● 2a59 · 28 ◐ 4a12

APR 1984: 1 ● 7a10 · 5 O 6a45 · 8 ◑ 11p52 · 12 O 8a56 · 15 ◑ 2p11 · 18 ● 7p27 · 26 ◑ 10p 1 · 30 ◐ 3p 6

MAY 1984 – DEC 1984

	MAY 1984	JUN 1984	JUL 1984	AUG 1984	SEP 1984	OCT 1984	NOV 1984	DEC 1984
⊙ →	♊	♋	♌	♍	♎	♏	♐	♑
	20 3p58	21 12a 3	22 10a59	22 6p 1	22 3p34	23 12a46	21 10p11	21 11a24

☽ → SIGNS

MAY 1984: 2 ♊ 11a 2 · 4 ♋ 6p26 · 6 ♌ 11p43 · 9 ♍ 3a 2 · 11 ♎ 4a54 · 13 ♏ 6a22 · 15 ♐ 8a50 · 17 ♑ 1p43 · 19 ♒ 9p56 · 22 ♓ 9a 9 · 24 ♈ 9p40 · 27 ♉ 9a14 · 29 ♊ 6p23

JUN 1984: 1 ♋ 12a54 · 3 ♌ 5a19 · 5 ♍ 8a27 · 7 ♎ 11a 4 · 9 ♏ 1p49 · 11 ♐ 5p27 · 13 ♑ 10p33 · 16 ♒ 6a41 · 18 ♓ 5p18 · 21 ♈ 5a41 · 23 ♉ 6p44 · 26 ♊ 5a38 · 28 ♋ 1p55 · 30 ♌ 12p30

JUL 1984: 2 ♍ 2p28 · 4 ♎ 4p27 · 6 ♏ 7p29 · 9 ♐ 12a 3 · 11 ♑ 6a23 · 13 ♒ 2p42 · 16 ♓ 1a11 · 18 ♈ 1p26 · 21 ♉ 2a 2 · 23 ♊ 12p10 · 25 ♋ 6p44 · 27 ♌ 9p42 · 31 ♎ 11p 3

AUG 1984: 1 ♍ 1a 4 · 3 ♎ 5a30 · 5 ♏ 12p25 · 7 ♐ 8a13 · 10 ♑ 8a13 · 12 ♒ 8p28 · 14 ♓ 7p28 · 17 ♈ 8p32 · 19 ♉ 9a21 · 22 ♊ 4a21 · 24 ♋ 8a33 · 26 ♌ 7a57 · 28 ♍ 8a23

SEP 1984: 1 ♐ 11a30 · 3 ♑ 5p55 · 6 ♒ 3a12 · 8 ♓ 2p25 · 11 ♈ 2a47 · 13 ♉ 3p33 · 16 ♊ 3a26 · 18 ♋ 12p36 · 20 ♌ 5p49 · 22 ♍ 7p19 · 24 ♎ 6p41 · 26 ♏ 6p 4 · 28 ♐ 7p32

OCT 1984: 1 ♑ 12a28 · 3 ♒ 8p20 · 5 ♓ 8p 9 · 8 ♈ 9a29 · 10 ♉ 9a14 · 13 ♊ 9p 0 · 16 ♋ 6a47 · 18 ♌ 1p12 · 20 ♍ 4a56 · 22 ♎ 5a32 · 24 ♏ 5a 8 · 27 ♐ 9a 5 · 29 ♑ 4p13

NOV 1984: 2 ♒ 2a50 · 4 ♓ 3p21 · 7 ♈ 3a54 · 9 ♉ 3p11 · 12 ♊ 12a32 · 14 ♋ 7a34 · 16 ♌ 12p 8 · 18 ♍ 2p30 · 20 ♎ 3p31 · 22 ♏ 4p34 · 24 ♐ 7p18 · 27 ♑ 1a 6 · 29 ♒ 9a50

DEC 1984: 2 ♓ 10p42 · 4 ♈ 11a21 · 6 ♉ 10p24 · 9 ♊ 6a57 · 11 ♋ 1p 9 · 13 ♌ 5p36 · 15 ♍ 8p52 · 17 ♎ 11p28 · 20 ♏ 1a59 · 22 ♐ 5a21 · 24 ♑ 10a48 · 26 ♒ 7p19 · 29 ♓ 6a50 · 31 ♈ 7p37

☽ PHASES

MAY 1984: 4 ● 5p46 · 8 O 6a50 · 11 ◑ 3p17 · 14 ◐ 11p29 · 18 ● 1p37 · 22 O 12p45 · 26 ◑ 3p 2 · 30 ◐ 11a48

JUN 1984: 3 ● 1a39 · 6 O 11a42 · 9 ◑ 9p17 · 13 ◐ 4a13 · 16 ● 9p20 · 20 O 6a10 · 24 ◑ 8p 5 · 28 ● 10p19

JUL 1984: 2 ● 7a29 · 5 O 4p 5 · 9 ◑ 4a13 · 12 ◐ 9p20 · 16 O 8p25 · 20 ● 11p 2 · 24 ◑ 8p 5 · 31 ● 12p44

AUG 1984: 3 O 9p33 · 7 ◑ 12a54 · 11 ◐ 10a44 · 14 O 4a43 · 19 ● 2p41 · 23 ◑ 7a36 · 26 ● 2p26 · 29 O 6p56

SEP 1984: 2 O 5a30 · 5 ◑ 12a54 · 10 ◐ 4a31 · 14 ● 10a21 · 18 O 5p 7 · 21 ◑ 5p11 · 24 ● 9p50 · 28 O 3a21

OCT 1984: 1 ◑ 4p53 · 5 ● 3p54 · 8 ◐ 8p47 · 11 O 11a 0 · 14 ◑ 9p14 · 17 ● 2a21 · 20 O 7a 9 · 24 ◑ 7a 9 · 27 ● 2p50 · 31 O 8a 8

NOV 1984: 4 O 10a 2 · 8 ◑ 12p 0 · 10 O 10a41 · 14 ◑ 11a 2 · 18 ● 2p57 · 22 ◐ 5p36 · 27 O 7p18 · 30 O 3a 1

DEC 1984: 4 O 6a20 · 8 ◑ 5a54 · 11 O 10p30 · 15 ◑ 10a26 · 18 ● 8p10 · 22 ● 6a47 · 25 ◐ 11p18 · 30 O 12a28

JAN 1985 – AUG 1985

JAN 1985	FEB 1985	MAR 1985	APR 1985	MAY 1985	JUN 1985	JUL 1985	AUG 1985
☉ -> ♒ 19 9p58	☉ -> ♓ 18 12p 8	☉ -> ♈ 20 11a14	☉ -> ♉ 19 10p26	☉ -> ♊ 20 9p43	☉ -> ♋ 21 5a45	☉ -> ♌ 22 4p37	☉ -> ♍ 22 11p36

D->SIGNS

JAN 1985	FEB 1985	MAR 1985	APR 1985	MAY 1985	JUN 1985	JUL 1985	AUG 1985
3 ♊ 7a 1	2 ♋ 12a59	1 ♋ 10a24	2 ♍ 5a25	1 ♎ 4p22	2 ♐ 2a34	1 ♑ 1p22	2 ♓ 7a34
5 ♋ 3p18	4 ♌ 6a 2	3 ♌ 4p28	4 ♎ 5a54	3 ♏ 4p17	4 ♑ 3a34	3 ♒ 4p36	4 ♈ 4p43
7 ♌ 8p28	6 ♍ 8a10	5 ♍ 6p43	6 ♏ 5a11	5 ♐ 3p56	6 ♒ 6a52	5 ♓ 10p40	7 ♉ 4a42
9 ♍ 11p40	8 ♎ 9a11	7 ♎ 6p48	8 ♐ 5a18	7 ♑ 5p12	8 ♓ 1p47	8 ♈ 8a21	9 ♊ 5p32
12 ♎ 2a14	10 ♏ 10a49	9 ♏ 6p47	10 ♑ 7a57	9 ♒ 9p38	11 ♈ 12a24	10 ♉ 8p44	12 ♋ 4a29
14 ♏ 5a 8	12 ♐ 2p 9	11 ♐ 8p29	12 ♒ 2p 2	12 ♓ 4a56	13 ♉ 1p12	13 ♊ 9a24	14 ♌ 11a57
16 ♐ 8a48	14 ♑ 7p27	14 ♑ 12a55	14 ♓ 11p31	14 ♈ 5p26	16 ♊ 1a46	15 ♋ 7p55	16 ♍ 4p15
18 ♑ 1p29	17 ♒ 2a11	16 ♒ 8a11	17 ♈ 11a19	17 ♉ 6a24	18 ♋ 12p16	18 ♌ 3a25	18 ♎ ,6p44
20 ♒ 7p39	19 ♓ 11a38	18 ♓ 5p51	20 ♉ 12a13	19 ♊ 7p 1	20 ♌ 8p32	20 ♍ 8a30	20 ♏ 8p52
23 ♓ 4a 2	21 ♈ 5a21	21 ♈ 5a21	22 ♊ 1p 1	22 ♋ 6a 5	23 ♍ 2a33	22 ♎ 12p10	22 ♐ 8p43
25 ♈ 3p 5	24 ♉ 11a28	23 ♉ 6p 7	25 ♋ 12a26	24 ♌ 2p54	25 ♎ 6a48	24 ♏ 3p16	25 ♑ 3a25
28 ♉ 3a54	27 ♊ 12a12	26 ♊ 7a 2	27 ♌ 7a 2	26 ♍ 9p 7	27 ♏ 9a38	26 ♐ 6p13	27 ♒ 8a32
30 ♊ 4p 1		28 ♋ 6p14	29 ♍ 2p24	29 ♎ 12a41	29 ♐ 11a31	28 ♑ 9p21	
		31 ♌ 1a52		31 ♏ 2a 8		31 ♒ 1a26	

D PHASES

JAN 1985	FEB 1985	MAR 1985	APR 1985	MAY 1985	JUN 1985	JUL 1985	AUG 1985
3 O 2a55	1 O 9p41	3 O 1p12	2 O 1a11	1 O 10a10	2 O 10p51	2 O 7a 9	4 O 11a17
6 O 9p16	5 O 10a19	6 O 9p13	5 O 6a33	4 ♐ 2p53	6 O 8a14	5 O 8p43	8 O 1p29
10 O 8a33	8 O 5p34	10 O 2a23	8 O 11a31	7 O 9p20	10 O 3a19	9 O 7p50	12 C 1p58
13 O 6p27	13 C 2a57	13 O 12p34	11 O 11p42	11 O 12p34	14 ● 6a58	13 C 10p36	16 ● 6a 6
17 C 6a16	15 C 5p41	17 C 6a40	15 C 9p19	15 C 1p23	18 ● 6a58	16 ● 6p57	19 O 2p19
20 ● 9p29	19 ● 1p43	21 ● 6a59	20 ● 12a22	19 ♐ 4p42	22 D 1a11	21 D 8a14	22 O 11p36
24 D 7p 4	23 D 3p28	25 D 10a42	24 D 3a 5	23 D 3p49	26 O 10p51	24 O 6p39	26 O 11a47
28 O 10p29	27 O 6p41	29 O 11a12	27 O 11p25	27 O 7a56		28 O 4a41	30 O 4a28
				30 O 5p 2		31 O 4p41	

SEP 1985 – APR 1986

SEP 1985	OCT 1985	NOV 1985	DEC 1985	JAN 1986	FEB 1986	MAR 1986	APR 1986
☉ -> ♎ 22 9p 8	☉ -> ♏ 23 6a23	☉ -> ♐ 22 3a52	☉ -> ♑ 21 5p 0	☉ -> ♒ 20 3a47	☉ -> ♓ 13 5p58	☉ -> ♈ 20 5p 3	☉ -> ♉ 20 4a13

D->SIGNS

SEP 1985	OCT 1985	NOV 1985	DEC 1985	JAN 1986	FEB 1986	MAR 1986	APR 1986
1 ♓ 12a42	3 ♊ 12a28	2 ♌ 3a31	1 ♌ 8p 0	2 ♎ 3p46	1 ♏ 1a20	2 ♐ 9a52	2 ♒ 10p11
3 ♈ 12p28	5 ♋ 8p59	4 ♍ 2p 4	4 ♍ 4a14	4 ♏ 7p44	3 ♐ 4a32	4 ♑ 12p56	5 ♈ 4a 1
6 ♉ 1a27	8 ♌ 6a34	6 ♎ 9p19	6 ♎ 9a34	6 ♐ 9p47	5 ♑ 7a 2	6 ♒ 4p43	7 ♉ 12p12
8 ♊ 1p11	10 ♍ 12p10	9 ♏ 12a52	8 ♏ 11a57	8 ♑ 10p42	7 ♒ 9a35	8 ♓ 9p48	9 ♊ 10p36
10 ♋ 9p28	12 ♎ 2p12	11 ♐ 1a31	10 ♐ 12p41	10 ♒ 12a 2	9 ♓ 1p33	11 ♈ 5a 4	12 ♋ 10a51
13 ♌ 1a53	14 ♏ 2p13	13 ♑ 12a53	12 ♑ 12p45	13 ♓ 3a39	11 ♈ 8p21	13 ♉ 3p 4	14 ♌ 11a42
15 ♍ 3a34	16 ♐ 2p 6	15 ♒ 12a53	14 ♒ 1p46	15 ♈ 11a 3	14 ♉ 6a38	16 ♊ 3a23	17 ♍ 11a10
17 ♎ 4a17	18 ♑ 3p35	17 ♓ 3a26	16 ♓ 5p50	17 ♉ 10p14	16 ♊ 7p17	18 ♋ 4p 5	19 ♎ 7p24
19 ♏ 5a41	20 ♒ 7p55	19 ♈ 9a43	19 ♈ 1a43	20 ♊ 11a12	19 ♋ 7a39	21 ♌ 4a 5	21 ♏ 11p50
21 ♐ 8a50	23 ♓ 3a28	21 ♈ 7p43	21 ♉ 1p31	22 ♋ 11p15	21 ♌ 5p25	23 ♍ 1p41	24 ♐ 1a16
23 ♑ 2p12	25 ♈ 1p48	24 ♉ 8a 7	24 ♊ 2a34	25 ♌ 8a48	23 ♍ 11p58	25 ♎ 7p23	26 ♑ 1a16
25 ♒ 9p51	28 ♉ 2a 0	26 ♊ 9p 8	26 ♋ 2p 8	27 ♍ 3p51	26 ♎ 4a 7	27 ♏ 9p 6	28 ♒ 1a41
28 ♓ 7a43	31 ♊ 2p59	29 ♋ 9a23	29 ♌ 9a33	29 ♎ 9p10	28 ♏ 7a 6	29 ♐ 8p28	30 ♓ 4a 6
30 ♉ 7p35			31 ♍ 9a44			31 ♑ 6p26	

D PHASES

SEP 1985	OCT 1985	NOV 1985	DEC 1985	JAN 1986	FEB 1986	MAR 1986	APR 1986
3 O 3a59	2 O 10p 8	1 O 4p19	1 O 9a 4	3 O 2p48	1 O 11p41	3 O 7a18	1 O 2p30
7 O 7a16	7 O 12a 4	5 O 3p 7	5 O 4a 2	7 C 12a26	5 C 9a33	6 C 6p38	5 C 4a38
11 C 3a53	10 C 4p29	9 C 4a29	9 C 4a 2	10 ● 7a22	8 ● 7p56	10 ● 9a52	9 ♀ 1a 9
14 ● 2p20	13 ● 11p34	12 ♐ 9a21	11 ● 7p55	13 D 6p58	12 D 12p58	14 D 8a19	13 D 3a20
17 D 8p46	17 D 4a39	15 D 2p42	15 D 3a25	17 O 5p14	16 O 2p55	18 O 11a39	17 O 5a35
21 O 4a 0	20 O 3p13	19 O 4a 4	18 O 8p58	21 O 8p59	20 O 4p43	22 O 9a42	20 O 11p26
24 O 10a37	23 O 10a37	23 O 10a37	22 O 11p55	24 O 10a 3	24 O 10a 3	25 O 10p 2	24 ♀ 7a47
28 O 7p 9	28 ♀ 12p38	27 O 7a42	27 O 2a31	29 O 11a27		29 O 5a33	27 O 12p55
			30 O 11p30				30 ● 10p22

MAY 1986 – DEC 1986

MAY 1986	JUN 1986	JUL 1986	AUG 1986	SEP 1986	OCT 1986	NOV 1986	DEC 1986
☉ -> ♊ 21 3a28	☉ -> ♋ 21 11a30	☉ -> ♌ 22 10p25	☉ -> ♍ 23 5a26	☉ -> ♎ 23 3a 0	☉ -> ♏ 23 12p15	☉ -> ♐ 22 9a45	☉ -> ♑ 21 11p 3

D->SIGNS

MAY 1986	JUN 1986	JUL 1986	AUG 1986	SEP 1986	OCT 1986	NOV 1986	DEC 1986
2 ♈ 9a31	3 ♊ 10a45	3 ♋ 5a32	2 ♌ 1a 4	3 ♍ 5a 6	2 ♎ 8p 3	1 ♏ 9a20	2 ♐ 8p29
4 ♉ 6p 1	5 ♋ 11p27	5 ♌ 6p20	4 ♍ 12p27	5 ♎ 11a34	4 ♏ 11p36	3 ♐ 10a19	4 ♑ 8p23
7 ♊ 4a59	8 ♌ 12p16	8 ♍ 5a56	6 ♎ 9p 5	7 ♏ 4p12	7 ♐ 3a53	5 ♑ 12p29	6 ♒ 10p49
9 ♋ 5p26	11 ♍ 12a12	10 ♎ 3p50	9 ♏ 5a 5	9 ♐ 7p41	9 ♑ 3a53	7 ♒ 4p30	9 ♓ 4a49
12 ♌ 6a18	13 ♎ 10a 1	12 ♏ 11p06	11 ♐ 10a36	11 ♑ 10p28	11 ♒ 4p30	9 ♓ 4p30	11 ♈ 2p11
14 ♍ 6p15	15 ♏ 5p38	15 ♐ 4a59	13 ♑ 2p17	14 ♒ 4a23	13 ♓ 11a 4	11 ♈ 11a 1	11 ♈ 1a42
17 ♎ 3a46	17 ♐ 9p37	17 ♑ 7a35	15 ♒ 4p23	16 ♓ 6a44	15 ♈ 1a36	14 ♉ 8a25	16 ♊ 2p11
19 ♏ 9a41	19 ♑ 8a10	19 ♒ 8a18	17 ♓ 7p52	18 ♈ 9a34	18 ♉ 1a36	17 ♊ 7p27	19 ♋ 2p44
21 ♐ 12p 3	21 ♒ 10p 0	21 ♓ 8a18	19 ♈ 11p32	20 ♉ 5p26	20 ♊ 12p16	19 ♋ 7p46	21 ♌ 2p31
23 ♑ 11a57	23 ♓ 9p50	23 ♈ 9a59	22 ♉ 12a27	23 ♊ 4a14	23 ♋ 12a38	21 ♌ 8p25	24 ♍ 12a 5
25 ♒ 11a15	26 ♈ 12a13	25 ♉ 3p 3	24 ♊ 8a37	25 ♋ 4p45	25 ♌ 1p 3	24 ♎ 7a46	26 ♎ 8a20
27 ♓ 12p 0	28 ♉ 6a35	28 ♊ 12a19	26 ♋ 8p 5	28 ♌ 4a40	28 ♍ 3p59	26 ♏ 3p59	28 ♏ 8a20
29 ♈ 3p55	30 ♊ 4p55	30 ♋ 12p19	29 ♌ 8a40	30 ♍ 1p58	30 ♎ 11p20	28 ♐ 9p14	30 ♐ 7a54
31 ♉ 11p43			31 ♍ 8p 9			30 ♐ 9p 8	

D PHASES

MAY 1986	JUN 1986	JUL 1986	AUG 1986	SEP 1986	OCT 1986	NOV 1986	DEC 1986
4 C 4p17	3 C 5a54	2 C 9p 9	1 O 1p23	4 O 2a11	3 ♏ 1p55	1 ● 1a 2	1 O 11a43
8 ● 5p10	7 ● 9a 1	6 ● 11p55	5 O 8p 3	7 D 1p30	5 D 7a13	5 D 7a13	4 D 4p12
12 D 8p27	11 D 10a52	10 D 10p35	8 D 8a 4	11 O 2a41	10 O 8a29	7 O 4p11	8 O 3a 2
16 O 8p 0	15 O 7a 0	14 O 3p10	12 D 10a26	14 O 12p19	13 O 8p42	12 O 7a12	11 O 11p42
20 O 10a 4	18 O 6p10	18 O 12a26	16 O 6a 2	18 O 12a34	17 O 2p22	16 O 7p 0	16 O 5a16
23 O 3p45	21 O 10p42	21 O 2p52	19 O 1p55	21 ● 5p26	21 ● 5p26	20 O 11a51	20 O 4a17
26 O 8p15	28 O 7p54	24 O 2p52	23 ● 3a57	25 O 10p18	25 O 5p26	24 C 11a51	24 O 4a17
30 O 7a55		28 O 2p52	26 ● 3a39	29 C 10p24	29 C 2p11	28 C 4a43	27 ● 5p25
		31 C 5a58	31 C 5a58				31 ● 10p10

JAN 1987

☉ -> ≈ 20 9a41

D->SIGNS
1 ≏ 6a54
3 ♏ 7a36
5 ♐ 11a51
7 ♑ 8p13
10 ≈ 7a40
12 ♓ 8p19
15 ♈ 8a45
17 ♉ 8p15
20 ♊ 6a10
22 ♋ 1p31
24 ♌ 5p36
26 ♍ 6p43
28 ≏ 6p17
30 ♏ 6p25

D PHASES
3) 3a17
6 ○ 5p35
10 ○ 6p 5
14 ○ 9p31
18 ○ 10p35
22 ○ 5p46
26 (4a 0
29 ● 8a45

FEB 1987

☉ -> ♓ 18 11p51

D->SIGNS
1 ♐ 7a37
4 ♑ 3a53
6 ≈ 2p24
9 ♓ 2a55
11 ♈ 3p22
14 ♉ 2a26
16 ♊ 11a45
18 ♋ 7p 5
21 ♌ 12a 9
22 ♍ 2a57
25 ♏ 4a 9
27 ≈ 5a 7

D PHASES
1) 4p48
5 ○ 11a21
9 ○ 2p 3
13 ○ 3p58
17 ○ 12p58
21 ○ 3a56
24 (12p48
27 ● 7p51

MAR 1987

☉ -> ♈ 20 10p53

D->SIGNS
1 ♐ 7a37
3 ♑ 1p12
6 ≈ 10p27
9 ♓ 10a25
11 ♈ 10p55
14 ♉ 9a56
16 ♊ 6p34
19 ♋ 12a57
20 ♌ 5a32
22 ♍ 3a49
25 ≏ 11a18
27 ♏ 1p46
29 ♐ 7a46
30 ♑ 10p46

D PHASES
3) 8a28
7 ○ 6a59
11 ○ 9a53
15 ○ 8a13
19 ○ 12a 2
22 ○ 11a22
25 (8p40
29 ● 7a46

APR 1987

☉ -> ♉ 20 9a58

D->SIGNS
2 ♊ 7a17
4 ♉ 6p34
7 ♊ 7a 4
9 ♋ 6p28
12 ♌ 3a 6
14 ♍ 8a41
16 ≏ 12p 2
18 ♏ 2p21
20 ♐ 4p45
22 ♑ 8p 2
25 ≈ 12a41
27 ♓ 7a 6
29 ♈ 3p43

D PHASES
2) 1a28
6 ○ 2a48
10 ○ 4a 4
13 ○ 9p31
17 ○ 8a13
20 ○ 5p16
24 (4a38
27 ● 8p35

MAY 1987

☉ -> ♊ 21 9a10

D->SIGNS
2 ♉ 2a39
4 ♊ 3p 7
7 ♋ 3a 8
9 ♌ 6p10
11 ♍ 8p41
13 ≏ 9p37
15 ♏ 10p43
20 ♈ 1a24
22 ♉ 6a23
24 ♊ 1p39
27 ♋ 10p56
29 ♌ 10a 0
31 ♍ 10p26

D PHASES
1 ○ 6p49
5 ○ 9p26
9 ○ 7p35
13 ○ 7a51
16 ○ 2p32
20 ○ 11p 3
23 (1p38
27 ● 10a14
31 ○ 11a43

JUN 1987

☉ -> ♋ 21 5p11

D->SIGNS
3 ♊ 10a57
5 ♋ 9p25
8 ♌ 4a 7
10 ♍ 6a53
12 ≏ 7a 5
14 ♏ 6a45
16 ♐ 7a55
18 ♑ 11a57
20 ≈ 7p 9
23 ♓ 4a55
25 ♈ 4p22
28 ♉ 4a52
30 ♊ 5p34

D PHASES
4 ○ 1p53
8 ○ 8a 0
11 ○ 3p49
14 ○ 8p22
18 ○ 6a 3
22 ● 12a37
26 ● 12a37
30) 3a33

JUL 1987

☉ -> ♌ 23 4a 7

D->SIGNS
3 ≏ 4a55
5 ♏ 5p 6
8 ♌ 5p44
10 ♍ 7a 5
12 ≏ 6a53
15 ♈ 7p 1
15 ♈ 7p 1
17 ♉ 1a 5
20 ♊ 10a33
22 ♋ 10a50
25 ♌ 10a50
30 ≏ 11a 0

D PHASES
4 ○ 3a35
7 ○ 5p35
10 ○ 10p33
14 ○ 3a 2
17 ○ 1p 7
21 (1p 7
25 ● 3p38
29) 5p52

AUG 1987

☉ -> ♍ 23 11a10

D->SIGNS
1 ♏ 8p10
3 ♐ 1a48
6 ♑ 3a52
8 ≈ 3a37
10 ♓ 3a 1
12 ♈ 4a10
14 ♉ 8a38
16 ♊ 4p59
19 ♋ 4a19
21 ♌ 4p58
24 ♍ 5a24
26 ≏ 4p36
29 ♏ 1a50
31 ♐ 8a20

D PHASES
2 ○ 2p24
6 ○ 1a 3
9 ○ 5a18
12 ○ 11a42
16 ○ 3a25
20 (4a11
24 ● 6a59
28 ● 6a19
31) 10p48

SEP 1987

☉ -> ≏ 23 8a46

D->SIGNS
2 ♑ 12p 4
4 ≈ 1p22
6 ♓ 1p37
8 ♈ 2p34
10 ♉ 5p57
13 ♊ 12a55
15 ♋ 11a21
17 ♌ 11p51
20 ♍ 12p13
22 ≏ 10p59
25 ♏ 7a30
27 ♐ 1p49
29 ♑ 6p 9

D PHASES
4 ○ 7a37
7 ○ 1p13
10 ○ 11p 6
14 ○ 6p45
18 (9p20
22 ♍ 10p 9
26) 4p50
30 ○ 5a39

OCT 1987

☉ -> ♏ 23 6p 2

D->SIGNS
1 ≈ 8p52
3 ♓ 10p40
6 ♈ 12a35
8 ♉ 3a58
10 ♊ 10a 4
12 ♋ 7p31
15 ♌ 7a34
17 ♍ 8p 9
20 ≏ 6a50
22 ♏ 2p42
25 ♐ 7p57
27 ♑ 11p33
29 ≈ 2a27
31 ♓ 5a20

D PHASES
3 ○ 2p28
6 (11p13
10 ○ 1p38
14 ○ 1p 6
18 (3p50
22 ● 12p28
26) 12p11

NOV 1987

☉ -> ♐ 22 3p30

D->SIGNS
2 ♈ 8a40
4 ♉ 1p 2
6 ♊ 7p16
9 ♋ 4a10
11 ♌ 3p45
14 ♍ 4a30
16 ≏ 3p16
19 ♏ 11p47
22 ♐ 4p17
24 ♑ 6a32
26 ≈ 5p10
29 ♓ 2p36

D PHASES
1 ○ 10p39
5 ○ 11a46
10 ○ 7a12
13 ○ 9a39
17 ○ 10a23
21 ● 1a33
24) 10a20
29 ○ 7p37

DEC 1987

☉ -> ♑ 22 4a47

D->SIGNS
1 ♈ 8p 6
4 ♉ 3a14
6 ♊ 12p20
8 ♋ 11p41
11 ♌ 12p30
14 ♍ 12a40
16 ≏ 9a42
18 ♏ 2p33
20 ♐ 4p 8
22 ♑ 4p20
24 ≈ 5p10
26 ♓ 8p 6
29 ♈ 1a37
31 ♉ 9a29

D PHASES
1 ○ 8a59
5 ○ 3a 1
10 ○ 3a 6
13 ○ 6a42
17 ○ 3a30
20 ● 1p26
24) 7p13
27 ○ 5a 1
30 ○ 9p55

JAN 1988

☉ -> ≈ 20 3p25

D->SIGNS
2 ♊ 7p17
5 ♋ 6a48
7 ♌ 7p35
10 ♍ 8a18
12 ≏ 6p40
15 ♏ 12a59
17 ♐ 3a16
19 ♑ 3a 2
21 ≈ 2a27
23 ♓ 3a31
25 ♈ 7a37
27 ♉ 3p 3
30 ♊ 1a12

D PHASES
3 ○ 8p52
7 ○ 11p54
12 ○ 2a 4
14 (6p11
19 ● 12a26
25) 5a18
30 ○ 1p32

FEB 1988

☉ -> ♓ 19 5a36

D->SIGNS
1 ♋ 1p 6
4 ♌ 1a55
6 ♍ 2p36
9 ≏ 1a42
11 ♏ 9a36
13 ♐ 1p50
15 ♑ 2p26
17 ≈ 1p44
19 ♓ 1p31
21 ♈ 3p51
24 ♉ 9p42
26 ♊ 7a12
29 ♋ 7p13

D PHASES
2 ○ 8p53
6 ○ 7p30
11 ○ 2a31
13 (10a55
17 ● 4p48
24) 4p48
28 ○ 7a21

MAR 1988

☉ -> ♈ 20 4a39

D->SIGNS
2 ♌ 8a 7
4 ♍ 8p32
7 ≏ 7a27
9 ♏ 3p59
11 ♐ 9p31
14 ♑ 12a12
16 ≈ 12a45
18 ♓ 12a25
20 ♈ 2a 5
22 ♉ 6a21
24 ♊ 2a28
27 ♋ 1a54
29 ♌ 2p49

D PHASES
3 ♐ 11a 1
8 ○ 11a58
11 (5a57
17 ○ 3p39
21 ● 9p 3
24) 11p42
29 ○ 2a16

APR 1988

☉ -> ♉ 19 3p45

D->SIGNS
1 ≏ 3a 5
3 ♏ 1p26
5 ♐ 9p29
8 ♑ 3a20
10 ≈ 7a11
12 ♓ 9a25
14 ♈ 10a47
16 ♉ 12p32
18 ♊ 4p10
21 ♋ 11p 5
23 ♌ 9a35
25 ♍ 10p16
28 ≏ 10a38
30 ♏ 8p40

D PHASES
2 ○ 4a22
6 ○ 12a28
9 ○ 2p21
12 (11p23
19 ● 7a 0
26) 7p26
30 ○ 5p32
27 ○ 8p41

MAY 1988

☉ -> ♊ 20 2p57

D->SIGNS
3 ♐ 3a53
5 ♑ 8a54
7 ≈ 12p37
9 ♓ 3p39
11 ♈ 6p24
13 ♉ 9p22
16 ♊ 1a32
18 ♋ 8a 6
20 ♌ 5p52
23 ♍ 6a13
25 ≏ 5a 7
28 ♏ 5a 7
30 ♐ 1p33

D PHASES
1 ○ 6p41
5 ○ 9a25
8 ○ 8p23
12 (6a 8
15 ○ 5p11
19 ○ 10p36
23 ○ 11a49
27 ○ 1p14
31 ○ 5a54

JUN 1988

☉ -> ♋ 20 10p57

D->SIGNS
1 ♑ 3p59
3 ♈ 6p34
5 ≈ 9p 1
8 ♈ 12a 4
10 ♉ 4a 3
12 ♊ 9a15
14 ♋ 4p19
16 ♌ 1a58
19 ♍ 2p 0
21 ≏ 1p53
24 ♏ 1p59
26 ♐ 9p18
29 ♑ 1a 9

D PHASES
3 ○ 4p 1
6 ○ 1a22
10 (12p54
13 ○ 4p53
18 ○ 2a18
22 ○ 2a10
26 ○ 3a11
29 ○ 2p46

JUL 1988

☉ -> ♌ 22 9a52

D->SIGNS
1 ≈ 2a30
3 ♓ 3a34
5 ♈ 5a37
7 ♉ 9a27
9 ♊ 3p16
11 ♋ 11p 9
14 ♌ 9a12
16 ♍ 9p18
19 ≏ 10a22
21 ♏ 10p13
24 ♐ 6a42
26 ♑ 11a 7
28 ≈ 12p25
30 ♓ 12p23

D PHASES
2 ○ 9p38
6 ○ 6a37
9 (8p49
13 ○ 4p53
17 ○ 6p50
21 ○ 9p15
24 ○ 2p43
28 ○ 10p26

AUG 1988

☉ -> ♍ 22 4p55

D->SIGNS
1 ♈ 12p53
3 ♉ 3p24
5 ♊ 8p43
8 ♋ 4a53
10 ♌ 3p21
13 ♍ 3a34
15 ≏ 4p52
18 ♏ 5a 8
20 ♐ 2p55
22 ♑ 8p49
24 ≈ 11p 5
27 ♓ 1a15
28 ♈ 10p29
30 ♉ 11p23

D PHASES
1 ○ 3a34
4 ○ 1p23
8 (7a 5
11 ○ 11p50
16 ○ 11a 7
20 ○ 10a52
24 ○ 12a28
27 ○ 5a56
30 ○ 10a54

SEP 1988

☉ -> ≏ 22 2p30

D->SIGNS
2 ♊ 3a12
4 ♋ 10a37
6 ♌ 9p15
9 ♍ 9a26
11 ≏ 10p51
14 ♏ 11a 8
16 ♐ 9p26
19 ♑ 4a45
21 ≈ 8a43
23 ♓ 9a51
25 ♈ 9a30
27 ♉ 9a40
29 ♊ 11a43

D PHASES
2 ○ 10p51
6 (1p24
11 ○ 11p50
15 ○ 2a15
18 ○ 10p19
22 ● 9a13
25 ○ 2p 7
28 ○ 8p32

OCT 1988

☉ -> ♏ 22 11p45

D->SIGNS
1 ♋ 5p39
4 ♌ 3a31
6 ♍ 4p 2
9 ≏ 5a 4
11 ♏ 5p 0
14 ♐ 2a58
16 ♑ 10a45
18 ≈ 4p 5
20 ♓ 6p59
22 ♈ 7p53
24 ♉ 8p23
26 ♊ 9p56
29 ♋ 2a29
31 ♌ 11a 4

D PHASES
2 ○ 11a59
6 (1p24
11 ○ 4p49
15 ○ 3p40
18 ● 8p23
22 ○ 9a12
24 ○ 1a22

NOV 1988

☉ -> ♐ 21 9p13

D->SIGNS
2 ♍ 11p 2
5 ≏ 11p47
7 ♏ 11p58
10 ♐ 9a 6
12 ♑ 4p13
14 ≈ 9p37
17 ♓ 1a34
19 ♈ 4a13
21 ♉ 6a19
23 ♊ 9a 2
25 ♋ 12p20
28 ♌ 7p52
30 ♍ 7p 2

D PHASES
2 ○ 5a12
5 (8a46
10 ○ 3a20
13 ○ 4p36
20 ● 2a10
24 ○ 10a54
30 ○ 1a22

DEC 1988

☉ -> ♑ 21 10a29

D->SIGNS
2 ♏ 7p56
5 ♐ 7a52
7 ♑ 4p56
9 ≈ 11p 7
12 ♓ 3a26
14 ♈ 6a53
16 ♉ 10a 3
18 ♊ 1p11
20 ♋ 4p43
22 ♌ 9p35
25 ♍ 4a58
27 ≏ 3p28
30 ♏ 4a10

D PHASES
1 ○ 1a50
5 (4a54
8 ○ 12a36
12 ○ 1p44
16 ○ 12a41
20 ○ 11a26
23 ○ 12a29
26 ● 8p40
30 ○ 11p57

JAN 1989 – AUG 1989

☉ ingresses:
- JAN 1989: ☉ → ♒ 19 9p 8
- FEB 1989: ☉ → ♓ 18 11a21
- MAR 1989: ☉ → ♈ 20 10a29
- APR 1989: ☉ → ♉ 19 9p39
- MAY 1989: ☉ → ♊ 20 8p54
- JUN 1989: ☉ → ♋ 21 4a54
- JUL 1989: ☉ → ♌ 22 3p46
- AUG 1989: ☉ → ♍ 22 10p47

D → SIGNS

JAN 1989	FEB 1989	MAR 1989	APR 1989	MAY 1989	JUN 1989	JUL 1989	AUG 1989
1 ♏ 4p34	2 ♑ 6p30	2 ♑ 3a58	2 ♓ 8p37	2 ♈ 6a51	2 ♊ 5p 3	2 ♋ 4a19	3 ♍ 2a19
4 ♐ 2a12	4 ♒ 9p51	4 ♒ 8a37	4 ♈ 8p51	4 ♉ 6a55	4 ♋ 7p17	4 ♌ 9a38	5 ♎ 1p28
6 ♑ 8a14	6 ♓ 10p52	6 ♓ 9a59	6 ♉ 8p 9	6 ♊ 7a 3	7 ♌ 12a28	6 ♍ 6p 5	8 ♏ 2p 3
8 ♒ 11a31	8 ♈ 11p18	8 ♈ 9a37	8 ♊ 8p31	8 ♋ 9a20	9 ♍ 9a30	9 ♎ 5a31	10 ♐ 2p 3
10 ♓ 1p31	11 ♉ 1p31	10 ♉ 9a25	10 ♋ 11p58	10 ♌ 3p23	11 ♎ 9p31	11 ♏ 6p 9	12 ♑ 11p17
12 ♈ 3p36	13 ♊ 4a23	12 ♊ 11a16	13 ♌ 7a31	13 ♍ 1a30	14 ♏ 10a11	14 ♐ 5a32	15 ♒ 4a59
14 ♉ 6p36	15 ♋ 10a40	14 ♋ 4p28	15 ♍ 6p40	15 ♎ 2p 8	16 ♐ 9p13	16 ♑ 2p 2	17 ♓ 7a46
16 ♊ 10p57	17 ♌ 7p33	17 ♌ 1a13	18 ♎ 7a32	18 ♏ 2a48	19 ♑ 5a42	18 ♒ 7p36	19 ♈ 8a59
19 ♋ 4a57	20 ♍ 6a35	19 ♍ 12p40	20 ♏ 8p14	20 ♐ 1p52	21 ♒ 11a57	20 ♓ 11p 7	21 ♉ 10a16
21 ♌ 1p 3	22 ♎ 7p 5	22 ♎ 1a24	23 ♐ 7a39	22 ♑ 10p54	23 ♓ 4p37	23 ♈ 1a41	23 ♊ 12p39
23 ♍ 11p33	25 ♏ 7a57	24 ♏ 2p11	25 ♑ 5p 4	25 ♒ 6a 1	25 ♈ 8p 6	25 ♉ 4a10	25 ♋ 5p14
26 ♎ 12p 2	27 ♐ 7p30	27 ♐ 1a54	28 ♒ 12a33	27 ♓ 11a13	27 ♉ 10p45	27 ♊ 7a15	28 ♌ 12a12
29 ♏ 12a49		29 ♑ 11a26	30 ♓ 5a 4	29 ♈ 2p26	30 ♊ 1a 9	29 ♋ 11a32	30 ♍ 9a30
31 ♐ 11a31		31 ♒ 5p45		31 ♉ 4p 0		31 ♌ 5p41	

D PHASES

JAN 1989	FEB 1989	MAR 1989	APR 1989	MAY 1989	JUN 1989	JUL 1989	AUG 1989
4 ☽ 12a 0	2 ☽ 4p48	4 ☽ 6a43	2 ● 5p35	2 ● 1a43	3 ● 2p53	2 ● 11p59	1 ● 11a 6
7 ● 2p23	6 ● 2a37	7 ● 1p19	5 ☽ 10p33	5 ☽ 6a47	7 ☽ 3a21	7 ☽ 5p43	5 ☽ 9a46
10 ☽ 11p23	9 ☽ 8a44	10 ☽ 6p 8	9 ○ 3a59	8 ○ 2p52	10 ○ 1a59	10 ○ 7p19	10 ○ 12p29
14 ○ 8a59	12 ○ 6p15	14 ○ 5a11	12 ○ 6p13	12 ○ 9a20	15 ○ 4a40	15 ○ 8p 1	13 ○ 10a 0
17 ○ 10p 8	16 ○ 10a58	18 ○ 2a 4	16 ○ 6p50	16 ○ 12p 4	18 ○ 1a58	18 ○ 12p42	17 ○ 10p 7
21 ○ 4p34	20 ☽ 10a32	22 ○ 4a58	20 ○ 10p14	20 ○ 1p17	22 ○ 4p58	22 ○ 11p22	20 ○ 5a11
25 ○ 5p40	24 ○ 2p 4	26 ☽ 7a51	24 ○ 10p 4	24 ○ 8a52	25 ☽ 4a 9	25 ☽ 8a32	24 ☽ 0p41
29 ☽ 9p 3	28 ☽ 3p 8	30 ☽ 5a22	28 ☽ 3p46	27 ☽ 11p 1	29 ☽ 1p18	28 ☽ 7p28	27 ☽ 3a53
				31 ○ 7a53			31 ☽ 2a45

SEP 1989 – APR 1990

☉ ingresses:
- SEP 1989: ☉ → ♎ 22 8p20
- OCT 1989: ☉ → ♏ 23 5a36
- NOV 1989: ☉ → ♐ 22 3a 5
- DEC 1989: ☉ → ♑ 21 4p23
- JAN 1990: ☉ → ♒ 20 3a 2
- FEB 1990: ☉ → ♓ 18 5p15
- MAR 1990: ☉ → ♈ 20 4p20
- APR 1990: ☉ → ♉ 20 3a27

D → SIGNS

SEP 1989	OCT 1989	NOV 1989	DEC 1989	JAN 1990	FEB 1990	MAR 1990	APR 1990
1 ♎ 8p48	1 ♏ 3p53	2 ♑ 9p47	2 ♒ 12p42	1 ♓ 1a10	1 ♉ 2p27	2 ♊ 10p38	2 ♋ 7a50
4 ♏ 9a23	4 ♐ 4a30	5 ♒ 7p48	4 ♓ 7p48	3 ♈ 5a57	3 ♊ 5p13	5 ♋ 2a 3	3 ♌ 12p50
6 ♐ 9p51	6 ♑ 3p46	7 ♓ 1p25	7 ♈ 12a12	5 ♉ 9a 4	5 ♋ 8p27	7 ♌ 7a25	5 ♍ 8p42
9 ♑ 8a13	9 ♒ 12a 7	9 ♈ 4p 8	9 ♉ 1a59	7 ♊ 11a42	8 ♌ 12a52	9 ♍ 2p47	8 ♎ 6a45
11 ♒ 3p 2	11 ♓ 4a38	11 ♉ 4p10	11 ♊ 2a15	9 ♋ 12p52	10 ♍ 7a13	12 ♎ 12a 9	10 ♏ 6p18
13 ♓ 6p38	13 ♈ 5a42	13 ♊ 3p51	13 ♋ 2a49	11 ♌ 4p 3	12 ♎ 4p 3	14 ♏ 11a25	13 ♐ 7a15
15 ♈ 6p37	15 ♉ 4a53	15 ♋ 3p19	15 ♌ 5a42	13 ♍ 9p58	15 ♏ 3a35	16 ♐ 11p56	15 ♑ 7p53
17 ♉ 6p23	17 ♊ 4a19	17 ♌ 6p 1	17 ♍ 12p20	16 ♎ 7a18	17 ♐ 4p 3	19 ♑ 12p 2	18 ♒ 5a33
19 ♊ 7p16	19 ♋ 6a10	20 ♍ 0p46	20 ♎ 10p46	18 ♏ 7p16	20 ♑ 3a31	21 ♒ 9p32	20 ♓ 12p57
21 ♋ 10p51	21 ♌ 11a48	22 ♎ 11a19	22 ♏ 11a19	21 ♐ 7a44	22 ♒ 11a53	24 ♓ 3a 9	22 ♈ 3p59
24 ♌ 5a45	23 ♍ 9p15	25 ♏ 4a14	24 ♐ 11p37	23 ♑ 6p28	24 ♓ 4p50	26 ♈ 5a16	24 ♉ 4p 3
26 ♍ 2p35	26 ♎ 9a11	27 ♐ 9a 7	27 ♑ 10a11	26 ♒ 2a25	26 ♈ 7p17	28 ♉ 5a27	26 ♊ 3p39
29 ♎ 3a15	28 ♏ 9p56	30 ♑ 3a27	29 ♒ 6p38	28 ♓ 7a51	28 ♉ 8p43	30 ♊ 5a42	28 ♋ 3p49
	31 ♐ 10a23			30 ♈ 11a34			30 ♌ 7p 9

D PHASES

SEP 1989	OCT 1989	NOV 1989	DEC 1989	JAN 1990	FEB 1990	MAR 1990	APR 1990
4 ● 2a50	3 ☽ 8p 2	2 ☽ 12p32	3 ☽ 3a34	2 ○ 5a41	2 ○ 1p33	3 ○ 9p 5	2 ○ 5a24
8 ☽ 4a50	7 ○ 7p53	5 ● 8p26	5 ● 8p26	7 ○ 2p46	6 ● 12a10	7 ● 10a42	5 ● 10p46
11 ○ 10p41	11 ○ 10a 9	9 ○ 9a11	9 ○ 5a48	10 ☽ 11p57	9 ☽ 2p16	11 ☽ 5a59	10 ☽ 10p19
15 ○ 6a51	14 ○ 3p32	13 ○ 12a52	13 ○ 12a52	14 ○ 3p37	14 ○ 11a 8	15 ○ 6a46	14 ○ 1a 5
18 ○ 11a39	17 ☽ 7p58	16 ○ 11p44	16 ○ 6p55	18 ○ 4p18	17 ○ 1p48	17 ○ 9a31	18 ○ 2a 3
21 ☽ 9p10	21 ☽ 8a19	19 ☽ 11p44	19 ☽ 9p53	22 ☽ 1p30	21 ☽ 1p30	21 ☽ 5a20	21 ☽ 5p34
25 ☽ 3p39	25 ☽ 7a 9	23 ● 10p20	23 ● 10p13	26 ● 2p20	24 ● 3a55	26 ● 2p49	24 ● 11p28
29 ● 4p47	29 ● 10a27	27 ● 4p22	27 ☽ 10p20	30 ☽ 3a21	28 ☽ 12p15	29 ☽ 8p 4	28 ☽ 3a49
			31 ☽ 4p34				

MAY 1990 – DEC 1990

☉ ingresses:
- MAY 1990: ☉ → ♊ 21 2a38
- JUN 1990: ☉ → ♋ 21 10a33
- JUL 1990: ☉ → ♌ 22 9p22
- AUG 1990: ☉ → ♍ 23 4a21
- SEP 1990: ☉ → ♎ 23 1a56
- OCT 1990: ☉ → ♏ 23 11a15
- NOV 1990: ☉ → ♐ 22 8a48
- DEC 1990: ☉ → ♑ 21 10p 8

D → SIGNS

MAY 1990	JUN 1990	JUL 1990	AUG 1990	SEP 1990	OCT 1990	NOV 1990	DEC 1990
3 ♍ 2a18	1 ♎ 6p31	1 ♏ 1p 1	2 ♑ 9p 9	1 ♒ 3p51	1 ♓ 8a43	2 ♉ 12a32	2 ♊ 11a23
5 ♎ 12p29	4 ♏ 6a22	3 ♐ 1a36	5 ♒ 7a19	3 ♓ 11p 6	3 ♈ 12p42	4 ♊ 12a36	4 ♋ 11a17
8 ♏ 12a23	6 ♐ 7p 0	6 ♑ 1p40	7 ♓ 2p55	6 ♈ 3a23	5 ♉ 2p 6	6 ♋ 1a24	6 ♌ 2p39
10 ♐ 12p56	9 ♑ 7a12	9 ♒ 12a 7	9 ♈ 8p13	8 ♉ 5a56	7 ♊ 2p47	8 ♌ 4a24	9 ♍ 2p39
13 ♑ 1a21	11 ♒ 6p 9	11 ♓ 8a30	11 ♉ 11p55	10 ♊ 7a47	9 ♋ 4p30	10 ♍ 10a 2	11 ♎ 11a23
15 ♒ 12p31	14 ♓ 3a 0	13 ♈ 2p24	14 ♊ 2a42	12 ♋ 10a53	11 ♌ 8p17	12 ♎ 4p 7	14 ♏ 8p28
17 ♓ 8p54	16 ♈ 8a55	15 ♉ 6p29	16 ♋ 5a13	14 ♌ 2p 8	14 ♍ 2a21	15 ♏ 2a32	16 ♐ 8a28
20 ♈ 1a32	18 ♉ 11a43	17 ♊ 8p32	18 ♌ 8a12	16 ♍ 8p19	16 ♎ 10a27	17 ♐ 2p40	19 ♑ 9p55
22 ♉ 2a43	20 ♊ 12p10	19 ♋ 9p44	20 ♍ 12p33	19 ♎ 4a56	18 ♏ 8p24	20 ♑ 3a32	22 ♒ 9p48
24 ♊ 2a 0	22 ♋ 12p10	21 ♌ 11p29	22 ♎ 7p17	21 ♏ 1p 6	21 ♐ 8a10	22 ♒ 4p 9	24 ♓ 10p16
26 ♋ 1a25	24 ♌ 1p25	24 ♍ 3a18	25 ♏ 4a56	24 ♐ 1a37	23 ♑ 9p 3	25 ♓ 2a 9	27 ♈ 6a22
28 ♌ 3a29	26 ♍ 5p42	26 ♎ 10a19	27 ♐ 4p58	26 ♑ 2p 8	26 ♒ 9a14	27 ♈ 9a 7	29 ♉ 11a38
30 ♍ 9a 8	29 ♎ 1a47	28 ♏ 8p40	30 ♑ 5a23	29 ♒ 12a54	28 ♓ 6p22	29 ♉ 11a38	31 ♊ 1p36
		31 ♐ 9a 0			30 ♈ 11p15		

D PHASES

MAY 1990	JUN 1990	JUL 1990	AUG 1990	SEP 1990	OCT 1990	NOV 1990	DEC 1990
1 ○ 3p18	4 ○ 3a16	3 ○ 7p 6	1 ○ 11a28	1 ○ 3a46	1 ○ 7a 2	2 ● 4p49	2 ● 2a50
5 ● 12p28	8 ● 6a 0	7 ● 8p24	6 ● 9a20	4 ● 8p46	4 ● 7p32	9 ☽ 9p33	5 ☽ 7a54
9 ☽ 2p31	12 ☽ 6a10	11 ☽ 6a 4	10 ☽ 12a18	8 ☽ 6a54	7 ☽ 7p19	13 ☽ 3a 5	9 ☽ 9p 4
13 ○ 5p 3	15 ○ 11p48	15 ○ 6a14	13 ○ 10a55	11 ○ 11p43	11 ○ 10p32	16 ○ 4a51	13 ○ 3a 5
17 ○ 2p45	19 ○ 8a59	18 ○ 10p55	17 ○ 8p15	16 ○ 5a39	14 ○ 1p43	21 ○ 7a51	16 ○ 11p22
21 ☽ 6a48	22 ☽ 1p55	22 ☽ 8p15	21 ☽ 7a39	18 ☽ 12p39	18 ☽ 10a37	25 ● 8a12	21 ● 2a 0
24 ● 6a48	25 ☽ 10p38	25 ● 5a 8	24 ● 1a22	22 ● 12p39	22 ● 12p39	28 ☽ 9p52	24 ☽ 10p16
27 ☽ 12p26	29 ○ 5p 8	29 ○ 9a 2	28 ○ 2a35	26 ○ 6p 7	26 ○ 3p27		31 ○ 1p36
31 ○ 3a11				30 ○ 7p16	30 ○ 9a23		

JAN 1991

☉ -> ≈   20   8a48

☽ -> SIGNS

1	♏	9p55
3	♐	11p57
6	♑	5a34
8	♒	3p 0
11	♓	3a 7
13	♈	4p 1
16	♉	4a 5
18	♊	2p24
20	♋	10p28
23	♌	4a 1
25	♍	7a 7
27	♎	8a23
29	♏	9a 4
31	♐	10a44

☽ PHASES

3	○	8p50
7	◐	1p36
11	●	3p32
15	◑	6p50
19	○	5p31
23	◐	9a22
26	○	6p35
30	●	1a10

FEB 1991

☉ -> ♓   18   10p59

☽ -> SIGNS

2	♎	3p 3
4	♏	11p 2
6	♐	10a24
9	♑	11p16
11	♒	11a17
14	♓	8p59
17	♈	4a12
19	♉	9a25
21	♊	1p11
23	♋	3p57
25	♌	6p13
27	♍	8p50

☽ PHASES

2	◐	12p 4
6	●	8a53
10	◑	12p21
14	○	12p32
18	◐	5a44
21	●	5p59
25	○	3a32
28	●	1p25

MAR 1991

☉ -> ♈   20   10p 3

☽ -> SIGNS

2	♎	1a 4
4	♏	8a 9
6	♐	6p35
9	♑	7a14
11	♒	7p31
14	♓	5a11
16	♈	11a38
18	♉	3p41
20	♊	6p 9
22	♋	9p28
25	♌	12a44
27	♍	4a41
29	♎	9a50
31	♏	5p 1

☽ PHASES

4	○	4a58
8	●	5a32
12	◑	12p21
16	●	3a11
19	◑	3p 2
23	○	1a 3
26	◐	12p13
30	●	3p59

APR 1991

☉ -> ♉   20   9a 9

☽ -> SIGNS

2	♐	2a59
5	♑	3p20
7	♒	4a 0
10	♓	2p18
12	♈	7p31
15	♉	12a 6
17	♊	1a41
19	♋	3a18
21	♌	6a 5
23	♍	10a30
25	♎	4p36
28	♏	12a34
30	♐	10a42

☽ PHASES

2	○	10p50
7	◑	1a46
11	●	1a16
15	◐	2p38
17	○	10p27
21	○	7a39
24	◐	9p17
28	○	3p59

MAY 1991

☉ -> ♊   21   8a21

☽ -> SIGNS

2	♑	10p55
4	♒	11a51
7	♓	11p 5
10	♈	6a35
12	♉	10a 8
14	♊	11a 2
16	♋	11a14
18	♌	12p30
20	♍	4p 1
22	♎	10p 8
25	♏	6a42
27	♐	5p21
30	♑	5a41

☽ PHASES

2	○	4p48
6	◑	7p47
10	●	2p49
14	◐	11p36
17	○	5a 8
20	○	2p46
24	○	7a31
28	○	6a37

JUN 1991

☉ -> ♋   21   4p19

☽ -> SIGNS

1	♒	6p42
4	♓	6a37
6	♈	3p26
8	♉	8p13
10	♊	9p37
12	♋	9p17
14	♌	9p11
16	♍	11p 3
19	♎	4a 2
21	♏	12p19
23	♐	11p16
26	♑	11a50
28	♒	12a48

☽ PHASES

1	○	9a48
5	◑	10a30
8	●	1a10
12	◐	7a 6
15	○	12p 2
18	○	11p20
22	○	7p40
26	●	9p59

JUL 1991

☉ -> ♌   23   3a12

☽ -> SIGNS

1	♓	12p51
3	♈	10p34
6	♉	4a52
8	♊	7a42
10	♋	8a 3
12	♌	7a35
14	♍	8a12
16	♎	11a34
18	♏	6p41
21	♐	5a17
23	♑	5p56
26	♒	6a49
28	♓	6p35
31	♈	4a21

☽ PHASES

1	○	12a50
4	◑	9p51
7	●	2p 7
11	◐	8p 1
14	○	8p 1
18	○	10a11
22	○	10a 5
26	○	1p25
30	○	9p21

AUG 1991

☉ -> ♍   23   10a14

☽ -> SIGNS

2	♉	11a32
4	♊	3p55
6	♋	5p47
8	♌	6p10
10	♍	6p35
12	♎	8p52
15	♏	2a14
17	♐	12p11
20	♑	12a35
22	♒	1p27
25	♓	12a52
27	♈	10a 1
29	♉	5p 0
31	♊	10p 3

☽ PHASES

3	○	6a26
6	◐	3p59
10	●	9p28
13	◑	5a55
17	○	12a 1
21	○	2a34
25	○	4a 8
28	○	11p33

SEP 1991

☉ -> ♎   23   7a49

☽ -> SIGNS

3	♋	1a20
5	♌	3a13
7	♍	4a35
9	♎	6a52
11	♏	11a42
13	♐	8p15
16	♑	8a 4
18	♒	8p58
21	♓	8a21
23	♈	4p56
25	♉	11p 0
28	♊	3a32
30	♋	6a59

☽ PHASES

1	○	1p17
4	◐	10p25
8	●	6a 1
11	◑	6p31
15	○	5p 2
19	○	8p12
23	○	5p40
27	○	8a13
30	◐	7p30

OCT 1991

☉ -> ♏   23   5p 6

☽ -> SIGNS

2	♌	9a59
4	♍	12p45
6	♎	4p 1
9	♏	9p 0
11	♐	4a58
13	♑	4p11
16	♒	5a 5
18	♓	4p53
21	♈	1a33
23	♉	6a56
25	♊	10a 9
27	♋	12p37
29	♌	3p21
31	♍	6p47

☽ PHASES

4	◐	5a28
7	●	4p39
11	◑	10a24
15	○	12p33
19	○	11p52
23	◐	6a 9
26	○	4p23
30	●	2a11

NOV 1991

☉ -> ♐   22   2p37

☽ -> SIGNS

2	♎	11p13
5	♏	5a 9
7	♐	1p22
10	♑	12a17
12	♒	1p 7
15	♓	1a34
17	♈	11a 8
19	♉	4p49
21	♊	7p 1
23	♋	8p26
25	♌	9p38
28	♍	12a 1
30	♎	4a47

☽ PHASES

2	◐	2p 9
6	●	6a11
10	◑	5a20
14	○	9a 2
18	○	10a42
21	◐	3p43
25	○	12a57
28	○	10a22

DEC 1991

☉ -> ♑   22   3a54

☽ -> SIGNS

2	♏	11a33
4	♐	8p33
7	♑	7a41
9	♒	8p27
12	♓	9a20
14	♈	8p 7
17	♉	3a10
19	♊	6a22
21	♋	6a55
23	♌	6a39
25	♍	7a24
27	♎	10a38
30	♏	5p 4

☽ PHASES

2	◐	2p 9
4	●	1a28
10	◑	10p57
14	○	4a32
18	○	9p46
21	○	5a24
24	◐	10a34
28	●	8p55
31	◑	4p 9

JAN 1992

☉ -> ≈   20   2p33

☽ -> SIGNS

1	♐	2a30
3	♑	2p 9
6	♒	3a 0
8	♓	3p52
11	♈	3a23
13	♉	12p 1
15	♊	4p55
17	♋	6p26
19	♌	5p57
21	♍	5p22
23	♎	6p43
25	♏	11p32
28	♐	8a20
30	♑	8p 8

☽ PHASES

1	●	6p10
8	◑	10p 7
16	○	11a13
19	○	4p29
22	○	9p31
26	○	10a28
30	●	9a58

FEB 1992

☉ -> ♓   19   4a44

☽ -> SIGNS

2	♒	9a 9
4	♓	9p51
7	♈	9a15
9	♉	8p26
12	♊	1a 8
14	♋	4a47
16	♌	5a16
18	♍	4a47
20	♎	5a22
24	♏	3p27
26	♐	3p34
29	♑	3p34

☽ PHASES

3	○	2p 0
7	◑	3p45
11	●	11a15
14	○	10p 7
18	○	3a 5
22	○	9p31
25	◑	5a35

MAR 1992

☉ -> ♈   20   3a49

☽ -> SIGNS

3	♓	4a11
5	♈	3p 7
8	♉	12a 5
10	♊	7a 4
12	♋	11a50
14	♌	2p21
16	♍	3p14
18	♎	3p55
20	♏	6p20
23	♐	12a13
25	♑	10a 9
27	♒	10p45
30	♓	11a24

☽ PHASES

4	◐	8a23
8	●	5a55
11	◑	9p36
15	○	7a 2
18	○	10p18
22	○	12a 4
25	○	9p30
30	◐	12a58

APR 1992

☉ -> ♉   19   2p57

☽ -> SIGNS

1	♈	10p 4
4	♉	6a18
6	♊	12p33
8	♋	5p19
10	♌	8p46
12	♍	11p 9
15	♎	1a11
17	♏	4a10
19	♐	9a41
21	♑	6p20
24	♒	6a39
26	♓	7p20
29	♈	6a14

☽ PHASES

3	◐	12a 2
6	●	4p43
10	◑	2p20
13	○	4p39
17	○	11p43
20	○	9a39
24	○	4p40
28	◐	6p30

MAY 1992

☉ -> ♊   20   2p13

☽ -> SIGNS

1	♉	2p10
3	♊	7p29
5	♋	11p10
8	♌	2a 8
10	♍	4a56
12	♎	8a 5
14	♏	12p15
16	♐	6p22
19	♑	3a13
21	♒	2p44
24	♓	3a26
26	♈	2p53
28	♉	11p17
31	♊	4a19

☽ PHASES

2	○	12p45
6	◑	12a48
9	●	10a44
12	○	9p 8
16	○	11a 3
20	○	8a13
24	◑	10a54
28	◐	9a30
31	●	10p57

JUN 1992

☉ -> ♋   20   10p15

☽ -> SIGNS

2	♋	6a58
4	♌	8a35
6	♍	10a28
8	♎	1p34
10	♏	6p27
13	♐	1a29
15	♑	10a50
17	♒	10p19
20	♓	11a 0
22	♈	11p 4
25	♉	9a 3
27	♊	2p14
29	♋	4p42

☽ PHASES

4	◑	7a 7
7	●	3p47
11	◑	2p26
14	○	11p50
18	○	5p 0
23	○	3a12
26	◐	8a21
30	●	7a18

JUL 1992

☉ -> ♍   22   9a 9

☽ -> SIGNS

1	♌	5p15
3	♍	5p38
5	♎	6p46
7	♏	11p54
10	♐	7a18
12	♑	5p16
15	♒	5a 3
17	♓	5p45
20	♈	6a 8
22	♉	4p36
24	♊	11p45
27	♋	3a 9
29	♌	3a40
31	♍	3a 2

☽ PHASES

3	◑	12p47
6	●	9p44
10	◑	2p26
14	○	2p 7
18	○	5p 0
23	○	5p13
26	◐	8a21
31	◑	3a 6

AUG 1992

☉ -> ♎   22   4p11

☽ -> SIGNS

2	♎	3a17
4	♏	6a16
6	♐	12p57
8	♑	10p11
11	♒	11a11
13	♓	11p51
16	♈	12p12
18	♉	11p10
21	♊	7a37
23	♋	12p37
25	♌	2p37
27	♍	1p47
29	♎	1p11
31	♏	2p39

☽ PHASES

1	◑	7p 1
5	●	5a59
9	○	3a28
13	○	7a46
17	○	7a28
21	◑	5p 3
24	◐	6p 2
29	●	9p42
31	◑	3a 6

SEP 1992

☉ -> ♎   22   1p43

☽ -> SIGNS

2	♐	7p50
5	♑	5a 6
7	♒	5p 9
10	♓	5a56
12	♈	6p 3
15	♉	4a47
17	♊	1p40
19	♋	7p59
21	♌	11p19
24	♍	12a 8
26	♎	12a12
28	♏	1a11
30	♐	4a34

☽ PHASES

3	●	5p39
7	○	6p17
11	○	9p17
15	○	9p 3
19	◑	2p53
23	◐	12a42
26	●	5a41
29	◑	2p10

OCT 1992

☉ -> ♏   22   10p58

☽ -> SIGNS

2	♑	12p29
4	♒	11p53
7	♓	12p38
10	♈	1a 0
12	♉	10a49
15	♊	7p 9
17	♋	1a36
19	♌	6a 1
21	♍	8a28
23	♎	9a40
25	♏	11a 5
27	♐	2p29
29	♑	9p18

☽ PHASES

3	○	9a12
7	○	11a59
11	○	1p 3
15	○	8a52
19	◐	11p12
22	●	4p10
25	◑	3p34
29	○	4a53

NOV 1992

☉ -> ♐   21   8p27

☽ -> SIGNS

1	♒	7a44
3	♓	8p13
6	♈	8a20
8	♉	6p19
11	♊	1a50
13	♋	7a19
15	♌	11a23
17	♍	2p29
19	♎	5p 3
21	♏	7p52
23	♐	12a 1
26	♑	6a39
28	♒	4p14

☽ PHASES

2	○	4a12
6	○	7a 1
10	○	4a21
13	○	7p23
17	◐	6a39
20	●	4p22
24	◑	4a12
27	◑	11p 4

DEC 1992

☉ -> ♑   21   9a44

☽ -> SIGNS

1	♓	4a24
3	♈	4p49
6	♉	3a17
8	♊	10a33
10	♋	3p 6
12	♌	5p56
14	♍	7p56
16	♎	10p33
19	♏	2a20
21	♐	7a43
23	♑	3p 5
26	♒	12a43
28	♓	12p28
31	♈	1a 7

☽ PHASES

2	○	1a17
6	○	6p41
9	○	6p41
13	○	6a39
16	◐	2p13
20	●	2a26
23	◑	7p43
27	◑	7p26
30	○	10p39

JAN 1993
☉ -> ♒ 19 8p24

☽->SIGNS
- 2 ♏ 12p30
- 4 ♐ 8p42
- 7 ♑ 1a11
- 9 ♒ 2a50
- 11 ♓ 3a21
- 13 ♈ 4a31
- 15 ♉ 7a42
- 17 ♊ 1p31
- 19 ♋ 9p47
- 22 ♌ 8a 1
- 24 ♍ 7p48
- 27 ♎ 8a28
- 29 ♏ 8p37

☽ PHASES
- 4 ○ 8p11
- 8 ○ 7a38
- 11 ◑ 2p 1
- 14 ◐ 11p 2
- 18 ◑ 3p 2
- 22 ● 1p27
- 26 ◒ 4p 9
- 30 ◓ 6p20

FEB 1993
☉ -> ♓ 18 10a36

☽->SIGNS
- 1 ♊ 6a15
- 3 ♋ 11a57
- 5 ♌ 7p42
- 7 ♍ 1p29
- 9 ♎ 12p59
- 11 ♏ 2p24
- 13 ♐ 7p 8
- 16 ♑ 3a21
- 18 ♒ 2p 6
- 21 ♓ 2a12
- 23 ♈ 2p51
- 26 ♉ 3a12
- 28 ♊ 1p53

☽ PHASES
- 3 ○ 11a44
- 6 ○ 6p56
- 10 ○ 11p22
- 13 ○ 9a57
- 17 ◐ 6a 8
- 21 ● 8a 6
- 25 ◒ 11a22

MAR 1993
☉ -> ♈ 20 9a41

☽->SIGNS
- 2 ♋ 9p17
- 5 ♌ 12a41
- 7 ♍ 2a53
- 8 ♎ 11p47
- 10 ♏ 11p40
- 13 ♐ 2a34
- 15 ♑ 9a28
- 17 ♒ 7p53
- 20 ♓ 8a11
- 22 ♈ 8p52
- 25 ♉ 9a 0
- 27 ♊ 7p48
- 30 ♋ 4a14

☽ PHASES
- 1 ○ 10a47
- 5 ○ 12a 5
- 8 ○ 4a46
- 11 ○ 9a37
- 15 ◐ 1p17
- 18 ◐ 11p 1
- 23 ● 2a15
- 27 ● 3a43
- 30 ● 11p10

APR 1993
☉ -> ♉ 19 8p50

☽->SIGNS
- 1 ♌ 9a22
- 3 ♍ 11a11
- 5 ♎ 10a55
- 7 ♏ 10a32
- 9 ♐ 12p10
- 11 ♑ 5p24
- 14 ♒ 2a36
- 16 ♓ 2p33
- 19 ♈ 3a15
- 21 ♉ 3p 8
- 24 ♊ 1a27
- 26 ♋ 9a46
- 28 ♌ 3p40
- 30 ♍ 7p 0

☽ PHASES
- 3 ○ 9a18
- 6 ○ 1p44
- 9 ○ 9p 9
- 13 ○ 2p39
- 17 ◐ 9a57
- 21 ● 6p49
- 25 ◒ 1a50
- 28 ◒ 1p22
- 30 ○ 10p 6

MAY 1993
☉ -> ♊ 20 8p 2

☽->SIGNS
- 2 ♎ 8p20
- 4 ♏ 8p58
- 6 ♐ 10p35
- 9 ♑ 2a51
- 11 ♒ 10a44
- 13 ♓ 9p51
- 16 ♈ 10a25
- 18 ♉ 10p17
- 21 ♊ 8a 8
- 23 ♋ 3p38
- 25 ♌ 9p 3
- 28 ♍ 12a47
- 30 ♎ 3a18

☽ PHASES
- 2 ○ 4p13
- 6 ○ 10p34
- 9 ○ 10a 5
- 13 ○ 7a20
- 17 ◐ 9a57
- 21 ● 9a 7
- 24 ◒ 7a41
- 28 ○ 1p22
- 31 ○ 10p 6

JUN 1993
☉ -> ♋ 21 4a 0

☽->SIGNS
- 1 ♏ 5a23
- 3 ♐ 8a 2
- 5 ♑ 12p27
- 7 ♒ 7p40
- 10 ♓ 5a57
- 12 ♈ 6p14
- 15 ♉ 6a20
- 17 ♊ 4p12
- 19 ♋ 11p 5
- 22 ♌ 3a27
- 24 ♍ 5a46
- 26 ♎ 8a46
- 28 ♏ 11a38
- 30 ♐ 3p28

☽ PHASES
- 4 ○ 8a13
- 8 ○ 12a17
- 12 ○ 3a36
- 16 ◐ 2a14
- 19 ● 8p53
- 23 ◒ 8a32
- 26 ◒ 4p18
- 30 ○ 4a18

JUL 1993
☉ -> ♌ 22 2p51

☽->SIGNS
- 2 ♑ 8p49
- 5 ♒ 4a15
- 7 ♓ 2p10
- 10 ♈ 2a11
- 12 ♉ 2p38
- 15 ♊ 1a 7
- 17 ♋ 8a 8
- 19 ♌ 11a48
- 21 ♍ 1p24
- 23 ♎ 2p40
- 25 ♏ 5p 0
- 27 ♐ 9p13
- 30 ♑ 3a27

☽ PHASES
- 3 ○ 6p46
- 8 ○ 9p35
- 11 ◐ 5p49
- 15 ◐ 4p54
- 19 ● 6a24
- 22 ◒ 1p55
- 25 ◒ 10p26
- 29 ○ 12p 1

AUG 1993
☉ -> ♍ 22 9p51

☽->SIGNS
- 1 ♒ 11a37
- 3 ♓ 9p44
- 6 ♈ 9a40
- 8 ♉ 10p23
- 11 ♊ 9a35
- 13 ♋ 5p47
- 15 ♌ 9p44
- 17 ♍ 10p41
- 19 ♎ 10p36
- 21 ♏ 11p28
- 24 ♐ 2a46
- 26 ♑ 8a58
- 28 ♒ 5p42
- 31 ♓ 4a19

☽ PHASES
- 2 ○ 7a10
- 6 ○ 7a46
- 10 ○ 10a20
- 14 ◐ 5a38
- 17 ● 2p29
- 20 ◒ 7p31
- 23 ◒ 4a58
- 27 ○ 10p15
- 31 ○ 9p33

SEP 1993
☉ -> ♎ 22 7p23

☽->SIGNS
- 2 ♈ 4p21
- 5 ♉ 5a10
- 7 ♊ 5p16
- 10 ♋ 2a37
- 12 ♌ 7a52
- 14 ♍ 9a21
- 16 ♎ 8a44
- 18 ♏ 8a15
- 20 ♐ 9a54
- 22 ♑ 2p54
- 24 ♒ 11p19
- 27 ♓ 10a13
- 29 ♈ 10p37

☽ PHASES
- 5 ○ 12a26
- 9 ◐ 1a27
- 12 ◐ 4p33
- 15 ● 10p11
- 19 ◒ 2a45
- 22 ○ 2p33
- 26 ○ 11a38
- 30 ○ 1p54

OCT 1993
☉ -> ♏ 23 4a38

☽->SIGNS
- 2 ♉ 11a14
- 4 ♊ 11p27
- 7 ♋ 9a43
- 9 ♌ 4p34
- 11 ♍ 7p36
- 13 ♎ 7p48
- 15 ♏ 7p 1
- 17 ♐ 7p24
- 19 ♑ 10p42
- 22 ♒ 5a49
- 24 ♓ 4p18
- 27 ♈ 4a40
- 29 ♉ 5p21

☽ PHASES
- 4 ○ 4p51
- 8 ○ 2p36
- 12 ◐ 2a 7
- 15 ● 6a36
- 18 ◒ 12p43
- 22 ○ 3a53
- 26 ○ 4a21
- 30 ○ 7a38

NOV 1993
☉ -> ♐ 22 2a 8

☽->SIGNS
- 1 ♊ 5a13
- 3 ♋ 3p25
- 5 ♌ 11p 7
- 8 ♍ 3a48
- 10 ♎ 5a43
- 12 ♏ 6a 0
- 14 ♐ 6a11
- 16 ♑ 8a35
- 18 ♒ 2p 8
- 20 ♓ 11p28
- 23 ♈ 11a31
- 25 ♉ 11p46
- 28 ♊ 11a48
- 30 ♋ 9p18

☽ PHASES
- 3 ○ 8a 1
- 7 ○ 1a36
- 10 ◐ 11a 2
- 13 ● 4p35
- 17 ◒ 1a55
- 20 ○ 9p 4
- 24 ○ 11p53
- 29 ○ 1a31

DEC 1993
☉ -> ♑ 21 3p27

☽->SIGNS
- 3 ♌ 4a33
- 5 ♍ 9a43
- 7 ♎ 1p 4
- 9 ♏ 3p 5
- 11 ♐ 5p40
- 13 ♑ 9p 6
- 15 ♒ 11p52
- 17 ♓ 7a59
- 20 ♈ 7p19
- 23 ♉ 8a 5
- 25 ♊ 7p46
- 28 ♋ 4a46
- 30 ♌ 11a 0

☽ PHASES
- 2 ○ 9p10
- 6 ○ 10a49
- 9 ◐ 8p 0
- 13 ● 4a27
- 17 ◒ 1a55
- 20 ○ 5p26
- 24 ○ 8p43
- 28 ○ 6p 6

JAN 1994
☉ -> ♒ 20 2a 8

☽->SIGNS
- 1 ♏ 3p15
- 4 ♐ 6a15
- 6 ♑ 9p33
- 8 ♒ 9p29
- 10 ♓ 4a16
- 12 ♈ 4a16
- 14 ♉ 5p 4
- 17 ♊ 3a42
- 19 ♋ 4p22
- 22 ♌ 11p28
- 24 ♍ 5a48
- 26 ♎ 8a28
- 28 ♏ 9a 6
- 31 ♐ 12a34

☽ PHASES
- 1 ○ 8a11
- 4 ○ 7p 1
- 8 ◐ 5a34
- 11 ● 6p11
- 15 ◒ 1p 1
- 19 ○ 3p27
- 23 ○ 4p42
- 27 ○ 8a23
- 30 ○ 5p37

FEB 1994
☉ -> ♓ 18 4p22

☽->SIGNS
- 2 ♐ 2a50
- 4 ♑ 6a15
- 6 ♒ 9p29
- 8 ♓ 5p17
- 11 ♈ 1a23
- 13 ♉ 1a50
- 16 ♊ 5p 4
- 18 ♋ 10p28
- 20 ♌ 5p48
- 23 ♍ 5a48
- 25 ♎ 9a 6
- 27 ♎ 9a 6

☽ PHASES
- 3 ○ 3a 7
- 6 ◐ 4p 8
- 10 ● 9a30
- 14 ◒ 12p48
- 18 ○ 12p48
- 22 ○ 8p16
- 25 ○ 8p16

MAR 1994
☉ -> ♈ 20 3p29

☽->SIGNS
- 1 ♐ 9a44
- 3 ♑ 11a54
- 5 ♒ 4p25
- 7 ♓ 11p15
- 10 ♈ 8a10
- 12 ♉ 6p59
- 15 ♊ 7a28
- 17 ♋ 8p29
- 20 ♌ 7a54
- 22 ♍ 3p40
- 24 ♎ 7p47
- 26 ♏ 7p15
- 28 ♐ 7p 0
- 30 ♑ 7p42

☽ PHASES
- 1 ○ 2a20
- 4 ◐ 11a54
- 8 ● 4a 2
- 12 ◒ 2a 5
- 16 ○ 5a 2
- 20 ○ 11p36
- 23 ○ 11p36
- 27 ○ 6a30
- 30 ○ 11a 1

APR 1994
☉ -> ♉ 20 2a37

☽->SIGNS
- 1 ♒ 10p38
- 4 ♓ 4a46
- 6 ♈ 1p51
- 9 ♉ 1a 9
- 11 ♊ 1p48
- 14 ♋ 2a48
- 16 ♌ 2p41
- 18 ♍ 11p45
- 21 ♎ 4a58
- 23 ♏ 6a41
- 25 ♐ 6a19
- 27 ♑ 5a49
- 29 ♒ 7a 5

☽ PHASES
- 2 ○ 9p55
- 6 ◐ 5p32
- 10 ● 7p18
- 14 ◒ 10p54
- 18 ○ 9p35
- 22 ○ 2p45
- 25 ○ 2p45
- 28 ○ 8p11

MAY 1994
☉ -> ♊ 21 1a49

☽->SIGNS
- 1 ♓ 11a35
- 3 ♈ 7p47
- 6 ♉ 7a 2
- 8 ♊ 7p51
- 11 ♋ 8a44
- 13 ♌ 8p27
- 16 ♍ 5a12
- 18 ♎ 12p31
- 20 ♏ 3p55
- 22 ♐ 4p51
- 24 ♑ 4p43
- 26 ♒ 5p17
- 28 ♓ 8p19
- 31 ♈ 3a 4

☽ PHASES
- 2 ○ 9a33
- 6 ◐ 8a38
- 10 ● 12p 7
- 14 ◒ 1p27
- 18 ○ 7a50
- 21 ○ 5p39
- 24 ○ 10p40
- 28 ○ 6a13
- 31 ○ 11p 3

JUN 1994
☉ -> ♋ 21 9p48

☽->SIGNS
- 2 ♉ 1p32
- 5 ♊ 2a14
- 7 ♋ 3p 9
- 10 ♌ 2a22
- 12 ♍ 11a29
- 14 ♎ 6p17
- 16 ♏ 10p48
- 19 ♐ 1a20
- 21 ♑ 2a33
- 23 ♒ 3a37
- 25 ♓ 6a10
- 27 ♈ 11a45
- 29 ♉ 9p 7

☽ PHASES
- 5 ◐ 12a58
- 9 ● 3a27
- 12 ◒ 12a28
- 16 ○ 2p57
- 20 ○ 11p50
- 23 ○ 6a34
- 26 ○ 5p37
- 29 ○ 2p31

JUL 1994
☉ -> ♌ 22 8p42

☽->SIGNS
- 2 ♊ 9a18
- 4 ♋ 10p13
- 7 ♌ 9a18
- 9 ♍ 5p44
- 11 ♎ 11p49
- 14 ♏ 4a15
- 16 ♐ 7a35
- 18 ♑ 10a10
- 20 ♒ 12p51
- 22 ♓ 3p39
- 24 ♈ 8p57
- 27 ♉ 5a31
- 29 ♊ 5p13

☽ PHASES
- 4 ◐ 5p36
- 8 ● 9p38
- 12 ◒ 8a37
- 16 ○ 8p12
- 19 ○ 11a49
- 22 ○ 3p16
- 26 ○ 6a59
- 29 ○ 7a41

AUG 1994
☉ -> ♍ 23 3a44

☽->SIGNS
- 1 ♋ 6a 5
- 3 ♌ 5p23
- 6 ♍ 1a31
- 8 ♎ 6a43
- 10 ♏ 10a 7
- 12 ♐ 12p56
- 14 ♑ 3p53
- 16 ♒ 7p18
- 18 ♓ 11p34
- 21 ♈ 5a28
- 23 ♉ 1p55
- 26 ♊ 1a14
- 28 ♋ 2p 8
- 31 ♌ 2a 0

☽ PHASES
- 3 ◐ 9a42
- 7 ● 3a46
- 10 ◒ 3p 8
- 15 ○ 2a58
- 17 ○ 11a49
- 21 ○ 1a47
- 24 ○ 10p40
- 29 ● 1a41

SEP 1994
☉ -> ♎ 23 1a20

☽->SIGNS
- 2 ♌ 10a38
- 4 ♍ 3p34
- 6 ♎ 7p26
- 8 ♏ 9p26
- 10 ♐ 11p10
- 12 ♑ 12a45
- 15 ♒ 3p53
- 17 ♓ 2p32
- 19 ♈ 9p30
- 22 ♉ 8a48
- 24 ♊ 9p10
- 27 ♋ 10a12
- 29 ♌ 7p56

☽ PHASES
- 2 ◐ 12a35
- 5 ● 10p56
- 9 ◒ 9p24
- 13 ○ 6a34
- 15 ○ 7a24
- 19 ○ 3p 1
- 23 ○ 4p24
- 27 ○ 7p24

OCT 1994
☉ -> ♏ 23 10a37

☽->SIGNS
- 2 ♍ 1a40
- 4 ♎ 3a57
- 6 ♏ 4a22
- 8 ♐ 4a47
- 10 ♑ 6a44
- 13 ♒ 11a10
- 15 ♓ 6p35
- 17 ♈ 3a57
- 19 ♉ 3p35
- 22 ♊ 4a28
- 24 ♋ 5p16
- 27 ♌ 4a 5
- 29 ♍ 11a22
- 31 ♎ 2p47

☽ PHASES
- 2 ◐ 2p 8
- 5 ● 10p56
- 11 ◒ 2p18
- 13 ○ 10p39
- 15 ○ 7a24
- 19 ○ 7a18
- 23 ○ 11a 1
- 30 ○ 11a45

NOV 1994
☉ -> ♐ 22 8a 7

☽->SIGNS
- 2 ♏ 3p20
- 4 ♐ 2p46
- 6 ♑ 3p 2
- 8 ♒ 5p49
- 11 ♓ 12a12
- 13 ♈ 9a44
- 15 ♉ 9p44
- 18 ♊ 10a42
- 20 ♋ 10a33
- 23 ♌ 11p21
- 25 ♍ 7p 9
- 27 ♎ 9p29
- 30 ♏ 2a22

☽ PHASES
- 3 ◐ 8a36
- 6 ● 1p36
- 10 ○ 10p39
- 13 ○ 10p39
- 18 ○ 10p42
- 22 ○ 2a 4
- 26 ◐ 1p50
- 29 ◐ 12a10

DEC 1994
☉ -> ♑ 21 9p24

☽->SIGNS
- 2 ♐ 2a13
- 4 ♑ 1a43
- 6 ♒ 2a52
- 8 ♓ 7a25
- 10 ♈ 4p 4
- 13 ♉ 3a56
- 15 ♊ 5p 0
- 18 ♋ 5a25
- 20 ♌ 4p13
- 23 ♍ 1a 1
- 25 ♎ 7a28
- 27 ♏ 12p46
- 29 ♐ 12p58
- 31 ♑ 12p58

☽ PHASES
- 2 ● 6p55
- 6 ○ 12a59
- 9 ○ 4p 7
- 13 ○ 5p33
- 18 ○ 9p18
- 21 ○ 8p51
- 25 ○ 2p 7
- 29 ◐ 12a10

JAN 1995	FEB 1995	MAR 1995	APR 1995	MAY 1995	JUN 1995	JUL 1995	AUG 1995
☉ → ≈ 20 8a 1	☉ → ♓ 18 10p11	☉ → ♈ 20 9p15	☉ → ♉ 20 8a22	☉ → ♊ 21 7a35	☉ → ♋ 21 3p35	☉ → ♌ 23 2a30	☉ → ♍ 23 9a36
☽→SIGNS 2 ≈ 1p39 4 ♓ 4p49 6 ♈ 11p57 9 ♉ 10a59 11 ♊ 11p58 14 ♋ 12p20 16 ♌ 10p37 19 ♍ 6a40 21 ♎ 12p54 23 ♏ 5p33 25 ♐ 8p37 27 ♑ 10p27 30 ≈ 12a 3	**☽→SIGNS** 1 ♓ 3a 5 3 ♈ 9a13 5 ♉ 7p 9 8 ♊ 7a44 10 ♋ 8p17 13 ♌ 6a32 15 ♍ 1p52 17 ♎ 7p 1 19 ♏ 10p56 22 ♐ 2a13 24 ♑ 5a11 26 ≈ 8a14 28 ♓ 12p16	**☽→SIGNS** 2 ♓ 6p30 5 ♈ 3a51 7 ♉ 1p30 10 ♊ 1a56 12 ♋ 3p29 15 ♌ 1a47 17 ♍ 10p55 19 ♎ 5a53 21 ♏ 7a58 23 ♐ 10a32 25 ♑ 2p51 27 ♒ 7p18 30 ♈ 2a26	**☽→SIGNS** 2 ♉ 11a59 3 ♊ 11p49 6 ♋ 12a16 9 ♌ 8a39 11 ♍ 1p21 13 ♎ 3p13 15 ♏ 3p52 17 ♐ 4p54 21 ♑ 7p38 24 ≈ 12a51 26 ♓ 8a42 28 ♉ 6p53	**☽→SIGNS** 1 ♉ 6a54 3 ♊ 7p45 6 ♋ 7a55 8 ♌ 5p34 10 ♍ 11p31 13 ♎ 1a54 15 ♏ 1a59 17 ♐ 1a36 19 ♑ 2a14 22 ≈ 6a40 24 ♓ 2p47 26 ♉ 1p 7 28 ♉ 1p 7 31 ♊ 2a 0	**☽→SIGNS** 2 ♋ 2p17 5 ♌ 12a47 7 ♍ 7a55 9 ♎ 12p 4 11 ♏ 12p50 13 ♐ 12p 5 15 ♑ 11a52 17 ≈ 2p14 19 ♓ 8p29 22 ♈ 6a36 24 ♉ 7p 3 27 ♊ 7a57 29 ♋ 8p 2	**☽→SIGNS** 2 ♍ 6a36 4 ♎ 2p56 6 ♏ 8p19 9 ♐ 10p38 11 ♑ 10p44 13 ≈ 10p21 15 ♓ 11p37 17 ♈ 4a23 19 ♉ 1p21 22 ♊ 1a24 24 ♋ 2p18 27 ♌ 2a 7 29 ♍ 12p12 31 ♎ 8p24	**☽→SIGNS** 1 ♍ 2a30 3 ♎ 6a14 5 ♏ 7a52 7 ♐ 8a28 9 ♑ 9a47 11 ≈ 1p41 13 ♓ 9p26 16 ♈ 8a40 18 ♉ 9p24 21 ♊ 9a13 23 ♋ 6p51 28 ♌ 2a15 30 ♍ 7a52
☽ PHASES 1 ● 5a56 8 ◐ 10a27 16 ○ 3p27 23 ◑ 11p58 30 ● 5p48	**☽ PHASES** 3 ◐ 7a46 7 ◐ 7a55 15 ○ 11a 3 18 ○ 8p59 21 ◑ 8a 4 25 ◑ 6p23	**☽ PHASES** 1 ● 6a48 5 ◐ 2a23 9 ◐ 5a14 16 ○ 8p26 20 ○ 1p23 23 ◑ 3p10 27 ◑ 3a33 30 ● 9p 9	**☽ PHASES** 3 ◐ 9p32 7 ○ 4p44 11 ○ 8p44 15 ◑ 7a 9 18 ◑ 1p23 25 ◑ 1p59 29 ● 12p37	**☽ PHASES** 3 ○ 3p35 7 ○ 4p44 11 ○ 8a50 14 ○ 3p49 17 ○ 3p49 21 ◑ 2a19 25 ◑ 2a19 29 ● 4a28	**☽ PHASES** 2 ◐ 7a21 6 ○ 5a26 9 ○ 6p 8 12 ○ 11p 4 16 ○ 3a54 19 ● 5p 1 23 ◑ 4p35 27 ● 7p50	**☽ PHASES** 1 ◐ 8p27 5 ○ 3p 3 9 ○ 1a14 12 ○ 5a50 15 ◑ 6a10 19 ◑ 6a10 23 ◑ 10a13 31 ● 7a 9	**☽ PHASES** 3 ○ 10p16 7 ○ 7a 6 10 ○ 1p16 14 ○ 12a28 17 ◑ 10p 4 22 ◑ 12a55 26 ● 11p31 29 ● 4p 2

SEP 1995	OCT 1995	NOV 1995	DEC 1995	JAN 1996	FEB 1996	MAR 1996	APR 1996
☉ → ♎ 23 7a14	☉ → ♏ 23 4p32	☉ → ♐ 22 2p 2	☉ → ♑ 22 3a18	☉ → ≈ 20 1p53	☉ → ♓ 19 4a 2	☉ → ♈ 20 3a 4	☉ → ♉ 19 2p11
☽→SIGNS 1 ♎ 11a57 3 ♏ 2p45 5 ♐ 4p48 7 ♑ 7p 8 9 ≈ 11p14 12 ♓ 6a22 14 ♈ 4p49 17 ♉ 5a16 19 ♊ 5p20 22 ♋ 3a 2 24 ♌ 9a50 26 ♍ 2p21 28 ♎ 5p31 30 ♏ 8p11	**☽→SIGNS** 2 ♐ 11p 0 5 ♑ 2a36 7 ≈ 7a42 9 ♓ 3p 5 12 ♈ 1a10 14 ♉ 1p20 17 ♊ 1a47 19 ♋ 12p12 21 ♌ 7p16 24 ♍ 12a57 26 ♎ 12a57 28 ♏ 1a16 30 ≈ 4a24	**☽→SIGNS** 1 ♓ 8a18 3 ♈ 2p21 5 ♉ 10p36 8 ♊ 8a55 10 ♋ 8p57 13 ♌ 9a38 15 ♍ 9p 3 18 ♎ 5a18 20 ♏ 9a41 22 ♐ 10a57 24 ♑ 10a49 26 ≈ 11a16 28 ♓ 1p59 30 ♈ 7p51	**☽→SIGNS** 3 ♉ 4a40 5 ♊ 3p35 8 ♋ 3a45 10 ♌ 4p25 13 ♍ 4a27 15 ♎ 2p 4 17 ♏ 8p 7 21 ♐ 10p14 23 ♑ 9p55 25 ≈ 9p45 28 ♈ 10a21	**☽→SIGNS** 1 ♊ 9p30 4 ♋ 9a56 6 ♌ 10p31 9 ♍ 10a30 11 ♎ 8p55 14 ♏ 4a30 16 ♐ 8a25 18 ♑ 9a 7 20 ≈ 8a15 22 ♓ 10a37 24 ♈ 5p17 29 ♊ 3a43 31 ♋ 4p11	**☽→SIGNS** 3 ♌ 4a46 5 ♍ 4p23 8 ♎ 2a30 10 ♏ 10a36 12 ♐ 3p59 14 ♑ 6p30 16 ≈ 7p 0 18 ♓ 7p 3 20 ♈ 8p59 23 ♉ 2a 6 25 ♊ 11a14 27 ♋ 11p11	**☽→SIGNS** 1 ♌ 11a48 3 ♍ 11p13 6 ♎ 8a41 8 ♏ 4p 6 10 ♐ 9p33 13 ♑ 1a 8 15 ≈ 3a16 17 ♓ 4a51 19 ♈ 7a16 21 ♉ 11a59 23 ♊ 8p 0 28 ♍ 7p37 31 ♍ 7a15	**☽→SIGNS** 2 ≈ 4p27 4 ♓ 10p57 7 ♈ 3a22 9 ♉ 6a31 11 ♊ 9a10 13 ♋ 12p 0 15 ♌ 3p43 17 ♍ 9p 6 20 ♎ 4a55 22 ♏ 3p25 25 ♐ 3a45 27 ♑ 3p49 29 ≈ 1a28
☽ PHASES 2 ○ 4a 4 5 ○ 12p58 8 ○ 10p37 12 ○ 3p 6 16 ◑ 4p10 20 ◑ 10a11 24 ● 11a55 27 ● 11p57	**☽ PHASES** 1 ○ 9a36 4 ○ 8p13 8 ◐ 10a52 11 ○ 8a36 16 ○ 11a26 20 ◑ 10a11 23 ● 11p57 27 ◑ 7a30 30 ● 4p17	**☽ PHASES** 3 ○ 6a12 7 ○ 2a21 11 ○ 4a 0 15 ◑ 6a40 19 ◑ 1a44 22 ● 10a43 25 ● 3p52 28 ◐ 1a29	**☽ PHASES** 2 ○ 7p44 6 ○ 8p27 10 ○ 11p48 15 ◑ 12a32 18 ◑ 3p40 21 ● 9p23 25 ● 1a51 28 ◐ 2p 7	**☽ PHASES** 1 ○ 12p41 5 ○ 3p51 9 ○ 6p22 13 ◑ 3p46 17 ● 3a24 20 ● 7a51 23 ● 2p 3 27 ◐ 6a14 31 ○ 7a57	**☽ PHASES** 4 ○ 10a58 8 ○ 8p19 12 ◑ 2p59 18 ● 6p31 22 ● 4a29 26 ● 12a53	**☽ PHASES** 1 ○ 3a53 5 ◑ 4a23 8 ● 11p13 12 ● 12p15 15 ◑ 9p 4 19 ◑ 5a45 22 ● 8p38 26 ● 8p31 30 ○ 10p52	**☽ PHASES** 3 ◐ 7p 7 7 ● 8a33 10 ● 6p36 14 ◑ 4a38 17 ◑ 5p49 21 ● 1p37 25 ● 3p41 29 ○ 3p42

MAY 1996	JUN 1996	JUL 1996	AUG 1996	SEP 1996	OCT 1996	NOV 1996	DEC 1996
☉ → ♊ 20 1p24	☉ → ♋ 20 9p24	☉ → ♌ 22 8a19	☉ → ♍ 22 3p24	☉ → ♎ 22 1p 1	☉ → ♏ 22 10p20	☉ → ♐ 21 7p50	☉ → ♑ 21 9a 7
☽→SIGNS 2 ♏ 7a43 4 ♐ 11a 5 6 ♑ 12p31 8 ≈ 2p39 10 ♓ 5p29 12 ♈ 10p 1 15 ♉ 4a35 17 ♊ 12p48 19 ♋ 11a28 24 ♎ 11a59 27 ♏ 10a34 29 ♐ 5p31 31 ♐ 8p43	**☽→SIGNS** 2 ♑ 9p29 4 ≈ 9p45 6 ♓ 11p20 9 ♈ 3a23 11 ♉ 10a11 13 ♊ 7p16 16 ♋ 6a 8 18 ♌ 6p22 21 ♍ 7a 7 23 ♎ 6p38 26 ♏ 2a54 28 ♐ 7a 2 30 ♑ 7a47	**☽→SIGNS** 2 ≈ 7a 6 4 ♓ 7a 7 6 ♈ 9a42 8 ♉ 3p44 11 ♊ 12a33 13 ♋ 12p 8 16 ♌ 12a32 18 ♍ 1p17 21 ♎ 1a16 23 ♏ 10a43 25 ♐ 4p18 27 ♑ 6p18 30 ≈ 7a47	**☽→SIGNS** 1 ♓ 6p 5 4 ♈ 10p34 6 ♉ 6a49 9 ♊ 5p58 12 ♋ 6a29 14 ♌ 7p 8 17 ♍ 6a56 19 ♎ 4p51 21 ♏ 11p49 24 ♐ 3a22 26 ♑ 4a11 28 ≈ 3a49 30 ♓ 4a15	**☽→SIGNS** 1 ♈ 7a20 3 ♉ 2p 9 6 ♊ 12a30 8 ♋ 12p54 11 ♌ 1a46 13 ♍ 1p52 16 ♎ 10p20 18 ♏ 5a31 20 ♐ 10a13 23 ♑ 12p40 25 ≈ 2p36 27 ♓ 2p46 30 ♉ 11p 2	**☽→SIGNS** 3 ♉ 8a15 5 ♊ 8p12 8 ♋ 8a49 10 ♌ 8p 1 13 ♍ 4a46 15 ♎ 11a 3 17 ♏ 3p38 20 ♐ 6p52 22 ♑ 9p22 26 ≈ 3a12 28 ♊ 8a35 30 ♋ 4p57	**☽→SIGNS** 2 ♌ 4a16 4 ♍ 4p58 7 ♎ 4a29 9 ♏ 1p 2 11 ♐ 6p27 13 ♑ 9p44 15 ≈ 3a 0 17 ♓ 7a51 20 ♈ 12p10 22 ♉ 11a12 25 ♊ 5p20 27 ♋ 1a38 29 ♌ 12p30	**☽→SIGNS** 1 ♍ 1a11 4 ♎ 1p24 6 ♏ 10p39 9 ♐ 3a59 11 ♑ 6a15 13 ≈ 7a14 15 ♓ 8a44 17 ♈ 11a56 20 ♉ 5p10 22 ♊ 12a18 26 ♌ 8p 9 28 ♍ 8p45 31 ♎ 9p32
☽ PHASES 3 ● 6a49 6 ○ 3p30 10 ● 12a 4 13 ◑ 12p45 17 ◑ 6a47 21 ● 9a14 25 ○ 5a39	**☽ PHASES** 1 ○ 3p47 4 ○ 9p16 8 ◐ 6a 6 11 ◑ 9a47 15 ◑ 8p36 19 ● 2p11 24 ○ 12a24 27 ○ 4p38 30 ○ 10p59	**☽ PHASES** 3 ○ 3a15 7 ○ 1p55 11 ◑ 9a47 15 ◑ 11a15 19 ● 2p11 23 ○ 1a11 30 ○ 5a36	**☽ PHASES** 2 ○ 10a43 4 ○ 2p 7 9 ◑ 11p38 14 ◑ 2a34 18 ● 3p50 21 ● 10p37 25 ○ 8a16 28 ○ 12p53	**☽ PHASES** 4 ○ 2p 7 8 ◐ 3p36 12 ◑ 3p36 16 ◑ 3p 1 20 ● 10p18 26 ● 9a40	**☽ PHASES** 4 ○ 7a 5 8 ◐ 10a 2 12 ◑ 1a36 16 ◑ 1p10 19 ● 10p35 22 ○ 10p53 30 ○ 1a51	**☽ PHASES** 2 ○ 2a51 5 ◐ 1a 7 10 ◑ 11p17 14 ◑ 10a28 17 ● 8p 9 20 ● 7a51 24 ● 1p10 28 ○ 8p48	**☽ PHASES** 3 ○ 12a 6 6 ◐ 11p17 10 ◑ 11a57 13 ● 7p 9 17 ◑ 4a31 20 ● 7p26 24 ● 3p41 28 ○ 5p28

JAN 1997 – AUG 1997

JAN 1997
☉ → ≈ 19 7p43

☽→SIGNS
3 ♏ 8a 2
5 ♐ 2p28
7 ♑ 4p55
9 ≈ 5p 0
11 ♓ 4p51
13 ♈ 6p22
15 ♉ 10p40
18 ♊ 5a54
20 ♋ 3p29
23 ♌ 2a50
25 ♍ 3p27
28 ♎ 4a22
30 ♏ 3p48

☽ PHASES
1 ○ 8p46
5 ◑ 9p26
8 ● 11p26
12 ◐ 4a34
15 ○ 3p 3
19 ◑ 9p37
23 ● 10a11
27 ◐ 1p59
31 ○ 2p41

FEB 1997
☉ → ♓ 18 9a52

☽→SIGNS
1 ♐ 11p51
3 ♑ 3a45
6 ≈ 4a22
8 ♓ 3a34
10 ♈ 3a30
12 ♉ 5a57
14 ♊ 11a54
16 ♋ 9p13
19 ♌ 9a31
21 ♍ 9p39
24 ♎ 10a23
26 ♏ 9p57

☽ PHASES
4 ◑ 4a47
7 ● 10a 7
10 ◐ 3p14
14 ○ 3a58
18 ◑ 2a12
22 ● 5a27
26 ◐ 8a12

MAR 1997
☉ → ♈ 20 8a55

☽→SIGNS
1 ♐ 7a 1
3 ♑ 12p39
5 ≈ 2p55
7 ♓ 2p57
9 ♈ 2p33
11 ♉ 3p38
13 ♊ 7p49
16 ♋ 3a51
18 ♌ 3p 9
21 ♍ 4a 0
23 ♎ 4p36
26 ♏ 3a42
28 ♐ 12p40
30 ♑ 7p 7

☽ PHASES
2 ○ 4a38
5 ◑ 3p25
8 ● 8p51
12 ◐ 4p 8
15 ○ 7p 7
18 ◑ 8p27
23 ● 11p46
27 ◐ 10p40
31 ○ 2p39

APR 1997
☉ → ♉ 19 8p 4

☽→SIGNS
1 ≈ 10p59
3 ♓ 12a43
6 ♈ 1a20
8 ♉ 2a21
10 ♊ 5a28
12 ♋ 12p 4
15 ♌ 10p 9
17 ♍ 11a 1
20 ♎ 11p37
22 ♏ 10a19
24 ♐ 6p52
27 ♑ 12a33
29 ≈ 4a51

☽ PHASES
3 ◑ 11p50
7 ● 6a 2
10 ◐ 4p 8
14 ○ 12p 0
18 ◑ 7p 7
22 ● 3p34
25 ◐ 4p46
29 ○ 9p38

MAY 1997
☉ → ♊ 20 7p19

☽→SIGNS
1 ♓ 7a51
3 ♈ 10a 0
5 ♉ 12p 5
7 ♊ 3p21
9 ♋ 9p13
12 ♌ 6a33
14 ♍ 6p44
17 ♎ 7a27
19 ♏ 6p12
22 ♐ 1a51
24 ♑ 6a52
26 ≈ 10a21
28 ♓ 1p18
30 ♈ 4p18

☽ PHASES
3 ◑ 6a48
7 ● 3p47
10 ◐ 6a13
14 ○ 5a56
18 ◑ 8a34
22 ● 4a14
25 ◐ 4p46
29 ○ 2a52

JUN 1997
☉ → ♋ 21 3a21

☽→SIGNS
1 ♉ 7p29
3 ♊ 11p55
6 ♋ 5a 2
8 ♌ 2p58
10 ♍ 2a43
13 ♎ 3p36
16 ♏ 2a51
18 ♐ 10a40
20 ♑ 3p 3
22 ≈ 5p21
24 ♓ 7p 9
26 ♈ 9p39
29 ♉ 1a24

☽ PHASES
1 ◐ 1p15
5 ● 2a 4
9 ◑ 9p26
12 ○ 11p52
16 ◑ 11p50
20 ◐ 2p 9
23 ● 10p40
27 ◑ 7p43
30 ● 8p17

JUL 1997
☉ → ♌ 22 2p16

☽→SIGNS
1 ♊ 6a36
3 ♋ 1p33
5 ♌ 10p45
8 ♍ 10a22
10 ♎ 11p21
13 ♏ 11a21
15 ♐ 8p 3
18 ♑ 12a46
20 ≈ 2a29
22 ♓ 3a 0
24 ♈ 4a 3
26 ♉ 6a54
28 ♊ 12p 5
30 ♋ 7p39

☽ PHASES
4 ● 1p40
9 ◑ 1p39
12 ○ 12p38
16 ◑ 10p21
20 ◐ 4a17
23 ● 7p43
26 ◑ 5a 7
30 ○ 7p39

AUG 1997
☉ → ♍ 22 9p20

☽→SIGNS
2 ♌ 5a27
4 ♍ 5p16
7 ♎ 6a17
9 ♏ 6p51
12 ♐ 4a45
14 ♑ 10a43
16 ≈ 12p59
18 ♓ 1p 1
20 ♈ 12p45
22 ♉ 1p58
24 ♊ 5p57
27 ♋ 1a11
29 ♌ 11a19
31 ♍ 11p27

☽ PHASES
3 ● 3a14
6 ◐ 6a16
10 ○ 7a43
14 ◑ 11p23
18 ● 5a56
21 ◐ 10a49
24 ○ 9p49
27 ◑ 4p52

SEP 1997 – APR 1998

SEP 1997
☉ → ♎ 22 6p57

☽→SIGNS
3 ♎ 12p30
6 ♏ 1a10
8 ♐ 11a55
10 ♑ 7p24
12 ≈ 11p11
15 ♓ 12a14
17 ♈ 11p25
18 ♉ 11p22
21 ♊ 1a39
23 ♋ 7a33
25 ♌ 5p13
28 ♍ 5a28
30 ♎ 6p33

☽ PHASES
1 ● 6p52
5 ◐ 10p19
9 ○ 9p32
13 ◑ 8a49
16 ● 1p51
19 ◐ 7p14
23 ○ 8a36
27 ◑ 8a 6

OCT 1997
☉ → ♏ 23 4a16

☽→SIGNS
3 ♏ 6a58
5 ♐ 5p43
8 ♑ 2a 4
10 ≈ 7a29
12 ♓ 10a10
14 ♈ 10a25
16 ♉ 10a16
18 ♊ 11a27
20 ♋ 3p46
23 ♌ 12a10
25 ♍ 12p 0
28 ♎ 1a 5
30 ♏ 1p16

☽ PHASES
1 ● 11a52
5 ◐ 12p58
9 ○ 7a23
12 ◑ 5p35
16 ● 10p46
19 ◐ 6a23
23 ○ 11p49
27 ◑ 2a32
31 ● 5a 2

NOV 1997
☉ → ♐ 22 1a49

☽→SIGNS
1 ♐ 11p27
4 ♑ 7a31
6 ≈ 1p34
8 ♓ 5p35
10 ♈ 7p44
12 ♉ 8p57
15 ♊ 10p 5
17 ♋ 1a33
19 ♌ 8a38
21 ♍ 7p 4
24 ♎ 8a30
26 ♏ 8p44
29 ♐ 6a29

☽ PHASES
1 ◐ 1a48
7 ○ 4p44
10 ◑ 2a12
14 ● 9a12
17 ◐ 8p 2
21 ○ 6p58
25 ◑ 9p14
29 ● 11a57

DEC 1997
☉ → ♑ 22 3p 8

☽→SIGNS
1 ♑ 1p39
3 ≈ 6p58
5 ♓ 11p 8
8 ♈ 2a24
10 ♉ 5a 0
12 ♊ 7a35
14 ♋ 11a25
16 ♌ 5p58
19 ♎ 4a 0
21 ♏ 4p35
24 ♐ 3p 8
26 ♑ 9p49
28 ≈ 9p49
31 ♓ 1a59

☽ PHASES
3 ◐ 1p 1
7 ○ 1a10
10 ◑ 11a 8
13 ● 9p38
17 ◐ 2p40
21 ○ 4p44
25 ◑ 6p41
29 ● 11a57

JAN 1998
☉ → ≈ 20 1a47

☽→SIGNS
2 ♈ 4a56
4 ♉ 7a44
6 ♊ 10a53
8 ♋ 2p42
10 ♌ 7p43
13 ♍ 2a43
15 ♎ 12p32
18 ♏ 12a45
20 ♐ 1p35
23 ♑ 12a26
25 ≈ 7a40
27 ♓ 11a27
29 ♈ 1p 9
31 ♉ 2p21

☽ PHASES
1 ◐ 11p 6
5 ○ 9a19
8 ◑ 8p59
12 ● 12p24
16 ◐ 11a 2
20 ○ 12p41
24 ◑ 12p50
28 ● 1a 1
31 ◐ 8a33

FEB 1998
☉ → ♓ 18 3p56

☽→SIGNS
2 ♊ 4p25
4 ♋ 8p10
7 ♌ 1a58
9 ♍ 9a57
11 ♎ 8p10
14 ♏ 8a13
16 ♐ 9p18
19 ♑ 9a13
21 ≈ 5p30
23 ♓ 10p11
25 ♈ 11p43
27 ♉ 11p43

☽ PHASES
3 ○ 5p54
7 ◑ 8a31
11 ● 5a23
15 ◐ 10a27
19 ○ 10a27
21 ◑ 5p30
26 ✗ 12p26

MAR 1998
☉ → ♈ 20 2p55

☽→SIGNS
2 ♊ 12a 1
4 ♋ 2a15
6 ♌ 7a27
8 ♍ 3p46
11 ♎ 2a36
13 ♏ 2p58
16 ♐ 3a51
18 ♑ 3p57
21 ≈ 1a44
23 ♓ 8a 5
25 ♈ 10a43
27 ♉ 10a43
29 ♊ 10a 7
31 ♋ 10a38

☽ PHASES
1 ◐ 5p44
5 ○ 3a41
9 ◑ 7p10
13 ● 10p13
17 ◐ 3a 7
21 ○ 2a38
24 ◑ 4p35
27 ● 10p14
31 ◐ 3a 3

APR 1998
☉ → ♉ 20 1a57

☽→SIGNS
3 ♌ 2p10
5 ♍ 9p36
8 ♎ 8a11
10 ♏ 8p38
13 ♐ 9a35
15 ♑ 9p53
18 ≈ 9p42
20 ♓ 6p 6
22 ♈ 9p31
24 ♉ 9p 9
26 ♊ 8p53
29 ♋ 1p 3

☽ PHASES
3 ○ 3p19
7 ◑ 1p57
11 ● 7p 6
15 ◐ 2p53
19 ○ 2p53
23 ◑ 1a56
26 ● 6a42
29 ◐ 1p 3

MAY 1998 – DEC 1998

MAY 1998
☉ → ♊ 21 1a 6

☽→SIGNS
2 ♌ 4a50
4 ♍ 2p47
7 ♎ 3a19
9 ♏ 4p11
12 ♐ 3a48
14 ♑ 1p39
16 ≈ 9p57
19 ♓ 3a 4
21 ♈ 6a 6
23 ♉ 7a 7
25 ♊ 7a26
27 ♋ 8a59
29 ♌ 1p38
31 ♍ 10p21

☽ PHASES
3 ○ 5a 4
7 ◑ 6a50
11 ● 9a30
15 ◐ 4p36
18 ○ 11p36
22 ◑ 8a52
25 ● 2p33
29 ◐ 12a23

JUN 1998
☉ → ♋ 21 9a 3

☽→SIGNS
3 ♎ 10a17
5 ♏ 11p 6
8 ♐ 10a35
10 ♑ 7p51
13 ≈ 3a 3
15 ♓ 8a32
17 ♈ 12p23
19 ♉ 2p48
21 ♊ 4p27
23 ♋ 6p40
25 ♌ 11p 4
28 ♍ 6a55
30 ♎ 6p 5

☽ PHASES
1 ○ 8p46
5 ◑ 11p42
9 ● 11p19
13 ◐ 4p54
17 ○ 5a39
20 ◑ 2p25
23 ● 10p51
27 ◐ 1p36

JUL 1998
☉ → ♌ 22 7p56

☽→SIGNS
3 ♏ 6a46
5 ♐ 6p24
8 ♑ 3a28
10 ≈ 9a53
12 ♓ 2p23
14 ♈ 5p45
16 ♉ 8p34
18 ♊ 11p19
21 ♋ 2a43
23 ♌ 7a49
25 ♍ 3p34
28 ♎ 2a15
30 ♏ 2p45

☽ PHASES
1 ○ 1p43
5 ◑ 3p42
9 ● 11p19
13 ◐ 12a 4
16 ○ 10a14
19 ◑ 7p59
23 ● 8a44
27 ◐ 4a46
30 ○ 7a 6

AUG 1998
☉ → ♍ 23 3a 0

☽→SIGNS
2 ♐ 2a48
4 ♑ 12p18
6 ≈ 6p32
8 ♓ 10p 5
11 ♈ 12a11
13 ♉ 2a 5
15 ♊ 4a46
17 ♋ 8a56
19 ♌ 2p57
21 ♍ 11p22
24 ♎ 10a 2
26 ♏ 10p26
29 ♐ 10a56
31 ♑ 9p23

☽ PHASES
4 ○ 6a30
7 ◑ 9p10
11 ● 6a 8
14 ◐ 2p49
18 ○ 3a 4
21 ◑ 9p 4
25 ● 9p29
30 ○ 12a 7

SEP 1998
☉ → ♎ 23 12a38

☽→SIGNS
3 ♓ 4a21
5 ♈ 7a48
7 ♉ 8a53
9 ♊ 9a17
11 ♋ 10a41
13 ♌ 2p21
15 ♍ 8p48
18 ♎ 5a52
20 ♏ 5p22
23 ♐ 5a31
25 ♑ 6p 0
28 ≈ 5a31
30 ♓ 1p54

☽ PHASES
2 ○ 8p 5
6 ◑ 6a22
9 ● 12p14
12 ◐ 8p58
16 ○ 6a11
20 ◑ 2p 2
24 ● 7p 2
28 ○ 9p37

OCT 1998
☉ → ♏ 23 10a 0

☽→SIGNS
2 ♈ 6p24
4 ♉ 6p13
6 ♊ 6p58
8 ♋ 6p44
10 ♌ 8p49
13 ♍ 2a26
15 ♎ 11a32
17 ♏ 11p 3
20 ♐ 11a37
22 ♑ 12a17
25 ≈ 12p 5
27 ♓ 9p45
30 ♈ 3a59

☽ PHASES
2 ○ 8a27
5 ◑ 3p12
9 ● 6a11
12 ◐ 12a43
16 ○ 6a11
20 ◑ 5a10
24 ● 8a12
28 ◐ 6a47
31 ○ 7p37

NOV 1998
☉ → ♐ 22 7a35

☽→SIGNS
1 ♉ 6a28
3 ♊ 6a13
5 ♋ 5a11
7 ♌ 5a40
9 ♍ 9a33
11 ♎ 5p37
14 ♏ 4a58
16 ♐ 5p41
19 ♑ 6a13
21 ≈ 5p46
24 ♓ 3a44
26 ♈ 11a15
28 ♉ 3p44
30 ♊ 4p53

☽ PHASES
4 ◑ 12a19
8 ● 5a20
11 ◐ 4p28
14 ○ 8p 0
18 ◑ 11p27
23 ● 12a22
30 ○ 7p23

DEC 1998
☉ → ♑ 21 8p58

☽→SIGNS
2 ♊ 4p30
4 ♋ 4p28
6 ♌ 6p56
9 ♍ 1a22
11 ♎ 11a44
13 ♏ 11p56
16 ♐ 12p48
18 ♑ 11p56
21 ≈ 9a17
23 ♓ 4p45
26 ♈ 10p 4
28 ♉ 1a 5
30 ♊ 2a22

☽ PHASES
3 ○ 10a20
6 ◑ 6p17
10 ● 12p54
14 ◐ 3p48
18 ○ 5p43
22 ◑ 2p40
26 ● 5a46
29 ○ 2p47

JAN 1999 – AUG 1999

	JAN 1999	FEB 1999	MAR 1999	APR 1999	MAY 1999	JUN 1999	JUL 1999	AUG 1999
☉ ->	♒ 20 7a38	♓ 18 9p48	♈ 20 8p47	♉ 20 7a47	♊ 21 6a53	♋ 21 2p50	♌ 23 1a45	♍ 23 8a52

☽ -> SIGNS

JAN	FEB	MAR	APR	MAY	JUN	JUL	AUG
1 ♌ 3a15	1 ♍ 8p38	1 ♍ 5a 5	1 ♏ 7a49	2 ♐ 2a37	3 ♒ 8a37	2 ♓ 11p35	1 ♈ 11a47
3 ♌ 5a31	4 ♎ 4a56	3 ♎ 1p35	4 ♐ 8p 8	4 ♑ 3p12	5 ♓ 6p 1	5 ♈ 6a22	3 ♉ 4p 9
5 ♍ 10a49	6 ♏ 4p 7	6 ♏ 12a23	6 ♑ 8a39	7 ♒ 2a41	8 ♈ 12a 8	7 ♉ 10a22	5 ♊ 6p58
7 ♎ 7p53	9 ♐ 4a39	8 ♐ 12p46	9 ♒ 7p25	9 ♓ 11a17	10 ♉ 2a44	9 ♊ 12p 0	7 ♋ 8p53
10 ♏ 7a49	11 ♑ 4p10	11 ♑ 1a19	11 ♓ 2a35	11 ♈ 3p54	12 ♊ 2a49	11 ♋ 12p28	9 ♌ 10p56
12 ♐ 8p24	14 ♒ 12a57	13 ♒ 10a32	13 ♈ 5a47	13 ♉ 4p57	14 ♋ 2a14	13 ♌ 1p 0	12 ♍ 2a22
15 ♑ 7a29	16 ♓ 6a40	15 ♓ 4p10	15 ♉ 6a 8	15 ♊ 4p 8	16 ♌ 3a 8	15 ♍ 4p39	14 ♎ 8a24
17 ♒ 4p12	18 ♈ 10a 7	17 ♈ 7p13	17 ♊ 5a39	17 ♋ 3p40	18 ♍ 7a12	17 ♎ 11p20	16 ♏ 5p40
19 ♓ 10p40	20 ♉ 12p29	19 ♉ 8p 9	19 ♋ 6a28	19 ♌ 5p37	20 ♎ 3p11	20 ♏ 9a31	19 ♐ 5a32
22 ♈ 3a25	22 ♊ 2p54	21 ♊ 9p 6	22 ♌ 10a 6	21 ♍ 11p16	23 ♏ 2a19	22 ♐ 9p44	21 ♑ 6p 0
24 ♉ 6a53	24 ♋ 6p 9	23 ♋ 11p34	24 ♍ 5p 5	24 ♎ 8a30	25 ♐ 2p52	25 ♑ 10a 9	24 ♒ 4a50
26 ♊ 9a30	26 ♌ 10p45	26 ♌ 4a23	27 ♎ 2a47	26 ♏ 8p 5	28 ♑ 3a12	27 ♒ 9p55	26 ♓ 12p50
28 ♋ 11a57		28 ♍ 11a35	29 ♏ 2p13	29 ♐ 8a38	30 ♒ 2p20	30 ♓ 5a28	28 ♈ 6p10
30 ♌ 3p16		30 ♎ 8p50		31 ♑ 9p 6			30 ♉ 9p41

☽ PHASES

JAN	FEB	MAR	APR	MAY	JUN	JUL	AUG
1 ○ 9p50	4 ○ 5a12	2 ○ 1a59	4 ○ 7p43	4 ○ 12p50	3 ○ 3a24	2 ○ 3p 8	1 ○ 12a16
5 ○ 10a32	8 ○ 6a58	6 ○ 6a58	8 ○ 9p51	8 ◑ 12p29	6 ◑ 11p20	6 ◑ 6a57	4 ○ 12p27
9 ◑ 9a22	12 ◑ 8a20	10 ◑ 3a41	12 ◑ 3p43	12 ◑ 2a10	10 ◑ 9a43	9 ◑ 3p34	7 ◑ 9p 4
13 ◑ 12p30	16 ● 1a39	14 ● 1a44	15 ● 11p22	15 ● 7a 6	13 ● 2p 3	13 ● 9p25	11 ● 6a 9
17 ● 10a47	19 ● 12p23	17 ● 1p48	19 ● 3a57	18 ● 11a46	16 ● 8p52	16 ● 7a53	14 ● 9p10
21 ◐ 2a39	26 ◐ 9p43	20 ◐ 8p30	22 ◐ 2p 2	22 ◐ 12a35	20 ◐ 2p16	20 ◐ 1p13	18 ◐ 8p47
24 ◐ 2p16		24 ◐ 5a18	26 ◐ 9a 3	25 ◐ 11p 2	24 ◐ 2p16	24 ◐ 6a25	22 ◐ 10p57
27 ○ 1p49		27 ○ 8p31	30 ○ 9a55	30 ○ 1a40	28 ◐ 4p38		26 ○ 6p48
31 ● 11a 7		31 ○ 5p49					30 ○ 7a33

SEP 1999 – APR 2000

	SEP 1999	OCT 1999	NOV 1999	DEC 1999	JAN 2000	FEB 2000	MAR 2000	APR 2000
☉ ->	♎ 23 6a32	♏ 23 3p53	♐ 22 1p26	♑ 22 2a45	♒ 20 1p24	♓ 19 3a34	♈ 20 2a36	♉ 19 1p40

☽ -> SIGNS

SEP	OCT	NOV	DEC	JAN	FEB	MAR	APR
2 ♊ 12a25	1 ♋ 8a32	1 ♍ 11p 8	1 ♎ 12p30	2 ♐ 4p32	1 ♑ 12p10	2 ♒ 8a15	1 ♓ 3a13
4 ♋ 3a10	3 ♌ 12p14	4 ♎ 6a57	3 ♏ 10p36	5 ♑ 5a24	4 ♒ 12a47	4 ♓ 6p31	3 ♈ 10a22
6 ♌ 6a29	5 ♍ 5p40	6 ♏ 4p46	6 ♐ 10a28	7 ♒ 5p53	6 ♓ 11a 2	7 ♈ 1a55	5 ♉ 2p29
8 ♍ 10a57	8 ♎ 1a 2	9 ♐ 4a15	8 ♑ 11p14	10 ♓ 4a 6	8 ♈ 7p18	9 ♉ 7a 1	7 ♊ 4p59
10 ♎ 5p16	10 ♏ 10a 2	11 ♑ 5p 1	11 ♒ 11a59	12 ♈ 1p49	11 ♉ 1a 8	11 ♊ 10a46	9 ♋ 7p16
13 ♏ 2a19	12 ♐ 9p19	14 ♒ 5a46	13 ♓ 11p18	14 ♉ 7p38	13 ♊ 5a23	13 ♋ 1p52	11 ♌ 10p16
15 ♐ 1p35	15 ♑ 10a 1	16 ♓ 4p21	16 ♈ 7a31	16 ♊ 10p25	15 ♋ 7a45	15 ♌ 4p44	14 ♍ 2a19
18 ♑ 2a14	17 ♒ 10p58	18 ♈ 10p58	18 ♉ 11a46	18 ♋ 11p 1	17 ♌ 9a12	17 ♍ 7p49	16 ♎ 7a36
20 ♒ 1p39	20 ♓ 7a33	21 ♉ 1a14	20 ♊ 12p29	20 ♌ 10p59	19 ♍ 10a54	19 ♎ 11p57	18 ♏ 2p36
22 ♓ 9p52	22 ♈ 1a14	23 ♊ 1a14	22 ♋ 11a53	23 ♍ 12a 8	21 ♎ 2p22	22 ♏ 6a18	21 ♐ 11p58
25 ♈ 4a51	24 ♉ 2p26	25 ♋ 12a29	24 ♌ 11a32	25 ♎ 4a10	24 ♏ 8p58	24 ♐ 3p43	23 ♑ 11a48
27 ♉ 4a51	26 ♊ 2p34	27 ♌ 1a19	26 ♍ 1p35	27 ♏ 12p 2	26 ♐ 7p 5	27 ♑ 3a51	26 ♒ 12a42
29 ♊ 6a21	28 ♋ 3p10	29 ♍ 5a11	28 ♎ 7p15	29 ♐ 11p18	28 ♑ 7p46	29 ♒ 4p35	28 ♓ 12p31
	30 ♌ 5p48		31 ♏ 4a37				30 ♈ 7p55

☽ PHASES

SEP	OCT	NOV	DEC	JAN	FEB	MAR	APR
2 ● 5p18	1 ◐ 11p 3	4 ◐ 12a10	3 ◐ 3p 8	2 ◐ 9a27	1 ◐ 5a50	2 ◐ 2a18	4 ◐ 1p13
6 ◐ 3a35	5 ◐ 12p17	8 ◐ 10p54	7 ◐ 5p32	6 ● 1p14	5 ● 8a 4	6 ● 12a17	11 ● 11p 3
9 ○ 5p 3	9 ○ 6a35	11 ○ 9p12	11 ○ 9p12	10 ● 2p22	12 ○ 6p22	13 ○ 1a59	14 ○ 8a31
13 ◑ 12p52	13 ◑ 6a46	15 ◑ 7p51	15 ◑ 7p51	14 ◑ 8a35	16 ◑ 12p 7	19 ◑ 1p45	18 ◑ 12p42
17 ● 3p 6	17 ● 10a 0	19 ● 2a54	19 ● 2a54	20 ○ 11p41	16 ○ 11a27	23 ○ 5p31	22 ○ 11a17
21 ○ 6a24	20 ○ 6a24	22 ○ 12p32	22 ○ 12p32	24 ○ 8a25	23 ● 12a20	27 ● 7p21	30 ◐ 12p 4
25 ● 5p52	23 ● 4p 3	25 ● 6p23	25 ● 6p23	28 ● 2a57	26 ● 10p54	31 ◐ 8p49	
28 ○ 2p11	27 ○ 9p32	29 ● 9a 5	29 ● 9a 5				
	31 ● 6a 4						

MAY 2000 – DEC 2000

	MAY 2000	JUN 2000	JUL 2000	AUG 2000	SEP 2000	OCT 2000	NOV 2000	DEC 2000
☉ ->	♊ 20 12p50	♋ 20 8p48	♌ 22 7a43	♍ 22 2p49	♎ 22 12p28	♏ 22 9p48	♐ 21 7p20	♑ 21 8a38

☽ -> SIGNS

MAY	JUN	JUL	AUG	SEP	OCT	NOV	DEC
2 ♉ 11p51	1 ♊ 11a35	2 ♌ 9p38	1 ♍ 8a28	2 ♏ 12a56	1 ♐ 5p50	3 ♒ 1a41	2 ♓ 10p23
5 ♊ 1a24	3 ♋ 11a30	4 ♍ 10p19	3 ♎ 10a32	4 ♐ 9a 9	4 ♑ 4a43	5 ♓ 2p13	5 ♈ 9a18
7 ♋ 2a14	5 ♌ 11a46	7 ♎ 1a47	5 ♏ 4p31	6 ♑ 8p48	6 ♒ 5p34	8 ♈ 12a 3	7 ♉ 4p27
9 ♌ 4a 2	7 ♍ 1p58	9 ♏ 8a49	8 ♐ 1a31	9 ♒ 9a45	9 ♓ 5a37	10 ♉ 6a12	9 ♊ 7p51
11 ♍ 7a42	9 ♎ 6p56	11 ♐ 7p 6	10 ♑ 1p43	11 ♓ 9p35	11 ♈ 2p52	12 ♊ 9a28	11 ♋ 8p49
13 ♎ 1p28	12 ♏ 2a55	14 ♑ 7a28	13 ♒ 2a43	14 ♈ 7p 1	14 ♉ 9a28	14 ♋ 11a22	13 ♌ 9p24
15 ♏ 9p17	14 ♐ 1a27	16 ♒ 8p27	15 ♓ 2p44	16 ♉ 7p23	16 ♊ 4a37	16 ♌ 4p16	15 ♍ 10p30
18 ♐ 7a10	16 ♑ 1a27	19 ♓ 8a45	18 ♈ 1a15	18 ♊ 7p23	18 ♋ 6a35	18 ♍ 8p35	18 ♎ 2a 1
20 ♑ 7p 2	19 ♒ 2a52	21 ♈ 7p10	20 ♉ 8p55	20 ♋ 11p16	20 ♌ 10a33	20 ♎ 8a12	20 ♏ 8a12
23 ♒ 8a 1	21 ♓ 2p52	24 ♉ 2a44	22 ♊ 1p55	22 ♌ 1a 2	22 ♍ 2p30	22 ♏ 4p58	22 ♐ 4p58
25 ♓ 8p 4	24 ♈ 12a 1	26 ♊ 7p19	24 ♋ 4p17	25 ♍ 2a 1	24 ♎ 6a22	25 ♐ 3a54	24 ♑ 3a54
28 ♈ 5a 8	26 ♉ 7p19	28 ♋ 8a30	26 ♌ 6p17	27 ♎ 2p54	26 ♏ 10a30	27 ♑ 4p26	27 ♒ 4p26
30 ♉ 10a 3	28 ♊ 10p10	30 ♌ 9p10	28 ♍ 6p56	29 ♏ 6a17	29 ♐ 2a41	29 ♒ 9p27	29 ♓ 4p14
	30 ♋ 10p10		30 ♎ 8p33		31 ♑ 1p 2		

☽ PHASES

MAY	JUN	JUL	AUG	SEP	OCT	NOV	DEC
2 ● 11p13	2 ● 7a14	1 ● 2p20	3 ◐ 4a15	1 ◐ 3p23	1 ◐ 5a38	4 ○ 2a27	3 ○ 10p56
7 ◐ 5a48	5 ◐ 12p19	4 ◐ 7p30	10 ○ 9p 2	5 ○ 11a28	5 ○ 4a 6	7 ○ 2a16	6 ○ 6p32
10 ○ 3p 1	8 ○ 10p30	8 ○ 7a53	13 ◑ 12a13	7 ◑ 2p38	10 ◑ 4a27	11 ◑ 4p15	10 ◑ 4a 3
14 ◑ 5a54	12 ◑ 4p45	10 ◑ 4a56	18 ● 10p18	16 ● 2p 8	13 ● 3a53	11 ● 11p41	11 ● 12p36
18 ● 2a35	16 ● 5p28	16 ● 5a50	25 ◐ 11p 6	20 ○ 8p29	16 ○ 10a55	15 ○ 6p12	17 ○ 7p42
22 ○ 4a44	20 ○ 8p50	20 ○ 10a46	29 ● 5a20	24 ● 5a53	23 ● 1p44	23 ● 4a33	21 ● 12p36
29 ◐ 11p56	24 ● 8p 1	24 ● 6a 3		27 ● 2p54	27 ● 2a59	25 ● 7p25	25 ● 12p22
	28 ◐ 9a 4	27 ◐ 4p28			30 ● 11p15		29 ● 4p14
		30 ● 9p26					

Avoid situations where others try to hurry you. At the same time, recognize that occasionally you probably do need a good shove. Feel satisfied that your habit patterns are correct for you, but try new ways of doing things once in awhile just for variety.

If Your Moon Sign Is Gemini ♊

You are known for your nervous energy. This can express itself in sparkling wit as well as a tendency to talk a little too much. You are forever searching for something new. Your feelings can change as swiftly as a chameleon, and you have an instinctive talent for expressing and communicating these feelings. In fact, you have a drive to communicate whatever comes to your mind, although you may not be as consciously aware of this as a Gemini Sun sign. Fortunately, you are equally as interested in the ideas of others.

You might try practicing meditation to "de-jitter" your nerves and to increase your attention span. However, be happy with your driving energy and your versatility.

If Your Moon Sign Is Cancer ♋

You are very sensitive to the feelings of others. Your moods are strong and fluctuating although you usually don't let them show and may not be as consciously aware of them as a Cancer Sun sign. But you are always aware of the undercurrents in a situation. You know when something doesn't "feel right," although you may not be able to put these feelings into words.

There are times when you should learn to let the feelings of others flow around you without being compelled to absorb them like a sponge. Avoid a tendency to brood, and try to bring some of your emotions into the open. However, always trust your basic instincts.

If Your Moon Sign Is Leo ♌

You are by nature cheerful and warm, and this gives you an instinct for raising the spirits of others, even "down" people. You don't mind showing your feelings. You enjoy the attention of others and in turn can be very considerate and often entertaining. You never lose your spirit of playfulness.

A Leo **Sun sign** usually realizes he or she enjoys the spotlight. But you, as a Leo Moon sign, may tend to monopolize the spotlight without realizing you are doing it. Also, you may need to cultivate more flexibility in your habit patterns. In any event, be thankful for your sunny disposition.

If Your Moon Sign Is Virgo ♍

You are very attentive to the many details of life. The terms **conscientious** and **fastidious** describe your character. Added to this is a basic practicality and natural sense of order. This also means that you like to think things out before acting.

You are somewhat reserved in your relationships with others, but you have a natural instinct toward helping them whatever way you can.

Try to cultivate calmness and guard against your tendency to "overthink," a tendency you may not be as aware of as a Virgo Sun sign is. Try to balance your critical ability with an acceptance of imperfection. Be aware that broader issues can also be important. However, don't forget that your greatest ability is to be able to bring into focus and to put into order all the various parts that make up the whole.

If Your Moon Sign Is Libra ♎

You are gifted with a gentle manner, tact and a natural charm. In addition, your consideration for others leads to many happy social contacts. You are able to balance thinking and feeling, and you have a constant awareness of beauty.

You have a tendency to go along with whatever viewpoint is being presented at the moment, without realizing this as consciously as a Libra Sun sign would. There are times when you need to assert your own views. There are even times when it is necessary to take a strong stand (or take definite action) concerning something you believe in, even if it makes waves. However, be grateful for your ability to create harmony around you.

If Your Moon Sign Is Scorpio ♏

You have strong, passionate desires. You are persistent in the pursuit of your aims. Also, you are able to sense the hidden currents of thought and underlying motivations of others. You have very intense moods, but you tend to conceal the extent of your feelings from others.

Guard against a tendency to "use" people, sometimes done so subtly that you may not even realize it yourself as consciously as a Scorpio Sun sign would. Try not to hold grudges. Focus on the positive side of human nature. But try to preserve your determination to get at the truth, even when it hurts.

If Your Moon Sign Is Sagittarius ♐

You are naturally cheerful and optimistic. Your enthusiasm is infectious. You enjoy being around people and very often love to put on a show, although you may not be as conscious of this tendency as a Sagittarius Sun sign. Also, there is a restless side to your nature which may be expressed in a variety of interests and activities or in a love of sports or travel.

Realize that there are times when you may need to restrain your excessive optimism, especially when it involves glossing over necessary details or avoiding responsibilities. Try to develop a sense of depth as well as breadth in your interests. However, don't let your free spirit be stifled.

If Your Moon Sign Is Capricorn ♑

You have a natural reserve and apparent seriousness which gives you an air of control and confidence. Some of this may just be an outward facade, but the fact is that you tend to be stable and practical and very seldom go to pieces in an emergency. Also, you are capable of hard work and will stick to any aim that you have set for yourself.

Try to soften your sense of detached superiority by consciously broadening your feelings of affection toward others. This will, in turn, minimize your fears of isolation and your tendency toward melancholy, which you might be less conscious of than a Capricorn Sun sign. However, treasure your instinctive sense of dignity.

If Your Moon Sign Is Aquarius ♒

Your main qualities are independence and inventiveness. Above all, you are your own person and cannot be molded, or easily influenced by

others. You make up your own mind. In addition, you keep a strict
sense of objectivity, both in personal relationships and life situations.

Even though you have a natural interest in human problems, particularly in a general sense, you may need to exert an effort to bring
these feelings down to a personal level. Your independent ways of thinking can often make you seem erratic, and you must remember that this
is often unsettling to others. You may not be as aware of this unsettling quality as an Aquarius Sun sign. However, never lose your basic
independence and talent for producing the unexpected.

If Your Moon Sign Is Pisces ♓

You are gifted with compassion and extreme sensitivity, both to your
environment and to the feelings of others. You understand instinctively that true communication with others is to be able to identify totally
with their reality. This is a built-in function of the Piscean Moon. In
addition, you have a vivid imagination and sense of fantasy.

Your fantasies can sometimes seem more real to you than the mundane world. This can lead you to escapist tendencies. Therefore, you
need to develop a strong inner direction to keep from confusing fantasy with reality and the needs of others with your own. However, you
should never lose your profoundly sympathetic nature.

Your Moon Phase

Your astrological Moon **sign** (Moon in Libra, etc.) indicates what sign
of the zodiac (as seen from Earth) the Moon was in when you were
born. Your Moon **phase**, however, refers not to any particular sign of
the zodiac, but simply to **how much of the bright side of the Moon
could be seen from Earth at the time you were born**. This is caused
by the dynamic interaction between the Sun, Moon and Earth. The
Moon **sign** and Moon **phase** are two independent but superimposed
cycles.

Your Moon phase indicates your **characteristic way of approaching
relationships**. It indicates the manner in which your conscious and your
instinctual characteristics interact.

For directions in finding your Moon phase in the calendar in this
book, turn to page 85. Below are descriptions of the meaning of each
Moon phase.

IF YOU WERE BORN UNDER A NEW MOON ●

You tune into the beginning of cycles, approaching life from an extremely subjective standpoint. Your emotions and instincts are very keen, and you are quite sensitive to the impressions you are receiving and what they mean to you.

IF YOU WERE BORN UNDER A CRESCENT MOON ☽

You are interested in new ideas and can assert yourself with confidence. You enjoy a challenge and find yourself thinking up new ways to do things. You have a strong need to express yourself.

IF YOU WERE BORN UNDER A FIRST QUARTER MOON ☾

You have a strong need for action, which can sometimes appear as impatience. Potentially, you have a lot of enterprise and are interested in building for the future without fear of leaving the past behind.

IF YOU WERE BORN UNDER A GIBBOUS MOON ○

You are highly aware of the meaning of what is going on around you. You do not accept anything at face value, but look for what can make your understanding clearer.

IF YOU WERE BORN UNDER A FULL MOON ○

You approach life from a highly objective standpoint, looking to see the larger picture as it covers not just yourself but people in general. You prefer to think in absolutes and can be quite a perfectionist. You often feel pulled in contrary directions.

IF YOU WERE BORN UNDER A DISSEMINATING MOON ○

Your mind integrates whatever you have learned into overall meanings that you then like to share with others. You can teach what you have learned in such a way that others can understand it.

IF YOU WERE BORN UNDER A THIRD-QUARTER MOON ☽

You can focus on the need for change based on ideals which not everyone seems to understand. You have a strong sense of future directions.

IF YOU WERE BORN UNDER A BALSAMIC MOON ☾

Your vision of the future is very important to you, and at times you can be somewhat prophetic. You are willing to work for what you believe in, sometimes rather fanatically.

Moon Phases

New: Subjective ●	youthful in spirit, introspective, impulsive, receptive
Crescent: Innovative ☽	projective of new ideas, confident, creative, assertive
First Quarter: Enterprising ◐	impatient, strong-willed, fearless, action oriented
Gibbous: Aware ◐	intellectual, skeptical, mature in attitude, revealing
Full: Objective ○	oriented toward wholeness, thinking in absolutes, perfectionistic, socially conscious
Disseminating: Integrative ◑	a teacher (in a broad sense), disseminating (of ideas), a popularizer, a synthesizer
Third Quarter: Inventive ◑	unconventional, future oriented, a maverick (in ideas), a reformer
Balsamic: Visionary ☾	mystic, prophetic, fanatic, a crusader

Eclipses

WERE YOU BORN ON THE DAY OF AN ECLIPSE?
You can determine whether you were born on the day of an eclipse by checking your birthday on the calendar beginning on page 89. If you were born on a solar eclipse, instead of the usual new-Moon symbol "●," you will find "●̸." If you were born on a lunar eclipse, instead of the usual full-Moon symbol "○," you will find "◓." The nearer your birth time is to the time of an eclipse, the more important the symbolism.

IF YOU WERE BORN CLOSE TO AN ECLIPSE OF THE SUN:
You can develop a particularly strong interaction between your conscious (Sun) self and your instinctual (Moon) self. This can be an advantage in that your conscious and instinctual natures have less tendency to work against each other, as they do in many people. However, you must watch that your conscious aims are not obscured by your instinctual reactions.

IF YOU WERE BORN CLOSE TO AN ECLIPSE OF THE MOON:
You may have a strong restlessness in your nature. Your relationships, particularly those with the opposite sex, are likely to be intense. You may need to develop a sense of what your instincts are telling you, as your consciousness has a tendency to override them.

CHAPTER FIVE

SUN-MOON COMBINATIONS

Your Sun Sign-
Moon Sign Combination

SUNSIGN

MOON SIGN	Aries ♈	Taurus ♉	Gemini ♊	Cancer ♋	Leo ♌	Virgo ♍	Libra ♎	Scorpio ♏	Sagittarius ♐	Capricorn ♑	Aquarius ♒	Pisces ♓
Aries ♈	141	142	143	145	146	147	149	150	152	153	155	156
Taurus ♉	141	142	143	145	146	147	149	150	152	153	155	156
Gemini ♊	141	142	143	145	146	148	149	150	152	153	155	156
Cancer ♋	141	142	144	145	146	148	149	151	152	154	155	156
Leo ♌	141	142	144	145	146	148	149	151	152	154	155	156
Virgo ♍	141	142	144	145	146	148	149	151	152	154	155	156
Libra ♎	141	143	144	145	147	148	149	151	152	154	155	157
Scorpio ♏	141	143	144	145	147	148	150	151	153	154	155	157
Sagittarius ♐	141	143	144	145	147	148	150	151	153	154	155	157
Capricorn ♑	142	143	144	146	147	148	150	151	153	154	156	157
Aquarius ♒	142	143	144	146	147	149	150	151	153	154	156	157
Pisces ♓	142	143	144	146	147	149	150	152	153	154	156	157

SUN IN ARIES/MOON IN ARIES ☉♈ ☽♈

Your thinking is incisive, your perceptions are instantaneous, and your energy is high. Curb self-centered and rash impulses.

SUN IN ARIES/MOON IN TAURUS ☉♈ ☽♉

You combine forcefulness with an affectionate nature, and you can channel your energies. Check a tendency to be too sure of yourself.

SUN IN ARIES/MOON IN GEMINI ☉♈ ☽♊

You can talk your way in and out of most anything, and find a different topic every day. Learn not to exaggerate and to appreciate the value of silence.

SUN IN ARIES/MOON IN CANCER ☉♈ ☽♋

You can combine daring and caution, self-assurance and sensitivity. Use your sense of perspective to balance out your mood changes.

SUN IN ARIES/MOON IN LEO ☉♈ ☽♌

You have an air of warmhearted confidence that draws people to you. Don't become overlydramatic or let your need for recognition misuse your creativity.

SUN IN ARIES/MOON IN VIRGO ☉♈ ☽♍

You analyze as easily as you breathe, probing always for what makes things tick. Learn to appreciate the broad stroke as well as the fine detail, and don't judge too harshly.

SUN IN ARIES/MOON IN LIBRA ☉♈ ☽♎

You can combine the ability to act with decision with a sensitivity to the needs of others. Keep in touch with your own center and keep daydreaming in proportion.

SUN IN ARIES/MOON IN SCORPIO ☉♈ ☽♏

You are strongly self-sufficient and can be quite magnetic. Learn to balance out your turbulent nature and let yourself (and others) be in peace.

SUN IN ARIES/MOON IN SAGITTARIUS ☉♈ ☽♐

With your natural enthusiasm you can inspire others with a sense of principles which should be acted upon. Curb restlessness and learn not to scatter energies.

SUN IN ARIES/MOON IN CAPRICORN ⊙♈ ☽♑
Your ambition and drive are strong, and people sense your leadership ability. Keep within proportion your power drive and your tendency to dominate.

SUN IN ARIES/MOON IN AQUARIUS ⊙♈ ☽♒
Your mind is clear and original and you combine a sense of independence and adventure with a good social sense. Soften your touch of abruptness.

SUN IN ARIES/MOON IN PISCES ⊙♈ ☽♓
Your thoughts are deeper than you can easily express to others. Recharge your energies in solitude, but don't let yourself brood.

♉ SUN IN TAURUS/MOON IN ARIES ⊙♉ ☽♈
Your impression on others is powerful, and you can be persistent in pursuing what you want. Avoid arrogance and learn to view yourself objectively.

SUN IN TAURUS/MOON IN TAURUS ⊙♉ ☽♉
You have built-in practicality and determination and can follow through on long-term plans. Don't be too attached to your possessions, keep your stubbornness in check, and don't harbor anger.

SUN IN TAURUS/MOON IN GEMINI ⊙♉ ☽♊
You have a stable base within yourself from which you like to move around, both physically and ideawise. Keep your mind well fed to maximize contentment.

SUN IN TAURUS/MOON IN CANCER ⊙♉ ☽♋
You are sensitive and reserved, with a good imagination and a natural diplomacy. Don't lose track of your own point of view.

SUN IN TAURUS/MOON IN LEO ⊙♉ ☽♌
You have a clearly defined personality and let people know where you stand. Learn to be flexible in your point of view and don't exaggerate.

SUN IN TAURUS/MOON IN VIRGO ⊙♉ ☽♍
You have lots of common sense and a good critical ability combined with charm. Keep learning and don't rest on your laurels.

SUN IN TAURUS/MOON IN LIBRA ☉♉ ☽♎

Your heart rules your head, and you have a keen sense of what is beautiful. Learn self-reliance and the knack of soothing your nerves.

SUN IN TAURUS/MOON IN SCORPIO ☉♉ ☽♏

Your will and independence are prominent, as are your emotions. Keep your passionate approach to life in proportion and learn to let your head and heart communicate.

SUN IN TAURUS/MOON IN SAGITTARIUS ☉♉ ☽♐

Your principles are important to you and you are basically an optimist. Watch an extremist streak in yourself as well as a tendency to be judgmental.

SUN IN TAURUS/MOON IN CAPRICORN ☉♉ ☽♑

You can plot a practical course for yourself and push right on until you get there. Don't let the need for security blind you to the beauty of out-of-this-world dreams.

SUN IN TAURUS/MOON IN AQUARIUS ☉♉ ☽♒

You have excellent concentration and a natural ability to work with people. Keep yourself flexible and don't be opinionated or let your natural self-confidence become egotism.

SUN IN TAURUS/MOON IN PISCES ☉♉ ☽♓

Your sympathetic awareness of the needs of others is always present, as well as your strong aesthetic sense. Don't let others impose upon you.

♊ SUN IN GEMINI/MOON IN ARIES ☉♊ ☽♈

Your mind (and sometimes your tongue) is sharp and your wit is quick. Learn that some of your initial impulses need control, and cultivate steadiness and sympathy.

SUN IN GEMINI/MOON IN TAURUS ☉♊ ☽♉

You can be both flexible and dependable, seeing the intricacies of people and situations, and yet being loyal. Don't neglect some self-expression in the arts to develop your emotional sensitivity.

SUN IN GEMINI/MOON IN GEMINI ☉♊ ☽♊

You are exceedingly clever, with much variety in your thought, and you can express yourself instantly and in detail. Tune in on your feeling as well as your thinking. Learn to relax.

SUN IN GEMINI/MOON IN CANCER ☉♊ ☽♋
You are sensitive to everything that goes on around you, and your mind is comprehensive and retentive. Learn how to concentrate and to insulate yourself from impressions you don't need.

SUN IN GEMINI/MOON IN LEO ☉♊ ☽♌
You are lively, friendly and witty, with an endearing warmth and a lot of imagination. Don't fret over not being able to express everything you know is inside.

SUN IN GEMINI/MOON IN VIRGO ☉♊ ☽♍
You are versatile and analytical and keep all sorts of ideas going in your head at once. Practice concentration and pull out of worry moods by not allowing yourself to rehash what is unnecessary.

SUN IN GEMINI/MOON IN LIBRA ☉♊ ☽♎
You are high on imagination and idealism and can express yourself gracefully and well. Learn not to be too long-winded and to calm your restlessness.

SUN IN GEMINI/MOON IN SCORPIO ☉♊ ☽♏
Your personality is magnetic and your mind and perceptions sharp and critical. Watch oversensitivity and don't let your ability to argue turn to sarcasm.

SUN IN GEMINI/MOON IN SAGITTARIUS ☉♊ ☽♐
You love to move around, both in the physical and the mental world, and can express yourself vividly. Learn to discipline your mind and distinguish between facts and fancy.

SUN IN GEMINI/MOON IN CAPRICORN ☉♊ ☽♑
You combine a strong sense of direction with flexibility, and you can develop a good memory. Don't be too serious, and develop warmth in your nature.

SUN IN GEMINI/MOON IN AQUARIUS ☉♊ ☽♒
You have a lot of originality and ability to see into people and situations. Don't be too erratic, and keep your visions in touch with reality.

SUN IN GEMINI/MOON IN PISCES ☉♊ ☽♓
You are intuitive and a dreamer, and your thinking has the flavor of fantasy about it. Learn to be comfortable in the world as it is, and don't feel that it's always necessary to explain yourself.

SUN IN CANCER/MOON IN ARIES ☉♋ ☽♈

You can start things and then follow through on them; your mind is quick and your memory good. Keep your rebelliousness where it belongs, and don't let your emotions and impulses go to extremes.

SUN IN CANCER/MOON IN TAURUS ☉♋ ☽♉

You can combine charm, practicality and perseverance with an unusual imaginative touch. Don't brood or allow your sympathetic nature to let you be too affected by others.

SUN IN CANCER/MOON IN GEMINI ☉♋ ☽♊

You are sensitive to everything going on around you and also quite adaptable. Don't let your openness make you indecisive.

SUN IN CANCER/MOON IN CANCER ☉♋ ☽♋

You are affectionate and aware, with a natural diplomacy and creativity. Don't let your need for solitude become aloofness.

SUN IN CANCER/MOON IN LEO ☉♋ ☽♌

Your feelings are intense and warm, with a touch of the dramatic. Watch yourself for a bent toward sensationalism and a tendency to go to extremes.

SUN IN CANCER/MOON IN VIRGO ☉♋ ☽♍

You are aware of many nuances of feelings and like to help others. Develop the ability to be decisive, and rid yourself of the worry habit.

SUN IN CANCER/MOON IN LIBRA ☉♋ ☽♎

You are quite tuned into other people, and you also have a pronounced sense of the beautiful. Don't let yourself become overly sentimental.

SUN IN CANCER/MOON IN SCORPIO ☉♋ ☽♏

Your personality commands the awareness of others, and you can be rather dramatic. Don't use your concentration powers in a negative direction or become a martyr.

SUN IN CANCER/MOON IN SAGITTARIUS ☉♋ ☽♐

You have high aims and ideals combined with warmheartedness and sensitivity. Learn to accept that your reach will always exceed your grasp.

SUN IN CANCER/MOON IN CAPRICORN ☉♋ ☽♑

Your nature combines a practical and shrewd side with much sensitivity. Develop the ability to express your inner feelings.

SUN IN CANCER/MOON IN AQUARIUS ☉♋ ☽♒

You can be accurate in your thinking and can convince others of your viewpoint. Don't let ego tendencies make you an opportunist.

SUN IN CANCER/MOON IN PISCES ☉♋ ☽♓

You have a built-in sense of the subtle changes in emotional atmospheres and you adapt almost automatically. Get some solitude, and don't get lost in the past or let sensitivity close you to others.

♌ SUN IN LEO/MOON IN ARIES ☉♌ ☽♈

You have courage and enthusiasm to spare, and you are both loyal and self-reliant. Don't overdramatize, learn the importance of objectivity, and look at a broader scope than merely the personal.

SUN IN LEO/MOON IN TAURUS ☉♌ ☽♉

You are good-natured, practical and firm in your point of view. Learn some diplomacy and to recognize when it is advisable to compromise.

SUN IN LEO/MOON IN GEMINI ☉♌ ☽♊

You have both a lot of ideas and the energy to put them in action: your head and your heart can work together. Keep in touch with some form of the arts, and be your sociable self without always trying to impress people.

SUN IN LEO/MOON IN CANCER ☉♌ ☽♋

You have a lot of affection and strong protective instincts for those you love. Keep your emotions in control and your sentimentality in perspective.

SUN IN LEO/MOON IN LEO ☉♌ ☽♌

You have a strong presence and combine an affectionate nature with independence. Don't let your sense of broader perspectives keep you from being introspective.

SUN IN LEO/MOON IN VIRGO ☉♌ ☽♍

You are resourceful and can combine analytical ability with strength of conviction. Learn to quiet your anxieties and also to be tactful.

SUN IN LEO/MOON IN LIBRA ☉♌ ☽♎

You are idealistic, companionable and compassionate, with a vivid imagination and love for the beautiful. Learn to appreciate solitude and to see group needs in proportion to needs of the individual.

SUN IN LEO/MOON IN SCORPIO ☉♌ ☽♏

You have intense vitality, passionate enthusiasms and an instinct for the dramatic. Learn to see a point of objectivity beyond your personal needs.

SUN IN LEO/MOON IN SAGITTARIUS ☉♌ ☽♐

You are fiery and adventurous, loving variety and having a warm heart. You can be very persuasive. Learn restraint and how to harness your abundant energies.

SUN IN LEO/MOON IN CAPRICORN ☉♌ ☽♑

You are ambitious and intense, with controlled energies and organizational ability. Develop some softness and don't let your power drive override the rights of others.

SUN IN LEO/MOON IN AQUARIUS ☉♌ ☽♒

You have a strong will and ability to judge human nature, and you combine independence with sociability. Develop flexibility and practicality.

SUN IN LEO/MOON IN PISCES ☉♌ ☽♓

You like to do something about what you believe in, and have both sensitivity and courage. Learn to accept that your dreams will not always manifest in reality.

SUN IN VIRGO/MOON IN ARIES ☉♍ ☽♈

You have a keen mind and a good wit, and can express yourself with much dynamism. Don't oversell your abilities and learn to tune in on other people's feelings.

SUN IN VIRGO/MOON IN TAURUS ☉♍ ☽♉

You are gentle and easygoing, practical and intuitive, with a touch of poetry in your nature. Avoid a tendency to coast through life and to be overcautious.

SUN IN VIRGO/MOON IN GEMINI ☉♍ ☽♊
Your mind is always active, gathering information from many sources and sifting through all of its intricacies. Keep in touch with your feelings and don't be too detached.

SUN IN VIRGO/MOON IN CANCER ☉♍ ☽♋
You are quiet, adaptable and sensitive to others, with an interest in how to help. Overcome a tendency to be defensive and too particular about things.

SUN IN VIRGO/MOON IN LEO ☉♍ ☽♌
You have a strong ethical sense as well as generosity and appreciation of beauty. You may need to develop initiative and independence.

SUN IN VIRGO/MOON IN VIRGO ☉♍ ☽♍
Your mind is always in evidence, discriminating, precise and accurate, and you are a good worker. Don't let yourself mill around in your mind and learn to see the broad sweep of things as well as the details.

SUN IN VIRGO/MOON IN LIBRA ☉♍ ☽♎
You think for yourself, enjoy learning, and possess natural tact and good taste. Practice sharpening up your ability to make decisions, and learn to put up with people who lack your fastidiousness.

SUN IN VIRGO/MOON IN SCORPIO ☉♍ ☽♏
You are quite intuitive and like to delve into what's really going on. You can also be quite persuasive. Learn to be impersonal and less critical.

SUN IN VIRGO/MOON IN SAGITTARIUS ☉♍ ☽♐
You approach life philosophically and with warmth, and you can also be practical. Try to get these twin sides of your nature together and curb overimpulsiveness.

SUN IN VIRGO/MOON IN CAPRICORN ☉♍ ☽♑
You can think things out thoroughly and seriously, and you have good ability to get work done. Don't overemphasize materiality, and lighten up with humor.

SUN IN VIRGO/MOON IN AQUARIUS ☉♍ ☽≈

Your impressions are quick, your mind is ingenious and you learn easily. Develop warmth and restrain a tendency to be calculating.

SUN IN VIRGO/MOON IN PISCES ☉♍ ☽♓

You have both a good mind and strong intuitions, and your nature is quite sympathetic. Calm some of your restlessness and learn to deal with others in a straightforward manner.

♎ SUN IN LIBRA/MOON IN ARIES ☉♎ ☽♈

You are both gentle and independent, with a good and balanced mind. Watch a touch of impatience, and don't let your interest in new ideas lead you in directions that are too far afield.

SUN IN LIBRA/MOON IN TAURUS ☉♎ ☽♉

Your nature is harmonious and affectionate, with a strong appreciation for all things beautiful. Don't be too influenced by others, and don't let your sentimentality get out of hand.

SUN IN LIBRA/MOON IN GEMINI ☉♎ ☽♊

You express yourself well and with charm, and you combine good taste with a quick mind. Find your center of stability, and don't neglect deepening your thoughts.

SUN IN LIBRA/MOON IN CANCER ☉♎ ☽♋

Your perceptions into others are quick and you have an excellent capacity for making people feel at home. Don't let amiability keep you from following your own direction.

SUN IN LIBRA/MOON IN LEO ☉♎ ☽♌

You are idealistic and romantic, with a pronounced aesthetic sense and a lot of charm. Don't let your trusting nature lead you to be unrealistic about others.

SUN IN LIBRA/MOON IN VIRGO ☉♎ ☽♍

Your nature is reasonable and charming, with both analytical ability and a sense of proportion. Find ways to strengthen your ability to make decisions.

SUN IN LIBRA/MOON IN LIBRA ☉♎ ☽♎

You are sensitive and romantic, with great delicacy of feeling and kindliness. You will need to work on the ability to stand your ground in spite of what others think.

SUN IN LIBRA/MOON IN SCORPIO ☉♎ ☽♏

You are quite ambitious, with a penetrating mind and the ability to make your way through a variety of situations. Keep a balance between your drive and your more gentle side.

SUN IN LIBRA/MOON IN SAGITTARIUS ☉♎ ☽♐

You are very sociable, with a love of adventure and a mind which sees the overall perspective. You have a strong sense of justice. Develop practicality and don't be reckless.

SUN IN LIBRA/MOON IN CAPRICORN ☉♎ ☽♑

You have good discipline and a strong sense of purpose, combined with tact. Curb a touch of opportunism and develop your sense of social as well as individual needs.

SUN IN LIBRA/MOON IN AQUARIUS ☉♎ ☽♒

Your nature is both dramatic and romantic, with insight into human nature and a sense of the future. Keep your imagination in the proper channels.

SUN IN LIBRA/MOON IN PISCES ☉♎ ☽♓

You have much charm, combined with excellent observational ability which can enable you to understand what human beings are about. Develop self-sufficiency and don't let others impose on your sympathetic nature.

SUN IN SCORPIO/MOON IN ARIES ☉♏ ☽♈

Your character expresses itself passionately, courageously and with resoluteness, and you have plenty of drive. Watch yourself for excessive assertiveness and jealousy, and try to develop some humility.

SUN IN SCORPIO/MOON IN TAURUS ☉♏ ☽♉

You can plan on a large scale and follow through with determination. You combine practicality with an artistic sense. Learn flexibility and how to be graceful about it when you lose.

SUN IN SCORPIO/MOON IN GEMINI ☉♏ ☽♊

You have an excellent sense of honor, shrewdness, and a mind both flexible and deep. Don't be an extremist, and keep your cynicism to a minimum.

SUN IN SCORPIO/MOON IN CANCER ☉♏ ☽♋
You have keen intuition and much emotional sensitivity, and your personality has a magnetic quality. Guard against being too impressionable and perhaps overly suspicious.

SUN IN SCORPIO/MOON IN LEO ☉♏ ☽♌
You can make quite an impression on people, for your personality is intense. You have the ability to follow plans through. Don't overdo your imagination, and learn to be detached when your emotions become too intense.

SUN IN SCORPIO/MOON IN VIRGO ☉♏ ☽♍
Your mind digs to the bottom of things and you have plenty of insight into how to improve them. Watch a tendency to have a sharp tongue and to pry into other people's affairs.

SUN IN SCORPIO/MOON IN LIBRA ☉♏ ☽♎
You have a natural poise and potential for developing unusually keen insights into others. Don't expect everyone to approach life with the same understanding that you have.

SUN IN SCORPIO/MOON IN SCORPIO ☉♏ ☽♏
Your nature is intense, self-reliant, magnetic, passionate and capable of tremendous creativity. Keep your power drive where it belongs, and learn to respect the space of other people rather than to dominate them.

SUN IN SCORPIO/MOON IN SAGITTARIUS ☉♏ ☽♐
You are sincere about your principles and approach life with much vitality. Watch a streak of impulsiveness, and don't blurt things out without gauging their effect.

SUN IN SCORPIO/MOON IN CAPRICORN ☉♏ ☽♑
You have independence, intense drive and the ability to sustain a direction you have set. Develop flexibility, and avoid self-indulgence.

SUN IN SCORPIO/MOON IN AQUARIUS ☉♏ ☽♒
You approach life with vision and with independence, and you usually know your own mind. Learn tolerance, and don't let yourself be irritable.

SUN IN SCORPIO/MOON IN PISCES ☉♏ ☽♓
You tune in intuitively to people and situations immediately and intensely. Don't let your imagination run away with you, and don't let your sense of your own (or other people's) pain cause you to build a shell around yourself.

SUN IN SAGITTARIUS/MOON IN ARIES ☉♐ ☽♈
You have enough energy, enthusiasm, and spirit of adventure for two people, and you are never devious in your approach to life. Develop restraint and calmness.

SUN IN SAGITTARIUS/MOON IN TAURUS ☉♐ ☽♉
You are affectionate and idealistic, with a natural devotion, a sense of humor, and the capacity for faith. Keep your idealism grounded in practical application, and develop your artistic side.

SUN IN SAGITTARIUS/MOON IN GEMINI ☉♐ ☽♊
You are a very active person, highly aware of what's going on around you and able to express yourself well. Learn to relax and center yourself.

SUN IN SAGITTARIUS/MOON IN CANCER ☉♐ ☽♋
Your imagination and intuition are paramount, and you can blend intellectual understanding with feeling. Get to the roots of things rather than letting yourself be carried away by their glamor.

SUN IN SAGITTARIUS/MOON IN LEO ☉♐ ☽♌
You have a warmth, loyalty and sense of honor which can endear you to others. Don't be showy, and keep track of the practicalities.

SUN IN SAGITTARIUS/MOON IN VIRGO ☉♐ ☽♍
You have a mind which grasps both broad principles and the realistic details, and you can express yourself with both warmth and detachment. Don't let yourself become judgmental.

SUN IN SAGITTARIUS/MOON IN LIBRA ☉♐ ☽♎
You are active, full of ideas, and have a generous nature. You have a strong sense of proportion and appreciate beauty intensely. Be sure to keep at least one foot on the ground.

SUN IN SAGITTARIUS/MOON IN SCORPIO ☉♐ ☽♏

You know your own mind, and look at life from a broad standpoint, but also with depth and humor. Channel your nervous energy, and avoid sarcasm.

SUN IN SAGITTARIUS/MOON IN SAGITTARIUS ☉♐ ☽♐

You see everything that happens in terms of its larger meaning, and you love to broaden your experience, both in travel and in new points of view. Relaxation techniques and music can help quiet your restlessness.

SUN IN SAGITTARIUS/MOON IN CAPRICORN ☉♐ ☽♑

You are able to see everything in terms of principles and an overall order, and you can express yourself with charm and humor. Don't jump to conclusions.

SUN IN SAGITTARIUS/MOON IN AQUARIUS ☉♐ ☽♒

You see the broad horizons of life and are ready to defend your point of view eloquently. Don't overdo, and learn not to defend yourself with too many words.

SUN IN SAGITTARIUS/MOON IN PISCES ☉♐ ☽♓

You have a natural awareness of influences from the spirit, as well as much sympathy and charitable feelings for others. Find the source of initiative in yourself, and learn not to worry.

♑ SUN IN CAPRICORN/MOON IN ARIES ☉♑ ☽♈

You chart your own course and then go full steam ahead to get there. Develop gentleness, and learn to let your mind rest.

SUN IN CAPRICORN/MOON IN TAURUS ☉♑ ☽♉

There is a dependable, down-to-earth quality about you that can endear you to others, and you have the ability to think things out to their end result. Don't sulk if things aren't always going your way for a time.

SUN IN CAPRICORN/MOON IN GEMINI ☉♑ ☽♊

You are both ingenious and methodical, with a good imagination and the ability to express it. Don't be carried away by your need to express yourself.

SUN IN CAPRICORN/MOON IN CANCER ☉♑ ☽♋

You are sensitive and look deeply into yourself and others, although not always expressing what you see. Avoid situations of nervous tension, yet don't live in a shell.

SUN IN CAPRICORN/MOON IN LEO ☉♑ ☽♌

You have an air of authority about you which combines stability with vigor and a strong will. Develop the warmth in your nature, and don't become too materialistic.

SUN IN CAPRICORN/MOON IN VIRGO ☉♑ ☽♍

Your capacity for methodical thinking and work is great, and you can keep your feet on the ground. Learn to center yourself so you can make decisions calmly, and don't let yourself be a snob.

SUN IN CAPRICORN/MOON IN LIBRA ☉♑ ☽♎

You have balance and foresight, and you can envision the ideal direction that events should take. Learn not to be gullible and to check your plans for soundness.

SUN IN CAPRICORN/MOON IN SCORPIO ☉♑ ☽♏

You have firmness, a clear sense of direction, and the drive to reach your goals. Don't be judgmental, and develop some flexibility in your point of view.

SUN IN CAPRICORN/MOON IN SAGITTARIUS ☉♑ ☽♐

You have humor, a lot of energy, and the capacity to work toward broad goals. In order to handle your nervous energy, you must get exercise and also learn to relax.

SUN IN CAPRICORN/MOON IN CAPRICORN ☉♑ ☽♑

You are self-controlled, thorough, and wonderfully organized, with a natural reserve and tact. Open yourself to relationships, and don't let yourself be despondent.

SUN IN CAPRICORN/MOON IN AQUARIUS ☉♑ ☽♒

You are an organizer, with a lot of drive and an ability to think big and with originality. Don't be unrealistically optimistic.

SUN IN CAPRICORN/MOON IN PISCES ☉♑ ☽♓

You have quietness and depth, with much intuition, understanding and sympathy for people. Learn to trust yourself and calm your apprehension about the future.

SUN IN AQUARIUS/MOON IN ARIES ☉♒ ☽♈
You can be emotionally detached, with a probing yet broad understanding combined with determination. Don't let yourself be smug, and learn to open to the feeling side of your nature.

SUN IN AQUARIUS/MOON IN TAURUS ☉♒ ☽♉
You have steadiness and purpose to your character, with loyalty to your friends and tolerance of their quirks. Curb stubbornness, and develop flexibility.

SUN IN AQUARIUS/MOON IN GEMINI ☉♒ ☽♊
Your nature is studious, and you have the ability to express yourself dramatically and with originality. Learn to persevere and that it's not always greener in the other field.

SUN IN AQUARIUS/MOON IN CANCER ☉♒ ☽♋
You enjoy companionship and have plenty of insight into other people, with excellent potential for balancing your mind and your emotions. However, don't let your emotional attachment to unique ideas take you too far from the practical.

SUN IN AQUARIUS/MOON IN LEO ☉♒ ☽♌
Your nature is romantic and warm, with imagination, creativity, and an active mind. Find quietness in yourself, and avoid unconsciously hogging attention.

SUN IN AQUARIUS/MOON IN VIRGO ☉♒ ☽♍
You are able to analyze objectively and express yourself eloquently and with subtlety. Don't give in to self-pity, and learn to express your feelings.

SUN IN AQUARIUS/MOON IN LIBRA ☉♒ ☽♎
You have intuition, balanced judgment, and the ability to look ahead. You are both sociable and charming. Learn to enjoy some solitude.

SUN IN AQUARIUS/MOON IN SCORPIO ☉♒ ☽♏
You have a strong presence, self-confidence, and the ability to influence others. Learn to respect the viewpoints of others, and curb irritability.

SUN IN AQUARIUS/MOON IN SAGITTARIUS ☉♒ ☽♐
You are independent and forthright, with a strong social consciousness and a liking for many people. Watch yourself for too impulsive speech and action.

SUN IN AQUARIUS/MOON IN CAPRICORN ☉♒ ☽♑
You are responsible and serious, with foresight and imagination, and you can achieve the common touch with people. Don't lose track of your feelings.

SUN IN AQUARIUS/MOON IN AQUARIUS ☉♒ ☽♒
You naturally accumulate knowledge and look at it with originality and to see its broader implications. Learn to relate personally as well as idealistically.

SUN IN AQUARIUS/MOON IN PISCES ☉♒ ☽♓
You have the inspiration to blend the thinking and feeling parts of your nature. Don't let your sense of fantasy take over where reason is necessary.

♓ SUN IN PISCES/MOON IN ARIES ☉♓ ☽♈
You have much energy and self-reliance, a quick comprehension, and a kind heart. Develop persistence and self-control.

SUN IN PISCES/MOON IN TAURUS ☉♓ ☽♉
You are sociable and can get along with anyone. You also have an aesthetic bent to your nature. Learn to be more sure of yourself and not to be influenced by flattery.

SUN IN PISCES/MOON IN GEMINI ☉♓ ☽♊
You are very flexible, learn easily, and express yourself well. Learn to steady your direction and your idea flow, and avoid tackling too much.

SUN IN PISCES/MOON IN CANCER ☉♓ ☽♋
You are sensitive, sympathetic, and considerate, with imagination and a sense of the dramatic. Learn detachment from the reactions of others and also how to even out your moods.

SUN IN PISCES/MOON IN LEO ☉♓ ☽♌
You have a generous nature and an imagination which can project you into far and fantastic horizons. Don't go overboard on how things appear, and keep in touch with practicalities.

SUN IN PISCES/MOON IN VIRGO ☉♓ ☽♍
You combine seriousness with a sense of humor and can blend your intuitions with logic. Learn self-confidence, and don't let your head go around in worry circles.

SUN IN PISCES/MOON IN LIBRA ☉♓ ☽♎

You have an inborn aesthetic quality to everything you do, with a particular connection to the world of fantasy. Keep aware of the reality principle, and don't get so focused on others that you lose touch with your own flow.

SUN IN PISCES/MOON IN SCORPIO ☉♓ ☽♏

You are both intuitive and perceptive, with a sense of whimsy and a taste for the unusual. Combat morbidity or depression by cultivating your awareness of the ludicrous side of human situations.

SUN IN PISCES/MOON IN SAGITTARIUS ☉♓ ☽♐

You see vast horizons and long-range directions, and you enjoy moving around. Learn to focus on specifics and practicalities, and don't let yourself be too touchy.

SUN IN PISCES/MOON IN CAPRICORN ☉♓ ☽♑

You have both vision and practicality, with a quiet sensitivity and good driving power. Don't be too secretive or let yourself give way to despondency.

SUN IN PISCES/MOON IN AQUARIUS ☉♓ ☽♒

You are a friendly person and want to help things become better in the world. Don't lose tolerance for people with different viewpoints.

SUN IN PISCES/MOON IN PISCES ☉♓ ☽♓

You are deeply introspective, with an active imagination and tremendous sensitivity. Learn to not be overly influenced by others, but don't become withdrawn.

CHAPTER SIX

THE PLANETS

In addition to the Sun sign and Moon sign, the positions of the planets in the zodiac signs at the time of your birth can give information about you. Besides the Earth, there are eight known planets going around the Sun. For convenience, the Sun and Moon are usually called "planets" as well, lumping them with the other bodies to form an **energy pattern** which characterizes you.

Each planet corresponds to a different **function** in your life, for instance: Mercury relates to how you think; Venus to your likes and dislikes; Mars to your energy and assertiveness. Each planet is influenced by the zodiac sign it is in, what astrological **house** it occupies (to be explained), and its connections with other planets (**aspects**).

At times the planets are spread out, each in a different sign of the zodiac, and at other times they are grouped together with several in the same sign. If you were born with a number of planets in the same sign (called a **stellium**), you are much more typical of that sign than someone whose planets are more spread out. If your Sun is in one sign, say Sagittarius, and you have a stellium in another sign, say Capricorn, you might, perhaps, be mistaken for a Capricorn.

Each planet is considered the **ruler** of one sign (sometimes two). This means that the planet functions particularly strongly when it happens to be placed in this sign. Even when in another sign, it seems to have a connection with the sign it rules and any planets therein. The modern trend in astrology is to understand just how the different signs relate to each planet rather than to label any combination "good" or "bad."

For example, here is a typical planetary spread through the zodiac:

Aries: no planets	Libra: Moon
Taurus: no planets	Scorpio: Mercury
Gemini: Pluto	Sagittarius: Sun; Uranus
Cancer: Neptune	Capricorn: Mars; Jupiter; and Saturn
Leo: no planets	Aquarius: Venus
Virgo: no planets	Pisces: no planets

To find where in the zodiac Jupiter, Saturn, Uranus, Neptune, and Pluto were when you were born, see page 176. Because Mercury, Venus and Mars change zodiac signs so often, space limitations prevented us from giving their positions.

In the next few pages we will describe what each planet means. Beginning on page 163, we will describe how each planet works in each of the signs.

Mercury ☿ Rules Gemini ♊ and Virgo ♍

The position of Mercury in your chart tells much about how your mind works, more specifically the rational, concrete thought processes. It shows how you communicate, the kinds of words and expressions which particularly convey your thoughts, the kinds of ideas you focus on and remember. It is also one indication of whether you talk slow or fast, much or little.

Mercury also relates to the tone of your nervous system, both in general and more particularly as it relays the messages of your senses.

Mercury is the closest known planet to the Sun. As seen from Earth, it is always close to the Sun; therefore it is either in your Sun sign or the sign immediately before or immediately after your Sun sign.

Venus ♀ Rules Taurus ♉ and Libra ♎

The position of Venus is a strong indication of your sense of beauty and what you value — what attracts you and what you draw to you. Therefore it indicates your affections — who and what you are fond of — and your tastes. It is a strong component in the kind of creativity and emotional qualities you manifest.

Like the Moon, Venus has a feminine quality. In a man's chart its position (as well as that of the Moon) indicates what traits in a woman will attract him. In fact, if he is not comfortable with his own feminine side, he may allow the women around him to express the kind of beauty, sensuality and sweetness indicated by the position of his Venus.

Like Mercury, Venus is closer to the Sun than the Earth is. Venus always appears in your Sun sign, the sign immediately before or immediately after your Sun sign, or, although rarely, two signs away on either side.

Mars ♂ Rules Aries ♈, co-rules Scorpio ♏

The position of Mars relates to the amount and expression of your energy, and indicates forcefulness, assertiveness and courage. It is related to your passion, sex drive and what kind of temper you have. It is prominently placed in the charts of people who love active sports.

Like the Sun, Mars has a masculine quality and its position is one of the indications in a woman's chart of what qualities in a man will attract her. If she is not comfortable with the masculine side of her nature, she may repress personal expression of the position of Mars and let the man in her life express it for her.

Mars is the first of the planets whose orbits are farther out from the Sun than that of Earth, and therefore your Sun sign gives no indication of what sign contains Mars. It takes almost two years to go through all the signs of the zodiac.

Jupiter ♃ Rules Sagittarius ♐, co-rules Pisces ♓

Jupiter, the largest of the planets, relates to expansive influences in your life and the enlargement of your frame of reference. Its position characterizes the direction of your enthusiasms, your philosophical outlook, your religious bents and where your loyalties lie. Just as Mercury indicates your more concrete thought processes, Jupiter indicates your more abstract thoughts. It shows what you are optimistic about and how lucky you are.

Depending on its position, Jupiter can signify abundance in such diverse forms as more money, more ideas — or more weight. Jupiter takes about twelve years to circle the zodiac and stays in each sign about a year. Find Jupiter's position in your chart on page 177.

Saturn ♄ Rules Capricorn ♑ , co-rules Aquarius ♒

Whereas Jupiter is connected with expansion, Saturn, the second largest planet, is connected with contraction. The position of Saturn indicates what you tend to be practical and serious about, your comprehension of the structures and restraints in life. Also, the areas which call for discipline, your capacity for organization and form, and your time sense are all indicated by where Saturn is in your chart.

The directions and strength of your ambitions, your qualities of responsibility, endurance and caution are connected with Saturn. Although the qualities represented by Saturn are necessary and, in a larger sense, beneficial in our lives, human nature often prefers the flowering expansion of Jupiter rather than the pruning contraction of Saturn.

Saturn takes almost twenty-nine years to circle the zodiac, staying about two and a half years in a sign. Find Saturn's position in your chart on page 177.

Uranus ♅ Rules Aquarius ♒

The position of Uranus indicates the type of independence you manifest and the kind of inventiveness and originality that come naturally to you. It denotes your intuition and your tendency toward genius. It is as if Uranus breaks through outworn Saturnian structures with a new, and unexpected, direction.

The planets up through Saturn were known to the ancients, as they are clearly visible to the naked eye. However, it took the invention of the telescope to find Uranus in 1781. Once its orbit was known, its position was plotted in birth charts of many people (born both before and after its discovery). Thus astrologers were able to deduce its significance.

Uranus takes eighty-four years to circle the zodiac, spending about seven years in each sign. Since everyone born in that seven-year period has Uranus in the same sign, it serves to tie in certain characteristics of that age group. However, its aspects and house position (see page182) change with every chart. It is more important in some individual charts than in others.

On page 179 you can find out what sign Uranus was in when you were born.

Neptune ♆ Rules Pisces ♓

Neptune is the planet of inspiration, indicating our connection with that ideal realm from which come imagination, dreams, fantasy and illusion. The illusion enters only when you forget that the perfection represented by the ideal Neptunian dream can never be totally realized in the limited physical world.

Neptune is connected less with the intellect and more with the aesthetic sense. The highest level of art carries the imprint of Neptune, but it may be expressed through the more personal aesthetic manifestations of Venus.

Neptune was discovered in 1846 and takes 165 years to go around the zodiac, spending about 14 years in a sign. Therefore its sign position shows certain qualities common to the dreams and ideals of almost a generation. Its position by aspect and by house will indicate in what areas and how strongly it is significant in an individual chart.

On page 177 you can find out what sign Neptune was in when you were born.

Pluto ♇ Rules Scorpio ♏

How you relate to group energy patterns is shown by the position of Pluto in your chart. This can be as seemingly superficial as, for instance, the fashions you relate to, or as deep as the underlying points of view you share with the groups with which you identify.

Unless Pluto is strongly placed by house and aspect, it denotes drives predominantly below the surface of consciousness, unquestioned and compelling. It indicates the potentiality for basic change (reformulation) of your life patterns, as well as areas of your potential contribution to society.

Pluto was the last planet to have been discovered, having been located in 1930. It goes around the zodiac in 248 years. Because of its eccentric orbit, the number of years in each sign varies, but the average is 20. In a sense, people born with Pluto in the same zodiac sign constitute a generation, and there is an underlying similarity in their approach to life that can be correlated to the characteristics of Pluto's sign.

On page 177 you can find out what sign Pluto was in when you were born.

CHAPTER SEVEN

PLANET-SIGN COMBINATIONS
PLANETARY KEYWORDS

Sun: Individuality ☉ vitality, self, power, sense of "I", conscious aim
Moon: Instincts ☽ feelings, moods, sensitivity, receptivity, habits, bodily functions
Mercury: Intellect written and verbal communication, active, intelligence, memory, senses
Venus: Affections ♀ personal relationships, disposition, romance, aesthetics, emotions, values
Mars: Forcefulness ♂ assertiveness, courage, aggression, passion, sex drive, initiative, sports
Jupiter: Enthusiasm ♃ expansion, optimism, abstraction, philosophy, religion, wisdom, loyalty
Saturn: Practicality ♄ self-discipline, organization, time sense, endurance, restraint, ambition, caution
Uranus: Independence ♅ new directions, inventiveness, originality, intuition, freedom, genius
Neptune: Inspiration ♆ idealism, vision, compassion, sympathy, devotion, mysticism, illusion
Pluto: Basic Change ♇ group dynamics, reformulation, regeneration, compulsion, collective energy

☿ MERCURY IN ARIES ☿♈

Your wits are quick and sharp (and your tongue can be also). You have plenty of new ideas, often expressed as soon as they come to you. Develop follow-through in your thinking, and curb a tendency to argue.

MERCURY IN TAURUS ☿♉

You have a common-sense and practical approach and tend to think deliberately and in depth. You can concentrate and have good powers of visualization. Avoid clinging to ideas just because you are used to them.

MERCURY IN GEMINI ☿♊

You have a lot of curiosity and easily see many points of view. You also have a way with words, and probably with languages. Try not to "overtalk." Learn how to soothe your nervous energy.

MERCURY IN CANCER ☿♋

You are more intuitive than logical. You often learn better by doing than by theorizing first. Your memory is probably good. Watch for a tendency to let emotional influences cloud your thinking.

MERCURY IN LEO ☿♌

You think in a broad scope and can concentrate and follow through with your plans. You express yourself dramatically but with warmth. Work on keeping your ideas flexible, and don't ignore details.

MERCURY IN VIRGO ☿♍

You are highly analytical and take into into consideration all the details. You think in practical terms and can express yourself with precision. Avoid cluttering your mind and a tendency to be excessively critical.

MERCURY IN LIBRA ☿♎

You consider various points of view before making up your mind and have a strong sense of justice. You express yourself with grace and sensitivity to others. You may need to develop decisiveness.

MERCURY IN SCORPIO ☿♏

You have a penetrating and intuitive mind and seldom express your thoughts without good reason. You naturally dig down to the causes underneath the surface, and you can size up people well. Avoid fixity in your judgments.

MERCURY IN SAGITTARIUS ☿♐

You look at facts from the standpoint of how they fit into overall viewpoints. Your mind is flexible but not particularly concerned with logic. You express yourself frankly. Practice concentration to improve your memory, and avoid conclusion-jumping.

MERCURY IN CAPRICORN ☿ ♑

You think methodically and with concentration. Your ideas are practical and clearly structured, and you can handle detail. You may need to allow your imagination more freedom and learn to lighten your manner of expression.

MERCURY IN AQUARIUS ☿ ≈

You have some very original inventive thoughts and an impersonal viewpoint. You can express yourself well and enjoy working in groups. Watch out for too much abruptness in your speech and some stubbornness in clinging to opinions.

MERCURY IN PISCES ☿ ♓

It is easier for you to think in pictures than in words. Dry facts and pure logic don't interest you. You can be either very quiet or very talkative, and you can express yourself poetically. Avoid undue influence of others on your thoughts, and don't lose control of your imagination.

VENUS IN ARIES ♀ ♈

You can take the initiative in going after that which attracts you, whether objects or persons. You have a lively social personality. Learn to relate to people on a deep enough level so you don't lose interest if they don't always give you a lot of personal attention.

VENUS IN TAURUS ♀ ♉

You are affectionate and loyal to those whom you love. You have a strong appreciation for beautiful things and like comfort. Your voice has a pleasing quality. Guard against a tendency to be possessive (of things and people).

VENUS IN GEMINI ♀ ♊

You are friendly and affectionate toward a lot of people and like to move around freely in a variety of social situations without being pinned down. You have a good wit. Learn to reach your own emotional depths.

VENUS IN CANCER ♀ ♋

You are deeply attached and sensitive to the people you love: family, friends and romantic relationships. You love your home and have a strong instinct to take care of people. Guard against clinging too strongly to security and a tendency toward oversentimentality.

VENUS IN LEO ♀♌

You are warmhearted and loyal in your affections and also have a bent toward the dramatic in your relationships. You love company. Your aesthetic tastes run toward the strong and vivid. Watch a tendency to be overly demanding of attention to yourself.

VENUS IN VIRGO ♀♍

You love order and perfection, not only in objects but also in your relationships. You enjoy serving people whom you are fond of. Learn to let your emotions flow spontaneously and to live with a certain amount of imperfection.

VENUS IN LIBRA ♀♎

You have a lot of charm and seek harmony, both in your surroundings and in your relationships, which are very important to you. You are likely to have talent in some form of the arts. Avoid agreeing with people merely to keep peace, and don't be too fickle.

VENUS IN SCORPIO ♀♏

Your emotions are intense and deep, and you can be very magnetic. You are loyal, but can end a relationship with finality if deeply hurt. Curb a tendency toward jealousy, and learn to live and let live in your emotions.

VENUS IN SAGITTARIUS ♀♐

Your affections are strong and outgoing, and include many people. You are both open and idealistic about your feelings. In your tastes you appreciate a touch of the flamboyant. Cultivate an awareness of when a delicate touch is needed in your emotional reactions.

VENUS IN CAPRICORN ♀♑

You are serious about your emotional relationships but may tend to be reserved about expressing your feelings. In music and art you are drawn toward those forms with a definite structure. Conquer your fears of being hurt, and allow your emotions to flow more freely.

VENUS IN AQUARIUS ♀♒

You are outgoing and affectionate to many people. Although you can be loyal to the people you love, you don't like to be emotionally fenced in. Your aesthetic tastes tend toward the original and unusual. Guard against letting your mind be too involved in your emotions.

VENUS IN PISCES ♀♓

Your emotions are deep and compassionate, and you feel sympathy toward many people as well as an innate understanding of their feelings. Your aesthetic sense is strong, with a preference for expressions of a dream world. Learn to avoid overdependence emotionally.

♂ MARS IN ARIES ♂♈

You are self-starting and can shift immediately into high gear. Your physical and mental energy can help others overcome inertia. Curb your tendencies toward impulsiveness and combativeness as well as starting more projects than you can handle.

MARS IN TAURUS ♂♉

It's sometimes hard for you to get going, but once started on any activity, you are capable of sustained energy flow, patience and determination. You are quite practical, but may emphasize your material needs a bit too much. Watch a tendency toward stubbornness and a slow burn when things don't go your way.

MARS IN GEMINI ♂♊

Physically and mentally, your energy darts from one thing to another. This gives you a sparkling wit and enables you to juggle many activities at once. However, you need to learn to channel energy more efficiently and sometimes curb your tongue.

MARS IN CANCER ♂♋

Your energies are closely tied to your feelings. When your physical or emotional security is involved, you can work with quiet tenacity to achieve your aims. Develop positive outlets for emotion to counter a bottling-up tendency.

MARS IN LEO ♂♌

Your driving energy is strong and sustained, both for yourself and as a focal point for others. You are naturally high-spirited and confident, excellent qualities so long as you do not become overbearing and have difficulty admitting when you are wrong.

MARS IN VIRGO ♂♍

You are industrious and exacting in whatever you do and are motivated to pay attention to all the details. You analyze and plan your activities in a practical way. Your craftsmanlike energies can accomplish much so long as you don't fuss too much over every little thing.

MARS IN LIBRA ♂ ♎

You prefer to use your energies in cooperative ventures rather than purely on your own. Although you are not aggressive, you can be very competitive. Watch a tendency to argue, and develop the ability to balance your desires and those of others.

MARS IN SCORPIO ♂ ♏

Your energies well up intensely from deep inside and, when rightly channeled, give you the power to push through strong obstacles and persevere in working toward your goals. Don't bottle up anger and learn to accept compromise when necessary.

MARS IN SAGITTARIUS ♂ ♐

Your energies are based in your ideals, but also have a restless, adventurous quality. You enjoy active sports and the outdoors. Don't expect to win everyone to your viewpoint, and learn to keep your goals realistic.

MARS IN CAPRICORN ♂ ♑

You are capable of organizing and directing your energies very effectively. You can act decisively and practically, preferring to plan ahead. Don't let your strong goal orientation cause you to lose track of the human factors.

MARS IN AQUARIUS ♂ ♒

Your energies work best when you can function somewhat independently and at your own erratic pace. Nevertheless, you enjoy teamwork and can be motivated by social ideals, although with your own original touch. Watch that your originality doesn't become rebellion for rebellion's sake.

MARS IN PISCES ♂ ♓

The key to your energy flow is the state of your emotions. Your driving force is not aggressive but springs from your "feel" of the situation. You are quite adaptable but must learn to stabilize your direction, when necessary, through changing circumstances.

♃ JUPITER IN ARIES ♃ ♈

You take initiative in expanding your horizons and can also spark others to seek broader viewpoints. You can be optimistic and you almost certainly enjoy exploring. Watch your tendency to be overly optimistic and extravagant.

JUPITER IN TAURUS ♃♉

You particularly enjoy good material things and are practical in handling your resources. You are capable of seeing a philosophic meaning in the everyday events of life. Watch a tendency toward excessive indulgence, and keep your viewpoints flexible.

JUPITER IN GEMINI ♃♊

Your mind naturally collects bits of information and ideas from many different fields and tries to fit the assortment into a total framework. You can communicate well, but learn not to talk too much and to deepen your understanding as well as broaden it.

JUPITER IN CANCER ♃♋

Your nurturing instincts expand to include many people. You can see the personal experiences of yourself and others in a broader context. Avoid excessive sentimentality in your idealism and also a possible tendency to overeat.

JUPITER IN LEO ♃♌

Whatever you do, you like to do it on a big scale. You can be generous in sharing not only your possessions but also your understandings. Your sense of dignity is strong. Avoid too much pride and ostentation.

JUPITER IN VIRGO ♃♍

Your philosophy has a definitely down-to-earth quality and you tend to distrust points of view when you cannot see their practical application. You value service and meticulousness. Make room sometimes for some beautiful, even though impractical, dreams and don't make mountains out of molehills.

JUPITER IN LIBRA ♃♎

Your sense of justice and fair play is very strong, as is your sense of the beautiful. You usually have good relationships with others and are considerate and cooperative. However, don't try to please everybody or promise more than you can deliver.

JUPITER IN SCORPIO ♃♏

You look for the real truth behind any point of view presented to you. You can be uncompromising in your adherence to the underlying reality as you see it. Don't use unfairly your potential for controlling others.

JUPITER IN SAGITTARIUS ♃♐

You see all the parts of your life, and that of others, as they relate to a larger whole. You like to travel, both physically and in thought, to broaden your perspective. Calm your excess restlessness, and don't expect everyone to see your point of view.

JUPITER IN CAPRICORN ♃♑

You value integrity, responsibility and the proper use of resources. You are conscientious and ambitious, and willing to work for what you believe in. Sometimes your point of view may need broadening.

JUPITER IN AQUARIUS ♃♒

Your values are distinctly humanitarian, and you have much tolerance for other points of view. You like to work with others for improvements in society. Learn to focus your interests, and keep an eye on the practical.

JUPITER IN PISCES ♃♓

Your compassion is strong for those who need help. Your emotional depths often touch mystical levels. Allow yourself seclusion sometimes, and balance your service to, with your dependence on, others.

♄ SATURN IN ARIES ♄♈

You have the ability to be self-reliant and to follow through on the projects you tackle. You can be resourceful in your methods. Learn cooperation, and don't overdo self-justification. Keep active physically.

SATURN IN TAURUS ♄♉

You can have great patience and persistence in pursuing your goals, which usually emphasize the practical. You can be a good manager of resources since security is important to you. Watch a tendency toward stubbornness and collecting more things than you really need.

SATURN IN GEMINI ♄♊

You have a natural bent toward mental discipline and logical problem solving. Your thinking is practical and clear, and you can help others think things out. Guard against negative thinking, and keep a sense of the value of nonsense.

SATURN IN CANCER ♄♋

You are very sensitive to any attempt to impose emotional restrictions on you, and you require respect as an individual. Work on both opening up the flow of your own emotions and on self-discipline.

SATURN IN LEO ♄♌
Your will is strong, as is your need to be recognized. It is natural for you to control your personal environment, and you can also give leadership, so long as you restrict your tendency to be an autocrat and respect the need of others for independent action.

SATURN IN VIRGO ♄♍
You have great capacity for methodical work with careful attention to all details. You can be patient, practical and analytical. Learn to discriminate between the important and unimportant elements, and keep your sense of humor handy.

SATURN IN LIBRA ♄♎
You have a firm sense of justice and the importance of cooperative efforts. Tact and timing come naturally to you, as well as the ability to organize and plan ahead. Never forget that the **spirit** of justice is more important than its strict interpretation.

SATURN IN SCORPIO ♄♏
You value responsibility and diligence both in yourself and in others. Your drive to succeed is intense and you coordinate the hidden as well as the obvious elements in any situation. Learn to forgive injustices done to you, and use properly your ability to hatch plots.

SATURN IN SAGITTARIUS ♄♐
You have a natural sense of how to apply general principles in a practical and personal manner, both in your own life and in teaching others. You are inclined to speak out for what you believe. Watch undue pride and a tendency toward self-righteousness.

SATURN IN CAPRICORN ♄♑
Your ambition is strong, as is your need to secure your place in life and your ability to organize. You are capable of discipline, patience and foresight. Keep your sense of humor, and develop the ability to flow with events even when they run counter to your plans.

SATURN IN AQUARIUS ♄♒
You are a practical idealist with a scientific approach which can be both logical and intuitive. You have a strong structural sense and ability to concentrate, with a potential bent toward mathematics. Watch a tendency toward limiting your viewpoint and becoming opinionated.

SATURN IN PISCES ♄ ♓

You have a natural understanding of the emotions of others and are not limited in your approaches toward helping. You also have a bent toward meditation and need periods of solitude. Do not become immersed in fears and problems either of others or of yourself.

♅ URANUS IN ARIES ♅ ♈

In some area or other you have a pioneering bent to your thinking. When your sense of independence is touched, you can be outspoken. Watch impulsiveness and a preference for something new just because it is different.

URANUS IN TAURUS ♅ ♉

You are intrigued by new ways to deal with practical matters or material resources. You can also be interested in new approaches to the arts. Don't disrupt old habit patterns unless the change is really worth it.

URANUS IN GEMINI ♅ ♊

You are interested in all sorts of new ways of thinking, particularly when logic and intuition come together. Your mind can range in many directions, looking for the unexpected twist. Learn to curb your restlessness and develop follow-through.

URANUS IN CANCER ♅ ♋

You don't like any attempt to corral your feelings. You are also not an emotional hypocrite — sooner or later you express what you feel. Realize that your mood changes don't always stem from the level of your true feelings.

URANUS IN LEO ♅ ♌

Freedom of self-expression is important to you. Your creativity tends toward the nontraditional, and your will to pursue your own line of endeavor can be strong. Don't try to be a law unto yourself.

URANUS IN VIRGO ♅ ♍

You can be resourceful and inventive in your approach to work. You can analyze what is wrong with old thought patterns and what new approaches can be incorporated in such fields as science, education and health. Avoid scattering your energies.

URANUS IN LIBRA ♅ ♎

You are able to sense new forms of beauty which break away from the traditional. You also have the ability to break away from outmoded habit patterns in relationships. Learn to see the merit in traditional forms while you are revising them.

URANUS IN SCORPIO ♅ ♏

You have an instinct for probing in unexpected ways what goes on beneath the surface. You believe in acting decisively to root out what needs correction. Keep aware that destruction should make way for new construction.

URANUS IN SAGITTARIUS ♅ ♐

You can find your horizons suddenly broadened by unexpected breakthroughs in understanding. Insights in one area of your life will throw light on something in another area. Don't discard all your old beliefs in your enthusiasm for the new.

URANUS IN CAPRICORN ♅ ♑

You have the ability to take the established patterns in your life and find new outlets for them. Potentially you can combine a respect for the status quo with a practical sense of how it can be adapted to new circumstances. Don't let yourself be overly ambitious.

URANUS IN AQUARIUS ♅ ♒

You are open to new ideas and can develop a good intuition. You have your own mind and also a strong respect for the truth. There is a humanitarian side to your nature. Don't go overboard on freedom for freedom's sake, and keep your eccentricity realistic.

URANUS IN PISCES ♅ ♓

You have the potential for seeing through and discarding outmoded emotional patterns and helping others to do the same. Your intuition can have a mystical turn. Keep your idealism practical, and dream without escaping into your dreams.

 NEPTUNE IN CANCER ♆ ♋
Your highest ideals are expressed in feelings that you cannot easily put into words but that embody deep compassion, sympathy and a mutual nurturing between people. If you are not in touch with the depths of this feeling, however, it can come out as mere sentimentality and emotional attachment.

NEPTUNE IN LEO ♆♌

Consciously or unconsciously you are always searching for the true center in yourself and in others. You are a romantic when it comes to love. Learn to accept the faults in everyone while aiming toward the ideal.

NEPTUNE IN VIRGO ♆♍

You can picture a world in which, in a spirit of humanitarian service, each person gives according to what he or she can do best. You understand that clearing up things on a practical level is an important step to a better world. Keep a vision of the whole, and don't let your critical ability get lost in the details.

NEPTUNE IN LIBRA ♆♎

You have high ideals about what relationships between people could be, and you understand that mutual responsibility and a strong sense of justice are key factors. You also have an intense appreciation of beauty in many forms. Learn to accept a certain amount of imbalance in the short term, balancing things out in the long term.

NEPTUNE IN SCORPIO ♆♏

You understand that strong desire energies are the raw material for strong spiritual energies, and you see the need for such energy transformation in the world. Keep your energies strong without getting lost in impure expressions of them.

NEPTUNE IN SAGITTARIUS ♆♐

You can envision a world united in its spiritual beliefs, in which the exchange of ideas and cultures takes place on a common foundation. Keep deepening your sense of cosmic law while knowing that it cannot be confined to any one person or set of beliefs.

NEPTUNE IN CAPRICORN ♆♑

You strive to bring your dreams down to Earth, seeking the perfect forms which express your ideals. Learn to accept that not every fantasy can be made concrete and that efficiency and structure are important in daily life.

NEPTUNE IN AQUARIUS ♆♒

You can visualize ideal cooperation in families, communities, nations and the world. You seek freedom from outmoded structures and new ways of understanding yourself and the world. Don't discard traditional dreams just because they have been around awhile.

PLUTO IN GEMINI ♇♊

The most profound changes in your life can come from a reformulation of some of the ideas which you had accepted as almost self-evident. Learn that your familiar ways of thinking may not be exactly the way things actually are.

PLUTO IN CANCER ♇♋

Potentially the area of greatest release in your life can come when you can give up those early-developed emotional patterns to which you cling simply because they are familiar. Learn the beauty in letting your emotional flow take unaccustomed channels.

PLUTO IN LEO ♇♌

The change which you seek is to move your center of action from your more superficial self to your deeper self. This will release power which is now blocked. Don't let your energies settle on trivial goals.

PLUTO IN VIRGO ♇♍

The perfection you are looking for can become more meaningful when you deepen your understanding of what perfection means. Don't get bogged down in habitual work patterns.

PLUTO IN LIBRA ♇♎

Meaningful change for you involves a reformulation of your relationships so that they are based on responsibility and freedom rather than any level of contention and compulsion. Realize that the sense of balance you are looking for is related to your inner center rather than a more superficial point.

PLUTO IN SCORPIO ♇♏

You seek to change yourself and your world at the roots, where action can be most effective. When your direction is set, your will can be powerful. It is important that this will does not operate from a purely ego level.

PLUTO IN SAGITTARIUS ♇♐

You want to make basic changes in the way your world is organized, in accordance with your deepening understanding of its meaning. Realize that progress does not depend on everyone fitting into the same mold.

CHAPTER EIGHT

PLANET CALENDARS (1911–2000)

The following charts and the information on page 180 will enable you to find out what signs Jupiter, Saturn, Uranus, Neptune, and Pluto were in when you were born. Find your birth year across the top of the charts. Follow this column down until you find a planet line. Look horizontally to the left to see which sign it was in. Where a planet line crosses the bottom line of the space indicating a zodiac sign, the planet made its **ingress** (entrance) into that sign. The following graphs will assist you in determining approximately when these planets entered the various signs.

   More specific dates are given on page 180. Ingresses of Jupiter, Saturn, Uranus, Neptune and Pluto are listed. Note that planets sometimes go back into a previous sign temporarily. The dates given here will cover those cases as well.

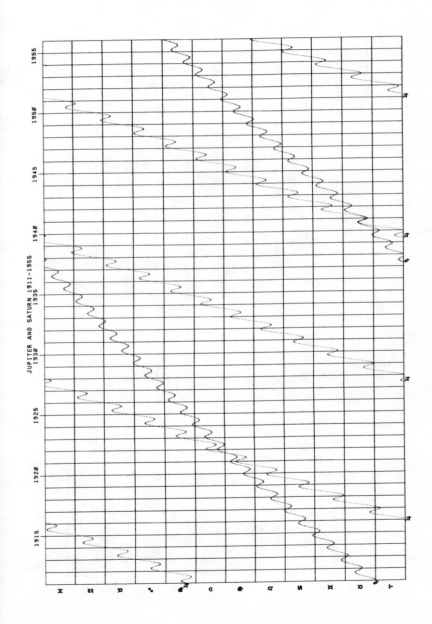

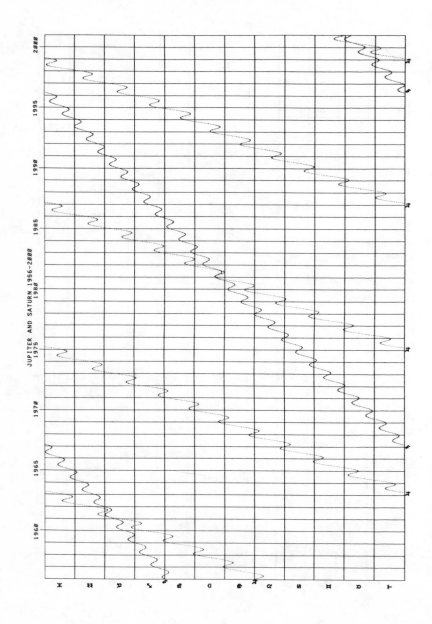

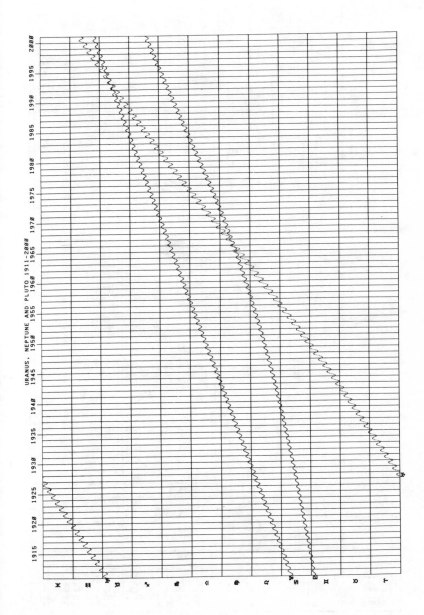

URANUS, NEPTUNE AND PLUTO 1911-2000

JUPITER INGRESSES

```
1911 DEC 10 ♐  6a35   1939 OCT 29 ♓R  7p46   1960 JUN  9 ♐R  8p51   1976 OCT 16 ♉R  3p23
1913 JAN  2 ♑  2p46   1939 DEC 20 ♈  12p 3   1960 OCT 25 ♑  10p 2   1977 APR  3 ♊ 10a43
1914 JAN 21 ♒ 10a13   1940 MAY 16 ♉   2a54   1961 MAR 15 ♒   3a 2   1977 AUG 20 ♋  7a44
1915 FEB  3 ♓  7p44   1941 MAY 26 ♊   4p46   1961 AUG 12 ♑R  3a51   1977 DEC 30 ♊R  6p48
1916 FEB 12 ♈  2a12   1942 JUN 10 ♋   5a36   1961 NOV  3 ♒   9p51   1978 APR 11 ♋  7p14
1916 JUN 25 ♉  8p32   1943 JUN 30 ♌   4p46   1962 MAR 25 ♓   5p 8   1978 SEP  5 ♌  3a32
1916 OCT 26 ♈R 9a52   1944 JUL 25 ♍   8p 4   1963 APR  3 ♈  10p20   1979 FEB 28 ♌R  6p31
1917 FEB 12 ♉ 10a59   1945 AUG 25 ♎   1a 6   1964 APR 12 ♉   1a53   1979 APR 20 ♌  3a33
1917 JUN 29 ♊  6p51   1946 SEP 25 ♏   5a20   1965 APR 22 ♊   9a33   1979 SEP 29 ♍  5a25
1918 JUL 13 ♋ 12a54   1947 OCT 23 ♐  10p 0   1965 SEP 20 ♋   5p45   1980 OCT 27 ♎  5a12
1919 AUG  2 ♌  3a39   1948 NOV 15 ♑   5a38   1965 NOV 16 ♊R 10p 6   1981 NOV 26 ♏  9p21
1920 AUG 27 ♍ 12a29   1949 APR 12 ♒   2p18   1966 MAY  5 ♋   9a53   1982 DEC 25 ♐  8p59
1921 SEP 25 ♎  6p10   1949 JUN 27 ♑R  1p29   1966 SEP 27 ♌   8a20   1984 JAN 19 ♑ 10a 5
1922 OCT 26 ♏  2p16   1949 NOV 30 ♒   3p 8   1967 JAN 15 ♍R 10p48   1985 FEB  6 ♒ 10a36
1923 NOV 24 ♐ 12p31   1950 APR 15 ♓   3a58   1967 MAY 23 ♌   3a22   1986 FEB 20 ♓ 11a 6
1924 DEC 18 ♑  1a25   1950 DEC  1 ♓   2p58   1967 OCT 19 ♍   5a52   1987 MAR  2 ♈  1p42
1926 JAN  5 ♒  8p 1   1951 APR 21 ♈   9a57   1968 FEB 26 ♍R 10p31   1988 MAR  8 ♉ 10a45
1927 JAN 18 ♓  6a44   1952 APR 28 ♉   3p50   1968 JUN 15 ♍   9a45   1988 JUL 21 ♊  7p 0
1927 JUN  6 ♈  5a13   1953 MAY  9 ♊  10a34   1968 NOV 15 ♎   5p45   1988 NOV 30 ♉R  3p54
1927 SEP 10 ♓R10p44   1954 MAY 23 ♋  11p44   1969 MAR 30 ♍R  4p34   1989 MAR 10 ♊ 10p27
1928 JAN 22 ♈  9p54   1955 JUN  9 ♌   7p 8   1969 JUL 15 ♎   8a32   1989 JUL 30 ♋  6p51
1928 JUN  3 ♉ 11p50   1955 NOV 16 ♍  11p 1   1969 DEC 16 ♏  10p57   1990 AUG 18 ♌  2a31
1929 JUN 12 ♊  7a20   1956 JAN 17 ♌R  9p 2   1970 APR 30 ♎R  1a42   1991 SEP 12 ♍  1a 2
1930 JUN 26 ♋  5p42   1956 JUL  7 ♍   2p 2   1970 AUG 15 ♏   1p 0   1992 OCT 10 ♎  8a28
1931 JUL 17 ♌  2a52   1956 DEC 12 ♎   9p18   1971 JAN 14 ♐   3a50   1993 NOV 10 ♏  3a17
1932 AUG 11 ♍  2a17   1957 FEB 19 ♍R 10a35   1971 JUN  4 ♏R  9p10   1994 DEC  9 ♐  5a56
1933 SEP 10 ♎ 12a11   1957 AUG  6 ♎   9p12   1971 SEP 11 ♐  10a35   1996 JAN  3 ♑  2a24
1934 OCT 10 ♏ 11p56   1958 JAN 13 ♏   7a53   1972 FEB  6 ♑   2p38   1997 JAN 21 ♒ 10a14
1935 NOV  8 ♐  9p56   1958 MAR 20 ♎R  2p12   1972 JUL 24 ♐R 11a37   1998 FEB  4 ♓  5a53
1936 DEC  2 ♑  3a39   1958 SEP  7 ♏   3a53   1972 SEP 25 ♑   1p23   1999 FEB 12 ♈  8p24
1937 DEC 19 ♒ 11p 5   1959 FEB 10 ♐   8a47   1973 FEB 23 ♒   4a29   1999 JUN 28 ♉  4a29
1938 MAY 14 ♓  2a45   1959 APR 24 ♏R  9a10   1974 MAR  8 ♓   6a12   1999 OCT 23 ♈TR12a49
1938 JUL 29 ♒R10p 3   1959 OCT  5 ♐   9a41   1975 MAR 18 ♈  11a49   2000 FEB 14 ♉  4p41
1938 DEC 29 ♓  1p34   1960 MAR  1 ♑   8a11   1976 MAR 26 ♉   5a46   2000 JUN 30 ♊  2a36
1939 MAY 11 ♈  9a 7                           1976 AUG 23 ♊   5a26
```

SATURN INGRESSES

```
1911 JAN 20 ♉  4a26   1932 AUG 13 ♑R  6a10   1956 MAY 13 ♏R 10p41   1978 JUL 26 ♍  7a 6
1912 JUL  7 ♊  1a13   1932 NOV 19 ♒   9p12   1956 OCT 10 ♐  10a14   1980 SEP 21 ♎  5a52
1912 NOV 30 ♉R 1p16   1935 FEB 14 ♓   9a10   1959 JAN  5 ♑   8a36   1982 NOV 29 ♏  5a33
1913 MAR 26 ♊  8a 8   1937 APR 25 ♈   1a31   1962 JAN  3 ♒   2p 5   1983 MAY  6 ♎R 2p23
1914 AUG 24 ♋ 12p28   1937 OCT 17 ♓R 10p37   1964 MAR 23 ♓  11p21   1983 AUG 24 ♏  7a 0
1914 DEC  7 ♊R 1a47   1938 JAN 14 ♈   5a34   1964 SEP 16 ♒R  3p57   1985 NOV 16 ♐  9p14
1915 MAY 11 ♋  4p24   1939 JUL  6 ♉  12a48   1964 DEC 16 ♓  12a45   1988 FEB 13 ♑  6p57
1916 OCT 17 ♌ 10a36   1939 SEP 22 ♈R 12a14   1967 MAR  3 ♈   4p35   1988 JUN 10 ♐R12a15
1916 DEC  7 ♋R 2p20   1940 MAR 20 ♉   4a43   1969 APR 29 ♉   5p26   1991 FEB  6 ♒  4a31
1917 JUN 24 ♌  8a54   1942 MAY  8 ♊   2p41   1971 JUN 18 ♊  11a11   1991 FEB  6     1p56
1919 AUG 12 ♍  8a52   1944 JUN 20 ♋   2a50   1972 JAN  9 ♉R 10p34   1993 MAY 21 ♓ 12a15
1921 OCT  7 ♎ 12p22   1946 AUG  2 ♌   9a44   1972 FEB 21 ♊  10a 2   1993 JUN 30 ♒R 3a10
1923 DEC 19 ♏ 11p26   1948 SEP 18 ♍  11p37   1973 AUG  1 ♋   5p38   1994 JAN 28 ♓  6p49
1924 APR  6 ♎R 3a34   1949 APR  2 ♌R 10p34   1974 JAN  7 ♊R  3p22   1996 APR  7 ♈  3a54
1924 SEP 13 ♏  5p 1   1949 MAY 29 ♍   8a 3   1974 APR 18 ♋   5p38   1998 JUN  9 ♉  1a14
1926 DEC  2 ♐  5p36   1950 NOV 20 ♎  10a53   1975 SEP 17 ♌  12a 0   1998 OCT 25 ♈R 1p33
1929 MAR 15 ♑  8a52   1951 MAR  7 ♍R  7a10   1976 JAN 14 ♋R  8a11   1999 FEB 28 ♉  8p34
1929 MAY  4 ♐R11p14   1951 AUG 13 ♎  11a46   1976 JUN  5 ♌  12a12   2000 AUG  9 ♊  9p38
1929 NOV 29 ♑ 11p24   1953 OCT 22 ♏  10a37   1977 NOV 16 ♍   9p49   2000 OCT 15 ♉R 7p34
1932 FEB 23 ♒  9p49   1956 JAN 12 ♐   1p49   1978 JAN  4 ♌R  7p36
```

URANUS INGRESSES

```
1912 JAN 30 ♒  5p40   1934 OCT  9 ♈R  7p32   1956 JUN  9 ♌   8p52   1981 FEB 17 ♐  4a34
1912 SEP  4 ♑R11a48   1935 MAR 27 ♉  10p 1   1961 NOV  1 ♍  11a 3   1981 MAR 20 ♏R 5p43
1912 NOV 12 ♒  3a42   1941 AUG  7 ♊   2a54   1962 JAN 10 ♌R 12a50   1981 NOV 16 ♐  7a13
1919 MAR 31 ♓  8p47   1941 OCT  4 ♉R  8p56   1962 AUG  9 ♍   8p21   1988 FEB 14 ♑  7p35
1919 AUG 16 ♒R 5p 5   1942 MAY 14 ♊  11p10   1968 SEP 28 ♎  11a 9   1988 MAY 26 ♐R 7p50
1920 JAN 22 ♓  1p33   1948 AUG 30 ♋  10a50   1969 MAY 20 ♍R  3p54   1988 DEC  2 ♑ 10a52
1927 MAR 31 ♈ 12p28   1948 NOV 12 ♊R  8p47   1969 JUN 24 ♎   5a33   1995 APR  1 ♒  8a 4
1927 NOV  4 ♓R 5a25   1949 JUN  9 ♋  11p13   1974 NOV 21 ♏   4a32   1995 JUN  8 ♑R 7p44
1928 JAN 13 ♈  3a52   1955 AUG 24 ♌   1p 7   1975 MAY  1 ♎R 12p45   1996 JAN 12 ♒  2a39
1934 JUN  6 ♉ 10a45   1956 JAN 27 ♋R  8p52   1975 SEP  8 ♏  12a18
```

NEPTUNE INGRESSES

```
1914 SEP 23 ♌  3p26   1929 JUL 24 ♍  10a 8   1957 JUN 15 ♎R  3p52   1984 NOV 21 ♑  6a46
1914 DEC 14 ♋R 3p37   1942 OCT  3 ♎  11a59   1957 AUG  6 ♏   2a43   1998 JAN 28 ♒  7p35
1915 JUL 19 ♌  8a35   1943 APR 17 ♍R  5a57   1970 JAN  4 ♐   2p 2   1998 AUG 22 ♑R11p19
1916 MAR 19 ♋R10a18   1943 AUG  2 ♎   2p 9   1970 MAY  2 ♏R  9p37   1998 NOV 27 ♒  4p47
1916 MAY  2 ♌  5a51   1955 DEC 24 ♏   9a56   1970 NOV  6 ♐  10a48
1928 SEP 21 ♍  7a 7   1956 MAR 11 ♎R  9p22   1984 JAN 18 ♑   8p22
1929 FEB 19 ♌R 6a18   1956 OCT 19 ♏   4a13   1984 JUN 22 ♐R 10p15
```

PLUTO INGRESSES

```
1912 SEP 10 ♋ 11a20   1937 NOV 25 ♋R  4a 5   1957 AUG 19 ♍  11p32   1983 NOV  5 ♏  4p42
1912 OCT 20 ♊R 3a32   1938 AUG  3 ♌  12p58   1958 APR 11 ♌R  9a39   1984 MAY 18 ♎R 8a33
1913 JUL  9 ♋  5p20   1939 FEB  7 ♋R  7a55   1958 JUN 10 ♍   2p 8   1984 AUG 28 ♏ 12a39
1913 DEC 27 ♊R11p22   1939 JUN 13 ♌  11p48   1971 OCT  5 ♎   1a31   1995 JAN 17 ♐  5a53
1914 MAY 26 ♋  3p38   1956 OCT 20 ♍   1a24   1972 APR 17 ♍R  2a23   1995 APR 20 ♏R 8p 4
1937 OCT  7 ♌  7a15   1957 JAN 14 ♌R  9p29   1972 JUL 30 ♎   7a 4   1995 NOV 10 ♐  3p14
```

CHAPTER NINE

YOUR HOROSCOPE

What zodiac signs the planets (including the Sun and Moon) were in when you were born shows only part of your astrological picture. A complete horoscope is an astrological map (usually in a circular form) which shows the interrelationships between the planets **as seen from your birthplace at your exact birth time**.

A complete horoscope must be cast (which means calculated) by an astrologer or astrological computer service. If you have not had your chart cast, see Appendix A for information on obtaining a personal chart, cast by a computer. You will also find, in Appendix B, addresses of national astrological organizations which can help you find an astrologer in your area. On page 210 you can read about how to evaluate an astrologer.

You will learn in the following pages how to understand for yourself some of the basic meaning of an astrological chart and how it can be used as a kind of personal weather forecast.

What can a knowledge of your horoscope tell you? It can give you a variety of information about:

- your personality, your talents, your temperament;
- what comes easily for you and what requires more work;
- the kind of environment in which you function best;
- how you relate to various people;
- the type of activities or work you will find most fulfilling;
- potential problem areas and how these can be turned into strengths.

In other words, your horoscope is useful background material to aid you in meeting life's challenges. It is also possible with your chart to achieve a better understanding of changing conditions in your life.

Sometimes people are afraid that their astrological chart will reveal unchangeable problems or character defects which they are stuck with for life. Many of the older astrological books only reinforced these fears by implying darkly that with certain patterns of the planets you were bound to end up either on the gallows or in the darkest of dungeons. However, modern astrologers understand that the pattern of the planets is simply a mirror of the **pattern of energies** within you. How this pattern of energies is **used** determines whether the outcome is "good" or "bad." Total prediction of what to expect is not possible just from knowing your chart. There are still many unknown factors, not the least of which is that which we call freedom.

Your Rising Sign and Houses

Your rising sign is the beginning of your First **House**. This house shows how you approach life. All twelve houses (or **sectors**) of your horoscope show **areas of your life**, such as your finances, your home, creative expression, relationships. The next few pages will describe these areas in more detail.

There are **two different ways** in which the same 360-degree circle of the zodiac is cut up into a twelve-slice pie:

1. The twelve signs of the zodiac, which are twelve absolutely regular slices of 30 degrees each
2. The twelve houses, which can be irregular sizes, some houses having more degrees than others. Also, a house doesn't have to begin at the beginning of a sign but can start on any degree of the zodiac. How the houses are determined is described below.

An example of the two "patterns" of slices can be seen on page 183.

Each of the 360 degrees of the zodiac is a **specific point in the sky**, sometimes inhabited by a "fixed" star, but more often "empty" space. If you stood looking east for twenty-four hours, you would see each of the 360 degrees of the zodiac rise — every four minutes a different degree appears, and every two hours a different sign appears. **Your rising sign**, or ascendant, **is the zodiac sign which was coming up over the eastern horizon at the particular time and place you were born**. A child born at the same place but a different **time** would have a different

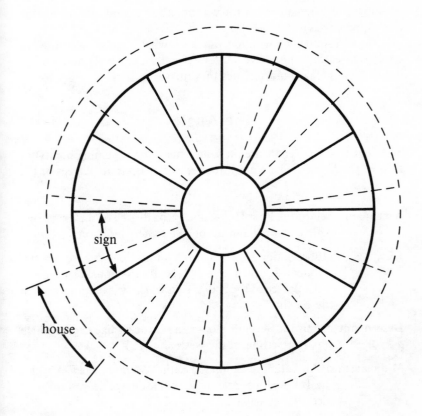

rising sign (or at least a different degree of the same sign rising). This would also be true of a child born at the same time but a different **place**.

As we have said, the rising sign (or rather the point of the ascendant) always begins the First House. In an astrological chart it is placed on the left side of the circle and, as you have seen, can be any degree of the zodiac. Going **counterclockwise**, the Second House begins thirty degrees more or less farther on, and so on through the twelve houses. There are several systems for determining exactly where each house begins, which is an important point (its **cusp**). Except for the equal house system, the number of degrees in each house varies depending on how far away from the equator you were born. Accurate calculation of the rising sign and other house cusps must be done on the basis of both the longitude and latitude of your birthplace, as well as with the use of mathematical tables called **tables of houses**. These calculations are complex and beyond the scope of this book. You can get any competent astrologer to calculate them for you or order a computer horoscope (see Appendix A).

In the following pages you will learn what areas of your life are covered by each of the twelve houses. After this, you will find out what are the particular characteristics of your rising sign.

The Angles

The **angles** of your chart are the house cusps (or beginning points) of four of the houses. These mark four specific, separate degrees of the zodiac:

Ascendant begins the First House and is the degree of the rising sign which was coming up on the eastern horizon;

I.C., (abbreviation for the Latin *"Imum Coeli"* — sometimes erroneously called "Nadir") begins the Fourth House and is the degree of the zodiac sign which was deepest through the Earth;

Descendant begins the Seventh House and is the zodiac degree which was just setting in the west;

Midheaven, or M.C. (abbreviation for Latin *"Medium Coeli"*) begins the Tenth House and is the zodiac degree nearest to being directly overhead.

The Houses

FIRST HOUSE
The First House (particularly the ascendant point in the rising sign) characterizes how you most naturally approach life and the **personality** (or image) with which you relate to the outside world. It also indicates your physical appearance and mannerisms as well as your constitution. (This is distinguished from the Sun sign, which denotes your conscious sense of self.)

SECOND HOUSE
The Second House relates to your **personal resources** — on every level. This includes money, possessions and talents. It characterizes your attitude toward your resources, how money and possessions come to you, and how you handle them.

THIRD HOUSE
The Third House indicates your **concrete learning experiences and your communications**. It also shows how you relate to your immediate environment, including neighbors and relatives (except parents and spouse). It includes travel around your more immediate and familiar environment.

FOURTH HOUSE
The Fourth House (particularly the I.C. point) indicates your **personal foundations**, both of physical reality and of the psyche. Therefore, it refers to conditions in your home (originally and at present), your mother (in some cases your father instead), and the roots of your psyche into which you dig psychologically and in meditation.

FIFTH HOUSE
The Fifth House is the house of **creative self-expression**. This includes creations of the body (your children) and creations of the emotions and mind — not only works of art, writing, theater, but also play: hobbies, entertainment and the pursuit of pleasure. It includes speculation, romance and pets (purely for pleasure, not working animals).

SIXTH HOUSE
The Sixth House includes techniques and **working patterns** which you develop, both for expressing your Fifth House inspirations and for other work or service. It includes working conditions and relationships with people who work for you. It also refers to health conditions, particularly of a passing nature rather than chronic. It relates to "working" animals, such as watchdogs.

SEVENTH HOUSE
The Seventh House (particularly the descendant point) indicates **point-to-point relationships**: marriage, partnerships, the **you** in any I-you connection. This can apply both to people who balance your own personality and those with whom you feel conflict as opposites. The signs and any planets in the Seventh House characterize the way you tend to see others. The cusp (called the **descendant**) is particularly important in this respect.

EIGHTH HOUSE
The Eighth House relates to **resources of your relationships**, such as joint funds, or money and goods which come from your spouse or by inheritance. The Eighth House also includes sex, and it marks the point

of **transformation** in your life cycle into a larger whole, death (both of periods in your life and physical death) and regeneration.

NINTH HOUSE
The Ninth House is the house of **expansion into larger meaning**. This includes your philosophy and religion, higher or more abstract education, and long journeys which enlarge your understanding of the world. It relates to inspiration and dreams, and a comprehension of law, both of legal systems and the laws of the universe.

TENTH HOUSE
The Tenth House (particularly the midheaven point) indicates the nature of your **potential contribution to society,** including your public image. It is often called the house of profession, the "statement" you make as a person. It also relates to your father (in some cases your mother).

ELEVENTH HOUSE
The Eleventh House is connected with the **creative objectives which you share with groups**. This can include organizations for the betterment of human conditions or simply clubs with a common interest. It is therefore your house of hopes and wishes (particularly in a social sense) and of friends and acquaintances to whom you relate in a more impersonal manner.

TWELFTH HOUSE
The Twelfth House relates to the **summing-up of your life experiences** and the consequences of your actions. This can be in either a negative or a positive sense. It includes both your service in connection with the shared creative objectives of the Eleventh House and your withdrawal from activity to consolidate your understanding. It is also connected with chronic illness or chronic health.

Your Rising Sign

IF YOUR RISING SIGN IS ARIES ♈
You have much energy and approach life as a challenge. Learn tact and how to follow through.

IF YOUR RISING SIGN IS TAURUS ♉
You move fairly slowly and don't push yourself into situations. Don't let your love of beautiful things make you possessive.

IF YOUR RISING SIGN IS GEMINI ♊
You are high-strung and quick in your movements, friendly and you love to talk. Cultivate calmness and confidence in yourself.

IF YOUR RISING SIGN IS CANCER ♋
You feel a situation out before projecting yourself into it. You can overcome timidity and a tendency to let people upset you.

IF YOUR RISING SIGN IS LEO ♌
Your personality is sunny and extroverted, yet dignified. Learn not to dominate situations where it's not called for.

IF YOUR RISING SIGN IS VIRGO ♍
Your personality has a delicate, unassuming quality, combined with a quickness and awareness. Learn relaxation.

IF YOUR RISING SIGN IS LIBRA ♎
You express yourself with charm and are quite sociable, with a love of beauty. Learn to appreciate solitude.

IF YOUR RISING SIGN IS SCORPIO ♏
You are intense and strong-willed, with emotional reserves that don't usually show. Don't brood on injustices.

IF YOUR RISING SIGN IS SAGITTARIUS ♐
You are outgoing and optimistic and enjoy meeting many people. Don't let yourself be too restless and too talkative.

IF YOUR RISING SIGN IS CAPRICORN ♑
You are serious and somewhat reserved, with a methodical patience. Learn to express your warmth and to play.

IF YOUR RISING SIGN IS AQUARIUS ♒
You are outgoing, friendly and intuitive, as well as fun-loving. Keep in touch with your feelings and don't be overly rebellious.

IF YOUR RISING SIGN IS PISCES ♓
You are supersensitive to your surroundings, and your dream world can be very vivid. Keep in touch with practicalities.

CHAPTER TEN

CONSTRUCTING A HOROSCOPE

How does an astrologer go about constructing a horoscope? First, he or she will need to know the year, month and day, as well as the exact time you were born and the place. The next step is to consult a special astrological calendar, called an **ephemeris**, which will give, among other information for the date of your birth, the **sidereal time** (meaning "star time") for that particular date in Greenwich, England. For our purposes, it is only necessary to understand that, since sidereal time, like the zodiac, is reckoned with the spring equinox as a starting point, it connects the day of your birth with the zodiac in such a way that the astrologer can use it as the basis for calculating your **sidereal time of birth**, after he or she has corrected the given (clock) time of your birth so as to apply to the longitude of your birthplace.

The astrologer will then use a **table of houses** which, on the basis of your sidereal time of birth and the latitude of your birthplace, will give the zodiac sign and degree of your house cusps. To do this accurately, the astrologer will adjust the nearest figures in the tables to your exact sidereal time and the latitude of your birthplace.

Then the astrologer will return to the ephemeris to find, on the date of your birth, the zodiac signs and degrees for the Sun, Moon and each planet. Again, this will require an adjustment for your time and place of birth from the information given in the ephemeris, which is always for midnight or noon in Greenwich, England, the point of beginning for time zones around the world.

After making all of these calculations, the astrologer will put the figures on a circular chart form something like the following one. He or she will place the ascendant degree of the rising sign on the left side

of the chart form and then put the signs of the zodiac in order, beginning with the rising sign, around the circle in a counterclockwise direction. The other house cusps will be marked in and the planets will be
put in their proper positions. Then the astrologer will be ready to study
and interpret the chart.

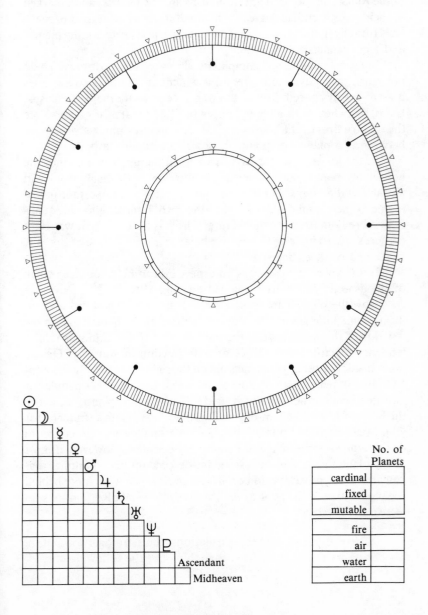

No. of Planets

cardinal	
fixed	
mutable	

fire	
air	
water	
earth	

In the chart form on page 189 all 360 degrees are marked in on the rim of the wheel, with short lines ending in small black circles every 30 degrees. Each 30-degree sector will indicate a sign of the zodiac. The astrologer will mark whatever zodiac sign is rising at the left of the wheel; it will be followed counterclockwise by the next sign in the order of the zodiac, and so on. The house cusps and the planets can be marked in their specific zodiac degrees. The small inner wheel is used to mark lines (usually in different colors) indicating aspects between the planets and from planets to important points.

Many astrologers and computer services use chart forms which do not mark the individual degrees but which already have twelve lines drawn, evenly spaced around the wheel, to indicate the house cusps. Using the wheel with all 360 degrees indicated makes it easier to see the relative sizes of the houses and also to count the number of degrees between two planets or points in order to recognize aspects.

In the lower right corner of this form there is space to indicate how many planets and important points are in cardinal, fixed and mutable zodiac signs. If there are more planets and important points in one of these qualities than in the other two, it means that this quality is more dominant in your nature. There is also, in the lower right corner, space to indicate the relative balance in your nature of fire, air, water and earth zodiac signs.

In the lower left corner is an **aspect grid** to help you keep track of the aspects, which are explained on page 191.

How the planets are spread around the chart wheel can also indicate something about your nature. If most of the planets are on the left side of the wheel (left of the midheaven-I.C. line), this denotes a tendency toward independence or self-direction in your life. On the other hand, if most of the planets are on the right side of the midheaven-I.C. line, it means that in some manner you look to other people for direction in important areas of your life. If most of the planets are above the horizon (the ascendant-descendant line), it suggests a tendency for your life to be more "public" (whether in a small or in a larger group) or that you are objectively or community oriented. However, if most of the planets are below the ascendant-descendant line, it implies that you are a more private person or, if well known, you work more behind the scenes than in the public eye. This can also symbolize a more subjective approach.

CHAPTER ELEVEN

ASPECTS

An **aspect** is a kind of harness between two planets or other important points (such as the midheaven) in your horoscope. For example: if your Mars (energy) is in the same degree of the zodiac as your Mercury (expression), you express yourself energetically. On the other hand, if Mars and Mercury are across the zodiac circle from each other (180 degrees apart), you probably enjoy a good argument. As you can see, different aspects between planets or important points (or between a planet and an important point) make for different effects, as described in the following pages.

To determine the aspects in your chart, you need to know the exact degree of each planet or important point. In other words, your chart must be cast using an astrological **ephemeris**, which is a calendar telling the exact positions of the planets on the day of your birth. An aspect is found by counting how many degrees apart the two planets or important points are. Not every separation is equally effective. The table below shows the major aspects and some of the minor ones:

	Name	Symbol	Fraction of Circle	No. of Degrees Apart
Major Aspects	Conjunction	☌	1/1	0
	Square	□	1/4	90
	Trine	△	1/3	120
	Opposition	☍	1/2	180
Minor Aspects	Sextile	✳	1/6	60
	Quintile	Q	1/5	72
	Semisquare	∠	1/8	45
	Semisextile	⊻	1/12	30
	Quincunx (or Inconjunct)	⊼	5/12	150

Aspects can be counted from any point on the circle going in either direction around it. They are most important when the two points are separated by the exact number of degrees of the particular aspect. However, they are also significant (although less so) if they are a few degrees more or less than exact. Major aspects have a range (called **orb**) of roughly 6–9 degrees, and minor aspects an orb of 2–4 degrees. For instance, a square is strongest if the two points are exactly 90 degrees apart, but it is still worth noting if the two points are between 81 degrees and 99 degrees apart.

In counting aspects, remember that there are 30 degrees in each zodiac sign and that the numbering of these degrees runs counterclockwise. Below is an example of two aspects. Pluto (♇) at 17 degrees Gemini (17♊) is 179 degrees away from Uranus (♅) at 16♐. This is just 1 degree away from an exact opposition (☍), which would be 180 degrees. Jupiter (♃), at 15♑, is 29 degrees (a semisextile ⊻) from Uranus and 152 degrees (a quincunx ⚻) from Pluto.

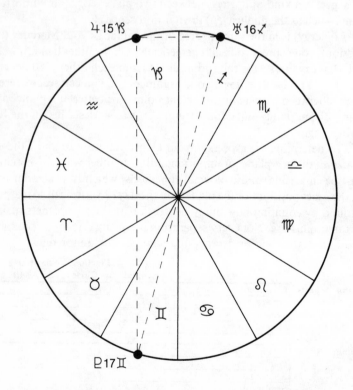

The ancients referred to the music of the spheres, and there is increasing indication that astrological aspects are harmonics of the circle. A piano string will resonate its whole length, one-half its length, one-third its length, etc. The simple divisions of the zodiac circle, such as one half (180 degrees) or one third (120 degrees), seem to "resonate" in a similar way. The aspects also seem to be related to the angles in which a light ray passes through a prism to cause the various colors.

Meaning of the Aspects

Major Aspects
CONJUNCTION ☌ 0°
The two energies are **harnessed together,** working as a team. How this manifests depends, of course, on the planets involved. As mentioned above, Mercury conjunct (harnessed with) Mars shows you have an energetic way of expressing yourself. On the other hand, Mercury working hand in hand with Venus would indicate an affectionate quality to your manner of expression; in certain signs, such as Libra (which is ruled by Venus), this would be more pronounced than in other signs, such as Capricorn.

SQUARE □ 90°
An aspect in which the two energies are **contrasted** with each other. Sometimes this is expressed in inner conflict and you are challenged to make choices between the two energies, or, more positively, it can be expressed as an increased awareness of the proper use of each energy.

TRINE △ 120°
A flowing aspect in which the two energies relate easily to create a **harmonious interplay.** The benefits of a trine usually happen so automatically that you are unaware of the factors involved.

OPPOSITION ☍ 180°
A challenging aspect in which the two energies are **polarized** — either pulling apart in conflict or else creating a dynamic equilibrium. If you have not resolved an opposition in your chart, you are very likely to project it onto other people.

Minor Aspects
SEXTILE ✶ 60°
A flowing aspect which can produce a **harmonious interplay** much like a trine, but it must be consciously developed.

QUINTILE Q 72°
An aspect which increases **understanding** of the two energies involved.

SEMISQUARE ∠ 45°
A mildly challenging aspect, **contrasting** the energies. It is something like a square, but does not operate as strongly.

SEMISEXTILE ⊻ 30°
An aspect which calls for the integrating of two quite different energies.

QUINCUNX ⊼ 150°
An aspect which relates the energies involved in unexpected manners, sometimes in a smooth flow and sometimes in a challenging manner.

CHAPTER TWELVE

SIGN CLASSIFICATIONS

Sign	Element	Quality	Extroverted or Introverted	Planetary Ruler
Aries ♈	fire	cardinal	extroverted	Mars ♂
Taurus ♉	earth	fixed	introverted	Venus ♀
Gemini ♊	air	mutable	extroverted	Mercury ☿
Cancer ♋	water	cardinal	introverted	Moon ☽
Leo ♌	fire	fixed	extroverted	Sun ☉
Virgo ♍	earth	mutable	introverted	Mercury ☿
Libra ♎	air	cardinal	extroverted	Venus ♀
Scorpio ♏	water	fixed	introverted	Pluto & Mars ♇ ♂
Sagittarius ♐	fire	mutable	extroverted	Jupiter ♃
Capricorn ♑	earth	cardinal	introverted	Saturn ♄
Aquarius ♒	air	fixed	extroverted	Uranus & Saturn ♅ ♄
Pisces ♓	water	mutable	introverted	Neptune & Jupiter ♆ ♃

Fire: operates mainly from enthusiasms.
Air: focuses on the need to understand.
Water: operates from emotions.
Earth: orients toward practicalities and concrete results.

Cardinal: initiates action.
Fixed: follows through on action.
Mutable: keeps the action moving and steers it through changes.

Extroverted: more outgoing, social and assertive.
Introverted: more introspective, sometimes shy, less assertive.

CHAPTER THIRTEEN

INTERPRETATION OUTLINE

This outline will help you find all the interpretation paragraphs in this book which apply to you. With this book alone you can find all of the data necessary for you to fill in Part I. However, for Part II it will be necessary for you to have your horoscope accurately calculated by either an astrologer or an astrological computer service (see Appendices A and B).

Part I

Look in the calendar beginning on page 89 and fill in, for nos. 1, 2, 3 and 4 in this outline, your Sun sign, Moon sign and Moon phase, as well as their symbols. Then fill in the page numbers on which they are described.

Read all of the indicated paragraphs earlier in this book. Now think about how all this information fits together to describe you and how you are now using these characteristics of your nature. Think also about other ways in which these characteristics can be well used.

1. Your Sun sign is ___Libra___ (/7).
   Find your Sun sign in the Sun sign list on page 16 and read the key words associated with this zodiac sign. Read about it in more detail on page _//_ (This section begins on page 5.)

2. Your Moon sign is _Capricorn_ (_116_).
   Read about this Moon sign on page _136_. (This section begins
   on page 88.)

3. Read about how a _Libra_ Sun combines with a
   Capricorn Moon on page _150_. (This section
   begins on page 140.)

4. You were born under a _crescent_ Moon phase. (See
   instructions on finding your Moon phase on page 85). Read about
   this Moon phase on page _138_. (This section begins on page 137.)

5. For each of the following planets fill in the zodiac sign positions.
   The information you will need to do this begins on page 176. Then
   read the paragraphs indicated by page numbers in the column "Function of Planet." For each planet think about how the energy now
   operates in your life and how you can best use it. Also read
   "Planetary Keywords" on page 163. This short summary will give
   you key words to help fix the meaning of each planet in your mind.

   Finally, discover how each sign position modifies a planet begi-
   niing on page 168.

Planet	Sign	Function Of Planet	How Sign Position Affects Planet (begins on page 168)	
Jupiter ♃	♊	page 160	page _169_	Gemini
Saturn ♄	♓	page 161	page _172_	Pisces
Uranus ♅	♍	page 161	page _172_	Virgo
Neptune ♆	♏	page 162	page _174_	Scorpio
Pluto ♇	♍	page 162	page _175_	Virgo

Part II

(For this information you will need to have your complete horoscope
calculated.)

6. Fill in the zodiac sign positions for each of the following planets.
   Then fill in the proper page numbers as above and read the
   paragraphs indicated. Again, for each planet, think about how the
   energy now operates in your life and how you can best use it. Look
   to the "Planetary Keywords" on page 163 to help fix the meaning
   of each planet in your mind.

Planet	Sign	Function Of Planet	How Sign Position Affects Planet (begins on page 163)
Mercury ☿		page 159	page _____
Venus ♀		page 159	page _____
Mars ♂		page 160	page _____

7. **Aspects**: Under each aspect listed below fill in any pair of planets or planet and important point) which are within orb of the indicated aspect. (See page 191 for how to do this.) Then read the paragraphs which describe the meaning of each aspect. In considering the meaning of each aspect, take into account what you have previously learned about the sign positions of the planets or important points involved.

CONJUNCTION ☌ (page 193)	OPPOSITION ☍ (page 193)	SQUARE □ (page 193)	TRINE △ (page 193)
SEXTILE ✳ (page 193)	SEMISQUARE ∠ (page 194)	SEMISEXTILE ⊻ (page 194)	QUINCUNX ⚻ (page 194)

8. **House positions**: Fill in the signs on the cusp (beginning) of each house (going counterclockwise around your chart). Then read both the paragraph describing each house and the paragraph describing the sign on its cusp. For the rising sign (ascendant) read also the section beginning on page 186.

House	Areas Of Life Indicated	Sign On Cusp	Description (begins page 6)	Planets In This House
1 (rising sign)	page 184			
2	page 184			
3	page 185			
4 (I.C.)	page 185			
5	page 185			
6	page 185			
7 (descendant)	page 185			
8	page 185			
9	page 186			
10 (midheaven)	page 186			
11	page 186			
12	page 186			

Think about how all of these astrological patterns are presently being expressed in your life and also about other possibilities. **Creative use of astrology takes the basic themes in a chart and sees the many different ways these themes can be expressed, emphasizing their constructive use.**

Interpreting A Horoscope

On the next page is the horoscope of Walt Disney, set up for the time and place he was born. This is his **natal chart** and expresses the fundamental characteristics of his whole life. It is like taking a snapshot of the planetary positions at the exact moment of birth. Of course, the planets are continuously moving, and their shifting positions must be constantly compared with the original pattern in order to tell what is happening at any given time. (You will learn more about this in the chapter on Predicting.)

On the left of the chart Walt Disney's First House begins at 24 degrees of Virgo (24 ♍) (the rising sign or ascendant) and runs through the rest of Virgo and the beginning of Libra (♎) to 24 degrees of Libra (24 ♎). (Both the signs of the zodiac and the houses run **counterclockwise**.) His Second House begins at 24 ♎ and runs to 23 degrees of Scorpio (23 ♏), and so on through the twelve houses.

Each planet is positioned in the appropriate pie slice according to its zodiac degree. For instance, at the time of his birth, the Sun (☉) was in 12 degrees of Sagittarius (12 ♐), placing it in the Third House. The Moon (☽) was in 9 ♎ in the First House.

We would look first to the Sun, Moon and rising sign as the most important elements. His consciousness (Sun) was expansive and adventurous (Sagittarius) and concerned with communication (Third House). His Moon in Libra in the First House would indicate that his personality (First House) was instinctively (Moon) oriented toward the arts (Libra). Moon in the First House also suggests a touch of moodiness in the personality. The rising sign (beginning of the First House) was Virgo, which would show that he would approach anything with a careful attention to details.

Walt Disney's movies showed his Sagittarian love of entertainment, adventure and the outdoors, as well as of animals. (In fact, centaurs, the symbol of Sagittarius, cavorted in *Fantasia*.) His Sagittarian Sun was also evident in his love of vivid colors, his enthusiasm, and the continual expansion of his aims. At the same time, he expressed this through an art form (Libra Moon) and with the infinite attention to

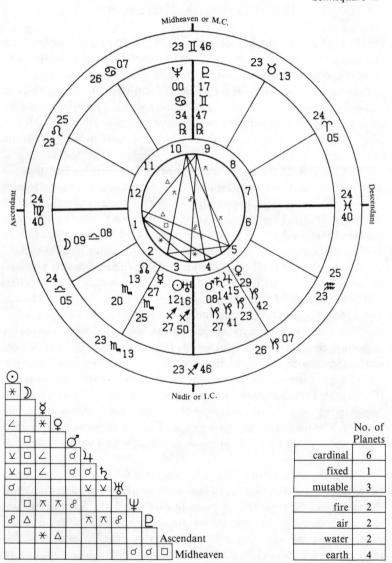

Walt Disney
December 5, 1901
Approx. 12:30 a.m.
Chicago, Illinois

Conjunction ☌
Square □
Opposition ☍
Trine △
Sextile ✶
Quincunx ⊼
Semisextile ⊻
Semisquare ∠

No. of Planets

cardinal	6
fixed	1
mutable	3

fire	2
air	2
water	2
earth	4

detail (Virgo rising) that is necessary in the making of animated cartoons. Virgo rising indicated he worked always for technical perfection and was a stickler for neatness. He also set standards of extreme cleanliness for the maintenance of Disneyland.

We next note that he had had four planets in Capricorn: Mars, Saturn, Jupiter and Venus. These included both the ruler of his Sun sign (Jupiter) and the ruler of his Moon sign (Venus). All this puts strong emphasis on Capricorn in his chart, evident in his capacity for hard work (a characteristic of both Capricorn and Virgo), his drive and his ambition. He showed not only the Capricorn capacity for business organization, but also its structural sense which, combined with the Sagittarian awareness of the overall picture, enabled him to pick the important elements out of any story and combine them into a meaningful whole. He also had the Capricorn stick-to-itiveness when the going got rough.

Three of his Capricorn planets were in the Fourth House, emphasizing his drive to establish firm foundations for himself. Venus, however, was in the Fifth House, indicating that his personal creativity (Fifth House) was expressed in an art form (Venus). This gives added strength to the indication that he would use art as a means of expressing his personality, shown also by the Moon in Libra in the First House.

All but two of the planets in Walt Disney's chart were below the horizon (the ascendant-descendant line). This often indicates a person who is more likely to work behind the scenes than up front. This was evident in his case in that he was known not for his personal image but for his work.

The sign on the midheaven was Gemini ($\mathrm{I\!I}$), a sign emphasizing communication. He had Neptune (Ψ) in the Tenth House in 0 degrees of Cancer ($\mathfrak{S}$), so his profession involved communicating in many different ways (Gemini midheaven) the feeling (Cancer) of a fantasy world (Neptune) to the public (Tenth House). In addition, he had Pluto (P) conjunct the midheaven, though in the Ninth House of inspiration and dreams. Pluto tied in with the midheaven indicates the mass appeal of his work, since Pluto is an indicator of group patterns rather than more personal expressions.

A study of other planetary aspects in Walt Disney's chart gives more information about him. Mercury in Scorpio (M) in the Third House would indicate that his penetrating and intuitive mind would dig underneath the surface and be engaged in communication. Mercury is sextile ($\divideontimes$) to Venus ($\mathfrak{P}$) in Capricorn ($\mathfrak{F}$) in the Fifth House (his creative expression). This sextile means he had talent for self-expression in an art form. Mercury and Venus both form quincunxes (⊼) to Neptune (♆) in the Tenth House. This three-way aspect pattern (a sextile and two quincunxes) has been called a "finger of fate" or, in more ancient astrological terminology, a "finger of God," and indicates a special sensitivity or task for the person's life in connection with the planet which is quincunx to the other two, in this case Neptune. Certainly he expressed this in his bringing of Neptunian wonder and make-believe to the public.

Another aspect in his chart is Sun conjunct Uranus (♅) (innovation) in Sagittarius in the Third House. This was shown in a talent for technological innovation, the exploring (Sagittarius) of new ways to communicate (Third House).

In this interpretation of Walt Disney's chart we have not gone into the characteristics of all of the houses or all of the aspects. If a house has no planets in it, it does not mean that there is no action in this area of the person's life but merely that you must consider the **planet which is associated with the sign on the house cusp** to give you indications of what to expect in this house. In other words, although Walt Disney had no planets in the Second House, which indicates his personal resources and money, the sign on the cusp is Libra, which is ruled by Venus, which is in his Fifth House of creative self-expression. Thus, his resources were strongly connected to his creative self-expression.

Like any complex art or science, understanding how all the factors in an astrological chart fit together is not simple. It takes study, thought and practice. It is important that you use your common sense to know what conclusions can be drawn from a chart by a beginner and what interpretations require an experienced professional astrologer. The beginner must be very careful not to jump to conclusions that are too simple, based on a few elements in the chart, such as only the Sun sign. Always remember that human beings are extremely complex and that **any astrological chart can be expressed in thousands of different ways. Whether you use your chart negatively or positively is up to you.**

CHAPTER FOURTEEN

ASTROLOGICAL AFFINITIES

The connections indicated between the various signs of the zodiac and the categories on this list do not necessarily mean that if you are an Aries, for example, you should wear only bright red and diamonds, grow geraniums, flavor everything with garlic and move to Iceland. However, you might feel a special affinity for the colors, gems, flowers, etc., which correspond to your Sun sign or Moon sign. On the other hand, if you feel you are lacking in the qualities of a certain sign, you might want to cultivate them by surrounding yourself with the colors, etc., which correspond to that sign.

This list has been collected from several traditional sources. As they are far from being in agreement, you will find some items appearing under more than one sign, or you may run across a different sign association in another source. In some cases the item is associated more with the sign's ruling planet than the sign itself.

Zodiac Sign	Colors	Gems	Flowers
Aries ♈	bright red	diamond, ruby, bloodstone, garnet, amethyst	anemone, poppy, geranium
Taurus ♉	red-orange, yellow, pink, citron, pastels	moss agate, emerald, jade, alabaster	violet, daisy, daffodil, apple blossom, lily, rose, columbine
Gemini ♊	orange, violet, pale blue, yellow	aquamarine, beryl, chrysolite, crystal	lavender, wildflowers, lily-of-the-valley, woodbine
Cancer ♋	orange-yellow, green, russet, silver, iridescent hues	crystal, emerald, moonstone, opal, pearl	white rose, honeysuckle, water lily
Leo ♌	yellow, orange, gold	diamond, ruby, amber, carbuncle, cat's eye	marigold, sunflower, orange blossoms, heliotrope, poppy
Virgo ♍	yellow-green violet deep blue	sardonyx, pink jasper, hyacinth, agate	narcissus, wildflowers, mignonette, lavender, lily-of-the-valley
Libra ♎	green, yellow, blue	emerald, chrysolite, diamond, cornelian, coral, opal	violet, lily, pansy, rose, myrtle,
Scorpio ♏	blue-green, brownish red, luminous colors	bloodstone, ruby, malachite, topaz, jasper	heather, thistle, cactus flower
Sagittarius ♐	blue, purple, deep red, olive, rich, full hues	turquoise, carbuncle, zircon, garnet	red rose, lime flower, daisy, dandelion
Capricorn ♑	indigo, dark brown, deep blue-black, sage green	jet, onyx, garnet, moonstone	pansy, magnolia, quince blossom, black poppy
Aquarius ♒	indigo, sky blue, mixtures	sapphire, opal, amber, chalcedony	fruit tree blossoms, pansy
Pisces ♓	violet, blue-green, glistening white	aquamarine, peridot, jade, tourmaline, amethyst	orchid, water lily, lotus blossom

	Herbs & Spices	Foods
♈	garlic, mustard, pepper, nettle, cayenne, ginger, wild cherry bark	dates, sunflower seeds, lychee nuts, wheat germ, bran, onion
♉	sage, thyme, rosemary, yarrow, burdock, marjoram, coltsfoot, tansy, horseradish	chard, spinach, celeryroot, radish, turnip, kohlrabi
♊	flax, tansy, comfrey leaves, licorice, parsley	melons, summer squash, cucumber, blueberry, strawberry, pineapple, dulse
♋	plantain, chickweed, wintergreen, hyssop, hazel, purslane	carrots, parsley, collards, cabbage, kale, kelp, watercress, spinach,
♌	bay leaves, camomile, eyebright saffron, angelica, cinnamon, wild rue, mints	almonds, walnuts, banana, peanuts, cashews, bran, soybeans, plum, orange
♍	caraway seeds, parsley, dill, savory, fenugreek, licorice, fennel, skullcap	cranberry, parsley, green beans, avocado, Brazil nuts, currants, apple, peach, peas, pineapple
♎	celery tops, spearmint, burdock, dandelion, mugwort	sunflower seed, coconut, wild rice, meat, sweet corn, green beans, brown rice, all whole grains, figs
♏	basil, rue, horehound, garlic, mustard, tarragon, sarsaparilla, pepper, ginger, horseradish	broccoli, cabbage, kelp, watercress, cauliflower, kale, brussels sprouts, carrots
♐	marjoram, nutmeg, cloves, anise, betony, chicory	lettuce, parsnips, onion, cucumber, artichoke, cabbage, asparagus, scotch oats
♑	wintergreen, flaxseed, mullein, slippery elm, comfrey root, Solomon's seal	Brazil nuts, soybeans, pistachios, almonds, sesame seeds, milk, esp. goats milk, cheese
♒	sea holly, horehound, valerian, bayberry, dragonwort, snakeroot, spikenard	olives, beets, water chestnuts, mangos, figs, tomatoes, seaweeds, celery, chard
♓	vervain, woodruff, German chamomile, seaweed, Irish moss	sauerkraut, seaweeds, wheat germ, raisins, molasses, apricots, dry beans

	Flavors	Metals Minerals	Parts of Body	Places
♈	sharp, acid	iron, potassium phosphate	head	England, Germany, Denmark, Israel, Iceland, Syria
♉	sweet	copper, sodium sulfate	neck	Netherlands, Ireland, Greenland, Asia Minor, Australia, Tasmania
♊	mildly astringent	mercury, potassium chloride	arms & hands, lungs	Belgium, Venezuela, Northeast coast of Africa, Lower Egypt
♋	insipid	silver, aluminum, calcium fluoride	stomach, breasts	Africa, United States, Scotland, Netherlands, Paraguay
♌	sweet & pungent	gold, magnesium phosphate	heart, spinal column	Alps, France, Italy, Sicily
♍	mildly astringent	mercury, potassium sulfate	intestines, alimentary canal	Switzerland, Brazil, Turkey, Crete
♎	sweet	copper, sodium phosphate	kidneys,	China, Japan, Burma, Argentina, Tibet, Upper Egypt
♏	sharp, acid, aromatic	iron, steel, calcium sulfate	sex organs, colon	Algeria, Syria, Norway, Morocco, Korea, Paraguay
♐	fragrant, bland	tin, silica	hips, thighs	Arabia, Spain, Australia, Czechoslavakia, Hungary, Chile
♑	sour	lead, calcium phosphate	knees, bones, hair	Afghanistan, Bulgaria, Albania, Antarctica, Mexico, India, Greece
♒	brackish	lead, uranium, sodium chloride	calves of legs, ankles	Arabia, Syria, Cyprus, Iran, Sweden, Russia
♓	subtle	tin, platinum, iron phosphate	feet	Europe, Scandinavia, Portugal, Samoa

CHAPTER FIFTEEN

ASTROLOGICAL PREDICTING

You might think of your basic horoscope, set up for the time of your birth, as a pattern of colors. Since that time the planets, in their ever-changing positions, have been like a pattern of colored light beams moving around on the basic horoscope. This interaction can help you achieve a better understanding of the changing conditions you have faced and will be facing in the future.

This is done by several methods. The most important is comparing the positions of the planets at a certain time, say today, with the positions of the planets at your birth.

If, for example, the Sun at your birth was in that fixed point of the sky which is five degrees of Libra (5 ♎) that degree, for you, always carries the imprint of the Sun, your focus of consciousness. If today the Moon (or any planet) passes over 5 ♎, this influence, called a **transit**, can affect your consciousness.

An influence can also be determined if a transiting planet is in opposition aspect to 5 ♎, 180 degrees away on the zodiac at 5 Aries (♈). Besides the conjunction and opposition, other transiting aspects to 5 ♎ will also influence your Sun, particularly squares and trines, although the minor aspects are less important. And the natal position of the Moon and each of the other planets can be similarly affected by transits.

For a transit to be effective, the transiting planet has to be in close aspect to a natal planet (or other natal point). In other words, a transit is not often felt until the transiting planet is within two degrees **before** reaching an exact aspect to a natal planet. Its effect continues until it passes about one degree **past** exact aspect. For this reason the faster moving planets have much shorter effects than the slower moving ones.

Symbolism of the Moon

The Moon moves about a degree every two hours, so its transiting effects (often noticed as mood changes) are over in a few hours. Since the Moon circles the zodiac a little faster than once a month, each transit of the Moon will happen at least once a month.

With this book you can begin to understand transits by following the Moon sign changes through several months and noticing how they relate to your own mood changes and those of family and friends. Although with this book you cannot determine the exact time when the Moon passes over important degrees in your chart, nevertheless you can begin to recognize the different general effects of the Moon in the various signs of the zodiac.

In addition, with this book you can note new moons, a good time to start projects. The new moons marked ☌ (eclipses of the Sun) are, however, not considered the best time for beginnings. You can also note full moons, high-energy periods with some restlessness. This is particularly true of full moons marked ☍, which are lunar eclipses.

Whenever a solar eclipse or a lunar eclipse occurs in your Sun sign, your Moon sign or the sign opposite either of these in the zodiac, it signifies a particular opportunity in your life. Of course, whether this opportunity is well used or poorly used depends upon you.

Also, each month, we experience a lunar birthday when the phase of the Moon coincides with the phase under which we were born. At this time, perhaps more than any other time of the month, we are "resonating with the spheres," as the ancients used to say. We can, unconsciously at least, feel in tune with the rhythms of the universe.

Symbolism of the Other Planets

The slowest-moving planets (Saturn, Uranus, Neptune and Pluto) have the most lasting patterns when operating as transits. Uranus, for instance, moves so slowly that its transits can be effective for several months. Since it takes eighty-four years to go around the zodiac, each transit aspect of Uranus is likely to happen only once a lifetime.

If you have had your astrological chart cast, you can follow the transits with an astrological calendar or ephemeris, which is a book giving exact positions of the planets every day. There are several astrological calendars available for the current years and an ephemeris available as far ahead as the year 2000.

The art of interpreting a transit depends upon an understanding of the basic meaning of the planets involved. For instance, if Jupiter (expansion) were transiting your natal Mercury (ideas and communication), you could expect to be bursting with ideas and possibly be more talkative than usual.

The best way to learn about the meaning of transits in your chart is to look back to what was happening in transits during previous important events. But remember that, as in interpreting a natal chart, prediction with the use of transits is a complex matter and is to be approached with common sense — **don't jump to conclusions on the basis of a couple of planetary indications.**

CHAPTER SIXTEEN

EVALUATING ASTROLOGERS

An increasing number of astrologers and astrological computing services are available to cast and interpret your chart. The fee can depend upon time involved, how complex an interpretation is desired, and how much in demand the astrologer is.

As in any field where there is increasing interest, some people will set themselves up as astrologers with inadequate preparation. The mathematics necessary to set up a chart accurately is no more complex than that for computing your income tax, but there are enough intricacies to leave plenty of room for error if it is not done conscientiously. A properly programmed computer can set up a chart rapidly and without error, providing the basic data is fed into it accurately.

Astrologers are by nature an independent breed, and this fact, coupled with the present rapid growth in astrological knowledge, means that we are not likely to soon see generally accepted standards and widespread licensing of astrologers. This means that you must judge an astrologer or an astrological computing service in the same way you would many other services — by asking about their study and experience and by their reputation.

The less you know about astrology, the more you may tend to feel (consciously or unconsciously) that anything an astrologer tells you comes directly from the stars, who are up there pulling our strings like gigantic puppeteers. In reality, your astrological chart shows psychological themes, not set events, and it is so complex that no astrologer can interpret with absolute certainty. However, much information can be given which has a strong degree of probability. For instance, if you have inherited a stocky build and a large frame, this genetic "given" would indicate that you are not suited to become a jockey, where lightness counts. Certain astrological indications are just as clear-cut; however, at least in the present state of the art, other astrological indications can give only more general direction.

Making predictions is complex also. If you are starting out on a journey in the middle of a snowstorm, it can be accurately predicted that it will take longer to reach your destination. It can also be said that the likelihood of an accident is increased — but not certain. A responsible astrologer, in making your personal astrological "weather forecast," is aware that astrological patterns can be used in many different ways — **none is in itself either good or bad**.

Therefore, **avoid** an astrologer who makes **too-simple** definite statements about either your natal chart or what to expect, such as: "You'll never get along with Aquarians." "You will become a world-famous musician." "You can never hold your temper." "Your marriage is bound to end in divorce." "You will die of heart disease."

Some computers are programmed to give the meanings of certain astrological combinations. Many of these computer "interpretations" can be quite useful. However, astrology is an art as well as a science. A total computer interpretation of an astrological chart, like computer-composed music, lacks the human factor, the intuitive touch which a live person can give in tying the whole chart together in its personal meaning for you.

Books on astrology are also to be approached with care. There are hundreds available, ranging from simple to highly technical. Many, of course, are written by knowledgeable and responsible astrologers, but there are also quite a few by people whose astrological knowledge is not well-rounded and who have emphasized the sensational aspects of astrology. Some of these can be dangerously misleading, particularly those which give highly negative interpretations of certain planetary positions and combinations. Again, remember that any planetary position or combination can be used constructively or destructively. Let your common sense be your guide.

APPENDIX A

We have arranged with a well-qualified astrological computer service to send you an accurately cast natal chart and an accompanying sheet which tells you just which pages and paragraphs in this book apply to interpreting your chart. In ordering this chart the following information must be given:

1. Name
2. Address
3. Place of birth: town (if small, give nearest larger town), state and country
4. Date of birth: month, day, year
5. Time of birth as exactly as possible, AM or PM
6. Ask for the *Instant Astrology* option.

Send a total of $4.00 ($2.00 for chart and $2.00 handling) in check or money order (don't send cash) to:

> Astro Computing Services, Inc.
> P.O. Box 16430
> San Diego, CA 92126-0430

Price subject to change

APPENDIX B

Listed are national and international astrological organizations which
may be able to recommend competent astrologers in your area. (As
we have said, however, there are good astrologers who are not members
of any of these groups.) These organizations may also be able to give
you information about study centers for astrology and where to pur-
chase astrology books in your area.

NASO (National Astrology Society)
c/o Barbara Somerfield
205 Third Ave., #2A
New York, N.Y. 10003

National Council for Geocosmic Research, Inc.
78 Hubbard Ave.
Stamford, CT 06905

NOTES

NOTES

NOTES

6 Cardinal: Libra, Cancer, Aries, Capricorn
initiate action (rather than ~ fixed ||
sustain + mutable || keep it moving)

For People Who Look Ahead!

CHART CALCULATIONS

Natal Chart wheel with planet/sign glyphs. 2.00
Arabic Parts All traditional parts and more 1.00
Asteroids ⚳ ⚴ ⚵ ⚶ in wheel + aspects/midpoints 50
Asteroids ⚳ ⚴ ⚵ ⚶ + 15 new ones for 20th century only . 1.00
Astrodynes Power, harmony and discord 2.00
Concentric Wheels Any 3 charts available in wheel format may be combined into a '3 wheeler' 3.00
Deduct $1.00 for each chart ordered as a separate wheel.
Fixed Stars Robson's 110 fixed stars with aspects 50
Fortune Finder 97 ancient, 99 modern Arabic Parts 2.00
Graphic Midpoint Sort highlights groupings. **Specify integer divisions of 360°** (1 = 360°, 4 = 90°, etc.) 1.00
Harmonic Chart John Addey type. **Specify harmonic number** 2.00
Harmonic Positions 30 consecutive sets. **Specify starting harmonic #** 1.00
Hindu Style natal chart (square format) 2.00
Shad Bala planetary strengths 1.00
Heliocentric Charts Sun-centered positions 2.00
Horary Report Based on *The Horary Reference Book* 3.00
House Systems Comparison for 9 systems 50
Local Space Planet compass directions (azimuth & altitude) 50
Locality Map USA, World, Europe, S. Amer., Far East, Austl., Middle East and Africa map — choice of rise, set, and culmination lines or Asc., Desc., MC, IC lines for each map 6.00
Midpoint Structures Midpoint aspects + midpoints in 45° and 90° sequence 1.00
Rectification Assist 10 same-day charts. **Specify starting time, time increment, e.g., 6 AM, every 20 minutes** 10.00
Relocation Chart Specify original birth data & new location 2.00
City Azimuths listing of azimuth figures for major cities (US & world) 1.00
Azimuth Aspect Ranges listing of the azimuth figures making aspects to natal planets 1.00
Planets on City Lines listings of cities which conjunct planetary lines 1.00
Uranian Planets + halfsums 50
Uranian Sensitive Points (includes Uranian Planets) 3.50

INTERPRETATION REPORTS

Planetary Profile . . . . (Complete) 20-30 pages 18.00
Both include natal chart. . . . (Concise) about 15 pages 12.00
A major breakthrough in an integrated natal interpretation report.
Astrological Annotation gives astrological factors used (if requested) . . . . N/C
Each of the following sections of the Planetary Profile may be ordered separately: basic identity, overview, work & career, mind, relationships, values & beliefs, sex, money, children, parents, growth areas, future themes. . . . . each 2.00
Comparison Profile Specify coworker, relative, mother/child, father/child, romantic partner, friend 18.00
Sexual Expression & Enrichment Report 6.00
Interpretive Romance Report Specify natal data for 2 births. Romance oriented. See **Themes for Two** for other relationships. 8.00
Themes for Two report includes composite chart. Specify natal data for two births and location. Suitable for any relationship. 8.00
Interpretive Transits. Specify starting month
Outer Planets ♃♄♅♆♇ Hard aspects only ☌☍□∠⚼ . . . . 12 mos. 8.00
Outer Planets ♃♄♅♆♇ Soft & hard aspects △✶⚻☌☍□∠⚼ . . . . 12 mos. 10.00
9 Planets Hard aspects only . . . . . 6 mos. 15.00/12 mos. 25.00
9 Planets Soft & hard aspects . . . 6 mos. 18.00/12 mos. 30.00

HUMAN RELATIONSHIPS

Chart Comparison (Synastry) All aspects between the two sets of planets plus house positions of one in the other 1.50
Composite Chart Rob Hand-type. **Specify location** 2.00
Relationship Chart Erected for space-time midpoint 2.00

COLOR CHARTS

4-Color Wheel Any chart we offer in new, aesthetic format with color-coded aspect lines 2.00
Local Space Map 4-color on 360° circle 2.00
Custom 6″ Disk for any harmonic (laminated, you cut out) overlays on our color wheel charts 4.00

COLOR CHARTS (continued)

Plotted Natal Dial Use with custom 6″ Disk. **Specify harmonic #** 2.00
Plotted 2 Ring-Concentric Wheel 3.00
Custom Graphic Ephemeris in 4 colors. **Specify harmonic, zodiac, starting date.** . . . . varied prices
Dynamic Astrology Graph . . . . 1 year 3.00

FUTURE TRENDS

Progressed Chart Secondary, quotidian, tertiary or minor. **Specify progressed day, month and year** 2.00
Secondary Progressions Day-by-day progressed aspects to natal and progressed planets, ingresses and parallels by month, day and year. **Specify starting year, MC by solar arc (standard) or RA of mean Sun**
5 years 3.00
10 years 5.00
85 years 15.00
Minor or Tertiary Progressions Minor based on lunar-month-for-a-year, tertiary on day-for-a-lunar-month. **Specify year, MC by solar arc (standard) or RA of mean Sun** . . . . 1 year 2.00
Progressed Lifetime Lunar Phases a la Dane Rudhyar . . . 5.00
Solar Arc Directions Day-by-day solar arc directed aspects to the natal planets, house and sign ingresses by month, day and year. **Specify starting year.** Asc. and Vertex arc directions available at same prices
1st 5 years 1.00
Each add'l 5 years .50
Primary Arc Directions (Includes speculum) . . . . . . 5 years 1.50
Specify starting year Each add'l 5 years .50
Transits by all planets except Moon. Date and time of transiting aspects/ingresses to natal chart. **Specify starting month.** Moon-only transits available at same prices. . . . . 6 mos. 7.00
12 mos. 12.00
Summary only . . . . 6 mos. 3.50
Summary only . . . . 12 mos. 6.00
Calendar Format (9 planets OR Moon only) . . . . 6 mos. 7.00
Calendar Format (9 planets OR Moon only) . . . . 12 mos. 12.00
Calendar Format (Moon & planets) . . . . 6 mos. 12.00
Calendar Format (Moon & planets) . . . . 12 mos. 20.00
Returns in wheel format. All returns can be precession corrected. **Specify place, Sun-return year, Moon-return month, planet-return month/year.** Solar, Lunar or Planet 2.00
13 Lunar 15.00

ALL ABOUT ASTROLOGY

Booklets to explain options. (Cal. residents add 6% sales tax)
What Are Astrolocality Maps? 2.00
What Are Winning Transits 1.50
The Zodiac: A Historical Survey 2.00
The Eastpoint and the Anti-Vertex 2.00
Interpreting Composite and Relationship Charts 1.50
The Art of Chart Comparison 2.00
The Comet Halley Ephemeris 2.00
How to Use Dials (color illustrations) 3.00
Working With Local Space 2.00

POTPOURRI

Winning!! Timing for gamblers, exact planet and transiting house cusps based on Joyce Wehrman's system. Specify location, dates of speculation, natal data. 1-7 days (per day) 3.00
8 or more days (per day) 2.00
Winning Overview Planetary transits with + and − for planning speculation . . . . 6 mos. 12.00/12 mos. 20.00
Biorhythms Chart the 23-day, 28-day and 33-day cycles in . . . . Printed { per mo. .50 / 12 mos. 4.00 }
black/white graph format.
4-color graph on our plotter . . . . Color 6 mos. 2.00
Custom House Cusps Table Specify latitude ° ′ ″ or city 10.00
Custom American Ephemeris Page Any month, 2500 BC-AD 2500. **Specify zodiac (sidereal includes RA & dec.)**
One mo. geocentric or two mos. heliocentric 5.00
One year ephemeris (**specify beginning mo. yr.**) 50.00
One year heliocentric ephemeris 25.00
Fertility Report The Jonas method for 1 year 3.00
Specify starting month.
Lamination of 1 or 2 sheets (Back to back) 1.00
Transparency (B/W) of any chart or map.
Ordered at same time 1.00
Handling charge per order 2.00
In Canada & Mexico 3.00

SAME DAY SERVICE — Ask for Free Catalog
ASTRO COMPUTING SERVICES, Inc.
P.O. BOX 16430
SAN DIEGO, CA 92116-0430
NEIL F. MICHELSEN
(Prices Subject to Change)